Recht im Kontext

edited by

Dieter Grimm
Alexandra Kemmerer
Christoph Möllers

Volume 5

Dieter Grimm/Alexandra Kemmerer/
Christoph Möllers (eds.)

Human Dignity in Context

Explorations of a Contested Concept

Supported by the Berlin Senate Department for Economics, Technology and Research, and by the Dräger Foundation.

Die Deutsche Nationalbibliothek lists this publication in the Deutsche Nationalbibliografie; detailed bibliographic data is available in the Internet at http://dnb.d-nb.de

ISBN   978-3-8487-2356-0 (Print)
       978-3-8452-6458-5 (ePDF)

British Library Cataloguing-in-Publication Data
A catalogue record for this book is available from the British Library.

ISBN: HB (Hart)   978-1-78225-621-2

Library of Congress Cataloging-in-Publication Data
Grimm, Dieter / Kemmerer, Alexandra / Möllers, Christoph
Human Dignity in Context
Explorations of a Contested Concept
Dieter Grimm / Alexandra Kemmerer / Christoph Möllers (eds.)
637 p.

Includes bibliographic references and index.

ISBN   978-1-78225-621-2   (hardcover Hart)

1st Edition 2018
© Nomos Verlagsgesellschaft, Baden-Baden, Germany 2018. Printed and bound in Germany.

This work is subject to copyright. All rights reserved. No part of this publication may be reproduced or transmitted in any form or by any means, electronic or mechanical, including photocopying, re-cording, or any information storage or retrieval system, without prior permission in writing from the publishers. Under § 54 of the German Copyright Law where copies are made for other than private use a fee is payable to "Verwertungsgesellschaft Wort", Munich.

No responsibility for loss caused to any individual or organization acting on or refraining from action as a result of the material in this publication can be accepted by Nomos or the editors.

Recht im Kontext. The Series.

Recht im Kontext is the series of the project *Recht im Kontext* (Law in Context) at the Wissenschaftskolleg zu Berlin (Institute for Advanced Study Berlin). The series features research presented and discussed in the framework of the project's various formats, from conferences and talks to blog symposia and seminars. *Recht im Kontext* aims to create an enhanced re-contextualization of the law among its neighboring disciplines and seeks to advance German legal scholarship's *aggiornamento* in a global context. From a genuinely legal perspective, the project cooperates with individual and institutional partners and initiates new forms of dialogue with the goal of creating discursive structures between the law, the humanities and social sciences. Under a twofold agenda, *Recht im Kontext* advances transnationalisation and interdisciplinarity of legal scholarship in Germany. The project explores the foundations and contexts of law in a plural world where competitive and complementary multiplicities of legal and normative orders are part of social reality. To us, *Recht im Kontext* stands for a style of discourse, an exchange on current issues in legal scholarship, for interdisciplinary encounters, and for dialogues within wider national as well as transnational public spheres we hope to foster.

Dieter Grimm
Alexandra Kemmerer
Christoph Möllers

Acknowledgements

Most of the chapters assembled in this volume had their origin in two conferences held at the Wissenschaftskolleg zu Berlin in November 2011 and June 2013. It has been a long process which led us from the presentation of original research, from multidisciplinary and transregional encounters, and from lively conference discussions to publication of the present book. A project of this scope incurs many debts of gratitude.

We are very grateful for the authors' willingness to contribute their specific expertise, and for their patience. In addition to the contributors, many other speakers and participants have also offered important insights into the chosen theme of the conferences. Particular thanks go to *Samantha Besson, Heiner Bielefeldt, Edward J. Eberle, Michaela Hailbronner, Jeff King, Jeffrey Rosen, Julika Rosenstock, Kim Lane Scheppele, Frank Schorkopf, and Lea Ypi*.

As an experiment in comparative constitutional law in context, this project has been realized within the framework of *Recht im Kontext* at the Wissenschaftskolleg zu Berlin. Initially funded by the Land Berlin (*Berlin Senate Department for Economics, Technology and Research*) and the Wissenschaftskolleg, the project advances transnationalization and interdisciplinarity of legal scholarship in Germany.

The *Dräger Foundation* generously supported the two conferences. We are grateful to *Rudolf Mellinghoff, Petra Pissulla*, and to the late *Dieter Feddersen* (1935-2016) who was a legal practitioner, philanthropic entrepreneur and passionate facilitator of transatlantic encounters in academia and judicial networks at the highest level.

The Wissenschaftskolleg zu Berlin provided a unique venue for our multidisciplinary and transregional conversations, on snowy Grunewald days in November 2011 as well as in the sweltering heat of June 2013. We remain grateful to *Luca Giuliani, Joachim Nettelbeck* and *Thorsten Wilhelmy* as well as to the entire WiKo staff. Our thanks to *Lucy Chebout, Christine Hofmann, Kerstin von der Krone* and *Thea Schwarz* for their superb organization of the conferences.

We wish to warmly thank *Marlene Teichmann, Nils Weinberg* and *Maike Voltmer* for their excellent editorial assistance, *Justus Quecke* for his translation assistance and *Janet Mindes* for her expert language editing.

Acknowledgements

We are grateful to *Johannes Rux*, *Peter Schmidt*, and the team at Nomos for their patience and a sustained cooperation which guided us through the publishing process, and to *Sinead Moloney* at Hart Publishing. Our home institutions, past and present – Humboldt-Universität zu Berlin, Wissenschaftskolleg zu Berlin and the Max Planck Institute for Comparative Public Law and International Law – provided support in the preparation of this volume.

Last, but by no means least, our heartfelt thanks go to *Sylvi Paulick*, project assistant at *Recht im Kontext* and assistant editor of this book, for her many invaluable contributions to the project. We are immensely grateful for her hard work, her diligence and grace.

Berlin, December 2017

Dieter Grimm
Alexandra Kemmerer
Christoph Möllers

Table of Contents

Recht im Kontext. The Series. — 5

Acknowledgements — 7

Table of Contents — 9

Dieter Grimm, Alexandra Kemmerer, Christoph Möllers
Human Dignity in Context. An Introduction — 13

Part I: Foundations — **23**

Christopher McCrudden
On Portraying Human Dignity — 25

Ino Augsberg
'The Moral Feeling Within Me': On Kant's Concept of Human
Freedom and Dignity as Auto-Heteronomy — 55

Ingolf U. Dalferth
Religion, Morality and Being Human:
The Controversial Status of Human Dignity — 69

Stephan Schaede
For the Sake of Human Dignity, Ban Reified Concepts of 'Man
Made in the Image of God': Some Theological Perspectives — 107

Table of Contents

Susannah Heschel
'Wherever You See the Trace of Man, There I Stand Before You':
The Complexities of God and Human Dignity Within Judaism   129

Russell A. Miller
Literature *as* Human Dignity: The Constitutional Court's
Misguided Ban of the Novel *Esra*   163

Part II: Developments   **191**

Christoph Goos
Würde des Menschen: Restoring Human Dignity in Post-Nazi
Germany   193

Matthildi Chatzipanagiotou
Hermeneutic and Literary Remarks on the *Objektformel* as a Tool
of Critical Reflection in Practicing the Law of Human Dignity   211

Nils Teifke
Balancing Human Dignity: Human Dignity as a Principle and as a
Constitutional Right   225

David Dyzenhaus
Dignity in Administrative Law: Judicial Deference in a Culture of
Justification   239

Jochen von Bernstorff
The Dispute About Human Dignity and Ethical Absolutism in the
Field of Fundamental and Human Rights Protection: Defending a
Deontic Understanding of Rights   267

Roger Brownsword
Developing a Modern Understanding of Human Dignity   299

Eric Hilgendorf
Problem Areas in the Dignity Debate and the Ensemble Theory of
Human Dignity ... 325

Tim Wihl
Towards Progressive Human Dignity ... 345

Part III: Variations ... **367**

Alexander Somek
The Question of Self-Repair: On Discrimination and Dignity ... 369

Morag Goodwin
Architecture, Choice Architecture and Dignity ... 393

Stefan Huster
The Universality of Human Dignity and the Relativity of Social
Rights ... 415

Nora Markard
What's in a Label? Transatlantic Reflections on Health Insurance
and Dignity ... 421

Rehan Abeyratne
Socioeconomic Rights, Human Dignity, and Constitutional
Legitimacy in India ... 445

Conor O'Mahony
The Dignity of the Individual in Irish Constitutional Law ... 469

Christoph Goos
Grandma's Dignity: Technology and the 'Elderly' ... 499

Table of Contents

Marion Albers
Biotechnologies and Human Dignity — 509

Tatjana Hörnle
How to Define Human Dignity, and the Resulting Implications for Biotechnology — 561

Bibliography — 583

Contributors — 621

Index — 625

Human Dignity in Context. An Introduction

Dieter Grimm, Alexandra Kemmerer, Christoph Möllers

Human dignity is a complex topic. It is a philosophical, a theological as well as a legal concept with a long and manifold intellectual history – a history it brought to the human rights context, to which it has been applied only rather recently. Within the legal world, it remains a gateway for ethical arguments. And as such it has received increased attention in recent years. Equally, when the prohibition of torture was called into question during the so-called war on terror or when the ethical limits of biotechnology became more relevant in the face of disappearing practical boundaries, these issues were debated in dignity-based language both within and outside the legal world. Human dignity arguments thus transcend disciplinary boundaries.

In confronting this phenomenon, as the book's title indicates, we are here attempting to put human dignity in context. On the one hand, bringing context to universal concepts is an ambivalent undertaking. As our arguments claim to be universal when we evoke human dignity, they defy the very idea of context. On the other hand, given the abstractness of the concept and its application to various fields, we run the risk of missing something if we ignore the different contexts. In fact it may often be easier to agree on the violation of human dignity in a specific context than on the notion's abstract meaning. It is no coincidence therefore that German constitutional lawyers, following *Günter Dürig*, approach dignity cases not by abstractly conceptualizing what is protected under Article 1 (1) Basic Law but by determining acts of infringement instead.

This volume is the result of two conferences on human dignity convened by the editors and held at the Wissenschaftskolleg zu Berlin (Institute for Advanced Study Berlin) on 16-18 November 2011 and 19-21 June 2013. As exercises in comparative constitutional law in context, both events brought together a wide array of scholars from various disciplinary and regional backgrounds.

Each of the conferences was preceded by a keynote lecture, open to the general public, and based on reflections that have been published elsewhere.

Avishai Margalit, in his 2011 lecture, outlined two genealogies of human dignity: one based on the deification of the human person (to him, apparently only of limited relevance in a secular age), the other on moral 'kitsch', on an exaggeration of sentimentality, stressing the capacity of suffering, shared by all human beings.[1] For *Margalit*, the latter genealogy carries the risk of a victimization culture where every human being is seen as a (potential) victim and where respect for human beings is linked to victimhood. In order to dignify the victim, the victim is to be seen as necessarily pure and innocent. For *Margalit*, however, the very purpose of respecting the human being, of human dignity as a concept, is to exclude the need to verify the individual's innocence and 'nobility'. All human beings, even the most despicable ones, deserve moral respect – not for what they do, but for who they are: members of the Family of Man.

In his 2013 keynote lecture, *Hans Joas* offered an alternative to the two dominant narratives on the history of human rights: the mostly secularist view that traces human rights back to the French Revolution and its roots in Enlightenment thinking, and the mostly Catholic view of human rights as an outgrowth of the personalist understanding of God. The alternative 'genealogy' which *Joas* proposed deals with human rights as the product of a profound cultural transformation for which he uses the term 'sacralization of the person'.[2] The empirical cases he discussed concerned the abolition of torture and of slavery and the codification of human rights in the late eighteenth century and in the years following the Second World War. Expanding his argument in a global perspective, *Joas* shed new light on the connection between the emergence of moral universalism in the Axial Age and the history of human rights in the last few centuries.

A number of authors in this volume have engaged with the work of *Avishai Margalit*[3] and *Hans Joas*,[4] and readers will find aspects of their

---

1   A Margalit, 'Human Dignity Between Kitsch and Deification' in C Cordner and R Gaita (eds), *Philosophy, Ethics, and a Common Humanity: Essays in Honour of Raimond Gaita* (London, Routledge, 2011) 106.
2   H Joas, *Slavery and Torture in a Global Perspective. Human Rights and the Western Tradition* (Leiden, Brill, 2014). On the history of human rights and universal human dignity, and their justification, see also H Joas, *The Sacredness of the Person. A New Genealogy of Human Rights* (Washington, Georgetown University Press, 2013).
3   See *Hilgendorf, Hörnle*, and *McCrudden* (in this volume).
4   See *von Bernstorff, McCrudden*, and *Wihl* (in this volume).

contributions to contemporary legal and philosophical discourses reflected and discussed throughout the book.

The 23 chapters of this book capture a rich and multifaceted glimpse into current understandings of and conversations about human dignity. While we cannot (and do not intend to) provide a detailed sketch of all aspects canvassed by the authors, we want to leave readers with a sense of how the volume may be read and used. In putting together this collection we have approached the topic of human dignity from three different angles: foundations, developments, and variations. These can be seen as three steps in a multidisciplinary conversation that has been convened and curated, as has the resulting collection, from a genuinely legal perspective. While the editors focus on human dignity as a legal concept, the authors also draw upon various other disciplines and traditions of dignity to investigate conceptual implications for many different fields of application.

The book begins at the beginnings – with explorations into the foundations of human dignity. This includes not only philosophical and theological reflections, but also the wider fields of arts and humanities.

Taking a closer look at Diego Velázquez's *Las Meninas*, Christopher McCrudden engages in a retrospective justification of the painting's use in the dignity context – and, more broadly, in a conversation on the relevance of art forms such as literature and painting for an understanding of complex concepts in law and moral philosophy. In *McCrudden's* reading, *Las Menina*s conveys an experience that encourages us to engage in reflexive conversations with others.

In deconstructing and reconstructing Kant's idea of human freedom and dignity, *Ino Augsberg* provides a fresh reading of one of the core philosophical foundations of the concept of human dignity in the German constitutional tradition. *Augsberg* questions Kant's supposedly clear-cut distinction between autonomy and heteronomy and argues that 'Kant's moral philosophy, and in particular his concept of *Achtung*, undermines the classical dichotomy between Christianity and Judaism, between letter and spirit, between individual right and mitzvah, between Western and non-Western legal tradition'.

Ingolf U. Dalferth analyzes the controversial status of human dignity in legal, political, moral, philosophical and theological debates from a Christian perspective and proposes a 'dynamic personalist understanding of dignity', grounded in respect for each other that is intertwined with the respect of God for everyone 'as his neighbor'. *Dalferth* outlines 'the dignity of human persons as the humane mode of living a human life in the presence of God'.

From a perspective informed by the complex history of theological concepts, *Stephan Schaede* takes further the Protestant critique of essentialist conceptualizations of human dignity and voices a strong plea for a ban on reified concepts of 'man made in the image of God'. His chapter offers insights into the resistance of nineteenth-century Protestant theology against addressing the problem of dignity, an overview of various semantic antecedents of dignity in Latin, and a Christological reading of dignity discourses which leads to a dynamic understanding of human dignity as relationship to God.

Susannah Heschel explores the complexities of human dignity within Judaism, taking her readers from biblical origins and classical rabbinical texts to the American civil rights movement and present-day decisions of secular Israeli courts. According to *Heschel*, 'perhaps the most radical shift in Jewish thought occurred when theologians of the modern period expanded the point of reference of human dignity to include all human beings'. But *Heschel* also demonstrates that 'reconciling religious belief with human equality or democratic pluralism is not a new problem, but a tension already inherent in the earliest strata of rabbinic thought'.

Concluding the first part of the book, *Russell A. Miller*, drawing upon literary theory, brings us back to law and humanities and shifts the focus to how art is not only a potential means to better understand concepts of human dignity, but how art is itself a form of human dignity. In his passionate critique of the German Federal Constitutional Court's decision in the *Esra* case, *Miller* emphasizes the 'dignitarian potential of the literary acts of reading and writing'.

The second part of the volume is concerned with developments in the human dignity discourse. Or, more precisely: with developments in legal human dignity discourses. A special emphasis is placed here on the German constitutional protection of human dignity as enshrined in Article 1 (1) Basic Law.

Christoph Goos reconstructs the long-neglected genealogy of Article 1, its 'original meaning' and the intentions of the fathers and mothers of the 1949 German constitution. *Goos* rebuts the widely-held assumption that the dignity article is 'a specific result of Catholic and Kantian thought', and he argues that the meaning of the term 'dignity of man' is to be defined 'as a real capacity of human beings that had been proven highly vulnerable during the Nazi regime: the inner freedom'.

The *Objektformel* (object formula) doctrine, deduced from Kantian ethics and shaped by Günter Dürig and Josef Wintrich, has long been a prevailing pattern of conceptual interpretation of human dignity. In taking a closer look at the Federal Constitutional Court's *Aviation Security Act Case* (2006), *Matthildi Chatzipanagiotou* shows how 'the *Objektformel* doctrine operates as a tool of critical reflection'. Her hermeneutic and literary approach serves as 'a lens through which to look at the *Objektformel* as a recurrent feature of human dignity practice'.

The past few years have seen a heated and still ongoing debate among German constitutional law scholars about the claim to absoluteness of Article 1 (1) Basic Law, triggered in 2003 by the new commentary on this clause by Matthias Herdegen, Professor of Public Law at the University of Bonn, and the following criticism of Ernst-Wolfgang Böckenförde, former Justice at the German Federal Constitutional Court and Professor Emeritus of Public Law at the University of Freiburg. For the first time since 1949, the fundamental axiom of German constitutional law and culture was put into question.

In this section, *Nils Teifke* discusses the absoluteness of human dignity on the basis of Robert Alexy's Theory of Principles. The absoluteness of human dignity, *Teifke* argues, exists only as an idea. 'As an overarching principle, human dignity is both absolute as an idea and relative in legal practice. This is the double character of human dignity which combines the real with the ideal dimension.'

Reaffirming the claim to absoluteness and defending a deontic understanding of rights, *Jochen von Bernstorff*, in his contribution, takes the contrary position. *Von Bernstorff* contextualizes the incorporation of Article 1 into the German Basic Law with the origins of the universal human rights movement during the 1940s. Against the background of these genealogies, he develops an understanding of the human dignity clause as inspired by Emmanuel Lévinas' concept of the vulnerability of the individual. He interprets Article 1 as 'a provision that requires constitutional organs to erect and respect boundaries in what the executive powers can do to human beings'.

David Dyzenhaus takes us from Germany to apartheid South Africa of his student days and from there to contemporary Canada – and he takes us on a journey from constitutional to administrative law. Comparing the 'much too interesting' administrative law in apartheid South Africa ('a direct result of the country's bad health on the dignity scale') with the 'boring nature of Canadian administrative law', *Dyzenhaus* argues that 'this right to dignity is at the core of administrative law – the law to which officials are subject in making decisions that carry the authority of state and law'.

Other authors in the second part of this volume discuss the conceptual conundrum of human dignity on a more abstract level, not explicitly linked to particular times, traditions and regions.

Roger Brownsword looks for common ground between a rights-centered understanding of human dignity as empowerment and a duty-centered understanding of human dignity as constraint. If there is an Archimedean point in the conceptual landscape of human dignity, he suggests, it is to be found in a Gewirthian theory of rights. *Brownsword* stresses that 'in an age when regulators are discovering a new repertoire of technological tools, we need to keep an eye on the complexion of the regulatory environment'. It is here, he argues, that human dignity has an important role to play 'as a critical benchmark for the use of techno-regulation'.

Eric Hilgendorf deplores the often highly disordered and unstructured way in which debates on human dignity are conducted. In his contribution, he identifies key questions in the human dignity debate, providing lawyers and philosophers with 'both a sort of road map of the key issues, and with something of a legal-philosophical toolbox containing instruments for analysis, arguments and possible solutions'. With his aim of defining the concept of human dignity in a way that allows for an effective anchoring of normative differences in pluralist societies in a foundation of commonly held values, *Hilgendorf* proposes an 'ensemble theory of human dignity', based on a set of core rights which are considered to be absolute.

Finally, drawing from different philosophical theories of truth, *Tim Wihl* develops a progressive 'consensus' idea of human dignity that is distinct from the prevailing conservative 'correspondence' and the liberal 'coherence' approaches. *Wihl* encourages German doctrine to adopt 'more progressive-republican elements' and argues that 'structural progressivism demands a sublation of conservative and liberal visions of dignity in a democratic-republican perfection of equal liberty'.

A rich and diverse collection of variations of our topic then forms the third part of the volume. Here, legal human dignity arguments and their concrete implications are investigated and analysed in different contexts. These range from the fast-changing and contested field of biotechnologies, from choice architecture informed by behavioral economics to social rights arguments in general and the socioeconomic rights jurisprudence of the Indian Supreme Court, to human dignity in Irish constitutional law as well as to constitutional discourses on health insurance in the United States of America and in Germany more specifically. The chapters pose questions that aging societies must face, explore the links between dignity, freedom and discrimination and criticize inconsistent uses of the concept of dignity.

Alexander Somek explores the twisted connections between dignity, freedom and discrimination in a competitive world where 'individual agility and adaptability are virtues that individuals are generally expected to develop' – a world 'not for the depressed and inflexible'. *Somek* traces the postmodern-neoliberal path to self-perfection where 'the question of self-repair' easily turns into a matter of Kierkegaard's 'despair' if the individual fails to come up with a 'socially suitable personal identity'. His proposed reconstruction of discrimination allows for 'self-constitution in the medium of the play between choices and tinkering with identities', prompts ironic breaks and concludes with a forceful reminder that 'living a life in dignity requires more than legal protection from discrimination'.

In her chapter, *Morag Goodwin* responds to the dignitarian challenges posed by the various tools that have been developed based on insights from behavioural economics in order to move the citizen towards more 'reasonable' conduct. *Goodwin* states that 'nudging' undermines our status as social and political agents and 'betrays an understanding of individuals as morally weak', as incapable of taking morally responsible action. Her paper inspired our further interest in a constitutionalist perspective on choice architectures and behaviorally informed regulation, and has now also become part of the edited volume *'Choice Architecture in Democracies. Exploring the Legitimacy of Nudging'* (Alexandra Kemmerer, Christoph Möllers, Maximilian Steinbeis, Gerhard Wagner, eds., Recht im Kontext 6).

Stefan Huster explores the complex connection between human dignity and social (human) rights and contrasts the universality of human dignity with the relativity of social rights. *Huster* stresses that both the content and the applicability of social rights are relative – and, in his view, rightly so: 'If human dignity is aimed at equal belonging, and the substance of inclusion is oriented to the relevant conception within a particular society, then social rights depend on this conception.'

In her comparative transatlantic reflections on health insurance and dignity, *Nora Markard* describes how health insurance relies on solidarity in the United States and Germany and outlines constitutional issues in terms of federal authority and fundamental rights. *Markard* examines in particular the role of human dignity and liberty for minimum entitlements and solidarity, tracing a discontinued line of dignity jurisprudence in the US. In a concluding critical comparative move, she argues that 'human dignity, by virtue of its inviolability, has proven a reliable line of defence for those forgotten by political process'.

Rehan Abeyratne examines the concept of human dignity in Indian constitutional law, with a focus on socioeconomic rights. Drawing upon the work of Frank Michelman, *Abeyratne* looks at two objections to constitutional social human rights (as developed in the 'activist' judicial decision-making of the Indian Supreme Court) that are not substantial in nature, but focus on how political and legal institutions should function under a democratic constitutional scheme. He explains that a 'democratic' objection can be overcome in light of India's history and the dysfunctionalities of its elected government, while, to him, a 'contractarian' objection seems justified – but could be avoided if the Court 'limited itself to adjudicating only the reasonableness of government schemes, much like the South African Constitutional Court'.

The Irish Constitution of 1937 was one of the earliest constitutional documents to invoke human dignity as a foundational principle, but it is only in recent years that human dignity began to play an ever more significant, but not very consistent role in Irish constitutional case law. *Conor O'Mahony* critically analyzes the various guises in which human dignity has appeared in Irish constitutional adjudication and he calls for a more consistent use of the principle, restricted 'to the role of a background principle that acts as a normative justification for and interpretive aid to rights provisions, by reference to the equal treatment and respect that should be afforded to all human beings'.

Christoph Goos urges a 'more inclusive, more realistic, more holistic understanding of human dignity' in order to adequately cope with the challenges of aging societies. In his case-study on three current examples of assistive and surveillance technologies specifically designed for older people with dementia, he argues that 'dependence, vulnerability and limitations, change, loss and death, messiness, helplessness and uncertainties' should be integrated into 'a contemporary understanding of human dignity as a legal concept'.

With their potential for bringing about radical transformations, advanced biotechnologies are prompting a reconfiguration of the normative concepts of human rights, rights of the individual and human dignity. *Marion Albers* provides a detailed overview of significant biotechnological fields and visions as well as of essential discussions concerning those fields referring to human dignity. She examines 'legal contexts of human dignity', in particular texts and documents enshrining human dignity, legislation, the reasoning of courts and scientific discourses. *Albers* stresses the need to develop a contextualized and differentiated concept of human dignity – an idea that is 'probably more obviously than ever before a social construction as well as an extraordinarily complex legal concept'.

Tatjana Hörnle discusses the strengths and weaknesses of different approaches to defining human dignity and the implications of these approaches for judgements regarding new developments in the area of human reproduction. In her view, human dignity needs to be clearly defined. As a meaningful concept, she argues, it cannot be defined positively, but only negatively, i.e. by defining violations of human dignity. According to *Hörnle*, one should not invoke human dignity as an objective value, or point to *Gattungswürde* ('dignity of the human species') because she identifies 'an underlying socio-psychological need for "naturalness" that is rooted in ill-reflected fears and quasi-religious feelings'. As a relational concept, human dignity presupposes interactions with other people. This understanding has profound implications for the assessment of new technologies in the area of human reproduction, as *Hörnle* demonstrates using the example of surrogate motherhood.

Where does this wide variety of complex, often conflicting and contradictory understandings of human dignity leave us? What did we take from the conversations, the dialogues and controversies we had at the Wissenschaftskolleg? And what can readers take from this book?

As has been said, this volume does neither offer a comprehensive picture of human dignity discourses in the early twenty-first century, nor is it intended to do so. The present book is a kaleidoscope of legal, philosophical and theological perspectives on the concept of human dignity, and we invite readers to explore the scholarship assembled here from a position of reflexive situatedness and disciplinarity, engaging with their own discipline, formation, profession, and habitus.

Despite an often deplored 'dignity fatigue', despite a sometimes voiced plea to 'move on' and leave behind a concept that to some observers seems vague, empty and 'oversqueezed' – the chapters of this book confirm the relevance and salience of comparative and contextual engagements with human dignity. 'Dignity is here to stay!', as *Samantha Besson* confidently stated in her general comments at the end of our first conference.

The very notion of human dignity opens spaces to discuss and renegotiate competing, conflicting, sometimes incommensurable but sometimes also overlapping legal, philosophical and theological concepts and ideas. It is indeed a notion inviting us to explore and better understand the internal tensions of liberal constitutionalism. What could be more timely?

Part I

Foundations

On Portraying Human Dignity

Christopher McCrudden[*]

I. Introduction

There is a well-known scene in *The Simpsons*, which is an American cartoon show for the over-16s, when Kirk and Luanne are playing Pictionary.[1] This involves players guessing the word or phrase as it is being 'drawn' by their partner. Kirk is seen drawing what looks to the viewer like a random set of squiggles on the board and saying to his partner, Luanne, somewhat testily: 'Ah, come on Luanne, you know what this is.' Luanne says: 'Kirk, I *don't* know what it is.' Kirk sighs and says: 'It could not be more *simple*, Luanne. You want me to show this to the *cat*, and have the cat tell you what it is? 'Cause the cat's going to get it.' After a lot of argument between the two of them, Kirk gives up in frustration at Luanne's inability to 'get' it, and says: 'It's *dignity*! Don't you even know *dignity* when you see it?'

But Luanne is dismissive of Kirk's efforts. He challenges her: 'Okay, genius,' he says to her, 'why don't *you* draw dignity.' She goes to the drawing board, and sketches something. Everyone gasps in recognition, but we, the viewers, can't see it because it's hidden from our sight. We're none the wiser, but we're supposed to be left with the idea that if only we were able to see the picture that Luanne had drawn, we too would gain an insight into dignity. Or, at least that is the *initial* idea we are supposed to take from the scene. But, of course, the joke is actually a lot deeper than that, as it nearly always is in *The Simpsons*: in fact, it's a critique of the idea that one picture is worth a thousand words.

So, from the ridiculous to the sublime. What I want to consider is whether Diego Velázquez (1599-1660) succeeded in doing in *Las Meninas*

---

[*] An earlier version was presented at the Straus Institute, New York University Law School, where I was a Fellow in the academic year 2013-14. I am particularly grateful to Alexandra Kemmerer, Emily Kidd White, Aden Kumler and David Freedberg for commenting on an earlier version.

[1] *The Simpsons*, episode 6, season 8: 'A Milhouse Divided', first broadcast December 1, 1996.

what Kirk in *The Simpsons* wasn't able to do, and whether Velázquez has indeed conveyed several aspects of the idea of human dignity in ways that do not just echo some aspects of contemporary philosophical and legal analysis, but transcend them, bringing into our understanding aspects of dignity, and the controversy surrounding it, that otherwise might be underestimated.

II. The Aims of this Chapter

When I chose *Las Meninas* as the cover of a recent edited book of essays on human dignity, I was blissfully unaware of the extent to which the painting had been viewed by countless others in multiple settings. *Las Meninas,* painted in 1656, has intrigued pretty much everyone who has ever seen it.[2] I know it did me when I first saw it in the Prado in Madrid in the early 1990s. In drawing on *Las Meninas* to make a broader point in philosophy, I am following in the illustrious, if controversial,[3] steps of none other than Michel Foucault.[4] Foucault has an extensive discussion of the painting in the first chapter of his 1966 book,[5] but he uses the painting in a way that differs from my use. For Foucault, the painting usefully problematizes issues of representation through its use of mirrors and screens; for me, it provides insights into ways of thinking about human dignity. As we shall see, however, the approach that Foucault adopted, focusing on the complex perspectives embedded in the painting, and our position as spectators in the painting, are also important for my project.

My purpose in this article is partly, therefore, to engage in a retrospective justification of the use of the painting in the dignity context. At the time I included the painting on my book cover, I thought that making the connection between dignity and *Las Meninas* was an original idea; I

---

2   The scholarly literature on Velázquez, and the paining is, of course, immense. For an introduction to the former, see SL Stratton-Pruitt, 'Introduction: A Brief History of the Literature on Velázquez' in SL Stratton-Pruitt, *The Cambridge Companion to Velázquez* (Cambridge, Cambridge University Press, 2002). For an introduction to the literature on the paining, see SL Stratton-Pruitt, 'Velázquez's *Las Meninas*: An Interpretive Primer' in SL Stratton-Pruitt, *Velázquez's* Las Meninas (Cambridge, Cambridge University Press, 2003).

3   See Y Greslé, 'Foucault's Las Meninas and Art-Historical Methods' (2006) 22 *Journal of Literary Studies* 211.

4   I am grateful to Robert Yelle, who first pointed this out to me.

5   M Foucault, *Les mots et les choses (*trans as *The Order of Things).*

should have known better, of course. Andrew Edgar had already linked the painting to the representation of dignity, in his 2003 article.[6] Indeed, Edgar had already argued, as I shall here, that

> [f]undamental questions about the very notion of dignity lie at the core of much of Velázquez's work, and indeed it may be suggested that they find their culmination in *Las Meninas*.[7]

He also usefully documents how others have seen strong connections between the painting and conceptions of dignity. I want to continue that conversation. To help in this endeavor, I will draw on recent work by Avishai Margalit[8] and Hans Joas,[9] both of whom have presented their work as lectures associated with the two conferences of dignity at the Wissenschaftskolleg zu Berlin, from which this volume draws.

More broadly, I want to continue a conversation in the *legal* academy (I am, after all, a legal scholar) on how far resort to art forms such as literature and painting may help us understand problematic concepts in law and moral philosophy.[10] Iris Murdoch has famously claimed that great art 'is the most educational of all human activities and a place in which the nature of morality can be *seen*. Art gives a clear sense to many ideas which seem more puzzling when we meet them elsewhere.'[11] She continues:

> we may be able to learn more about the central area of morality if we examine what are essentially the same concepts more simply on display elsewhere.[12]

---

6   A Edgar, 'Velázquez and the Representation of Dignity' (2003) 6 *Medicine, Health Care and Philosophy* 111.
7   ibid.
8   A Margalit, 'Human Dignity, Between Kitsch and Deification' in C Cordner (ed), *Philosophy, Ethics, and a Common Humanity: Essays in Honour of Raimond Gaita* (London, Routledge, 2011).
9   H Joas, *Die Sakralität der Person. Eine neue Genealogie der Menschenrechte* (Berlin, Suhrkamp, 2012), trans as *The Sacredness of the Person: A New Genealogy of Human Rights* (Washington DC, Georgetown University Press, 2013).
10 I am thinking, in particular, of the debate in the legal academy over the use of literary texts since JB White's *The Legal Imagination: Studies in the Nature of Legal Thought and Expression* (Boston, Little, Brown and Co., 1973), in which the use of literature is seen as a valuable means of illuminating law by stimulating critical thought.
11 I Murdoch, *The Sovereignty of Good* (London, Ark Paperbacks, 1985) 87 f. I am grateful to Emily Kidd White for drawing this to my attention.
12 ibid 89.

This aspect of the article is, however, a secondary element, and one that I shall only hint at in addressing my primary concern.

Figure 1: Diego Velázquez, *Las Meninas,* Museo del Prado

III. Looking at Las Meninas

Let's turn to look at the painting itself. It's a complex painting. Here is *one* way of viewing what is going on, although this interpretation is contested.[13] What we seem to see is a self-portrait of Velázquez, painting the king and queen of Spain, King Philip IV and his second wife Mariana of Austria, who are standing where we, the spectators, are placed. The king and queen are seen reflected in a mirror at the back of the room. Looking at the king and queen as they are being painted, and looking at us, the spectators, is a group composed from among the royal household—the extended 'family' of the royal couple; indeed, the painting was originally known by a title that reflected this 'family' element.[14] The apparent centerpiece of this group is a young girl, the five-year-old Infanta, Doña Margaret Theresa, their daughter. She is with two of her ladies-in-waiting, or *meninas*, on either side of her. On the right of the painting is Doña Isabel de Velasco. On the left of the painting is Doña Maria Agustina Sariento, who is offering the Infanta something to drink, in a red cup on a silver tray. They form the main group. It looks like the Infanta is perhaps playing up, because the *meninas* look as if they are trying to surround her, dancing attendance on her, even perhaps trying to control her.

Outside this group, there is an additional collection of people. To the right of the painting as we look at it, there is what looks like a young boy, but whom we know is Nicolasito Pertusato, who is actually a dwarf. He is prodding what appears to be a sleeping dog, possibly playing with it, or trying to provoke it. Next to him, there is another dwarf; she is Mariabárbola. Behind the two dwarfs are two other people, one apparently dressed in religious garb, Doña Marcela de Ulloa, the Infanta's chaperone (or *guardamujer*). She is talking to an unidentified soldier or bodyguard. And last, there is a courtier at the back of the painting, standing in the doorway. He is Don José Nieto Velázquez, the queen's chamberlain. So, what is it about 'human dignity' that causes me to feel I should resort to choosing art to help our understanding, and why does *Las Meninas* help in this regard?

---

13   On the variety of possible interpretations, see R Wicks, 'Using Artistic Masterpieces as Philosophical Examples: The Case of *Las Meninas*' (2010) 68 *Journal of Aesthetics and Art Criticism* 259.

14   It was originally known as *El Cuadro de la Familia*, then as *La Familia de Filipe IV*.

IV. Relating Las Meninas to Dignity

One of the current problems with 'dignity-talk', at least in some jurisdictions, is what has been termed 'dignity-fatigue', which I understand to mean that the current ubiquity of the concept is leading to its degradation. Dignity is now so commonplace that it ceases to have the power that it once had in pointing to important fundamentals. This degradation is important, not least because 'human dignity' has been identified as *a*, if not *the*, central principle on which human rights are based; if 'dignity' becomes degraded, then so too will human rights. Here, perhaps, is where other media can assist—in confronting the spectator directly, without the 'corrupting' effect of an overused word.

There are several further functions that *Las Meninas* might play initially in understanding the idea of dignity. One important debate in our current attempts to understand the concept concerns the *history* of the concept: there is an debate between those who see the use of human dignity in earlier times as having a significant degree of continuity of meaning with its use in later times, as opposed to those who see the history of dignity as one of significant discontinuities in meaning.[15] Does dignity have a relatively similar meaning in different historical contexts? And what are the implications if it doesn't? In thinking further about this debate, we might look at *Las Meninas* as a historical artifact and think about what it tells us about the evolution of the meaning of dignity in the Spanish court of the 17th Century, in much the same way as Lynn Hunt and Joseph Slaughter attempt to do with the concept of 'human rights' by examining novels.[16]

Second, we might look at *Las Meninas* not from the historical perspective but more broadly: as a way of articulating (representing?) something of universal significance that is true across space and time, helping us to understand how dignity is to be understood as a principle that transcends historical contingency. For example, a powerful understanding of dignity is that it expresses the idea that a person should be accorded respect due to

---

15 Contrast the approaches adopted by S Moyn, 'The Secret History of Constitutional Dignity' in C McCrudden (ed), *Understanding Human Dignity* (Oxford, Oxford University Press, 2013) and R Scott, 'Dignité/Dignidade: Organizing Against Threats to Dignity in Societies after Slavery' in McCrudden, *Understanding Human Dignity*.
16 L Hunt, *Inventing Human Rights: A History* (New York, WW Norton, 2008); JR Slaughter, *Human Rights, Inc: The World Novel, Narrative Form, and International Law* (New York, Fordham University Press, 2007).

their status, as opposed to the view that dignity involves the deeper issue of what it means to be human. Terms like 'equal moral worth', or in German '*Menschenwürde*,' capture this idea. The problem in undertaking this second approach is that we may feel that in seeing the universal represented in the painting all we do is to find our current understanding; that all perspectives of dignity, perhaps, are necessarily contingent and context specific. (We might even think that this is true of all supposed universal principles: that we simply translate whatever is current into that principle.) Dignity (and this painting) is conceived to be an empty vessel into which each generation pours its own understandings.

I should say immediately that I do not think that Velázquez intended *Las Meninas* to represent 'Dignity', in the sense that those in the tradition of iconology that preceded him sought explicitly to 'represent' particular virtues.[17] But I do partly engage here in what Suzanne Stratton-Pruitt has termed an 'emblematic reading' of the painting, by which she means a reading of a painting that sees it as 'representing' something additional to the subjects that form the ostensible basis of the painting.[18] In my case, I want to explore the extent to which *Las Meninas* can usefully be seen as emblematic, even if unintentionally, of 'dignity'. But perhaps it is better to say that I adopt what Denis Donoghue has described as 'interpretation as exemplification', where 'someone analyses a work of art not for its own sake but to offer it as an example, proof, or illustration of some argument he wants to make'.[19] All this is by way of entering a caveat: this chapter is emphatically *not* an attempt at art history or art criticism, as those disciplines are traditionally conceived.

V. Dignity as Rank and Honor

How does the painting relate to dignity? To begin with, there is a very clear picture of one understanding of dignity captured in the form of the Infanta. If ever there was someone conscious of her dignity, in the sense of her honor and her rank, it is she. This is the sense in which EH Gombrich could write that the royals in Velázquez's paintings 'were men and women

---

17   See, eg, Cesare Ripa Perugino, *Iconologia* (1618), in which Dignity is portrayed in the guise of a woman bearing [bearing up?] under a heavy load.
18   Stratton-Pruitt, *Velázquez' Las Meninas* 126.
19   D Donoghue, quoted by Stratton-Pruitt, *Velázquez' Las Meninas* 134.

who insisted upon their dignity'.[20] And those dancing attendance are also clearly conscious of the difference in rank, not only in focusing on the Infanta (the lady-in-waiting to her left is kneeling), but also (in the case of the second lady-in-waiting) in being careful to keep a close eye on the king and queen, seeming to check with them what she needs to do. The painting presents the different ranks in the royal household.[21] So, we clearly have a strong representation of dignity in the sense of rank, honor, and social status. And we are quite able to understand this, and appreciate its advantages (after all, it resulted in Velázquez painting this scene, didn't it?), at the same time as worrying about the inequality and hierarchy on which it was based.[22]

The idea of dignity as honor remains highly important in some legal contexts, particularly in the law of countries influenced by Roman Law.[23] That use is, however, a remnant. Some argue that the way we should understand the modern conception of dignity is to build on this idea of dignity as status, but to democratize it, introducing an egalitarian element into the equation. Jeremy Waldron suggests that modern democratic dignity accords to every person that which formerly only aristocrats were accorded.[24] And this has, indeed, some persuasive force.[25] So, we can quite easily imagine (at least those of us fortunate enough to have daughters) how we might want the Infanta's self-confidence and poise to be something all little girls of her age develop. As a general proposition, however, Waldron's argument simply doesn't work. In particular, borrowing from Don

---

20   EH Gombrich, *The Story of Art*, 5th edn (London, Phaidon, 1989) 320, quoted in Edgar, 'Velázquez and the Representation of Dignity' 112.
21   Edgar, 'Velázquez and the Representation of Dignity' 119.
22   The advantages of hierarchy in producing great art are highlighted in G Katab, *Human Dignity* (Cambridge, Mass, Harvard University Press, 2012).
23   'In a Roman context, *dignitas* very much meant rank or status. Individuals were endowed with different degrees of *dignitas*, and the delict *inuria* could be said to have at its core the disruption of this hierarchy; *inuria* was committed whenever the defendant willfully raised himself above, or brought the claimant below, the status granted to them by society.' E Descheemaeker, 'Solatium and Injury to Feelings: Roman Law, English Law and Modern Tort Theory' in E Descheemaeker and H Scott (eds), *Inuria and the Common Law* (Oxford, Hart Publishing, 2013) 94.
24   J Waldron, *Dignity, Rank, and Rights* (M Dan-Cohen ed, Oxford, Oxford University Press, 2012).
25   Similar arguments have been made by KA Appiah, *The Honor Code: How Moral Revolutions Happen* (New York, WW Norton, 2011) 130.

Herzog and Michael Rosen's critiques of Waldron,[26] the Infanta's dignity depends on others *not* having the same status as she has. Indeed, not all of the many advantages possessed by her, and the aristocratic class of which she is a member, *should* be accorded to everyone. Generalizing or equalizing the privilege to everyone would hardly fit modern ideas of human dignity.

We can also test Waldron's understanding of dignity by turning back to *Las Meninas*, and considering the figure of Velázquez himself. One of the most striking features of this figure is the presence of a red cross on his tunic. This represents the Cross of St James of the Order of Santiago, and the consensus among art historians is that this must have been added later, since he only received the honor after the painting had been completed.[27] To be made a knight of this Order required the consent of a commission established to enquire into the purity of the candidate's lineage. The aim of these enquiries was to prevent the appointment of anyone found to have even a taint of 'heresy' in their background, a broad concept that included having a trace of Jewish or Moorish blood; Velázquez's possible Jewish heritage[28] had to be waived aside. How can we generalize to everyone the anti-Semitism and hypocrisy on which this system of dignity depends? The honor bestowed depended on its being exclusive and exclusionary.

VI. Dignity of Art, and Dignity of Work

There is, however, an additional interpretation of the figure of Velázquez in the painting that gives a different meaning also to the inclusion of the Cross of the Order of Santiago on Velázquez's chest. To become a member of the Order, it was also necessary that a candidate establish that he was not contaminated by engagement with trade or commerce on either side of the family. Velázquez's plebeian origins, and his occupation as an artist engaged in the commerce of being paid to paint, were therefore important barriers to gaining membership. In this interpretation, the painting represents part of Velázquez's claim that he was worthy to be included in

---

26 Don Herzog's critique is contained as a comment in Waldron, *Dignity, Rank, and Rights* 99. M Rosen's critique along similar lines is to be found at 79.
27 S Alpers, 'Interpretation Without Representation, or, the Viewing of *Las Meninas*' (1983) 1 *Representations* 31, 41 fn 5.
28 Wicks, 'Using Artistic Masterpieces as Philosophical Examples' 272 fn 24.

the Order because engaging in artistic production was meritorious, and was worthy of praise and honor, an honor subsequently recognized by the award of the Order. Seen from this perspective, the painting is an attempt by Velázquez to assert 'the dignity of his art'.[29]

Was this also a way of asserting the 'dignity of work', that later 19th Century trade unionists and others loudly proclaimed? Some have seen this broader implication in the painting. Bryon Hamann's study of *Las Meninas* seeks to 'restore visibility to men and women who cannot be directly seen within the painting itself',[30] by focusing on the silver tray on which the red ceramic cup is placed, together with the deep red curtains hanging over the heads of the king and queen. Each of these, he argues, derived in one way or another from Spain's American colonies. For Hamann, applying a materialist postcultural interpretation, these objects 'can be read as reflections of the value-producing labor of men and women' in these colonies, and therefore as introducing into the painting a recognition of what would later be called 'the dignity of labor'.[31]

However, as Emily Umberger and Francesca Bavuso observe in their response to Hamann, there is no evidence that either Velázquez or his European audience was 'particularly conscious' of these implications.[32] Indeed, rather than trying to hint at the dignity of labor of the sort that produced the objects included in the painting, Velázquez 'was distancing himself from lower-class artists and craftsmen'.[33] For Alpers, the painting is a

> claim for the nobility of painting as a liberal art and … a personal claim for nobility on the part of Velázquez himself. In short, Las Meninas is now interpreted as a visual statement of the social rank desired by the painter.[34]

After all, associating his work with that of the laboring classes would have further discouraged the award of the honor of membership of the Order.

---

29 J Brown and C Garrido, *Velázquez, The Technique of Genius* (New Haven, Yale University Press, 1998) 27, quoted in Edgar, 'Velázquez and the Representation of Dignity' 120.
30 B Hamann, 'The Mirrors of *Las Meninas*: Cochineal, Silver, and Clay' (2010) 92 *The Art Bulletin* 6, 29.
31 ibid.
32 E Umberger and F Bavuso, 'Reflections on Reflections' (2010) 92 *The Art Bulletin* 54, 57.
33 ibid 56.
34 S Alpers, 'Interpretation Without Representation' 33.

The existence of such a strong distinction between labor and production, on the one hand, and artistic endeavor, on the other, does, however, point to a different conclusion regarding the 'dignity of labor'. By the late eighteenth century, as Umberger and Bavuso point out, the changes in economic thought regarding labor and production were beginning to be reflected in art, but not in the time of Velázquez.[35] 'What we see in the seventeenth century are ... steps in the development of such concerns.' In other words, our understanding of what constitutes 'dignity' changes over time and builds on what has gone before, spreading the net of empathy wider and wider. The logic of dignity seems to lead to it escaping the boundaries we seem to place on it. Velázquez's own *oeuvre* hints at this. An extraordinary, 1650 portrait in New York's Metropolitan Museum depicts Velázquez's Moorish slave, Juan de Pareja, who served as an assistant in his workshop, and whom he later freed. Here is someone who clearly possesses dignity, despite his origins and status, and his manual labor. Velázquez may have wanted to distinguish the dignity of the artist from productive labor in *Las Meninas*, but in his portrait of Juan de Pareja, this distinction is subtly undermined.[36]

---

35   ibid.
36   Historically, too, there is a connection between the 19th Century emancipation movement, and the development of the idea of the dignity of labor.

Figure 2: Diego Velázquez, *Juan de Pareja,* The Metropolitan Museum of Art

VII. The King's Two Dignities

The ambiguity that we see comparing Velázquez's paintings is reflected also in *Las Meninas* itself, although in a different way. There is, in the painting itself, a certain degree of ambiguity about dignity. We obtain some inkling of this by thinking more about the portrayal of the king and queen. In this period, and indeed later, 'dignity' was often associated with the office that a person held. This understanding of 'dignity', as something associated with the status of office, goes back to Roman times. The king is in a particularly interesting position in this regard. The dignity of the king, *qua* king, had long been recognized. In England, for example, Elizabethan judges recognized the king as possessing a 'Body politic, which contains his royal Estate and Dignity'.³⁷ But this gave rise to a problem: how should we regard the king otherwise?

To solve this problem, the king was recognized as having 'two bodies', the Body politic and the Body natural. For Ernst Kantorowicz, the fascinating contortions that this gave rise to provided endless interest, but for our purposes one in particular is pregnant with meaning for understanding the development of dignity. We see in the portraiture of the royals in the Spanish court of the 16th Century a similar understanding of the dual nature of kingship, both office and person at the same time. For Erasmus of Rotterdam, it was the king's 'inner virtues, not the symbols of power and authority' that 'made a truly good king'. The king's 'prestige, his greatness, his regal dignity must not be established and preserved by noisy displays of privileged rank but by wisdom, integrity, and right action'.³⁸ We begin to see, therefore, the development of the idea of 'dignity' as arising not from holding a particular office, but from possessing particular qualities.

Antorio Feros argues that the Spanish royals, at the time of Velázquez,

> sought to cultivate this Erasmian iconographic model of the ideal monarch, privileging a pictorial representation ... of the king as an individual who embodied the virtues of a good ruler ...³⁹

Velázquez depicted the royals as virtuous, paternalistic, and benevolent rulers'.⁴⁰ What better way to do this than to portray the king and queen, as in *Las Meninas*, as surrounded by his 'family', which for many years was regarded as a metaphor for the people as a whole?⁴¹ By emphasizing the king's Body natural, his true dignity as king arises from his individual virtues. It is a relatively small step from seeing dignity arising from particular human qualities to seeing dignity arising from the quality of being human, another way in which dignity seems able to escape its boundaries. We can see a hint, therefore, of the parallel understanding of dignity that had emerged earlier, one not based in the status of office, but based rather in

---

37   Quoted in EH Kantorowicz, *The King's Two Bodies* (Princeton, Princeton University Press, 1957) 9.
38   Quoted in A Feros, '"Sacred and Terrifying Gazes": Languages and Images of Power in Early Modern Spain' in Stratton-Pruitt, *Cambridge Companion to Velázquez* 83.
39   ibid.
40   ibid 86.
41   JM Blythe, 'Family, Government, and the Medieval Aristotelians' (1989) 10 *History of Political Thought* 4.

one's position as a person. Kantorowicz credits Dante with the essence of the same idea in his description of 'Man' in the *Inferno*, and with it the idea of Dignity attaching to a person by virtue of being a 'Man', an understanding reflected also in Pico's famous oration, often seen as one of the earliest articulations of a humanistic understanding of dignity.[42] In this context, dignity is understood as the inestimable value we regard human persons as having, simply in virtue of the basic human qualities they possess as humans.

VIII. Dignified Behavior

We shall return to this point subsequently, but before doing so, we need to complicate things a little more, by introducing a further understanding of dignity as 'dignified behavior', especially in the face of trial and adversity. We say that a person acts with dignity, for example, when they don't collapse when someone close to them dies. Terms like fortitude, forbearance, acting with restraint in the face of adversity, are all associated with this idea.

With that idea in mind, let's turn to another, for me perhaps the most noteworthy feature of *Las Meninas*. Apart from the Infanta, what is particularly striking about the scene presented to us is the inclusion of the two dwarfs. That the dwarfs are included in the family group at all is highly significant. Dwarfs had been included in numerous paintings prior to Velázquez, but

> they were almost never depicted as autonomous beings; rather they are shown as decorative elements situated at the fringes of the lives of others more important than themselves.[43]

Velázquez, however, painted at least ten portraits of dwarfs, which transcend this tradition. *Las Meninas* is, apparently, one of the first examples in modern portraiture of servants being painted literally on the same level as the master. The dwarf to the left of the picture is probably achondroplastic, which accounts for her size and shape. But, significantly, she is portrayed as taller than the Infanta. Also, as Janet Ravenscroft points out,

---

42 Kantorowicz, *The King's Two Bodies* 493.
43 BM Adelson, *The Lives of Dwarfs: Their Journey from Public Curiosity Towards Social Liberation* (New Brunswick, NJ, Rutgers University Press, 2005) 146.

she 'is not actively serving the young princess, but rather stands and gazes confidently out at the viewer' (and, of course, at the King and Queen also).[44]

One of the attractive qualities of Velázquez's paintings is his willingness to paint some of the most excluded parts of human society. Let's turn first to another of Velázquez's dwarf paintings also now in the Prado, the 1645 portrait of the dwarf Sebastián de Morra, who was a jester at the court of Philip. Velázquez portrays his whole body, sitting on the ground, wearing a rich cloak but with his short legs pointing forward in an inelegant position reminiscent of a marionette. He looks directly at the viewer. His hands are motionless, but they appear to be tightly clenched. With this painting, we should also revisit Velázquez's painting of his slave, Juan de Pareja, who exudes a quiet confidence, an inner strength.

---

44 J Ravenscroft, 'Invisible Friends: Questioning the Representation of the Court Dwarf in Hapsburg Spain' in W Ernst (ed), *Histories of the Normal and the Abnormal: Social and Cultural Histories of Norms and Normativity* (London, Routledge, 2006) 46.

Figure 3: Diego Velázquez, *The Buffoon Sebastián de Morra,* Museo del Prado

One way of viewing these dwarfs and the slave is as examples of dignified behavior in the face of adversity: the noble slave, proud and unbowed despite his slavery; the suggestion in Sebastián de Morra's expression of a barely suppressed frustration at his physical condition and an implicit denunciation of the court's humiliating treatment of him and other dwarfs.[45] Or, we might see something deeper, of Velázquez's attempt to capture something in the human person that transcends their temporal status. So, JP Dominguez has written that Velázquez painted them 'with humanity' showing them to be 'as human as their masters'. He concludes: 'He respected their dignity as human beings and delineated their individual personalities.'[46] Why is his portrait of the slave so striking? Not because the slave was equal in status to Velázquez, he clearly isn't, but because the human in the slave is so clearly recognized and recognizable. We see the slave's humanity, *in spite* of his servitude; *in spite* of his inequality, *in spite* of his lowly position in the hierarchy. And so it is with Sebastián de Morra and the dwarfs in *Las Meninas*. But why?

IX. Dignity and Autonomy

One explanation may lie in the fact that several of those portrayed look out at us from the painting. As Edgar observes, Morra 'stares back at the spectator'.[47] We earlier used the word 'gaze' to describe what the subjects in *Las Meninas* are doing. The word 'gaze' is important here. Svetlana Alpers distinguishes between a gaze and a glance. The gaze, as is the case in this painting, 'signals from within the picture that the viewer outside the picture is seen and in turn it acknowledges the state of being seen'.[48] Our eyes meet, and we are on the same level. The Morra painting,

---

45   A point made by Edgar, 'Velázquez and the Representation of Dignity' 117. See further Adelson, *The Lives of Dwarfs* 149 (discussing the views of others who made similar observations). The portrayal of dwarfs in *Las Meninas* is now a subject of interest in disability studies, see, for example, M Davidson, The Rage of Caliban: Missing Bodies in Modernist Aesthetics, available at: www.northumbria.ac.uk/static/5007/fadss/Lect_3_Rage_of_Caliban.pdf.
46   JP Dominguez, 'El niño de Valladares [Francisco Lezcano]' (1989) 261 *Journal of the American Medical Association* 496.
47   Edgar, 'Velázquez and the Representation of Dignity' 118.
48   Alpers, 'Interpretation Without Representation' 32.

... in effect demands that the spectator interacts with Morra as an equal. That is to say that Morra is necessarily attributed the rights of a competent and equal participant in social interaction.[49]

He exercises agency; he is an autonomous individual.

Velázquez's portrayal of the dwarfs is in marked contrast to other depictions. Those who have seen *The Wolf of Wall Street*[50] will remember vividly the scene in which the traders, masters of the universe, New York gods we might say, are discussing the hiring of a dwarf to be used as a human dart, to be fitted with Velcro and thrown against a huge dart board. It is significant that in the film, the traders continually refer to the dwarf they will hire as 'it'. Not he, not she; but 'it'. A thing, not a person. Something to be instrumentalized in the crudest way. And readers who know the jurisprudence on dignity, will know well that one of the most famous cases deals with dwarf-throwing and the compatibility of this activity with the idea of human dignity.[51] Mr Manuel Wackenheim complained to the United Nations Human Rights Committee that, when France banned dwarf throwing, he was put out of a job which he regarded as rewarding, particularly given the difficulties he faced in getting other employment. France argued that the ban was in the interests of protecting human dignity. Wackenheim argued that putting him out of a job infringed his *autonomy*; indeed, some view this idea of autonomy as itself what dignity is about, and the ban on dwarf throwing as moralistic paternalism.

X. Sense and Sensibility Towards the Human Person

But *France* won in the Human Rights Committee, not Mr Wackenheim. Unlike Edgar, the Committee did not accept that *Menschenwürde* is equivalent to the exercise of autonomy and reason. An individualistic, autonomy-based understanding of dignity did not capture its meaning; in-

---

49 Edgar, 'Velázquez and the Representation of Dignity' 118.
50 *Wolf of Wall Street*, 2013, based on the autobiographical account by J Belfort of his own rise and fall, see *The Wolf of Wall Street* (New York, Bantam, 2007).
51 *Wackenheim v France*, Communication No 854/1999, U.N. Doc. CCPR/C/75/D/854/1999 (2002). Similar decisions have resulted in several different jurisdictions, eg in Germany, see Beschluss des VG Neustadt vom 21.05.1992 - Aktz: 7 L 1271/92, available at: http://www.saarheim.de/Entscheidungen/VG%20Neustadt%20-%207%20L%201271aus92.htm.

stead, we find a relational understanding of dignity, where Mr Wackenheim's willingness to be thrown, his willingness to be humiliated, had to be seen as having adverse effects on others, notably other dwarfs. There is an additional problem with interpreting dignity as 'autonomy'. Edgar argues that the paintings of the slave, or the dwarfs, *because* they emphasize autonomy and reason, fall short of portraying the value of the human simply in virtue of their humanity, and that this is shown by the absence of equivalent dignity being accorded to those portrayed in two other paintings by Velázquez, the paintings of Calabazas and Francisco Lezcano.[52] In these paintings, two other court jesters are portrayed, both of them mentally disabled. In neither of these paintings does Edgar find the dignity that is present in the painting of Morra. Although all the subjects gaze back at us, the two court jesters do not interact with us in the way that the others do. For this reason, he argues, there is 'not yet dignity as *Menschenwürde*, for there is no clear identification of such grounding human capacities of autonomy and reason'.[53]

---

52   Edgar, 'Velázquez and the Representation of Dignity' 120.
53   ibid.

Figure 4: Diego Velázquez, *El bufón Calabacillas,* Museo del Prado

On Portraying Human Dignity

Figure 5: Francisco Lezcano, *El Niño de Vallecas,* Museo del Prado

If the idea of dignity we get from the painting isn't satisfied by a status-based approach, or one based on the idea of the dignified person suffering in silence, or autonomy, what else is there? I've suggested earlier that a core meaning of dignity is the idea that the individual person has dignity simply by virtue of being human, and that this is an understanding of the

45

human in relation to others. For me, what comes from the portraits of the dwarfs is the same deep impression that we get from the portrait of the slave, a sense of him as a person, not a thing, and the same goes for the representation of the dwarfs, and of the jesters.

One way of capturing this specialness is to think of the human as in some way 'sacred'. For Hans Joas, the connecting thread in the history of human rights is in this 'sacralization of the person'.[54] The belief in human rights and universal human dignity is, he argues,

> the result of a specific process of sacralization—a process in which every single human being has increasingly, and with ever-increasing motivational and sensitizing effects, been viewed as sacred, and this understanding has been institutionalized in law.

Whilst acknowledging the importance of Lynn Hunt's work, he distinguishes her idea of the 'expansion of empathy' from his idea of the 'progressive sacralization of the person'. For Joas, the 'dimension of sacralization' seems 'more fundamental than that of empathy'. People choose whether to 'allow their capacity for empathy ... to come into operation'; it needs something to get it going.[55] Empathy depends, he suggests, on the sacralization of the person for its effectiveness in practice, because the sacralization of the person 'motivates us to show empathy; empathy alone does not engender the sacralization of the person, of all persons.'[56]

Joas then asks: 'Why do people experience certain things as sacred? And how do we get to a point where each person becomes sacred ...?'[57] The answers to these questions, he suggests, lie in

> a theory of the genesis of values, an investigation into value-constitutive experiences and especially those experiences that may give rise to an affective attachment to values rooted in moral universalism.[58]

He portrays the genesis and development of human rights 'as a history of the relocating' of 'subjective certainty, the sense of self-evidence and affective intensity of the kind characteristic of the sacred'.[59] This process 'straddles the sphere of practices, values, and institutions'.[60]

---

54 Joas, *The Sacredness of the Person* 5: 'the history of human rights is a history ... of the sacralization of the person'.
55 ibid 59.
56 ibid 60.
57 ibid 153.
58 ibid 153.
59 ibid 173.
60 ibid 173.

Joas demonstrates this by detailed studies of specific historical changes, considering how, in the case of torture, it was transformed from being widely practiced and acceptable before the 18th Century, to being largely unacceptable by the mid-19th Century. The changes that occurred in the 18th Century involved, he argues, a 'profound cultural shift in which the human person became a sacred object', which meant the 'integration of those—such as criminals ... —who had not been self-evidently included within this concept' previously.[61] So too, he sees 'the demand for the abolition of slavery' in the 19th Century as 'another radical movement for inclusion'.[62] He describes the movement for abolitionism as a 'morally informed movement' that saw the world 'from the perspective of others and not just those with whom we are linked by established affective ties ...'.[63] Armed with this insight, we can return, yet again, to *Las Meninas*. What is its relevance to Joas' argument? Martha Nussbaum has suggested that the added value that literature and, by extension, art bring to the philosophical, political, and legal controversy is not sense (meaning rationality) but sensibility, an orientation towards the human person.[64] She doesn't call this dignity, but there is a strong resemblance. Velázquez, painting in 17th Century Spain, seems to provide an earlier, if limited, example of the phenomenon that Joas describes, but, in doing so, he also provides a portrait that continues to speak to us in these terms.

XI. Does Art Help or Hinder?

We need to be careful however. Both Emmanuel Levinas and Avishai Margalit have warned, in different but related ways, of potential problems that can make the use of visual representations for the purpose of understanding dignity a parlous exercise. For Levinas, the problem is that the use of such representations threatens to weaken, if not destroy, the humanity that it aims to capture.[65] Levinas grounds the phenomenon of the hu-

---

61 ibid 49.
62 ibid 63. This is examined in detail in ch 3.
63 ibid 91.
64 MC Nussbaum, '"Finely Aware and Richly Responsible": Moral Attention and the Moral Task of Literature' (1985) 82 *Journal of Philosophy* 516.
65 This account draws heavily from the excellent discussion by J Zimmermann, 'Levinas's Humanism of the Other' in id, *Humanism and Religion: A Call for the Renewal of Western Culture* (Oxford, Oxford University Press, 2012).

man (including human dignity) in the personal, transcendent, ethical demand of another human being. Being human means having concern for others. Encountering the 'other' face-to-face becomes the most foundational structure of human reality. But art has a tendency to distort face-to-face relationships. Art, he argues, consists in substituting an *image* for the object it is portraying. Art's image-making no longer maintains a living relationship to the concept portrayed but freezes it in the image. The image not only objectifies the 'other', but also ensnares the spectator. Images encourage spectators to think of themselves as mere objects among other objects. As a result, he suggests, art encourages passivity and thus diminishes our sense of responsibility. Art not only does not have the human quality of the living instant, it can also enchant with its beauty. Art's beauty lures us into a world without suffering and justice, again encouraging the evasion of responsibility. Art places its own representation between the person viewing the picture and reality, becoming a barrier to a real encounter. In a painting, the represented elements do not serve as symbols by which one gains access to a reality; rather, their presence bars the way to a living reality.

For Levinas, however, art is not necessarily irredeemable, but it requires the voice of the art critic to free the ethical from the freezing effect of the artistic method. Criticism integrates the inhuman work of the artist back into the human world, by re-attaching the artist and his work to its socio-political influences, to real history. But the art critic needs the help of the philosopher, for philosophy understands the larger and deeper sources of the emergence of art. Only ethical transcendence carried out by art critics, assisted by philosophy, prevents art from becoming mere images of reality or idolatrous vehicles of pleasure. Ethical transcendence restores our encounter with, and responsibility to, others, in whose proximity we can detect the trace of a just God.

We can leave to one side whether this understanding is convincing more generally, and focus on whether it captures what happens when we view *Las Meninas*. On the one hand, it is clear that we are drawn into the painting, and on one view at least we are encouraged to think of ourselves as sharing in the status of the King and Queen. But does this render the viewer passive, and dull our sense of responsibility? And is the top-down, elitist view that we need the art critic and philosopher to understand it correct? In these respects at least, Levinas fails to convince. Indeed, Velázquez seems to have gone out of his way to prevent us, the viewer, settling into the role of passive object, and encouraged us to explore our role. As Leo Steinberg has observed, there is a 'kind of reciprocity':

Something we bring to the picture—the very effectiveness of our presence—ricochets from the picture, provokes an immediate response, a reflex of mutual fixation ...[66]

The perspectival complexity of the painting means that we are constantly challenged to locate where we stand.[67] Are we standing together with the King and Queen, thus appearing to be accorded their status and perspective?[68] Or, rather, as careful geometric analysis of the painting has suggested, has the audience an eye level of about 4½ feet, which indicates we may be the same height as one of the dwarfs, with a very different perspective from that of the King and Queen? The effect, therefore, is to require us to think carefully about who we are, and what our perspective is (literally and figuratively). This does not support a Levinasian interpretation; rather the opposite.

XII. Dignity and Kitsch

For Margalit, there is a different, but equally unfortunate, tendency in the discussion of human dignity in the secular context: to conceive of the individual in highly sentimentalized terms, and it is on this aspect of portraying dignity through art that I want to focus now. Human rights activism is especially prone to the tendency towards this sentimentality, or *kitsch*. In order to promote the cause of the moment, we seek to construct a narrative of a pure victimhood (preferably in the shape of a child), one who has suffered something abominable, but is without anger or motives of revenge, and certainly defenseless, without deadly weapons with which to respond. Seeking an understanding of what it means to be human from art may encourage, I think, a particular tendency towards *kitsch* of the type that Margalit identifies. And when we combine art with human rights, this tendency is particularly on display; think of the powerful impact of photographic images in human rights campaigning.

Strategically, of course, sentimentality may have a critically important role to play in bringing about a degree of sensibility towards others, even a degree of empathy. But we shouldn't mistake the strategy and its effects

---

66 L Steinberg, 'Velázquez' *Las Meninas*' (1981) 19 *October* 45, 50.
67 See the discussion in Wicks, 'Using Artistic Masterpieces as Philosophical Examples' 265–68.
68 As Foucault, *Les Mots et Les Choses* 15, appeared to believe.

for a foundational concept strong enough to ground human rights. Empathy, as Joas argues, must be based on something more grounded if it is to be anything other than ephemeral. The question is whether the concept of human dignity supplies that need. Is it a concept we can rely on to provide both sense and sensibility, but without losing the critical importance of actual people, and without descending into *kitsch* sentimentality?

XIII. Dignity and Animals

Look at the dog in *Las Meninas*. Would the dog be included within the scope of dignity? Probably not. But *why* not? Something deeper must be going on. Note, first, that one of the dwarfs has his foot on the dog, and is possibly kicking it, demonstrating his mastery over the dog, an echo perhaps of the famous passage in the *Book of Genesis*, in which God gives Man mastery over all living things.[69] Note also that unlike all the humans in the picture the dog has its eyes closed. As Foucault observed, the dog lying on the floor is 'the only element in the picture that is neither looking at anything nor moving, because it is not intended ... to be anything but an object to be seen'.[70]

What is it that distinguishes the human person, someone with human dignity, from something else that doesn't? Some consider that differences in capacities and capabilities are what distinguish the human from the non-human,[71] whilst others (I'm among them) think that this approach may create more problems than it solves. We consider the jesters human, do we not, despite their obviously limited capacities? So too, animals share some capacities with humans, whereas those humans in a permanent vegetative state have far fewer capacities. Why are animals not included within human dignity, and those permanently incapacitated included? For Margalit, the problem in discussions of dignity is the reverse of that identified by Levinas: a tendency to deify the human person, to turn the person into the creator of all things, the center of the universe, and representations may encourage this tendency. It is not merely coincidental that the same pas-

---

69   *Genesis*, ch 1, verse 28 (Authorized Version).
70   Foucault, *Les Mots et Les Choses* 14.
71   See, eg, C Tollefsen, 'The Dignity of Marriage' in McCrudden, *Understanding Human Dignity*.

sage in Genesis in which Man is given mastery of the earth also refers to Man being made in the Image of God.

XIV. Dignity and Religion

Here is where another important debate is central. How far does human dignity have religious and theological presuppositions embedded in it and, if so, is that a problem?[72] The idea of humans being made 'in the image of God' is the common Judeo-Christian way of capturing the idea that the individual is in some sense sacred, different from the rest of creation, and given mastery over it. The implications this has for the possibility of dialogue between those who share and those who do not share these presuppositions is extraordinarily important. How far can arguments based on the mystery of human personhood permit engagement with secular philosophers or lawyers? Is dignity viewed in this way simply a conversation stopper? Even if there is an added value that theological reflection brings to dignity, does it have a valid political or legal role to play? We shall return to consider this in a moment.

XV. The Pluralism of Meanings of Dignity

Before doing so, however, we need to step back and draw breath. So far, we have touched on at least five understandings of dignity: dignity as hierarchy, dignity as equal status, dignity as respect, dignity as dignified behavior, and dignity as the equal moral worth of human persons. These understandings are likely to conflict in significant respects. The conflict between religious and secular understandings of human dignity is only one set of conflicts apparent. There are various, sometimes overlapping, conflicts between the five understandings discussed.[73] As Joas puts it, what if, as happens in practice, 'one person's subjective sense of self-evidence diverges from another's or collides with it'? 'How then do we deal with

---

72　Contrast J Rivers, 'Justifying Freedom of Religion: Does Dignity Help?' in McCrudden, *Understanding Human Dignity*, with M Rosen, *Dignity: Its History and Meaning* (Cambridge, Mass, Harvard University Press, 2012).
73　See further the introductory chapter 'In Pursuit of Human Dignity: An Introduction to Current Debates' by C McCrudden in McCrudden, *Understanding Human Dignity*.

such disagreement when it comes to values?'[74] For Joas, it is possible to reach agreement on new areas of common ground. The character of this process can best be termed, following Parsons, 'value generalization'.[75] Parsons defines this as

> the inclusion, under a single legitimizing value-pattern, of components which are not only diverse and differentiated from each other, but many of which have, historically, claimed some sort of an 'absolutistic' monopoly of moral legitimacy.[76]

For Joas, Parsons's concept has two particularly important elements that distinguish it from other similar approaches: 'a dynamic process of mutual modification' and 'attention to the deeper layers of value systems and religions'.[77] Religious values and understandings have a role to play in the conversation, but not as a conversation-stopper.

We have seen that there are significant disputes between those who see human dignity as having particular core substantive meanings (and I've talked about the different varieties of these substantive meanings), and between those who consider dignity to have religious underpinnings and those who do not (and I've asked whether a reconciliation between these viewpoints can take place). Importantly, there is a debate among theologians and others as to how far how far religious traditions should be open to the world, how far secular thinking can inform, even change, religious understandings of dignity, or how far the relationship should always flow from religion to society, and never the other way. Joas encourages us to consider that understanding may best come from openness on all sides to the other.

XVI. Conclusion: An Unfinished Project and the Open Door

With that in mind, let's return to *Las Meninas* one last time and observe two further aspects of the painting that we haven't mentioned so far. We should pay some attention to the painting that Velázquez is pictured beside, paintbrush in hand. This is clearly unfinished. Carlos Fuentes, in an interesting aside, considers the implications of this. 'Does it not', he asks,

---

74   Joas, *The Sacredness of the Person* 173.
75   ibid 174.
76   ibid 179.
77   ibid 181.

raise the possibility that everything in the world—this paining, but also this history, this narrative—is unfinished? And that, more specifically, we are unfinished ourselves, men and women who cannot be declared 'complete,' enclosed within boundaries of finitude and certainty ...[78]

Let's now look at the chamberlain at the back of the room, in front of the open doorway. Without the doorway, drawing our gaze to the light, it would be an intensely closed, even claustrophobic, scene. There is only one other source of light from the window at the right of the painting, throwing light onto the Infanta. Because of its geometric position, the viewer is placed opposite this open doorway, looking through it to the light beyond.[79] The significance of the open doorway is greater, however, because of the figure of the Chamberlain. We aren't sure, are we, whether he is coming or going? But in any event, what is important is that the openness of the doorway shows us that there is an outside, a world beyond, and the light of that world is available, if we just draw aside the curtain, as the Chamberlain has done. There is a relatively clear symbolic importance that we can discern, with the open doorway and the light beyond symbolizing 'genuine enlightenment beyond the social order'.[80] As Robert Wicks suggests, 'only the painting's audience is in the position to see through the open, brightly illuminated doorway, beyond the painting's worldly realm and conceivably into the realm of the divine'. He continues that the message conveyed is that 'only by "standing outside of oneself"— in this case, only by standing outside of the painting—is the path to enlightenment discernable'.[81]

Combine the two elements: the unfinished canvas, and the open door leading to the light. From what I have suggested thus far, *Las Meninas* serves (literally) as a canvas on which the varieties of current debates about dignity can be illustrated and played with. It also has a 'distancing' function, helping us not only to depict and play with current debates, but also to break disciplinary boundaries current in the conduct of these debates.[82] Leaving the religious symbolism to one side, the open door in *Las*

78	C Fuentes, *The Buried Mirror: Reflections on Spain and the New World* (Boston, Houghton Mifflin, 1992) 182.
79	Wicks, 'Using Artistic Masterpieces as Philosophical Examples' 265.
80	ibid 268.
81	ibid 269.
82	See A Kemmerer, 'Dignified Disciplinarity: Towards a Transdisciplinary Understanding of Human Dignity' in McCrudden, *Understanding Human Dignity*.

Meninas can serve to symbolize another strand of thinking about dignity, one that has come to the fore relatively recently. This views dignity as having utility primarily as a functionally useful device, rather than necessarily one with a particular substantive meaning. Some consider that the concept of human dignity may be useful primarily for allowing a dialogue to continue between those who fundamentally disagree about what it is to be human.[83]

What the Chamberlain is doing, perhaps, is inviting us to join an unfinished conversation in which others outside the room are engaged. On this reading, what *Las Meninas* provides, ultimately, is an experience which encourages us to 'share the ethical framework' of other people, as Anil Gomes suggests great art may do.[84] In doing so, it seems a near perfect medium for better understanding the current dilemmas and debates over dignity; for in experiencing the painting we are pointed to the importance of what Murdoch called 'unselfing', 'the capacity to go beyond the personal prejudices arising from my own ego'.[85] It inculcates a capacity for standing in another person's shoes, a capacity that is at the core of reflexivity, the 'perception of other as individual'.[86] It is not unique in doing this, but it is nevertheless important, particularly when words that provide the language for expressing that perception begin to lose their power to move us, as threatens to be the case with 'dignity'.

---

[83] See, eg, R Siegel, 'Dignity and the Duty to Protect Unborn Life' in McCrudden, *Understanding Human Dignity* and P Carozza, 'Human Rights, Human Dignity, and Human Experience' in McCrudden, *Understanding Human Dignity*.

[84] A Gomes, 'Iris Murdoch on Art, Ethics, and Attention' (2013) 53 *British Journal of Aesthetics* 321.

[85] ibid 334.

[86] C Sedmak, 'Human Dignity, Interiority, and Poverty' in McCrudden, *Understanding Human Dignity* 562.

'The Moral Feeling Within Me': On Kant's Concept of Human Freedom and Dignity as Auto-Heteronomy

Ino Augsberg

I.

Taking a look at popular compendiums commenting on the German Basic Law and its fundamental idea that 'Human Dignity shall be inviolable', we find that according to the prevalent view presented in these books the philosophical foundations of this concept are threefold: the idea is based, first, on the ancient Stoa, second, on renaissance humanism,[1] and third and most importantly, on the philosophy of Enlightenment,[2] namely on the ideas of Immanuel Kant.[3] To be more precise, Kant's influence on the concept is highlighted with regard to two connected issues: the idea of autonomy on the one side[4] and the so-called 'object formula', that is to say the necessity to treat a human being not only as a means to achieve a certain aim, but always also as an end in herself or himself, on the other. While the second aspect is particularly important for the practical judicial implementation of the concept (though its connection with Kant's concept of human dignity is also disputed[5]), the more fundamental issues are associated with the first aspect. This holds true not only from a philosophical perspective, but also (as Alain Ehrenberg has recently shown with regard

---

1 See the contributions in R Gröschner, S Kirste and OW Lembcke (eds), *Des Menschen Würde – entdeckt und erfunden im Humanismus der italienischen Renaissance* (Tübingen, Mohr Siebeck, 2008).
2 See for a telling example F Hufen, *Staatsrecht II. Grundrechte* (Munich, C. H. Beck, 2007) 135 f.
3 See in more detail RA Lorz, *Modernes Grund- und Menschenrechtsverständnis und die Philosophie der Freiheit Kants* (Stuttgart, Boorberg, 1993) 119 ff.
4 See J Braun, 'Selbstbestimmung und Fremdbestimmung. Über die Schwierigkeit autonomen Handelns in einer heteronom bestimmten Gesellschaft' (2012) 43 *Rechtstheorie* 159, 159 f.
5 See D von der Pfordten, 'Zur Würde des Menschen bei Kant' in id (ed), *Menschenwürde, Recht und Staat bei Kant. Fünf Untersuchungen* (Paderborn, Mentis, 2009).

to our contemporary society[6]) from a sociological point of view. For the idea of the autonomous person exercising his or her free will is the basic premise of Kant's moral philosophy as well as of today's society and its legal framework. In a certain contrast to scholarly endeavours asserting the irrelevance of philosophical reflections on human dignity for the legal system—in fact a point Karl-Heinz Ladeur and I myself have tried to make[7]—and despite the fundamental differences which Kant himself states between moral and legal philosophy[8] one may assume, therefore, that a re- or deconstruction of this premise could tell us something about our contemporary concept of law.

With this in mind, in what follows I want to attempt a re-reading of some passages from Kant's most famous texts on practical philosophy. More precisely, I will focus on an aspect which Martin Heidegger, in his Marburg lecture in the summer of 1927—the year *Being and Time* was published—qualified as 'the most lucid phenomenological analysis of the phenomenon of morality that we find in Kant'[9]: the so-called 'moral feeling' of *Achtung*. By scrutinising this feeling in some detail I intend to demonstrate that both autonomy and dignity are highly ambivalent concepts in Kant's moral philosophy. As a comparative perspective on human dignity, this close reading of the philosophical tradition functions as a critical reminder: If the legal discourse refers to these concepts as a possible source of explanation for its own conceptions, it should at least recognise their complex and ambiguous structure in the original context.

II.

As is well known, Kant's entire moral philosophy is based on the fundamental distinction between the empirical sphere of the senses and corresponding inclinations on the one side and the transcendent realm of pure

---

6   See A Ehrenberg, *La société du malaise* (Paris, Odile Jacob, 2010).
7   See KH Ladeur and I Augsberg, *Die Funktion der Menschenwürde im Verfassungsstaat. Humangenetik – Neurowissenschaft – Medien* (Tübingen, Mohr Siebeck, 2008).
8   See D von der Pfordten, 'Kants Rechtsbegriff' in id (ed), *Menschenwürde, Recht und Staat bei Kant. Fünf Untersuchungen* (Paderborn, Mentis, 2009).
9   M Heidegger, *Die Grundprobleme der Phänomenologie. Marburger Vorlesung Sommersemester 1927. Gesamtausgabe Bd. 24*, 2nd edn, edited by FW von Herrmann (Frankfurt am Main, Klostermann, 1989) 189.

reason on the other. In order to safeguard its status as a truly universal commandment a priori, the moral law must not depend on any empirical, contingent event. It has to be conceived of as a purely rational construction, and that is to say, as the form of the law itself, devoid of any material aspects. Thus, the moral imperative is not merely effective in a hypothetical way, that is to say, valid only insofar as certain preconditions are fulfilled. Rather, its validity is unconditioned and absolute. Kant famously calls this kind of imperative 'categorical'.[10]

In the history of the reception of Kant's ideas, it is this aspect of his moral philosophy which has faced the most severe critique.[11] Critics have emphasised the 'emptiness' of this purely formal concept of law.[12]

However, viewed against the background of this general concept, a closer look at the development of Kant's ideas reveals a remarkable finding. For as Kant explains in the first part of the *Foundations of the Metaphysics of Morals*, we cannot get to know the moral law and its commandment by means of pure reason alone. Rather, what enables this insight is a strange hybrid, a 'moral feeling'[13] which is, according to Kant, nothing sensual, but a purely rational phenomenon, and therefore 'is regarded as an object neither of inclination nor of fear', and yet as 'something analogous to both'.[14] Kant calls this feeling *Achtung*, respect.[15] Its important role within the framework of Kant's concept becomes evident in the definition Kant gives of duty. Duty, Kant states, 'is the necessity to do an action from respect for law.'[16] On the one side, any moral obligation has to be met not only in accordance with, but because of the law, that is

---

10 See I Kant, *Foundations of the Metaphysics of Morals*, 2nd edn, translated by LW Beck (Upper Saddle River/NJ, Prentice-Hall, 1997) 30 f (*Grundlegung zur Metaphysik der Sitten*, BA 39 f).
11 See, eg, M Scheler, *Der Formalismus in der Ethik und die materiale Wertethik. Gesammelte Werke Bd. 2*, 5th edn (Bern, Francke, 1966) passim, esp 171 f.
12 See F Rosenzweig, *Der Stern der Erlösung* (Frankfurt am Main, Suhrkamp, 1988) 239; G Deleuze, 'On Four Poetic Formulas That Might Summarize the Kantian Philosophy' in id (ed): *Essays Critical and Clinical*, translated by DW Smith and MA Greco (London, Verso, 1998); G Deleuze, 'Sacher-Masoch und der Masochismus' in L von Sacher-Masoch (ed), *Venus im Pelz* (Frankfurt am Main, Insel, 1980) 233; on this, see S Žižek, *The Ticklish Subject. The Absent Centre of Political Ontology* (London, Verso, 1999) 364 ff.
13 Kant, *Foundations of the Metaphysics of Morals* 78 (*Grundlegung zur Metaphysik der Sitten*, BA 122).
14 ibid 17 (*Grundlegung zur Metaphysik der Sitten*, BA 16).
15 See ibid 16 f (*Grundlegung zur Metaphysik der Sitten*, BA 15 f).
16 ibid 16 (*Grundlegung zur Metaphysik der Sitten*, BA 14).

to say, action has to be taken not only according to duty, but from duty.[17] On the other side, 'law itself ... can be an object of respect *and thus* a command'.[18] Hence it is only *Achtung* which reveals the law as commandment, as a binding imperative, and thus enables obedience toward the law. Respect transforms the objective law into a subjective duty which is felt and has to be felt as an indomitable constraint (*Nötigung*) since the finite human will, exposed to the inclinations, 'is not by its nature necessarily obedient'.[19] What is more: since all 'respect for a person is only respect for the law',[20] our ability to recognise another human being as a moral person also depends on that moral sentiment.

Hence at a central point of his moral philosophy Kant confronts us with a phenomenon that does not fit well into the usual distinction between sensual and rational. Though respect is explicitly called a feeling, it is, according to Kant, 'not one received through any [outer] influence but is self-wrought by a rational concept'.[21] As such, it is evidently a challenge for the consistency of Kant's theory. In a way it transcends or undermines the borders of the philosophical framework. The least one can say is that it is hard to deduce from its premises. Kant himself repeatedly states that this feeling is inexplicable.[22] What is more, he explicitly calls it a 'paradox'.[23]

How can we deal with this paradox, then? How can we meet the challenge it presents to moral theory? One way is to attempt to get rid of this strange and vexing feeling by simply ignoring it.[24] Another way is to assert that it is simply misplaced. It should, as some scholars claim, be discussed as a phenomenon of empirical psychology, not of pure rationality.[25] Yet this strategy is not convincing. For the analysis of *Achtung* does

---

17   See ibid 12 ff (*Grundlegung zur Metaphysik der Sitten*, BA 8 ff).
18   ibid 16 (emphasis added) (*Grundlegung zur Metaphysik der Sitten*, BA 14).
19   ibid 29 (*Grundlegung zur Metaphysik der Sitten*, BA 37).
20   ibid 18 (*Grundlegung zur Metaphysik der Sitten*, BA 17).
21   ibid 17 (*Grundlegung zur Metaphysik der Sitten*, BA 16).
22   See, eg, ibid 77 f, 79 f (*Grundlegung zur Metaphysik der Sitten*, BA 121 f, 125).
23   ibid 56 (*Grundlegung zur Metaphysik der Sitten*, BA 84).
24   See, eg, von der Pfordten, *Menschenwürde, Recht und Staat bei Kant* (2009); G Prauss, *Kant über Freiheit als Autonomie* (Frankfurt am Main, Klostermann, 1983).
25   See, eg, HJ Paton, *The Categorical Imperative: A Study in Kant's Moral Philosophy* (Philadelphia, University of Pennsylvania Press, 1971) 63 ff; on this

not only take place within the *Foundations of the Metaphysics of Morals*. On the contrary, the topic is reconsidered and discussed at length in the *Critique of Practical Reason*. In fact, here Kant basically devotes an entire chapter 'On the incentives of pure practical reason' to dealing with *Achtung*.[26] Hence, despite its obscure status, *Achtung* obviously plays a distinct and pivotal role in the constitution of morality. In turning to this chapter, we can elucidate in more detail this function of respect within the framework of Kant's moral philosophy.

III.

However, a first look at this chapter seems to be rather disillusioning. The first sentences seem to underline the classical dichotomy of reason and feelings. Kant writes:

> What is essential to any moral worth of actions is *that the moral law determine the will immediately*. If the determination of the will takes place *conformably* with the moral law but only by means of a feeling, of whatever kind, that has to be presupposed in order for the law to become a sufficient determining ground of the will, so that the action is not done *for the sake of the law*, then the action will contain *legality* indeed but not *morality*.[27]

Thus Kant begins his explanation by stating once again that the moral law and the obedience to it cannot be based on empirical inclinations. Quite the contrary, these inclinations have to be overcome. And yet—and with this the perspective starts to change—even the pure will apparently needs some form of incentive (*Triebfeder*). The 'objective determining ground' (*objektiver Bestimmungsgrund*) needs some form of correlative 'subjective determining ground' (*subjektiv-hinreichender Bestimmungsgrund*),[28] though of course it cannot be an empirical, sensual one. The challenge, then, is to find an incentive which has nothing to do with sensual motives but functions in an opposite way, as a rejection of all empirical inclinations. This incentive constitutes the core of the problem Kant elaborates

---

and similar misunderstandings see B Recki, *Ästhetik der Sitten* (Frankfurt am Main, Vittorio Klostermann, 2001) 282 ff with further references.

26   See I Kant, *Critique of Practical Reason*, translated by M Gregor (Cambridge, Cambridge University Press, 1997) 62 ff (*Kritik der praktischen Vernunft*, [*KpV*] A 126 ff).

27   ibid 62 (*KpV* A 126 f).

28   ibid 62 (*KpV* A 127).

upon. His analysis sways characteristically to and fro, leaving it unclear whether this feeling forms the necessary precondition for the overcoming of empirical interests or is but its expression.

On the one hand, Kant asserts that morality can be based on nothing else than the law itself.

> What is essential in every determination of the will by the moral law is that, as a free will—and so not only without the cooperation of sensible impulses but even with rejection of all of them and with infringement upon all inclination insofar as they could be opposed to that law—it is determined solely by the law.[29]

Consequently, the law itself has to be the incentive, and *Achtung* can be nothing more than its consequence, a product of pure practical reason. This perspective obviously fits into the general scheme: The law is a self-given product of practical reason, as such it suppresses and supersedes all empirical inclinations, and this suppression itself can then be felt, it constitutes the feeling of respect for the law and its capacities. Yet because of the finitude of human cognitive faculties, this analysis can only take the form of an *ex negativo* approach; it cannot explain the mechanisms of practical reason in a positive way. In Kant's own words:

> For how a law can be of itself and immediately a determining ground of the will (though this is what is essential in all morality) is for human reason alone an insoluble problem and identical with that of how a free will is possible. What we shall have to show a priori is, therefore, not the ground from which the moral law itself supplies an incentive, but rather what it effects (or, to put it better, must effect) in the mind insofar as it is an incentive.[30]

On the other hand, however, Kant apparently also admits that this feeling has to be something else and something more than merely the product of the moral law. This analysis deals with the problematic, supposedly inaccessible 'positive' aspect of the moral feeling called *Achtung*. Though he once again insists that *Achtung* has nothing to do with any 'pathological' inclination, caused by an empirical object, it still must be conceived of as something like an interest, for, as Kant asserts in his *Critique of Practical Reason*, thereby silently following Spinoza,[31] every feeling can only be overcome by another feeling. 'For, all inclination and every sensible impulse is based on feeling, and the negative effect on feeling (by the in-

---

29   ibid 63 (*KpV* A 129).
30   ibid 62 f (*KpV* A 128).
31   See Heidegger, *Grundprobleme der Phänomenologie* (1989) 189.

fringement upon the inclinations that takes place) is itself a feeling.'[32] In this perspective, the feeling is not only a derivative phenomenon. Feeling comes first; it precedes rational understanding, paving its way by suppressing the opposing inclinations.

Yet the function of the moral sentiment is not limited to this negative aspect of suppressing the opposing inclinations alone. Using a different perspective, we can try to elaborate on another reason for the idea that, as Heidegger remarks with regard to Kant's concept, *Achtung* is 'the way in which the law as law becomes accessible at all'.[33] In order to be perceived as an authoritative, truly binding commandment, the law, according to the rational paradigm nothing but the self-given product of pure practical reason, has to be something that transcends the freedom of one's own will. It is this aspect which can be more easily connected with feeling than with the pure *ratio*. In every sentiment there is something uncanny and uncontrollable that lies beyond the grasp of reason. As Martin Heidegger famously put it in *Being and Time*: 'A mood assails us. It comes neither from "outside" nor from "inside", but arises out of Being-in-the-world, as a way of such Being.'[34] Kant's analysis shows precisely this uncanny status of the moral sentiment when it comes to discussing the respect not only for the law itself, but for other human beings as subjects to the moral law. Kant repeatedly states that we have to acknowledge, involuntarily, the moral quality in others. '*Respect* is a *tribute* that we cannot refuse to pay to merit, whether we want or not; we may indeed withhold it outwardly but we still cannot help feeling it inwardly.'[35] *Achtung* assails us, thus producing obedience toward the law.

In contrast to the first approach, this second analysis appears less motivated by the leading idea of theoretical consistency. Rather, it answers to a certain aspect of morality which presents itself as everyday life experience. In this sense, we can now better understand why Heidegger labelled this aspect of Kant's philosophy as its 'most lucid phenomenological analysis': Indeed we find something rather more descriptive than speculative in these passages. Yet this everyday experience should not be taken too lightly. Kant himself repeatedly underlines its importance. Since free-

---

32   Kant, *Critique* 63 (*KpV* A 128 f).
33   Heidegger, *Grundprobleme der Phänomenologie* (1989) 191.
34   M Heidegger, *Being and Time*, translated by J Macquarrie and E Robinson (New York, Harper and Row, 1962) 176.
35   Kant, *Critique* 66 (*KpV* A 138).

dom as a transcendent idea can never be proven as 'reality', our everyday knowledge of morality is one way of getting access to it. As a footnote to the preface of the *Critique of Practical Reason* states, the moral law is the *ratio cognoscendi* for freedom, though freedom is its *ratio essendi*.[36] And the moral law is said to be deducible from our usual idea of the moral good. Thus there is a characteristic tension between a speculative and a phenomenological approach in Kant's moral philosophy, and this tension becomes particularly evident in his analyses of *Achtung*.

IV.

This tension cannot be sufficiently explained by simply pointing to the dichotomy between the world of the *homo noumenon* and the *homo phaenomenon*. True, man is a finite being belonging to both worlds, and only for this reason the need arises that the law must be understood as an imperative whose commandment is directed against the countercurrent of the sensual inclinations.[37] Yet the apparently clear distinction between the two worlds cannot hide the fact that the actual problem consists in their relation. Although freedom can never be a part of the empirical reality, it cannot be separated completely from it, either. Even though the moral good will does not depend upon successfully accomplished actions,[38] it must at least have possible consequences, for a will that can never lead to action at all would be just as self-contradictory as the famous example of the promise no one intends to keep.[39] The same applies to the opposite direction: although all material incentives are rejected in order to give way to the pure form of the law, the form itself thereby adopts the functional role of

---

36   ibid 4 (*KpV* A 5).
37   See Kant, *Foundations of the Metaphysics of Morals* 29 f (*Grundlegung zur Metaphysik der Sitten* BA 39).
38   See ibid 9 ff (*Grundlegung zur Metaphysik der Sitten* BA 1 ff).
39   On the importance of promising see W Hamacher, 'The Promise of Interpretation: Remarks on the Hermeneutic Imperative in Kant and Nietzsche' in id (ed), *Premises. Essays on Philosophy and Literature from Kant to Celan*, translated by P Fenves (Stanford, Stanford University Press, 1996) 97: 'A promise is in fact more than just another example of the autonomy of practical reason: it is the legislation of reason itself, a speech act in which language gives itself a law and thus constitutes itself as language in the first place. This act does not have a merely empirical character but is constitutive of every will and every language—a transcendental speech act.'

material reasons. We may call this transformation from form to matter (or content) the decisive act of an 'ethical transsubstantiation'.[40] Its manifestation is the moral sentiment of *Achtung*. *Achtung* conceptualises the uncanny and strangely paradoxical movement which according to Kant is so characteristic of mankind. The human will is free in the sense that it is not bound by pathological drives. Yet at the same time it needs an incentive that drives morality. The 'moral law within me',[41] constituting man as moral person, becomes accessible and effective only because of the moral feeling within me. 'The respect for the law is the outside, the exteriority of the law. ... Respect is the way in which the law presents itself.'[42] As Kant explicitly states: 'such a feeling is inseparably connected with the representation of the moral law in every finite rational being'.[43]

Therefore, man's fundamental dilemma is based on his status as a subject to the law in the double sense of being both its author, as law-giver, and its subordinate, as observant recipient of the moral imperative.[44] The law-giving reason is the reason of the subject – and yet as commandment it presents itself as something else, something different from the subject.[45] Thus any simple identification of law and subject is bound to fail.[46] The analysis of the moral feeling reveals this problem with remarkable clarity,

---

40 See A Zupančič, *Das Reale einer Illusion. Kant und Lacan* (Frankfurt am Main, Suhrkamp, 2001) 26 f.
41 Famous of course in combination with 'the starry heavens above me' (see Kant, *Critique* 133 [*KpV* A 288]); on this twin motive from the perspective of the history of ideas see P Probst, *Bestirnter Himmel und moralisches Gesetz. Zum geschichtlichen Horizont einer These Immanuel Kants* (Würzburg, Königshausen & Neumann, 1994).
42 HD Gondek, 'Vom Schönen, Guten, Wahren. Das Gesetz und das Erhabene bei Kant und Lacan' in HD Gondek and P Widmer (eds), *Ethik und Psychoanalyse. Vom kategorischen Imperativ zum Gesetz des Begehrens: Kant und Lacan* (Frankfurt am Main, Fischer, 1994) 148.
43 Kant, *Critique* 68 (*KpV* A 142).
44 See, eg, Kant, *Foundations of the Metaphysics of Morals* 49 f, 57 (*Grundlegung zur Metaphysik der Sitten* BA 70 f, 86 f).
45 See T Vesting, 'Die innere Seite des Gesetzes. Symbolische Ordnung, Rechtssubjektivität und der Umgang mit Ungewissheit' in I Augsberg (ed), *Ungewissheit als Chance. Perspektiven eines produktiven Umgangs mit Unsicherheit im Rechtssystem* (Tübingen, Mohr Siebeck 2009) 43.
46 See R Bernet, 'Subjekt und Gesetz in der Ethik von Kant und Lacan' in Gondek and Widmer (eds), *Ethik und Psychoanalyse* (1994) 51, who is however pointing to Lacan's critique against Kant rather than to Kant's conception itself.

and it insists that the problem cannot be resolved or overcome in any easy way. Kant is very clear on this point.

> We are indeed lawgiving members of a kingdom of morals possible through freedom and represented to us by practical reason for our respect; but we are at the same time subjects in it, not its sovereign, and to fail to recognise our inferior position as creatures and to deny from self-conceit the authority of the holy law is already to defect from it in spirit, even though the letter of the law is fulfilled.[47]

This also holds true beyond the theological dimension of the argument. The ethical act, as obedience to the law, does not prevail over the split between *homo noumenon* and *homo phaenomenon*. Rather, the moral subject, as subject to the law in the above-mentioned double sense, is constituted by this very split. In this way, the moral act proves the subject's nonidentity with itself. The ethical act does not abandon the 'pathological' subject. In contrast to Lacan's reading, Kant's subject is not only 'a subject longing to overcome its inner divisiveness and, as pure will, to wish for the law alone'.[48] Obedience to the law does not mean leaving the finite human existence and becoming part of an angelic sphere. 'The Freedom, the subject's only freedom, is the freedom to be split, and to choose its own splitting.'[49]

By introducing the concept of *Achtung* in his philosophy Kant implicitly recognises this split. At the same time he recognises that there is something beyond autonomy in the sense of pure spontaneity of reason alone, that at the very heart of autonomy we find something like heteronomy. The moral subject is not only actively creating its own commandments, it is also—and maybe primarily—responding to them. In this sense, 'respect' is an insufficient translation for the Kantian concept. For *Achtung* includes also an almost epistemological aspect. *Achten*, in German, means not only to respect someone, but also to be attentive to someone or something. Hence *Achtung* is a movement of paying both respect and attention to the law whose commandment makes itself heard.

Kant makes this double connotation explicit when he comes to explain the phenomenon of conscience, within the 'Doctrine of Virtue' in his *Metaphysics of Morals*. Conscience is an 'original intellectual and (since it is

---

47 Kant, *Critique* 70 (*KpV* A 147).
48 Bernet, 'Subjekt und Gesetz in der Ethik von Kant und Lacan' 50, summarising Lacan's perspective.
49 Zupančič, *Das Reale einer Illusion* (2001) 31.

the thought of duty) moral predisposition'[50] whose voice speaks to us 'involuntarily and unavoidably'.[51] Conscience imposes on the subject a strange indirect duty which does not actually substitute but rather supplements the moral duty in the strict sense.

> The duty here is only to cultivate one's conscience, to sharpen one's attentiveness [*Aufmerksamkeit*] to the voice of the inner judge, and to use every means to obtain a hearing for it (hence the duty is only indirect).[52]

At the same time Kant emphasises very clearly the uncanny character of this 'fearful voice':[53]

> Every human being has a conscience and finds himself observed, threatened and, in general kept in awe [*Respekt*] (respect [*Achtung*] coupled with fear) by an internal judge, and this authority [*Gewalt*] watching over the law in him is not something that he himself (voluntarily) *makes*, but something incorporated in his being. It follows him like his shadow when he plans to escape.[54]

It is in the conscience that the split in the subject becomes manifest. While conscience enacts a trial, inner court proceedings, is also reveals that it would be an 'absurd way of representing a court' if

> a human being who is *accused* by his conscience as *one and same person* as the judge; since then the prosecutor would always lose. —For all duties a human being's conscience will, accordingly, have to think of *someone other* than himself (i.e. other than the human being as such) as the judge of his actions, if conscience is not to be in contradiction with itself.[55]

In order to avoid this contradiction and achieve unity, the subject has to oppose a 'merely ideal person that reason creates for itself',[56] that is to say it has to construct a spectral doppelganger of itself which at the same time differs from the subject. Its own voice must become unfamiliar in order to realise its latent normative contents. Once again the result of Kant's analysis is that it is only its inner split which constitutes the moral subject.

What Kant here explicitly ascribes to the inner court proceedings applies just as well for inner law-making. Notwithstanding all the assertions

---

50 I Kant, *The Metaphysics of Morals*, edited and translated by M Gregor (Cambridge, Cambridge University Press, 1996) 189 (*Metaphysik der Sitten* [MdS] A 99).
51 ibid 161 (*MdS* A 39).
52 ibid.
53 ibid 189 (*MdS* A 99).
54 ibid.
55 ibid 189 (*MdS* A 100).
56 ibid.

of its non-empirical, non-pathological character, the moral feeling implies a trace of heteronomy. However, it is a heteronomy which has to be conceived of as a 'pure', non-empirical form. It does not oppose autonomy in the sense of a subsequent event, but rather precedes it. The subject 'belongs to the moral law before it belongs to itself'.[57] Consequently, if we conceive of dignity as closely connected to the idea of autonomy (and in fact this is what Kant does, who hardly ever talks about specifically *human* dignity, but refers far more often to the dignity of moral, and that is to say: autonomous beings in general[58]), then 'human dignity' becomes a rather ambivalent concept. Given the double auto-heteronomous character of the moral subject, the concept now also has to be understood as a form of attentionality and responsivity.[59] Thus it corresponds to something that Emmanuel Levinas has underlined as the decisive aspect of the ethical act: this act is all about 'an obedience that precedes any hearing about the commandment'.[60]

Against the background of this analysis, one might be tempted to draw a parallel to another legal tradition which also emphasises the point that to observe the law does not necessarily mean to understand it first.

> The desire first to know whether it is worthwhile to listen to the voice of the law is the inversion of an original order passed on in the exclamation: *na'asseh ve nishma!*—'we will first act and then listen (think about it)'. With this exclamation the Israelites have, according to Talmudic doctrine, guessed the 'Secret of the Angels': They know that the obligation to the law is older than reason. Hence law and reason are not identical; reason reacts with regard to the law like an answer to a question which is, like tradition itself, older than one's own thinking.[61]

V.

Let me conclude with some brief remarks on the possible outcome of this debate for our current concept of law. In a small essay on 'Obligation' as a 'Jewish Jurisprudence of the Social Order', Robert Cover has argued that

---

57 Vesting, 'Die innere Seite des Gesetzes' 47.
58 See von der Pfordten, 'Zur Würde des Menschen bei Kant' (2009).
59 On the concept of responsivity see B Waldenfels, *Schattenrisse der Moral* (Frankfurt am Main, Suhrkamp, 2006) 106 ff.
60 E Lévinas, *Jenseits des Seins oder Anders als Sein geschieht* (Freiburg, Alber, 1992) 325.
61 AS Bruckstein, *Die Maske des Moses. Studien zur jüdischen Hermeneutik*, 2nd edn (Berlin, Philo, 2007) 162 f.

the Western legal tradition is characterised by its founding myth of the social contract, or autonomy, and therefore it conceives of the law basically as 'rights', while the Jewish legal tradition is characterised by the founding myth of the revelation at Sinai, and thus conceives of the law basically as 'obligation', and that is to say: as heteronomy.[62] As it turns out, the concept of *Achtung* undermines this clear-cut dichotomy. *Achtung*, so it seems, reveals the concept of specifically *human* dignity as both a self-given law, and thus as an individual right, and as a fundamental obligation.

Looking at the classical borderline between the Jewish and the Christian tradition as constituted by the Pauline distinction between the 'letter' and the 'spirit' of the law,[63] one could say that Kant's moral philosophy is more legalistic, more obliged to the law and maybe even to the 'letter of the law', than Kant himself would like to admit. This degree of proximity of Kant's thinking and the Jewish tradition was already noticed by Kant's contemporaries and his philosophical followers. The general insight is expressed in Schopenhauer's ugly, anti-Semitic comment on Kant's 'Jewish smell'.[64] In fact we can read Kant's moral philosophy as a hidden commentary on St. Paul's epistles.[65] Kant repeatedly sets his distinction of acting not only according to but from duty parallel to the Pauline letter-and-spirit-dichotomy, thus apparently claiming the Christian heritage for his own project.[66] And yet at the same time he does not abandon the idea of the law completely, as St. Paul did, who in his epistle to the Romans famously talks of the 'end of the law'.[67] By contrast, Kant explicitly main-

---

62 See R Cover, 'Obligation: A Jewish Jurisprudence of the Social Order' in M Minow, M Ryan and A Sarat (eds), *Narrative, Violence, and the Law. The Essays of Robert Cover* (Ann Arbor, University of Michigan Press, 1993).
63 See 2 Cor 3:6.
64 See A Schopenhauer, 'Die beiden Grundprobleme der Ethik' in *Kleinere Schriften, Werke in fünf Bänden Bd. III* (Ludger Lüdkehaus ed, Zürich, Haffmans, 1988) 605: 'One sees that all times and all countries have indeed recognized the source of morality: except in Europe, for which the *foetor Judaicus* which pervades everything and everything is alone to blame: to be a moral law, an imperative, in short an order and command, that is parried: of that they cannot let go und refuse to accept, that the like can ever only have egoism as its foundation.'
65 For a parallel in general between the Kantian and the Pauline anthropology see also Probst, *Bestirnter Himmel und moralisches Gesetz* (1994) 38 ff.
66 See Kant, *Critique* 62, 70 (*KpV* A 128, A 147).
67 See Rom 10:4.

tains the metaphor of the 'yoke of the law'[68] which we have to bear—only that now, since the law is conceived of as self-given, the yoke can be identified as 'a mild one'.[69] Human dignity, in this perspective, is part of the yoke.

In this sense, we cannot take Kant's idea of human freedom and dignity and present it as the solid fundament of our legal tradition. Rather, this idea challenges some of the most common assumptions of modern legal theory. By subverting the supposedly clear-cut difference between autonomy and heteronomy, Kant's moral philosophy, and in particular his concept of *Achtung*, undermines the classical dichotomy between Christianity and Judaism, between letter and spirit, between individual right and mitzvah, between Western and non-Western legal tradition.

---

68   See Acts 15:8.
69   Kant, *Critique* 72 (*KpV* A 152).

Religion, Morality and Being Human: The Controversial Status of Human Dignity

Ingolf U. Dalferth *

I. A Controversial Issue

In recent years human dignity has become a central and controversial issue in legal, political, moral, philosophical, and theological debates. Some take human dignity to be the fundamental 'right to have rights' that underpins all our other rights and duties, whether laid down in a written constitution or not.[1] Others dismiss it as a useless and harmful notion that adds nothing substantive to the understanding of our rights but rather obfuscates the ideas of human rights, freedom, justice, and equality.[2] In democratic societies

> our rights are constrained by respect for the rights of others. My rights correlate with your duties; your rights correlate with my duties. So when rights are equal, each person has duties in regard to the rights of others.[3]

This correlation of rights and duties among members of modern society is an important insight. But all we need to state and justify it are the ideas of freedom, justice, and equality, but not, however, the 'Reappraisal of an Ancient Legal Concept' such as human dignity.[4] We can do without it; and we should.

---

*   This chapter was originally published in P Jonkers and M Sarot (eds), Embodied Religion. Proceedings of the 2012 Conference of the European Society for Philosophy of Religion (Utrecht, *Ars Disputandi Supplement Series,* Vol. 6, 2013, 143-179). Reprint with generous permission of the author and the editors.
1   cf D Dyzenhaus, 'Dignity in Administrative Law: Judicial Deference in a Culture of Justification' (October 1, 2011) *23rd McDonald Lecture* (2011), http://ssrn.com/abstract=2029818, 2. Also in this volume.
2   R Macklin, 'Dignity Is a Useless Concept. It Means No More than Respect for Persons or Their Autonomy' (2003) 327 *British Medical Journal* 1419–1420; S Pinker, 'The Stupidity of Dignity', http://richarddawkins.net/articles/2567.
3   J Waldron, 'Dignity, Rights, and Responsibilities' (May 2010) *Max Weber Lecture EUI* 4, http://ssrn.com/abstract=1710759.
4   S Hennette-Vauchez, 'A Human *Dignitas*? The Contemporary Principle of

However, the history of human rights discourse in the 20th century tells a different story. Respect for human dignity is a central idea in *The Universal Declaration of Human Rights*. It plays a foundational role in a growing number of national constitutions, most notably in Article 1 (1) of the German Basic Law. It lies at the center of many contemporary debates in bioethics, the ethics of war, or the ethics of care. It plays the key role 'in the emerging international biomedical law.'[5] And it is invoked by human rights groups and networks across the world who

> wish to stimulate systemic change, globally and locally, to open space for dignity and mutual respect and esteem to take root and grow, thus ending humiliating practices and breaking cycles of humiliation throughout the world.[6]

The history of the idea reaches back through the enlightenment (Immanuel Kant) and renaissance humanism (Pico della Mirandola) to Roman antiquity (*dignitas, honor, potestas, maiestas, decus*). It did not function centrally in the Christian tradition before the 20th century. But since the Second World War it has won growing public momentum by playing a major role in constitutions and international legal declarations.[7] This is where we must start if we want to understand the contemporary debates about human dignity. What exactly is the role it plays in those constitutional documents, and what does 'human dignity' mean there?

II. A Right to Dignity vs. Rights Based on Dignity

The answer is not easy. There is no clear legal definition of the term in any of these documents,[8] and the way they refer to it is ambiguous. In the preamble of *The Universal Declaration of Human Rights* the 'recognition

---

    Human Dignity as a Mere Reappraisal of an Ancient Legal Concept', http://ssrn.com/abstract=1303427.

5   R Andorno, 'Human dignity and human rights as a common ground for a global bioethics' (2009) 34 *Journal of Medicine and Philosophy* 223–40, esp. 226.

6   Human Dignity and Humiliation Studies: http://www.humiliationstudies.org.

7   cf the UNESCO Universal Declaration on Bioethics and Human Rights (October 19, 2005): http://portal.unesco.org/en/ev.php-URL_ID=31058&URL_DO=DO_TOPIC&URL_SECTION=201.html.

8   BM Knoppers, *Human Dignity and Genetic Heritage: Study Paper* (Ottawa, Law Reform Commission of Canada, 1991) 2: 'Those provisions concerning human dignity have not been authoritatively interpreted or applied by any of the competent, independent, international institutions.'

of the inherent dignity and of the equal and inalienable rights of all members of the human family' is called 'the foundation of freedom, justice and peace in the world.'[9] Similarly Article 1 states:

> All human beings are born free and equal in dignity and rights. They are endowed with reason and conscience and should act towards one another in a spirit of brotherhood.[10]

But then we are also told to make every effort to safeguard the inherent dignity of human beings and make it the fundamental right of rights, the right that grounds all others.[11] Thus, on the one hand, dignity 'is what some of our rights are rights *to*,' on the other hand, 'dignity is also what grounds all of our rights.'[12] Human rights are said to, 'derive from the inherent dignity of the human person,'[13] but people are also held to have a right to be protected against 'degrading treatment' and 'outrages on personal dignity.'[14]

To some this 'blurring of the distinction between content ("a right to dignity") and justification ("rights based on dignity")'[15] looks like an equivocation similar to the one Jeremy Bentham made fun of with respect to 'liberty.' To quote a recent commentator:

Defenders of natural rights would say that men are born free, Bentham observed, but then complain in the name of rights that so many of them were born into slavery. If challenged to justify their demands for liberty, they would cite human liberty as the ground of these demands. But liberty, which they were citing as an existent justification for rights, was also what they were demanding, and because they thought they had to demand it, they were acknowledging that men were not free. So what became of the alleged justification for their claim? 'Men ought to be free because they

---

9   *The Universal Declaration of Human Rights*, Preamble, http://www.un.org/en/documents/udhr/index.shtml.
10 ibid Article 1.
11 According to K Dicke, 'The Founding Function of Human Dignity in the Universal Declaration of Human Rights' in D Kretzmer and E Klein (eds), *The Concept of Human Dignity in Human Rights Discourse* (Leiden, Kluwer Law International, 2002) 111, 'dignity' conveys 'a formal, transcendental norm to legitimize human rights claims': it is the right to have rights and as such grounds (all) other rights.
12 J Waldron, 'Dignity, Rank, and Rights: The 2009 Tanner Lectures at UC Berkeley', http://papers.ssrn.com/sol3/papers.cfm?abstract_id=1461220, 5.
13 The International Covenant on Civil and Political Rights, Preamble.
14 Geneva Conventions, Common Article 3.
15 Waldron, 'Dignity, Rank, and Rights' 4.

are free, even though they are not' – was that the claim? Such reasoning, which Bentham called 'absurd and miserable nonsense,'[16] seemed to veer between the incoherent and the tautological. And the dual usage of 'dignity' appears to partake of this logic... As Bentham said (not specifically about dignity but in an analogous context):

> It is from beginning to end so much flat assertion: it neither has anything to do with reason nor will endure the mention of it. It lays down as a fundamental and inviolable principle whatever is in dispute.[17][18]

But this dispute is spurious. It is perfectly possible to understand human dignity as a fundamental right (the right of rights) on which other rights are based without falling into inconsistency, but whether one can or should claim that *all* other rights are based on dignity is a different matter. But rights can only function as rights if they are clearly defined: Unclear formulations and vague terms make an alleged right pointless. If we do not know what the statement of an alleged right means or involves, we cannot use it in legal practice or in deciding cases. However, the term 'dignity' or 'human dignity' is not defined in the legal documents cited nor does there seem to exist a canonical definition of the term in the law.[19]

III. Human Dignity vs. the Dignity of Human Beings

This has been lamented as a highly problematic deficiency (especially by criminal lawyers and judges who have to decide cases), or defended as an important feature of the functioning of the term in a constitutional context (especially by constitutional lawyers who look at the moral foundation and political role of constitutions in state and society). The German *Grundgesetz*,[20] one of the first and most influential constitutions using the term

---

16   J Bentham, 'Anarchical Fallacies' in J Waldron (ed), *Nonsense upon Stilts: BenthamBurke and Marx on the Rights of Man* (London, Routledge, 1987) 50.
17   Ibid 74.
18   Waldron, 'Dignity, Rank, and Rights' 4–5.
19   O Schachter, 'Human Dignity as a Normative Concept' (1983) 77 *American Journal of International Law* 849: 'We do not find an explicit definition of the expression "dignity of the human person" in international instruments or (as far as I know) in national law. Its intrinsic meaning has been left to intuitive understanding, conditioned in large measure by cultural factors.'
20   For the following cf C Goos, *Innere Freiheit. Eine Rekonstruktion des grundgesetzlichen Würdebegriffs* (Göttingen, V&R Unipress, 2011).

'human dignity,' states without much ado in Article 1 Paragraph 1: 'Human dignity shall be inviolable. To respect and protect it shall be the duty of all state authority.'[21] The German version puts it even more categorically by using indicative language: 'Die Würde des Menschen ist unantastbar. Sie zu achten und zu schützen ist Verpflichtung aller staatlichen Gewalt': 'Human dignity [the dignity of the human being] *is* inviolable [or 'untouchable' or 'non-negotiable']. To respect and protect it *is* the duty of all state authority.' It is clear that the first sentence states an absolute principle in a categorical way. However, we are not told what 'human dignity' means.

There was conflict about this from the beginning. Carlo Schmid, one of the most influential members of the Parliamentary Council that drafted the Constitution, insisted that the term 'should be defined.'[22] Theodor Heuss, on the other hand, the first president of the republic, defended the first sentence as a 'non-interpreted thesis.'[23] The term, he insisted, should not be defined. He declared that 'Human dignity must rest in itself. It must not be derived from any governmental position.'[24]

This opened the door to an ongoing dispute in German constitutional scholarship and jurisprudence.[25] In 1952 Günter Dürig argued that 'Hav-

---

21   I follow the official translation of the *Basic Law for the Federal Republic of Germany* published by the Bundestag in October 2010 (80201000.pdf).
22   He understood it to be 'a quality, an attribute that determines the human and that distinguishes humans from other creatures.'
23   T Heuss in *Parlamentarischer Rat. Akten und Protokolle*, vol. 5, 72; cf C Goos, 'Wie die Würde des Menschen zum bedeutungslosen Rechtsbegriff wurde – und wie sie eigentlich gemeint war ...', http://www.jura.unibonn.de/.../Goos_Thesenpapier_Menschenwuerde_Goettingen_1._Juni_2011.pdf.
24   Heuss, ibid: 'No one in power should have the prerogative to define it. Definitions are ruled or governed by interests, and it is better to leave the term "human dignity" undefined than to tailor it to the interests of a government.'
25   M Schreiter, 'Gehorsam für automatische Farbzeichen. Ein Beitrag zum Roboterproblem,' (1956) *Die öffentliche Verwaltung* 692–694; J Wintrich, 'Die Bedeutung der "Menschenwürde" für die Anwendung des Rechts' (1957) *Bayerische Verwaltungsblätter* 137–140; B Giese, *Das Würde-Konzept. Eine normfunktionale Explikation des Begriffes Würde in Art. 1 Abs. 1 GG* (Berlin, Duncker & Humblot, 1975); C Starck, 'Menschenwürde als Verfassungsgarantie im modernen Staat' (1981) *JZ* 457–464; N Hoerster, 'Zur Bedeutung des Prinzips der Menschenwürde' (1983) *JuS* 93–96 ; W Graf Vitzthum, 'Die Menschenwürde als Verfassungsbegriff' (1985) *JZ* 201–209; id, 'Die Spur zu verfolgen, wo er seinen Weg nahm' in P Lerche et al (eds), *Zum Gedenken an Professor Dr. iur. Günter Dürig 1920-1996* (Tübingen, Tübinger Universitätsreden N.F. Bd. 27, 1999) 37ff; EW Böckenförde and R Spaemann (eds), *Men-*

ing dignity means: being a personality,' and a person becomes a personality by affirming and serving the basic values of being related to the eternal 'you' of God, the 'you' of others, and the 'we' of the community.[26] Ten years later, in 1964, Peter Badura criticized this interpretation because it did not see human beings as they are but as they should be according to the ideal of an autonomous personality.[27] This had the unfortunate effect that one had to give reasons for somebody being an autonomous person in this sense in order to be a subject of dignity, and this made it difficult for

---

schenrechte und Menschenwürde. Historische Voraussetzungen – säkulare Gestalt – christliches Verständnis (Stuttgart, Klett-Cotta, 1987); K Stern, 'Die Menschenwürde als Fundament der Grundrechte' in id (ed), *Staatsrecht,* Vol. III/1 (Munich, C.H. Beck, 1988), § 58; W Holzhüter, *Konkretisierung und Bedeutungswandel der Menschenwürdenorm des Artikels 1, Absatz 1 des Grundgesetzes* (Darmstadt, DDD, 1989); T Geddert-Steinacher, *Menschenwürde als Verfassungsbegriff* (Berlin, Duncker & Humblot, 1990); H Hofmann, 'Die versprochene Menschenwürde' (1993) 118 *AöR* 353–377; RA Lorz, *Modernes Grund- und Menschenrechtsverständnis und die Philosophie der Freiheit Kants* (Stuttgart et al, Boorberg, 1993); P Häberle, 'Die Menschenwürde als Grundlage der staatlichen Gemeinschaft' in J Isensee and P Kirchhoff (eds), Handbuch des Staatsrechts der Bundesrepublik Deutschland, Vol. 1, 2nd edn (Heidelberg, Müller, 1995) § 20; W Höfling, 'Die Unantastbarkeit der Menschenwürde' (1995) *JuS* 857–862; K Bayertz, 'Die Idee der Menschenwürde: Probleme und Paradoxien' (1995) 81 *ARSP* 465–481; C Enders, *Die Menschenwürde in der Verfassungsordnung. Zur Dogmatik des Art. 1 GG* (Tübingen, Mohr Siebeck, 1997); H Dreier, 'Art. 1' in id (ed), *GG-Kommentar* (Tübingen, Mohr Siebeck, 1998); M Kloepfer, 'Leben und Würde des Menschen,' P Badura and H Dreier (eds), *Festschrift 50 Jahre Bundesverfassungsgericht. Bd. 2: Klärung und Fortbildung des Verfassungsrechts* (Tübingen, Mohr Siebeck, 2001) 77–104; T Veit, 'Würde als absoluter und relationaler Begriff' (2001) 87 *ARSP* 299–310; FJ Wetz, 'Die Würde des Menschen – Ein Phantom?' (2001) 87 *ARSP* 311–327; EW Böckenförde, 'Menschenwürde als normatives Prinzip' (2003) *JZ* 809–815; D Jaber et al (eds), *Über den mehrfachen Sinn von Menschenwürdegarantien,* (Frankfurt and London, Fouque London Publishing, 2003); H Dreier, 'Menschenwürde in der Rechtsprechung des Bundesverwaltungsgerichts' in E Schmidt-Aßmann et al (eds), *Festgabe 50 Jahre Bundesverwaltungsgericht* (Köln et al, Heymann, 2003) 201–222; K Seelmann (ed), *Menschenwürde als Rechtsbegriff* (Stuttgart, Steiner, 2004); M Nettesheim, 'Die Garantie der Menschenwürde zwischen metaphysischer Überhöhung und bloßem Abwägungstopos' (2005) 130 *AöR* 71–113.

26 G Dürig, 'Die Menschenauffassung des Grundgesetzes' (1952) *JR* 259–263; id, 'Der Grundrechtssatz von der Menschenwürde' (1956) 81 *AöR* 117–157; C Groos, 'Human dignity and the German Basic Law – a historical perspective' (unpublished paper at Berlin, Wissenschaftskolleg, November 17, 2011).

27 P Badura, 'Generalprävention und Menschenwürde' (1964) *JZ* 336–344.

precisely those who were most in need of it to claim the protection of Article 1 of the Basic Law (little children, the mentally disabled, people suffering from Alzheimer's disease, the unborn and the deceased). Badura therefore suggested what came to be called 'the negative interpretation method': One should concentrate on injuries of human dignity and clear violations but not try to define it positively. It is easier to agree on what the principle of human dignity excludes and prohibits than on what it states or defends. For to agree on violations of human dignity is possible even where we differ in our positive accounts of it.

However, the debate is confused because it does not distinguish between two different readings of the term 'human dignity' (Würde des Menschen). One is to take it to mean a complex property *human dignity* that can truly be predicated of everything that fulfills the conditions summarized in its definition: 'human dignity' = def. XYZ. The other is to construe it as referring to the *dignity of human beings*, i.e. to a particular aspect of human beings called 'dignity.' In the first case we talk about a complex property (human dignity), in the second case about a particular aspect or characteristic of human beings[28] (the dignity of human beings). However, the property *human dignity* can be meaningfully defined whether or not there is somebody of whom it can truly be predicated, and so can *dignity*. But to speak affirmatively of the *dignity of human beings* is to assume that there are human beings who have dignity or to claim that if there are human beings, then they have dignity. The claim is not that they have *human dignity*: *For every x, if x is a human being, then it has human dignity*, but rather: *For every x, if x is a human being, then it has dignity*.

The first sentence of Article 1 of the Basic Law is not about a property *human dignity* that is said to be inviolable. Rather it starts from the fact that there are human beings, it ascribes dignity to them, and it strictly prohibits any violation of it to anybody, not only to the state. The dignity of human beings is non-negotiable for anyone in any situation and under any circumstances. The point of this principle is not the mistaken claim that bearers of this dignity (i.e. persons) cannot be harmed (they can), nor the highly ambiguous claim that a person's dignity cannot be violated what-

---

28 As I shall argue below, it is not a property in the sense of a defining characteristic of human beings but rather an indicator of how we ought to relate to them, that is, how we ought to determine ourselves to behave towards human beings: in a way that is not in conflict with our common humanity. Because human beings qua human beings have dignity, we ought to determine ourselves to treat them (and us) with dignity.

ever one may do to a person (even if human dignity cannot be violated directly or *per se,* it is violated indirectly by harming the bearers of it). However, the first sentence of the Basic Law does not speak of human beings (the bearers of dignity) but of their dignity (an essential characteristic which they cannot lose). It is not stated that *only* human beings have or can have dignity.[29] But the term 'dignity' is not defined. It cannot be used to identify those to whom it is rightly applied but rather presupposes that those to whom it is applied are rightly identified as human beings – whatever this may mean. Human beings are bearers of a dignity which is said to be inviolable. Thus, in an important sense the principle is not about *human dignity* but about *human beings* who have dignity: What is at stake is not a property but the bearer of it. And the property human beings are said to have in an inviolable way is not *human dignity* but *dignity* – the dignity that is characteristic of human beings *as* human beings.

IV. Predicate vs. Designation

Thus, the descriptive phrase 'die Würde des Menschen' (the dignity of the human being) must not be confused with the predicate phrase 'Menschenwürde' (human dignity). The second is a predicate that can (in principle) be defined by enumerating the features that together characterize the property *human dignity*; and this property can be predicated of something (wrongly) or somebody (truly) in propositions such as 'Peter has human dignity' or 'There is an x and x possesses human dignity.' The first, on the contrary, is not a predicate but a condensed predication or proposition 'Human beings have dignity' or 'Human beings *qua* human beings possess dignity' which cannot be predicated of something else because it is not a property but a proposition used as a designation[30] to refer to those who are said to have this dignity: human beings.[31] It is true to say that

---

29 Kant used it not for human beings but for the moral law or morality: 'Morality, and humanity as capable of it, is that which alone has dignity.' I Kant, *The Metaphysics of Morals,* (edited by A Diem and D Lane, Walnut, 208), 58. And Pope Benedikt XVI has used it recently not merely for human beings but for the earth when he spoke of 'the dignity of the earth'.

30 cf B Russell, 'On Denoting' (1905) 14 *Mind* 479–493; M Devitt, *Designation* (New York, Columbia University Press, 1981).

31 Whereas it is meaningful but false to say 'Chimps possess human dignity' (ie that which we mean by the predicate 'human dignity') because Chimps may

human beings have this dignity, whatever may happen to them or whatever they may do. Hence, whatever we may do to other human beings or to ourselves must not conflict with the fact that we all possess this dignity – not because of what makes us different from other beings (being human) or from other human beings (being a particular human being) but by the sheer fact of existing as human beings.

But what exactly does this mean? Are we said to have this dignity because we are *human beings* or because we *exist* as human beings? Is the ascription of dignity tied to *what* or *who* we are (our essence[32]) or to the fact *that* we are (our existence)? In the first case even a merely possible human being would possess dignity: To possess dignity would be analytically true of anybody who is human. In the second case the possession of dignity would be contingent on actually existing as a human being: To possess dignity would be synthetically true only of those human beings who exist (have existed or will exist).

The latter understanding seems to be closer to our actual practice. Existence seems to be an essential requirement for ascribing dignity to human beings. Someone who doesn't exist cannot claim a right to have rights. The claim is not that if x is a human being, then x possesses dignity, but rather that if x is a human being *and exists*, then x possesses dignity. The ascription of dignity does not depend on being human, but on existing as a human being.[33] That is to say, the dignity of human beings is

---

possess dignity, but not human dignity, it is meaningless to say 'Chimps possess that which we mean by the proposition 'Human beings have dignity.' *Human dignity* is a property that can be predicated of someone, and so is *dignity*, but *the dignity of the human being* is an abbreviated proposition used as a designation that cannot be predicated of something else. It does not refer to a specific *human dignity* (that can only be ascribed to humans) but to a *dignity* (not necessarily only of human beings) ascribed to human beings; and it is stated that the truth that humans possess this dignity is seen and accepted as a principle that must never be violated by anybody.

32   I use the term in a broad sense to signify everything that provides a defensible answer to the question 'What are human beings?'.

33   If we construe *dignity* as an essential property of human beings (ie as *human dignity*) then it belongs to the set of determinations of what humans are so that it is impossible for anyone to be human and not to possess human dignity – whether he or she exists or not. If, on the other hand, we construe *dignity* not as a property of what humans are but of the fact that they are (if they are), then it is impossible for any human being to exist and not to have this dignity. Possible human beings do not possess any dignity but at best possible dignity: If they exist, then they have dignity, if they don't, then they don't. Actual beings,

not a particular human dignity which they have insofar as they are *humans* ('If x is a human being, then *x has human dignity*') but rather the dignity they have insofar as they *exist* as humans ('If x is a human being *and exists*, then *x has dignity*' or 'If x is a human being, then x has dignity, if x exists'). It is not an analytic truth that humans have this dignity but a synthetic truth that if they exist, then they have it: their dignity comes with their existence, not with their essence. Merely possible human beings have at best a possible dignity. Only actual human beings, i.e. human beings who exist, have dignity.

V. Who We Are vs. that We Are

This allows for a different way of distinguishing between *human dignity* and *the dignity* we have as human beings: If the dignity of human beings comes with their existence (the fact that they are), not with their essence (that which they are), then their dignity should not be construed as a necessary property of their essence (human dignity) but as a contingent property of their existence (the dignity of humans). This dignity (whatever it is) need not be restricted to humans (the dignity only of humans). Rather, the term 'human dignity'– and this is a different reading from the one discussed above – may be an abbreviation of the *human way or mode* in which human beings have dignity: They do not possess a special human dignity but they have the dignity they have in a special human way. The decisive point of this special way is that humans have this dignity not simply by being human but by being human beings *who exist*. Dignity is not a feature of their humanity *per se* (their essence) but rather of their *existence* as human beings (their actual presence with others in situations of communication and interaction). That is to say, it is impossible for human beings to be and not possess this dignity but not because their *being human* analytically implies this property but because it is impossible for them *to be* and not to have this dignity. We do not need to know what this dignity involves, nor what exactly we mean by 'human being,' but we can say that human beings (whatever that may mean) have dignity (whatever that may mean) not because of *who or what* they are (human beings) but

---

on the other hand, are not human beings because they possess human dignity but rather they possess *dignity* (not human dignity) because they are *human beings who exist*.

because of the fact *that* they are: 'For every x, if x is a human being, then it has dignity *if it exists.*'

VI. Denials of Humanity, Denials of Existence, and Denials of Personhood

If we start from here, then we must distinguish not merely between *human dignity* and the *dignity of humans* but also between three ways of denying the dignity of humans: denials of their humanity, denials of their existence, and denials of their personhood. If we construe *human* dignity as an essential property of human beings, then to be human is a necessary and sufficient condition for having this property: To be human is to have human dignity, and to deny it someone is to deny that she or he is human. We may still see them as something interesting or useful for us, but we would not treat them as humans, i.e. as one of us. On the other hand, if we construe *dignity* as a property tied to the existence of human beings, then to be human is neither necessary nor sufficient for having it: Other beings may have dignity as well, and humans have it only if they exist (have existed or will exist). However, if they exist, then they exist *as human persons*, i.e. as beings who deserve to be treated in the same way as we and all other persons want to be treated. A person is a being that exists as a member of a community of persons, i.e. by communicating and interacting with other persons as persons, and a human person is a being that lives his or her humanity in communicating with and interacting with other human persons, i.e. as a member of the community of those with whom we interact as persons. Thus, to be a person is to put a demand on other persons to be treated as a person, and it involves a commitment, obligation, or duty to treat other persons as persons. We cannot see someone as a person and deny the demand on us to treat him or her as a person. And we cannot see ourselves as persons and deny the duty to relate to other persons as persons. We may fail to do so, but this failure is not merely a failure with respect to the other, but also with respect to ourselves: We fail to be true to who we are as persons.

A denial of dignity is then not merely or always a denial of being human (at least not necessarily so) but a refusal to see someone as a human being that actually exists together with us or to refuse to relate to somebody as a person who lives as a person among us: It is not his or her humanity that is ignored but the fact that he or she exists as a member of our community of persons. We deny their existence and personhood, not necessarily that they are humans. Just as in the first case we do not take them to be humans but mistake them for something else, so in the second case we ignore that they exist at all (existence) or that they are present to us as one of us (person): We treat them like the dead, i.e. someone who is no longer with us, or like fictional characters, i.e. someone who was never with us, or like a thing or object that we use, but we do not relate to them as partners with whom we may or should or could communicate and interact as persons among persons.

All these are ways of mistreating the other. But it is one thing to be mistaken for something else (not a human being), another to be simply ignored (a non-existing entity) or to be excluded from the community of persons by being treated as an unperson or non-person. If we construe violations of human dignity as an offense against the humanity of a person, then we treat him or her not as a human being: We de-humanize the other by ignoring his or her humanity. If we construe violations of human dignity as a denial of the existence of a person, then we treat him or her as a non-existent entity, or as a non-person: We de-personalize the other by excluding him or her from the community of those who exist and with whom we communicate as persons. In the first case we act as if there were not a human being but only something else. In the second we act as if there were nobody or nothing at all or no person with whom we would and ought to interact as a person. All these are inhuman ways of relating to others: to deny what they are (their humanity), to ignore that they are (their existence), or to disregard who they are (persons). All this is incompatible with the dignity of human beings. However, none of this can do away with the fact (if it is a fact) that the other is a human being, that he or she exists, and that he or she is present to us as a person. We may deny the one, ignore the other, and disregard the third. We may behave in ways that flatly contradict them. But we cannot do away with them.

VII. Violating Persons vs. Violating Dignity

Is this the meaning of the first sentence of the German Basic Law 'The dignity of the human being is inviolable'? Hardly. It is true: Nobody ceases to be human by being treated in inhuman ways or by living under inhumane conditions. Human beings do not stop being human by being treated in ways that contradict their dignity or by being forced to live under conditions that are inhumane. But these ways and conditions are incompatible with their irrevocable dignity as human persons. A state that prides itself on serving and protecting the welfare of its citizens cannot put up with this.

Thus, although the first sentence in German uses the grammatical indicative, i.e. *is* rather than *shall*, it states a norm, not merely a fact – or perhaps one could say: it states a norm with respect to human beings and a fact with respect to their dignity: You can violate the first (human beings) but not the second (their dignity), yet you ought not to violate the first because of the second. Dignity is indeed not something that can be 'touched;' only things, bodies, animals or human beings can. And whereas you can touch a human being, you cannot, at least not in the same sense, touch his or her dignity. But this is not to say that Article 1 allows us to do what we want to human beings because their dignity will stay untouched. On the contrary, just because the human bearers of dignity are violable, the principle of the inviolability of the dignity of human beings states that this shall not be the case: The *human bearers of dignity* – not the *bearers of human dignity* – must not be touched in a way that conflicts with their dignity as human persons. The principle is not about *human dignity* (Menschenwürde) but about the *dignity* human beings have in an irrevocable way if and insofar as they exist as persons among persons (Würde des Menschen), and their dignity defines the scope and limit of what is acceptable, or not acceptable, in our dealings with human beings. Just because human beings are violable, and indeed are violated often to a shocking degree, the principle states that everybody must respect the dignity of human beings in dealing with them. Not only must the state do so, but also each individual must respect the dignity not only of others but also of him- or herself.

Therefore, the German constitution commits the German people axiomatically to the absolute principle of not violating the dignity of human beings, i.e. of not treating human bearers of dignity in ways that are incompatible with their dignity as human persons. This implies negatively not to allow, or put up with, any violation of those who are human bearers of dignity that conflicts with their dignity as human persons. And it implies positively to do everything to create conditions for humans to live their lives among and together with others as bearers of this dignity. This is clear from the second paragraph of Article 1: 'The German people therefore acknowledge inviolable and inalienable human rights as the basis of every community, of peace and of justice in the world.' The dignity of human beings is not the same as human rights. But as the 'therefore' indicates, human rights are guaranteed because of the dignity of human beings, and they are necessary to protect human beings against violations that conflict with and are contrary to their dignity. The right to have rights is restricted to human bearers of this dignity, i.e. to human persons. Human beings who exist cannot lose their dignity even when they are treated in inhumane ways. Since they cannot lose it as long as they live, and even beyond (because if they have been persons, it will always be true that they have been persons), they will always be bearers of the fundamental human rights that unfold the normative content and point of their dignity. This dignity is said to be inviolable just because its bearers can be, and often are, violated.

In this sense the first sentence of Article 1 states an absolute principle not to be violated by anybody. To torture anybody is strictly prohibited, even if it may help to save the lives of many. Torture of whatever sort harms not merely the body but contradicts the dignity of a person. The same principle has been invoked in decisions of the German Federal Constitutional Court against life imprisonment without the possibility of parole, the shooting down of aircrafts that are used as weapons by terrorists, abortion of embryos, peep shows where the performer cannot see those who are watching, or horror movies and video games such as the Mortal Kombat series. Actions of this sort are strictly forbidden not only to the state but to anyone.

The second sentence addresses the state explicitly and states two public duties that require action: The state has to respect the dignity of human persons, i.e. has to design the entire legal system in a manner that does not conflict with the dignity of persons. And it also has to protect this dignity, i.e. has to take appropriate measures if other people or poor living conditions endanger or undermine the dignity of persons. Whereas the prohibition of violations of the dignity of human persons in the first sentence of Paragraph 1 Article 1 is strict and without exception, the state duties mentioned in the second sentence are such that they require consideration of all interests affected, all parties concerned, and even of political preferences. Here balancing is not merely a possibility but a duty, whereas all balancing of principles is excluded in the first sentence.[34] The dignity of human persons is not something that can be relativized in any way. It is not a relative but an absolute value.

---

34 cf N Teifke, *Das Prinzip Menschenwürde. Zur Abwägungsfähigkeit des Höchstrangigen* (Tübingen, Mohr Siebeck, 2011).

VIII. Value vs. Dignity

But is it? If it is a value it cannot be absolute because all value or worth (*Wert*) is the polar opposite of worthlessness or non-value (*Unwert*) and thus can come by degrees: it has more or less value as its price indicates. But this is not so with dignity as Kant emphasized:

> In the kingdom of ends everything has either value or dignity. Whatever has a value can be replaced by something else which is equivalent; whatever, on the other hand, is above all value, and therefore admits of no equivalent, has a dignity.
>
> Whatever has reference to the general inclinations and wants of mankind has a market value; whatever, without presupposing a want, corresponds to a certain taste, that is to a satisfaction in the mere purposeless play of our faculties, has a fancy value; but that which constitutes the condition under which alone anything can be an end in itself, this has not merely a relative worth, i.e., value, but an intrinsic worth, that is, dignity.
>
> Now morality is the condition under which alone a rational being can be an end in himself, since by this alone is it possible that he should be a legislating member in the kingdom of ends. Thus morality, and humanity as capable of it, is that which alone has dignity...This estimation therefore shows that the worth of such a disposition is dignity, and places it infinitely above all value, with which it cannot for a moment be brought into comparison or competition without as it were violating its sanctity.[35]

Dignity is here explicitly contrasted to and distinguished from all value discourse. Something may be more or less valuable, and no value can be absolute because it is always positioned on a scale between 0 and 1. Values are necessarily relative because the value of something depends on comparison and a particular judgment of that thing. Not so with dignity. Dignity is absolute, its ascription is not based on comparison, and it does not come by degrees. Either one has it, or one doesn't, and if one has it, one has it in exactly the same way and to the same extent as everybody else who has it. Dignity is not a relative value but an absolute, exclusive and complete distinction: If any human being has it, every human being has it. But human beings have it not because of any empirical trait or biological characteristic but only in so far as they are moral beings, i.e. capable of autonomy – of determining their own will (i.e. themselves) independent of any actual context according to the maxim of the good will.

---

35 Kant, *The Metaphysics of Morals*; cf I Kant, *Groundwork of the Metaphysics of Morals* (edited and translated by M Gregor, Cambridge, Cambridge University Press, 1996) 42–43.

For to be autonomous in the Kantian sense is not merely to be able to choose between available options or courses of action in terms of what is more pleasant, or more useful, or more conductive to a greater happiness of many. Rather it is to be able to determine oneself to will only that which is willed by anybody who determines herself or himself to will only that which is willed by anybody who determines herself or himself to will only that which … – in short, to be one who wills nothing that cannot be willed by anyone who puts not his own interests but the requirements of our common humanity first. Kantian autonomy does not hinge on the capacity for deciding or choosing between options – this is something we find in one way or other everywhere among living beings. Nor is it to be identified with the specifically human capacity for rational decision, that is, for deciding between options motivated by reasons and not merely by desires, interests, or conventions – this distinguishes humans from other beings only by degree. Rather, it hinges on the moral capacity for deciding *how* to decide, or willing *how* to will, or choosing *how* to choose, *in terms of the good*, that is, by orienting the way one decides how to decide to the (morally) good, which is not defined by the individual interests of those who choose but which is the same for everyone. I am autonomous not because I can choose between options for reasons but because I can choose *how* to choose and determine the *how* of my choosing by orienting it to the good which is universally valid for everyone (the moral law). In choosing how to choose I am not determined by the actual options at hand, or by what I think or perceive to be the options in a given situation, or by reasons that appeal to some end that I desire. Rather, I can determine my way of choosing how to choose independently of the contingent (causal) actualities of a given situation and subjective interests in a situation by orienting it to the (morally) good. For the morally good does not vary with different situations or subjective interests but is the same, and motivates *per se* in the same way, in all possible situations of human choosing, deciding, and acting.[36]

---

[36] There is nothing in the much-discussed Libet experiments that comes close to the complexity of Kantian autonomy or could be construed as an objection to it.

IX. The Dignity of Morality

Therefore – and this is perhaps the most important point which Kant makes about dignity – dignity is not ascribed to human beings *qua* rational animals, at least not primarily and directly, but to *morality*, and through morality to *humanity*: 'morality, and humanity as capable of it, is that which alone has dignity.' Morality has dignity in an absolute sense: There is not morality without dignity, and no dignity that is not tied to morality. Humanity, on the other hand, has dignity in a relative sense *in so far as* it is capable of being informed by morality: Humanity, i.e. that which characterizes human beings and distinguishes them from all other beings, can be viewed and thematized in many different ways: from empirical, biological, psychological, sociological, historical, philosophical or theological perspectives. But only if we regard humanity from a moral perspective as something capable of morality can we ascribe dignity to it. Morality has dignity under any description, humanity only when viewed from a moral perspective.

For Kant this is not the only perspective for understanding human beings but it is an indispensable one if we really want to be true to the way we experience our lives and ourselves. From the moral perspective, to be human is to be capable of orienting one's life to the good, that is to say, to be able to live in a morally good or morally evil way. However, we are not merely capable of living a moral life but we cannot avoid doing so: A morally neutral life is not one of our options. As human beings it is possible for us to choose between good and evil (we can determine our willing or choosing by orienting it to the good, or by not doing so) but we also *must* do so and hence always in fact do: It is not possible for us *not* to choose between good and evil. If we can choose, we must choose, and there is nobody, as Kant elaborates in his doctrine of radical evil, who will not have to admit upon careful examination that he or she has in fact chosen not to live in a morally good but rather in a morally evil way.

Without going into detail, we may summarize Kant's account of human personhood as follows: Human beings are *persons*. As *persons* they are a moral beings capable of orienting their willing how to will to the good, or of not doing so, and as *human* persons they are not capable of not orienting their willing in either of these two ways: It is impossible for humans to live in a morally neutral way. To be *human* is to be capable of morality: It is impossible to be human and not to be able to live a moral life. And to be a human *person* is necessarily to actualize this capability: It is impossible to live as a human person and not to live in either a morally good or a morally evil way. As it happens, all of us in fact actualize our human capacity for morality in a way that misses the possibility of the good. We all live in fact by not orienting our lives to the good, or to the good only, or primarily to the good. We all live in fact in a way that is morally problematic, far from perfect, or outright evil.

X. The Dignity of Being Capable of Morality

However, this does not infringe on our dignity. We do not possess dignity because we live a morally good life but because we have the potential and capacity to do so. The *capability* of morality, not the actuality of a morally good life is Kant's basis for ascribing unrestricted dignity to human persons. The ascription of dignity is not restricted to those who live a morally good life, or denied to those who live in a morally evil way. It is tied to our capacity to live morally, and since every human person necessarily actualizes this capacity in a positive or negative way, there is no human being who cannot rightly be viewed and judged from a moral perspective.

Thus, Kant's account of dignity has two important implications. First, since dignity is ascribed to human beings in terms of the moral capacity of our common humanity, it does not allow us to distinguish between human beings or to classify human beings into groups, sets or classes of those who have or don't have dignity: Dignity is not a concept that defines a class of human beings but a general feature of human beings as such. Human beings *qua* human beings have dignity, i.e. the right to be treated with dignity by everybody because every human being is capable of morality and in fact lives a morally good or evil life. Recourse to dignity does not allow us to draw a distinction between different sorts, groups, ranks, or classes of human beings (one group of humans vs. another group of humans) but only to distinguish humans from non-human beings in terms of the capacity for morality that humans share with all other moral beings.

However, and this is the second point, dignity is not a property that together with others defines our common humanity. Whatever we take to be the essence of humanity, i.e. the set of properties that together constitutes our common humanity, it will not include dignity but only our capacity for morality. This capacity is the basis for ascribing dignity to us, but dignity is not identical with it. Dignity is not a defining feature of humanity but rather humanity is capable of manifesting morality that alone has dignity. It does so because we cannot enact our humanity concretely without in fact living in a moral way, whether good or evil. However, our dignity does not depend on *how* we live in fact, but on the fact *that* we can live in a morally good or evil way and cannot live without in fact living in the one way or the other. Since we can orient our lives to the morally good we ought to do so, but even if we fail to do so and miss our end as moral beings we still have dignity because, as humans, we are *capable* of morality. Whereas morality *has* dignity, we partake in it by living a morally good or a morally evil life. As humans we can do this because we, and we alone among all living animals, are capable of morality and thus can live in a humane (morally good) or inhumane (morally evil) way. We are moral ends in ourselves, and this is true of us even if we fail to live in a humane way. The dignity of humans as moral beings is that they are faced with the challenge and task of existing as persons, that is, not merely as means to an end but as moral ends in themselves. Kant makes the point explicitly:

> Now I say that the human being and in general every rational being *exists* not merely as a means to be used by this or that will at its discretion; instead he must in all his actions always be regarded *at the same time as an end*.[37]

In short, dignity is not a feature of what we are (humans) but of the way in which we live as human beings who can and must determine themselves morally (moral beings or persons). Not our actual moral self-determination (how we in fact orient our lives) but the possibility and necessity of such a determination is decisive for our dignity: As finite moral beings (human persons) we are capable of orienting our lives to the good or of not doing so, and at the same time we are not capable of not orienting our lives either to the good or not to the good. In this sense, dignity hinges not on our actual moral character but on the possibility of having a moral character (as *humans*) and on the impossibility of not actually having a positive or negative moral character (as *persons*). Here as elsewhere Kant puts the emphasis on our real possibility (we are capable of morality) and not on our concrete actuality as moral beings (we in fact live in a morally evil or in a morally good way). Thus for Kant, to be human is, from an empirical perspective, not to be a rational animal (*animal rationale*) but an animal *capable* of rationality (*animal rationabile*) and, from a moral

---

37   Kant, *Groundwork* (1996) 79. Not humanity *per se* (ie that which makes us human beings) nor any other essential determination (such as the one of rational beings) but only the inescapably moral way of existing or living our common humanity as persons among persons is the basis for ascribing dignity to us: Dignity is true of us not because of our common humanity (essence) but only because we are able to live our common humanity in a moral way (mode of existence).

perspective, not *to be* morally good or *to be* morally evil but to be *capable* of morality. Human beings manifest the dignity of morality by living as moral beings, ends in themselves, or persons. They may fail to live up to their full potential as persons in their actual way of living by not orienting themselves to the good, and in one way or other we all in fact fail to do so. But this does not stop us from being persons who manifest the dignity of morality. If we can live in a morally good way, then we ought to do so. And we know that we can precisely because the moral law tells us that we ought to exist in this way by orienting our life to the good.

XI. Rational vs. Accountable Being

It is obvious that Kant does not argue within the parameters of the classical definition of the human being as *rational animal* (*animal rationale*) or *embodied rationality*.[38] He does not merely discriminate between our *animality*, which we share as our *genus proximum* with other living beings, and our *rationality*, which is the *differentia specifica* that marks us off from other living beings; nor does he merely discriminate from a reverse perspective between our *rationality*, which is the *genus proximum* that we share with all rational beings, and our *animality*, which is the *differentia specifica* that makes us embodied creatures in the realm of rational beings. Rather, Kant operates with a threefold distinction with respect to what we are between our biological (animality), rational (humanity) and moral dimensions (personality) which corresponds to his distinctions between *sensuality* (Sinnlichkeit), *understanding* (Verstand), and *reason* (Vernunft): We are not merely *living beings* (our 'predisposition to animality'), nor merely living and *rational beings* (our 'predisposition to humanity') but rational and *at the same time accountable beings* (our 'predisposition to personality').[39] The traditional duality between our animal and rational natures is thus incorporated into a new duality between our phenomenal (animality and rationality) and noumenal side (accountability or personality). We are individuals as organisms (biological animality) and rational agents

---

38 cf IU Dalferth, *Umsonst. Eine Erinnerung an die kreative Passivität des Menschen* (Tübingen, Mohr Siebeck, 2011).
39 I Kant, 'Religion within the boundaries of mere reason' 6:26-28, in: *Religion and Rational Theology*, trans. and ed. by AW Wood and G di Giovanni (Cambridge, Cambridge University Press 2001) 74-76.

(rationality), but we are necessarily members of a moral society as persons (moral accountability). Persons are not particulars of a shared commonality or general nature (humanity or rationality) but singular beings in a society of singular moral beings.[40] As *living beings* we belong to the system of nature or, more precisely, to the physical realm of animals. However, compared with other animals we are not excellent and outstanding but rather a weak, vulnerable and endangered kind of animal. On the scale of physical values we do not figure very high:

> Man in the system of nature (homo phaenomenon, animal rationale) is a being of slight importance and shares with the rest of the animals, as offsprings of the earth, a common value (pretium vulgare).[41]

This is not much different when we turn to our much-praised rationality. As *rational agents* we can set ends for ourselves and rationally choose between options because of our capacities of understanding and will. However, as such we are still part of the animal world and only relatively but not in principle different from other living beings.

> Although man has, in his reason, something more than they and can set his own ends, even this gives him only an *extrinsic* value in terms of his usefulness (pretium usus). This extrinsic value is the value of one man above another – that is, his *price* as a ware that can be exchanged for these other animals, as things. But, so conceived, man still has a lower value than the universal medium of exchange, the value of which can therefore be called pre-eminent (pretium eminens).[42]

Only in the third respect, i.e. as *persons*, we radically differ from other animals:

> But man regarded as a *person* – that is, as the subject of morally practical reason – is exalted above any price; for as such (homo noumenon) he is not to be valued as a mere means to the ends of others or even to his own ends, but as an end in himself. He possesses, in other words, a *dignity* (an absolute inner worth) by which he

---

40   This also enlarges and deepens the notion of 'human embodiment' (the metaphor is problematic because it wrongly suggests that 'we' – whoever we may be – live *in* our bodies, that is, are distinct from our bodies in such a way that our bodies are only the contingent temporal manifestation of our true eternal reality). But we are bodies, not merely in a biological sense but also, and in many contexts more importantly, in a social, cultural, moral, religious or political sense. To be part of a moral (religious, cultural, social, political, ecclesial) community is to be a body of a particular sort, and as human persons we cannot be who we are without being such a body. In this sense, we do not merely have a body but *are* bodies – in more than one respect.
41   Kant, *The Metaphysics of Morals*, 186.
42   ibid.

exacts *respect* for himself from all other rational beings in the world: he can measure himself with every other being of this kind and value himself on a footing of equality with them.[43]

That is to say, *persons* are not just rational agents who can set ends for themselves. Humans are not merely rational deciders and individual agents but persons who are *accountable* to others, i.e. who can be held responsible by others for what they do or fail to do or, even more importantly, how they do what they do and how they will what they will and do. As rational deciders and agents we can be compared with other animals or other humans according to the degree of efficiency in which we achieve our ends. Humans are generally more efficient than most other animals, and some humans are more efficient than others. As persons, however, we cannot be compared with others, whether animals or humans. With regard to personhood, we are not 'higher animals' than others (speciesism) and some of us do not rank 'higher' than others (elitism). Accountability is not a matter of degree, and it is not ascribed on the basis of comparing our effectiveness as rational deciders with that of other species (great apes, chimps, rats, dolphins) or other members of our own species (the educated vs. the uneducated, the rich vs. the poor, those in power vs. those without power, the aristocrats vs. the herd-people). Its ascription is based on a simple and absolute alternative: Are we able to live a moral life, or aren't we? We, and we alone among all living beings, have the capacity to do so, and since we can, we must because we cannot live in a morally neutral way. For Kant, morality is not a system of values based on gut feelings but on our capacity for autonomy, i.e. our potential to determine ourselves independently from any stimuli in our actual environment or state of our feelings by the maxim of the good will alone; and this capacity is such that we cannot live without in fact exercising it by either living, or failing to live, a moral life.

This potential for autonomy is the basis for the absolute respect we owe each other – a respect that does not depend on our rationality, physical strength, attractiveness, sociability or anything else that comes in degrees, i.e. can be increased or decreased, but on the mere capacity to live as moral beings according to the practical law. We are not merely rational animals (*Verstandeswesen*) but *persons* (*Vernunftwesen*). As such we are intrinsically related to a community of persons (rational spirits) who can hold us accountable for how we determine ourselves and live our lives,

---

43   ibid.

and who therefore owe us the same respect which we owe them. As *Vernunftwesen* we are not merely rational individuals but singular members of a moral society of persons or spirits. This moral society of free spirits does not coincide with anything in the physical world of animal life or the rational world of human knowers, deciders, and agents. As rational beings we differ from other animals only by degree. But as moral beings or *persons* we differ from them absolutely or qualitatively.

XII. Elitist vs. Universal Conceptions of Dignity

For Kant, dignity can only be predicated of moral beings, i.e. of beings capable of autonomy, and no moral being, whether finite or infinite, can be excluded from having it. Thus, with respect to humans the concept of dignity is intrinsically universal: If it is true of any person, then it is true of every person. You cannot be a person and not have dignity.[44] Moreover, dignity does not come in degrees: Either one has it or one doesn't. Either you are a person, or you are not. Dignity is an absolute, exclusive and complete distinction of persons. The concept of dignity does not allow us to draw distinctions between human beings or classify humans into groups, sets or classes (those who have dignity and those who don't). Kant's conception of dignity is *strictly universal*.

The contrary is true for Nietzsche. Following ancient elitist conceptions he sees an 'order of rank between man and man,'[45] and a gap between those few human beings who have true worth (rulers) and the average human being (slaves). For him, dignity is not the highest human value shared by all human beings. His understanding derives from the ancient notions of *dignitas, auctoritas, maiestas* or *nobilitas*. Dignity is not an intrinsic human value but rather an earned nobility. In the past one had it by being born into the right social class, and today one gets it by breaking away from the democratic egalitarianism of modern resentment driven herd culture through radical self-making, i.e. the willingness to stand in solitude over against the corrupt moral majority of the many. 'Morality is the *herd-*

---

44 This is not restricted to *human* persons but true of each and every person, whether human or other.
45 F Nietzsche, *Beyond Good and Evil. Prelude to a Philosophy of the Future* (translated by W Kaufmann, New York, Vintage Books, 1989) § 228.

instinct in the individual,'[46] not that which distinguished persons from all other beings. 'We, "the few and true ones" want to become those we are – human beings who are new, unique, incomparable, who give themselves laws, who create themselves.'[47] In short, dignity is not a universal character-trait of human beings but rather an indicator of social class (nobility vs. herd culture) that is not applicable to everybody.

It is easy to see how this can be found in religious and cultural traditions as well, especially where questions of religion and questions of national identity are so closely intertwined as in the Jewish tradition. As Susannah Heschel has pointed out, where human dignity is seen as a distinction or an honor of a particular group or nation (such as Israel) or of a particular group of people within a nation (such as male Jews) it is used in fact as an elitist concept that is not applicable to women and gentiles. In Judaism, as in most religious traditions, dignity, like religion itself, is not universal.[48]

This is Nietzsche's view, not Christianity's – at least not in an ideal world. It is precisely because it can be (mis)understood in this elitist way that Protestant theologians in the 19th century have shied away from using this category.[49] 'Image of God' was their term for expressing the universal characteristic of human persons, whereas 'dignity' was used only, if at all, when addressing a general non-Christian audience, as in Schleiermacher. Only against the backdrop of such an elitist conception of dignity does it make sense to say that claims that base human dignity on God and divine creation or imago Dei make human rights derivative, rather than primary.[50] And only then does it makes sense to denounce dignity discourse as 'a religious foundation clothed in secular garb,' by insisting that 'What must be primary is the human being as such, period.'[51] The point of modern dignity discourse is precisely to make the human being primary – the very fact of being human and not the possession of a particular quality or

---

46   Friedrich Nietzsche, *The Gay Science* (translated by W Kaufmann, New York, Vintage Books, 1974) § 116.
47   ibid § 266.
48   S Heschel, '"Wherever you see the trace of man, there I stand before you": The Complexities of God and Human Dignity within Judaism' in this volume, 129.
49   cf S Schaede, 'For the sake of human dignity, ban reified concepts of 'man made in the image of God': Some theological perspectives' in this volume 108-119.
50   Heschel, '"Wherever you see the trace of man, there I stand before you": The Complexities of God and Human Dignity within Judaism' 152.
51   ibid.

the belonging to a particular religious, political, or social group, class or orientation.

But then, what exactly is this universal distinction of human beings called dignity?

XIII. The Failure of the Factor X Approach

A.

In 2002, Francis Fukuyama searched for that 'Factor X' which makes us human, without which, he believes, human dignity can't have a foundation.[52] In 'the political realm we are required to respect people equally on the basis of their possession of Factor X.'[53] He is not satisfied with either the religious answer that all souls are equal before God,[54] nor with Kant's answer that right is based on our capacity to make rational choices,[55] (which isn't Kant's answer) nor with the Darwinian position 'that species do not have essences' as a species is merely a snapshot at the moment between what came before and what will come afterwards.[56] Rather, he argues,

> Factor X cannot be reduced to the possession of moral choice, or reason, or language, or sociability, or sentience, or emotions, or consciousness, or any other quality that has been put forth as a ground for human dignity. It is all these qualities coming together in a human whole that make up factor X.[57]

It is not clear whether he uses the term 'human dignity' as a short formula of this complex set of features, or whether he understands the set of features to be the necessary (and/or sufficient?) condition for applying the term 'human dignity' to a being. But it is clear, that for him there must be a set of features that mark off humans from other beings if the ascription of dignity is to have a legitimate foundation.

---

52 F Fukuyama, *Our Posthuman Future: Consequences of the Biotechnology Revolution* (New York, Picador, 2002) 149.
53 ibid 152.
54 ibid 150.
55 ibid 151 – which isn't Kant's answer as we have seen.
56 ibid 152.
57 ibid 171.

B.

A year later, in 2003, Ruth Macklin, professor of medical ethics at the Albert Einstein College of Medicine in New York, argued that 'Dignity is a useless concept. It means no more than respect for persons or their autonomy.'[58] 'Why,' she asked, 'do so many articles and reports appeal to human dignity, as if it means something over and above respect for persons or for their autonomy?'[59] And she concludes: 'Although the aetiology may remain a mystery, the diagnosis is clear. Dignity is a useless concept in medical ethics and can be eliminated without any loss of content.'[60]

C.

Another 5 years later, in 2008, the President's Council on Bioethics tried to put dignity on firmer conceptual ground in a 555-page report, titled *Human Dignity and Bioethics*. The report came under heavy fire, especially from the *Richard Dawkins Foundation for Reason and Science*. Steven Pinker attacked it in a paper on 'The Stupidity of Dignity' as 'conservative bioethics' latest, most dangerous ploy.'[61] 'The problem is that "dignity" is a squishy, subjective notion, hardly up to the heavyweight moral demands assigned to it.'[62] He criticizes that many of the 28 essays are written by 'vociferous advocates of a central role for religion in morality and public life,'[63] and that some 'align their arguments with Judeo-Christian doctrine' which he finds shocking in a secular context.[64]

It comes as little surprise when Pinker concludes that 'the concept of dignity remains a mess.'[65] For him, dignity has three features that undermine any possibility of using it as a foundation for bioethics. First, *dignity is relative*. One doesn't have to be a scientific or moral relativist to notice that ascriptions of dignity vary radically with the time, place, and behold-

---

58   R Macklin, 'Dignity Is a Useless Concept' (2003) 327 *BMJ* 7429: 1419–1420, http://www.ncbi.nlm.nih.gov/pmc/articles/PMC300789/.
59   ibid.
60   ibid.
61   S Pinker, 'The Stupidity of Dignity' 1.
62   ibid 2.
63   ibid.
64   ibid 2–3.
65   ibid 5.

er. Second, *dignity is fungible*. The Council and Vatican treat dignity as a sacred value, never to be compromised. In fact, every one of us voluntarily and repeatedly relinquishes dignity for other goods in life. ... Third, *dignity can be harmful.* ... Indeed, totalitarianism is often the imposition of a leader's conception of dignity on a population, such as the identical uniforms in Maoist China or the burqas of the Taliban ... So is dignity a useless concept? Almost. The word does have an identifiable sense, which gives it a claim, though a limited one, on our moral consideration. Dignity is a phenomenon of human perception ... certain features in another human being trigger ascriptions of worth. These features include signs of composure, cleanliness, maturity, attractiveness, and control of the body. The perception of dignity in turn elicits a response in the perceiver. Just as the smell of baking bread triggers a desire to eat it, and the sight of a baby's face triggers a desire to protect it, the appearance of dignity triggers a desire to esteem and respect the dignified person.[66]

Dignity is clearly seen here as a descriptive concept, and an elitist one.

This explains why dignity is morally significant: We should not ignore a phenomenon that causes one person to respect the rights and interests of another. But it also explains why dignity is relative, fungible, and often harmful. Dignity is skin-deep: it's the sizzle, not the steak; the cover, not the book. What ultimately matters is respect for the person, not the perceptual signals that typically trigger it. Indeed, the gap between perception and reality makes us vulnerable to dignity illusions. We may be impressed by signs of dignity without underlying merit, as in the tin-pot dictator, and fail to recognize merit in a person who has been stripped of the signs of dignity, such as a pauper or refugee.[67]

'Exactly what aspects of dignity should we respect?'[68] Pinker gives two answers, one positive, the other negative.

For one thing, people generally want to be seen as dignified. Dignity is thus one of the interests of a person, alongside bodily integrity and personal property, that other people are obligated to respect. We don't want anyone to stomp on our toes; we don't want anyone to steal our hubcaps; and we don't want anyone to open the bathroom door when we're sitting on the john... There is a second reason to give dignity a measure of cautious respect. Reductions in dignity may harden the perceiver's heart and

---

66   ibid 5–6.
67   ibid 6.
68   ibid.

loosen his inhibitions against mistreating the person. When people are degraded and humiliated, such as Jews in Nazi Germany being forced to wear yellow armbands or dissidents in the Cultural Revolution being forced to wear grotesque haircuts and costumes, onlookers find it easier to despise them. ... Note, though, that all these cases involve coercion, so once again they are ruled out by autonomy and respect for persons. So, even when breaches of dignity lead to an identifiable harm, it's ultimately autonomy and respect for persons that gives us the grounds for condemning it.[69]

Thus, according to Steven Pinker, dignity is a psychologically (or scientifically) useless concept: everything we want to say can be expressed by autonomy talk; it is a category of religious fanatics; and it is a phenomenon of human perception (what we conceive as 'dignified') that can bar us from seeing what is really important about persons. For all those reasons we should not continue dignity-discourse but rather decry this neoconservative idea as a scientifically useless notion.

D.

In 2010, Peter Augustine Lawler, a member of the President's Council on Bioethics attacked by Pinker, replied in his *Modern and American Dignity: Who We Are as Persons, and What That Means for our Future*[70] by drawing a sharp distinction between the 'modern' and the 'American' view of dignity. The 'modern' view of dignity, as he calls it, denies what's good about who we are by nature, understanding human dignity to mean moral autonomy (freedom *from* nature) or productivity (asserting our mastery over nature by devising ingenious transformations). This new understanding of dignity stands at odds with the 'American' view, which depends on the self-evidence of the truth that we are all created equally unique and irreplaceable. The American view, which is indebted to classical, Christian, and modern sources, understands that free persons are more than merely autonomous or productive beings—or, for that matter, clever chimps. It sees what's good in our personal freedom and our technical

---

69   ibid 6–7.
70   PA Lawler *Modern and American Dignity: Who We Are as Persons, and What That Means for our Future* (Wilmington, Intercollegiate Studies Institute, 2010).

mastery over nature, but only in balance with the rest of what makes us whole persons—our dignified performance of our 'relational' duties as familial, political, and religious beings.

The modern view, as Lawler calls it, is based on a problematic methodological prejudice.

It seems clear enough that human dignity must consist in what is unique about man as compared with other beings. That is to say, we must *compare* human beings with something else. Now, in a culture which has little or no conception of the supernatural, man cannot avoid comparing himself primarily with other visible beings (as opposed to invisible or spiritual beings) in determining where his uniqueness lies. Especially in a scientific culture, preoccupied as it is with natural studies and the alleviation of natural problems, it is not hard to see why many would reasonably conclude that what is unique about us humans is our ability to reflect on and alter our own nature. Animals cannot do this. You will never find even the noblest ape attempting to do things that it cannot do given its natural (or material) constitution (to fly, for example, or to develop electronic means of communication), nor will an ape attempt to make itself something other than it is by nature. Yet because of our unique abilities for intellection and self-reflection, we humans do extend our abilities beyond what nature has equipped us to do (that is, our physical limitations), and we also dream of improving ourselves in other ways, including overcoming our own mortality. Human persons, in other words, have a strong tendency to find their uniqueness precisely in their *autonomy* with respect to nature, including their own nature.[71]

Thus, for all his differences from Pinker, Lawler also agrees that dignity is a descriptive notion whose ascription is to be based on comparison. Not, however, on the comparison with other animals but on the comparison with supernatural beings. Since our culture has lost touch with this tradition, we look for dignity where it cannot be found (in our freedom from nature) instead of concentrating on what is good about who we are by nature. We need to be more Aristotelian and less modernist in our understanding of dignity if we want to defend it against the attack and criticism of empiricist and naturalist philosophers.

---

71 J Mirus, 'Human Dignity?', http://www.catholicculture.org/commentary/otc.cfm?id=819.

XIV. Descriptive vs. Orienting Conceptions

However, Lawler shares too much common ground with the views he repudiates. He construes dignity as a descriptive concept based on comparison just as his opponents do, and he criticizes his critics only for arguing from a wrong naturalist comparison with animals instead of from a comparison with supernatural beings. But this ties the problem to the problematic distinction between naturalism and theism and forgoes the opportunity to benefit from the Kantian insight that is neither naturalistic nor theistic. For Kant, 'dignity' is not a descriptive but an *orienting concept*. What does this mean?

Descriptive concepts can be predicated of subjects, defined, and used to classify phenomena into sets on the basis of particular features, traits, or characteristics. The traditional definition of 'human being' as 'rational animal' (*animal rationale*) is a case in point: It describes humans as animals, and it marks them off from other animals by their rationality as their distinguishing characteristic.[72]

Orienting concepts, on the other hand, cannot be defined because they have no semantically fixed meaning but only a pragmatic use whose rules or grammar can be described. They provide a *scheme of orientation* in terms of a set of distinctions and a *means of locating ourselves and others by using that scheme* that allow us to orient ourselves and others in real or symbolic spaces. Thus, we use *schemes of spatial distinctions* (left/right; above/ below; in front/behind etc.) to orient ourselves in space; or *schemes of temporal distinctions* (past/present/ future; earlier/later than etc.) to orient ourselves in time; or *schemes of communication* (personal pronouns) to orient ourselves in communicative contexts; or *schemes of salutary distinctions* (healthy/unhealthy; good/bad; medicine/ poison; etc.) to orient ourselves in health situations; or *schemes of emotional distinctions* to orient ourselves in bodily situations (pleasant/unpleasant; frightening/reassuring; etc.); or *schemes of moral distinctions* (good/evil) to orient ourselves in moral contexts; or *schemes of interpersonal behavior* (dignity/value) to orient ourselves in the mode of relating to others. These schemes are different and each has its own internal logic. For example, the spatial distinction between left and right can only be applied from a neutral position that is neither left nor right, whereas the temporal distinctions between past, present, and future can only be applied by being places in

---

72 cf Dalferth, *Umsonst* (2011) chap 1.

the present and not in the past or the future. But for all these differences, they have a common set of pragmatic functions that can be summarized as follows:

These distinctions are not descriptive distinctions 'in the world' but orienting distinctions in how we relate to the world: There is no 'here' and 'now,' 'left' or 'right,' 'present' or 'past,' 'good' or 'evil' in the world, but only with respect to us as we relate to the world around us in these ways.

These distinctions orient by not allowing for degrees or exceptions: If anything is present, past, or future in a given discourse, everything is present, past, or future.

These distinctions are only relevant, i.e. effective, by being used: Unless we orient ourselves in space in terms of left and right, there is no 'left' or 'right.'

One cannot use any one of these distinctions without using the whole scheme: Nobody can say 'I' or 'you' without being able to say 'he,' 'she,' 'it,' 'we,' 'you' and 'they' as well. Take one element of the scheme away and the whole scheme stops functioning.

One cannot use these distinctions without at the same time applying them to oneself, i.e. to locate oneself and others within the scheme: We cannot say 'you' without using (implicitly or in fact) 'I' or 'we' for us; and we cannot use 'dignity' for us without using it of others, and vice versa.

Thus, whereas elitist conceptions of dignity are either rank- or hierarchy-relative (as in Nietzsche or – in a different and more complex way – in Thomas) or description based, i.e. require a particular set of features to be instantiated by someone to whom they are applied legitimately, dignity used in a Kantian sense is *not* a generalized description or universalized elitist conception (i.e. an elitist conception with unrestricted scope) but an orienting device for a particular practice of human life, i.e. the practice of relating to others in moral contexts, in communication, and in other forms of social interaction. The basis for a legitimate ascription of dignity is not a 'Factor X', whether understood as a single feature or a complex set of features, but a practice of (moral) communication. We ascribe dignity to those with whom we communicate as human beings: If they are human persons, we treat them with dignity. This we do not because of any particular feature or set of features in them, but solely because *we commit ourselves* in principle to view and relate to anyone who is a human person in such a way that certain types of behavior are not acceptable (negative notions of dignity), whereas others are appropriate, desirable, required, or imperative (positive notions of dignity). How we conceptualize dignity changes over time and from culture to culture, but to use dignity as a basic device or idea for orienting our ways of relating to those who communicate with us in human interactions and practices is or can be (relatively) stable over time.

What is important here is that practice comes first, not dignity. Without a humane practice of living together with other persons, there is no dignity. We destroy or harm this practice if we ascribe dignity only to us and not to others as well, or only to some humans, and not to all, or only sometimes, and not always, or not only to humans but also to other animals. Conversely, we further this practice if we commit ourselves to viewing and treating every human being, not merely family and friends but also strangers and enemies, as human persons with an untouchable dignity. In this sense, dignity is an orienting concept of a particular human practice – the practice of living a humane rather than an inhumane life together with others (before God – as Christians, Jews, or Moslems will add). The rule of dignity defines a practice that encompasses all human beings to whom we can or could relate in communicative interactions as persons, it comprises all dimensions of our lives from the biological and corporeal through the social and political to the moral and religious,[73] and it states that we commit ourselves to relate to other persons in the same way as we relate to ourselves as persons. To be a human person is enough for sharing this dignity – not to be human in a particular way, or to be genetically close or very similar to humans. The ascription of dignity is not based on comparison, and it is not relative to or dependent on a set of features in a human being, but merely on the fact that we see and identify the other as a human person[74] with whom we interact in a common practice with other human persons.

---

[73] We are bodies not merely in a narrow biological sense but in a rich and complex sense that comprises all dimensions of human life, biological and physical as well as social, cultural, economic, political, moral and religious. In all these dimensions we can suffer and be hurt, and in all these dimensions we can live in humane or inhumane ways by the way we and others orient our lives.

[74] Pinker is right in understanding dignity as a phenomenon of human perception: how we see others and ourselves determines how we relate to others and ourselves. But he misconstrues this insight in a narrowly empiricist way as an occasion that triggers certain ascriptions of worth instead of conceiving it as indicating a human practice based on an ethics of seeing as Arne *Grøn* has developed it. Cf A *Grøn*, 'Ethics of Vision' in IU Dalferth (ed), *Ethik der Liebe. Studien zu Kierkegaard's 'Taten der Liebe'* (Tübingen, Mohr Siebeck, 2002) 111–122.

XV. Three Dimensions of Dignity Discourse

Thus, if we construe dignity discourse as orienting discourse, then the basic problem is not how to define dignity (in a naturalistic or theistic, a modern or an American way), but rather who is to count as a human person so that he or she is a potential partner of human dignity practice. For empiricists this seems to be primarily a biological problem, but it is not. Throughout Western history the character and identity of human beings has been explored by drawing on three basic contrasts or comparisons: the biological contrast between humans and non-humans (humans vs. other animals); the theological contrast between humans and super-humans (humans vs. gods); and the anthropological contrast between humans and humans (inhumane vs. humane ways of living).

Against the backdrop of these approaches three distinct sets of differences have been used to determine the content and function of the concept of dignity. For many it 'seems clear enough that human dignity must consist in what is unique about man as compared with other beings.'[75] However, this can be spelled out in naturalistic, theistic or anthropological terms.

Naturalists understand dignity to be a relative distinction based on a set of biological features that can be found more or less clearly in (some) humans and to some degree also in (some) other great apes; and sometimes more clearly in apes than in humans. Dignity can legitimately be ascribed to those who manifest these features, whether human or not.

Theists, on the other hand, base their account of dignity on a comparison of humans with deities or the divine. Whereas humans are deficient with respect to perfect being, they are more perfect than any other non-divine beings because of their sense of the divine – a sense allegedly unique to them (*sensus divinitatis*).[76]

---

75 Mirus, 'Human Dignity?'.
76 cf GE Lessing, 'Die Religion. Fragment (1753)' in *Gesammelte Werke,* Vol. 1 (3rd edition, Berlin, Aufbau-Verlag, 1968): 'Der Mensch? Wo ist er her? / Zu schlecht für einen Gott; zu gut fürs Ungefähr.' Humans are betwixt and between the divine and non-human creatures and hence in a dangerous if not impossible and paradoxical position: too good to be merely a product of blind chance, as Lessing put it, and not good enough to be divine or angelic. Thus, dignityis ascribed to all and only humans because and insofar as they differ from all other creatures in possessing a sense of the divine.

Anthropological accounts of dignity, finally, compare humans with other humans and understand dignity as a distinct mode of living a human life – a mode that differentiates between inhuman und humane ways of living. The ascription of dignity here depends on a conception of the good life that serves as the touchstone for judging the actual life of humans if they live up to this standard or fail to do so. Those, and only those, who live their lives in a humane way, however this may be defined, manifest dignity.

Thus, whereas naturalistic accounts ascribe dignity to some humans and some other apes, theistic accounts ascribe it to all humans and only to humans, and anthropological accounts ascribe it to those humans who live their lives in a particular way.

XVI. Dignity as a Distinction of Persons

In the anthropological sense, dignity is not a natural property or trait, nor a set of natural properties or traits that can be identified in an organism (naturalism), but a moral category: It is a short formula for the human self-determination to treat other persons with the respect they deserve because of our common humanity.

However, what is this common humanity? Answers differ widely. Biological accounts elaborate the differences between humans and other animals. But this by itself will never be enough. It will always result in identifying merely gradual differences, and this is not enough for the absolute ascription of dignity because it misses the moral point and orienting function of dignity discourse.

In order to avoid the naturalistic fallacy of searching for a Factor X in Fukuyama's sense, moral answers understand our being human not simply as a natural fact but as a way of basing our lives on a normative decision about what we want to be and how we want to live as humans. We can live, or fail to live, our lives in a humane (as opposed to an inhumane) way, and if we can, then we should. From a moral perspective the decisive feature of being human is not to be what one is, but rather to have the potential, the duty and the obligation to *become* what one can be as a human being by living a humane rather than an inhumane life.

The religious answer goes beyond the moral answer by defining a humane way of life in a specific way, i.e. by viewing, placing, or locating human life in relation to God. The theological argument behind this can briefly be summarized as follows: We are all different, but as the different individuals we are, we are all equal before the law. However, the set of those who are equal before the law comprises those, and only those, who are equal before God. Equality before God is the non-natural distinction we all share as persons, and this is the basis for the ascription of dignity to us. Personhood and equality are not something that can be ascribed to humans on the basis of a comparison, but rather are presupposed in comparing humans with others. The logic of comparing requires reference to a third in order to compare two: to compare A with B is to compare A to B with respect to C. From a religious perspective, humans are equal with respect to the law *because* they are equal with respect to the presence of God; and they are equal with respect to God not because they chose to live in the presence of God but rather because God freely becomes their loving neighbor and in doing so opens the space and time for humans to live their lives in a humane way – or to fail to do so.

That is to say, dignity is not ascribed to us *tout court* but to us *as persons*, and not just in any sense of 'person' but *in so far as we as persons manifest or express the presence of God*. As persons we are more than we appear to be: We are signs that point beyond ourselves to the presence of the one without whom we would not be, and we can become signs that manifest the presence of God to others, not necessarily by intentionally trying to do so but rather, and normally, without knowing it, or learning about it only retrospectively. To be able to signify God's presence to others is what distinguishes us from other beings. As persons we are *personae* of God's presence.

Thus, to respect the dignity of persons is to respect the presence of God in the other and myself. This is more than the Kantian principle that human beings should never be treated merely as a means, but always as ends in themselves. It is to insist that we – each and every one of us – are more than we appear to be because we are *personae dei*, i.e. somebody in and through whom God makes his presence manifest to others. Persons in this sense are not only the powerful and rich, as a misconceived doctrine of analogy might suggest, but even more so the poor and oppressed, those without rights and possession, those whom we don't like, even our enemies: They are all potential occasions of the manifestation of God's presence to us, and hence should be treated with the respect those deserve who are dignified by God to become occasions for manifesting his presence.

That is to say, everybody, *simply by being a human person,* is dignified to become an occasion of manifesting God's presence to others. This is the Christian origin and foundation of the universalist idea of human dignity *with respect to humans*, which is based on an elitist understanding of dignity *with respect to God*: *Dignity* is first and foremost the dignity of God the creator, maker of heaven and earth. God's dignity is transferred and extended to the creature when and in so far as God makes them bearers and revealers of his presence to others. It is a dignity in which creatures participate by receiving it as a gift of God without ever possessing it. And since they do not possess it, they cannot lose or be robbed of it. This is why the dignity of human persons is universal and untouchable, and yet they can be treated in ways that ignore and contradict it. Their dignity can be offended by treating them in inhumane ways. But this offends the dignity of the source and origin of all dignity, i.e. the one who has chosen to make human beings his representatives and to manifest his presence to us in and through each and every human person, not merely, as the elitist notion has it, through some of us but not others.

XVII. Property Essentialism vs. Dynamic Personalism

The three basic contrasts for comparing human beings result in three different approaches to human dignity. The first concentrates on comparing humans and non-humans (animals), and seeks to explicate dignity as an indicator of biological excellence. But this approach is a failure. Naturalism is no help in understanding dignity.

The third concentrates on comparing humans with humans and sees the real difference at stake not in the biological difference between humans and other animals but rather in the anthropological difference between humane and inhumane ways of living a human life. Dignity here indicates a *mode* of human living – a *humane* as distinct from an *inhumane mode* of living. This is the proper locus of dignity discourse as developed in the 20th century.

The central question then becomes what we mean by a 'humane way of living a human life.' Here the second approach as worked out in the Christian tradition offers two importantly different answers.

The first is property essentialism: Dignity is a property that distinguishes humans (and angels) from other creatures or distinguishes a religious view of the world as creation (Pope Benedict XVI: 'dignity of the earth') from secular views. Thus humans have dignity because they are rational beings or at least beings who have the potential of being rational beings. They are rational souls in a body, and whereas the latter signifies their commonality with other creatures, the former signifies their (analogical) commonality with their Creator. The problem of this approach is that it collapses two distinctions into one: the distinction between God and creature, and the distinction between human and other creatures. *Reason* or *rationality* are taken to constitute the decisive difference between humans and other creatures on earth, and they are at the same time taken to be that which show us, and only us, to be related to God. The feature or property that singles humans out among creatures is at the same time that which singles humans out in their relationship to God. But this is in no way obvious and results in an over-determined notion of reason: Reason is what distinguishes us from other animals (animal *rationale*) and as such constitutes our (relative) sameness with God according to the analogical difference between God as the source of reason and dignity and humans as the created occasions of reason and dignity. However, why should that which distinguishes us from other animals be at the same time that which manifests our special relationship with God? Property essentialism uses the theological comparison between the human and the divine to interpret or elucidate the biological difference between humans and other animals. It gives a theological answer to a biological problem, and in doing so it fails to locate the problem of dignity where it ought to be located: in the difference between humane and inhumane ways of living a human life.

The second and very different answer is given by a dynamic personalism: Dignity is seen as divine gift that empowers us to become what we can be because of the gift given to us. It is a distinction that enables us to become the persons we can be by living up to who we are as persons: God's freely chosen neighbors. We are all born as humans who can live as persons, and we do this in the fullest sense open to us if we orient our lives to the way God relates to us. By relating to us as our neighbor, God gives us the potential to become what we cannot become from our own powers: humans who live a humane life as persons among persons before God. The theological contrast between human and divine is used here not to elucidate the contrast between humans and animals but rather the anthropological or ethical contrast between humane and inhumane ways of living our life. The point of departure is not what humans are, do, or have but rather what God does to and for them. From a human perspective this means emphasizing the basic passivity, dependency or (in more positive terms) enrichment and empowerment of human life by the way God relates to and becomes present in it. Dignity is and remains God's property and hence cannot be taken away from us who participate in it as a divine gift. This gift can be spelled out without reference to dignity. Indeed, this category may explicitly be avoided because it lends itself to naturalist or essentialist misunderstandings, i.e. as signifying something in our biological, natural or cultural make-up that marks us off from other creatures. But the point of the dynamic personalist understanding of dignity is that we are unique not in what *we* are but in what we become *empowered* to *show* or *indicate about God* (creator) – i.e. that God is present to his creation in a particular way, a way spelled out as *love* in the Christian tradition. Thus, the criterion of a properly humane humanity is to accept one's basic passivity, i.e. our empowerment to mediate and manifest the presence of God to others. This empowerment is something beyond our control: we cannot give it to anyone nor can we take it away from anyone: It is a pre-given of all our acting and doing. This in turn grounds our respect for each other – a respect that is always a respect for the respect of God for others. That is to say, we respect others because we respect that God respects everyone as his neighbor, not merely those who belong to a particular nation, group, or tradition, but unrestrictedly everyone: God is the *neighbor of everybody*. This constitutes the *dignity of human persons* as the *humane mode of living a human life in the presence of God*. Humans acknowledge and respect this, as Christians say, by living according to the rule of love: To live in this way is to see God (or God's presence) in everybody and hence tailor what we do not merely to our own interests or the requirements of the other but also, and even more so, to the gift that he or she represents as much as we do: to be those whom God has chosen to be his neighbors.

For the Sake of Human Dignity, Ban Reified Concepts of 'Man Made in the Image of God': Some Theological Perspectives

Stephan Schaede

Dignity? Should we expect any relevant contribution by Protestant theology worth mentioning? 'Of course!' a representative of a Protestant ethics commission should answer. 'Man's Dignity has as its deep foundation that man was made in the image of God. To be thus is free for everybody. Completely automatically man is an image of God, and therefore dignity is universal and for free. This is a God who is generous toward everybody.' Is there any other perspective so clear, so sharp, so simple? Then might the secularist mocker not agree, saying: 'Absolutely! Dignity based on the image of God may be for free, but also is useless.'

A historical, passably informed Protestant position has to come to a different judgment. This position might suggest: 'You should sequester the concepts of dignity and image of God for the time being.' Why? Because both are – candidly, agreeing with Elisabeth Anscombe – very loosely defined, kitchen-sink concepts, so called 'rag-bag categories' (cf. G.E.M. Anscombe, The first person). Everybody projects without hesitation onto the blank screen of the concepts dignity and image of God a broad framework, later to be fleshed out by profound argumentation. Sometimes it is reason, sometimes it is spirit, sometimes it is love, sometimes it is natural domination which is to constitute the image of God. Sometimes dignity is merited, sometimes it is acquired, sometimes it is bound to specific qualities, to entities or to prayer. Sometimes dignity is mystifying in its elusiveness. Therefore arguments and motives cited with good cause, or only contingently with reference to European traditions, remain rather obscure for philosophical masterminds as well.

To remain silent on the question of dignity – that is worth mentioning. Remarkably, this exactly was the 19th century Protestant position. During the 19th century, the concept of dignity was nearly completely absent from the anthropological chapters of relevant dogmatics. Martin Luther had dreaded to consider the problem of dignity in a constructive manner. Characteristically, he employs this concept negatively. Unfortunately modern Protestant thinkers prefer to suppress this aspect of Luther's intellectual biography. Therefore, it would be particularly worthwhile to set out the history and fortunes of the ancient Christian concept of dignity across the 20th century and into the 21st. Not less, it would be worthwhile to write a systematic article to address the question, what would be gained if dignity had been a Christian concept since Saint Paul wrote his letters? Is dignity therefore automatically a viable concept?

Hopefully the reader will not be desperately disappointed, but may well be quite surprised, to learn that neither the history nor the systematic exploration of the concept of dignity has been written up to now. Therefore parts one and two of this paper are contributions to a terminological virgin territory. Part one offers insight into the resistance against addressing the problem of dignity in 19th century theology. A short commentary concerning when dignity was rediscovered in Protestant anthropology also is included.

Part two provides a short overview of various Latin semantic antecedents of dignity. Dignity has always been a so called 'pollachos legomenon' (said in many ways), a concept belonging to many categories. That explains why varied connotations resonate whenever the concept of dignity is invoked. Collectively, these many connotations legitimate and allow us to comprehend dignity as a dowry passed down to us, as well as an intellectual and theological effort at defining dignity for the benefit of contemporary society.

A short third part will free dignity from its semantic 'wilderness'. This is because a Protestant theologian never ever should end his explorations without touching the cross of Jesus Christ. We have learned this from Saint Paul. He hammered into the Corinthians: We are preaching no person other than Jesus Christ, the crucified.

What was helpful for the Corinthians shouldn't hurt the Berliners.

I. 'Resistance' Against Dignity in 19th Century Protestant Theology

A. Friedrich Daniel Ernst Schleiermacher: The Human Person Beyond the Image of God and Beyond Dignity

At the beginning of the 19th century the concepts of dignity and image of God come under fire. Criticism is first and especially verbalized by the most important Protestant theologian of the century, *Friedrich Daniel Ernst Schleiermacher*. The concept of dignity fades out from Schleiermacher's anthropology. At the same time Schleiermacher criticizes the concept of the image of God. This concept is too trivial and 'folksy'. It does not convincingly explain what it purports to explain: The exceptional position of humankind in God's creation.

The young Schleiermacher, in his first speech about religion (1809), writes passionately about 'dignity of humankind' to win his readers for 'morality, right and freedom'; in his classical work 'Glaubenslehre' (The Christian Faith in Outline) (1831), he avoids speaking about dignity entirely. Beyond that, he fundamentally criticizes the concept of image of God, and argues as follows: The concept of image of God has to 'reveal human nature in its superiority to other creatures.' This intention is acceptable. But the concept of the image of God cannot realize this intention, as 'image of God' denotes a relation of similarity. Schleiermacher asks: Which kind of similarity could be meant? There are two possibilities: 1. The whole world is to God as our organism is to our highest mental faculty. In that case God has to become one with the world. Hence the world is his body. This conclusion implies for Schleiermacher pantheism. That is unworthy of discussion. The second possibility also is out of the question: 2. God in himself ought to have an element corresponding to our physical organism. But assuming this means God is 'contaminated,' given his deity. Therefore Schleiermacher prefers to describe explicitly the exclusive and unique qualities of human beings in comparison with all other living beings. Schleiermacher identifies as one important quality 'the continuous vitality of consciousness of God.' In this regard God is *immanent* in a human person without being identical with this person in a pantheistic sense.[1] Schleiermacher's Glaubenslehre can be regarded as an approach which develops this thesis for all aspects of Protestant theology.

B. Alois Biedermann: Inquiries on the Utility of Dignity and Image of God

A second important theological witness of the 19th century is Alois Emanuel Biedermann. Biedermann, Swiss theologian and freethinker, chooses a controversial theological approach to the question of the image of God. His crucial point is: Either the image of God will be defined in a

---

1   See FDE Schleiermacher, 'Der christliche Glaube. 2. Auflage (1830-31)', § 61, 4 in R Schäfer (ed): *Kritische Gesamtausgabe*, vol 13 (Berlin/New York, De Gruyter, 2013) 381-387.

way which can be understood also in a secular context, but then the contribution of theology is completely boring. Or, the image of God will be defined incisively in the theological sense of the word, but then it can't be attributed to all human beings – without creating a semantic-pragmatic disorder. That is not worthy of discussion.

Developing this crucial point, Biedermann identifies a problem which is structurally interesting for the concept of dignity. This problem belongs to the theoretical level of specific theological descriptions within a universal philosophical anthropology. The problem is: Either the discourse will be quite specific, but then suffers from a loss of universal validity. Or the universal validity is obvious, but then the discourse lacks any theological point.

Biedermann exposes this problem as follows: For the Catholic theologian the image of God consists in the pure mental capacity of human beings. For the Protestant theologian, however, the image of God consists in the relation between human beings and God. Because *'the elevation of a human being beyond its naturalness is the center of its pure nature.'*[2]

This contrast clarifies much: The Catholic definition has the advantage of attributing the image of God universally to all human beings. In this context every agnostic or atheistic intellectual is an image of God due to the fact that he has intellect at his disposal. This argumentation succeeds at the expense of religious relevance. The relation to God is not essential for the concept of the image of God. This relation to God only is added by grace as a gift which enhances and lends meaning to human existence.

Let us now transform this theological history and argument into the interdisciplinary discourse of dignity: All human beings have dignity. The theorem which shows that is extra-theological. It could be developed just as well by a secular philosophy which esteems the intellect as a central human faculty. That which theology adds is a pure *donum superadditum*. Therefore theology is irrelevant for an interdisciplinary discourse of dignity; yet, the interdisciplinary contribution adds next to nothing. Why? Because the intellectual should realize that he will be wiser thanks to the theological discussion on dignity. However, why and how he becomes wiser is difficult to set out.

Protestantism also is in a bind, but in a rather specific different way. The image of God is an essential classification of a human being. A hu-

---

[2] See AE Biedermann, *Christliche Dogmatik*, Vol. 2 (Berlin, Dietrich Reimer Verlag, 1885) 287, 290.

man being is an image of God precisely when conforming to God, and lives and deals justly and according to that ideal. This is – judged from a theological standpoint – attractive. But what about an intellectual who is an irreligious nonconformist? The 'consistent' Protestant has to judge as follows: This intellectual has become lost as a human being. In exactly this manner Flacius Illyricus argued. Outside the Christian religion, a human being is an image of the devil. From a secular point of view this construct is out of the question.

That's why the Lutheran and Reformed theologians have formulated a *'Cave consequentariis!'* against Flacius Illyricus. But then the question is: How can the Protestant dogmatic theology manage the fact that God's own likeness *de facto,*[3] with a few paltry exceptions, has been lost.

Simply put, to resolve this problem Biedermann identifies in the Reformed and the Lutheran theology a specific denominational predecessor of a theory of development of the image of God:

The Lutherans with their *'simul iustus et peccator'* argue:

1. The image of God is originally present in a human being. But it is actually, effectively lost.[4] 2. It is not present in the human being by itself. But by grace alone God makes this correspondence possible. God relates to a human being as if this human being would be as an image of God. However, not until the human being is resurrected to eternal life will it be an inviolable image of God.[5]

The Reformists emphasize the difference between potentiality and actuality.

In a first step the image of God is potentially violable. In a second step it is violated because of human frailty This violated image of God is present at every moment of life. So it is a complete, but pale image.[6] In a third step the persistence of faith, which is a gift from above, shapes the inviolable reality of the image of God out of the violated potentiality of that image. It is a powerful image with depth of clarity and definition.

Biedermann notes, it is also intricate: The concept of image of God is a fragile term. What potentially is unachievable, cannot be lost; what is

---

3 See RA Lipsius, *Lehrbuch der Evangelisch-Protestantischen Dogmatik* (Braunschweig, Schwetschke, 1893) 348.
4 See Biedermann, *Dogmatik* (1885) 292.
5 ibid.
6 See FHR Frank, *System der christlichen Wahrheit* (Erlangen, Verlag von Andreas Deichert, 1885) 365.

achieved, can be lost.[7] Even August Vilmar has taken this inherent fragility – both of the dignity concept and of dignity itself – as his subject.

C. August Vilmar: Death and Freedom of Choice as the End of Dignity

The New Lutheran August Vilmar – although well-known for his attacks of piety[8] – nevertheless is deeply interesting for his discourse on dignity, because he underlines that the image of God will be lost in two situations: 1. During dying and death and 2. In the course of freedom of choice.

At 1: In distinction from all the other theologians he works out the following:

'The phrase "the death is a blessing or a benefit" exists in an infinite thoughtlessness Blasphemous or facile phrases invented to express modern cultural norms descend into a form of blindness.'[9] Death is the quintessence of bad finitude; all similar life situations (depression, loneliness, hatred etc.), as well. They diverge from all that which is meant by image of God. They reduce vital interchange, the presence of God and pleasure.[10] Vilmar's position is a characteristic Protestant one and prepares a line of argumentation which denies the possibility of dying with dignity and a dignified death. Both of them harm human dignity – dying as well as death.

At 2: It is completely absurd to interpret freedom of choice as a central moment of being an image of God. It is not possible that the privilege of human beings consists in being oblivious to the difference between good and evil. A human being ... cannot confirm its autonomy and independence merely by deciding occasionally between two options.'[11] Vilmar emphasizes: 'Freedom is the capacity to remain I,' but not to become 'Not-I.' Consequently freedom of choice is not an attribute of God.[12] Vilmar's reflections cast a critical light on positions which associate dignity with a high level or maximum of freedom of choice.

---

7   See Frank, *System* (1885) 565.
8   See AFC Vilmar, *Dogmatik. Akademik Vorlesungen*, after his death edited by KW Piderit (Gütersloh, Bertelsmann, 1874) 328.
9   See Vilmar, *Dogmatik* (1874) 338.
10 See Vilmar, *Dogmaik* (1874) 339
11 See Vilmar, *Dogmatik* (1874) 344 f.
12 ibid.

To judge from Vilmar's point of view, and even more so beyond Vilmar's point of view: Freedom of choice degrades dignity.

But now let us examine Isaak August Dorner. He was the first 19th century theologian to use the concept of value. Value in this context denotes the privilege of a human being within creation.

D. Isaak August Dorner: Image of God and Value of Life

Isaak August Dorner, inspired by Kant, Hegel and Schleiermacher,[13] has combined the concept of image of God with the concept of value of life. However, he has not yet spoken of human dignity. Dorner suggests: Something has a value only if it is closely related to an intention. This suggestion leads to the following conclusion: 'If it had been a matter of indifference to God whether there is a world or not, this would be to declare the world as waste and worthless. And this is against the opinion of the Holy Bible.'[14] 'But God', Dorner continues, 'is a lover of life. He loves the world so that he contributes value to it.' God has a good mind to reproduce, multiply and increase the love life of beings. Furthermore God has a good mind to a kingdom of love.' But why are human beings special images of God? This is because a human being is able to reflect on his/her life and to realize that the human ability to love others is a product of self-communication of divine love.[15]

This rather trivial justification of human life's value is not sufficient in the eyes of Dorner. Therefore Dorner becomes extraordinarily Christianly: A human being is an invaluable image of God not only because of the ability to receive the idea of God in an intellectual way; beyond this, human beings can completely receive God much as God communicates himself.[16] Thus it is for a human being (in opposition to Calvin's *Finitium non capax infiniti*). The finitude of creatures does not limit the infinite love of God.[17] That manifestation appears for the first time in Jesus Christ. Dorner further has no problem with universalizing this: In everyone can appear the infinite love of God. That is why Dorner refers to Saint Paul and

---

13 See IA Dorner, *System der christlichen Glaubenslehre*, vol 1 (Berlin, W.L. Hertz, 1879).
14 See Dorner, *System* (1879) 449.
15 See Dorner, *System* (1879) 453.
16 See Dorner, *System* (1879) 455.
17 See Dorner, *System* (1879) 456.

speaks of the 'vital temple', in which the holy God realizes his trinitarian existence.

In an absurd species-ism he continues: For the sake of these free beings, which are 'exclusive endearing autonomous objects of love.' the world was created. 'All the others are organs and resources and the arena for the kingdom of love.'[18]

Human beings must develop this dowry of the image of God during their 'natural life.'[19] Dorner integrates this issue into a theory of development: God as the promoter of life evolves and enhances human efforts. He evolves these human developmental efforts by generating in these beings an immortal image of himself. This thesis certainly is a theological one. It cannot be proved. But Dorner is convinced that it is necessary to risk this thesis. This is because 'the true concept of God – thanks to God's will to love the community of mankind –' holds up highly the 'value and the personality of a human being'. Hence God's will to love gives security for the immortality of mankind.' Therefore human beings have 'the potential' to live eternally.[20]

This is the place to make a structural observation: By emphasizing the essential significance the concept of an eternal image of God, Dorner tries to ensure in a theological manner what in later times will be ensured with rather different secular arguments proclaiming the centrality of the concept of an inviolable dignity.

But what is really remarkable is the fact that – apart from (ultra)orthodox Lutheran positions – all 19th century Protestant theologians subscribe to the view that the image of God is strictly a concept which describes a developmental trajectory, not an ontological status. This also has to be said for theological structures which prepare the justification for explicit use of the concept of human dignity. Richard Rothe has pointed out this insight. Rothe was one of the sharpest and wittiest of the so called 'Vermittlungstheologen' (theologians of mediation).

---

18   See Dorner, *System* (1879) 458.
19   See Dorner, *System* (1879) 520.
20   See IA Dorner, *System der christlichen Glaubenslehre*, Vol..2, part 2 (Berlin, W.L. Hertz, 1881) 922.

E. Richard Rothe: Developing Towards an Image of God, Dignity and Inviolable Law

There are two reasons why Rothe's arguments must be discussed in this context.

First aspect: Rothe – in a critical manner – accepts the theological premise that a human being is an image of God. But to be an image of God in the concrete sense of the word is pie-in-the-sky, impossible. A human person might find such an obligation frustrating, to try to live up to such an image or goal, given human imperfections and weaknesses. At the beginning of life there is nothing but pure ability. To become an image of God a person must dedicate his life to divine purpose.

Second aspect: Rothe refers only once, but that once explicitly, to the concept of dignity. His central point is: Dignity has to be orientated toward an *inviolable* law.

In detail: Rothe documents scholastically: In the Old Testament the meaning of the image of God firstly consists in ruling over the other creatures. Secondly, it consists of an original immortality, and thirdly, of special moral qualities of human beings (Sir. 17,5-8). In the New Testament the emphases will be changed. Now moral qualities are central, as is clear from the Sermon on the Mount (Mt. 5,48 etc.). But the most important issue is the following one: Jesus Christ becomes the embodiment and paragon of the image of God (2. Cor 4,4; Col 1,15 and Hebr 1,3). Thus a human being is challenged to become an image of God. But one will be an image of God in a distant future and will gain bit by bit this image by improving and perfecting one's moral capacities.[21] That view sheds a clear light on the first parents of world history. Adam and Eve, if they ever existed, should not be seen as nearly so unique and brilliant as church history has suggested. Adam and Eve, our original images of integrity ... Quite an overstatement! Intelligence, knowledge and volition were in a very terrifying stage in (the theological account of) human history. How can we understand them? Adam and Eve are taken in by the 'simple sophisms of the snake' and are adept immediately at lying. So they are scarcely anything like an image of God.[22] Therefore the classical dogmatical thesis is absurd – that justice was an original state present at the beginning of human affairs. Moreover justice has to be described as a morally acquired attribute.

---

21   See R Rothe, *Zur Dogmatik* (Gotha, F.A. Perthes, 1863) 261.
22   See Rothe, *Zur Dogmatik* (1863) 263

It emerges in specific cultural and social conditions. Hence justice never is a natural ability and is therefore not 'original'.

In the view of Rothe, the biblical history of creation advertises the actual *conditio humana*. Thus the theology of the Socinians, who rejected the concepts of original justice and original sin, will be relevant. Socinianism is no longer a heresy. That is the first central point.

The other central point is: Rothe emphasizes the 'essential equality of all members of the human species.' This equality for Rothe is 'of peculiar and immediate religious interest.' It does not have to be justified in a biological manner. It is of no importance to know if 'mankind comes from a unique human couple or from an unique troop of monkeys.'[23]

Why is that? Rothe clarifies this in an argumentation by referring at a certain point to the concept of dignity.

The 'universal concept of the human creation must be defined' as follows: The human creature is a 'terrestrial personal creature.' It is 'the immediate unity of a material body (natural organism) and a Self which results from a coordination of vital functions (personality). As a person a human being is essentially an *'individual being which is conceptually distinguished from all other beings.'* Wherever a being can be identified in a bodily manner in this way, we are discussing a human being. Therefore there is no need for a specific biological origin. The 'power of *self-determination*' is central.[24] Thus man is essentially a 'moral being', because he determines how to lead his life.[25]

How to live his life depends on his ability to relate his 'material nature to his immaterial I.' The two anthropologic 'elements' – material nature and immaterial I – have completely different dignity. In this connection dignity is a graduated concept. The immaterial I has the highest dignity. Therefore it has to define and guide material nature. If not there will be confusion of dignity. But as all human beings fundamentally are on a journey toward being an image of God, it is their life task to further actualize the dominance of I during their life. This life task will be formulated by an 'inviolable law.'[26] It is interesting how Rothe uses the three terms 'inviolable', 'law' and 'dignity'. Human dignity is not inviolable. The law is inviolable which guides human beings to fulfill the dignity of their I. In

---

23 See Rothe, *Zur Dogmatik* (1863) 265.
24 See Rothe, *Zur Dogmatik* (1863) 269.
25 See Rothe, *Zur Dogmatik* (1863) 270.
26 See Rothe, *Zur Dogmatik* (1863) 271.

addition, men themselves do not even possess dignity. Dignity will be more or less attributed only to their fundamental natural *'elements'*. Men have to sort out the natural disorder and confusion of their 'elements' to gain freedom. At the end of this process of liberation – Rothe emphasizes – immortality waits for men.[27]

F. Guaranteed Dignity (Verbürgte Würde) Beyond Nature and Culture. The Rediscovery of Dignity in 20th Century Theology in the Work of Martin Kähler

It was not in fact Federal President Gustav Heinemann – as often is maintained – inspired by the German constitution – who reintroduced into modern discourse the concept of human dignity, as rooted in Protestant theology. The Protestant theologian Martin Kähler is responsible, having revived this concept at the beginning of the 20th century. How did that come about? The reason is very clear. Kähler absorbed Kant and used Kant's ideas as he likes; he has transformed them somewhat idiosyncratically in the service of rather theological interests. His central point is: Human beings as vital self-purpose have a guaranteed dignity from God – beyond nature and culture.

And so it is set out in Kähler's 'science of Christian faith':

The lives of men are in their own hands. That is their God-given dowry. Because of this dowry everything around them is a means. A human being considers itself 'as the fundamental purpose of his existence' and treats himself accordingly.[28] Again, this self-determination is why a human being is an image of God.

Actually men do possess an ability to be such an image. To be an image of God is a task men have to fulfill.[29] But this task has to be fulfilled in an inconsistent, uncertain context delimited in the following sentence: 'Man is a created person.' What is created has its sources elsewhere. But a person is founded, built, by itself. This is the essential inconsistency of Christian theology. As a created person a human being is on the way from a

---

27 ibid.
28 See M Kähler, *Die Wissenschaft der christlichen Lehre* (Leipzig, A. Deichert'sche Verlagsbuchhandlung, 1905) 270.
29 See Kähler, *Wissenschaft* (1905) 270.

pure formal origin to the actual fulfillment of the desire and determination to be a person.[30]

Against this background Kähler develops a rather demanding nature-culture-theory. It is in this context that he has used the concept 'human dignity.'

Based on a natural instinct men preserve themselves. This instinct arranges human life so that men esteem themselves. This self-esteem cultivates men. Human culture serves the perfection of self-esteem. In perfecting self-esteem 'a structure of life-tasks' will be built which assert a certain ability to then resolve these life-tasks. Kähler judges very carefully: In resolving these tasks only 'sporadically'/'in patches' a 'similar human dignity' is maintained.[31]

But the bitter fact is: This similar human dignity 'beyond Christian history' was nowhere realized 'even in human insight and in legal regulation'.[32] Kähler admits: 'Man isolated from his concrete position in history' is a 'general concept held in vain '. In this context religion has to be criticized, too: Degradation of human persons and dedication to wrong purposes certainly are possible in a religious context.[33]

But then it has to be asked: How is dignity realized in the world? Thanks to a genuine theological insight: The world has the dignity to be the scene of reconciliation.[34] A human being has dignity in this world because he is in effect a 'citizen of two worlds.' To symbolize this the Sabbath was instituted. The Sabbath, Sunday in Christianity, is the day of dignity, because Sunday as resting day shows mankind quite plainly the self purpose of human life, that practical labor is not all, that 'man does not live by bread alone'. Therefore dignity is guaranteed as an expression of such self purpose of life, which cultural scholarship regularly misses.[35]

Finally it has to be emphasized: Kähler would reject the 20th century assertion of an intimate connection between dignity and image of God. In his eyes it is false to affirm: 'A human being has dignity because it is an image of God.' It is correct to say: 'A human being on the basis of its ability to become an image of God is able to preserve dignity.' Nothing else matters. The fundamental way to guarantee dignity is the following one: A

---

30 See Kähler, *Wissenschaft* (1905) 269.
31 See Kähler, *Wissenschaft* (1905) 306.
32 See Kähler, *Wissenschaft* (1905) 138.
33 See Kähler, *Wissenschaft* (1905) 183.
34 See Kähler, *Wissenschaft* (1905) 269
35 See Kähler, *Wissenschaft* (1905) 269.

clever altruism. A clever altruism first and foremost is interested in the dignity of the other without losing own dignity. This is only possible if the purpose of the other at the same time is my purpose and I by myself can remain my purpose.[36]

II. Short Overview of Various Latin Semantic 'Precursors' of Dignity

For Protestant ethics, the leading authority is Christian faith. Protestant ethics opens understanding to the moral direction of faith. And the power of judgment of Protestant ethics is geared towards the love that grows out of Christian faith. These judgments, however, are formulated by means of concepts and terms which always have non-Christian connotations as well. Christian ethos has gained cultural influence because of the fact that it also associated itself with non-Christian thinking.[37] Nevertheless, what matters is how confident Christian ethos is in its association with non-Christian thought. Is it only following behind or does it coin its own terms? The concept of human dignity is a prime example with which to examine this question.

In the following part is a rudimentary exploration of the origins of definitions of dignity, from the perspective of the history of ideas.[38] With regard to dignity, rather complex, reciprocal secular-Christian processes of inheritance have occurred in the past. Most probably, originally non-Christian conceptions of dignity have been incorporated into Christian theology. Theology has given them distinctive reinterpretations. And philosophy and law have then adapted the accordingly Christianized concepts of dignity anew.

The term dignity has eight precedents when looking at its Latin history alone. Apart from dignitas, the terms auctoritas, honestas, honor, decus, gravitas, maiestas and nobilitas ought to be mentioned.[39] I will quickly describe the Roman origins of these terms and explain at the same time what changed in the transition from their profane [or, pagan] to the specifically

---

36 See Kähler, *Wissenschaft* (1905) 600.
37 See J Fischer, *Theologische Ethik. Grundwissen und Orientierung* (Stuttgart, Kohlhammer, 2002) 47.
38 See S Schaede, 'Würde – eine ideengeschichtliche Annäherung' in P Bahr and H-M Heinig (eds), *Menschenwürde in der säkularen Verfassungsordnung* (Tübingen, Mohr Siebeck, 2006) 7-72.
39 See Schaede, 'Würde'.

Christian usage. Through this historical process, the concept of dignity is gaining systematic poignancy as will be shown below.

1. *Dignitas* is conditioned by the freedom of man.[40] *Dignitas* is the marker of a particular social group. In this privileged social group, there are other, different and varied levels of dignity. This means: Only some people have *dignitas*. Those who have *dignitas* can possess more or less of it.[41] *Dignitas* strives for societal appreciation and protection. Ambrosius of Milan delved into *dignitas* and initially formulated the claim that for a Christian, it does not pose a problem to lose his *dignitas*, as long as that loss happens in the name of Jesus Christ.[42] According to Ambrosius, the fruit of *dignitas* is hollow and the question whether there are different levels of dignity collapses where God shows his presence.[43]

In contrast to this reckoning with the Roman concept, Ambrosius formulated a pointedly different, Christian understanding of dignity. He said: The ideal state of human life is where all of mankind shares the same dignity.[44] Ambrosius of Milan was the first to link dignity in the sense of *dignitas* with the maxim of equality. He arrived at this link neither through general cultural theoretical nor through naturalistic arguments. On the contrary, he tried to understand the account of creation in the first book Moses.

The Venerable Bede, however, suddenly restarted the talk of levels or distinctions of dignity (*gradus dignitatis*). Bernard de Clairvaux claimed that dignity was something which any man might gain through certain attitudes.[45] This is why Martin Luther sharply condemned talking about *dignitas personae*. Acquired dignity was an absurdity to him!

2. *Decus* makes that which dignitas is, tangible in a person's behavior and appearance. It renders it visible. A person's charisma is *decus*. This is the appeal, the force of dignity which can be so affecting and potent as to become indestructible. In order to realize *decus* one must meet a person face to face.[46] A person's dignity depends on being perceived by some-

---

40 See Cicero, *Pro C. Rabirio perduellionis reo* 16.
41 See Cicero, *De re publica II*, 27, 43 with *De oratore II*, 48,198.
42 See Ambrosius, *Explanatio psalmorum XII*, Psalmus 43: 70,1.
43 See Ambrosius, *Expositio euangelii secundum Lucam IV*, 28.
44 See Ambrosius, *Exameron*, dies 5, 15, 52.
45 See Schaede, 'Würde' 32 f.
46 See Cicero, *De officiis I*, 34, 124 with Cicero, *In M. Antonium orationes Phlippicae oratio III*, 14, 36 and Ovid; *Epistulae ex Ponto*, lib. II, carm. 5 v. 27-30.

body other than him. This is a very important motive which will be picked up by theology.

3. *Gravitas* signifies the weight and momentum of a person's dignity. *Gravitas* simply is. It does not need other people's appreciation. If a person has *gravitas*, people will notice him as soon as he enters a room. His presence fills the room. *Gravitas* also is the subjugating power of dignity.[47] This, too, is a motive of dignity which will become influential for theology. People emanate dignity by simply being there, without doing or refraining from something. This is constitutive for the Protestant teachings of vindication, which say that man becomes just – and thus does justice to and in his life – exclusively through faith and trust in God.

4. *Honestas* is the self-sufficient form of dignity. A fellow human who noiselessly but unabashedly commits himself to a society's *bonum commune* has *honestas*.[48] *Honestas* is a person's inner dignity, and thus is an important element necessary to guarantee the inviolability of dignity, beyond the fact of how a person is treated.

5. *Nobilitas* is an even more strongly exclusive title of a certain social class. The Roman senate's political opponents would later even use the term as abuse. This term in particular has caused a lot of controversy in theology. The reasons for this have not yet been researched. Gregory the Great said: God heightens man to his *nobilitas*. In the process, he continued, man accepts Christ – not only all mankind (!) – as God's image and tries to emulate him.[49] Later on, Christian theology would develop teachings about different levels and intensities of dignity from and through *nobilitas*. A hierarchy of dignity was developed with regard to the biological classification as well as the differing capabilities of all beings. A bird is more dignified than a worm. Man is more dignified than an animal. Perceiving is more dignified than eating. Thinking is more dignified than perceiving. With increasing dignity, a being's and its life's complexity are growing, too. A human being who eats and drinks a lot but does not think that much defrauds his very own existence of the adequate usage of his talents.

At this point, Aristotle's biological writings are referred to and boldly combined with the Bible's remarks on creation – thus, this is an attempt to

---

47 See Ovid, *Metamorphosen IX*, 39-41.
48 See Seneca, *De beata vita IV*, 3.
49 See Gregory the Great, *Moralia in Iob XX*, 16, 41.

combine 'scientific' and Biblical derivations of dignity.[50] Bonaventure, noting the high number of natural abortions in the early stages of development, argues without restraint – and he is not alone in this – that dignity (*nobilitas*) had been increasing during the course of a pregnancy in animals as well as humans. Those who claimed differently had to accuse God of letting a dignified form (*tam nobilis forma*) perish without any justified reason. To argue thus, however, was considered downright impious.[51]

6. *Auctoritas* is dignity as a power phenomenon. *Auctoritas* is the basis for the power to devise living conditions of others as well as the self. Those who are endowed with *auctoritas* determine themselves and the conditions in which they are living; they are content with themselves and their lives.[52]

7. Dignity as *maiestas* is superior dignity. In his *Fasti*, Ovid lets the Goddess *maiestas* appear as the daughter of honor and *reverentia*. Having just been born, *maiestas* has already grown up, is displaying strong charisma and occupying the throne on Olympus, dressed in purple robes.[53] Originally attributed to God, *maiestas* was predominantly a characteristic of the Roman people; only later was it transferred to the people's representatives.[54] Christian theology has used *maiestas* in the exact other way around. Christ has *maiestas*, and everybody who believes in him is indirectly reinforcing his own *maiestas*. *Maiestas* is the special dignity of Christians.[55]

8. *Honor* can, like *honestas* and *dignitas*, be acquired through merits (*merita*) and virtues (*virtutes*). *Honor*, unlike all other definitions of dignity, requires tangible signs of appreciation.[56] This definition is central for the double status of dignity, which is supposed to be inviolable but at the same time can be destroyed. Anselm of Canterbury, in his writing *Cur deus homo*, has performed this for God's dignity (*dignitatis honor*). For An-

---

50 See for instance Albertus Magnus, *De animalibus XVI* tr. 1 c. 1 and 13. Extensively on this: Schaede, 'Würde' 40-45.
51 See Bonaventura, *II Sent*, dist 18 a. 2 q. 3 contra 6.
52 See Cicero, *Brutus I*, 2, 7 with H Rabe, 'Art. Autorität' in J Ritter et al (eds): *Historisches Wörterbuch der Philosophie*, Vol. 1 (Basel, Schwabe Verlag, 1971) col. 727.
53 See Ovid, *Fasti V*, 23ff.
54 See Cicero, *De oratore II*,164 with Horaz, *Epistulae*, lib. 2, Epistula 1, v. 257-259 and Codex Iustinianus I, 14, 12.
55 See Schaede, 'Würde' 25 f.
56 See Schaede, 'Würde' 26 f with the lecture by Thomas of Aquin, *summa theologiae IIa IIae*, q. 103 a 1 ad 3.

selm, dignity is a relative term. It is always dignity of somebody. God, with regard to his dignity, relates only to himself. He is His own dignity. Therefore, it is true that God could never lose his dignity. But with regard to God's external dignified relation towards creation, dignity can be violated. People are contemptuous of God and belittle him. But such debasement of God could never affect his inner dignity. In this way, Anselm has described a dialectical definition of dignity for God, which is of great importance for modern definitions of dignity.

Giving this an anthropological and psychological turn, however, does by no means suggest that because a person can relate to himself, his dignity cannot be taken from him. External debasement can humiliate a person to such an extent that he gives himself up and loses all self-possession. The inviolability of human dignity is protected differently.

This is the point where it is appropriate to at least briefly touch on theology's task to understand dignity.

Dignity as a concept of Christian ethos consonant with Protestant theology can only be clarified by explaining in what way faith in Jesus Christ incorporates dignity, and to what extent man is imbued with dignity. This clarification has to stand the test of a hermeneutically differentiated dialogue on the texts of the New Testament. For such a clarification, the space of an entire book would be necessary.[57] The conclusions, however, can be understood all the same from a much briefer discussion.

III. Some Principal Theological Remarks

In one paragraph:

According to Biblical texts, dignity constitutes that God acts antecedent to people. Dignity simply constitutes that God loves humankind (see for instance John 3,16). Nowhere does this show as clearly as in the life and death of Jesus of Nazareth. He is, according to 1. Cor 2, 8, a master who is determined by dignity, and master of dignity (*kyrios tes doxes*). He has received his dignity from God (Rom 6,4). It is a dignity which is not verifiable in a simple, obvious, empirical way. It can be overlooked. For instance, those who crucified him have massively overlooked the dignity of Jesus of Nazareth. In fact, it was damaged terribly at the cross. Jesus' crucifixion explicitly testifies to the terrible reality that to be human is to be

---

57   See Schaede, 'Würde' 60-67.

always vulnerable to being violated in one's dignity, and this fact is at the center of the meaning of the crucifixion. But at the same time, the cross turns into a real symbol for the fact that people's dignity can never be damaged in such a way that it is completely destroyed. Jesus seemed debased; he had grown radically lonely. The tale of his death stresses that all his friends had deserted him. Only God remained. This documents that nobody, no situation in this world can prevent God from appreciating a person through his love.

Since Jesus received his dignity from God, it was not created through the mere appreciation of others. Rather, His dignity creates something in others; it creates trust in God and thus arranges for a unique appreciation of life in the world. This kind of protection of dignity through God is symbolized by the talk of God's spirit.[58] In his spirit, God is so close to a human that the latter keeps his dignity even if he has given himself up entirely in the midst of profound suffering.

These few remarks will have to suffice in the present context. They outline how Protestant theology communicates the design of life against the background of the concept of dignity. It is true that this rationale's claim to truth can only be understood by those who believe in God. The validity of this dignity, however, does not expire at the borders of faith. The protection of human dignity holds universal validity.

Therefore, there are three main points of this Christian definition of dignity which Christian ethos will argue for when confronting general ethics:

1. All humans, regardless of which culture, regardless in which condition of life or state of faith, *have dignity*.

2. All humans have *the same* dignity.

3. Nobody *has to work for or acquire* dignity. A human being has dignity without having to do anything to obtain it. We therefore owe all persons adequate treatment.

IV. Closing Remarks

Every academic discipline, any religious or a-religious attitude regarding questions of dignity and personality, all are characterized by presumptions which influence the respective perspectives. Therefore, one could say: Be-

---

58   See for instance Paul, *Epistle to the Romans*, Chapter 8.

cause this is so, we may listen to varied perspectives, be content with congruencies, and cry about divergences. We cannot, however, change anything about them, since all perspectives are equal and their claim to truth cannot be proven.

I do not believe that this is true. On the contrary, the proffered concepts can very well be scrutinized on the basis of those contexts of life which are shared by humans, and the specifics in which they occur. Does not the concept of dignity suit the aim to properly describe and fashion our contexts of life? If it doesn't, the concept is obsolete.

This survey of the origins and usefulness of the concept of dignity on the basis of life contexts has to consider that every academic discipline works with its own system of symbolization. It would be absurd to want to scrutinize utterances about human dignity which stem from Protestant theology *directly* by means of jurisprudential methods.

Nevertheless, Protestant theology can refer to research results that do not contradict its convictions without wrongly crossing the borders of systems of symbolization. Here is only one example:

There is no way to prove the primacy of dignity as presumed by Protestant theology by means of the natural sciences. There are no empirical methods through which the fact that God loves a human being even before the latter has started to live could be indicated or even proven. When people are trying to justify a life in dignity primarily for humans, there are analogies from the material world or the philosophy of life on which to base these attempts, at best. – In a good case, the creation of human life is preceded by the future parents' love and strong desire to have children. The question as to whether I will be born in the first place is independent of my individual decision, my will.

Observations like this do not form the basis of Christian convictions. They confirm their plausibility – not more, but no less either.

Beyond this, theology will say: Dignity is decisive in constituting that God relates to a human being.

It will say that all social relations are founded in God. It is important to realize: Saying that God's social relations with the world *were* the social world relations of a human being would lead to a deification of human beings themselves, to a confusion of the created with the creator. This does not even make sense. The net of social relations of human beings, the love of parents, the more or less pronounced love-hate-relationship between siblings or the love between colleagues can hardly be equated with God's love expressed toward humans. At least even in Berlin at the WiKo, which is, hopefully, characterized by a strong professional love among colleagues, the respective fondness of one professor for another can still easily be distinguished from the love of God. Painful differences are likely to arise every now and again, at the least.

Theology cannot elucidate in terms of functional empirics, how God naturally, socially and culturally arranges for human dignity by coming to and being in, with and amongst all these relations in the world. It does not have the prophetical power that would be necessary for this. Theology will, however, claim that it is nevertheless true.

God as the God of love is *also* the God of nature, but not only that. Because dignity, according to Christian conviction, arrives at its core in that which Paul has called the new life in 2. Cor 5f. or Rom 6. New life is reconciliated life; reconciliated life, however, is not a natural but a cultural phenomenon. The Christian faith and tradition rightly perceive this as one of the secrets of life. Nevertheless: In order to maintain academic legitimacy, Christians are better off not claiming to have the prophetical power to identify dignity precisely at this or that particular instance. This is even important for the intention to develop quite clear criteria to identify and describe dignity.

Sometimes poetry can encapsulate truth better than any academic proclamation: 'When you lay your eyes on me, I become beautiful.' The first line of the poem 'Shame' by Gabriela Mistral has understood a fundamental truth. To be lovingly gazed at engenders dignity. And accordingly, Protestant theology refers to the deeper insight of faith, that God already regards a human with love, before the latter can actively form his life through any emotion, impulse or design. A human's dignity is the reason that God, by looking and regarding, creates life again and again, that he makes life which had seemed lost beautiful.

Therefore even Protestant theology should warn against the term image of God, if it is chronically and colloquially used and taken for granted. A human person should not hold in the mind in actuality a definite image of itself. These images are misleading. We should impose a ban on these images. This declaration of a need to ban defined, reified concrete images, image referents and concepts of dignity may reflect a fundamental lack of clarity concerning the anthropology of man's relationship to God. And this lack of clarity has permeated 20th century discourse on dignity, and kept it at a mostly superficial level.

A human being is not the king of the castle. But it also has not delegated its sovereignty, its *gravitas* and *auctoritas* to dark powers, to blind wishes and forces. Still, the person delegates its sovereignty to an omnipresent inherently flawed reality. This reality creates a socially and affectively embedded person.

Yet beyond this inherently flawed reality, because of God's regard, we are removed from ourselves – but to our own advantage. Nobody can separate a human person from this regarding. This is exactly the reason why dignity becomes inviolable. True inviolable human dignity should never be reified, and can never be constituted as concretely defined anthropological imagery.

In our discourses on human dignity, and responses to threats to human dignity, which proliferate daily in every place, we would do well to ban concrete imagery and referents and instead focus on the fundamentally abstract nature of our human dignity as a continually developing capacity and relationship to God.

'Wherever You See the Trace of Man, There I Stand Before You': The Complexities of God and Human Dignity Within Judaism

Susannah Heschel[1]

One of my favorite students, Dierre Upshaw, who graduated from Dartmouth College several years ago, returned to the College to be my research assistant for the summer term of 2013. To thank him for his efforts, I asked him to join me when I was invited to a formal reception at the White House, hosted by President Obama, for Civil Rights leaders and their families. The evening was spectacular: we had the opportunity to meet and speak with heroes of the Civil Rights movement, major political members of Congress, writers, artists, and, of course, the President. My student, who is African-American, was thrilled by the experience. Ten days later, back in a small town in rural Vermont, he was purchasing gasoline for his car when a group of white men drove up and started shouting racist epithets at him, both offending and frightening him. He immediately jumped in his car and drove off, but was shaken by the experience.

Notable is the juxtaposition: to be a guest at the White House, where he was treated with respect and dignity as part of a select and honored group, and shook hands with President Obama, and then ten days later subjected to ugly racial harassment and threat. How quickly dignity can be granted

---

[1] TB: Talmud Bavli (Babylonian Talmud); TJ: Talmud Yerushalmi (Palestinian Talmud); M: Mishnah. The quotation comes from a classical Midrashic text, Mechiltah de'Rabbi Ishmael, Tractate Vayassa, chapter seven, ed. JZ Lauterbach and D Stern (Philadelphia: Jewish Publication Society, 2010) 253.
I would like to thank Alexandra Kemmerer for inviting me to participate in the colloquium on Human Dignity that she organized at the Wissenschaftskolleg zu Berlin in the fall of 2011, and for stimulating my interest in this important topic. I would also like to thank Professor Penina Lahav, Boston University Law School, for calling my attention to several important articles on the Israeli judicial system, and Professor Anat Biletzki, Quinnipiac University, for important conversations about human rights in Israel and the Occupied Territories.

to someone and then denied, and how fragile dignity can be when confronted with social constructs of race and threats of physical violence provoked by racism.

Human dignity is proclaimed with an implied understanding that it has universal validity: there cannot be human dignity for some, but not others. In reality, however, religious texts, political circumstances, and the biases created by race, money, and gender modify the universal claim of human dignity, often distorting the nature of the dignity, or establishing hierarchies in which the dignity of some people receives greater protection than that of others. Even more troubling, human dignity at times comes into conflict with other claims, including the rights of the individual, so that at times human dignity functions rhetorically in legal, political, and intellectual settings to protect traditional prerogatives or oppressive political regimes rather than the human rights that dignity purportedly upholds.

Studies of human dignity within the classical texts of Judaism generally derive the concept from the passage in Genesis 1:27 claiming that all human beings are created in the image (literally, 'form') of God (*tselem Elohim*). The verse functions to provide an alliance between the human and God, though the nature of that alliance has been debated: that all human beings are derived from that original creation, and hence elevated to the same status, and that God holds a correspondence to the human, suggesting that God, too, is corporeal. Despite ambiguity of the verse in Genesis, its link to human dignity is widely taken for granted.[2]

That all human beings are equal, possessed of an inviolable, immutable dignity, is a religious vision that almost immediately came into conflict within the Bible itself, with a variety of political claims, religious hierarchies, and tribal conflicts (e.g., Judges 19). Basing human dignity on a monogenesis of *imago Dei* has led Jewish thinkers to argue that God is the originating point and ultimate guarantor of ethical behavior. The term *tselem* and the Akkadian salmu (form), from which it is derived, are associated with physicality, both in the Bible and in rabbinic literature, linking human dignity with respect for the body as a physical manifestation of God, and thus assuming a corporeal or anthropomorphic God, an understanding reinforced in biblical texts, such as Ezekiel's visions, and subse-

---

2   See, for example, A Barak, *Human Dignity: The Constitutional Value and the Constitutional Right* (Cambridge, Cambridge University Press, 2015) 18-21.

quent rabbinic and mystical literature.³ Thus, to harm the human body is to injure God, so that torture and execution are severely restricted, though not outlawed, in rabbinic literature, and treating the corpse with respect conveys dignity to the human being. While the emphasis on *tselem Elohim* as a physical manifestation of God implies that God is corporeal, the gendered nature of that divine body is not specified in biblical or rabbinic literature. The physical nature of the human image of God, and the corporeality ascribed to God, was not acceptable to many in the Jewish philosophical tradition, nor in the Christian and Islamic philosophical tradition, and their exegeses of the biblical and rabbinic passages required a very different outcome.⁴

Concomitant is the theological claim that dignity is inherent in all human beings, rather than constructed by society and conveyed through human action. On the private, individual level, dignity is conveyed by virtue of being created in the image of God; on the social level, however, dignity requires a recognition that is enacted and not simply self-evident. Judaism recognizes that human dignity is not only an innate quality, but also an attribute that is constructed and acquired by social context and religious law, as well as constituted by individual behavior and actions that perform 'dignity.' Much of Jewish law is concerned with preserving dignity and protecting it against its inverse, shame. In either case, dignity (or shame) is not necessarily fixed and static, an innate aspect of being human, but rather is an economy that is remarkably slippery, modified by gender, class, race, and other variables. Human dignity does not transcend political and ideological powers, but is modified by them for its own purposes.

Classical Jewish religious texts speak frequently of the dignity of human beings, but the application of human dignity to particular circumstances is at times constrained within the texts by conflicting religious obligations and by the elevated status of Jewish law (*halakha*) over moral principles (*aggada*). Rabbinic Judaism affirms the concept of 'human dignity' in passages such as 'Great is the [principle of] human dignity, for it overrides a negative precept of the Torah' (Berakhot 19b). However, such statements are relegated to the category of *aggada* (legendary, mythic, or

---

3   Note that the Septuagint translates 'tselem' as eikon and the Vulgate as imago, both carrying the meaning of likeness or semblance.
4   See, for example, T Aquinas, *Summa Theologica* ST I, q.93, a.6, 'Whether the image of God is in man as regards the mind only.' Aquinas distinguishes 'imago' (image) from vestigium (trace): 'the very shape of the human body represents the image of God in the soul by way of a trace (vestigium).'

hortatory comments) rather than *halakha* (law), and have not carried determinative authority in Jewish legal rulings.[5] Aggada is not regarded as a 'normative category' within the rabbinic world, although some scholars of rabbinic literature have challenged the division between *aggada* and *halakha*, arguing that *aggada* functions as the non-legal body of norms and principles that inform *halakha*.[6]

Jewish law, which functioned for two thousand years in circumstances in which Jews lacked autonomous political regimes, now informs decisions in the very different political context of Jewish sovereignty in the State of Israel. The result is a drastic difference: ancient religious Jewish legal concepts that developed in an era of Jewish minority status and limited communal autonomy are now informing a secular Jewish state that gives Jews political control and power over both Jews and Gentiles. Apart from matters of family law and personal status, such as marriage, divorce, and conversion, which are regulated by the Orthodox rabbinate, the State of Israel is governed by secular laws as interpreted by a secular judicial system. Still, Jewish religious tradition is often invoked in court decisions, especially when the law and the judiciary interpret difficult questions of human dignity in conflicts between Gentiles and Jews, women and men, Jews of wealth and Jews without money. Does the dignity of Jews take precedence over the dignity of Christians and Muslims, Arabs and Druze, within a Jewish state? Should the rights of Jewish women be limited to preserve the dignity of Jewish men? Does the right of the individual take precedence over the dignity of Jewish tradition in a Jewish state?

Human dignity is affirmed in the Bible, and subsequent rabbinic texts go further, mandating not only the recognition of human dignity, but also the obligation to protect and enhance the dignity of other people, thus recognizing that dignity is not simply an inherent quality, but one that is socially mediated, conveyed, and performed. For example, Jewish law recognizes that displays of wealth can enhance one's dignity in the eyes of others, while leaving those without wealth feeling ashamed. In response, rabbinic law attempts to ameliorate some of the inequities by insisting that

---

[5] A Altmann, 'Homo Imago Dei in Jewish and Christian Theology,' *Journal of Religion* 48:3 (July 1968) 235-259.

[6] The challenge extends from Leopold Zunz, Abraham Geiger, Zecharias Frankel, among others, in the nineteenth century, to Gershom Scholem, Abraham Joshua Heschel, and Moshe Halbertal in the twentieth. For the most recent discussion, see Y Lorberbaum, *In God's Image: Myth, Theology, and Law in Classical Judaism* (Cambridge: Cambridge University Press, 2014) 76ff.

wealth not be displayed at crucial moments, such as burial; all Jews are buried in a pine coffin or shroud, and expensive coffins are forbidden. Through such religious laws and practices, dignity becomes not merely acknowledged, but actively enhanced. In such circumstances, dignity is dependent for its very existence by being conveyed and recognized by others, and not displayed through wealth or pomp. Yet even in circumstances in which dignity is denied, and public humiliation occurs through social standing or bias, a person may feel a strong sense of his or her own dignity, as described, for example, in slave narratives and holocaust memoirs, suggesting that dignity may be experienced as an inherent attribute that cannot be destroyed even in the most degrading circumstances.[7]

The relationship between human dignity and human rights is not always clear-cut in legal systems, including Jewish law. The dignity we experience at one moment may be abruptly withdrawn; it is not static, but slippery, and it can be invoked both to protect human liberties and to deny them. Doron Shultziner and Guy Carmi, in their review of national constitutions, conclude that human dignity may be invoked to protect individual rights, but may also be used to suppress those rights. They note that the term 'human dignity' appears frequently in constitutions composed by emerging states in recent decades, and that the term has been invoked to end discriminatory and even bodily violation practices in many countries. For example, Uganda outlawed female genital mutilation on the grounds of human dignity, and courts in India have acted to protect women's inheritance rights on similar grounds.[8] However, Shultziner and Carmi warn that human dignity has also been invoked arbitrarily, limiting individual freedoms and rights to protect the 'dignity' of the collective. For example, the constitution of Laos states, 'All cultural and mass media activities which are detrimental to national interests or to the traditional culture and dignity of Lao people are prohibited', language that finds parallels in the

---

7   Steven Pinker challenges the meaningfulness of 'dignity' on this very point: how can dignity be claimed as inherent when it is also treated with utter contempt: 'we read that slavery and degradation are wrong because they take someone's dignity away. But we also read that nothing you can do to a person, including enslaving or degrading him, can take his dignity away.' S Pinker, 'Dignity' *The New Republic* (May 28, 2008). See also R Macklin, 'Dignity Is a Useless Concept,' *British Medical Journal* 327 (December 20, 2003) 1419-1420.

8   D Shultziner and GE Carmi, 'Human Dignity in National Constitutions: Functions, Promises and Dangers' (2014) 62 *American Journal of Comparative Law* 490.

constitutions of Montenegro, Moldova, Gabon, Saudi Arabia, Romania, among many others.[9] Invoking human dignity in such circumstances functions as a rhetorical device employed for purposes of persuasion in support of a pre-determined political position; it is not a term that guarantees individual liberties, but may severely limit a range of liberties, including free expression.[10] Moreover, some commentators have noted that dignity can be invoked to justify totalitarian regimes; Nazi Germany claimed that the dignity of German Aryans was violated and required restoration.

Within Jewish texts, human dignity functions similarly, as a rhetorical device that does not necessarily guarantee individual rights or liberties within Jewish law, but may even function to limit them by pitting the dignity of one group against another. The Catholic philosopher Teresa Iglesias distinguishes between fixed and universal understandings of dignity, those that link dignity to status and those that claim a universal dignity of all human beings.[11] Examples of both can be found in classical Jewish texts. As with state constitutions, human dignity functions in Jewish legal texts as a universal attribute of all human beings, linking them to God, yet that shared human dignity does not necessarily guarantee the rights of human beings in relation to one another. There is no single, uniform Jewish understanding of human dignity, nor of its applicability, and the multiplicity of meanings have been used both to guarantee liberties and to restrict them, as have state constitutions. For example, human dignity has been applied in some Jewish texts to all human beings, while in others it is applied to men. The dignity of women is mentioned explicitly in reference to the female corpse, which rabbinic law insists must be treated with the same dignity as the male corpse and given a proper burial (M Moed Katan 3:8, TB Niddah 9:16). While the dignity of women's dead bodies is protected, living women do not always have the same rights as men. For example, the 'dignity of the congregation' (TB Megillah 23a) is invoked in the Talmud to prevent women from being called to the Torah in the syna-

---

9   ibid 484.
10 In some cases, human dignity is invoked to 'to place positive obligations on the state' in caring for its citizens, especially women, children, the elderly, and the disabled, but, as Shultziner and Carmi make clear, human dignity can also be 'used as a limitation on fundamental rights' (483). These limitations may include freedom of expression, on the grounds that it may offend the dignity of others or of the state.
11 T Iglesias, 'Bedrock Truths and the Dignity of the Individual' (2001) 4 *Logos: A Journal of Catholic Thought and Culture* 120.

gogue; in that case, the 'dignity of the congregation' is actually the dignity of men. The ruling is based on the assumption that women would violate men's dignity by being called to the Torah, although no reason is given for that assumption. What we observe in that ruling is that dignity is a social construct: the dignity of men is created by excluding women from synagogue leadership. That women's dignity might be violated through the exclusion is not a consideration in the Talmud, which was composed by men.

What is perhaps unique to Judaism's religious teachings is that dignity applies not only to human beings, but also to abstract ideas, such as the Sabbath and Jewish holidays (BT Taanit 26b), and to religious objects, such as the Torah scroll (BT Yoma 70a; Gittin 60a). Moreover, dignity is not simply received, but conveyed; indeed, conveying dignity is a central aspect of Jewish ritual. Dignity is conveyed to other human beings not only because it is their due, but more importantly because the act of conveying dignity is a commandment. The recipients of dignity may or may not be cognizant of it; for example, dignity is conveyed to a corpse, to the synagogue, to the Sabbath, and to holidays, with the primary purpose being the act of conveying the dignity.

I. Biblical Creation of Human Dignity

Much of the affirmation of human dignity rests on the claim that all humans were created equal by God, or were created as the image of God. That claim comes as an inversion of race theory, which began its appearance by challenging monogenesis. The decline in the seventeenth century of the authority of Scripture, argues the historian Colin Kidd, 'opened up an ideological space for the uninhibited articulation of racialist sentiments.'[12] Racism rejected monogenesis and claimed that humans form a hierarchy, with whites at the top. Racism was not an attack on theology, but the outcome of the decline of religious belief in divine creation. In an inverse sense, human dignity began to be asserted in the late 1930s and 40s, while Nazi racism was at its zenith, by reactionary Catholic theologi-

---

12   C Kidd, *The Forging of Races: Race and Scripture in the Protestant Atlantic World, 1600-2000* (Cambridge, England: Cambridge University Press, 2006) 19. See also S Heschel, *The Aryan Jesus: Christian Theologians and the Bible in Nazi Germany* (Princeton, NJ: Princeton University Press, 2008).

ans eager to reestablish church authority in the face of communism, Nazism, and secular capitalism.[13] If the decline in Scriptural authority opened the door to race as a powerful legal, political, and cultural force in society, assertions of human dignity as resting in Scriptural claims to monogenetic divine creation could renew the power of Scripture, support the conservative social order that the church desired.

God's creation of human beings in the 'image of God (*tselem Elohim*)' appears three times in the Bible (Genesis 1:26-28; 5:1-3; 9:6), although the term *tselem* appears even more often in a negative context, referring to idolatry.[14] The biblical word '*kavod*,' which can be translated as dignity, honor, or glory, stems from a common Semitic root meaning 'heavy', and is found in all the classical Semitic languages, including Babylonian, Old South Arabian, Ethiopic, Arabic, Phoenician, and Hebrew. The link between 'heavy' and 'honor' is likely an association similar to the Latin 'gravitas'.

The concept of dignity is initially introduced in the Bible as an attribute of God. Moses asks God to see his '*kavod*', and God responds by agreeing to show Moses his back (Exodus 16:7). In this context, the *kavod* of God is usually translated as 'divine glory' and is linked to the divine corporeality that is elsewhere denied, as the Bible forbids images of God, and Judaism's rabbis insist it is an aniconic tradition. God's corporeal existence is denied in the Jewish philosophical tradition and affirmed in the Jewish mystical tradition, and anthropomorphisms pervade Jewish texts, beginning with the Bible. While verbal descriptions of the divine appearance abound in Judaism, the aniconic tradition bans visual images of God, with the exception of human beings, who are said to have been created in God's image, *b'tselem Elohim*. It is precisely anthropomorphism that creates the centrality of human dignity in rabbinic Judaism, according to Yair Lorberbaum, who argues that because the human body is a physical representation of God's own corporeality, the rabbis of the Talmud severely restricted the conditions of execution, despite its prevalence in the Bible. Executing a human being who is an image of God would be tantamount to deicide, in their view, unless the human being had committed the supreme crime of murder, in which case he or she forfeited the status of *imago Dei*.

---

13   S Moyn, *Christian Human Rights* (Philadelphia: University of Pennsylvania Press, 2015).
14   Numbers 33:52; I Samuel 6:5, 6, 11; II Kings 11:18; Ezekiel 7:20; 10:17; 23:14; II Chronicles 23:17.

Execution is not simply a violation of the moral dignity of human beings, but an expression of the rabbinic understanding of theurgy, the impact of human action on God.[15]

While the term *kavod* appears frequently in the Hebrew Bible, applied both to humans and to God, the Bible gives no precise definition over what constitutes the dignity of either. *Kavod* as 'dignity' is not simply an attribute shared with God, but an attribute bestowed upon the human being by God, according to Psalm 8:6: 'You have crowned him (man) with glory and honor (*kavod v'hadar*).' Although not always explicitly evoked, human dignity hovers over biblical thought, including the prophetic injunctions against injustice and economic exploitation, and also the Levitical proscriptions regarding incest. In all of these cases, it is the physical body that is viewed as most vulnerable to violations of dignity. If the body was understood in rabbinic literature as an icon of divinity, God's presence within the human, sexual conduct involving the penetration of one human by another presumably would also carry theurgic connotations and require legal regulation, as in the case of execution: necessary, perhaps, but restricted. Precisely what constitutes human dignity and its violation is presumed, but its full parameters are never entirely defined. Even more important: to which human beings is 'dignity' bestowed in rabbinic Judaism; is it restricted to Jews? To men? To adults? To monotheists? While torture and execution seem obvious examples of violating dignity, sexual penetration and other forms of physical contact seem less obviously linked to dignity or its violation.

II. Rabbinic Affirmations of Human Dignity

Jewish theology and practice are shaped not only by the Hebrew Bible, believed by Jews to be the divine revelation given by God to the Jewish people at Mt. Sinai, but also by the vast corpus of rabbinic literature, composed by rabbis over the course of six centuries, in Palestine and Babylonia, that they claim represent an orally-transmitted revelation that was received at Mt. Sinai along with the Bible. Rabbinic Judaism codified and consolidated Jewish law, shifting from a post-70 CE Temple-based wor-

---

15   Yair Lorberbaum, op. cit. Lorberbaum's argument stands in contrast to M Halbertal, *Interpretative Revolutions in the Making* (Jerusalem: Hebrew University Magnes Press, 1977).

ship, based on sacrifice and administered by a hereditary priesthood, to a synagogue-based oral worship administered by rabbis versed in Jewish law. Rabbinic literature developed the Judaism that is practiced to this day, and expounded moral and theological teachings, rooted in biblical texts or allusions.

Rabbinic Judaism uses the expression, '*kavod ha-adam*', dignity (or honor) of the person, when speaking of the dignity of individuals, usually Jews, and applies the broader term, '*kavod ha-briot*', dignity of created beings, to all human beings in the collective, including Gentiles and sometimes animals as well.[16] The latter term, however, plays a limited role in Jewish legal thought, and at times it is used to indicate 'glory' rather than honor or dignity, as in the glory of Aaron, the priest.[17] The concept can be invoked both within the Talmud and within contemporary Jewish legal thought as a basic principle that can override proscriptions. Within the Talmud, for example, it is permissible to walk in a former graveyard (where graves have been disturbed and bones may be scattered) when accompanying a mourner because the imperative to accompany a mourner takes precedence over the prohibition against walking among human remains: 'Great is human dignity since it overrides a negative precept of the Torah' (TB Berachot 19b). Similarly, the rabbinics scholar Tzvi Marx calls attention to Jewish legal authorities overriding religious prohibitions out of respect for the dignity of a disabled person who might otherwise be banned from certain rituals.[18]

Within classical rabbinic texts, the inherent dignity of all human beings is occasionally affirmed, while at the same time recognizing that dignity requires affirmation, particularly in cases when dignity might not be automatically conveyed. That is, dignity is both an essential, intrinsic aspect of being human, while at the same time it is created through appropriate behavior and societal acknowledgment. Dignity may be inviolable, but it is also dependent upon recognition and action by others to be brought into existence. The intrinsic dignity of human beings is established by the fundamental conviction that humans were not only created by God, but were created to bring honor to God. The earliest stratum of rabbinic literature,

---

16   On Gentiles, see Berakhot 19b and I Rosen-Zivi and A Ophir, 'Goy: Toward a Genealogy' (2011) 28 *Dine Israel* 69-112.

17   GJ Blidstein, '"Great is Human Dignity": An Analysis of the History of a Halakha' (Hebrew) (1982-83) 15 *Shnaton ha-Mishpat ha-Ivri* [Annual of the Institute for Research on Jewish Law] 127–86.

18   TC Marx, *Disability in Jewish Law* (New York, Routledge, 2002) 27.

the Mishnah, states: 'All that God created in His world He created exclusively for His *kavod* (honor or glory)' (M Avot 6:11). Indeed, God's love of humanity is exemplified in the creation of human beings as images of God, according to a statement in the Mishnah (M Avot 3:14). Moreover, the dignity of others should be considered as important as one's own: 'Let the honor of your fellow human being be as precious to you as your own' (M Avot 2:10).

Such general rabbinic statements concerning human beings as created by God and the consequent intrinsic nature of human dignity are applied above all to the deceased human body. Dignity is central to the compilation of rabbinic laws regulating the respect owed to a dead human body. A corpse, male or female, may not be disfigured, all of its body parts must be buried, and the corpse itself is washed, placed in a shroud, and not left alone prior to burial, but accompanied at all times by someone reciting psalms. Indeed, it is striking that desecration of a corpse is strongly forbidden, with clear rules about treating the dead body with dignity, whereas a human embryo can be discarded by a laboratory without arousing rabbinic condemnation.[19] Also striking is that the dignity of the corpse is not linked to the subjective experience of the recipient, since the corpse is unaware of how it is treated.

How a corpse is treated carries its own performative implication: my dignity is demonstrated by the respect I show a corpse; in conveying dignity to a corpse, I am dignifying God and myself. In biblical law, for example, a person who is hanged as a punishment for crime must be lowered immediately: 'For an impaled body is an affront to God: you shall not defile the land that the Lord your God is giving you to possess' (Deuteronomy 21:23). In his extensive study of rabbinic views of human dignity, Yair Lorberbaum notes that rabbinic literature comments that the body of a person who is hanged is viewed as an identical twin of God. Precisely in order to refrain from damaging the image of God, the body must be lowered immediately after the hanging.[20] Rabbinic law suggests that hanging is reserved for those who commit blasphemy and idolatry.[21] Disfiguration of

---

19 See the discussion of the embryo in M Barilan, 'Judaism, Human Dignity, and the Most Vulnerable Women on Earth' (2009) 1 *The American Journal of Bioethics* 35.
20 Y Lorberbaum, 'Blood and the Image of God': in D Kretzmer and E Klein (eds), *The Concept of Human Dignity in Human Rights Discourse* (The Hague, Kluwer Law International, 2002) 55.
21 TB Sanhedrin 6:5; Tosefta Sanhedrin 9:7; Sanhedrin 46a.

the body, such as castration, is a serious offense; an immoral act can be repaired through repentance, but once the body is disfigured, it is permanent, according to Talmudic law (TB Baba Batra 154a). Underlying the concern with disfiguration is a religious doctrine: in the messianic era, God will resurrect the dead, but a disfigured or amputated body will not be restored.

Although God is understood to be the creator of the entire world, including all human beings, human dignity in Judaism is not understood as operative on an equal basis. Hierarchical distinctions exist in Jewish law among men, women, slaves, the pious and learned, children, and idolaters, and yet invocations of dignity at times override those hierarchies. The honor of the poor, *kavod ha-aniyim*, is invoked to assure that all funerals be conducted in identical fashion, without distinction between rich and poor, so as not to detract from the dignity of the poor. When hierarchies are invoked, they stem not from a denial that women and Gentiles (as well as male Jews), for example, were created by God, but from the rabbinic assumption that dignity is created or performed by piety and religious learning.[22] That assumption, in turn, leads to distinctions between male and female dignity, and even the worth of male versus female life. Thus, a man who is a 'mamzer' (born of a forbidden union) but learned in Jewish law takes precedence over a high priest (a hereditary position) who is unlearned. And while Gentiles are distinguished from Jews, the Talmud obligates Jews to care even for idolaters:

> We are obliged to maintain the poor of idolaters, attend to their sick and bury their dead, as we do with those of our own community, for the sake of peace, for the whole of Judaism is for the sake of peace, her ways are pleasant and her paths are peace (Proverbs 3), as it is written, 'God is good to all and His mercy extends to all creatures' (Psalms 145:9) (M Gittin 5:9; BT Gittin 59b).

Jewish law and tradition recognize that dignity is conveyed (or not) and is thus dependent upon human will and human actions. Actions that convey dignity are essential requirements of Jewish law, which recognizes that dignity is received from acts performed by other people, and also that the act of conveying dignity to another person also brings dignity to the one who is conveying it. In that sense, dignity is not fixed, but depends upon actions and recognition; it is created through performance. Piety and religious learning, for example, enhance dignity, although since religious

---

22 Within a strain of esoteric Jewish mystical literature the bodies of Jews and Gentiles are regarded as ontologically distinct.

learning was traditionally open only to men, women's dignity was more narrowly circumscribed. Despite these variables, dignity is a central component of the cultic and ethical laws of Judaism, invoked, for example, in the regulations governing public worship, and also in the laws governing charity.

Rabbinic Judaism goes a step further than simply asserting that human beings are created in the image of God and are entitled to dignity. Rabbinic thought also asserts that God is in need of human beings (*'zoreh gavoha'*) and that observance of Jewish religious commandments gives strength to God. That tradition was given centrality in medieval Kabbalah, which claimed that God is in need of redemption, and that human actions can serve to redeem God. The theurgic tradition was opposed by the medieval rationalist philosophical tradition; indeed, the most important rabbinic authority and philosopher of the Middle Ages, Moses Maimonides, asserted that only a person with a perfected intellect was an image of God.[23]

III. Shame as the Central Challenge to Dignity

Human dignity is not simply 'recognized' in rabbinic texts, but is created by the laws of those texts. All Jewish texts, from the Bible onward, assert that human dignity is intrinsic to human beings, but derived from a transcendent divinity: human beings are the creation of God, and for that reason bear and deserve dignity. At the same time, dignity is presented as a performative act, one with wide ranging meanings that vary according to social status, gender, ethnicity, and so forth. In addition, as the incident with my student illustrates, dignity may be easily interrupted by societal prejudices such as racism and misogyny that render the recognition and performance of dignity irrelevant. That, too, is recognized in rabbinic law by the sharp prohibitions against public humiliation. Nakedness, for example, is considered a greater violation of women's dignity than of men's, so that clothing should first be provided to a woman, then to a man, since women are thought to be more easily shamed than men. Yet such regulations serve not simply to protect women's dignity but to invent and enshrine the social construction of women's bodily shame, hidden from view

---

[23] Y Lorberbaum, 'Human Dignity in the Jewish Tradition' in: *The Cambridge Handbook of Human Dignity: Interdisciplinary Perspectives*, ed. Marcus Düwell et. al. (Cambridge: Cambridge University Press, 2014) 141.

by a claim to 'protect' women's dignity. Shame, like dignity, is not an intrinsic experience shared equally by all people, but is the creation of laws that invent, impose, and regulate subjective emotion through their disciplinary regimes.

This is exemplified by the rabbinic rulings that extend hierarchies of dignity to Jews and Gentiles, and to life itself. Jewish law evaluates a situation in which the lives of men and women are simultaneously threatened. In that case, saving the life of the man takes precedence over saving the woman, and he must be rescued first (M Horayot 3:7). Later commentaries explain that the man has more commandments to fulfill, making his life more important. Learning also accords greater importance: the life of a learned mamzer (child of a forbidden union) takes precedence over the life of an uneducated priest (M Horayot 3:8). That particular teaching indicates that status for men does not come automatically with birth, but with study and piety; since traditional study is closed to women, elevating their status is not possible through learning.

Other hierarchies of life are delineated in rabbinic law. Sabbath prohibitions on work may be violated to save the life of a Jew, but rabbinical opinions differ whether it is permissible to violate the Sabbath to save the life of a Gentile. Indeed, Gentiles are frequently deprived of dignity by being compared to animals, such as donkeys, while Jews are presented as equal to angels. Non-Jews are permitted to engage in incest because they are like horses and donkeys, according to a relative obscure Midrash. In a Talmudic passage, Gentiles are said to eat and drink like bears, with flesh swollen like that of a bear, long hair like a bear, and restless like a bear.[24] Such comments are intended to emphasize that the commandments of God, which are incumbent upon Jews, convey the dignity that raises Jews above the level of animals. The use of animals to convey the superiority of a group of people is not an uncommon construction in Western thought; although animals were created by God, they are not in the 'image of God', as are human beings. However, despite occupying a lower status than human beings, animals are granted a day of rest on the Sabbath, and must be fed before the humans that own them.

Violation of dignity requires reparation, according to rabbinic law, but that principle gave rise to conflicts among the rabbis regarding how to de-

---

24 TB Megillah 11a; TB Kiddushin 72a. For a discussion of these and many other relevant rabbinic sources, see S Stern, *Jewish Identity in Early Rabbinic Writings* (Leiden, Brill, 1994) 33–39.

termine both the extent of the violation and the proper compensation for it. For example, Rabbi Meir insists that all victims of a particular assault are entitled to the same redress; what determines the reparation is the nature of the assault. Other rabbis disagreed, arguing that the status of the individual who was targeted should determine the extent of the compensation, since the reparation is for the degree of suffering experienced, and that can vary with social status (TB Baba Kamma 86a). The latter argument came to be the accepted principle. At the same time, rabbinic law made it clear that no person was without dignity when determining compensation; Maimonides ruled, 'One who embarrasses even a resident alien or a slave is liable for damages.'[25]

Rabbinic texts view shame as the opposite of dignity, and shaming another person in public as a major sin, tantamount to murder. For instance, a bride must be told she is beautiful, even if she is not, to avoid shaming her (BT Ketubot 16b-17a). Preventing shame is considered sufficient cause to override certain rabbinic laws; some rabbis permit abortion when pregnancy would result in public shaming, such as cases of rape or adultery.[26] At the same time, a woman's claim to have experienced an incidence of public shame cannot be overridden by a man's claim that she does not possess sufficient dignity to experience the incident as shaming.[27] By comparing public humiliation to murder, rabbinic law recognizes that just as a murdered person cannot be brought back to life, a person who has been shamed may be affected by the experience forever, regardless of preferred apologies. Dignity is so crucial that its destruction through public

---

25 M Maimonides, *Mishneh Torah*, Assault and Damages 3.7.
26 D Feldman, *Birth Control in Jewish Law: Marital Relations, Contraception, and Abortion as Set Forth in the Classic Texts of Jewish Law* (New York, New York University Press, 1968).
27 Mishnah Baba Kama 8:6: Rabbi Akiva ruled that a man who exposed a woman's hair should pay her a huge sum of money in damages for disgrace. The man protested: woman is of low social status, and has no dignity that could be offended. Rabbi Akiva replied: all Jews are children of the patriarchs and deserve respect as princes. The man then said that this woman had exposed her own hair once when trying to save oil from spilling, thus devaluing her own dignity below that of a bit of oil. Rabbi Akiva answered that only the person herself has the right to harm her own self (for her own private reasons), and this does not reduce the person's dignity and her right to compensation in situations of nonconsensual disgrace. Cited by YM Barilan, 'From Imago Dei in the Jewish-Christian Traditions to Human Dignity in Contemporary Jewish Law' (2009) 19 *Kennedy Institute of Ethics Journal* 231.

humiliation is considered tantamount to murder; according to the Talmud (TB Baba Metzia 58b): 'One who embarrasses another in public, it is as if that person shed blood.' The strength of that claim is further justified in a later Midrash:

> Rabbi Akiva states, 'Love your fellow as yourself.' This is the greatest principle in the Torah. You must not say, 'Because I have been humiliated, let my fellow also be humiliated'... For, as Rabbi Tanhuma pointed out, if you act thus, realize who it is that you have actually humiliated: 'He made him in the likeness of God' (Midrash Genesis Rabbah 24:7).

The public humiliation of a human being is thus viewed as a humiliation of God, a denial, as it were, of God's divinity. The theurgic element of human dignity implies the ability of human beings to affect God through their behavior; one Midrash says, I am God and you are my witnesses, and if you are not my witnesses, then I am not God. (Isaiah 43:10, Midrash Tehillim 123:2). This is based on the rabbinic understanding of *zoreh gavoha*, divine need, a doctrine that becomes even stronger in classical Kabbalah and Hasidism.

In an extensive review of the uses of *'kavod'* in rabbinic literature, the late rabbinics scholar Chana Safrai concluded that a hierarchy is established: *kavod ha-makom*, the dignity of God, takes priority over *kavod ha-briot*, the dignity of the community, which stands above *kavod ha-adam*, the dignity of the individual.[28] Dignity is not assumed to be a universal given, but the command to convey dignity remains incumbent. Michael Rosen points out that even the dignity of a child deserves protection from the state—and yet, he writes, 'what is less dignified than a two-year-old?'[29] Similarly, in rabbinic law, even when a person behaves without dignity, or is incapable of experiencing dignity, whether as a two year old or a corpse, the obligation to convey dignity remains.

IV. The Dignity of Women Versus Men

The hierarchy of male and female becomes significant in rabbinic law when a potential clash occurs between two of the categories, dignity and

---

28 C Safrai, 'Human Dignity in Rabbinical Perspective' in Kretzmer and Klein (eds), *The Concept of Human Dignity in Human Rights Discourse*, 99.
29 M Rosen, *Dignity: Its History and Meaning* (Cambridge, Harvard University Press, 2012) 77.

shaming, or between two categories of people, men and women. For example, in a ritual described in the Bible and adumbrated in the Talmud, a husband who suspects his wife of adultery brings her to the priest, who makes the woman, a '*Sotah*', undergo a humiliating ritual that is described in both the Bible and the Talmud. One rabbinic justification for the ritual is 'God pays attention to the *kavod* (dignity) of Israel' (Midrash Numbers Rabbah 9:33). That is, the dignity of the collective people of Israel, represented, presumably, by men whose wives do not commit adultery, takes precedence over the humiliating ritual inflicted on a female Jew, the wife suspected by her husband of adultery. Here it is women whose human dignity is sacrificed to the greater honor of the husbands.

At the same time, the biblically mandated ritual of the *Sotah* may 'protect' the wife by forcing adjudication by the priest, rather than allowing suspicions to fester and possibly lead to a so-called 'honor killing' by an enraged husband, father, or brother. Note, however, that the ritual of *Sotah* could only occur while the Jerusalem temple was standing, and administered by a priest. The *Sotah* ritual was ultimately canceled, not on the grounds that it violated a woman's dignity, but because there was supposedly too much adultery (or, more likely, too many suspicious husbands) to regulate. Still, the rabbinic leaders did not cancel biblical rituals (Deuteronomy 22:21) that mandate stoning for a betrothed woman who engages in sexual activity. Indeed, the Talmud adds that the crowd observing the stoning also shames her parents by calling out, "Look at the offspring you have raised!" (Ketubot 45a). Similar shaming of parents accompanies the immolation of a priest's daughter who commits adultery, another biblical mandate.[30] Yet while 'honor killings' are sanctioned under Jewish law, and receive approval in some medieval commentaries, there is no historical evidence that they were carried out, even when Jews lived in regions of the world in which honor killings were practiced by members of the surrounding non-Jewish culture.

---

30 I Rosen-Zvi points out that rabbinic law transfer the private Sotah ritual to the public domain; see *'The Sotah Spectacle' Ha-tekes she-lo haya: mikdash, midrash u-migdar be-masekhet Sotah* [The Rite that Was Not: Temple, Midrash and Gender in Tractate Sotah] (Jerusalem: Magnes Press, 2008); Leviticus 21:9: 'and the daughter of a priest becomes desecrated through adultery, she desecrates her father; she shall be burned in fire.' Talmud Sanhedrin 52a: 'If he had been treated as holy (before), he will now be treated as mundane; (if he had been treated with) honor, now he will be treated with disgrace, as they will say, cursed be the one who gave birth to this one, who raised this one.'

A contrasting position is present in rabbinic texts in Rabbi Akiva's ruling that we should accept a violation of God's dignity for the sake of sparing a person from serious suffering. The passage also reinforces a frequent rabbinic injunction that the violation of the human body is an offense to God's dignity. The link between the human body and God's dignity, according to Michael Barilan, is not found in patristic literature of the same era, which denies that the human body is an image of God; indeed, he notes, canon law accepts torture, viewing the body as subordinate to the spirit.[31] The link between divine and human dignity leads Maimonides to state that punitive torture should be restricted so as not to violate 'the dignity of persons' since it is also 'the dignity of God' (Mishne Torah, Sanhedrin 24:10).

Since human beings were created as individuals in the divine image, rather than as a collective divine image, recent claims to a collective honor as a nation or religious group run counter to traditional Jewish views. Indeed, it is precisely the uniqueness of each individual that is emphasized in discussions of dignity. In its broad, sweeping statements, the Talmud generally includes all humanity in its assertions of human dignity, even if certain laws contradict that assertion. The Talmud asserts the uniqueness and importance of each person as evidence for the oneness of God; to destroy one person is to destroy the whole world, according to the Talmud (TB Sanhedrin 37a).

V. Medieval Texts

In varying medieval philosophical and mystical commentaries, God's 'kavod' forms the basis for discussions of anthropomorphic images of God, or is explained as an emanation or creation of God, as a divine substance that provides spiritual sustenance to human beings, or as a divine entity that receives human prayers. That human beings are created in the image of God bears an association with the bodily, supporting the many injunctions not to mistreat the human body, whether alive or dead.

Given that Jews enjoyed only limited, internal self-governance, rather than political autonomy, residing within Christian or Muslim realms during the Middle Ages, questions of human dignity were generally limited to internal matters. Moreover, decisions regarding Jewish law were based on

---

31   Barilan, 'From Imago Dei to Human Dignity' 234.

principles of human dignity that were not always articulated as such. Maimonides, for example, expanded biblical regulations forbidding harsh treatment of Hebrew slaves to include all slaves. While he does not explicitly invoke the term 'human dignity', Maimonides bases his argument on its principles:

> It is permissible to treat a Canaanite slave with harshness. This is the law. But piety and reason oblige a man to be merciful and just toward his slave, not to overburden him with work, not to cause him grief, but let him share all food and drink taken by himself, as was the custom of our sages of old... He should not humiliate him by infliction of corporal punishment nor by words. He should not shout at him angrily, but talk to him quietly and listen to his arguments.

Maimonides justifies his decision on two grounds: a passage from Job 31:13-15 asserting monogenesis, and on *tselem Elohim*, writing that 'cruelty and brutality are characteristics of pagans and idolaters', whereas Jews, like God, practice mercy.[32]

Yet elsewhere Maimonides seems to suggest that a husband may use a rod to beat his wife when she fails to perform her household duties or when she engages in physical lovemaking with another woman.[33] Although sexual relations between two women are not considered homosexuality in Jewish law, Maimonides ruled that lovemaking between women might stimulate a wife to engage in adultery with a man, which is forbidden. Most English translations as well as medieval Hebrew commentaries understand Maimonides to be stating that a husband may compel his wife 'by scourging her with a rod'. If that is his intended meaning (the passage is slightly unclear), then this, too, would be a break with prior Jewish law, which does not condone wife beating, as well as strikingly inconsistent with Maimonides' distinct sensitivity to the dignity of a slave and his ruling against torture. The ambiguity of his position – no torture of slaves but beating of wives – will be reiterated, as we will see, in the Israeli Supreme Court's ruling regarding torture.

---

32   Maimonides, *Code of Jewish Law*, Book 12, 'Slaves', ch 9, para 8. The quotation from the Book of Job states, 'Have I ever disregarded the rights of my slave or those of my bondwoman, when they had an argument with me? ... My Creator has made me and him in one womb and has formed us in one womb' (Job 31: 13,15).

33   DES Stein, 'Did Maimonides Really Say That?' (2005) 6 *Journal of Religion and Abuse* 1–8. The passage appears in Maimonides, Mishne Torah, Ketubot, 21:10a. The translation is debated.

One of the most important limitations to the applicability of human dignity in Jewish thought concerns idolatry; those who are idolatrous are generally considered to stand outside the potential recipients of dignity. Idolatry is considered one of the great evils, and a Jew should die rather than engage in it; even business dealings with idolaters are forbidden. Within the medieval period, the question arose whether Christianity was a monotheistic religion and, hence, an ethical religion. Idolatry, argued the noted medieval rabbis in Ashkenaz, including Gershom Meor Hagolah and Menahem Ha-Meiri, necessarily leads to immorality.[34] The two rabbis differed on how they exempted Christianity from the category of an idolatrous religion. Rabbi Gershom argued that Christians were simply following the customs of their forefathers, while Meiri argued that Christians adhered to ethical principles and hence could not be considered idolatrous. The ramifications were important, given both the prohibitions in rabbinic law on Jews doing business with idolaters and because the principle of *kavod ha-adam*, human dignity, could now, theoretically, be applied to Christians along with *kavod ha-briot*.

VI. Human Dignity in the Modern Era

A universal concept of human dignity, applicable to all, was rarely invoked in European society prior to the mid-twentieth century, yet attributes associated with it shifted from the exclusive realm of the aristocracy and nobility to widespread claims at all social ranks, including the enslaved and disenfranchised. For the German philosopher Immanuel Kant, dignity was the natural outcome of human free will and having the capacity to make rational moral decisions. That capacity is precisely what guarantees dignity to all, argues the philosopher Michael Rosen in his recent book, *Dignity*. Yet Rosen recognizes that Kant's argument for an intrinsic, inviolable human dignity based on rational decision-making is insufficient, and he concludes his book with the (perhaps) apocryphal anecdote about the elderly, dying Kant rising from his bed to greet his physician. When admonished to rest and not rise, Kant is said to have replied, 'The

---

34 See the discussion of medieval Jewish thought on the link between idolatry and immorality in M Halbertal and A Margalit, *Idolatry* (Cambridge, Harvard University Press, 1992) 211 f.

feeling of human dignity has not yet left me.'[35] Denying his right to pay respect to his visitor—to perform a gesture of dignity—would deny Kant the dignity that constitutes his humanity. Here, too, dignity is performative, acquired by Kant through a gesture of respect for his physician. Yet denial of dignity is precisely what is accomplished through racist institutions and social attitudes, such as the treatment my African-American student, Dierre Upshaw, experienced from a group of white men who sought to harass, threaten, and perhaps harm him.

The attributes that constitute human dignity in rabbinic literature—and learning—continued in secularized Jewish rhetoric. Dignity was discussed in two general contexts by Jews in the modern era, one of accommodation to the European nation-states, the other of human dignity within Zionism and the State of Israel. In the European nation-states, as Jews struggled for emancipation and legal rights, dignity—though not named as such— became politicized: as in all movements of liberation, the dignity of Jews was supposed to be grounds for their social acceptance. For that reason, European Jews promoted the acquisition of '*Bildung*', signifying not only learning but also the cultivation of European cultural tastes and intellectual discernment. Synagogues, starting in the nineteenth century, formulated rules of decorum to create a dignified liturgical service. Dignified behavior was assumed to express an inner, intrinsic and inviolable dignity that elevates the oppressed, the slave, the marginalized, the colonized, etc., to a status deserving of respect and equality even when they are excluded on legal or prejudicial grounds from those who dominate the power structures. At times, even elevated social status does not accord members of a despised group from the dignity normally associated with that status. For example, along with women and peasants, Jews in Europe were generally excluded from the 'code of honor' that led Gentiles to dueling. Even the dignity of the office of President of the United States, to take a contemporary example, did not impede members of Congress and the Supreme Court from loud, verbal expressions of mockery during President Barack Obama's delivery of the State of the Union addresses, mockery that some observers have attributed to racism.[36]

---

35   M Rosen, *Dignity: Its History and Meaning* 160.
36   I am referring here to the unprecedented shout of 'You lie!' bellowed by Rep. Joseph Wilson of South Carolina as he sat in Congress listening to Pres. Obama's speech in January 2009, and 'Not true' mouthed in the middle of the president's speech by US Supreme Court Justice Samuel Alito, in 2010.

Societal norms regulating dignified behavior function to configure political expression, moderating political viewpoints and modes of expression. Just as the famous figure of 'Uncle Tom' in the eponymous novel by Harriet Beecher Stowe is an example of how the image of a dignified black slave inspired many nineteenth-century Americans to oppose slavery, the dignified image of Moses Mendelssohn, the late eighteenth-century Berlin Jewish philosopher, became a symbol that inspired similar attitudes of respect toward Jews among European Christians.[37] The claim to dignity was important in winning political rights and social acceptance over ideologies of race and anti-Judaism, and also was an important component of the nonviolent movements against colonialism. Tropes of dignity invoked by Gandhi, for instance, appealed to the British sense of honor, and were also used in the context of apartheid in South Africa and segregation in the United States, employed in the context of the nonviolent civil disobedience practiced by the American Civil Rights Movement during the 1950s and 60s.

Liberal movements within modern Judaism invoke human dignity in making some of their most significant changes in religious practice, yet there is no consistency in the invocation of dignity. Dignity is applied selectively and does not always overrule underlying social prejudices when invoking Jewish law. For example, when considering homosexuality, members of the Conservative movement's rabbinic law committee invoked human dignity both in support of, and in opposition to, the permissibility of homosexual relationships and membership in synagogues. In supporting the inclusion of gay and lesbian members of Conservative synagogues, the rabbis wrote,

> The rabbinic prohibitions that have been associated with other gay and lesbian intimate acts are superseded based upon the Talmudic principle of *kvod ha-briot* (dignity of created beings), our obligation to preserve the human dignity of all people.

Yet the Conservative rabbis also wrote: 'The explicit biblical ban on anal sex between men remains in effect. Gay men are instructed to refrain from anal sex.'[38] Since anal intercourse (which is permissible under Jewish law

---

37 A Altmann, 'Moses Mendelssohn as the Archetypical German Jew' in J Reinharz and W Schatzberg (eds), *The Jewish Response to German Culture* (Hanover, University Press of New England, 1985) 17.
38 EN Dorff, DS Nevins, and AI Reisner, 'Homosexuality, Human Dignity and Halakha: A Combined Responsum for the Committee on Jewish Law and Standards' *Law Committee of the Rabbinical Assembly of America*, ratified on

in a heterosexual context) is one of the main forms of sexual pleasure enjoyed by homosexual men, it seems as though this resolution, in the name of preserving 'human dignity', is only recognizing and welcoming homosexuals who are celibate—that is, homosexuals who do not practice homosexuality.

The same principle of dignity, *kavod ha-briot*, was invoked in a very different way by the Sephardic chief rabbi of Israel, Ovadiah Yosef (1920-2013), in a liberal ruling of Jewish law concerning *pidyon ha-ben*, redemption of the first-born son. The case involved a woman who had undergone an abortion prior to her marriage, but had not told her husband. Since the son she bore was not the first male issue of her womb, the ritual of *pidyon ha-ben* would not apply and its blessings would constitute a *bracha l'vatala* (a blessing said inappropriately, which is forbidden). Yet to help her conceal the abortion from the husband, Rav Yosef ruled that the *pidyon ha-ben* should take place nonetheless, with all the requisite blessings, in order to preserve the woman's dignity, writing that '*gadol kavod ha-briot shedochech lo ta'aseh b'Torah*' (Great is human dignity since it overrides a negative precept of the Torah).[39]

VII. Universalization of Human Dignity in Jewish Thought

Perhaps the most radical shift in Jewish thought occurred when theologians of the modern period expanded the point of reference of human dignity to include all human beings, not only Jews. That Jews were the exclusive 'chosen people' of God clashes with the biblical assertion of monogenesis and universal *imago Dei*. Rabbinic literature presents conflicting claims: 'Precious is *adam* (man) for he was created in the image [of God]. Precious is Israel who are called children of the Omnipresent.' (Mishnah Avot 3:14). Modern Jewish thinkers usually focus on the universal, seeking to define Judaism as a religion of 'ethical monotheism', and emphasizing an older Jewish tradition that only monotheism can guarantee ethical behavior. For the twentieth century German-Jewish philosopher Franz Rosenzweig, love rather than dignity becomes the central category. Love

---

6 December 2006, by a vote of 13 to 12; www.rabbinicalassembly.org/sites/default/files/public/halakhah/teshuvot/20052010/dorff_nevins_reisner_dignity.pdf 19.

39 RO Yosef, *Yabiat Omer*, vol 8, note 32.

of the neighbor stems from the love of and for God; God commands our love for God – "thou shalt love the Lord your God" – which Rosenzweig understands as evidence that God loves us because only someone who loves can demand love in return. Love of neighbor is thus derivative, not foundational, as Samuel Moyn has pointed out: 'the neighbor is a substitutional category'.[40] Judaism and Christianity are responses to God's love, though other religions are not; Rosenzweig's universalism applies to the future, not the present. The French Jewish philosopher Emanuel Levinas (1906-1995) emphasizes that it is the face of the other that makes ethics primary, and not the actions of the other nor rational moral reasoning nor God.[41] Indeed, he argues that freedom and reason are not guarantees to prevent racism, totalitarianism, and genocide. For Levinas, dignity is achieved only by assuming a prior ethical responsibility for the other, and he questions whether the legal guarantees of liberalism are sufficient for achieving 'authentic dignity' because treating others with dignity would remain a choice that can easily be withdrawn.[42]

The theologian Abraham Joshua Heschel spoke in a more traditional, religious Jewish idiom, emphasizing the uniquely Jewish teaching of divine pathos (*zoreh gavoha*), God's empathic responsiveness to human beings, which he traced in prophetic, rabbinic, and medieval texts, and the centrality of *tselem Elohim*. Heschel links dignity to holiness (Leviticus 19:2).[43] Human beings contain divinity because God "blew into his nostrils the breath of life" (Genesis 2:7).[44] At the same time, he expanded the traditional theurgic understanding of divine pathos, arguing that God responds not only to observance of ritual commandments, but also to commandments governing human relationships, and he included all human beings in the ethical admonitions of Judaism. In many of his writings, he cites a Midrashic commentary to Isaiah 43:12: 'I am God and you are my

---

[40] S Moyn, *Origins of the Other: Emanuel Levinas Between Revelation and Ethics* (Ithaca, Cornell University Press, 2005) 153.

[41] D Perpich, *The Ethics of Emanuel Levinas* (Stanford, Stanford University Press, 2008) 153 f.

[42] E Levinas, 'Reflections on the Philosophy of Hitlerism', (1990) 17 *Critical Inquiry* 62, 63.

[43] AJ Heschel, 'Sacred Image of Man' in id (ed), *The Insecurity of Freedom: Essays on Human Existence* (New York: Farrar, Straus and Giroux, 1966) 150-167.

[44] ibid 157.

witnesses; if you are not my witnesses, then I am, as it were, not God.' (Pirke d'Ray Kahane 12:6, 102b).[45]

The root of Nazi criminality, Heschel argued in an essay he wrote in September 1940, just months after arriving as a refugee in the United States, began with its commodification of human beings. This was aided, he claimed, by a long stream of social theorists and philosophers who defined not the uniqueness and greatness of the human spirit, but rather compared human beings to animals or machines, placing them within the order of nature. By contrast, he argued that Judaism insisted on human dignity as derived from the uniqueness of humans:

> 'It was the classical achievement of antique Judaism to have worked out the differentiation between nature and spirit, and God's standing over nature. The negation of the separate existence of the spirit by naturalism means a relapse into a time when nature and spirit could not be differentiated and the abolition of human dignity.'[46]

For Heschel, human dignity does not collide with individual human rights; on the contrary, in a 1957 essay, "The Individual Jew and His Obligations," he argued for the recognition of the human soul as both the guarantor of dignity and of the inviolable claim to the rights of the individual. Halakha, Jewish law, promotes religious practices incumbent on all Jews, while neglecting, he claimed, the individual and his or her personal anxieties, dilemmas, and spiritual problems.[47]

Heschel's engagement in political activism, including the Civil Rights movement, brought him to take public stances in issues involving Gentiles, not just Jews, making him both the most traditional of modern Jewish theologians and simultaneously the most universal. Divine need is served not only through performance of ritual commandments, but also through human behavior toward one another, and it also serves as a caution against placing humans in an abject position in relation to God. When Rabbi Akiva, one of the most important rabbinic authorities of the second century CE, ruled that one should even accept the violation of God's dignity for the sake of sparing a person serious suffering (TJ Nedarim 9:4), he meant all persons, in Heschel's interpretation. Perhaps most radical and

---

45 AJ Heschel, 'The Sacred Image of Man' *The Insecurity of Freedom*, 164.
46 AJ Heschel, 'Antwort an Einstein' (September 1940) 20 *Aufbau*.
47 AJ Heschel, 'The Individual Jew and His Obligations' in id (ed), *The Insecurity of Freedom* 187-211.

distinctive is Heschel's assertion that rabbinic laws regarding dignity apply to all human beings, not only to Jews.

Performance of dignity does not always conquer racism. The destruction of European Jews in the Holocaust is widely recognized as the event that catalyzed international attention to human dignity. The murder was accompanied by degradation and humiliation, an 'excremental assault', in the words of Terrence Des Pres.[48] Numerous memoirs by inmates of death camps report that the preservation of a sense of human dignity was essential to their survival, while others report the absolute obliteration of their dignity. The French philosopher Jean Améry writes,

> You do not observe dehumanized man committing his deeds and misdeeds without having all of your notions of inherent human dignity placed in doubt. We emerged from the camp stripped, robbed, emptied out, disoriented—and it was a long time before we were able even to learn the ordinary language of freedom. Still today, incidentally, we speak it with discomfort and without real trust in its validity.[49]

What may reconstitute the dignity of the perpetrators, if at all possible, has not been examined thus far.

VIII. Human Dignity and Honor in Zionist Thought

Zionism challenged the Jewish contract with European society. Not only was political integration rejected, dignity itself was questioned. A central tenet of most Zionist theorists was that the Jewish experience of exile had feminized Jewish men, depriving them of dignity. Establishing a Jewish state would overcome the degeneration caused by diaspora and its piety and learning, according to a major trend within Zionist thought. Spinoza, in his *Tractatus Theologico-Politicus*, published in 1670, had argued that Jewish religious piety emasculates Jewish men; the nineteenth century Hungarian Jewish physician and Zionist leader Max Nordau argued that Judaism had produced a 'degeneration' of Jewish men whereas Zionism would produce 'muscular Jews'; Theodor Herzl, the leader of political Zionism, who bore a scar from a duel he had engaged in as member of a stu-

---

48 T Des Pres, *The Survivor: An Anatomy of Life in the Death Camps* (New York, Oxford University Press, 1976).

49 J Améry, *At the Mind's Limits: Contemplations by a Survivor on Auschwitz and Its Realities* (New York, Schocken Books, 1986) 20.

dent fraternity, depicted a State of Israel that would restore such manly practices of honor to Jewish men; Vladimir Jabotinsky wrote with contempt of the despised, sickly, ugly, frightened 'Yid' who will be replaced through Zionism by the proud, independent 'Hebrew' of masculine strength and beauty who will both charm and command with pride.[50]

The emphasis on human dignity that is found in Zionist thinkers continued in the State of Israel's legal documents. Israel's Declaration of Independence, proclaimed in May 1948, promises

> complete equality of social and political rights to all its inhabitants irrespective of religion, race or sex; [and]... freedom of religion, conscience, language, education and culture.

Israel has never written a constitution, but enacted several Basic Laws that are supposed to ultimately inform a constitution whenever it may come to be written. Those Basic Laws, passed in 1992, do not speak of equality, but of *kavod ha'adam v'heruto*, the dignity of man and his liberty; equality was omitted as a concession to the religious parties, which reject equality of women and men. Those political party conflicts within the Knesset left the Basic Law without certain provisions that were ultimately extended by the Supreme Court, which invoked dignity in decisions such as freedom of religion and the right to equality.[51]

Honor and dignity assumed particular importance in the Zionist movement's effort to overcome the absence of political self-rule and the attendant persecutions and suffering of Diasporic existence. Zionists first asserted that Jewish life in diaspora had been humiliating to Jewish men, the result not only of not having political autonomy, but also the result of piety and study, rather than physical exertion and military prowess. Zionists then presented their movement as overcoming the shame and humiliation of Diaspora, with the State of Israel charged with protecting the Jewish collective. Israeli legal scholar Orit Kamir calls attention to the centrality of personal, masculine honor in Herzl's political Zionism and the contrasting emphasis on the dignity of the Jewish collective by Ahad Ha-Am, who advocated cultural Zionism. David Ben Gurion, Israel's first Prime

---

50 On Jabotinsky, see A Wolfe, *At Home in Exile: Why Diaspora is Good for the Jews* (Boston, Beacon Press, 2014) 17 f.
51 Kretzmer, in Kretzmer and Klein, 172.

Minister, united the two concepts of honor and dignity, Kamir argues, making human dignity and Jewish national honor 'almost synonymous'.[52]

IX. Human Dignity in the State of Israel

While Jewish law is not the governing law of the State of Israel, Jewish religious practice, ethical norms, and historical experience continue to influence court decisions as well as decisions made by the Knesset, the Israeli parliament. Human dignity was invoked by the Supreme Court of Israel even before adoption by the Knesset of the 1992 Basic Law on human dignity.[53] In accord with classical rabbinic texts, the Court has invoked dignity in decisions ranging from protecting animals from needless suffering and to protect the dignity of the human corpse. The Court has also limited freedom of expression on the grounds of human dignity, placing limits on pornography as potentially violating the dignity of women, and limiting speech promoting racial hatred.

Conflicting claims to dignity also mirror questions about the nature of the State itself: is it a state of individuals or a state representing the collective Jewish people or even Judaism? The distinctions are not embedded in law, but are rhetorically powerful as a measure of Israeli culture, which wavers between Israel as a Jewish state, a democratic state, a religious state, a secular state. The rhetoric functions within legal decisions in a manner analogous to the role of aggada in the Talmud. For example, a 1967 court ruling found that two Israeli citizens who had cut off the sidelocks of an Israeli Jew were guilty of attacking 'Jewish national honor'.[54] In a 1996 Supreme Court case regarding transportation on the Jewish Sabbath, Doron Shultziner reports that while Aharon Barak, a non-religious justice, ruled in favor of the rights of individuals to drive freely through Jewish religious neighborhoods on holidays that forbid automotive travel, religious justices ruled to the contrary. For Barak, human dignity upheld the autonomy granted by freedom of movement. However, the religious justice on that case, Tzvi Tal, asserted that freedom of movement on the

---

52 O Kamir, 'Honor and Dignity Cultures: The Case of *Kavod* and *Kvod Ha-Adam* in Israeli Society and Law' in Kretzmer and Klein *The Concept of Human Dignity in Human Rights Discourse* 231, 255.
53 D Kretzmer, Human Dignity in Israeli Jurisprudence, in Kretzmer and Klein, *The Concept of Human Dignity in Human Rights Discourse* 161, 163-165.
54 ibid 257.

Sabbath was of lesser importance than preserving respect for Jewish religious sentiments that regard the Sabbath as central to Jewish tradition; the issue of human dignity was defined by him not in terms of individual autonomy, but as the collective historical spirit of the Jewish people represented by the State of Israel. Thus, while rabbinic law does not govern Israeli court rulings, a murky and weakly delineated understanding of Jewish tradition does influence decisions. The invocation of Judaism and Jewish experience elevates the collective, and tends to weaken arguments for individual human rights as a protection for the individual since rabbinic law, as Heschel pointed out, neglects the individual Jew.[55]

The most difficult conflict has been the application of dignity to cases facing the High Court of Justice (HCJ) that adjudicates petitions against government actions and thus has a heavy caseload arising from the military administration of the Occupied Territories. Those appeals frequently invoke the Basic Law on human dignity and ask whether the human dignity of Palestinians can be invoked against claims to state security. The decisions of the HCJ underscore the ambiguity of the situation: it is unprecedented in international law to allow residents of an occupied territory access to the courts of the occupying nation, pointing to the reluctance of many leading political leaders in the State of Israel to speak of the West Bank as occupied.

The HCJ's cases operate at the heart of the conflict between human rights and claims to 'security,' with the Court acting at times as a restraint on military authorities and, at other times, as a legitimating force. The legal scholar David Kretzmer argues that the legitimating function dominates because the HCJ

> has not perceived itself as a judicial body that should play an expansive role in trying to protect basic rights against violation by government, but as a body that must support the foundation of military legislation in the Occupied Territories.[56]

The Israeli Supreme Court, too, has acted in concert with Israeli political policy, approving the establishment of civilian settlements in the West Bank on the grounds of military need, although the Geneva Convention

---

55   D Shultziner, 'A Jewish Conception of Human Dignity: Philosophy and Its Ethical Implications for Israeli Supreme Court Decisions' (2006) 34 *Journal of Religious Ethics* 663. AJ Heschel, 'The Individual Jew and His Obligations' *The Insecurity of Freedom* (New York, Farrar, Straus and Giroux, 1966) 187-211.

56   D Kretzmer, *The Occupation of Justice: The Supreme Court of Israel and the Occupied Territories* (New York, SUNY Press, 2002) 126.

prohibits the transfer of citizens of the occupying power to the occupied territory.[57] On the other hand, the Israeli Supreme Court ruled in 2005 against the use of targeted assassination of Palestinians suspected of terrorism in the Occupied Territories:

> unlawful combatants are not beyond the law. They are not 'outlaws'. God created them as well in his image; their human dignity as well is to be honored; they as well enjoy and are entitled to protection.[58]

Both courts waver between adhering to international law and state policy; the decision to permit settlements, for instance, contravenes the Geneva Convention, yet government lawyers, Kretzmer points out, plea at times in the name of the international law of belligerent occupation.[59] The very existence of the HCJ and the opportunity for civilian appeals against military actions opens the route to legal appeals and also acts as a mitigating influence, generating some degree of restraint by Israeli officials, creating what Kretzmer terms "in the shadow of the Court restraining influence."[60] Yet the decisions of the HCJ have also legitimated military actions against Palestinians, including house demolitions, confiscation of land, destruction of olive groves, and deportations, invariably in decisions that favor claims of state security over the human dignity of Palestinians.[61] The very existence of the HCJ provides "the oxygen that enables the occupation to operate," writes human rights lawyer Michael Sfard.[62] The tension between restraint and legitimation mirrors the difficult adjudication between human dignity and claims to superseding commitments, whether political regimes or ideological formations concerned with race, gender, or wealth.

Had the HCJ not acted as a force of restraint on the West Bank, allowing military control to engage in blatant violations of human rights, would the ensuing human abuse, Kretzmer asks, have 'made the occupation less

---

57   M Sfard, 'The Human Rights Lawyer's Existential Dilemma' *Israel Law Review* 38:3 (2005) 154-169, 162.
58   Public Committee against Torture in Israel v. Government of Israel, HCJ 769/02 (Supreme Court of Israel Sitting as the High Court of Justice) [December 11 2005]; cited by Christopher McCrudden, 'Human Dignity and Judicial Interpretation of Human Rights' *EILJ Working Paper* 2008/8, 37.
59   D Kretzmer, 'The Law of Belligerent Occupation in the Supreme Court of Israel' *International Review of the Red Cross* 94:885 (Spring 2012) 236.
60   Kretzmer, *Occupation of Justice*, passim.
61   Sfard, 'The Human Rights Lawyer's Existential Dilemma' 163.
62   Sfard, 'The Human Rights Lawyer's Existential Dilemma' 165.

palatable to Israeli elites,' thus forcing a political settlement that would have ended the occupation?[63]

Torture has been banned in a variety of international laws and covenants ratified since 1948, to which the State of Israel has been a signatory. Even more powerful is the explicit ban in those international conventions on the use of torture during states of exception, such as war or political instability. In examining the September 1999, ban on torture issued by the Israeli Supreme Court, the Israeli philosopher Anat Biletzki notes that while Israel had signed all the various international conventions of human rights, torture had continued under the rubrics of 'necessary for security' and described as 'pressure'.[64] Aharon Barak, President of the Court, when commenting on the Basic Law of dignity and liberty, proposed that the Knesset (Israeli parliament) pass laws permitting torture, if it so wished, writing

> It is there that the required legislation may be passed, provided, of course, that a law infringing upon a suspect's liberty befitting the values of the State of Israel, is enacted for a proper purpose, and to an extent no greater than is required.

The ambiguity is reminiscent of Maimonides' rejection of torture but approval of wife beating: the Court rejects torture unless it is for an undefined 'proper purpose' and no great than an undefined 'required.'

Although the Supreme Court's ruling on torture was ultimately equivocal, it nonetheless aroused outcries among right-wing Israeli Jews who supported torture of Palestinians and claimed that the Court was becoming imperial, undermining the State of Israel's security, and needed to be reined in by the government. Ultimately, the Knesset refused to legislate permission for torture, and although 'tentative and equivocal,' the Court's decision might be a harbinger, according to Biletzki, of the internal condemnation needed to secure human rights in Israel.[65] Of course, in considering who would be tortured, the Israelis who opposed in the court's ruling had in mind Palestinians suspected of terrorism. Reports of torture – 'pressure' – allegedly applied to Jews suspected of terrorism against Palestinians in December 2015, sparked a reversed outcry: right-wing Israeli Jews were now in opposition to torture. Like the society, Biletzki calls the court

---

63   Kretzmer, *Occupation of Justice*, 198.
64   A Biletzki, 'The Judicial Rhetoric of Morality: Israel's High Court of Justice on the Legality of Torture' (2001) *Occasional Papers of the School of Social Science, Paper no 9*.
65   Biletzki, 'The Judicial Rhetoric of Morality 16.

a 'schizophrenic court' for differentiating in a host of cases between Jewish and Arab applicants,

> between social-economic issues and political (i.e., Jewish-Arab conflict) ones: a liberal, rights-conscious court on the Jewish socio-economic side of things, a strict, security-minded one on the political conflict stage.[66]

Ultimately, the State of Israel, as a state for Jews, appeals to security as the state of exception that exempts Israel from various international legal obligations, whether those pertaining to nuclear disarmament or the occupation of conquered territories. In that respect, the State of Israel is in alignment with the United States, which, as Michael Ignatieff has argued, invokes American exceptionalism to exempt itself from applying the provisions of the international human rights conventions that it has signed, and denying jurisdiction to human rights law within its own domestic legal framework.[67] Nationalism influences the Israeli court's understanding of human dignity, making the universal understandings of the Bible and much of rabbinic literature secondary to the honor of Judaism, the Jewish people, and the State of Israel. On the one hand, universal claims to the inviolability of human dignity may be understood as upholding claims of liberty and personal autonomy, while on the other hand, human dignity may be invoked to uphold the rights of Judaism and the collective Jewish people, paralleling the findings of Shultziner and Carmi in their survey of courts that interpret the 'human dignity' of their national constitutions to uphold the collective or the national culture, even when denying individual human rights.

X. Conclusion

The different meanings of '*kavod*' that arose in biblical texts and became at times ambiguous in rabbinic literature continue to this day in the supposedly secular context of the Israeli courts. Human dignity, national honor, and divine glory each carry different political and cultural implications, as Orit Kamir wisely notes. Human dignity may be vested in human beings by God, but it does not exist without human action; dignity is granted to human society for cultivation. While dignity may be experienced sub-

---

66 Biletzki, 'The Judicial Rhetoric of Morality' 14.
67 M Ignatieff, *American Exceptionalism and Human Rights* (Princeton, Princeton University Press, 2005).

jectively, it requires continual recognition and performance by others. Despite Rabbi Meir's insistence in the Talmud that all victims deserve the same compensation, some societal distinctions of wealth, gender, ethnicity, and status became markers recognized in rabbinic law when determining both the nature of an offense against dignity and its recompense; the rabbis clearly recognized that the supposed universality of '*tselem Elohim*' did not function in all circumstances. Yet status markers conflict with the biblical claim of monogenesis, an equality of all human beings by virtue of divine creation, as well as the inviolability of human dignity as a reflection of God. Reconciling religious belief with human equality or democratic pluralism is thus not a new problem, but a tension already inherent in the earliest strata of rabbinic thought. The claims of dignity are not the same as the claims of rights, and the dignity of tradition, religion, or society may at times be given precedence over the dignity of an individual, especially if *kavod* is translated not as dignity, but as honor. The application of human dignity to Jews, rather than universally, could function when Jews held no political sovereignty over non-Jews. Israeli court decisions weighing human dignity against state security tend to retreat, especially when the dignity applies to Palestinians in the Occupied Territories; that is the inevitable outcome, perhaps, of an ethnically homogenous government ruling over members of outlying groups.

Even a relatively 'minor' offense against human dignity, whether as a racist threat against my African-American student, Dierre Upshaw, or a contemptuous comment directed against a president who is black, demonstrates the fragility of human dignity when confronted by systems of racism, structures of patriarchy, or other forms of societal hierarchies and privilege. Ultimately, both the legal system of rabbinic Judaism and contemporary legal jurisdiction in the secular courts of the State of Israel that are informed by Jewish historical experience agree that while human dignity is vested by God and remains an inviolable principle on a private level, dignity also depends upon the performance and recognition by other human beings to come into a social and legal existence that transcends regimes of race and gender.

Literature *as* Human Dignity: The Constitutional Court's Misguided Ban of the Novel *Esra*

Russell A. Miller*

I. Introduction

Maxim Biller's novel *Esra* ends with the line: 'The cave was empty, but it was filled with light.'[1] It is an achingly hopeful conclusion to a challenging, mostly dark work. Biller also would have been aware that those lines make a fair claim for the promise of literature. Empty words—mere inky-scribblings on a page—have the power to illuminate and enlighten life, the life of the author every bit as much as the lives of his or her readers. Biller's novel is profoundly conscious of its status as—and its participation in the project of—literature. But the lessons this smart and challenging book might have taught us were stillborn. In 2007 the German Federal Constitutional Court found no constitutional fault in the ban Germany's ordinary courts had imposed on the book.[2] And just like that, the light goes out.

---

* This text does not do him justice, but I wish to dedicate it to Professor John Ehrstine († 2016) who taught English literature at Washington State University from 1964-2000. Professor Ehrstine helped me to see that literature—more than law—is the best of what we are.

1 M Biller, *Esra* (Köln, Kiepenheuer und Witsch, 2007) 214 ('Die Höhle war leer, aber sie war voller Licht.') (All translations from *Esra* are by Russell Miller).

2 *Esra Novel Case*, 119 BVerfGE 1 (2007). All quotes and references are from the English-language translation produced by the Court and available at: https://www.bundesverfassungsgericht.de/entscheidungen/rs20070613_1bvr178305en.html. See K Bünnigmann, *Die Esra-Entscheidung als Ausgleich zwischen Persönlichkeitsschutz und Kunstfreiheit* (Tübingen, Mohr Siebeck, 2013); U Wittstock, *Der Fall Esra* (Köln, Kiepenheuer und Witsch, 2011); M Riedel, *Vermutung des Künstlerischen: Der Esra-Beschluss des Bundesverfassungsgerichts – Eine rechts-und literaturwissenschaftliche Untersuchung* (Tübingen, Mohr Siebeck, 2011); EI Obergfell, 'Der Fall Esra – Eine Neujustierung des Verhältnisses von Persönlichkeitsrecht und literarischer Kunstfreiheit?' (2010) 73 *Amsterdamer Beiträge zur neueren Germanistik* (Justitiabilität und Rechtmäßigkeit. Verrechtlichungsprozesse von Literatur und Film in der

Of course, in this age of hackers and scanners, it is still possible to read *Esra*. I was given a widely-circulating photocopy made from the edition that was published before the courts' injunction issued. The photocopy was made from a hardback print that sits on the shelves of the Universitätsbibliothek Paderborn, cataloged with the signature CSCB8728 under the keywords 'Romantic Relationship' and 'Novelist'.[3] The library's website says that normal borrowing rules apply.[4] Still, Kiepenheuer & Witsch (KiWi), Biller's publisher, does not name the novel alongside his other books in its list. At the KiWi website, there is an abbreviated reference to the ban—and a link to a related press-release—in an account of the boutique publishing house's history.[5] When I looked recently, two new copies of the book were for sale at Amazon.de, one for €299 and the other for €489. The cheapest of the seven used copies available was offered for €50. A single copy was listed at the online auction site Ebay for €220. This is what a 21st century book-ban looks like: just ten scandalously-priced copies of a ten year-old novel can be had in the whole World Wide Web.

    Moderne) 65; F Wittreck, 'Die aktuelle Entscheidung Esra, Mephisto und Salomo' (2010) 31 *JURA - Juristische Ausbildung* 128; O Jouanjan, 'Freedom of Expression in the Federal Republic of Germany' (2009) 84 *Ind. L.J.* 867; B Clark, 'Freedom of Art v. Personality Rights: Ban Upheld on the Real Life Novel Esra' (2008) 3 *Journal of Intellectual Property Law and Practice* 221; C Eichner and Y-G Mix, 'Ein Fehlurteil als Maßstab? Zu Maxim Billers Esra, Klaus Manns Mephisto und dem Problem der Kunstfreiheit in der Bundesrepublik Deutschland' (2007) 32 *Internationales Archiv für Sozialgeschichte der deutschen Literatur* 183; B von Becker, *Fiktion und Wirklichkeit im Roman: Der Schlüsselprozess um das Buch Esra* (Würzburg, Königshausen und Neumann, 2006).

3   See Universitätsbibliothek Paderborn, Katalog, available at www.katalog.ub.uni-paderborn.de/searches/ikxkc9/records/PAD_ALEPH000864882.
4   ibid.
5   Verlag Kiepenheuer and Witsch, *Chronik 2000-10*, www.kiwi-verlag.de/verlag/chronik.html ('Im Frühjahr erscheint der Roman *Esra* von Maxim Biller, gegen dessen Verbreitung durch den Verlag kurz nach der Veröffentlichung eine einstweilige Verfügung aus persönlichkeitsrechtlichen Gründen ergeht. Jahrelange Prozesse folgen, in denen Kiepenheuer und Witsch versucht, die Freiheit der Kunst gegen die persönlichkeitsrechtlichen Einsprüche zu verteidigen (bis zur endgültigen Entscheidung des Bundesverfassungsgerichtes im Herbst 2007).') For the press release, see Verlag Kiepenheuer and Witsch, *Vertagt: Verhandlung gegen Maxim Biller—Entscheidung in Karlsruhe wird abgewartet* (1 January 2007), available at www.kiwi-verlag.de/news/2007/vertagt-verhandlung-gegen-maxim-biller.html.

Biller was accused of having written a *Schlüsselroman*—a *Roman à clef*—in which the novel's characters and their circumstances are supposed to be thinly-disguised treatments of easily-recognized real people.⁶ From this perspective the book's protagonists—the lovelorn Jewish novelist addressing the reader as the first-person narrator named Adam; the narrator's ambivalent, indecisive and buffeted lover, the Turkish-German actress named Esra; and Esra's domineering mother, the Turkish-German human rights activist Lale—are obvious depictions of Biller, his one-time lover Ayse Romey, and Romey's mother Birsel Lemke. The novel's deeply personal narrative and honest voice treat some extremely private episodes in the characters' lives, including family interactions and sexual encounters. These are human, profoundly intimate, and sometimes terribly unflattering incidents—no less so for the narrator than for Esra and Lale. The courts imposed the ban because they were convinced that the personal elements of the novel were unavoidably attributable to Romey and Lemke, and that the novel would place the mother and daughter—and Romey's child—in a bad light. Sparing the plaintiffs these assumed ignominies, the ban was justified as a defense of Romey's human dignity at the price of a tolerable diminishment of Biller's artistic and literary freedom.⁷

The Constitutional Court's *Esra Case* poses some dreadful questions. Can the law, as a state-institutional phenomenon, advance human dignity better than literature, which is a profoundly human phenomenon? Worse, can the law advance any credible brand of human dignity at the expense of banning a book? The answer to these questions must be, I think, a resounding 'no.' It was a grave mistake for the Constitutional Court to endorse the ban on *Esra* because banning a book does more to erode human dignity than it does to promote it.

I will draw on literary criticism and theory to advance the critique that literature *is*—or is a *fuller form of*—dignity than anything the state's law

---

6   See C Clerc, 'History and Literature' in SR Serafin (ed), *The Continuum Encyclopedia of American Literature*, 2d edn (New York/London, The Continuum Publishing Company, 2003) 523-25; 'Roman à Clef' in I Ousby (ed) *Cambridge Paperback Guide to Literature in English* 332 (Cambridge, Cambridge University Press, 1996).

7   See Bundesgerichtshof [BGH] [Federal Court of Justice], *June 21, 2005*, (2005) 57 *Neue Juristische Wochenschrift* 2844 ('Die Klägerinnen müssen ein solches "Porträt" in Buchform nicht dulden. Ihre Beeinträchtigung wiegt so schwer, daß dem Schutz ihres allgemeinen Persönlichkeitsrechts der Vorrang vor der zugunsten der Beklagten streitenden Kunstfreiheit einzuräumen ist.').

can achieve. I am concerned here with the dignitarian potential of the literary acts of writing and reading books. From this perspective, banning a book can never be a vehicle for promoting human dignity. I maintain that, if the state feels itself obliged to negotiate apparent conflicts between literature and the state's legally constructed version of human dignity as it did in the *Esra Case*, then literature and not the dignity advanced by law should be given priority.[8] Literature has the greater human and humanizing potential. This is Adam's point when he declares in Biller's novel: 'I don't want to be told what I can and cannot write about. That would be like someone taking away the air I breathe.'[9]

II. The Book and the Judgment

A. The Book

To whom does the book *Esra* belong? By this I mean: whose story does the novel tell? From this point of view it is unquestionably Adam's book. The German-Czech-Jewish novelist in his mid-thirties is the book's first-person narrator. Across the slender volume's two-hundred pages he reflects upon and accounts for his trials as a lover, as a father, and as a writer. Adam struggles in all of these roles, but perhaps most painfully and profoundly in his relationship with Esra. As Adam reports it, despite some deeply emotive close-calls, the couple is never able to genuinely connect, to commit without static, misunderstanding or disillusion. They are equal contributors to this costly emotional misadventure. Adam will not give Esra the second child she seems determined to have. Esra cannot sufficiently disentangle herself from her former marriage and her family, and cannot summon the emotionality to give Adam all he seems to need from her. The pair's greatest rapprochement, hopeless as it is, comes when Esra is pregnant with another man's child. But the book is driven by Adam's

---

[8] See, eg A Peters, 'Humanity as the A and Ω of Sovereignty' (2009) 20 *European Journal of International Law* 513 f ('Consequently, conflicts between state sovereignty and human rights should not be approached in a balancing process in which the former is played off against the latter on an equal footing, but should be tackled on the basis of a presumption in favour of humanity.').

[9] Biller, *Esra* (2007) 17. ('Ich will nicht gesagt bekommen, worüber ich schreiben darf und worüber nicht. Das ist so, als nähme man mir die Luft zum Atmen.').

voice and he is determined to persuade us that he bears the damage of the couple's failed love more deeply. In the book's final pages, with Esra irrevocably lost to him, Adam calls his mother yearning for answers or absolution, and maybe a final ray of hope that he will be reunited with Esra. 'If you miss her so badly,' says his mother, 'then call her…'[10] Adam, however, would only use a phone call to try to punish Esra for her part in the couple's suffering. But nothing can dampen Adam's desperate need to be with Esra. Perhaps as a way of reminding Adam that he has other relationships from which he can draw some human fulfillment, during the phone call his mother asks about Adam's daughter—from a previous relationship—and about his daughter's mother. 'That doesn't interest me,' Adam exclaims.[11] 'What interests you then,' asks his mother.[12] 'Whether [Esra] was the right one,' Adam finally whispers, and the reader can feel that the words are breaking him.[13]

Even if they are given less attention, Adam's other challenges are no-less important. The scenes in which he describes his deep affection for his daughter, and the pain he endures as a result of their separation (she lives with her mother in another city) are powerfully and poignantly rendered. Adam's doubts about and disillusionment with his craft as a writer are portrayed with equal truth and force. The writer's tragic condition is conveyed by Adam's confession: 'if I didn't have to earn a living, sometimes I think I wouldn't write at all.'[14]

But the question, 'to whom does Esra belong,' might be taken as an altogether different inquiry, focusing on the book's eponymous character and not the novel itself. That would be an equally legitimate reading of the novel's program. If Adam cannot perfect his love for Esra, then to whom does she belong? The book is crowded with competing claimants. Esra's overbearing mother Lale has the claim with the longest tenure. Adam tells us that Lale neglected Esra as a child, that she pressed Esra into the role of care-giver to younger step-siblings, and that she continues to dominate Esra—through cruelty and passive-aggressive bouts of silence—even long after Esra has become an adult. It is possible that the wounds from this relationship so completely condition Esra's psyche that she really 'belongs'

---

10 ibid at 189 ('Wenn sie dir so fehlt … ruf sie an …').
11 ibid at 189-90 ('Wie geht's Stella? … Und Barbara?').
12 ibid at 190 ('Was interessiert dich dann?').
13 ibid ('Ob sie die Richtige war.').
14 ibid at 212 ('Wenn ich nicht Geld verdienen müßte, denke ich manchmal, würde ich vielleicht gar nicht schreiben.').

to her mother. In similar—but more conjectural terms—Esra might 'belong' to her grandfather. Adam thinks the patriarch sexually abused Esra as a young girl—with no intervention from Esra's mother or grandmother—leaving her emotionally damaged and withdrawn. Even Esra's daughter, from a youthful, failed marriage, competes with Adam for Esra's affection. Adam's disdain for this rival is underscored by his general lack of sympathy for the girl's serious, chronic illness. In an inexcusably egocentric tone Adam calls the sick child a 'tyrant,' imagines her as his tormentor, and accuses her of trying to disrupt his relationship with Esra.[15] Does Esra 'belong' to her daughter? Adam also has to contend with other lovers for Esra's devotion. Despite their divorce, Esra is not really free of her ex-husband Frido with whom she has to co-manage the care of their sick daughter and who has preserved a relationship with Esra's mother. And there is Thorben, an old suitor with whom Esra eventually has a brief affair and who fathers her second child. Esra might be said to 'belong' to these other men, too. But the more credible possibility is that Esra seems to be unhappily, impulsively driven into the arms of some man—occasionally Adam himself—for security and identity. Does she 'belong' to this psychological and abstract dependence on men?

This is a less redeemable narrative possibility for the book because, from this perspective, Biller comes dangerously close to portraying Esra as an object of others' interests and needs and not as an autonomous, intersubjective participant in the narrative. Of course, this says much about Biller and the utilitarian uses he makes of the character Esra, who functions as little more than a receptacle for Adam's chronic disaffection and a screen on which Adam projects a sexual-emotional fantasy. Indeed, it is a troublingly chauvinistic notion that Esra should 'belong' to anyone other than herself.

Another possibility for the novel is to read it as a contemporary treatment of the traditional biblical figures whose names Biller appropriates for his characters. Is the book a meditation on Adam's—and humankind's—alienated condition? Like his namesake, Adam has been banished from paradise, lost to love, lost to his family, and often joyless in his labors. The name 'Esra' also suggests the biblical 'Esra,' the high priest who waged a campaign for Jewish purity after the Israelis' return to Judea fol-

---

15   ibid at 63.

lowing the Babylonian exile.[16] This interpretation is supported by one of the book's subplots, which involves Adam in an international quest to confirm his suspicion that Esra has Jewish and not Turkish roots. This suspected ethnic bond helps Adam understand his single-minded passion for Esra. Does the book call on us to consider the claim that personal love can only be achieved as part of a broader project of cultural identity? This is a compelling possible arch for the book. It is a narrative as old as the *Bible*. It is the story of loss brought on by individuality and separation. And it is the story of salvation secured through selfless identification with a community.

There is another possibility for the novel. Adam and Esra might be seen as personifying the poles in literature's traditional fact/fiction dilemma. Adam would embody the rational and pragmatic spirit of fact. Esra would embody the irrational and dreamy spirit of fiction. In one scene the pair's love-making is irretrievably disrupted by Adam's insistence on using a condom. 'Why are you always so careful,' Esra demands, before accusing Adam of being 'very German.'[17] Adam responds, in turn, by declaring that Esra is 'very Oriental.' Adam demands: 'It isn't always all just fate.'[18] Throughout the novel Biller casts Adam as self-reflected and rational while Esra resides in an 'imaginary dream world.'[19]

Portentously (or—considering the book's legal fate—hubristically) the book engages explicitly with the fact/fiction problematic in literature. The usual disclaimer suggesting that the novel's characters are invented and that 'any similarities with living or dead persons are strictly accidental and not intentional' is prominently published on the book's copy-right page. Biller deepens his engagement with this theme as early as the book's third and fourth chapters in which Adam remarks that Esra once demanded that she never appear in one of his books.[20] In protest Adam asks if Esra be-

---

16 See B Becking, *Ezra, Nehemiah, and the Construction of Early Jewish Identity* (Tübingen, Mohr Siebeck, 2011); TA Bergren, *Sixth Ezra : The Text and Origin: The Text and Origin* (Oxford, Oxford University Press, 1989); CF Fensham, *The Books of Ezra and Nehemiah* (Michigan, William B. Eerdmans Publishing Co., 1982).
17 Biller, *Esra* (2007) 115. ('Warum bist du immer so vorsichtig? ... Manchmal bist du sehr deutsch.').
18 ibid ('Und du ... du bist sehr orientalisch. Es ist nicht immer alles Schicksal.').
19 See ibid at 133.
20 ibid at 14-16 ('Und die Bücher, die du sonst liest? ... Glaubst du, da ist alles ausgedacht?').

lieves that the other books she reads are 'completely constructed?'[21] Adam links Esra's insistence on her privacy with the scandal Thomas Mann's novel *Buddenbrooks* loosed in Lübeck society. 'Naturally,' Adam explains, 'I was on the side of Thomas Mann and the freedom of literature.'[22] Adam returns to the issue when he complains that, during a book tour, his readers insist on asking him how much his novel has to do with his life. Adam explains that 'I said very politely ... that life and the things a person makes of it when writing are like twins who are separated at birth.'[23]

The blurring of the real and the imagined involves Esra as well. Adam notes that Esra is frequently stopped by young Turkish-German women who identify strongly with the character she played in a successful film about a young Turkish-German woman's love affair with a German man. Inevitably, Adam also comes to conflate Esra's romantic dysfunction with the film character. 'In the end,' Adam concludes, 'Esra was exactly like Fatma, the girl from her film that had no right to her own free-will. Esra, too, cannot love who she chooses. Esra, too, must serve her family to the point of self-sacrifice.'[24]

Perhaps Biller is playing Adam in the novel, just as Esra played Fatma in the film (or Romey played Yasemin in a 'real' German/Turkish film by that name from 1988).[25] No one associated with the book is just one person, operating in just a single narrative space. Esra may be masquerading as Romey in the book, but Romey once masqueraded as Yasemin. Biller is a writer writing about a writer who is writing from his life's experience and contemplating the literary problems that involves. These are not mere gimmicks. The novel is fundamentally framed by this post-modern device. It is possible that these confounding loops through fact and fiction are the very point of the book. If that is true, then I cannot dismiss the possibility that Biller at least passively hoped for the legal proceedings triggered by

---

21   ibid.
22   ibid.
23   ibid 186 ('Ich sagte sehr höflich, das Leben und das, was man beim Schreiben daraus macht, seien wie Zwillinge, die bei ihrer Geburt auseinandergerissen wurden ...').
24   ibid 158. ('Sie war am Ende genau wie Fatma, das Mädchen aus ihrem Film, das kein Recht auf eigenen Willen hatte. Auch sie mußte bis zur Selbstverleugnung ihrer Familie dienen.').
25   See *Yasemin* (Hamburger Kino-Kompanie, Zweites Deutsches Fernsehen (ZDF) 1988).

the novel. In that case the Federal Constitutional Court's judgment would be the book's true final chapter.

B. The Judgment

The constitutional complaint before the Federal Constitutional Court had been brought by Biller's publisher, challenging the judgment of the Federal Court of Justice, which affirmed an injunction on the publication and distribution of *Esra* issued by the Munich courts. The publisher invoked the Basic Law's guarantee of artistic freedom in Article 5(3): 'Arts and sciences, research and teaching shall be free.'[26] The Constitutional Court concluded that the ordinary courts' ban had, for the most part, struck an acceptable balance between the competing constitutional interests in the case. On one hand, the Court found that the injunction on the book's publication and distribution resulted from an acceptable interpretation of Paragraphs 823 and 1004 of the *Bürgerliches Gesetzbuch* (BGB – German Civil Code),[27] which, in turn, help realize the constitutional protection of personality and dignity enshrined in Articles 2(1) and 1(1) of the Basic Law.[28] On the other hand, the Court held that the encroachment upon Biller's constitutionally guaranteed artistic freedom was justified and proportional.

Following its traditional, systematic formula, the Court began its analysis by trying to determine if Biller's novel was covered by the scope of Article 5(3). Was *Esra* even the kind of 'art' the constitutional right was

---

26 *Grundgesetz* [Constitution] [GG] art. 5(3) (F.R.G.). See H Jarass, 'Art. 5 – Freiheit von Kunst und Wissenschaft (Abs. 3)' in H Jarass and B Pieroth (eds) *Grundgesetz für die Bundesrepublik Deutschland – Kommentar*, 10th edn (Munich, C.H. Beck, 2009) 214-227. See also DP Kommers and RA Miller, *The Constitutional Jurisprudence of the Federal Republic of Germany*, 3rd edn (Durham, Duke University Press, 2012).

27 *Bürgerliches Gesetzbuch* [Civil Code] [BGB] Aug. 18. 1896, §§ 823, 1004 (F.R.G.).

28 *Grundgesetz* [Constitution] [GG] arts 1(1) and 2(1) (F.R.G.). See H Jarass, 'Art. 1 – Garantie der Menschenwürde' in H Jarass and B Pieroth (eds), *Grundgesetz für die Bundesrepublik Deutschland – Kommentar*, 10th ed (Munich, C.H. Beck, 2009) 39-57; H Jarass, 'Art. 2 – Freiheit, Leben, Unversehrtheit' in H Jarass and B Pieroth (eds), *Grundgesetz für die Bundesrepublik Deutschland – Kommentar*, 10th ed (Munich, C.H. Beck, 2009) 58-100. See also Kommers and Miller, *The Constitutional Jurisprudence of the Federal Republic of Germany* (2012).

meant to protect? Here the Constitutional Court sought to burnish its reputation as a force for enlightened liberalism, affirming the ordinary courts' conclusion that 'the novel *Esra* was a work of art.'[29] The accommodating definition applied by the Court, worked-out in earlier decisions, is that art consists in 'a free creative process whereby the artist in his chosen medium ... gives form to what he has felt, learnt or experienced.'[30] Because the objections to the novel were based on the claim that Biller had only thinly disguised reality, it might have been possible to remove the book from the protection of Article 5 altogether. According to this reasoning Biller's presentation of the facts did not involve a process of rendering his experiences in a newly created form. The Court dismissed this possibility. First, the Court reflected—once again—on the difficulty in finding a general definition for 'art' as an abstract concept.[31] Second, the Court reached the more specific conclusion that 'it is not possible with the help of a fixed demarcation line to distinguish art from non-art according to the degree to which there has been a successful artistic alteration of reality.'[32] It was clear in this case, the Court said, that it had been Biller's aim 'to present reality in an artistic manner.'[33]

Biller might be grateful that his novel qualified as the kind of 'art' that is owed the protection of Article 5(3). There is a strong temptation to credit the Court for its seeming refusal to be lured into the Orwellian (not to mention 'Nazi') business of defining 'art.' Except that this is precisely what the Court does. Of course, it is a tricky affair. And Biller slips through the gaps in the Court's fumbling definition. But already, at this point of its encounter with the case, we see that the Court embraces literature's subordination to the legal concepts it is charged with enforcing. *Esra* might survive the Court's scrutiny. But the very fact of the Court's scrutiny suggests that it is possible to imagine literary expression that does not count as 'art' for the purposes of Article 5(3) of the Basic Law.[34] Ra-

---

29   *Esra Novel Case*, 119 BVerfGE 1, 20-21 (2007). See M Stolleis (ed), *Herzkammern der Republik—Die Deutschen und das Bundesverfassungsgericht* (Munich, C.H. Beck, 2011); RC van Oyen and MHW Möllers (eds) *Das Bundesverfassungsgericht im politischen System* (Wiesbaden, Verlag für Sozialwissenschaften, 2006).
30   *Esra Novel Case*, 119 BVerfGE 1, 20-21 (2007) (citing BVerfGE 30, 173 (188-89); BVerfGE 67, 213 (226); BVerfGE 75, 369 (377)).
31   ibid.
32   ibid.
33   ibid.
34   See, eg *Titanic Case*, 86 BVerfGE 1, 9 (1992).

ther than praising the Court for adopting a permissive definition of 'art,' it would do more to insist that the Court recognize the illimitable human potential of literature by recusing itself from the definitional gambit altogether. The Court could simply presume the 'artistic' character of any work involved in an Article 5(3) challenge.

This need not lead to a problematic inflation of the force of Article 5(3), even if I could agree that there can be such a thing as 'too much constitutional protection of art.' If the Court is inclined to permit the regulation of this kind of human endeavor, then it can always find a basis for doing so in the remaining parts of its systematic constitutional analysis. After all, this is precisely what the Court did in the *Esra* case.

The Court found no violation of Biller's artistic freedom because the encroachment on that right—in this case the injunction prohibiting the book's publication—was 'justified.' The Court explained that the injunction was instituted pursuant to statutory authority. Significantly, the relevant Civil Code provisions aim to advance important, constitutionally protected interests, including the right to freely develop one's personality, which is secured by Article 2(1) of the Basic Law. It is through this door that human dignity entered the drama. The Court finds it no easier to define the right to personality secured by Article 2(1) than it does to define the artistic freedom secured by Article 5(3). But it recognizes that the kinds of interests that have merited the protection of Article 2(1) help form the core of human dignity,[35] including personal honor and reputational integrity.[36] Of course, human dignity is famously made 'inviolable' by the Basic Law's very first article. It is the nexus of these rights, the Court explained, that gives Romey's and Lemke's personality rights particularly high priority.

On the basis of this calculus—two weighty basic rights (Articles 1 and 2) opposed to just one (Article 5)—we cannot be surprised that the Court found that the encroachment upon Biller's artistic freedom was justified, even as the Court gestured towards the obligation to 'uphold the fundamental rights of both sides equally ... [doing] justice to the fundamental rights of both the artists and those affected by the work of art.'[37] But my

---

35   *Esra Novel Case*, 119 BVerfGE 1, 23-24 (2007).
36   'The general right of personality,' the Court explained, 'protects a person especially from false or distorted depictions which are not entirely true insignificant for the development of one's personality.' ibid 24.
37   ibid 23.

argument is that literature—the act of writing it as well as reading it—*is* or *profoundly helps form* the core of human dignity. Writing and reading are central to helping differentiate humans from other animals.[38] Writing and reading are two of the most fundamental means with which we form and express our identity and personality as humans.[39] Seen from this perspective, artistic freedom—literature in particular—lies at the 'core of human dignity' in a unique and important way that should have impelled the Court to place Articles 1 and 5 on Biller's side of the scale. The Court does not recognize the centrality of art to human dignity. Instead, it imposes a strict separation between dignity and literature, thereby placing a heavy finger on the personality and dignity side of the scale.

But the Court's recognition of the weighty personality and dignity rights opposing Biller's insistence on his artistic freedom merely obliged it to confront the controversial questions at the heart of the case. First, were the ordinary courts correct in concluding that Biller's novel served as an instrument for an encroachment on Romey's and Lemke's dignity? This, in turn, required the Court to ratify the ordinary courts' conclusion that Romey and Lemke were unavoidably recognizable as the models for the book's characters and that they had been more than minimally harmed by their association with the book. Second, had the ordinary courts given adequate consideration to Biller's artistic freedom when balancing the parties' competing constitutional interests?

The doctrinal innovation in the Constitutional Court's judgment resulted from the low threshold it applied to answering the first of these questions. In previous cases the Court had sought to shield novelists from petty attempts to restrain their resort to reality as a source for their fiction by insisting that a 'not insignificant readership' recognize the complainants as the characters in the book.[40] In essence, the Court required that many people—extending to the broad reading public—take offense to a book before the Basic Law's personality and dignity rights could be deployed to block

---

38 See J Gottschall, *The Storytelling Animal: How Stories Make Us Human* (Boston et al, Houghton Mifflin, 2012).
39 See, eg J Gray, *Straw Dogs: Thoughts on Humans and Other Animals* 56 (London, Granta Books, 2002) ('What is distinctively human is not the capacity for language. It is the crystallisation of language in writing.').
40 *Esra Novel Case*, 119 BVerfGE 1, 25 (2007) (citing *Mephisto Novel Case*, 30 BVerfGE 173, 196 (1971)).

its publication.[41] This gave the analysis important quantitative and objective elements because it would not be enough that the supposed victim of an alleged *Roman à clef* subjectively saw himself or herself as the basis for a character in a novel. Over a set of rare dissents (one authored jointly by Justices Hohmann-Dennhardt and Gaier, another authored separately by Justice Hoffmann-Riem) the Court adopted a more permissive and subjective standard in the *Esra Case*. Relying on the same test used by the ordinary courts' in their interpretation of the relevant statutory provisions, the Court asked only whether Romey and Lemke were recognizable as the characters in the novel 'by a more or less large circle of acquaintances.'[42] With this move the Court significantly reduced the scope of the required harm and opened the door for greater subjectivity in complainants' assertions of personality and dignity interests as a basis for chilling novelists' work. The Court justified this shift—no matter its cost for the human experience of writing and reading literature—as a way of democratizing the dignity protection provided by the Basic Law in circumstances such as these. The large-scale impact required by the earlier standard, the Court explained, would offer protection only to popular figures who are well-known to the broad reading public. While celebrities might enjoy protection of their dignity under that framework, the Court worried that the earlier standard left ordinary people exposed to constitutionally significant indignities and reputational harm at the level of their 'immediate circle of acquaintances.'[43] The Court insisted that this is the more meaningful form of dignity.

The new standard creates greater space for personality and dignity protection of the kind conceived of and enforced by the Court. But the Court's new standard can be characterized as expanding the protection of dignity only if literature's dignitarian character is significantly discounted (or ignored). The new standard profoundly reduces the scope for the kind of human dignity that is realized through literature. Now a limited and subjective claim for human dignity, on the basis of what the dissenting justices called an 'isolated instance of recognition,'[44] can subjugate the

---

41 See P Lerche, 'Kunstfreiheit inmitten aktueller Grundrechtskonzepte' in R Jacobs et al (eds), *Festschrift für Peter Raue* (Köln et al, Heymanns, 2006) 215; JF Henschel, 'Die Kunstfreiheit in der Rechtsprechung des BVerfG' (1990) 32 *Neue Juristische Wochenschrift* 1937.
42 *Esra Novel Case*, 119 BVerfGE 1, 25 (2007).
43 ibid.
44 ibid 39 (dissenting opinion of Justices Hohmann-Dennhardt and Gaier).

vast, human implications of a novel for both the writer and its readers. The lower threshold adopted by the Court is already having the feared chilling-effect. Uwe Wittstock reported in 2011 that publishers had begun to refuse to defend their authors against charges similar to those Biller faced.[45] The mere threat of legal action, Wittstock explained, led some publishers to abandon their publication plans altogether.[46] The distinct kind of dignity envisioned by the Court's interpretation of Articles 1 and 2 of the Basic Law is the clear winner in such cases. The human dignity achieved through literature, which ought to find its security in Article 5, is the clear loser.

Concluding its analysis under the first question, the Court largely deferred to the ordinary courts' factual determination that Romey and Lemke correctly saw in *Esra* 'a large accumulation of identifying factors,' and that, considering the intensely private nature of the incidents depicted in the novel, Romey and Lemke had suffered a serious encroachment upon their dignity. With respect to the former conclusion the Court agreed that the invented names assigned to the characters in the novel—and fictionalizing the names of awards those characters had received—had not been enough to overcome the 'continuing similarity' with Biller, Romey and Lemke.[47] The parallel details, the Court concluded, were simply too numerous to reach any other conclusion.

Turning to the second question, the Court found that the ordinary courts had—for the most part—given adequate consideration to Biller's artistic freedom before issuing the injunction. The Court agreed that the novel had done 'serious harm' to Romey's rights to personality and human dignity. That, however, had not been the case with respect to Lemke. Her portion of the lawsuit, involving what the Constitutional Court viewed as Biller's attempt to use the character Lale (perhaps standing-in for Lemke) for 'second level' literary purposes, involved less harm and more art. It is necessary to devote some attention to these distinct results—between Romey and Lemke—because they help illuminate the German courts' delicate and detailed task of balancing dignity and artistic freedom. Before turning to that effort, however, it must be noted that Biller's modest victory with respect to Lemke had no practical significance for literary freedom and its human potential. The Constitutional Court concluded, despite its

---

45 Wittstock, *Der Fall Esra* 8-10.
46 ibid.
47 *Esra Novel Case*, 119 BVerfGE 1, 26 (2007).

revision of the ordinary courts' judgment as it concerned Lemke, that the earlier decision in the case had 'rightfully imposed a total ban on the book.'[48] The constitutionally objectionable portions of the novel involving Romey were so important to the total concept of the work as to render any attempt at simply mitigating them seemingly impossible. And besides, the Court demurred, 'it is not the task of the courts to delete or modify certain passages so as to exclude a violation of rights.'[49] It is difficult to square the Court's endorsement of the total ban on *Esra* with its stated modesty when it comes to tinkering with the content of art and literature. Are we really meant to believe that a total ban is somehow *less intrusive* than an order requiring a novelist to remove or reframe constitutionally objectionable passages? Had the Court wanted to avoid upholding a book ban in this day and age, perhaps for shame if not out of recognition (as I urge) that literature is the better vehicle for advancing human dignity, then it had the chance to do so when choosing the remedy for the harm it believed Romey had suffered. Where is the Court's well-known instinct for proportionality? Again, the Court simply preferred its legalized notion of dignity over literature's dignitarian potential and chose the bluntest possible instrument to advance that position.

So why was it appropriate for the ordinary court's to conclude that *Esra* involved a serious harm to Romey's but not Lemke's personality and dignity rights? It was this result that justified the ultimate conclusion that Biller's constitutional interest in artistic freedom must yield. The Court explained that 'seriousness' should be determined by reference to context. On one hand, seriousness is a matter of the degree to which an author suggests—in the challenged work itself—a connection between his or her fictional endeavor and those who feel themselves harmed in reality. On the other hand, seriousness is a matter of the severity of the harm done in reality if a connection is made between the novel's characters and persons in reality. With respect to the first of these inquires, the Court emphasized that the novel should be presumed to be a work of fiction and censured for a connection to reality only if the characters and events had not benefitted from an adequate degree of 'fictionalization.' The Court explained that the presumption of fiction would not be overcome so long as the literary quality of the project's aspirations made it clear that it was more than just a 'report' and that the reader should see more than just the reality in the au-

---

48   ibid 35.
49   ibid.

thor's reliance on facts. This is the 'second level' or literary quality the Court found to exist with respect to Lale (perhaps standing-in for Lemke).[50] The character Lale, the Court explained, was more than just a representation of Lemke. She 'played an important role in the [narrator's] search for the person who is to blame for the failure of the relationship between Adam and Esra.'[51] Almost despite itself, the Court recognizes that Biller aimed for more than just a denigration of Lemke with the character Lale. Lale, the Court concluded, allows Biller to explore 'the question of blame and [emphasize] the difficult relationship between a man and his lover's mother.'[52] This, the Court said, 'indicates that the novel has a second level.'[53] For these reasons the connection between Lale and Lemke is not strong enough to support the conclusion that Lemke had suffered serious harm to her personality and dignity rights. Failing to reach that level of harm, the Court concluded, Lemke's personality and dignity rights do not supersede Biller's artistic freedom.

The problem with the Court's analysis is that it conflicts with the conclusion that the novel involves a clear connection between the character Esra and the person Ayse Romey. The Court does not seem to suggest, with respect to the Lale-Lemke constellation, that Lemke is not recognizable in the character Lale. After all, both are prize-winning Turkish human rights advocates, the mothers of the author's/narrator's love-interest, divorcees, and hoteliers. Once the literary project of reconstructing reality as fiction is dismissed, then it is hard to avoid the convergence of Lale and Lemke. But the Court found this connection to be mitigated by Biller's use of it to achieve 'second level' literary effects. In its analysis with respect to the Esra-Romey constellation, however, the Court seemed to dwell only on the poignancy of the connection between the character and the person. Romey is not just recognizable in the character Esra, the Court explained, but the novel suggests that the reader is to see Romey as the character Esra. The Court concluded:

> Her role in the novel relates to central events that occurred directly between her and the first-person narrator (who is not difficult to recognize as the author) during their relationship. [H]er intimate relationship with the author as well as her marriage, the illness of her daughter and her new relationship were more or less di-

---

50   ibid 31-32, 34.
51   ibid.
52   ibid at 31-32.
53   ibid.

rectly derived from reality so that ... the novel does not suggest to the reader that these events should be understood as fictional.[54]

Curiously, the Court does not consider the 'second level' literary use to which Biller puts the Esra-Romey constellation. Surely the literary exploration of failed love, sexuality, and the relationship between a man and his lover's children treat themes of equal 'second level' literary significance as the question of the relationship between a man and his lover's mother. In fact, Biller puts the character Esra to a remarkable range of literary uses. Many more uses, in fact, than the character Lale. To name just a few of these themes, the character Esra gives Biller a vehicle for exploring sexual and filial love; questions at the intersection of religious and racial identity and love; and the nature of literary production and they myth of the muse.

Having unconvincingly argued for a distinction in the literary quality of the connection the novel (may or may not) suggest for the Lale-Lemke constellation, on one hand, and the Esra-Romey constellation, in the other hand, the Court then affirmed the ordinary courts' conclusion that the connection resulted in severe harm to Romey's personality and dignity interests. Indeed, the Court's summary treatment of the first question and the strong language it used in addressing the second, suggests that this was the more grave concern. The Court found that Romey's rights were 'especially seriously affected' because the novel treats 'some of the most intimate details' in a realistic and detailed manner that was possible only due to the author's immediate experiences with Romey. Without saying so explicitly, the Court seems to especially have the sexual elements of the narrative in mind. Dissenting Justice Hoffmann-Riem seized on this, arguing that the Court's analysis risked making sexual matters a presumptively-protected literary taboo that are now susceptible to a 'basic ban.'[55] The Court disagreed. 'Sexual matters are not made taboo,' the Court explained, 'since an author is not prevented from describing intimate relations if he or she does not suggest to the reader that they should be connected with a certain person.'[56] This is a strange response to Justice Hoffmann-Riem's alarm. The Court suggests that sexuality—perhaps the most fundamental of literary themes—must be treated in highly stylized and thoroughly fictionalized terms. In any case, the Court's conclusion that Romey had suffered severe harm more explicitly hinged on the novel's account of the life-threatening

---

54 ibid at 34.
55 ibid 50 (dissenting opinion of Justice Hoffmann-Riem)
56 ibid 35-36.

illness of Esra's daughter. Romey also had a daughter with extreme health difficulties. That clear correspondence, the Court explained, constituted a serious violation of Romey's personality and dignity rights, especially 'in view of the special protection given to children and to the mother-child relationship' by the Basic Law.[57] The clear connection with Romey that is suggested by the novel, and the novel's grave intrusion on Romey's 'intimate sphere,' led the Court to conclude that the harm done to the core of her human dignity outweighed Biller's interest in artistic freedom.

It is clear that the Court's conclusion that Romey's 'intimate sphere' had been violated by the novel was a product of the book's portrayal of Esra's sexual and maternal interests. Assigning these to the Romey's 'intimate sphere' made the outcome of the Court's analysis a foregone conclusion. This is because the Court, in a number of cases,[58] has sought to guide its assessment of the proportionality of any intrusion on a claimant's Article 2 personality interests by reference to three concentric rings or 'spheres' of privacy and intimacy, with the inner-most sphere meriting the greatest constitutional protection.[59] This so-called 'theory of spheres' grants the 'intimate sphere'—involving a person's internal life with its feelings and ideas—absolute protection.[60] The intimate sphere enjoys this status, the Court has explained, for two reasons. First, it represents the unassailable essence of the personality protection secured by Article 2 of the Basic Law. That essence—as with the heart of every other fundamental right—is secured in general terms by Article 19(2) of the Basic Law.[61] Second, the intimate sphere—as already noted—is thought to be a part of the core of human dignity, which itself enjoys inviolable protection under

---

57   ibid 34.
58   See, eg *Esra Novel Case*, 119 BVerfGE 1, 29-30 (2007) (citing more than a dozen cases). See also *Caroline von Monaco I Case*, 97 BVerfGE 125 (1998); *Caroline von Monaco II Case*, 101 BVerfGE 361 (1999). The Caroline von Monaco cases are particularly relevant because they also involved the intersection of personality and family rights, which the Court found to operate in the inviolable 'intimate sphere'. *Caroline von Monaco II Case*, 101 BVerfGE 361, 385-386 (1999).
59   See C Bumke and A Voßkuhle, *Casebook Verfassungsrecht,* 5th edn (Munich, C.H. Beck, 2008) 81.
60   ibid.
61   *Diary Case*, 80 BVerfGE 367, 373 (2008). Article 19(2) of the Basic Law provides: 'In no case may the essence of a basic right be affected.' *Grundgesetz* [Constitution] [GG] art. 19(2) (F.R.G.).

Article 1(1) of the Basic Law.[62] Radiating outwards from the intimate sphere, the Court has given less vigorous protection to the 'private sphere' (involving non-public activities, family life and close friends) and still less protection to the outermost 'social sphere' (involving a person's public life).[63] Characterizing the themes treated by the novel as involving Romey's inviolable intimate sphere—without regard for their literary significance—left the Court with little choice but to ban the novel.

At nearly every step in this doctrinal analysis the Court chose a position favoring the law's vision of human dignity at the expense of a vision of human dignity as expressed through the acts of writing and reading literature. The Court marginalized literature by following the law's insistence that it engage in the highly-questionable practice of attempting to define art and literature. The Court marginalized literature by refusing to see artistic freedom as part of the 'core of human dignity,' thereby distinguishing—in the law—highly protected dignity interests in reputation and in one's intimate sphere from the less weighty interest in artistic freedom. The Court marginalized literature by adopting, in its systematic legal analysis, a more permissive standard for the assertion of personality and dignity rights against a literary work. The Court marginalized literature, again as part of its systematic legal analysis, by failing to grant Biller's treatment of Esra the fullest 'presumption of fiction.' Instead, the Court too readily saw a connection with reality in the Esra-Romey constellation. Finally, the Court marginalized literature in its systematic legal analysis by endorsing the most severe possible remedy: a total ban on the publication of the novel. The unifying argument across the whole of the Court's decision is that, in its noble struggle to secure human dignity, the law can do more to advance the human condition than can the free practice of the production and enjoyment of literature. It is to this deeply flawed position that I now turn my attention.

III. Literature as Dignity

The Constitutional Court's *Esra Case* seeks to promote human dignity by banning a book (or upholding the ban imposed by the ordinary courts).

---

62   *Diary Case*, 80 BVerfGE 367, 373 (2008).
63   C Bumke and A Voßkuhle, *Casebook Verfassungsrecht*, 5th edn (Munich, C.H. Beck, 2008).

That is strange medicine. Literature, after all, is an intrinsically human phenomenon. I will draw on literary criticism and theory to develop this claim, which argues that literature *is* human dignity, or is at least a *fuller form of* human dignity than anything the state's law achieved on behalf of Romey. I am concerned here with the dignitarian potential of the literary acts of writing and reading.

Literary critics have made grand, general claims for literature's uniquely human quality.[64] This is especially true for narrative fiction such as the novel *Esra*. From this point of view literature is seen as 'replicating humanity.' Scholes and Kellogg, for example, claimed that literature has two human (or humanizing) functions. On the one hand, in reading literature we encounter 'the human as it is lived today.'[65] On the other hand, in writing literature we express the uniquely human capacity for creativity and self-reflection. In this way literature becomes a 'symbol for the human spirit.'[66] These sweeping claims point to literature's human elements. One of these is *human autonomy*, which is realized in literature as the author's voice and as the reader's autonomous encounter with the literary text. Literary narrative's dependence on *character* is sometimes credited with having invented our notion of human personality. Critics as diverse as Nussbaum and Bloom have made versions of this claim.[67] The argument for the

---

64 See, eg S Sontag, The Truth of Fiction Evokes our Common Humanity, *Los Angeles Times* (April 7, 2014), at http://www.latimes.com/local/obituaries/la-122804sontag_archives-story.html#page=2 ('A great writer of fiction both creates a new, unique, individual world—through acts of imagination, through language that feels inevitable, through commanding forms—and responds to a world, the world the writer shares with other people but that is unknown or mis-known by still more people, confined in their worlds. Call that history, society, what you will. The writers who matter most to us are those who enlarge our consciences and our sympathies and our knowledge.'). See also MC Nussbaum, *Cultivating Humanity* (Boston, Harvard University Press, 1994); N Frye, *The Educated Imagination* (Bloomington, Indiana University Press, 1964); KS Prior, How Reading Makes Us More Human, *The Atlantic Monthly* (June 21, 2013), at http://www.theatlantic.com/national/archive/2013/06/how-reading-makes-us-more-human/277079/.

65 R Scholes and R Kellogg, *The Nature of Narrative* (New York, Oxford University Press, 1966).

66 ibid.

67 See, eg MC Nussbaum, *Poetic Justice: The Literary Imagination and Public Life* (Boston, Beacon Press, 1995); MC Nussbaum, *The Therapy of Desire: Theory and Practice in Hellenistic Ethics* (Princeton et al, Princeton University Press, 1996); H Bloom, *Shakespeare: The Invention of the Human* (New York, Riverhead Books, 1998); H Bloom, *The Anatomy of Influence: Literature as a*

human significance of character in literature emphasizes the way our contact with characters in literature promotes our human interiority. This inward existence is seen as a uniquely human condition that is uniquely reproduced and modeled in literature. Literature's reliance on *narrative and plot* is also thought to be distinctly human because it grapples with and reproduces the inexorable, unavoidable reality of life lived as a progression of time and successive incidents. The surrealist novelist and literary critic Kurt Vonnegut was particularly engaged with this feature of literature.[68] Finally, the grand claims for literature's humanity point to the special role of *meaning* in the literary endeavor. The act of producing literature is (as even the Constitutional Court seems to know) a process of negotiating the relation between fictional and real worlds. That, in turn, requires the author to struggle for meaning in both contexts. Meaning must be crafted in the fictional realm and meaning must be divined from our reality. The creation of meaning also is a fundamental part of the act of reading literature, especially in the straightforward sense that reading is often practiced as a search for human meaning in our identification with both the universals and the particulars we find in literature. Literature connects with these elements of the human condition in a singular way.

Albert Levi's essay 'Literature as Humanity' is a concentrated and accessible variation on the grand claim for literature's humanity.[69] Levi urged us to consider literature 'not as an indicator of social history, not as an exclusively formal structure, not as a weapon to secure social justice – but as humanity.'[70] He pointed to three elements that are definitive of literature as well as humanity: *communication; continuity;* and *criticism.* These elements, Levi explained, are grounded in the very nature of our

---

Way of Life (Yale, Yale University Press, 2011). Rita Felski anticipates and responds to the post-structural and post-modern critiques these claims for literature attract. R Felski, *Uses of Literature* (Oxford, Blackwell Publishing, 2008).

68 See, eg K Vonnegut, *A Man Without a Country* (New York, Random House Trade Paperbacks, 2005).

69 AW Levi, 'Literature as a Humanity' (1976) 10 *Journal of Aesthetic Education* 45. See AW Levi, 'Literary Truth' (1966) 24 *The Journal of Aesthetics and Art Criticism* 373; AW Levi, *The Humanities Today* (Bloomington, Indiana University Press, 1970); AW Levi, *Humanism and Politics—Studies in the Relationship of Power and Value in the Western Tradition* (Bloomington, Indiana University Press, 1969). See also JF Kavanaugh, 'Lived Humanism: The Aesthetic Education of Albert William Levi' (1991) 25 *Journal of Aesthetic Education* 21.

70 Levi, 'Literature as a Humanity' 50.

humanity and the conditions of our social life. The problems they seek to solve are rooted in the deepest needs and perplexities of the human person as he/she searches for identity, faces the challenges of communal existence, and seeks to ground meaning and value in a cosmos wider than the limits of the merely human horizon.[71]

With the term *communication* Levi meant the distinct human need for expression.[72] The language through which we produce literature, Levi argued, is the same language that embeds humans in webs of social meaning.[73] Language—and its practice as literature—are manifestations of the deeply-rooted human quest for expression and response.[74] Humans are determined to be, and the way we go about being is through our sharing.[75] This led Levi to the conclusion that communication—also in the form of literature—is an example of humankind's will-to-self. *Continuity*, the second of literature's three human elements, involves what Levi called 'the need for orientation in time.'[76] Literature, in the same way as human experience, is framed by a perception of the reality of time. This means that in literature—as in life—everything has conditions and consequences. Against this inexorable flow, humans search for anchors in time and history. The writer's work is an example of the human act of laying down roots. And the novel's characters remind and reassure the reader of the humanity of that search. Typically, we seek to resolve the inexorable flow of time with anchors that transcend our own time-bound reality, including social constructions such as family, religion or country.[77] Not surprisingly, Levi found these to be some of the most consequential themes in literature. Finally, Levi identified *criticism* as one of the human elements of literature. This is, Levi explained, the uniquely human search for rationality.[78] Again, literature contributes to this yearning both through the act of writing and through the answers it can suggest to readers. Literature participates in our empirical longing to understand our world by allowing us to test certain constellations of values and meaning in the realm of fiction. Through the expression of and encounter with certain attitudes in litera-

---

71 ibid 53.
72 ibid.
73 ibid.
74 ibid.
75 ibid.
76 ibid 54.
77 ibid.
78 ibid.

ture, Levi believed we can modify the conditions of our existence. This, Levi argued, is the critical and political character of literature and life.

Biller's novel—as much as any literary work that merits the designation—possesses each of Levi's literary-human elements. In fact, *Esra* engages with these elements to a profound degree. The Court could ignore the novel's great(er) potential for realizing human dignity only by neglecting these features.

The Court seemed to acknowledge the *communicative* significance of the novel. For example, when it concluded that *Esra* qualified for the protection of artistic freedom guaranteed by Article 5(3), the Court talked about both the artistic work itself and the 'effect it produces.'[79] The Court described this communicative impact—the novel's effect in the world—as 'the soil of artistic freedom.'[80] In finding that Romey (but not Lemke) would suffer harm from the publication of the novel, the Court implicitly acknowledged the work's success as a communicative endeavor. Biller claimed to have written the book only for Romey.[81] And if it is a *Schlüsselroman*, then *Esra* is a long—and complex—love letter. But there is so much more that Biller is communicating through this work. I mentioned some of the themes earlier, but they certainly include his attempt to embed himself in webs of social meaning with respect to issues such as love, sex, parenting, religious and ethnic identity, and (ironically) the act of producing literature. Biller wants to communicate, to be heard, on all of these (and other) points. And with Romey's lawsuit it seems Biller may have achieved that other fundamental feature of communication. He received Romey's (and the Court's) reply. In these ways the book participates in human communication: it is an example of the 'deeply-rooted human quest for expression and response.'

But, if the Court took the novel's communicative potential seriously and then used it against the book, the Court failed to see how the novel

---

79   *Esra Novel Case*, 119 BVerfGE 1, 21-23 (2007).
80   ibid.
81   'Although in the opinions of the author and the complainant [the publisher] the characters of the novel are fictitious, both conceded in the original proceeding that the author had been inspired by his love affair with the first plaintiff [Romey]. In the dedication in the copy of the book the author sent to the first plaintiff [Romey], he wrote: "Dear A. ..., this book is for you. I wrote it only for you, but I can understand that you might be afraid to read it. Perhaps you will read it when we are old—and will again see how much I loved you."' *Esra Novel Case*, 119 BVerfGE 1, 3 (2007) (quoting evidence presented in the original lawsuit).

functions as humanity by way of its engagement with *continuity* and *criticism*. These, however, are the novel's more significant human achievements.

The Court ignored the way the novel participates in the human search for *continuity*. This is reflected in Adam's detailed and painful accounts of his fractured family relations. It is reflected in Adam's preoccupation with his own and with Esra's (supposed) Jewish heritage. It is reflected in Adam's consciousness of his—and Esra's—status as immigrants in Germany. As Levi explained, literature's continuity typically involves struggles with family, religion or country. The book's expression of human continuity is also reflected in its acute awareness of life's unbreakable plodding momentum as it moves from conditions to consequences. In this regard, Adam is aware that his flawed and limited relationship with his daughter is a consequence of his separation from her mother. Adam is also desperate to construct a causal explanation for Esra's emotional detachment and he seizes on a suspicion that she had been abused by her grandfather when she was a child. Adam concluded that it must have been the grandfather. For what other reason, Adam wonders, did the grandfather and the grandmother break off communication with their beloved Esra, whom they had raised for years as their own daughter. For Adam it is obvious that the old man had began to feel shame for his actions, but he feared that Esra would inculpate him, and the grandmother took his side.[82]

Adam summarized this yearning for continuity and causality with the explanation that 'whoever has so much fear, must have once been terribly frightened.'[83] Biller's characters, especially Adam, look a lot like humans searching for roots amidst the bruising contingencies of time and history.

The Court also ignored the humanity involved in the novel's *critical* project. It did so despite signaling at least a superficial awareness of this element of the literary endeavor. The Court acknowledged, for example, that 'there is a particular danger that public criticism will be chilled' by its

---

82 Biller, *Esra* (2007) 45 ('Inzwischen denke ich, es war der Großvater. Warum sonst hatten er und die Großmutter aufgehört, mit der geliebten Enkelin zu sprechen, die sie jahrelang wie Eltern großgezogen hatten? ... Der alte Mann begann sich offenbar für seine Taten zu schämen, er hatte aber auch Angst, daß sie ihn beschuldigen würde, und die Großmutter hielt zu ihm.').
83 ibid 46 ('Wer aber so viel Angst hat, muß schon einmal fürchterlich erschreckt worden sein.').

enforcement of the right to dignity.[84] But the Court resolved this concern with its refined balancing analysis, insisting that an infringement of dignity must be severe if artistic freedom is to be limited.[85] A slight or purely conjectural harm to dignity, the Court explained, would not be enough to risk inhibiting literature's critical capacity. The Court ruled that this high standard was not fulfilled in the case of the Lale/Lemke constellation. Instead, the Court credited those parts of the novel for their critical force. At the very least, the Court explained, Adam's harsh disregard for Lale casts the narrator in such a negative light that it evolves into a critique of the narrator's weaknesses, shortcomings and broken relations. In this plausible reading the tension between Adam and Lale serves as the personification of the narrator's inner conflicts and petty jealousy.[86] With respect to the characters Adam and Lale, the Court also recognized the more straightforward critical project involving 'the question of blame and the emphasis on the relationship between a man and his lover's mother.' These interpretations of the book's treatment of the Lale/Lemke constellation, the Court explained, 'indicate that the novel has a second level.'[87] The Court accepted that, in these ways, the book contributed to the author's and the readers' human search for rationality.

The Court found, however, that the high standard for literature's critical character had not been met with respect to the Esra/Romey constellation. The Court concluded that Romey would be so severely harmed by the book's unfiltered treatment of Adam's and Esra's sexual intimacy that it justified the ban and the resulting infringement of Biller's artistic freedom.[88] The book would also produce a severe harm, the Court said, with its callous treatment of Esra's daughter.[89] In both cases, in light of the novel's realistic and detailed account of events, the harm would result because the character Esra could not be understood as fictional. The Court explained that the 'second level'—what Levi regarded as literature's critical function—had not been achieved with respect to Esra. But this analysis

---

84   'There is in particular a danger that public criticism and discussion of topics important for the public and society will be hindered by reference to the right of personality.' *Esra Novel Case*, 119 BVerfGE 1, 3 (2007) (citing BVerfGE 30, 173, 206-207 (1971) (dissenting opinion of Justice Stein).
85   ibid 29.
86   ibid 31-32.
87   ibid.
88   ibid 33-34.
89   ibid.

is hard to square with the balancing the Court did with respect to the Lale/Lemke constellation. First, the Court emphasized the likelihood that Esra would be recognized as Romey. Yet, it was no less true that Lale would be recognized as Lemke. Second, the Court credited the profound 'second level' or critical territory involved in the relationship between Adam and Lale. But it refused to recognize the deeply human nature of the issues raised by the novel's treatment of the relationship between Adam and Esra. The material surrounding that relationship critically explores the universal human questions of love, sex, parenthood, communication, jealousy, and family. The Court's dissenters were right to point out that the majority's opinion neglected the novel's critical (that is, its literary and human) potential. They explained that the book sought to express and deal with the many topics reflected in what Adam and Esra say and do. Alongside the themes just mentioned, the dissenters noted that the relationship between Adam and Esra also involves the author and reader in the search for meaning with respect to human atomization, loneliness, and cultural difference. It involves a search for identity in a multi-cultural world. The dissenters also recognized that the book's playful and pervasive engagement with the fiction/fact dichotomy (both as part of the novel's narrative and through the possible affinities between the characters and real people) serves as a critique of our perception of reality. In this interpretation, the novel involves a search for the meaning of reality by questioning whether 'real life' events should have a stronger claim on shaping our understanding of the world than 'fiction.' The dissenters credited this part of the book's critical project, concluding that, in *Esra* 'what used to be facts have dissolved into art.'[90]

Esra is no more likely to be seen as Romey than Lale is recognizable as Lemke. And it is hard to understand how the Court could conclude that Biller's critical project is more significant with respect to the Lale/Lemke constellation than it is with the Esra/Romey constellation.

In upholding the ban, the Constitutional Court found that it could promote a greater quantum of humanity by enforcing the legal construction of dignity than would be achieved by allowing the book to publish. To reach that conclusion the Court had to disregard literature's profoundly human qualities, including its distinct contribution to human communication and the unique way it contributes to our search for meaning and our struggle

---

90 ibid 47 (dissenting opinion of Justices Hohmann-Dennhardt and Gaier).

with life's continuity. But these features suggest that literature *is* humanity. And these are prominent features of the novel *Esra*.

IV. Conclusion

There is more human life in the novel *Esra* than the Court dares to perceive. The Court might be forgiven for this. After all, the justices are not trained literary critics—a fact that the dissenting Justices Hohmann-Dennhardt and Gaier lamented in their sharp rebuttal of the majority opinion.[91] The Court might be forgiven, except that it nonetheless chose to play the part of the most ruthless critic by upholding the ordinary courts' ban. I am haunted by the possibility that the Court might have disregarded the human potential of the book—and with it, all books—out of a self-interested and utterly unconscious fear of the loss of its definitive authority and role in administering human dignity for Germans. It—and not *human* writers and readers of the *human* phenomenon we call literature—is the better source human dignity! That concern leads me back to the rich human communication and continuity and criticism that operate across *Esra's* troubling narrative. These human conditions are inherently present in a truly human quantity and quality in literature in ways that they are not—and cannot be—in the Court's legal and institutional framing of the promise of human dignity. *Esra*—unlike the Court's dogmatic, institutional decision—is thick with the yearning and striving for all of these parts of the human experience. This is especially true *because* the novel might be fiction flirting with Biller's reality. That makes the narrator's pain and isolation more poignant because it is more tangible.

Biller, of course, knows that his passage along the metaphysical river that wends its way between our perceived realities and fictions, is the most literary facet of the work. Adam contemplates the complexities of the blurred space between fact and fiction, the uncertain territory between a novel and a life. But so do Romey and Esra. And so do we. This is where the Court most regrettably loses its way, failing to see that literature *is* human dignity.

---

91   ibid 45 (dissenting opinion of Justices Hohmann-Dennhardt and Gaier).

Part II

Developments

Würde des Menschen: Restoring Human Dignity in Post-Nazi Germany

*Christoph Goos**

I. A 'Non-Interpreted Thesis'

The genesis of the German Basic Law's human dignity article[1] has so far played a rather marginal role in the interpretation of this provision.[2] The numerous commentators have focused on the deeper philosophical or religious 'roots' of the concept.[3] However, hardly anybody has considered the question what the 'mothers and fathers of the Basic Law',[4] the 65 delegates from the State Parliaments assembled as Parliamentary Council in Bonn between September 1948 and May 1949,[5] could have meant by the term 'Würde des Menschen'.

---

* This article was originally published in C McCrudden (ed), *Understanding Human Dignity* (Oxford, Oxford University Press, 2013).

1 Article 1, paragraph 1 of the Grundgesetz für die Bundesrepublik Deutschland, 23 May 1949, Bundesgesetzblatt I, 1 (German Basic Law) states: 'Die Würde des Menschen ist unantastbar. Sie zu achten und zu schützen ist Verpflichtung aller staatlichen Gewalt.' – 'The dignity of man is inviolable. To respect and protect it is the duty of all state authority.'

2 See also M O'Malley, 'A Performative Definition of Human Dignity' in N Knoepffler et al (eds), *Facetten der Menschenwürde* (Freiburg and Munich, Karl Alber Verlag, 2011) 75: '[t]he principle's historical aspect is downplayed'.

3 See, most recently, J Isensee, 'Würde des Menschen', in D Merten and HJ Papier (eds), *Handbuch der Grundrechte in Deutschland und Europa, Vol. IV: Grundrechte in Deutschland: Einzelgrundrechte I* (Heidelberg, C.F. Müller, 2011) § 187 margin numbers 55–84; N Teifke, *Das Prinzip Menschenwürde* (Tübingen, Mohr Siebeck, 2011) 36–46; important clarifications at S Schaede, 'Würde – eine ideengeschichtliche Annäherung aus theologischer Perspektive', in P Bahr and HM Heinig (eds), *Menschenwürde in der säkularen Verfassungsordnung. Rechtswissenschaftliche und theologische Perspektiven* (Tübingen, Mohr Siebeck, 2006) 7.

4 BVerfGE (Entscheidungen des Bundesverfassungsgerichts) 103, 142, 158: 'Mütter und Väter des Grundgesetzes'.

5 See W Heun, *The Constitution of Germany. A Contextual Analysis* (Oxford, Hart Publishing, 2011) 9–24; MF Feldkamp, *Der Parlamentarische Rat 1948–*

There might be several reasons for this: First and foremost, the German Federal Constitutional Court held already in one of its very first decisions that not the subjective notions of the framers but the 'objectified will of the legislator' or the 'will of the law' was crucial for the interpretation of legal provisions.[6] Second, there was and there is still a widespread assumption that the records of the Parliamentary Council's proceedings were unproductive with regard to the meaning of the legal term of 'dignity of man'. Finally, these records were only partially published in 1949. The records of the proceedings of the 'Committee dealing with Basic Issues', where article 1 of the Basic Law was mainly and intensely discussed, were not published until 1993.[7] Until then, one had to manage with a summary, written by three staff members of the Parliamentary Council and published in the first volume of the new series of the Yearbook for Public Law in 1951.[8] This summary, entitled 'History of Origins of the Provisions of the Basic Law', is outstanding, and it is still a treasure chest for anyone who wants to learn more about the genesis of the Basic Law.[9] However, it is not exhaustive. The seven pages about Article 1 contain only one clue to a possible positive understanding of the term 'dignity of man': It is the famous but ambiguous dictum of Theodor Heuss that human dignity was a 'non-interpreted thesis'.[10] This statement was often quoted and taken as evidence that the framers had deliberately chosen a term that was meant to

---

1949. Die Entstehung des Grundgesetzes (Göttingen, Vandenhoeck & Ruprecht, 1998); EHM Lange, *Die Würde des Menschen ist unantastbar. Der Parlamentarische Rat und das Grundgesetz* (Heidelberg, Decker & Müller, 1993).

6   BVerfGE 1, 299, 312.

7   Deutscher Bundestag and Bundesarchiv (eds), *Der Parlamentarische Rat 1948–1949. Akten und Protokolle, Band 5, Ausschuss für Grundsatzfragen* (Boppard am Rhein, Harald Boldt Verlag, 1993).

8   KB von Doemming, RW Füsslein and W Matz, 'Entstehungsgeschichte der Artikel des Grundgesetzes', (1951) 1 *Jahrbuch des öffentlichen Rechts der Gegenwart* (new ed).

9   A 2nd edn, completed by a concise introduction written by Peter Häberle, has been published some years ago: P Häberle (ed), *Entstehungsgeschichte der Artikel des Grundgesetzes. Neuausgabe des Jahrbuch des öffentlichen Rechts der Gegenwart Band 1* (Tübingen, Mohr Siebeck, 2010).

10   von Doemming, Füsslein and Matz 'Entstehungsgeschichte der Artikel des Grundgesetzes' 49: 'Die Würde des Menschen stehe in seinem [Heuss'] Vorschlag als nicht interpretierte These.'

be freely interpretable or maybe even inaccessible to any kind of interpretation.[11] This false assumption did not remain without consequences.

II. Loss of Meaning

What is meant by 'Würde des Menschen', usually translated as 'dignity of man' or 'human dignity'?[12] 'Ironically, we do not know what human dignity is, but we know exactly whether human dignity is violated or not', states the author of a popular textbook on German constitutional law.[13] In the 1950s, things were different.[14] 'Having dignity means: being a personality', formulated Günter Dürig, maybe the most influential German constitutionalist at that time, in 1952.[15] In his opinion, a person 'ripens' to a personality by affirming and serving the values the person is 'essentially' related to, namely the eternal 'You' of God, the 'You' of the others and the 'We' of the community. The subject of the fundamental right guarantees of the Basic Law is, according to Dürig, 'always the responsible person, never the bondless individual'. None of the fundamental right guarantees protected the 'subhuman'.[16] Consequently, Dürig and others were convinced that the use of violence, drugs and psycho-technical means could be allowed and perhaps even constitutionally required in the interrogation of 'hardboiled' lawbreakers.[17] On the other hand, Dürig literally

---

11 See, for instance, J Limbach, 'Der Mensch wird nie ohne Makel sein', *Frankfurter Allgemeine Zeitung* of 25 February 2002, 51: 'non-interpretable thesis', my translation; D Schroeder, 'Human Rights and Human Dignity. An Appeal to Separate the Conjoined Twins' (2012) 15 *Ethical Theory and Moral Practice* 323, 326.
12 Martin O'Malley rightly emphasizes that 'Dignity is not simply Würde', see M O'Malley, 'Dignity in US Bio-Ethics Debate: Needs Würde' in C Baumbach and P Kunzmann (eds), *Würde – dignité – godnosc – dignity: Die Menschenwürde im internationalen Vergleich* (Munich, Herbert Utz Verlag, 2010) 253, 254–61.
13 F Hufen, *Staatsrecht II. Grundrechte*, 3rd edn (Munich, C.H. Beck, 2011) § 10 margin number 29, my translation.
14 For detailed references, see C Goos, *Innere Freiheit. Eine Rekonstruktion des grundgesetzlichen Würdebegriffs* (Göttingen, V&R unipress, 2011) 21–30.
15 G Dürig, 'Die Menschenauffassung des Grundgesetzes', (1952) 6 *Juristische Rundschau* 259, my translation.
16 ibid 261, my translation.
17 G Dürig, 'Der Grundrechtssatz von der Menschenwürde', (1956) 81 *Archiv des öffentlichen Rechts* 117, 128; F Klein in H von Mangoldt and F Klein, *Das*

195

'shuddered' to even think about issues like artificial insemination with the help of a sperm donor. Dürig had not the slightest doubt that such acts violated human dignity 'as such'.[18]

Dürig's deliberations shaped and dominated the interpretation of Article 1 of the Basic Law for years. Fundamental criticism did not emerge until the mid-1960s. In 1964, Peter Badura pointed out that the common value-based and personalistic interpretation of the first article of the Basic Law did not see men as they are but in the way they should be, according to the ethical ideal of the autonomous personality. However, those people not corresponding to this ideal because of their behavior or their constitution, needed to be protected. Paradoxically, the personalistic understanding of human dignity was forced to give reasons for the dignity of these people, as if they were a problematic borderline case. And even worse: this interpretation made it possible to exclude the most vulnerable people from the protection of Article 1 of the Basic Law. Badura therefore argued that one should no longer theorize about the moral personality of man but rather agree on a casuistry of clear infringements of human dignity.[19] His proposal was later called the 'negative interpretation method',[20] and it did not last long until Baduras' approach became the prevailing opinion. Günter Dürig, changeable as a chameleon, relented in the early 1970s and declared, as if he had never claimed anything else: 'One should not presume to interpret the principle of human dignity positively, but you can say what violates it.'[21]

A positive definition of human dignity was considered dispensable, because – this is how Dürig formulated it – 'after the experience of our people, there is a very precise consensus about how a political and social order should look and how it should not look.'[22] This assumption, however, soon proved illusory. In 1982, the first German test-tube baby was born,

---

	Bonner Grundgesetz, 2nd edn (Berlin and Frankfurt am Main, Franz Vahlen, 1957) Art. 1 Note III 5 a.
18	Dürig ibid 130.
19	P Badura, 'Generalprävention und Würde des Menschen', (1964) 19 *Juristen-Zeitung* 337, 340–41.
20	See HG Dederer, 'Die Garantie der Menschenwürde (Art. 1 Abs. 1 GG). Dogmatische Grundfragen auf dem Stand der Wissenschaft', (2009) 57 *Jahrbuch des öffentlichen Rechts der Gegenwart* 89, 105–07.
21	G Dürig, 'Zur Bedeutung und Tragweite des Art. 79 Abs. III GG' in H Spanner et al (eds), *Festgabe für Theodor Maunz zum 70. Geburtstag am 1. September 1971* (Munich, C.H. Beck, 1971) 41, 44–45, my translation.
22	ibid 44, my translation.

and it soon became apparent that it would be impossible to reach an agreement about the status of the embryo in vitro and the constitutional review of these new opportunities. Human dignity therefore was not the appropriate word, Peter Lerche concluded. According to him, human dignity could only defend its contours if one limited the use of this concept to those topics consented to by the community, and in vitro fertilization was, obviously, none of these cases.[23] In the mid-1990s, Horst Dreier proposed to 'free' the abortion debate 'from the heavy burden of Article 1, paragraph 1 of the Basic Law' as well, because, even in this case, there was no consensus in sight.[24]

In the first edition of his legal commentary on the Basic Law, which was published in 1996, Dreier listed slavery, servitude, deportation, stigmatization and torture as examples of self-evidently and universally consented violations of Article 1, paragraph 1 of the Basic Law.[25] Nevertheless, only a few years later, a German police officer threatened a kidnapper with considerable pain to find out the whereabouts of the kidnapped child. All the courts later concerned with this tragical case stated clearly and without exception that this was a violation of the kidnapper's dignity, even though the police officer had tried to save the life of an innocent child.[26] However, German constitutionalists began to discuss seriously if the so-called 'rescue torture' could be allowed by Article 1 of the Basic Law.[27] Critical observers anxiously diagnosed that the inviolability of human dignity seemed no longer as obvious as before. The findings of the

---

23 P Lerche, 'Verfassungsrechtliche Aspekte der Gentechnologie' in R Lukes and R Scholz (eds): *Rechtsfragen der Gentechnologie. Vorträge anläßlich eines Kolloquiums Recht und Technik – Rechtsfragen der Gentechnologie in der Tagungsstätte der Max-Planck-Gesellschaft 'Schloß Ringberg' am 18., 19. und 20. November 1985* (Köln, Carl Heymanns Verlag, 1986) 88, 100.

24 H Dreier, 'Menschenwürdegarantie und Schwangerschaftsabbruch', (1995) 48 *Die Öffentliche Verwaltung* 1036, 1040, my translation.

25 H Dreier in H Dreier (ed), *Grundgesetz. Kommentar, Band I, Artikel 1–19*, 1st ed (Tübingen, Mohr Siebeck, 1996) Art. 1 Abs. 1 margin number 80.

26 See, most recently, Oberlandesgericht Frankfurt/Main, 1 U 201/11 of 10 October 2012 at www.lareda.hessenrecht.hessen.de; European Court of Human Rights, Gafgen v. Germany, *European Human Rights Reports* 52 (2011) 1; Bundesverfassungsgericht, 1 BvR 1807/07 of 19 February 2008 at www.bverfg.de.

27 For discussion of this topic, see H Goerlich (ed), *Staatliche Folter: Heiligt der Zweck die Mittel?* (Paderborn, mentis Verlag, 2007); G Beestermöller and H Brunkhorst (eds), *Rückkehr der Folter. Der Rechtsstaat im Zwielicht?* (Munich, C.H. Beck, 2006).

Federal Constitutional Court concerning the dignity of innocent passengers on board a hijacked aircraft in the Aviation Security Act decision[28] were also discussed controversially.[29] A kind of 'tiredness with dignity' and a tendency to solve problematic cases without using Article 1 of the Basic Law could not be overlooked. 'After the knowing about the meaning of human dignity has faded away, it is now also becoming increasingly unclear to us why we still need it,' the German constitutionalist Uwe Volkmann remarked.[30]

III. Rediscovering the Original Meaning

What was meant by 'dignity of man'?[31] During the first meetings of the Plenary Assembly of the Parliamentary Council, rather nonspecific 'dignity-talk' prevailed: Delegates from all parties emphasized that freedom and dignity were the 'highest goods' and that it would be the main task of the Council to secure them again. However, some delegates already distinguished explicitly between 'freedom' and 'dignity'. Adolf Süsterhenn for instance, one of the most influential Christian Democratic members of the

---

28 BVerfGE 115, 118, 152–54.
29 For an overview, see O Lepsius, 'Human Dignity and the Downing of Aircraft. The German Federal Constitutional Court strikes down a Prominent Anti-Terrorism Provision in the New Air-transport security Act', (2006) 7 *German Law Journal* 761, 766–74; F Müller and T Richter, 'Report on the Bundesverfassungsgericht's (Federal Constitutional Court) Jurisprudence in 2005/2006', (2008) 9 *German Law Journal* 161, 184–93; both with further references.
30 U Volkmann, 'Nachricht vom Ende der Gewissheit', *Frankfurter Allgemeine Zeitung* of 24 November 2003, 8, my translation; see also T Wihl, 'Wahre Würde. Ansätze zu einer Metatheorie der Menschenwürdetheorien' in C Bäcker and S Ziemann (eds), *Junge Rechtsphilosophie* (Stuttgart, Franz Steiner Verlag, 2012) 187, 200: 'dispensable as a legal term', my translation.
31 Article 1 German Basic Law was mainly discussed during the 4th meeting of the Committee dealing with Basic Issues on 23 September 1948 (see Deutscher Bundestag and Bundesarchiv [eds.] *Der Parlamentarische Rat 1948–1949. Akten und Protokolle, Band 5, Ausschuss für Grundsatzfragen* 62–75) and during its 22nd and 23rd meeting on 18 November 1948 (see ibid 584–609). For further and more detailed references, see Goos *Innere Freiheit* 75–94. Compare also C Möllers, 'Democracy and Human Dignity: Limits of a Moralized Conception of Rights in German Constitutional Law', (2009) 42 *Israel Law Review* 416, 417–21; C Enders, 'A Right to Have Rights – The German Constitutional Concept of Human Dignity', (2010) 3 *NUJS Law Review* 253, 254–55; both with further references.

Council,[32] stated that human dignity, 'inner freedom' and the 'inner value' of the personality remained 'fine words' as long as the individuals had no possibility to make use of these capacities in their daily lives.[33] Helene Wessel, one of the two delegates of the Catholic Center party, emphasized in a very similar way the necessity to convey to the Germans the notion of 'true liberty', the freedom for individual development. She used the terms of 'human dignity' and 'freedom rights', differentiating between the ability to make one's own decisions and the freedom to act and to enter into relationships with others.[34]

The distinction between 'inner' and 'outer' freedom can also be found in the deliberations of the Committee dealing with Basic Issues that was responsible for the phrasing of the fundamental rights catalogue. The records of the proceedings of this committee show that the already mentioned dictum on human dignity as a 'non-interpreted thesis' was not at all meant to be a carte blanche for any arbitrary interpretation. Theodor Heuss[35] repeatedly criticized an early draft version of Article 1 ('The dignity of man rests on eternal, inherent rights.') for the very reason that he considered the reference to 'eternal, inherent rights' as too ambiguous.[36] He recalled his proposal ('The dignity of man is placed under the protection of the state order.')[37] and explained that the dignity of man was a 'non-interpreted thesis' in his proposal.[38] He added that he wanted to choose the wording of this Article in a way 'that one could comprehend theologically,

---

32 For further information, see C von Hehl, *Adolf Süsterhenn (1905–1974). Verfassungsvater, Weltanschauungspolitiker, Föderalist* (Düsseldorf, Droste Verlag, 2012).
33 Deutscher Bundestag and Bundesarchiv (eds), *Der Parlamentarische Rat 1948–1949. Akten und Protokolle, Band 9, Plenum*, rev Wolfram Werner (Munich, Harald Boldt Verlag, 1996) 185.
34 ibid 209.
35 For further information, see, most recently, J Radkau, *Theodor Heuss* (Munich, Carl Hanser Verlag, 2013); P Merseburger, *Theodor Heuss. Der Bürger als Präsident. Biographie* (Munich, Deutsche Verlags-Anstalt, 2012); EW Becker, *Theodor Heuss. Bürger im Zeitalter der Extreme* (Stuttgart, Kohlhammer Verlag, 2011).
36 Deutscher Bundestag and Bundesarchiv (eds) *Der Parlamentarische Rat 1948–1949. Akten und Protokolle, Band 5, Ausschuss für Grundsatzfragen* 67 and 72.
37 ibid 52 and 67, my translation.
38 ibid 72, my translation.

another philosophically, another ethically.'[39] Helene Weber, one of the four mothers of the Basic Law, agreed:

> The individual is free to take religious, ethical or historical insights as his or her starting point. However, it is most significant that we, at this historical moment, begin our Constitution with the concept of human dignity.[40]

Adolf Süsterhenn likewise declared:

> One sees human dignity rooted in humanity, another in the Christian conviction that men and women are created in the image of God. However, we agree in the concept of human dignity as the highest value in our worldliness.[41]

The members of the Committee dealing with Basic Issues agreed that the concept of human dignity has different roots and origins and that there are several good reasons for protecting human dignity constitutionally. With regard to its foundation, the human dignity article remained a 'non-interpreted thesis'.

However, the records also show that the mothers and fathers of the Basic Law did their very best to clarify the substantive meaning of the legal term of human dignity. Carlo Schmid, one of the most influential social democratic members of the Parliamentary Council,[42] demanded right at the beginning of the consultations: 'Dignity of man – that should be defined!'[43] The wording of Article 1 should be considered carefully, because 'in its systematic relevance, it is the key to the whole.'[44] Ludwig Bergsträsser contradicted immediately when Hermann von Mangoldt, the chairman of the Committee dealing with Basic Issues, complained that one could hardly get a concrete idea about the meaning of the legal term of human dignity:

> Human dignity forbids any compulsion to act against one's own conviction. For me, this seems to be one of the most important features of human dignity. Human

---

39   ibid 67, my translation.
40   ibid 69, my translation.
41   ibid 915, my translation.
42   For further information, see P Weber, *Carlo Schmid 1896–1979. Eine Biographie* (Frankfurt am Main, Suhrkamp Verlag, 1998); C Schmid, *Erinnerungen*, 3rd ed (Bern, Munich, Wien, Scherz Verlag, 1979).
43   Deutscher Bundestag and Bundesarchiv (eds) *Der Parlamentarische Rat 1948–1949. Akten und Protokolle, Band 5, Ausschuss für Grundsatzfragen* 66, my translation.
44   ibid 64, my translation.

dignity forbids that someone is beaten. Human dignity is, in other words, the freedom from compulsion to act against one's convictions.[45]

Theodor Heuss insisted: 'Human dignity must rest in itself. It must not be derived from any governmental position.'[46] Carlo Schmid called human dignity 'a quality, an attribute that determines the human and that distinguishes humans from other creatures.'[47] Schmid, well-versed in philosophy and theology, referred to Martin Luther's concept of the 'freedom of the Christian'[48] and the inherent dignity that, according to the late stoic philosopher Epictetus, remains even to the galley slave forged to his bench:[49] 'For me', Schmid explained, 'the dignity of man recognizes this attribute of man as an honour.'[50]

IV. Inner Freedom

This 'attribute' or capability Carlo Schmid referred to can be described as 'inner freedom'.[51] Martin Luther protested vehemently, as the German peasants demanded in 1525 in their *Twelve Articles* that they did not want to be serfs any longer because the scripture said that Christ had freed them. 'That is', declared Luther, 'making Christian freedom a completely physical matter.' 'A slave can be a Christian', Luther wrote in his famous *Admonition to Peace*, 'and have Christian freedom, in the same way that a

---

45	Deutscher Bundestag and Bundesarchiv (eds) *Der Parlamentarische Rat 1948–1949. Akten und Protokolle, Band 5, Ausschuss für Grundsatzfragen* 607.
46	ibid 588, my translation.
47	ibid 72.
48	Deutscher Bundestag and Bundesarchiv (eds), *Der Parlamentarische Rat 1948–1949. Akten und Protokolle, Band 14, Hauptausschuss*, rev Michael F. Feldkamp (Munich, R. Oldenbourg Verlag, 2009) 1290.
49	Deutscher Bundestag and Bundesarchiv (eds) *Der Parlamentarische Rat 1948–1949. Akten und Protokolle, Band 5, Ausschuss für Grundsatzfragen* 72; Deutscher Bundestag and Bundesarchiv (eds) *Der Parlamentarische Rat 1948–1949. Akten und Protokolle, Band 14, Hauptausschuss* 1290.
50	Deutscher Bundestag and Bundesarchiv (eds) *Der Parlamentarische Rat 1948–1949. Akten und Protokolle, Band 14, Hauptausschuss* 1290, my translation.
51	See Goos *Innere Freiheit* 95–157.

prisoner or a sick man is a Christian, and yet not free.'[52] Luther distinguished carefully between the 'inner' man and his liberty and the 'outward' man.[53] For the late-Stoic philosopher Epictetus, one's outer, external, social and political freedom is also not essential: If a liberated slave – to quote one of the examples he uses in his *Discourses* – falls in love with the wrong girl or makes himself dependent on other people for the sake of his professional advancement, he might fall into a far more abject slavery than the one he has escaped: 'Finally, when he crowns it off by becoming a senator, becoming a slave in fine company, then he experiences the poshest and most prestigious form of enslavement.'[54] For Epictetus, those are free who are able to distinguish between the things in their power and the things that are not in their power:

> I must die. But must I die bawling? I must be put in chains – but moaning and groaning too? I must be exiled; but is there anything to keep me from going with a smile, calm and self-composed?[55]

Liberal thinkers like Isaiah Berlin doubt that this inner freedom deserves the name of freedom at all because it is 'compatible with a very high degree of political despotism.'[56] One might also ask if 'inner freedom' really needs to be protected by law.[57] Isn't the galley slave, chained but free an-

---

52 Martin Luther, *'Admonition to Peace'*, trans. CM Jacobs, revised RC Schultz, in RC Schultz (ed), HT Lehmann (gen ed), *Luther's Works, vol. 46, The Christian in Society III* (Philadelphia, Fortress Press, 1967) 3, 39.

53 See C Goos, 'Wirtschaft und Freiheit in den Bauernkriegsartikeln. Verfassungshistorische Anmerkungen zu Artikel 2, 3, 11: Freiheit von Zehnt, Leibeigenschaft und Todfallabgaben' in GK Hasselhoff and D von Mayenburg (eds), *Die Zwölf Artikel von 1525 und das 'Göttliche Recht' der Bauern – rechtshistorische und theologische Dimensionen* (Würzburg, Ergon Verlag, 2012) 77, 94–97; M Heckel, 'Luthers Traktat "Von der Freiheit eines Christenmenschen" als Markstein des Kirchen- und Staatskirchenrechts' (2012) 109 *Zeitschrift für Theologie und Kirche* 122; E Jüngel, *Zur Freiheit eines Christenmenschen. Eine Erinnerung an Luthers Schrift* (Munich, Chr. Kaiser Verlag, 1991).

54 Epictetus, *'Discourses'* IV.1.39 in R Dobbin (trans and ed), *Epictetus. Discourses and Selected Writings* (London, Penguin Books, 2008) 177.

55 Epictetus, *'Discourses'* I.1.22, ibid 7; for further information, see eg AA Long, *Epictetus. A Stoic and Socratic Guide to Life* (Oxford, Clarendon Press, 2004) 207–30; R Sorabji, 'Epictetus on *proairesis* and Self' in T Scaltsas and AS Mason (eds), *The Philosophy of Epictetus* (Oxford, Oxford University Press, 2010) 87.

56 I Berlin, *Liberty. Incorporating Four Essays on Liberty* (Oxford, Oxford University Press, 2002) 32.

57 See, however, particularly instructively, Clemens Sedmak's reflections on 'interiority' and the uniqueness of the 'inner life' of human beings and the politi-

yway, the best example that the 'inner freedom' of man is inviolable in the truest sense of the word? In fact, there is still a dispute in the literature as to whether the first sentence of Article 1 ('The dignity of man is inviolable.') is to be understood descriptively or prescriptively.[58] 'It should be inviolable!' declared Ludwig Bergsträsser, as this question arose in the debates of the Parliamentary Council.[59] Hermann von Mangoldt said, and this was universally consented: 'After the things we have witnessed during the Nazi era, the legal protection of human dignity must be one of our main concerns.'[60]

The mothers and fathers of the Basic Law had experiences in mind like those transmitted by the later Hanoverian Bishop Hanns Lilje, the psychoanalyst Bruno Bettelheim and the psychiatrist and philosopher Viktor Frankl. Lilje, for instance, reports of a shocking encounter with the severely tortured Carl Friedrich Goerdeler: 'The Gestapo had made a ruin out of him. He made his comments in a mechanical, soulless manner, as if he said nothing but the things they taught him. His eyes had lost their former brightness, and they gave away that, in addition to the usual torture, even drugs and other bad things had done their work.'[61] After having spent approximately one year in the concentration camps at Dachau and Buchenwald, Bettelheim described it as being one of the goals of the Gestapo 'to break the prisoners as individuals'.[62] 'The last vestiges of personality were erased there', reported Viktor Frankl.[63] In a nightmarish study, the German philosopher Reinhold Aschenberg characterizes the Nazi concentration camps as 'institutions of de-subjectification': 'These laboratories emit large amounts, masses of human beings whose subjectivity slowly fades

---

cal dimension of interiority: C Sedmak, 'Human Dignity, Interiority, and Poverty', in C McCrudden (ed), *Understanding Human Dignity* (Oxford, Oxford University Press, 2013) 559.
58 See Teifke *Das Prinzip Menschenwürde* 73–74.
59 Deutscher Bundestag and Bundesarchiv (eds) *Der Parlamentarische Rat 1948–1949. Akten und Protokolle, Band 5, Ausschuss für Grundsatzfragen* 913, my translation.
60 ibid 52, my translation.
61 H Lilje, *Im finstern Tal* (Nürnberg, Laetare Verlag, 1947) 50, my translation.
62 B Bettelheim, 'Individual and Mass Behavior in Extreme Situations' (1943) 38 *The Journal of Abnormal and Social Psychology* 417, 418.
63 VE Frankl, 'Homo patiens' (1950) in id, *Der leidende Mensch*, 3rd ed (Bern, Verlag Hans Huber, 2005) 161, 176, my translation.

until they, while still alive, totally lose it.'[64] The Nazi system as a whole can be described as a major project of de-subjectifying man – in the concentration camps, the mass organizations, at school and in University, even at home, by a certain kind of infant education that caused avoidant personality disorders – with the well-known, devastating consequences.[65]

Only a few could preserve and prove their inner freedom under such circumstances. It can be shown that the desire for 'true intellectual freedom' was one of the motivations, the 'complete protection of freedom of spirit' one of the goals of the conspirators, especially for the students and professors around Sophie and Hans Scholl and Helmuth von Moltke and his Kreisau circle:[66] 'Delp, Gerstenmaier and I only thought,' Moltke wrote to his wife a few days before he was executed. 'And the Nazis fear the mere thought of these three lonely men so much that they want to cut off all that is infected with it.'[67] During the Nazi time, even freedom of thought, even inner freedom, had been threatened and proven to be fragile. For the fathers and mothers of the Basic Law there was no question that it had to be protected by law in the future. Not yet the Jewish tragedy, as Samuel Moyn rightly points out,[68] but this is the reason why they decided to begin with the sentence: 'The dignity of man is inviolable.'

Nevertheless, this conception might seem to be inadequate because it only applies to the 'inner' freedom of man. However, the inseparable connection between inner and outer freedom was not only intensely discussed in the Parliamentary Council. It is stated right in the following paragraph of Article 1 Basic Law:

> The dignity of man is inviolable. To respect it and to protect it is the duty of all state authority. The German people therefore acknowledge inviolable and inalienable human rights as the basis of every community, of peace and of justice in the world.

---

64   R Aschenberg, *Ent-Subjektivierung des Menschen. Lager und Shoah in philosophischer Reflexion* (Würzburg, Königshausen & Neumann, 2003) 278, my translation.
65   See Goos *Innere Freiheit* 127–38.
66   ibid 116–27.
67   HJ von Moltke, 'Letter of 10 January 1945' in G Brakelmann (ed), *Helmuth James von Moltke. Im Land der Gottlosen. Tagebuch und Briefe aus der Haft 1944/45* (Munich, C.H. Beck, 2009) 328, 334, my translation.
68   S Moyn, 'The Secret History of Constitutional Dignity', in C McCrudden (ed), *Understanding Human Dignity* (Oxford, Oxford University Press, 2013) 95.

Human dignity and human rights can be distinguished and they must be distinguished, but they must not be separated.[69] The basic rights are guaranteed for the sake of human dignity, 'since', according to Hermann von Mangoldt, 'every single article protects a bit of the freedom that is necessary to guarantee human dignity.'[70] It was precisely in this sense that Carlo Schmid stated it at the Hamburg SPD party Congress in May 1950:

> Epictetus once expressed that even the slave chained to his oar was free if he had the right attitude. But, comrades, we do not want to be satisfied with this freedom of the galley slave. We do not only want the opportunity to have this inner freedom. We also want to have the opportunity for a freedom that enables us to develop all human capacities in the outside world.[71]

V. Dignity and the 'Weak Subject'

However, one might ask if 'inner freedom' is not just another noble ideal that excludes many people, for example little children, the mentally disabled, people suffering from Alzheimer's disease, and, of course, the unborn and the deceased.[72] It is completely inconceivable that the mothers and fathers of the Basic Law wanted Article 1 paragraph 1 to be interpreted like this. To me, it therefore seems appropriate to further develop their conception in a way that these problematic cases can also be covered.[73] The records show clearly that the framers carefully chose the wording of

---

69   See Goos *Innere Freiheit* 205–09.
70   Deutscher Bundestag and Bundesarchiv (eds) *Der Parlamentarische Rat 1948–1949. Akten und Protokolle, Band 5, Ausschuss für Grundsatzfragen* 591, my translation.
71   C Schmid, in: *Protokoll der Verhandlungen des Parteitages der SPD vom 21. bis 25. Mai 1950 in Hamburg* (Frankfurt am Main, n.d.) 257, my translation.
72   Exactly the same problem arises with a Kantian understanding of dignity. See, most recently, Schroeder 'Human Rights and Human Dignity. An Appeal to Separate the Conjoined Twins' 329–31 ('The Kantian cul-de-sac'); C Foster, *Human Dignity in Bioethics and Law* (Oxford and Portland, Oregon, Hart Publishing, 2011) 38–39; C Dupre, 'Unlocking Human Dignity. Towards a Theory for the 21st Century', (2009) 2 *European Human Rights Law Review* 190, 193-94. Important clarifications at G Luf, 'Menschenwürde als Rechtsbegriff. Überlegungen zum Kant-Verständnis in der neueren deutschen Grundrechtstheorie', in: R Zaczyk et al (eds), *Festschrift für E.A. Wolff zum 70. Geburtstag am 1.10.1998* (Berlin, Springer, 1998) 307, 321; see also O Sensen, *Kant on Human Dignity* (Berlin and Boston, De Gruyter, 2011) 202–12.
73   See Goos *Innere Freiheit* 142–57.

Article 1 Basic Law. They discussed and discarded the wordings dignity of human 'existence', 'essence', or 'life' and unanimously decided for the dignity of 'man'. Helene Weber explained: 'This term covers everything and highlights neither the purely biological nor the purely spiritual. In short, it is exhausting.'[74] On the other hand, the records also indicate that the framers did not use the term 'Würde des Menschen' as a not further substantiated value attribution to the motto 'every human being is somehow valuable'. They used it to describe a very specific, vulnerable quality of man.

Considering this, it seems obvious to me that dignity as 'inner freedom' should be understood in the broadest possible sense. One should particularly avoid overemphasizing aspects like reason or rationality in positive definitions of the Basic Law's legal term of human dignity. The conception of the Italian Renaissance philosopher Giovanni Pico Della Mirandola, for instance, enthusiastically received by some German constitutionalists since the 1990s,[75] would not be adequate in describing the meaning of the Basic Law's human dignity article. For Pico, the human is characterized by the ability to lead his life according to his own design, to interpret and assimilate culture: 'its status was dignity, its nature was reason, and its consequence was autonomy.'[76] However, in practice, especially those people who are unable to think or do anything, not even to participate in culture, need to be protected.[77] In his remarkable book *Soul Hunger: The Feeling Human Being and the Life Sciences*, the Swiss psychiatrist Daniel Hell has pointed out that depressed people 'are often left with only a feeble experience of their corporeality. This experience cannot be turned into something positive, but it is the only thing of their own they have left.' Sometimes, though, depressed persons discovered 'unexpected avenues of experience' because of their depression:

---

74 Deutscher Bundestag and Bundesarchiv (eds) *Der Parlamentarische Rat 1948–1949. Akten und Protokolle, Band 5, Ausschuss für Grundsatzfragen* 73, my translation.

75 See, most recently, R Gröschner, S Kirste and O Lembcke (eds), *Des Menschen Würde – entdeckt und erfunden im Humanismus der italienischen Renaissance* (Tübingen, Mohr Siebeck, 2008).

76 C Foster *Human Dignity in Bioethics and Law* 34. See also M Lebech, *On the Problem of Human Dignity. A Hermeneutical and Phenomenological Investigation* (Würzburg, Königshausen & Neumann, 2009) 87–90.

77 Compare also Foster ibid: '[N]eat formulations don't do well when confronted with the messiness of real humans'; Dupre *Human Dignity in Bioethics and Law* 193.

They may sense that what made that possible was a first-person perspective that others don't know. ... A deeper understanding of depression may help in developing a passion for the 'weak subject', that is, to discard the image of a person who is weighted down by the excessive demands of the post-modern conception of man as creator, designer and engineer of reality. Seeing a totally independent and isolated ego as questionable, the subject must not perish. It may come to understand itself as a creature that, as a natural 'living being', depends on many necessities, but still senses that it has personal value or – in the ancient way of speaking – a soul.[78]

Hell concludes: 'Is it inconceivable that it is only the image of an ego perspective in another person that establishes the quality of humanness?'[79]

One can probably go even one step further: Dignity as first-person perspective in the broadest possible sense can be understood as something that an embryo already 'has' and that even survives the death.[80] Prenatal psychologists like Inge Krens and neurobiologists like Gerald Hüther emphasize that even the fertilized egg

> unites both physical and psychological components. A human organism is not created by cells initially forming a body and the soul later eventually joining this entity. Body and psyche differentiate simultaneously and undividedly.[81]

The already mentioned Viennese philosopher and psychiatrist Viktor Frankl points out in one of his books that the first-person perspective of another person is in the realm beyond physicality and sensuality even during their lifetime: 'We do not have it as we have an object, but we capture it because of sensory impressions.' Frankl uses the example of a famous opera singer: It does not matter if we listen to him in concert, on the radio or even to a recording after his death. In each of these cases we do not only hear sound waves, but – conveyed by them – the singer himself. His uniqueness, his 'magic' endures.[82] Not later than 1971, the German Federal Constitutional Court had ruled that it would be incompatible with the

---

78   D Hell, *Soul Hunger. The Feeling Human Being and the Life Sciences* (Einsiedeln, Daimon Verlag, 2010) 345–46.
79   ibid.
80   For further details, see Goos *Innere Freiheit* 148–57.
81   G Hüther and I Krens, *Das Geheimnis der ersten neun Monate. Unsere frühesten Prägungen* (Düsseldorf, Patmos Verlag, 2005) 36, my translation.
82   VE Frankl, 'Der unbedingte Mensch' (1949) in: id, *Der leidende Mensch*, 3rd ed (Bern, Verlag Hans Huber, 2005) 65, 132, my translation. Compare also Clemens Sedmak's reflections on 'mystery' as a fundamental feature of an approach to human dignity (C Sedmak 'Human Dignity, Interiority, and Poverty' 568).

guarantee of human dignity in Article 1 of the Basic Law if a person could be humiliated or degraded after his or her death.[83] The duty of all state authority to respect and to protect human dignity does not end in death. In my view, this jurisdiction is entirely as intended by the framers.

VI. Conclusion

We tend to assume that Article 1 German Basic Law is a specific result of Catholic and Kantian thought.[84] Indeed, the provision was interpreted like this very soon, especially and most influentially by the Catholic constitutionalist Günter Dürig in the 1950s. Decades later, Dürig admitted frankly and not without pride that he had successfully established a Christian-personalistic interpretation of the dignity article.[85] However, in this regard, Article 1 differs significantly from the dignity-references that can be found in the post-war constitutions of some German federal states. Although some Christian Democrats and National Conservatives in the Parliamentary Council tried to establish their idea of genuine, God-given freedom, phrasings like 'The dignity of man is founded on eternal, God-given rights' were repeatedly rejected by the other delegates.[86] Kant was not even mentioned during the framer's debates on Article 1.[87] The dignity debates were dominated by Carlo Schmid and Theodor Heuss, a secularist and a Protestant, both highly educated. The two could easily convince their colleagues that Article 1 should be formulated in a way 'that one

---

83   BVerfGE 30, 173, 194.
84   See, for instance, M Rosen, *Dignity. Its History and Meaning* (Cambridge, Massachusetts, and London, England, Harvard University Press, 2012) 80–90; RD Glensky, 'The Right to Dignity', (2011) 43 *Columbia Human Rights Law Review* 65, 96: 'clear Kantian overtones of the conceiving of dignity as "inviolable"'.
85   G Dürig, 'Dankrede am 65. Geburtstag', (1987) 36 *Jahrbuch des öffentlichen Rechts der Gegenwart* 91, 100.
86   See, in particular, the debate between the representatives Seebohm, Schmid, Heuss and Greve during the 42nd meeting of the Main Committee, Deutscher Bundestag and Bundesarchiv (eds) *Der Parlamentarische Rat 1948–1949. Akten und Protokolle, Band 14, Hauptausschuss* 1289–92. Compare also T Stein, *Himmlische Quellen und irdisches Recht. Religiöse Voraussetzungen des freiheitlichen Verfassungsstaates* (Frankfurt and New York, Campus, 2007) 308–09.
87   Compare also Möllers 'Democracy and Human Dignity' 427: 'When interpreting a constitutional text, it is maybe best to do without a house philosopher.'

could comprehend theologically, another philosophically, another ethically'. In contrast to this, the meaning of the term 'dignity of man' did not remain undefined. The framers agreed that the 'dignity of man' was neither a more or less vague value assignment nor just the sum of the following basic rights but a real capacity of human beings that had been proven highly vulnerable during the Nazi regime: the inner freedom. Unlike other legal systems, the German Constitution thereby focuses particularly on the inner self and accents the interior component of the human personality.[88] To me, the potential of this article in its original meaning has not been fully exploited yet.

---

88   Compare also, from a comparative law perspective, EJ Eberle, 'Human Dignity, Privacy, and Personality in German and American Constitutional Law', in N Knoepffler, P Kunzmann and M O'Malley (eds), *Facetten der Menschenwürde* (Freiburg and Munich, Verlag Karl Alber, 2011) 102.

Hermeneutic and Literary Remarks on the *Objektformel* as a Tool of Critical Reflection in Practicing the Law of Human Dignity

Matthildi Chatzipanagiotou

I. Abstract

The resurfacing of the *Objektformel* (object formula) doctrine in the famous *Aviation Security Act Case* (2006) of the *Bundesverfassungsgericht* (German Federal Constitutional Court, FCC) spurred scholarly debate, within and beyond Germany, on how the law of human dignity is to be practiced.[1] The practice of human dignity language in the *Aviation Security Act Case* is a panegyric on the *Objektformel,* and an illustrative instance of struggle over the term's meaning. How the objectification of human beings literally and figuratively eventuates in this case emphatically challenges the German Basic Law's *Menschenbild* (view of the human being, view of humanity) and the constitutional guarantee of human dignity under Art 1 sec 1 GG (*Grundgesetz,* Basic Law): shooting down a hijacked aircraft to prevent it from crashing on the ground in line with §14 sec 3 LuftSiG (*Luftsicherheitsgesetz,* Aviation Security Act) amounts to treating innocent passengers and crew on board as part of a weapon, that is, an object.[2] Practicing the *Objektformel* doctrine satisfies the guarantee of abso-

---

1 BVerfGE 115, 118 (161 ff.) (2006), First Senate of the FCC; Followed by a Plenary Decision on the 3rd of July 2012 (BVerfG, 2 PBvU 1/11 vom 3.7.2012, Absatz-Nr. (1-89)), which did not however deal with the fundamental rights issues raised in the judgment of the First Senate. The Aviation Security Act (*Luftsicherheitsgesetz*, LuftSiG) authorised the armed forces to shoot down aircrafts intended to be used as weapons.

2 See O Lepsius, 'Human Dignity and the Downing of Aircraft: The German Federal Constitutional Court Strikes Down a Prominent Anti-Terrorism Provision in the New Air-transport Security Act' (2006) 7 (9) *German Law Journal* 761, 771 ('The new decision of the Federal Constitutional Court, however, applies the dignity clause differently. Literally, the Court reasserts the conjunction of Articles 1 (1) and 2 (2). For its reasoning the Court does not need to draw upon the right to life at all, although it is mentioned in the judgment. The decision could have limited the reasoning to the human dignity clause alone

lute respect for and protection of human dignity in German constitutional law. Doctrine is, elementally, language. The hermeneutic and literary appreciation of objectification language permits the observation that the doctrine employed to detect and abjure objectification, introduces language that effectively materialises the images of the objectified human being on the one hand and of the state-perpetrator on the other. What does the surfacing of such images in FCC legal language games indicate about the *Objektformel*? How can we make sense of the presence of such images in legal language games?

The following remarks flow from a hermeneutic and literary approach to the practice of the law of human dignity and show how the *Objektformel* doctrine operates as a tool of critical reflection. The sources of impetus for this approach compose a landscape of multicollectivity. This pastiche suits, methodologically, the hermeneutic and literary project of carving a lens through which to look at the *Objektformel* as a recurrent feature of human dignity practice.[3] Exploring a dominant theme in the text of the

---

and could have let Article 2 (2) fall into oblivion. Hence it was not the rejection of the right to life but the mere treatment of individuals as objects without a proper legal protection at all that caused the unconstitutionality of the statute. The Court made an allusion to the older "object-formula" of the 1950s. This formula interprets the dignity clause without any references to individual human life; it only alludes to the abstract way human beings are treated by the legal order. Thus, it has the advantage of disconnecting life and dignity again, and, therefore, reversing a development in German constitutional interpretation that was never truly convincing, that created unforeseeable inconsistencies and contradicted the wording of the Basic Law, which clearly distinguishes between dignity (with absolute protection) and life (with limitable protection). The interesting development in the *Air-transport Security Act* case concerning Article 1 jurisprudence consequently can be summarized as follows. The Court practically gave up the long standing connection of life and dignity and reversed the jurisprudence it had been pursuing since the 1970s. Instead it invoked an older approach toward human dignity which seemed to have been overcome in the literature. However, the Court was either not courageous enough to declare so openly or it did not realize the remarkable shift away from the right to life that it was taking.' (footnotes omitted)).

3   See, on the hermeneutic approach, also, HG Gadamer, *Truth and Method*, rev 2nd edn (London, Continuum Publishing Group, 2004) 392 ('[W]ritten texts present the real hermeneutical task ... Overcoming it, reading the text, is thus the highest task of understanding. Even the pure signs of an inscription can be seen properly and articulated correctly only if the text can be transformed back into language. As we have said, however, this transformation always establishes a relationship to what is meant, to the subject matter being discussed.'); ibid 396 ('Everything written is, in fact, the paradigmatic object of hermeneutics.

Aviation Security Act Case through that lens proposes an alternative reading: unless understood as language kindling critical reflection by operating ex negativo, to wit by conjuring up the very violation of human dignity only to responsibly peruse whether that law is respected and protected, the presence of the *Objektformel* evokes images that embody the subversion of the absolute guarantee of human dignity in the Basic Law.

II. Objectification and the Experience of Deadlock

The *Objektformel* doctrine, originating in the ethics of Kant, the thought of Wintrich and Dürig's conceptualisation, has become a prevailing pattern of interpretation, and has not to date been displaced in its entirety by another interpretive approach to the meaning of human dignity violations.[4]

    … The horizon of understanding cannot be limited either by what the writer originally had in mind or by the horizon of the person to whom the text was originally addressed.'); See also, G Binder and R Weisberg, *Literary Criticism of Law* (Princeton, New Jersey, Princeton University Press, 2000) 133 ('Gadamer insists that because his hermeneutics both implicates and depends upon the interpreter, it should not be seen as a *method*. Instead, it is a challenging process of *Bildung* or self-cultivation.'); See, on the literary approach, also, ibid 4 ('Literature can offer a complex, multilayered experience that transcends rigid categories, alerting us to the plurality and dynamism of the meanings we attach to social life.'); ibid 5 ('[W]e may identify "the literary" narrowly with the work of a particular profession, or more broadly with imagination, complexity of perception, density of meaning, and the qualities of dramatic and aesthetic interest. If we conceive "the literary" in these broader terms, it becomes a meaning-making function that pervades social life.'); ibid 16 ('associations evoked when we are exhorted to experience law in a more literary way').

4   G Dürig, 'Der Grundrechtssatz von der Menschenwürde – Entwurf eines praktikablen Wertsystems der Grundrechte aus Art. 1 Abs. I in Verbindung mit Art. 19 Abs. II des Grundgesetzes' (1956) 81 *AöR* 117, 127; See M Herdegen, 'Art. 1 Abs. 1', in T Maunz & G Dürig (eds),. *Kommentar* (looseleaf collection since 1958, Munich, C.H. Beck, May 2009 (55.)) para 36; cp, A Schopenhauer, *The World as Will and Idea*, 7th edn, Vol. 1, trans. RB Haldane and J Kemp (London, Kegan Paul, Trench Trübner & Co., 1909; Project Gutenberg EBook 38427, release date: December 27, 2011) 447, 450 ('This proposition, so unweariedly repeated by all the Kantians, "Man must always be treated as an end, never as a means," certainly sounds significant, and is therefore a very suitable proposition for those who like to have a formula which saves them all further thought; but looked at in the light, it is an exceedingly vague, indefinite assertion, which reaches its aim quite indirectly, requires to be explained, defined,

In the text of the *Aviation Security Act Case*, objectification language operates on the borderline between the literal and the non-literal, metaphor and *le mot juste*.[5]

This opinion expresses in a virtually undisguised manner (*bringt geradezu unverhohlen zum Ausdruck*) that the victims of such an incident are no longer perceived as human beings but as part of an object, a view by which they themselves become objects (*dass die Opfer eines solchen Vorgangs nicht mehr als Menschen wahrgenommen, sondern als Teil einer Sache gesehen und damit selbst verdinglicht werden*). This cannot be reconciled with the Basic Law's concept of the human being and with the idea of the human being as a creature whose nature it is to exercise self-

---

and modified in every case of its application, and, if taken generally, is insufficient, meagre, and moreover problematical.'); J Wintrich, 'Über Eigenart und Methode verfassungsgerichtlicher Rechtsprechung' in A Süsterhenn (ed), *Verfassung und Verwaltung in Theorie und Wirklichkeit: Festschrift für Wilhelm Laforet* (Munich, Isar-Verlag, 1952) 235 ff ('[M]uß aber der Mensch auch in der Gemeinschaft und ihrer Rechtsordnung immer "Zweck an sich selbst" (Kant) bleiben, darf er nie zum bloßen Mittel eines Kollektivs, zum bloßen Werkzeug oder zum rechtlosen Objekt eines Verfahrens herabgewürdigt werden.'; 'Human beings must remain also in society and in a legal order always "ends in themselves" (Kant), and may never be degraded to bare means of a collectivity, to bare tools or right-less objects of a procedure.'); See P Schaber, *Instrumentalisierung und Würde* (Paderborn, Mentis, 2010); On the dominance of the *Objektformel* as a pattern of practice of the law of human dignity, see BVerfGE 9, 89 (95) (1959) (*Gehör bei Haftbefehl,* hearing on arrest warrant); BVerfGE 27, 1 (6) (1969) (*Mikrozensus,* micro-census); BVerfGE 28, 386 (391) (1970) (*Kurzzeitige Freiheitsstrafe,* short-term imprisonment); BVerfGE 45, 187 (228) (1977) (*Lebenslange Freiheitsstrafe,* life imprisonment); BVerfGE 50, 166 (175) (1979) (*Ausweisung I*; expulsion of alien convicted for illegal possession of weapons); BVerfGE 50, 205 (215) (1979) (*Strafbarkeit von Bagatelldelikten,* criminalisation of minor offenses); BVerfGE 57, 250 (275) (1981) (*V-Mann,* right to fair trial of the accused and limited reliability of anonymous informant as witness of 'hearsay'); BVerfGE 72, 105 (116) (1986) (life imprisonment); BVerfGE 87, 209 (228) (1992) (*Tanz der Teufel,* dance of the devil); BVerfGE 109, 279 (312f.) (2004) (*Großer Lauschangriff,* wiretapping); BVerfGE 117, 71 (89) (2006) (*Strafrestaussetzung.* suspension of sentence); BVerfGE 131, 268 (286ff.) (2012) (*Sicherungsverwahrung,* preventive detention).

5 S Greenblatt, *Renaissance Self-Fashioning: From More to Shakespeare* (Chicago, University of Chicago Press, 1980) 4 ('[T]he facts of life are less artless than they look, ... both particular cultures and the observers of these cultures are inevitably drawn to a metaphorical grasp of reality.').

determination in freedom [cited case omitted], and who therefore may not be made a mere object of state action.[6]

Harm as 'humiliation, branding, persecution, outlawing',[7] in other words 'injuring and annihilating'[8] human beings, is not the only conceivable kind of violence. Objectification is violence against human beings when they are forced into 'roles in which they no longer recognise themselves ... betray not only commitments but their own substance' or 'carry out actions that will destroy every possibility of action'.[9] The experience of deadlock consists in being subsumed under a totality from which there is no escape.[10] Objectification language vividly evokes the distortion of human beings as subjects, in particular, legal subjects. Deadlock renders passengers and crew 'objects not only of the perpetrators of the crime' but also of the state, 'which in such a situation resorts to the measures provided in §14 sec. 3 LuftSiG' thereby effectively treating them, argued the FCC, 'as mere objects of its rescue operation for the protection of others'.[11]

The assumption that the state shooting down the aircraft to save the lives of those on the ground totalises the passengers and the crew on board, ignores their status as subjects 'endowed with dignity and inalienable rights', and objectifies and deprives them of their rights begs scrutiny. The elusive passive voice framing, 'are no longer perceived as human beings but as part of an object', effectively conceals who the self charged with viewing the other as 'part of an object' is. This observation affirms the need for critical reflection on whether the state as the self with authori-

---

6   BVerfGE 115, 118 (158 f).
7   ibid (153).
8   E Levinas, *Totality and Infinity—An Essay on Exteriority*, trans. A Lingis (Pittsburgh, Pa., Duquesne University Press, 1969) 21.
9   ibid.
10   ibid 223 ('[V]iolence bears upon only a being both graspable and escaping every hold.'); John Wild, 'Introduction' in Levinas, *Totality and Infinity—An Essay on Exteriority*, trans. A Lingis (Pittsburgh, Pa., Duquesne University Press, 1969) 18 ('We do not *need* to know the other person (or thing) as he is in himself, and we shall never know him apart from acting with him. But unless we *desire* this, and go on trying, we shall never escape from the subjectivism of our systems and the objects they bring before us to categorize and manipulate.').
11   BVerfGE 115, 118 (154).

ty over the meaning comprised in legal language games is adequately depicted.[12]

III. Inviolability as a Tautological Proposition

The inviolability (*Unantastbarkeit*) of human dignity demands abstention from balancing (*Unabwägbarkeit*).[13] The linguistic-analytical pattern of inviolability is tautology;[14] the constitutional guarantee of inviolability essentially denotes that the dignity that human beings have by virtue of being human is absolutely guaranteed.[15] The tautological proposition of in-

---

12 R Alexy, *A Theory of Legal Argumentation—The Theory of Rational Discourse as Theory of Legal Justification*, trans. R Adler and N MacCormick (Oxford, Oxford University Press, 1989) 50 (characterizes moral and legal discourse language games *sui generis*).

13 H Dreier, 'Art. 1 Abs. 1' in id (ed), *Grundgesetz. Kommentar*, 3rd edn, Vol. 1, (Tübingen, Mohr Siebeck, 2013) para 46.

14 See the *Abortion II Case,* BVerfGE 88, 203 (252) ('Wo menschliches Leben existiert, kommt ihm Menschenwürde zu (vgl. BVerfGE 39, 1 (41)). Diese Würde des Menschseins liegt auch für das ungeborene Leben im Dasein um seiner selbst willen.' (Where human life exists, it is entitled to human dignity [*Abortion I Case* cited]. This dignity of being human lies also for unborn life in its existence for its own sake.)).

15 FCC jurisprudence recognizes both the prescriptive and descriptive character of the inviolability proposition under Art. 1 sec. 1 GG: human beings cannot be deprived of their human dignity, but their claim to respect springing from the guarantee can be violated. See BVerfGE 87, 209 (228) (1992) (*Tanz der Teufel*); *cf* Dreier, 'Art. 1 Abs. 1', para 128 (Dreier concurs with the dominant view in legal literature that the proposition of inviolability is prescriptive rather than descriptive); See also B Giese, *Das Würde-Konzept. Eine normfunktionale Explikation des Begriffs Würde in Art. 1 Abs. 1 GG* (Berlin, Duncker & Humblot, 1975) 46; W Krawietz, 'Gewährt Art. 1 Abs. 1 GG dem Menschen ein Grundrecht auf Achtung und Schutz seiner Würde?' in D Weber und H Wilke (eds), *Gedächtnisschrift für Friedrich Klein* (Munich, Franz Vahlen, 1977) 255 f.; H Müller-Dietz, *Menschenwürde und Strafvollzug* (Berlin, de Gruyter, 1994) 8; H Hofmann, 'Die versprochene Menschenwürde' in Hofmann, *Verfassungsrechtliche Perspektiven: Aufsätze aus den Jahren 1980-1994* (Tübingen, Mohr, 1995) 111 fn 36; 114 (Hofmann's thesis departs from an understanding of human dignity as a 'Seinsgegebenheit', a quality or characteristic of the individual).

violability does not correspond to a picture of reality,[16] because it 'allows every possible state of affairs'.[17]

> (4.462) ... In the tautology the conditions of agreement with the world—the presenting relations—cancel one another, so that it stands in no presenting relation to reality.
>
> (4.463) ... Tautology leaves to reality the whole infinite logical space; ...
>
> (4.464) The truth of tautology is certain, of propositions possible, of contradiction impossible. (Certain, possible, impossible: here we have an indication of that gradation which we need in the theory of probability.)[18]

The proposition of the law of human dignity is tautological and, precisely for that reason, holds true 'for all the truth-possibilities'.[19] Wittgenstein adds, '[t]he proposition shows what it says, the tautology and the contradiction that they say nothing'.[20] The tautology is unconditionally true, that is, 'has no truth-conditions' and 'without sense', still 'not senseless'.[21] Tautology 'is part of a symbolism'[22] and does not portray reality. Propositions of logic 'show in tautologies' the logic of the world.[23] Along similar lines, the '*absolute Metapher*' (absolute metaphor) characterisation of human dignity sheds light on how independence from reality can be tantamount to non-requirement of justification.[24]

> (5.142) A tautology follows from all propositions: it says nothing.[25]

As elucidating as this insight may be, the strictly linguistic-analytical reading of the law of human dignity in light of Ludwig Wittgenstein's propositions on tautology in the *Tractatus Logico-Philosophicus* cannot take legal

---

16 L Wittgenstein, *Tractatus Logico-Philosophicus,* ed. and transl. CK Ogden (London, Kegan Paul, Trench, Trubner & Co., New York, Harcourt, Brace & Company, 1922; Project Gutenberg EBook 5740, release date: October 22, 2010) (4.462).
17 ibid.
18 ibid (4.462), (4.463), (4.464).
19 ibid (4.46).
20 ibid (4.461).
21 ibid (4.4611).
22 ibid (4.4611).
23 ibid (6.22).
24 S Baer, 'Menschenwürde zwischen Recht, Prinzip und Referenz—Die Bedeutung von Enttabuisierungen' (2005) 4 *DZPhil* 571, 573.
25 Wittgenstein, *Tractatus* (1922) (5.142); See also Dreier, 'Art. 1 Abs. 1' para 55 (The *Objektformel* receives criticism for introducing a *Leerformel* (empty formula) or *leere Hülse* (empty shell).); ibid (Dreier observes the tautological structure of the *Objektformel*, noticing 'Menschen*würde* ist verletzt, wenn der Mensch herab*gewürdigt* wird' (human dignity is violated, when human beings are degraded or stripped of their human dignity), and associating this structure with the ascertainment of emptiness.).

actors too far with their reasoning. The law of human dignity has more than merely symbolic impact as practiced in FCC jurisprudence and as discussed in German legal doctrine. If legal actors only relied on the tautological proposition of inviolability to guarantee respect that human dignity is respected and protected, it is highly likely that the practice of that law would prove irrelevant to reality, understood here as the world of lived experience.[26]

As a linguistic and doctrinal tool of critical reflection, the *Objektformel* materialises the possibility of objectification at the level of language and meaning and, thus, effectuates a break with the tautological framing, only to assess whether inviolability is actually guaranteed. Whether the images springing from the application of the *Objektformel* are those of conventional and evident human dignity violations, or the imprint of 'all sorts of subjective valuations'[27] in an empty formula is of little importance here; for this hermeneutic and literary approach the crucial observation is that objectification language triggers confrontations with the world that extends before the constitutional judge.

Consistently with the all-permeating validity of the law of human dignity as the critical lens through which state actors look at the world, from a linguistic-analytical perspective, objectification language would have no place within the boundaries of FCC legal language games.[28] The appearance of objectification language in the sharing of a world that originates in the inviolability of human dignity[29], Art 1 sec 1 GG might seem paradoxical: the *Objektformel* materialises the possibility of objectification within legal language games as language and literary meaning, despite the fact that the vocabulary of the Basic Law forecloses such propositions, while, at the same time, as doctrine, prohibits the treatment of human beings as objects.[30]

---

26 Levinas, *Totality and Infinity* (1969), Wild, 'Introduction' 12.
27 Dreier 'Art. 1 Abs. 1'.
28 The tautological pattern of the proposition of inviolability ('*Unantastbarkeit*') corresponds and accounts for the all-permeating validity of the law of human dignity. Wittgenstein notes, in Wittgenstein, *Tractatus*, (4.463) 'Tautology leaves to reality the whole infinite logical space'.
29 Levinas, *Totality and Infinity* (1969), Wild, 'Introduction' 245 (The introduction of objectification language attests to the ethical choice of the speaking self to welcome the stranger.).
30 BVerfGE 115, 118 (153).

A hermeneutic and literary approach to the *Objektformel* might show how this doctrine opens up a plane of dissensus, an intersubjective space, and sets in motion a process of critical reflection within the totality structure of legal language games.[31] Critical reflection is essential for the de facto assessment and sound justification of violation or non-violation assertions; the Court as the speaking self is expected to satisfy those in order to demonstrate it has accorded human beings involved in the case a responsible answer.

IV. The Objektformel and the Ladder Metaphor[32]

An analogy can be drawn between the *Objektformel* as a tool of critical reflection and the ladder metaphor in Wittgenstein's *Tractatus*. Once the reflexive purpose of *Objektformel* language is fulfilled, this tool shall be discarded. Practicing the *Objektformel* triggers critical reflection and can stir real conversation and reinterpretation.[33] The literary meaning introduced thereby into human dignity legal language games shakes the certainty nurtured by the tautological form of the inviolability proposition and creates anew an intersubjective space[34].

Sharing, as the speaking self vis-à-vis the other, a world within which the risk of objectification manifests in propositions—that is, in linguistic-analytical terms, facts—breaks with the tautology of inviolability.[35] The *Objektformel* doctrine may hence be seen as a means of egress from the totality that the constitutional guarantee of inviolability institutes, making possible the all-important confrontation with the world of lived experience.[36] Delving into the world of lived experience is a fundamental inclination of infinitisers in Emmanuel Levinas' *Totality and Infinity*.[37] To be sure, totality traits on the one hand and gateways to infinity on the other

---

31 S Corcoran, 'Editor's Introduction' in J Rancière, *Dissensus on Politics and Aesthetics*, ed. and trans. S Corcoran (London and New York, Continuum International Publishing Group, 2010) 2 (Dissensus 'consists in the demonstration of a certain *impropriety* which disrupts the identity').
32 Wittgenstein, *Tractatus* (1922) (6.54).
33 Levinas, *Totality and Infinity* (1969), Wild, 'Introduction' 13.
34 Levinas, *Totality and Infinity* (1969), 290; See also Gadamer, *Truth and Method* (2004) 390 ('fusion of horizons').
35 Wittgenstein, *Tractatus* (1922) (4.462), (4.463), (4.464).
36 Levinas, *Totality and Infinity* (1969), Wild 'Introduction' 12.
37 ibid 17.

are equally important to the practice of the law of human dignity in a manner that ultimately serves human beings as ends, rather than, in autistic fashion, the law per se. Beyond the neutral, impartial, system of the eye and the field of sight simile, Levinas notes: '[T]he world as I originally experience it is not a logical system of this kind'.[38] Perceived as an initiator of critical reflection, the *Objektformel* may stand for the commitment of legal theory and doctrine to a constitutional order that, while framed as a totality structure, bespeaks infinity. The language introduced by the *Objektformel* doctrine causes a crack in the absolute guarantee of inviolability.

Correspondingly to a Wittgensteinian ladder, this doctrinal tool may guide legal actors, institutional and human at the same time, to ascend to an understanding; this ladder can then be discarded.[39] Wittgenstein metaphorically builds a ladder in his *Tractatus Logico-Philosophicus* to lead us to sense the limit of the world, that is, our world.[40] What cannot be expressed—hence nonsense if articulated—is so, using 'our world' perceived in terms of logic[41] as point of reference. Human dignity stands on the borderline between what can be 'said' and what cannot be 'said', but only 'shown' or sensed, thus constitutes the paradigmatic legal concept for exploring the notion of the limit. The colloquially put 'gut-feeling', which cannot be adequately expressed with words, vividly denotes how aspects of human dignity meaning can only be 'shown', and not 'said'. Propositions that grasp and utter 'nonsense', that is, 'say' what can only be 'shown', could, by analogy with a ladder, be put forward to assist our ascendance to an understanding. The ladder should then be discarded, argues Wittgenstein, to ensure the non-institution of a single such proposition that would totalize our understanding.

Unless the ladder is thrown away, the image of objectification would be instituted as *status quo* within the Court's legal language games. Confronting the possibility of objectification specifically on the part of the

---

38 ibid 12.
39 Wittgenstein, *Tractatus* (1922) (6.54).
40 ibid.
41 ibid (1.13) ('The facts in logical space are the world.'); This proposition intimates, for present purposes, first, how the world is conceived in philosophy of language and logic, that is, in purely linguistic-analytical terms, second, that the world of lived experience is larger than the world as the facts in logical space, and, ultimately, that the linguistic-analytical account alone does not suffice to portray the practice of the law of human dignity.

state is aligned with the commitment to guarantee de facto that the claim to respect for and protection of human dignity is not violated. A responsible answer to the other requires fuelling critical reflection with the findings of a reality check.[42] Reflection is key to sound justification as it renders the Court as the speaking self able to respond to the other, that is, the human being exposed to the constitutional judge's authority over meaning.

V. Portraying the Self

In the *Aviation Security Act Case,* state action is parallelised to the action of the perpetrators of the crime, not only apropos its consequences, but also re how innocent human beings on board the aircraft perceive of the attack.[43] Can shooting down an aircraft to avert an attack be analogised with using it as a weapon against the lives of human beings on the ground? Is, from the viewpoint of the passengers and the crew on board, an attack on the part of the state comparable to the actions of the perpetrators of the crime? From a hermeneutic perspective on law, the decisive question would be, who, the self or the other, or what, the action as such, is the critical determinant of meaning?[44]

Noticeably, the Court does not adequately and accurately portray the state as self in contrast to the perpetrators in the *Aviation Security Act Case,* who also act as self vis-à-vis the other, that is to say the innocent on board the aircraft. Why does the state shoot down the aircraft? How does the motivation of the state differ from that of the perpetrators, and does the Court concern itself with the disparity? How could the assertion that the victims of an attack are 'denied' the value of their lives on the part of the

---

42 Levinas, *Totality and Infinity* (1969), Wild 'Introduction' 14.
43 BVerfGE 115, 118 (154) ('... the state itself even encroaches on the lives of these defenseless people. Thus any procedure pursuant to § 14 sec 3 LuftSiG disregards, as has been explained, these people's positions as subjects in a manner that is incompatible with Art 1 sec 1 GG and disregards the ban on killing that results from it for the state.').
44 BVerfGE 115, 118 (157) ('[I]t is absolutely inconceivable under the applicability of Art 1 sec 1 GG to intentionally kill persons such as the crew and the passengers of a hijacked plane, who are in a situation that is hopeless for them, on the basis of a statutory authorisation which even accepts such imponderabilities if necessary.'); ibid (160) ('[T]he victims of an attack who are held in the aircraft are entitled to their lives being protected by the state.').

state be appreciated, given that de facto the state cannot protect the innocent passengers under the circumstances?

It bears noting that deferring to the viewpoint of the other for assessing the occurrence of objectification is attuned to phenomenological insights derived from *Totality and Infinity*. Instead of subsuming the other under a hermetically closed totality of meaning, the Court welcomes the other, attends to the experience of deadlock and gives precedence to the viewpoint of the other as the bearer of human dignity and fundamental rights.[45] The elusive passive voice framing in the above excerpt, 'that the victims of such an incident are no longer perceived as human beings but as part of an object', effectively conceals who the self-charged with viewing the other as 'part of an object' is. This, on the face of it, benign observation affirms the need for reflection on the adequacy and accuracy of the portrayal of the self.

VI. Concluding Remarks

In practicing the law of human dignity in the *Aviation Security Act Case,* the FCC associated 'being used as a means to save others' with being treated as an object. The leap is not self-evidently justified; unless reflected on, interpreted in light of context, and grounded on sound arguments, that leap might develop the totalising effects of oversimplification. Sound justification is material to the responsible practice of the tautological proposition. Responsibility as ability to respond to the other concerns both responsibility for cultivating that ability and the demonstration of soundness in the speaking self's reasoning. Critical reflection requires distancing as well as external to the legal language game points of reference or sources of insights.[46] The Court, in confronting the world of lived experience to assess whether objectification has eventuated, resorts to its field of sight that encompasses the subtotal of the legal language game. In the *Aviation Security Act Case,* the inclusion of a range of viewpoints on the nature of imponderabilities arising under the circumstances is evidence of such extroversion. The requirement of a responsible answer denotes the addressee, the other; an indicator of ability to respond is the tailoring of

---

45   Levinas, *Totality and Infinity* (1969) 300, 305.
46   cf Gadamer, *Truth and Method* (2004) 392 ('Writing is self-alienation.').

the answer to the facts of *ad hoc* cases.[47] The *Objektformel* doctrine calls, from a hermeneutic and literary perspective, for the demonstration of the speaking self's ability to respond to the other, responsibility.[48]

---

47   BVerfGE 115, 118 (162) ('situations are conceivable in which it can be reliably ascertained that the only people on board an aircraft which is involved in an aerial incident are offenders participating in such an incident, and in which it can also be assumed with sufficient certainty that a mission pursuant to §14 sec. 3 LuftSiG will not have consequences that are detrimental to the lives of people on the ground. Whether such a factual situation exists depends on the assessment of the situation in the individual case.').

48   Levinas, *Totality and Infinity* (1969), Wild 'Introduction' 14.

Balancing Human Dignity: Human Dignity as a Principle and as a Constitutional Right

Nils Teifke

In the field of human dignity the German Federal Constitutional Court has established that, in accordance with the principle of proportionality, no balancing is to take place. Does this mean that human dignity in legal practice is absolute — is not, in other words, amenable to balancing?

In the following (I.) the thesis of absoluteness shall be discussed first, followed by (II.) some considerations with respect to the structure of the norm of human dignity; (III.) the relationship between absoluteness and application leads, finally, to (IV.) considerations about the abstract priority of human dignity.

From this author's perspective, human dignity is not only a foundational value but also a constitutional right. It is doubtful whether these distinct functions can be combined in any simple way. In constitutional systems without a comprehensive catalogue of rights, dignity often serves as a generic conceptual source from which more specific rights like privacy are drawn.[1] Here, dignity is a very broad concept. By contrast, the definition of human dignity as a constitutional right has to be narrow. If not, one is in danger of having dignity drawn into the area of conflicting rights and balancing. On the other hand, if one defines dignity so narrowly that there is no need to balance it against other rights, it loses the broad meaning that makes it so useful as a foundational value.

Owing to this dilemma, I have tried to combine the different functions so that human dignity as a constitutional right with a narrow definition does not obscure or inappropriately constrain human dignity as a foundational value. I arrived at the result that in the application of law, the constitutional right of human dignity can be based on the broad meaning of human dignity as a foundational value.

---

1   cf J Habermas, 'Das Konzept der Menschenwürde und die realistische Utopie der Menschenrechte' in id, *Zur Verfassung Europas. Ein Essay* (Berlin, Suhrkamp, 2011) 16.

I. The Thesis of Absoluteness

Article 1(1), clause 1, of the German Basic Law engenders the impression of absoluteness: 'Human dignity is inviolable'. This opening sentence of the German Basic Law has scarcely given rise, over the years, to discussion. During the last few years, however, a debate about human dignity has been undertaken, and it has reached a breadth and depth that could hardly have been anticipated earlier. In view of the ever-greater intensity of the discussion, one can speak of a controversy over human dignity (This discussion of human dignity can be called a controversy in view of its ever-increasing intensity). Essentially, the controversy concerns the question of whether human dignity is absolute or amenable to balancing. If human dignity is absolute, then there is no way to limit it. According to this prevailing opinion, the impossibility of limiting the first sentence of the German Basic Law means that an infringement of human dignity is, at the same time, a violation of it. Therefore, an infringement of article 1(1), clause 1, Basic Law can never be justified. Thus the common practice of invoking the triad, consisting of first, the protected area, second, the infringement, and third, the limit[2] in the examination of constitutional rights, has no application to human dignity.[3]

Under ordinary circumstances an infringement of a constitutional right does not automatically mean a violation. There is a violation of a constitutional right only if the infringement cannot reasonably be justified. Whether an infringement of a constitutional right is justified can only be established definitively if the reasons justifying the infringement have been balanced against the reasons on behalf of non-infringement by means of a test of proportionality. Balancing can therefore be characterised as the core of the examination of constitutional rights. Human dignity, however, is to be withdrawn from the balancing process given the absolute protection it affords. The assertion that human dignity is capable of being balanced is not compatible with the thesis of absoluteness, according to which human dignity enjoys priority over all other constitutional principles and in all circumstances. Again, according to the thesis of absolute-

---

2 On the advantages of the triadic structure of the examination of constitutional rights, see R Alexy, *A Theory of Constitutional Rights* (Julian Rivers trans, Oxford, Oxford University Press, 2002) (1st edn in German 1985) 198.

3 cf K Möller, 'Balancing and the Structure of Constitutional Rights' (2007) 5 *ICON* 452, 467.

ness, human dignity cannot be limited.[4] Since every infringement of human dignity is at the same time a violation of it, every infringement in the protected area is already unconstitutional.[5] Thus it follows from the thesis of absoluteness that human dignity is not to be compromised under any circumstances and is not subject to balancing. Against this background, one sees that there is a relationship of exclusiveness between absoluteness and balancing.[6] If the structure of the norm respecting human dignity is our concern, what can be said on the matter by an appeal to the theory of principles?

In his theory of principles, Robert Alexy distinguishes between rules and principles and between two forms of the application of law: subsumption and balancing. The typical framework for the application of rules in the law is subsumption, and the typical framework for the application of principles in the law is balancing. According to Alexy's definition, 'principles are norms which require that something be realized to the greatest extent possible given the legal and factual possibilities'.[7] Principles are *'optimization requirements'*[8] and always have a prima facie character. 'By contrast, *rules* are norms which are always either fulfilled or not.'[9] They are *definitive* requirements and contain a decision about what is to happen within the realm of the legally and factually possible. Principles, by contrast, lack the inherent resources to determine their own extent in the light of competing principles and what is factually possible.[10] Principles are not

---

4   cf inter alii HD Jarass, 'Art. 1' in HD Jarass and B Pieroth, *Grundgesetz für die Bundesrepublik Deutschland. Kommentar*, 9th edn (Munich, C.H. Beck, 2007) para 16; W Höfling, 'Die Unantastbarkeit der Menschenwürde' (1995) *Juristische Schulung* 857, 859.
5   B Pieroth and B Schlink, *Grundrechte. Staatsrecht II*, 23th edn (Heidelberg, C.F.Müller, 2007) para 365; P Kunig, 'Art. 1' in I von Münch and P Kunig (eds), *Grundgesetz-Kommentar*, Vol. 1, 5th edn (Munich, C.H. Beck, 2000) para 4.
6   On the definition of an absolute right, see A Gewirth, 'Are There Any Absolute Rights?' (1981) 31 *The Philosophical Quarterly* 1, 2: 'A right is *absolute* when it cannot be overridden in any circumstances, so that it can never be justifiably infringed and it must be fulfilled without any exceptions'.
7   Alexy, *A Theory of Constitutional Rights* (2002) 47.
8   ibid 47.
9   ibid 48.
10   ibid 57. According to this definition, norms which contain only partially a decision about what is to happen within the realm of the legally and factually possible, are not principles but rules. Differently JR Sieckmann, *Regelmodelle und Prinzipienmodelle des Rechtssystems* (Baden-Baden, Nomos, 1990) 69,

only capable of being balanced but, indeed, stand at every turn in need of balancing. According to Alexy, every norm is either a rule or a principle.[11] Based on these premises, one can establish that article 1(1), clause 1 of the Basic Law is either amenable to balancing and stands also in need of balancing or is not amenable to balancing. Which of these is the case depends on whether the norm in question is a principle or a rule. This result seems to confirm the thesis of a relation of exclusiveness between absoluteness and balancing. The decisive point is the question of whether the normative sentence of article 1(1), clause 1, of the Basic Law expresses a rule or a principle. If it expresses a principle, can it be an absolute principle? A principle with absolute validity would enjoy priority in every case and in all circumstances. Its absoluteness would seem to preclude balancing. Since, however, a principle stands in need of balancing, the question can then be stated as follows: Is human dignity, representing an absolute value, to be understood according to the theory of principles as a rule rather than as a principle?

II. The Structure of the Norm of Human Dignity

If human dignity is not amenable to balancing, then, according to the norm-theoretic distinction at work here, it can only be a rule.

Alexy assumes that article 1(1), clause 1, of the Basic Law contains two norms, a rule of human dignity and a principle of human dignity.[12] This possibility exists owing to the general double-aspect of constitutional-

---

according to his distinction norms which contain no or only partially a decision about what is to happen within the realm of the legally and factually possible, are always principles, whereas norms which contain a complete decision are always rules. Again differently on the separate content of decision of rules and principles M Borowski, *Grundrechte als Prinzipien*, 2nd edn (Baden-Baden, Nomos, 2007) 101–04. According to the correct opinion of Borowski, a norm cannot be classified as rule or principle only on the basis of its content of decision. Though a norm which contains a complete decision is always a rule, and a norm without content of decision is always a principle, norms which contain only partially a decision could be either a rule or a principle (102). The deciding element is the dimension of weight (104).

11   Alexy, *A Theory of Constitutional Rights* (2002) 48.
12   ibid 64.

rights provisions.[13] Based on the distinction between a normative sentence and a norm which is constitutive for the semantic concept of a norm, constitutional-rights provisions are, in simple terms, the sentences contained in the text of the Constitution which express constitutional-rights norms. The double-aspect of a constitutional-rights provision consists in the fact that it can issue a principle as well as a rule.[14] Thus, a constitutional-rights provision has not merely issued a principle but also a rule whenever it makes some sort of decision relative to the requirements of competing principles.[15] The directly issued rule is usually an incomplete rule, for it is not applicable without some balancing test:

> To the extent that it is incomplete in this sense, constitutional adjudication must fall back on the level of principle with all its uncertainty. But this does not alter the fact that the decisions, to the extent that they apply, are to be taken seriously. The requirement to take seriously the decisions made in constitutional rights provisions, that is, the text of the Constitution, is one part of the postulate of the binding nature of the Constitution.[16]

In this sense, the formula of the inviolability of human dignity and the thesis that every infringement of human dignity necessarily counts as a violation of it, are representative of the level of rule of human dignity.

Alexy arrives at the conclusion that the principle of human dignity is not an absolute principle. He writes: 'If there are any absolute principles, then the definition of a principle must be emended'.[17] The reason for this is that if there are competing principles, the solution to their conflict consists in establishing not an *absolute* but a *conditional relation of priority* among the principles, in light of the circumstances of the case. The theory of competing principles would be inapplicable for absolute principles, for one cannot set any limit to them. Following Alexy, the reason for the impression of absoluteness rather arises from the fact

> that there are two human dignity norms, a human dignity rule and a human dignity principle, along with the fact that there is a whole host of conditions under which

---

13   On Alexy's definition of constitutional-rights provisions, see ibid 32: 'constitutional rights provisions are the statements formulated in articles 1 to 19 and those which guarantee the individual rights contained in articles 20(4), 33, 38, 101, 103, and 104 Basic Law'.
14   ibid 83.
15   ibid. In case of incomplete decisions, the issued norm is not necessarily a rule. cf above, n 10. The norm is only then a rule if it is not itself amenable to balancing, cf Borowski, *Grundrechte als Prinzipien* (2007) 103 f.
16   Alexy, *A Theory of Constitutional Rights* (2002) 83.
17   ibid 62.

we can say with a high degree of certainty that the human dignity principle takes precedence.[18]

The impression of absoluteness arises from a whole host of conditions under which one can say, effectively with certainty, that the principle of human dignity enjoys priority over all other principles, and ought not to be doubted here. The following objection, however, can be made to the existence of two norms of human dignity, a rule of human dignity and a principle of human dignity: The rule of human dignity, absolute in itself, would not be capable of being subsumed. Rather, the rule is dependent on the principle of human dignity, for the content of the rule of human dignity cannot be determined without balancing. If the rule of human dignity is supposed to be an independent norm, it ought to have the form of a rule under which one state of affairs or another can be subsumed. But how is such a subsumption to be understood if it is not clear what resources article 1(1), clause 1, of the Basic Law has for determining its own extent? Here, one might pose the question of how a violation of human dignity can be determined. A decision on the scope of human dignity must necessarily precede the determination of a violation of human dignity. Since the concept of human dignity is indeterminate, the rule of human dignity has, semantically, an open-structure. This area of open-structure gives rise to the need for still more discretion with respect to the decision concerning human dignity. In stating the circumstances, the possibility of balancing automatically arises.[19] For the purpose of a decision on the scope of the rule of human dignity, the principle of human dignity is balanced against other principles. The preference relation between the principle of human dignity and other principles competing with it determines the content of the rule of human dignity.[20] Therefore, the rule of human dignity is dependent on the principle of human dignity and has no independent meaning.[21] This finding calls into question the existence of two norms of hu-

---

18 ibid 64.
19 ibid 63. This is exemplified by comments of the German Federal Constitutional Court in the telephone tapping case, *Decisions of the German Federal Constitutional Court*, vol 30, 1 (BVerfGE 30, 1, 25): 'as regards the principle of the inviolability of human dignity laid down in article 1 Basic Law ... it all depends on establishing the circumstances under which human dignity might be violated. Clearly this cannot be stated in general terms, but only in the light of the concrete case'.
20 Alexy, *A Theory of Constitutional Rights* (2002) 64.
21 Differently C Goos, *Innere Freiheit. Eine Rekonstruktion des grundgesetzlichen Würdebegriffs* (Göttingen, Vandenhoeck & Ruprecht, 2011) 165.

man dignity—two norms that are both ostensibly established by the text of the Constitution. Thus, the rule of human dignity can only be a derivative constitutional-rights norm.

III. The Rule of Human Dignity as Derivative Constitutional-Rights Norm

One must distinguish between the norms directly established by the constitutional-rights provisions and the derivative constitutional-rights norms.[22] The latter are characterised as *derivative norms* because they are attributed to the norms directly expressed in the text of the Constitution. The directly expressed constitutional-rights norms are the bases of the derivative constitutional-rights norms. The latter stem from balancing principles following the Law of Competing Principles.[23] Therefore, according to Alexy, the following proposition applies:

> The result of every correct balancing of constitutional rights can be formulated in terms of a derivative constitutional rights norm in the form of a rule under which the case can be subsumed.[24]

According to Alexy, the rule of human dignity is a directly expressed constitutional-rights norm. That is, whereas the principle of human dignity is an *external-theoretic* right, the rule of human dignity might follow the *internal theory* of rights,[25] for the rule cannot be limited. According to the internal theory, no legal position can be limited, for it is not a matter of the right and its limit, but only the 'right which has a certain content'[26].

---

22   On the concept of derivative constitutional-rights norms, see Alexy, *A Theory of Constitutional Rights* (2002) 33–38.
23   The Law of Competing Principles goes: '(LCP) If principle $P1$ takes precedence over principle $P2$ in circumstances C: ($P1$ **P** $P2$) C, and if $P1$ gives rise to legal consequences Q in circumstances C, then a valid rule applies which has C as its protasis and Q as its apodosis: $C\ 5\ Q$' (Alexy, *A Theory of Constitutional Rights* (2002) 54).
24   Alexy, *A Theory of Constitutional Rights* (2002) 56.
25   On the distinction between 'the internal and the external theory', see Alexy, *A Theory of Constitutional Rights* (2002) 178 f; Borowski, *Grundrechte als Prinzipien* (2007) 34–39; id, 'Limiting Clauses: On the Continental European Tradition of Special Limiting Clauses and the General Limiting Clause of Art 52 (1) Charter of Fundamental Rights of the European Union' (2007) 1 *Legisprudence* 197, 202.
26   Alexy, *A Theory of Constitutional Rights* (2002) 179; cf Borowski, *Grundrechte als Prinzipien* (2007) 37.

According to the 'internal theory' of rights (*Innentheorie*), there is simply a right with its extension, whereas according to 'the external theory' of rights (*Außentheorie*), one can distinguish between the 'right in itself' (prima facie-right or *Recht an sich*) and the 'right as limited' (definitive right or *eingeschränktes Recht*). The 'right as limited' is what is left of the 'right in itself' once the limitation is in place.[27]

According to Alexy's conception, human dignity can be characterised as an external-theoretic right with an internal-theoretic concession to the text of the Constitution. Since balancing, however, takes place on the level of principles, the constitutionally immediate level of rules is not of concern.[28] Moreover, one can therefore consider the rule of human dignity as an absolute right, for it, in view of its semantic open-structure, stands in need of no limitation. Alexy argues:

> The advantage of this way of putting it is that on one hand no limiting clause needs to be read into the human dignity norm of the constitution, but that on the other hand the human dignity principle can still be balanced with other constitutional principles.[29]

Since absolute rights are rights that are not amenable to limitation, one can establish the following parallel distinctions:

> The above-mentioned distinction between rights according to the internal theory and the external theory is parallel to the distinction between 'absolute rights' and 'limitable rights'.[30]

In light of what has been asserted above, one can pose the question whether Alexy's conception of the existence of two directly expressed norms of human dignity is compatible with the theory of principles in general. An alternative construction here would simply be one constitutional-rights norm of human dignity with a double-aspect.

---

27 Borowski, 'Limiting Clauses' 202.
28 As regards the level of rules, one has to distinguish between the constitutionally immediate level of rules and the constitutionally mediate level of rules following from the Law of Competing Principles. On this distinction, see Borowski, *Grundrechte als Prinzipien* (2007) 86, fn 104.
29 Alexy, *A Theory of Constitutional Rights* (2002) 64, fn 69.
30 Borowski 'Limiting Clauses' 204.

IV. Constitutional-Rights Norm with a Double-Aspect?

Constitutional-rights norms have a double-aspect when they combine the immediate level of rules and the level of principles. 'Such a combination of both levels arises through the incorporation in a constitutional rights norm of a principled, and hence to-be-balanced, limitation clause.'[31] In this way, the constitutional-rights norm can formally be a rule, but substantively, owing to the to-be-balanced limiting clause, a principle. Thus, with respect to the norm of human dignity, the rule of human dignity and the principle of human dignity also could be combined in a double-aspect constitutional-rights norm. What would be left would be a single norm of human dignity as external-theoretic right. This would be, according to the theory of principles, a consistent construction. Alexy, however, sticks to two norms of human dignity, so that no limiting clause need be read into the rule of human dignity. This is the only way to maintain the thesis of absoluteness and impossibility of any limitation of human dignity, for it corresponds exclusively to an internal-theoretic structure of the norm of human dignity. According to a purely external-theoretic conception of human dignity, the thesis of absoluteness has a merely declarative significance. Should human dignity be absolute at the level of principles then it can only be an absolute principle. The concept of an absolute principle, however, is contrary to the definition of the concept of principles, here taken as a point of departure. The theory of competing principles would not be applicable to an absolute principle.[32] In the case of competing principles, there is no *absolute* relation of priority, which is established in light of the circumstances of the case, but only a *conditional* relation. Since absolute principles cannot be fulfilled to different degrees but can always only be fulfilled or not fulfilled, they are in actual fact rules—or at any rate the theory of competing principles does not lend itself to the distinction between absolute principles and rules.

One can establish that the conception of two norms of human dignity is appropriate to express the absoluteness of human dignity on the one hand, and the dependence of balancing on the absolute rule of human dignity on the other.[33] Nonetheless, on grounds of the dependence on the to-be-

---

31   Alexy, *A Theory of Constitutional Rights* (2002) 84.
32   ibid 62.
33   Another possibility in order to express this exceptional position of human dignity is to speak of a 'relative absoluteness', with this relative absoluteness re-

balanced principle, the rule of human dignity has no independent meaning. It has become clear that the content of the rule of human dignity cannot be determined without balancing. Thus, the abstract rule of human dignity can only be rendered concrete by balancing. The question is whether that rule can still be considered absolute.

V. Absoluteness and Application

An abstract norm must be rendered concrete in the course of its application. Thus, the abstract rule of human dignity also is applicable only if it is rendered concrete by means of further decisions. By contrast, a rule that falls under the principle of human dignity as result of balancing following the Law of Competing Principles is a concrete norm that lends itself to subsumption. However, conclusions cannot be drawn regarding the absoluteness of human dignity based on a concrete norm of this nature, for concrete norms address actual cases. A norm, however, is absolute only if it is applicable in all cases and under all circumstances. Hence, the thesis that only the concrete claim of dignity can be absolute[34] has to be rejected. Human dignity is not absolute if it is defined merely on the basis of (the) infringement.

The definition of human dignity on the basis of the infringement corresponds to the case law of the Federal Constitutional Court. The Federal Constitutional Court has not offered a positive definition of human dignity, but it has underlined 'the absolutely protected core area of private autonomy' in several cases.[35] An infringement of this absolutely protected core area is not allowed, for the core area is part of what is termed the inviolable human dignity. The Court writes:

> Even outweighing principles of the general interest cannot justify an infringement of the absolutely protected core area of private self-determination; balancing in accordance with the principle of proportionality does not take place.[36]

---

sulting from applying proportionality, see Borowski, *Grundrechte als Prinzipien* (2007) 280 f.

[34] M Herdegen, 'Art 1 (1)' in T Maunz and G Dürig, *Grundgesetz. Kommentar*, Vol. 1 (looseleaf collection, Munich, C.H. Beck) para 69. cf C Enders, *Die Menschenwürde in der Verfassungsordnung. Zur Dogmatik des Art. 1 GG* (Tübingen, Mohr Siebeck, 1997) 108.

[35] See BVerfGE 34, 238, 245,; 109, 279, 313.

[36] BVerfGE 34, 238, 245.

This sentence gives rise to problems of interpretation, as already pointed out by Alexy:

> Is it to be understood that the principle of human dignity takes precedence even in those cases when *from the perspective of constitutional law* a competing principle has greater weight? That would be illogical. To avoid this illogicality, the phrase 'outweighing principles of the general interest' must be understood to refer to interests which outweigh from some perspective which is not that of constitutional law. But then one can simply balance from the perspective of constitutional law and find the principle of human dignity more weighty.[37]

Therefore, nothing counts against balancing in accordance with the principle of proportionality.

If an infringement could not be justified under any circumstances as the thesis of absoluteness expresses it, then the area of protection would always be identical to the effective protection. If, however, they are not identical and if it is not the area of protection but only the effective protection or the definitive right that is defined by the concept of human dignity, then the thesis of absoluteness makes no sense. The thesis that the effective protection is absolute is redundant.[38] In this sense, the norm of human dignity does not differ from other norms, for the effective protection or the definitive right is always absolute.[39] If human dignity is really supposed to be absolute, it must be the area of protection that is absolute.

The fact that the area of protection of human dignity coincides in most cases with the definitive right does not mean that they coincide in all cases. At least, this fact engenders the impression of absoluteness of human dignity.

Finally, one can establish as a result that there is, according to the theory of principles, only one norm of human dignity, namely a principle of human dignity. It is not an absolute principle. Rather, it is, at least in theory, an external-theoretic and thus limitable right.

The absoluteness of the principle of human dignity is therefore only an apparent absoluteness. The impression of absoluteness arises, as already

---

37 Alexy, *A Theory of Constitutional Rights* (2002), fn 64.
38 cf D Jaber, *Über den mehrfachen Sinn von Menschenwürde-Garantien. Mit besonderer Berücksichtigung von Art. 1 Abs. 1 GG* (Frankfurt, Ontos, 2003) 315.
39 For a view that sees all rights as absolute, see R Shafer-Landau, 'Specifying Absolute Rights' (1995) 37 *Arizona Law Review* 209, 225. The programme of Shafer-Landau is 'specificationism' by reducing scope through the addition of exceptive clauses, while he argues against the prima facie and infringement theories.

mentioned, from the fact that there are a whole host of conditions according to which one can say, almost with certainty, that the principle of human dignity enjoys priority over all other principles.

VI. Abstract Priority of Human Dignity

The fact that there is a very large set of conditions of priority for the principle of human dignity, together with virtual certainty, namely that when these conditions obtain, the principle enjoys priority over competing principles,[40] is based on the fact that the abstract weight of human dignity reaches well beyond the abstract weight of other principles. This abstract weight of the principle of human dignity is so great that under ordinary circumstances, one can speak of protection in an absolute sense. Still, the thesis of absoluteness does not mean that in the most extreme circumstances the principle of human dignity cannot be outweighed.[41]

Finally, the question arises whether the abstract weight of human dignity is, at the very least, so great that one can speak of its enjoying an abstract *absolute* priority over all other principles. The assertion of an abstract priority of human dignity presupposes a priori that it is a principle. For in relations of preference—as well in abstract or unconditional relations of preference—there are only norms which have the dimension of weight. The dimension of weight is a classified criterion for the distinction between rules and principles.

An unconditional relation of preference is characterised by the fact that one of the competing principles always enjoys priority over the other independent of the circumstances of the particular case.[42] There are two possible types of preference:

(1) $P_1 \mathbf{P} P_2$: P_1 enjoys priority over P_2 under all circumstances.

(2) $P_2 \mathbf{P} P_1$: P_2 enjoys priority over P_1 under all circumstances.

---

40 cf Alexy, *A Theory of Constitutional Rights* (2002) 63.
41 Alexy, *A Theory of Constitutional Rights* (2002) 196, assumes in this context: 'The conviction that there must be rights which even in the most extreme circumstances are not outweighed – only such rights are genuinely absolute rights – may be held by any individual who is free to sacrifice himself for certain principles, but it cannot be maintained as a matter of constitutional law'.
42 Alexy, *A Theory of Constitutional Rights* (2002) 52; Borowski, *Grundrechte als Prinzipien* (2007) 81, fn 75.

By contrast, the abstract relation of preference gives evidence only about the question which principle has the greater abstract weight.[43] P_1 does not necessarily enjoy priority over P_2, although the abstract weight of P_1 is greater than the abstract weight of P_2.

From the perspective of constitutional law human dignity is the principle which has the greatest abstract weight.

Does this mean that there is now an abstract *absolute* priority of human dignity over all other principles? Contrary to the widely held opinion asserting the existence of an absolute priority, we have seen that according to the theory of principles there cannot be any absolute priority. Such a priority would have to be determined independently of the circumstances of an actual case. Since, however, there is no 'abstract balancing' in the application of law, applications of law are necessary, and the intensity of the infringements in this field of human dignity will always have to be determined concretely, the abstract priority of human dignity will have to be relativised in actual applications. Without any relation to a particular case, there is no competition and therefore no conflicting results. Thus, the weight of principles can never be determined absolutely.

Despite the great abstract weight of human dignity, the possibility remains that in an extreme case the significance of a competing principle is greater than the significance of human dignity. Therefore, one can speak of an abstract prima facie priority of human dignity. This prima facie priority is enhanced by virtue of the fact that in light of the great abstract weight of human dignity, a rule concerning the burden of proof will apply in its favour. This rule concerning the burden of proof does not, however, absolve one of the necessities of stating the set of conditions of priority in every actual case.

In summary, one can establish as a logical result that there is no absolute principle of human dignity. In addition, one can say that there is no rule of human dignity that is independent of the principle of human dignity and absolute. Rather, human dignity is simply a principle that is limitable but with a predominant abstract weight.

The absoluteness of human dignity exists only in the idea of the law. As an overarching principle, human dignity is both absolute as idea and relative in legal practice. This is the double character of human dignity, which combines the real with the ideal dimension.

---

43   Alexy, *A Theory of Constitutional Rights* (2002) 52, does not differentiate here between unconditional, 'abstract or absolute' relations of preference.

Dignity in Administrative Law: Judicial Deference in a Culture of Justification

David Dyzenhaus[1]

I. Introduction

My injection of 'dignity' into a talk on administrative law may seem a crude lure to entice you into the swamp of boredom,[2] especially when my alternative title was: 'The Healthy Boredom of Canadian Administrative Law'. However, this is not because a right to dignity is at home only in the constitutional law regime created by an entrenched bill of rights. Rather, to the extent that Canadian administrative law is boring, this is because the right to dignity is so entrenched in it that it is easy to forget not only its presence, but also that it animates the entire legal regime. For the right comes into clear view only on those occasions when an official makes an individual's life interesting in a bad way. In sum, the more boring the administrative law of a country, the healthier it is on the scale of dignity.

---

[1] This first draft of this article was written for the 23rd McDonald Lecture, given to the Faculty of Law of the University of Alberta in October of 2011. I thank the Centre for Constitutional Studies for the invitation and the hospitality, and all those present for the discussion. I also presented a draft at the conference 'The Concept of Human Dignity in a Transatlantic Perspective: Foundations and Variations', held at the Wissenschaftskolleg zu Berlin, and I thank all those who participated in that session. Finally, I thank Mark Walters for written comments on an earlier draft, Kenneth Chung for an initial, excellent memorandum on the topics to be canvassed, and Marcello Rodriguez Ferrere for extensive challenging comments on the penultimate draft.
This chapter appears by kind permission of the publishers of the Journal where it first appeared: (2012) 17 *Review of Constitutional Studies* 87-114.

[2] See A Scalia, 'Judicial Deference to Administrative Interpretations of the Law' (1989) *Duke Law Journal* 511: 'Administrative law is not for sissies—so you should lean back, clutch the sides of your chairs, and steel yourselves for a pretty dull lecture.'

I will argue that the right to dignity is more at home in administrative law than anywhere else.[3] This argument goes against the grain both of much constitutional scholarship and jurisprudence[4] where there is increasing interest in dignity as the foundational value and of recent work in political philosophy that invokes dignity as the right of rights—the right that grounds all others.

Note that dignity is a Roman law concept and in Roman law one's dignity varied according to one's official rank in society. For example, a punishment considered suitable for one class of society might not be considered suitable for another, because it would be an affront to the dignity of those in that class. Dignity thus might seem an unlikely basis for human rights, the rights that we supposedly have just because we are human beings. It becomes a more likely basis when we understand that one of the great transformative ideas in Western thought is that the law is no longer regarded as an instrument for sorting people into different classes of human beings, each with its legal and moral entitlements. Rather, human beings are regarded as members of just one class, and so every individual must be treated as a moral equal before the law.[5]

There are some obvious and difficult problems. First, the law is still used to draw morally and legally significant distinctions between classes, for example, children and adults, citizens and aliens, prisoners and those who enjoy full liberty. Second, there are persistent economic and other inequalities that make precarious a claim to equal human dignity, and which the law is often complicit in either creating or sustaining. Nevertheless, Western societies are officially committed to respecting dignity. And to point out that our societies fail to live up to an ideal is not a reason for abandoning it but rather a call for reform. So the commitment does make dignity seem more plausible as a basis for human rights.

My own tentative view is that we should resist the temptation to make dignity the right of rights. We should see it as the way of understanding our relationship as rights-bearing individuals with the state, a specifically

---

3   For a similar view from a leading US administrative lawyer, see JL Mashaw, *Due Process in the Administrative State* (New Haven, Yale University Press, 1985) 171 and ch 6.

4   Most prominently in Canada in *Law v Canada (Minister of Employment and Immigration)* [199] 1 SCR 497.

5   See J Waldron, 'Dignity, Rank, and Rights: The 2009 Tanner Lectures at UC Berkeley', available at papers.ssrn.com/sol3/papers.cfm?abstract_id=1461220, for illuminating discussion of such themes.

legal status most at home in administrative law. Put differently, the right to dignity is nothing more than the principle that individuals must be treated as equal before the law. Understood as such, dignity has a venerable presence in theories of constitutionalism.[6] But, as I will now argue, dignity is not merely a synonym for equality but a useful, perhaps even an essential, way of making precise the right to equality before law that is intrinsic to government according to law.[7]

II. Lucky to be Bored

My own attraction to administrative law started as a student in apartheid South Africa precisely because administrative law there was much too interesting—a direct result of the country's bad health on the dignity scale. I will spend some time on this topic, although my main theme is the boring nature of Canadian administrative law. For my claim is that we can only understand why we are lucky to be bored by administrative law if we appreciate when it becomes too interesting.

Apartheid laws created and maintained a system of radical inequality between white and black South Africans.[8] These laws were enacted by a Parliament that was, like the Canadian legislatures, modelled on the British parliamentary system, although there was the glaring difference that only whites had the vote. And just as in Canada prior to 1982, and the United Kingdom still today, there was no entrenched bill of rights that gave judges the authority to declare invalid laws inconsistent with rights. Legal challenges to the policy of apartheid laws could thus not challenge the laws themselves; they were confined to contesting the ways in which officials interpreted their authority to implement the laws.

---

6   Dicey said that it was the second meaning of the rule of law that all are equal before it: AV Dicey, *Introduction to the Study of the Law of the Constitution*, 8th edn (London, MacMillan, 1924) 189. For the most developed account of the rule of law in these terms, see TRS Allan, *Constitutional Justice: A Liberal Theory of the Rule of Law* (Oxford, Oxford University Press, 2001).

7   To limit the right to dignity in this way is not to preclude dignity playing a different role in constitutional law, as a value that informs in a quite general fashion the judicial interpretation of constitutionally protected rights. But I will not offer any opinion on that topic.

8   The basis of the argument in this section is set out in D Dyzenhaus, *Hard Cases in Wicked Legal Systems: Pathologies of Legality*, 2nd edn (Oxford, Oxford University Press, 2010).

Consider the Group Areas Act 1950, a statute that gave to officials the authority to set aside an area of South Africa for residence by one racial group and made it a criminal offence for members of other groups to reside there. The statute could not be challenged on the basis that it was invalid because of its violation of the right of all South Africans to equality since there was no bill of rights. However, when officials designated the biggest and best areas for white South Africans, their decisions could be and were challenged on the basis that the statute did not give officials the authority to act unreasonably by creating a situation of gross inequality for racial groups. In other words, unless the statute explicitly told officials that they did not have to respect the right of individuals to equal treatment in the way in which the law was administered, they were under a legal duty to respect that right.

This kind of challenge generally failed. On the few occasions when lower courts upheld the challenges, a higher court would overrule them. And a government that enjoyed the support of the great majority of its electorate could be counted on to use its grip on Parliament to ensure that the statute in question was amended to preclude further challenges, and that new statutes were drafted in ways that preempted similar challenges.

It might seem that the obvious conclusion to draw from the apartheid era is that a powerful government can use the law as an instrument of bad as well as good, to destroy the conditions necessary for human dignity as well as to create and sustain such conditions. But as a student in the late 1970s that conclusion did not seem altogether right to me. My intuition in this regard was largely responsible for a decision to remain a perpetual student of the law in a bid to explain why.

As I have indicated, administrative law provided the only basis in law for legal challenges to apartheid law. The principles of administrative law require in various ways that when officials decide how to implement the law that gives them authority to act in the name of the public, they make decisions that are reasonable in light of these principles. And it is an inherent feature of the judicial role that judges are entitled to review the officials' decisions to check that they are indeed reasonable in this light. Even when judges have no authority to declare a statute invalid, they have an authority—a jurisdiction—to declare when decisions are invalid because the officials have stepped outside of the limits of the authority given to them by Parliament. In cases like those about the Group Areas Act, judges thus had the opportunity to rely on administrative law principles to try to ensure that the administration of the law was to the greatest extent possible consistent with the right to dignity of all those subject to the law.

So while there is no denying that law can be used as an instrument of bad, it is also the case that law provides a basis for resistance to that use, more accurately, abuse of law. Something goes wrong, in short, when law is used to undermine or even destroy the conditions for individuals to live their lives with dignity. Put positively, law is most appropriately used in ways that respect human dignity, which is why when it is not so used we think of the use as an abuse. Hence we have the potential for a different conclusion from the apartheid experience: there is an intrinsic connection between government according to law and human dignity.

You may think that the example of the wicked legal system of apartheid South Africa clearly refutes this different conclusion. It shows that far from it being universally the case that there is an intrinsic connection between law and dignity, the connection is entirely contingent. For the example shows that a lot depends on which judge hears a dignitarian challenge and also, more importantly, that in many legal orders the government may and will opt to remove the basis for the challenges by making its intentions more explicit in the laws it enacts.

But, as I will now argue, far from helping to block the conclusion above, the fact that a government has to ensure that the Parliament does something explicit in its statutes helps to support it. For the Parliament has to adopt one or both of two methods.

First, the statute says altogether explicitly that the official is authorised to act unreasonably, for example, by setting aside areas that grossly discriminate against a racial group. Second, the statute incorporates a privative clause, a provision that explicitly deprives judges of their jurisdiction to review the decisions of the officials charged with implementing the statute.[9] Such provisions can be very general, for example, they might simply say that judges are not to review in any way the work of the officials. Alternatively, the clause can provide a version of the first method by saying that judges may not review on particular grounds, including that the official acted unreasonably in the light of one or other principle.

How does this support the conclusion that there is an intrinsic connection between government according to law and service to human dignity? Recall that judges have an inherent jurisdiction to ensure that state offi-

---

9   As I will point out in the next section, privative clauses are not necessarily designed to permit unbridled power; finality of decision-making and the certainty that comes with it are usually the ends Parliament is trying to achieve. Nevertheless, read literally, unbridled power is what they in fact achieve.

cials stay within the limits of the authority delegated to them by statute. It is in the nature of delegated authority both that there are such limits and that there is a body independent of the delegates to check that they stay within those limits, lest they become, in the words of the New Testament, 'a law unto themselves.'[10]

A Parliament that delegates authority to officials and announces that the authority is unlimited is guilty of two mistakes. There is a logical mistake about the nature of delegated authority. And there is a legal mistake about its task as a body that makes laws that permit those subject to the law to guide their behaviour. Judges have been able to use the logical error as a reason to sidestep a general privative clause, one that tells judges that they have no authority to review. They say in effect to Parliament:

> You cannot both give officials authority to carry out a particular mandate and tell them that they may do as they please, so we will ignore that part of your message that makes nonsense of the whole.

If one recalls the slogan that the rule of law provides us with something qualitatively different from the arbitrary rule of men, one can put this point in the following way: something goes wrong when a particular law seems to create an opportunity for completely arbitrary decision-making, so wrong that judges are entitled to ignore the problematic part of the law. The arbitrariness here is that the individual has no idea of what kind of decision to expect from officials. It is an affront to human dignity because it removes from those subject to the law the ability to plan their lives in advance, and the ability to plan one's life in this way is a necessary (though not a sufficient) condition for a life of dignity.

That Parliament makes both a logical and a legal mistake means that judges can correct the latter on the basis of the former. Things are different, however, when Parliament explicitly authorises officials to act unreasonably or tells judges that they may not review official action on the ground that it is unreasonable. Here there is no logical problem in that officials are given a limited and an unlimited authority by the same statute. Rather, there is a statutory license, even an invitation, to officials to act unreasonably. The arbitrariness arises because officials are directly empowered to inflict specific indignities on individuals, to treat them as less than worthy of equal concern and respect. But because there is no logical mistake, judges have not been able to sidestep this kind of statutory provi-

---

10   Romans 2:14: 'For when the Gentiles, which have not the law, do by nature the things contained in the law, these, having not the law, are a law unto themselves'.

sion in the absence of a written constitution. Nevertheless, their inability in this regard does not undermine the conclusion that there is an intrinsic connection between government according to law and human dignity.

Judges are under a duty to interpret the law that delegates authority to officials in light of the principles of administrative law until the point that Parliament forbids them to do so. That they are under such a duty tells us that the law implicitly claims to affect the lives of its subjects in ways that respect their dignity. When the law explicitly disavows that claim, something goes wrong not just morally speaking, but also legally speaking. Those subject to the law will have considerable difficulty in understanding why they should regard the law as an authority over them, and not simply as a brute force with sufficient power to enforce its will. In a legal order that has no entrenched bill of rights, judges will not be able to come to the aid of aggrieved individuals. But the order is in trouble legally speaking, something that is easier to appreciate in seeing that such a legal order is legally in more trouble than a slave-owning society.

A slave-owning society uses the law as an instrument of extreme injustice because it denies a whole class of human beings the status of being human; it deems them to be non-human things, to have no moral status at all. Things are used by human beings in the pursuit of their own ends and are not therefore capable of having dignity.[11] Such a society is in a great deal of moral trouble. But it will not be in trouble legally speaking, as long as the class of people who are deemed to be non-human is relentlessly consigned to a status in which no question arises of the capacity of an individual in that class to be, in Immanuel Kant's words, 'a lawgiving member in the kingdom of ends'.[12]

'As long as the class of people is relentlessly consigned ...' is, it must be emphasised, a big proviso. For slave-owning societies, societies in which the institution of slavery is constituted by law, usually experience immense difficulty in maintaining the enslaved group in a status beyond morality and law and therefore beyond dignity.[13]

---

11   See I Kant, 'Groundwork of the Metaphysics of Morals' in MJ Gregor (ed and trans), *The Cambridge Edition of the Works of Immanuel Kant: Practical Philosophy* (Cambridge, Cambridge University Press, 1996) 84.
12   ibid.
13   See, eg, WW Buckland, *A Text-Book of Roman Law from Augustus to Justinian* (Cambridge, Cambridge University Press, 1932) 62–66. Consider also the difficulties our society experiences with maintaining non-human animals—cows, dogs, pigs etc.—in the status of things, while giving them some legal

In contrast to a society that manages relentlessly to consign a group of people to the status of things, apartheid-era South Africa was a legal nightmare from the perspective of the rule of law, concerned with what it takes to maintain a society in good shape, legally speaking.[14] And it was so because the ideal that all South Africans were equal before the law—the specifically legal ideal of human dignity—was maintained as an abstract ideal of the legal order throughout the period, even as the particular apartheid laws made it ever clearer that the animating political ideology of the ruling party was one of white supremacy.

The reality of that nightmare was lived on a daily basis by black South Africans, as well as the other 'non-white' groups who were accorded privileges that put them somewhere in between black and white South Africans. But my focus is the way in which the nightmare played out in the law: in the convoluted attempts in statute law to ensure that the statutes would be interpreted in a fashion more consistent with the political ideal of white supremacy than with the legal ideal of human dignity; in the actual administration of the law by officials; and in the efforts by judges who took seriously the legal ideal of dignity to interpret the law in light of that ideal.

That the nightmare was played out within the law had the occasional advantage for those who used the law to challenge the political ideology of white supremacy. As I have suggested, sometimes the challenges succeeded. Indeed, in the 1980s a couple of challenges which went to the heart of apartheid policy were upheld by the highest court and were not overturned by the Parliament, perhaps because the government had come to the realisation that the political ideology was no longer workable. A further advantage was that the rule of law was taken seriously by many of the leaders of the opposition to apartheid, including the leaders of the armed struggle, so that out of the experience of that era came a commitment to government according to law, with both an independent judiciary in place

---

protection against various kinds of bad treatment because we recognize that they share certain attributes with us human animals, including the capacity to suffer. See, however, G Kateb, *Human Dignity* (Cambridge, Mass, Harvard University Press, 2011) who argues that suffering is the concern of morality whereas dignity is something existential.

14 See J Finnis, *Natural Law and Natural Rights* (Oxford, Clarendon Press, 1980) 270; and also N Simmonds, *Law as a Moral Idea* (Oxford, Oxford University Press, 2007).

to ensure that the rule of law is maintained and an entrenched bill of rights.

The lesson for other countries is one I can now formulate somewhat paradoxically: in the political situation in which there is widespread and explicit abuse of the law to undermine the legal ideal of human dignity, we discover an intrinsic connection between government according to law and that ideal. That ideal is a somewhat thin or formal one. It is the right to dignity—a right to equal treatment in the way in which the law is administered, a judgment internal to the legal regime created by the law. It is thus not a right to be treated in accordance with an external standard of political equality, by which I mean only external to that particular legal regime.

I do not want to claim that there is a bright line distinction. Consider a challenge to the validity of a statute that limits pension benefits to the 'opposite sex partners' of retired employees. If the statute says merely that the benefits go to the 'partners of retired employees', and those who administer the statute refuse to pay benefits to same-sex partners, an internal, administrative law challenge is possible. But if the statute explicitly says 'opposite sex partners', the legal challenge has to be external. It requires that some other legal document has primacy over that statute and lists a right to equality that makes possible that challenge.

The distinction is not a bright line one, first, because the two challenges are based on the same moral intuition—that discrimination on the basis of sexual orientation is wrong. Second, the point is not that the internal, administrative law challenge is uncontroversial politically while the external challenge is controversial. Those who suppose that discrimination on the basis of sexual orientation is perfectly justified will oppose both challenges.

But there is still a distinction because the internal challenge does not require a legal document as its basis that includes a right that might lead judges to conclude that a legislative decision violated some important principle. All it requires is that the political order is one of government according to law. In addition, while the intuition behind the challenges is the same, it does not operate in the same way or have exactly the same content.

The internal challenge does not operate in the same way as the external one because a violation of the right to dignity is detectable only in the context of the actual administration of a legal regime, while the violation of the right to political equality happens as soon as a statute is enacted that either explicitly treats a group with less than equal concern and respect or that cannot be implemented without resulting in such treatment. It does not have the same content because the right to dignity has a much more limited scope than its more abstract relation of the right to political equality.

Because of these differences in operation and content, an assertion of a novel interpretation of the right to dignity is less controversial than an assertion of the right to political equality, which explains, I think, the political strategy of much same-sex marriage litigation. Even when there is a bill of rights that entrenches a right to equality, it is easier to succeed by initially building public support through successful internal challenges to the administration of particular legal regimes than by launching the more dramatic external challenges to the validity of explicit statutory provisions.

I wish to highlight two more features of the right to dignity before turning to Canadian administrative law. The right is to government according to law, which is the right to have the administration of the law conform to the rule of law, in particular to the principle of equality before the law. It is not therefore a right to participate in choosing the body of lawmakers. Thus, a political order could conform closely to the rule of law without being democratic, if what we mean by democracy is the principle—endorsed by any plausible conception of the ideal of political equality—that legislation should be made by the representatives of an enfranchised adult population.

Conversely, as we are about to see, a political order can conform to the democratic principle and be something of flop when it comes to conformity to the rule of law. That the right to dignity can exist in the absence of conformity to the democratic principle, while the democratic principle cannot be a total flop when it comes to the rule of law is an issue worth further examination, a task I will come back to below.

Secondly, although the right to dignity does not entail the principle of democracy, the right to political equality does. And because the right to dignity is a kind of equality right, there is something jarring about a legal order that conforms to a considerable degree to the ideal of the individual as 'a lawgiving member in the kingdom of ends', but does not recognise the right of the same person to participate in the process of enacting the laws that provide the framework in which she make laws for herself. Even when the right to dignity of black South Africans was under continual assault, the fact that it was not entirely obliterated meant that there was a persistent tension within the policy of the ruling party between that right and the fact that ruling party was so intent on using law to deny political equality, including rights to participate in politics, to black South Africans.

It should by now be obvious why I think Canadian administrative law is boring and why that is a good thing. Canada is a society in which the democratic principle has been fairly fully observed for almost a century,[15] and legislatures have made great strides towards achieving equality in many areas of political and social life. Many factors, however, make the picture less than rosy. Among them: that great strides do not mean anything like complete success; that there is significant backsliding as the centre of Canadian politics seems to shift ever rightwards; and, most important, that for Canada's First Nations any claim about Canada's healthy record when it comes to either political equality or dignity is going to look very suspect. But Canada, warts and all, is the healthiest society I have encountered on the dignity scale and its health in that regard is directly related to its health on the political equality scale.

I have argued thus far that the internal tensions within a 'wicked legal system' illuminate the intrinsic connection between, first, law and dignity and, second, between dignity and political equality. As I will now show that, even in a decent legal system, one in which there is a serious commitment to using the law to serve the ideal of political equality so that the background conditions for dignity are in place, it is no easy matter to realise the right to dignity.[16]

---

15 'Status Indians' were accorded the right to vote only in 1960 and certain categories of prisoner were denied the right to vote until the 1980s. See the entry on 'Franchise' in the *Canadian Encyclopedia*, www.thecanadianencyclopedia. com/index.cfm?PgNm=TCE&Params=a1ARTA0003020.

16 Moreover, to the extent that there is backsliding from political equality, there will, as one would again expect, be echoes within administrative law, including, perhaps, in the procedural part of the Supreme Court's decision on deference doctrine which I discuss below—*Dunsmuir v New Brunswick* [2008] 1 SCR 190, paras 79–118. In my view, and despite its denial in paragraph 82, the Court retreated from the procedural advance in its decision in *Nicholson v Haldimand-Norfolk (Regional) Board of Commissioners of Police* [1979] 1 SCR 311, as developed in *Knight v Indian Head School Division No. 19* [1990] 1 SCR 653, and that retreat is plausibly understood as motivated by a shift in the societal commitment to political equality.

III. The 'Public Conscience' of the Law

One neglected item in my account so far is the extent to which the maintenance of a legal order in good shape requires judges who have the right mind-set. Recall that only a few of the apartheid-era judges were willing to uphold the kinds of rule-of-law challenge I described. But one should not conclude that as long as there are enough rule-of-law enthusiasts among the judiciary that the legal order will be in good shape. Besides the obvious and much more important consideration that a great deal depends on the moral character of those who make the law, a lot also depends on the judge's conception of the rule of law.

Note that the majority of apartheid-era judges had their own conception of the rule of law. On their understanding, the rule of law is the rule of rules made by Parliament, and the content of the rules is worked out by tests that rely exclusively on factual considerations that make it plausible to say: 'This is what the legislature as a matter of fact intended.' This 'plain fact' conception of the rule of law is consistent with the following understanding of the democratic principle: in a democracy the only legitimate mode of judicial interpretation is one that adopts plain fact tests, since only such a mode respects the authority of the representatives of the people to decide on the content of the laws. It thus differs from the mode of interpretation favoured by the minority of apartheid-era judges, since they tried to find a content to particular rules that was consistent with the right to dignity. For them the content of the law was in part determined not by factual tests, but by moral reasoning about what dignity requires.

But even if one favours a dignitarian conception of the rule of law, one has to take into account that such a conception has a contested content, and that one version of it creates vast problems for the administration of the law. This problematic version argues that the only way the state can serve human dignity is to make as little law as possible. The more law there is, the more decisions officials have to make about how to implement it; hence, the more potential there is for individuals to find that they are governed not in accordance with the rule of law but by the arbitrary decisions of particular officials. This conception of the rule of law fits snugly with a laissez-faire view of economics.[17]

---

17 For the most famous statement of this view, see FA Hayek, *The Road to Serfdom* (Chicago, University of Chicago Press, 1994).

Something like the latter version of the rule of law dominated judges in the late nineteenth century and well into the twentieth. To them the administrative state seemed lawless, a 'new despotism', as Lord Hewart said.[18] Such judges had two options when they were called upon to review official decisions. They could declare that what the officials were doing was not amenable to judicial supervision. Alternatively, they could try to curb the officials by interpreting the law so as to produce results friendly to the judges' laissez-faire view of the world. Often these judges veered from decision to decision between these options.

Because the second option threatened to derail the legislative reforms that set up the administrative state, reforms that were often in the service of political equality, legislatures felt compelled to curb what they regarded as the subordination of the democratic will of the people to judicial arbitrariness. Hence, it became common to insert privative clauses into statutes in order to make it clear to judges that they were not to second-guess official decisions.

In this context, the point of the clause is not the ignoble one of seeking to give officials unbridled power in order to permit them to make decisions that serve the policies of a wicked regime. Rather, the aim is finality of decision-making and the certainty that comes with it. However, the effect is the same for when officials are totally shielded from review, the ideal of political equality becomes detached from the ideal of human dignity. The officials become a law unto themselves, an affront to human dignity because it removes from those subject to the law the ability to plan their lives.

The remedy for this problem is, as we have seen, for judges to use as the basis for correcting Parliament's legal mistake its logical mistake in attempting to delegate an authority that is both limited and unlimited. However, if laissez-faire judges do this, we get one problem substituted for another—judicial arbitrariness for official arbitrariness; and judges' wanton circumvention of such clauses, on whatever basis, also affronts the right to dignity.

There is a way out of this conundrum, shown by Justice Ivan Rand in the Supreme Court in 1959 in *Roncarelli v Duplessis*,[19] a case which arose because Duplessis, the Premier and Attorney General of Quebec, had ordered the head of Quebec's Liquor Commission to revoke the liquor li-

---

18   L Hewart, *The New Despotism* (London, Ernest Benn Ltd, 1929).
19   *Roncarelli v Duplessis* [1959] SCR 121.

cense for Roncarelli's restaurant, thus causing Roncarelli's bankruptcy. Rand J's judgment provides the main ingredients of the solution to the unappealing choice between official and judicial arbitrariness and a more attractive version of a dignitarian conception of the rule of law.

Roncarelli was a Jehovah's Witness and Duplessis's order was one shot fired in the Quebec government's war against the missionary efforts of Jehovah's Witnesses in Quebec. Roncarelli's sin in the eyes of Quebec officials was that he has posted bail for missionaries who had been charged with the crime of contravening municipal by-laws that had been put in place especially to outlaw their efforts. Rand, along with the majority of the Court, found that the revocation was illegal and thus beyond the authority of the Liquor Commission. That cleared the way to the success of Roncarelli's claim against Duplessis for damages resulting from the loss of his business.

Roncarelli faced two obstacles.[20] First, Article 88 of Quebec's Civil Code seemed to bar his action for damages. It stated that no state official would be liable in damages 'by reason of any act done by him in the exercise of his public function or duty' unless notice were given within a certain period, which Roncarelli had failed to do. Thus one of the dissenting judges[21] reasoned that even had there been an illegal act it was protected because of the procedural bar in Article 88. Second, the statute that gave authority to the Liquor Commission said that the Commission 'may cancel any permit at its discretion', a provision that, as another dissenting judge reasoned, could be interpreted as giving to the Commission an unfettered or unlimited discretion to act; indeed, this judge said that the legislature had intended that the Commission be a 'law unto itself'.[22]

In sum, while the statute did not contain a privative clause—an instruction to judges not to review the decisions of the Commission—the combination of the procedural bar with the apparently limitless authority granted to the Commission seemed to have the same effect as such a clause for Roncarelli.

Rand's view of Article 88 was that Duplessis had not acted within the scope of his function but in a 'private capacity', for Duplessis had used the

---

20　See D Dyzenhaus, 'Rand's Legal Republicanism' (2010) 55 *McGill Law Journal* 491.
21　Fauteux J; for discussion, see R Leckey, 'Complexifying Roncarelli's Rule of Law' (2010) 55 *McGill Law Journal* 721.
22　Cartwright J, *Roncarelli*, 167 f.

'influence of his public office and power' to achieve a result that was altogether 'private'.[23] Rand did not say much about the distinction between 'public' and 'private' at this point of his judgment, so that his response to Article 88 might look a little brisk. However, it seems clear that the distinction is informed by the preceding, more elaborate part of his judgment, in which he dealt with the problem that the statute appeared to grant an unlimited authority.

First, Rand observed that economic life had become ever more regulated by law and that it was important to ensure that the officials in charge of the regulation served the purposes of the particular statute with 'complete impartiality and integrity'. While it was up to the Commission to decide whether to deny or cancel a license, that decision had to be 'based upon a weighing of considerations pertinent to the object of the administration'.[24]

Secondly, Rand said that no discretion is unlimited for no statute

> can, without express language, be taken to contemplate an unlimited arbitrary power exercisable for any purpose, however capricious or irrelevant, regardless of the nature or purpose of the statute.[25]

For example, even if the statute does not forbid fraudulent or corrupt decisions, such decisions will be regarded as outside the authority of the official. Thus discretion

> necessarily implies good faith in discharging public duty; there is always a perspective within which a statute is intended to operate; and any clear departure from its lines or objects is just as objectionable as fraud or corruption. Could an applicant be refused a permit because he had been born in another province, or because of the colour of his hair? The ordinary language of the legislature cannot be so distorted.[26]

Finally, Rand said that if the victim of such a decision had no legal remedy, the result would be:

> that an administration according to law is to be superseded by action dictated by and according to the arbitrary likes, dislikes and irrelevant purposes of public officers acting beyond their duty, would signalize the beginning of disintegration of the rule of law as a fundamental postulate of our constitutional structure.[27]

---

23   ibid 144.
24   ibid 140.
25   ibid.
26   ibid.
27   ibid 141 f.

Together, these three points contribute to a distinct and important conception of the idea of 'public' as used in contrast to 'private'. It helps us to understand why the greatest political philosopher to write in English, Thomas Hobbes, could talk of the qualities of the law as being such that it could be regarded as 'the publique Conscience, by which [the individual] ... hath already undertaken to be guided'.[28]

Individuals should accept the claim by the state to have authority over them, the claim that they should see their sovereign or his officials as making justified claims on them, when and only when the claims are put in general form in public laws, and the decisions of the officials as to how to implement the laws in particular cases comply with the dignity of the individuals subject to the decisions. For the decisions so to comply, they will have to be interpretable as consistent not only with the actual terms of the statutory mandate, but also with the principles of the rule of law.

Both constraints protect the right to dignity. The first does so by ensuring that the law can do its job of guiding individuals in advance of their own decisions. The second does so by ensuring that the guidance is intelligible to each individual as 'a lawgiving member in the kingdom of ends'. The second constraint also compensates for the fact that statutory guidance can never be total, and is sometimes left deliberately vague in order to permit officials to develop and adapt the law to changing circumstances. It protects dignity in such situations by ensuring that officials act in accordance with both a justifiable interpretation of the statute and the relevant principles of the rule of law. Thus while individuals in such situations cannot predict the exact content of the decision, they may expect that the content will bear a rational relationship to the purposes of the statute of the sort Rand describes and that it will be consistent with the rule of law.

These constraints do not, however, presuppose a commitment to any ideology about how an economy is best organised, let alone a laissez-faire one. It is for Parliament, the lawgiving body of the people, to make decisions about such issues. Nor do the constraints manifest any hostility to the fact that a vast administrative state has come into being. All they do is take seriously the fact that the decisions are expressed in a particular kind of public form—the legal form—and thus have to be implemented in accordance with both the actual terms stated in the law and with the requirements implicated in the commitment to governing through law.

---

28   T Hobbes, *Leviathan* in R Tuck (ed) (Cambridge, Cambridge University Press, 1997) 223.

It took exactly 40 years for the Supreme Court to elaborate the implications of these ideas in three further decisions, two in 1979 and the third in 1999.[29] I will now set out this elaboration and the way in which it has recently gone awry.

IV. Three Steps Forward, One Step Back

These three decisions elaborate the ideas in the central points from Rand's judgment: first, judges must defer to official interpretations of their legal mandate as long as these are reasonable, meaning adequately justified by reasons. Second, all delegations of authority to officials are limited both by the explicit law of the statute and by rule-of-law principles that are either stated explicitly in legal documents or are part of the unwritten tradition of the legal order.[30] Third, the rule of law is a constitutional fundamental so that its principles can only be overridden by express language.

The first decision responded to the problem that a privative clause seems to amount to express language to exclude review and thus accountability to the rule of law, but not by sidestepping the provision.[31] Rather, it understood the clause in the statute not as a negative prescription against any review but as a positive instruction to defer.[32] It thus staked out a middle ground between the bad options of judicial arbitrariness and official arbitrariness. On the one hand, the Supreme Court insisted on official accountability to the law, including the principles of the rule of law. On the other, it required that judges not second-guess the officials as long as their decisions were interpretable as reasonable understandings of their legal mandate.

In a paper on this and subsequent decisions, I argued that this kind of deference could not be understood according to the primary dictionary

---

29   *Canadian Union of Public Employees, Local 963 v New Brunswick Liquor Corporation* [1979] 2 SCR 177; *Nicholson*; *Baker v Canada (Minister of Citizenship and Immigration)* [1999] 2 SCR 817.
30   *Nicholson* put in place the basis for this proposition by providing that procedural protections applied to exercises of discretion that had hitherto been regarded as unreviewable on this basis. As I suggest above, in *Dunsmuir v New Brunswick* the majority of the Supreme Court might have retreated from this position.
31   *Canadian Union of Public Employees, Local 963*.
32   ibid 235 f.

meaning according to which one submits to the judgment of another. A stance of 'submissive deference' would be appropriate only if the privative clause were understood literally, according to a plain fact interpretation, as excluding altogether the judges' jurisdiction to review. Rather, we need the secondary meaning that deference requires not submission but respect: 'deference as respect' requires that judges pay 'a respectful attention to the reasons offered or which could be offered in support of a decision'.[33]

This formulation was adopted in the third decision—*Baker*—by Justice Claire L'Heureux-Dubé.[34] In addition, she held that where an official decision affects a legally protected interest, those affected are entitled to more than an opportunity to present their side of the case to the official; they are also entitled to the reasons from the official that purportedly justify the decision.[35]

The Supreme Court has on several occasions repeated its commitment to deference as respect, including in *Dunsmuir*, a 2008 decision in which it attempted to restate and refashion the Canadian approach to judicial review.[36] When the highest court of the land pays one the compliment of explicitly accepting one's position, it might seem churlish to complain that the commitment is less than whole hearted. But since the costs of a partial commitment seem to me to be high, I will register exactly that complaint.[37]

In the paragraph in which the quoted formulation is to be found, I framed the formulation with, on the one hand, the claim that submissive deference is the stance required by a plain fact understanding of the privative clause. Hence, if one were to reject that stance, one had to reject also the plain fact conception of the rule of law that lay behind it. On the other hand, I suggested that one of the advantages of deference as respect is that

---

33   D Dyzenhaus, 'The Politics of Deference: Judicial Review and Democracy' in M Taggart (ed), *The Province of Administrative Law* (Oxford, Hart Publishing, 1997) 286.
34   *Baker*, para 65.
35   ibid para 43.
36   *Dunsmuir* para 48.
37   I am greatly indebted in what follows to an unpublished paper by Mark D Walters, 'Respecting Deference as Respect', presented to a symposium on *Dunsmuir* at the Faculty of Law, University of Toronto, as well as to his magisterial 'Jurisdiction, Functionalism, and Constitutionalism in Canadian Administrative Law', in C Forsyth et al (eds), *Effective Judicial Review: A Cornerstone of Good Governance* (Oxford, Oxford University Press, 2010).

it is explicitly committed to the value of equality. I still stand by the claim in regard to the plain fact conception. But I wish to refine the suggestion about equality, in keeping with my argument, so that the commitment is understood to be in a direct relationship with dignity, but only an indirect one with political equality. That refinement does not remove political equality from the radar screen of administrative law. Rather, it moves it to the side since the relationship goes from administrative law through the right to dignity to political equality. I will start with the claim.

The plain fact conception of the rule of law is, as I have suggested, a plausible understanding of the democratic principle: the law should be made by exclusively by the people's representatives in Parliament, and the content of their judgments should be transmitted back to the people in such a way that decisions about what the law requires faithfully reflect the content of what the legislature in fact decided. But while plausible it also leads to a very serious problem, already partially identified.

In a complex administrative state where many officials have quite open-ended mandates to implement and develop the law of their regime, the plain fact conception substitutes rule by officials for rule by Parliament. We get the spectre of official lawlessness, which is only compounded if a privative clause attempts to shield the officials from judges. The point is not that officials will run amok without judicial supervision. Rather, it is the point much discussed in recent literature on 'Republicanism' that the slave with a benevolent master is as subject to domination and thus to arbitrary power as the slave whose master is malevolent. A benevolent dictator is still a dictator.[38]

But if we can see that problem, why should we think parliamentary dictatorship acceptable, albeit for limited periods so that we can vote in a new dictator if we do not like the old? The mistake here is in supposing that a parliamentary legal order amounts to serial dictatorship. However, just that view sometimes has a curious hold on judges, including the majority of the Supreme Court in *Dunsmuir*. For the majority asserted that there exists an

> underlying tension between the rule of law and the foundational democratic principle, which finds an expression in the initiatives of Parliament and legislatures to create various administrative bodies and endow them with broad powers.[39]

---

38   For discussion, see Dyzenhaus 'Rand's Legal Republicanism'.
39   *Dunsmuir v New Brunswick* [2008] 1 SCR 190, para 27.

Here the majority suggests that there is some plain fact in the content of Parliament's laws, determinable outside of the interpretative context constituted by the principles of the rule of law. But there is only such a tension if one supposes that it is possible to have parliamentary sovereignty without the rule of law. And there is a compelling argument that parliamentary sovereignty requires the rule of law.[40]

If Parliament is to be sovereign, the supreme lawmaker, it has to establish its supremacy over the executive, which requires an independent judiciary in order to ensure that the officials who make up the executive and who claim the authority of law for their decisions are in fact acting in accordance with the law. The supremacy of the supreme lawmaker is no more than the supremacy of law and thus of the rule of law. *Legal* subjects are subject to the rule of a positive framework of public laws.

In contrast, dictators may act as they please, malevolently or benevolently, as the whim takes them. It follows that even if one person is the sovereign, the fact that the sovereign is committed to ruling through law by itself distinguishes the situation of legal subjects from the situation of those subject to the whims of a dictator. That is why it is possible to have the rule of law in the absence of democracy. So parliamentary sovereignty is valuable only in part because it means that we are subject not to the arbitrary will of one or many individuals. The other part is that in a parliamentary legal order, representatives of an enfranchised adult population make law in accordance with democratic principles. But they must make law—establish a system of government according to law; and judges follow their duty to the parliamentary sovereign by interpreting particular provisions in statutes as though they were intended to be part of a system of legality. To do otherwise, Hobbes tells us, is a great insult to the sovereign.[41]

A parliament may introduce a tension into the legal order by relying on its place as supreme lawmaker to stipulate expressly that officials are to be a law unto themselves. But there is a world of difference between recognizing that fact and supposing, as did the Supreme Court, that there is an *underlying* tension between the 'foundational democratic principle' and

---

40   In my view, this argument is implicit in Dicey; see D Dyzenhaus, 'The "Organic Law" of *Ex Parte Milligan*' in A Sarat (ed), *Sovereignty, Emergency, Legality* (Cambridge, Cambridge University Press, 2010) 53 f.

41   Hobbes, *Leviathan* (1997) 194.

the rule of law. The only underlying tension is in the Court's own reasoning.[42]

That same tension manifests itself in the Court's treatment of deference. Canadian deference doctrine had, by the time of *Dunsmuir*, become quite complex. There were three different standards—correctness, reasonableness *simpliciter*, and patent unreasonableness. The Court had set out a list of criteria for determining which was appropriate. But it seemed to many that these criteria were so malleable that judges could avoid having to defer either by turning the issue into a correctness one if they so chose, or by hiding a judgment about correctness behind a smokescreen of reasonableness.[43] In addition, lawyers became understandably preoccupied with the issue of how to convince courts to adopt the standard most likely lead to the outcome that favoured their clients, which increased the complexity and thus the expense of litigation.

In *Dunsmuir*, the majority held that henceforth there would be only two standards:[44] correctness and reasonableness. Generally, the issue of which was appropriate could be ascertained by checking to see whether it had been settled by previous jurisprudence, but if it had not, a court would have to determine which of the two standards was appropriate.[45] Factors that would indicate that reasonableness was the appropriate standard would include the presence of a privative clause, a 'discrete and special administrative regime', and the 'nature of the question of law'.[46] In the last regard, the majority said that correctness review is always appropriate for an allegedly confined list of questions including constitutional law, the

---

42   It is true that the majority's preferred narrative in *Dunsmuir* is that they reject the plain fact conception and that Parliament cannot render executive decisions immune from review (para 52); the best Parliament can do is signal deference as respect (by way of a privative clause), and that this is totally justified because of the rule of law. But that narrative is undermined by the narrative that relies on a plain fact conception of how to interpret legislative intent.

43   Precisely the second charge was made against the majority of the Court by the dissenting judges in a decision prior to *Dunsmuir*; see *CUPE v Ontario (Minister of Labour)* [2003] 1 SCR 539, paragraph 46. Bastarache J, who wrote the dissenting judgment, went on to coauthor the majority judgment in *Dunsmuir*. In *Dunsmuir*, Binnie J, who wrote the majority judgment in that earlier case, wrote a minority opinion in which he sought to preserve to the extent possible his jurisprudential approach.

44   *Dunsmuir v New Brunswick* [2008] 1 SCR 190, para 45.

45   ibid para 62.

46   ibid para 55.

common law, 'general law', statutes other than the official's own statute, and a category called 'true jurisdiction'.[47]

The majority suggested that 'the rule of law is maintained because the courts have the last word on jurisdiction, and legislative supremacy is assured because determining the applicable standard of review is accomplished by establishing legislative intent'.[48] In addition, it held that deference is appropriate when the statute does not dictate 'one specific, particular result', in which case there would be a range 'of possible reasonable conclusions'[49] between which the official may choose.

Both of these statements presuppose the plain fact conception of the rule of law. As with the claim about underlying tension, the holdings assume that there is a fact of the matter about legislative intent that is determinable outside of the interpretative context constituted by rule-of-law principles. In order: there is a fact about what standard Parliament intended the courts to apply; about whether the statutory provision admits of only one meaning; and, if it does not, about whether the meaning arrived at by the officials falls within the range that judges should consider reasonable.

This array of claims is confusing. On the one hand, the majority could mean that a court should first determine what standard Parliament intended. It follows by definition that there is only 'one specific, particular result' if a court concludes that Parliament intended correctness and that there is a range of reasonable results only if a court concludes that Parliament intended reasonableness.

On the other hand, the majority could mean that a court should conclude that a reasonableness standard is appropriate if and only if it first concludes that the statutory provision in question does not in fact dictate 'one specific, particular result'. In contrast, if there is one such result (that is, if the judges suppose that they are able to arrive at a conclusion about what the law requires), the standard is correctness. And this last point raises particular problems.

Judges will usually presume that the law does provide an answer to the questions that are raised about its requirements. This is a regulative assumption of reasoning about the law for all legal officials charged with interpretation of the law, since they must seek to give an answer that is fully

---

47   ibid paras 58–61.
48   ibid para 31.
49   ibid para 47.

justified by legal reasons. As a result, if judges adopt a stance that permits them to ask whether there is such an answer in abstraction from the answer the official gave, so that they will consider deferring only if they cannot themselves determine an answer, they will rarely if ever find that they should consider deferring.[50]

The *Dunsmuir* majority thus far from simplifying and clarifying Canadian deference perpetuates a problem that plagued the Court since 1979. It has never managed to screw its courage to the sticking place of affirming once and for all that legislative intention is not the product of some plain fact test. To do that, the Court would not only have to resist the pull of declaring its allegiance to the plain fact conception of the rule of law. It would also have to embrace with all of its implications the idea that legislative intention is a normative construct—an interpretation of the statute in light of its purposes, including its more abstract purpose to be part of a scheme of public law that regulates the lives of legal subjects in ways that are intelligible to them as consistent with their right to dignity.

Macbeth's decision to take his wife's advice to stop dithering and reach the sticking place of his convictions was followed by disastrous consequences. And it might seem that disaster also looms if the Court jettison its plain fact tool kit, since that entails an assertion of its supremacy over Parliament in public law, even in cases where no constitutional question arises from either the Charter of Rights and Freedoms or the entrenched division of powers in the 1867 Constitution. However, as I have argued, the Court would be asserting not its supremacy but the supremacy of the system of public law that Parliament has made. It would then be in a position to accept the implications of deference as respect—of its duty to respect officials' decisions about how to understand and implement their statutory mandate, as long as the decisions are adequately justified by the reasons the officials gave.

V. Deference in the Culture of Justification

Courts who take seriously the idea of deference as respect start their inquiry not by looking for a fact about legislative intent, whether about the standard of review or about the meaning of a particular statutory provision. Rather, they inquire into the relationship between the official's rea-

---

50   For a similar point, see Scalia '*Judicial Deference*' 521.

sons and his or her conclusion. There is thus only one standard for all decisions—reasonableness—since jettisoning the plain fact conception requires jettisoning the correctness standard.

On the one hand, then, deference as respect may appear less intrusive than the *Dunsmuir* doctrine. But, on the other hand, it may appear more intrusive since an inquiry into whether the reasons adequately support the conclusion cannot avoid considering whether the official adequately weighed the reasons. Recall that Rand said that while it was up to the Liquor Commission to decide whether to deny or cancel a license, that decision had to be 'based upon a weighing of considerations pertinent to the object of the administration'. One does not weigh a pertinent consideration merely by mentioning it.

Consider an official who is asked to stay a deportation order on 'humanitarian and compassionate grounds' and who is under a duty to take into account the best interests of the children of the woman subject to the deportation order. If the official decides that the person should be deported despite the fact that her Canadian children will inevitably be affected by the deportation, he will have to show why the reasons in favour of deportation outweighed the impact on her children's interests. A court cannot scrutinise the reasons for adequacy without evaluating whether pertinent considerations were appropriately weighed, especially when the official's legal duty is to give a particular consideration—the best interests of the child—extra weight.

This example sets out a legal issue central to *Baker* and the Supreme Court's reasoning that the official's refusal to stay the deportation order was unreasonable hones in on the inappropriate consideration that the official gave to the interests of Baker's children. In contrast, the Court in *Suresh,* decided in the wake of 9/11, was captivated by the idea that when it comes to national security, state officials are omniscient; and so the Court proclaimed a taboo on reweighing. That taboo is now repeated mantra-like in its decisions on deference doctrine.[51]

The rationale for the taboo is that to reweigh is to review on the merits, to use the correctness standard, and thus reweighing is inappropriate if the legislative intent is that the court should deploy a reasonableness standard. However, as we have seen, that rationale presupposes that there is a plain fact as to legislative intention. Moreover, to the extent that the taboo is

---

51   *Suresh v Canada (Minister of Citizenship and Immigration)* [2002] 1 SCR 3, para 37.

impossible to observe, its repetition at the same time as a court engages in reweighing makes that court look bad. It will seem to be playing the old judicial game of cloaking correctness review with reasonableness rhetoric. Even worse, is that when the taboo is taken seriously, the duty to give reasons set out in *Baker* is largely gutted of its substantive point of ensuring the dignity of the individual affected by the decision. As L'Heureux-Dubé suggested, the normative basis of the duty is the dignity of the individual affected by the decision.[52]

The rule of law has to be more than the fiat of officials if it is to be explained in terms of a right to dignity. It establishes what during South Africa's transition to democracy an eminent public lawyer called a 'culture of justification':

> a culture in which every exercise of power is expected to be justified; in which leadership given by government rests on the cogency of the case offered in defence of its decisions, not the fear inspired by the force at its command.[53]

For officials to play their role in such a culture, they have to offer not only reasons to those affected by their decisions, but also reasons that do adequately justify their decisions. When, for example, an official makes a decision that negatively affects an individual's fundamental legal right, the official must regard that individual as someone to whom a duty is owed to justify why the right is legitimately limited. The individual is not going to be happy with the substantive outcome of the decision. But he or she will be able to distinguish between that feeling and the feeling that either the way the official decided or what the official decided violated his or her right to dignity.[54]

---

52   *Baker*, para 43.
53   E Mureinik, 'A Bridge to Where? Introducing the Interim Bill of Rights' (1994) 10 *South African Journal on Human Rights* 32.
54   If I am dismissed from my job because my employer thinks that I have been performing badly whereas I disagree, I will, of course, be unhappy. But my unhappiness is quite different from my sense of affront if I am dismissed without being given an opportunity—a hearing—to contest that judgment. It is also different from my sense of affront if I suspect or know that the real reason I was dismissed is that my employer had discovered that I am gay. When I am denied the opportunity to be heard, the decision is procedurally arbitrary. When I am dismissed because I am gay, the decision is substantively arbitrary. While curing the procedural problem is no guarantee that the decision will turn out not to be substantively arbitrary, it is the best hope that we have. My employer might want to get rid of me because I'm gay, and can find enough problems in my record at work to make a case for dismissing me on that basis, in

The subjective perception is important here both because it alerts us to an important distinction in the normative structure of our thought and because it is that perception that will trigger further action. However, the perception is not determinative. The question for a reviewing court is not whether the individual *felt* treated in a fashion inconsistent with her dignity, but whether she was *in fact* so treated.[55] And that she was so treated is important because there is a connection between appropriate process and substance.

Recall that individuals are treated arbitrarily when they are subject to the rule of officials who are a law unto themselves even when the officials make decisions that happen to be substantively good. A benevolent dictator, to repeat, is a dictator. But if all the official has to do to comply with the rule of law is to go through some cosmetic exercise that makes no difference to the substance of the decision, for example, ticking the box labelled 'Considered best interests of the children', the individuals subject to the official's power are no better off.

There has to be something to procedural duties that makes it more likely the decision-making exercise will result in decisions that are actually justified. For while many of the principles of the rule of law seem more procedural than substantive in nature, in that they pertain to the process of decision-making without measuring the decision against some external standard of political morality, they do condition the substance of the law.[56] Indeed, even the specifically legal right to dignity—the principle that individuals must be treated as equal before the law—is in a sense procedural. As we have seen, when dignity is in issue, equality is evaluated by standards internal to the particular legal regime, and not by reference to some conception of political equality.

The duty to give reasons is of particular importance here. It provides the lens through which compliance with the principle of equality before the law is evaluated. More generally, reasons provide to someone adversely affected by a decision a justification for the exercise of the coercive power

---

which case the hearing and reasons provided might make me even more affronted. But I will also have to take into account that my record did provide the basis for that case.

55 See SR Moreau, 'The Wrongs of Unequal Treatment' (2004) 54 *University of Toronto Law Journal* 291.

56 Consider the principle that one should get a hearing prior to a decision that affects an important interest, or the principle that the decision maker should not be biased.

of the state against him or her. They are a concrete manifestation of the official's view of how both the relevant procedural considerations and the substantive policy of the law bear on the particular decision. Hence, the question for the judge in a culture of justification is: 'Given those standards, has the official shown through his or her reasons that the individual has been treated in a way respectful of dignity?'

What is it that gives rise to the antecedent likelihood that a procedurally sound decision will also be substantively sound? The explanation is not simply that the principles of the rule of law help governments to exercise power effectively. Other ways of exercising power can be more effective, depending on what those with power want to achieve, which is why tyrants always want to keep open the option of behaving in an arbitrary fashion. Moreover, if the effective exercise of power were our concern, we would not take our bearings from efficacy as such. For our question is the extent to which the principles of the rule of law can be explained as helping the effective exercise of power through law.

To the extent efficacy is a concern, it is because effective guidance from the law is part of what it takes to treat legal subjects in a way that respects their right to dignity. But it is only a part, since it is also the case that the guidance has to be interpretable in a way that respects the right to be treated with dignity. A command that puts me in a condition of slavery, totally subjected to my master, makes it apparent how my conduct is to be guided—by master's whims. But the command radically violates my right to be treated as 'a lawgiving member in the kingdom of ends'.

I have argued that this right to dignity is at the core of administrative law—the law to which officials are subject in making decisions that carry the authority of state and law. An entailment of this argument is that there is a core of equality—the specifically legal status of equal dignity—to the public law order of any law-governed state. While this entailment might seem counterintuitive given the experience of wicked legal systems, my research suggests that this kind of experience supports the entailment. A government that wishes to eliminate this core of equality will find that it has to exercise power through means other than law. As the apartheid experience also suggests, such a government will have a wider political program, one that includes an assault on the right to political equality of a particular group. The assault will introduce tensions into the internal administration of the public law of the system as long as the core equality of the right to dignity is preserved, so that the core has to be eliminated if the assault is to succeed totally. That tells us that there is an intrinsic connection not only between law and the right to dignity, but also between law and political equality, though the former is direct and the latter indirect.

This explains why the initial formulation of deference as respect being explicitly committed to the value of equality has to be refined, since the commitment is directly to dignity, and only indirectly to political equality. A further modification, implicit in the argument so far, is to my claim that deference as respect requires 'a respectful attention to the reasons offered or which could be offered in support of a decision'. That claim was made before the Supreme Court had found a duty to give reasons. And with that duty in place, all that the judges need scrutinise are the actual reasons. But those reasons must justify the interpretation the officials have of the law when they claim to be acting according to law.

The judges on review must not ask the question required by the correctness standard, a question that would permit them to first work out the answer and then check to see whether the official's answer coincided without any need to inspect the reasons offered by the official. But they must ask whether the official's reasons do justify the conclusion, and that cannot be done, as I have suggested, without considering whether the official gave appropriate weight to important factors. That will lead to more or less intense scrutiny of the reasons, depending on the nature of the interest at stake. But even when the interest is a fundamental one, and so deserving of the most intense scrutiny imaginable, the issue remains whether the official justified the conclusion and not what the judge would have concluded in the absence of the official's reasons.[57]

Hence, the thought that deference as respect might be either less or more intrusive than *Dunsmuir* doctrine is misleading. For deference as respect requires of officials that they ensure that their reasons do justify their conclusions and of judges that that issue becomes their sole concern on review. If the inherent right of every individual to dignity presupposes a legal culture 'in which every exercise of power is expected to be justified', the legal decisions that most affect our lives, those of state officials, must be made in the spirit of that culture. But it follows that judges have to enter into that same spirit, which requires them to drop the plain fact conception of the rule of law and its corollary that judges have a monopoly on interpretation of the law.

---

57   See *Newfoundland and Labrador Nurses' Union v Newfoundland and Labrador* 2011 SCC 62.

The Dispute About Human Dignity and Ethical Absolutism in the Field of Fundamental and Human Rights Protection: Defending a Deontic Understanding of Rights

Jochen von Bernstorff[1]

Ten years ago a heated debate began among German constitutional law scholars about the guarantee of human dignity. The claim to absoluteness of the first sentence of Art. 1(1) German Basic Law, a fundamental axiom of German constitutional law, was for the first time subject to a profound controversy, which continues to this day. The following contribution contextualizes the incorporation of Art. 1 into the German Basic Law with the time of origin of the universal human rights movement during the forties of the 20th century. Against this background, an understanding of the human dignity clause will be developed that builds on the assumption of the vulnerability of the individual (Lévinas) and interprets the absolutist wording of Art. 1 German Basic Law as a provision which requires constitutional organs to erect and respect boundaries in what the executive powers can do to human beings.

I. The Controversy

A. Political Context and Development

The dispute was triggered in 2003 by the new commentary on this clause by Matthias Herdegen, Professor of Public Law at the University of Bonn, in the Commentary on the German Basic Law, published by Theodor Maunz and Günter Dürig, and the following criticism of Ernst Wolfgang Böckenförde, former Judge of the German Federal Constitutional Court

---

[1] This article was originally published in German under the title 'Der Streit um die Menschenwürde im Grund-und Menschenrechtsschutz' (2013) 19 *Juristenzeitung (JZ)*, 905-956. The text has been translated into English by Justus Quecke.

and Professor emer. of Public Law at University of Freiburg.[2] Herdegen's commentary replaced the epoch-making first commentary on this clause by Günter Dürig and argued for a gradual level of protection of Art. 1(1) German Basic Law that is to be determined case-by-case through balancing.[3] In this new commentary, Böckenförde saw a loss of categorical 'absolute requirements' set by the constitution, and criticized this step in a widely noted article in the Frankfurter Allgemeine Zeitung. Major constitutional law debates often have a practical political background; in this case the research on embryonic stem cells and the issue, whether Art. 1 German Basic Law imposes strict limits on the legislator in terms of destroying embryonic stem cells for genetic research and if so, where those limits are to be delineated from a constitutional law perspective.[4]

The debate about the claim to absoluteness of Art. 1(1) German Basic Law primarily concerned bioethical questions in the following years. However, a parallel discussion arose in the context of the suppression of Al-Qaeda-terrorism. Could the claim to absoluteness of the guarantee of human dignity still apply, if life-saving information could be extorted from suspects through police torture in order to prevent attacks?[5] Not later

---

2   EW Böckenförde, 'Die Würde des Menschen war unantastbar'; *Frankfurter Allgemeine Zeitung,* 03.09.2003, 33.

3   M Herdegen, 'Art. 1 Abs. 1 GG' in: T Maunz and G Dürig (eds), *Grundgesetz-Kommentar*, (Munich, looseleaf collection, February 2003) 56ff.

4   For the general debate about the guarantee of human dignity that initially was dominated by bioethical questions refer to C Starck, 'Behrendt, Gott im Grundgesetz' (1981*) JuristenZeitung* 457 ff; W Graf Vitzthum, 'Die Menschenwürde als Verfassungsbegriff' (1985) *JuristenZeitung* 201 ff; C Enders, 'Die Menschenwürde und ihr Schutz vor gentechnologischer Gefährdung' (1986) *Europäische Grundrechte-Zeitschrift* 241 ff; H Hofmann, 'Die versprochene Menschenwürde' (1993) 118 *Archiv des öffentlichen Rechts* 353 ff; E Picker, 'Menschenwürde und Menschenleben' in: HH Jakobs et al (eds), *Festgabe für Werner Flume* (Berlin et al, Springer, 1998) 155 ff; R Merkel, *Früheuthanasie. Rechtsethische und strafrechtliche Grundlagen ärztlicher Entscheidungen über Leben und Tod in der Neonatalmedizin* (Baden-Baden, Nomos, 2001); H Dreier, 'Art. 1' in id (ed), *Grundgesetz Kommentar*, 2nd edn, Vol. 1 (Tübingen, Mohr Siebeck, 2004) para 32 ff; EW Böckenförde, *Recht, Staat, Freiheit* (Frankfurt aM, Suhrkamp, 2006) 379-388; M Kettner (ed), *Menschenwürde und Biomedizin* (Frankfurt aM, Suhrkamp, 2004); M Nettesheim, 'Die Garantie der Menschenwürde zwischen metaphysischer Überhöhung und bloßem Abwägungstopos' (2005) 130 *Archiv des öffentlichen Rechts* 71 ff.

5   For the controversial debate concerning torture see instead of many: Brugger, W Brugger, *Menschenwürde, Menschenrechte, Grundrechte*, speech given on

than the decision of the German Federal Constitutional Court regarding the Aviation Security Act (Luftsicherheitsgesetz) in 2006, in which the Court restrained the legislator by using the dignity argument, the dispute around the claim to absoluteness shifted to matters of security.[6] Those concerned extreme circumstances in the area of suppression of terrorism and asked the question whether, with regard to Art. 1 (1) German Basic Law, collisions between claims to respect and claims to protect human dignity of different subjects may occur, and for that reason alone the claim to absoluteness should be indefensible.[7]

18.07.1996 (Baden-Baden, Nomos, 1997); F Wittreck, 'Menschenwürde und Folterverbot' (2003) 56 *Die öffentliche Verwaltung* 873 ff; M Hong, 'Das grundgesetzliche Folterverbot und der Menschenwürdegehalt der Grundrechte – eine verfassungsjuristische Betrachtung' in G Beestermöller and H Brunkhorst (eds), *Rückkehr der Folter. Der Rechtsstaat im Zwielicht?* (Munich, C.H. Beck, 2006) 24 ff; C Enders, 'Die Würde des Staates liegt in der Würde des Menschen – Das absolute Verbot von staatlicher Folter' 133 ff and H Bielefeldt, 'Das Folterverbot im Rechtsstaat' 95 ff, both in: P Nitschke (ed), *Rettungsfolter im modernen Rechtsstaat. Eine Verortung* (Bochum, Kamp, 2005); H Brunkhorst, 'Folter, Würde und repressiver Liberalismus' 88 ff; G Frankenberg, 'Folter, Feindstrafrecht und Sonderpolizeirecht. Anmerkungen zu Phänomenen des Bekämpfungsrechts' 55 ff.; F Hanschmann, 'Kalkulation des Unverfügbaren – Das Folterverbot in der Neu-Kommentierung von Art. 1 Abs. 1 GG in Maunz-Dürig' 130 ff, all three in G Beestermöller and H Brunkhorst (eds), *Rückkehr der Folter. Der Rechtsstaat im Zwielicht?* (Munich, C.H. Beck, 2006); J von Bernstorff, 'Pflichtenkollision und Menschenwürdegarantie. Zum Vorrang staatlicher Achtungspflichten im Normbereich des Art. 1 GG' (2008) 47 *Der Staat* 21 ff.

6   For the killing of the innocent in order to proctect other fundamental rights holders see W Höfling and S Augsberg, 'Luftsicherheit, Grundrechtsregime und Ausnahmezustand' (2005) *JuristenZeitung* 1080 ff; J Kersten, 'Die Tötung von Unbeteiligten' (2005) *NVwZ* 661 ff; D Winkler, 'Verfassungsmäßigkeit des Luftsicherheitsgesetzes' (2006) *NVwZ* 536 ff; R Merkel, '§ 14 Abs. 3 Luftsicherheitsgesetz: Wann und warum darf der Staat töten?' (2007) *JuristenZeitung* 373 ff; J Isensee, 'Menschenwürde: die säkulare Gesellschaft auf der Suche nach dem Absoluten' (2006) 131 *Archiv des öffentlichen Rechts* 173 ff; O Depenheuer, 'Das Bürgeropfer im Rechtsstaat' in id (ed), *Staat im Wort: Festschrift für Josef Isensee* (Heidelberg, C.F. Müller, 2007) 43 ff; EB Franz, 'Der Bundeswehreinsatz im Innern und die Tötung Unschuldiger im Kreuzfeuer von Menschenwürde und Recht auf Leben' (206) 45 *Der Staat* 501 ff; U Palm, 'Der wehrlose Staat?' (2007) 132 *Archiv des öffentlichen Rechts* 95 ff.

7   cf F Wittreck, 'Achtungs- gegen Schutzpflicht? Zur Diskussion um Menschenwürde und Folterverbot' in U Blaschke et al (eds), *Sicherheit statt Freiheit? Staatliche Handlungsspielräume in extremen Gefährdungslagen* (Berlin,

At the beginning of the current decade, the controversy was examined again at a more fundamental level. Now the endeavours focused on the analysis of the consequences of both debates for the interpretation of Art. 1(1) German Basic Law. Since then the classic interpretation of Art. 1(1) German Basic Law based on an absolutist understanding of the norm is still being challenged by some constitutional law scholars. Accordingly, the 'dogma of inviolability', as the proceedings of a conference on Art. 1 German Basic Law published by Lembcke and Gröschner are titled, is out-dated.[8] In the opinion of some scholars, as a result of the controversy, the guarantee of dignity should be lifted from its foundational constitutional position; henceforward, a right to dignity should be a fundamental right as any other fundamental right. Furthermore, 'inviolable' declared human dignity – so goes the criticism – had been sacralised by courts and jurisprudence through the claim to absoluteness. With regard to recent publications, an enduring uncertainty within the public law scholarship cannot be denied: One hardly finds the classical commitments to Art. 1 German Basic Law as 'supreme constitutional principle' or 'fundamental state norm' anymore. In addition, there remains an openly expressed discomfort regarding the claim to absoluteness.[9] It seems as if the former 'sacred' dignity-clause must now be completely rationalised. Claims to absoluteness are thereby rejected as irrational.[10] Supposedly there is no room

---

Duncker & Humblot, 2005) 161 ff; J von Bernstorff, 'Pflichtenkollision und Menschenwürdegarantie' (2008) 47 *Der Staat* 21 ff.

8 R Gröschner and OW Lembcke, 'Dignitas absoluta. Ein kritischer Kommentar zum Absolutheitsanspruch der Würde' in id (eds), *Das Dogma der Unantastbarkeit* (Tübingen, Mohr Siebeck, 2009) 1, 13; M Baldus, 'Menschenwürdegarantie und Absolutheitsthese' (2011) 136 *Archiv des öffentlichen Rechts* 551 ('but if the signs of the current debate do not deceive, the constitutional law practice and jurisprudence will not remain that much longer in this state. They will have to free themselves from the burdens of excessive idealistic thinking and to find the courage to more legal rationality, clarity and constitutional honesty when applying the dignity guarantee' – my translation –).

9 Gröschner and Lembcke, 'Dignitas absoluta'; with regard to the concept of 'sacral' in this context see U Haltern, 'Unsere protestantische Menschenwürde' in P Bahr and HM Heinig (eds), *Menschenwürde in der säkularen Verfassungsordnung* (Tübingen, Mohr Siebeck, 2006) 93.

10 Gröschner and Lembcke, 'Dignitas absoluta'; Baldus, 'Menschenwürdegarantie' 529 ff; G Dederer, 'Die Garantie der Menschenwürde' (2009) 57 *Jahrbuch des öffentlichen Rechts* 87, 113 f; KE Hain, 'Menschenwürde als Rechtsprin-

for the absoluteness of the human dignity clause in a 'rational' constitutional law[11] – further, it is portrayed as a German idiosyncrasy, a German 'Sonderweg'.[12] The ideologically neutral state should – according to the critics – cease using vague constitutional doctrines with ethical or religious origins, such as the inviolable dignity-doctrine as a judicial yardstick for concrete constitutional disputes.

B. The Dignity Topos in (International) Ascent

This discomfort of a growing number of German constitutional law experts regarding the human dignity standard is even more remarkable as the human dignity argument in recent years is clearly on the rise in international law and from a comparative law perspective. The latest UN Convention on Human Rights, for instance, the Convention on the Rights of Persons with Disabilities, holds the respect for dignity of persons with disabilities as a fundamental principle of the entire convention. Foreign and international courts use the dignity argument more frequently.[13] Like the German Basic Law the EU-Charter of Fundamental Rights places the 'inviolable' human dignity at the top of the EU's Bill of Rights, grasping even five separate articles under this clause. Ronald Dworkin, probably the most influential American legal philosopher, recently deceased, makes human dignity in his last book the key aspect of his fundamental and human rights theory.[14] Perhaps the post-war German human dignity-tradition is not an anachronism but a particularly valuable contribution to the global debate about the limits of restrictions on fundamental rights.

---

zip' in HJ Sandkühler (ed), *Menschenwürde* (Frankfurt aM et al, Lang, 2007) 87, 113 f.

11 Only by balancing a transparent and comprehensive application of Art. 1(1) German Basic Law is possible, cf Baldus, 'Menschenwürdegarantie' 548.

12 Herdegen sees the danger of 'parochial prejudice in exceedance of "German-legal" characteristics', Herdegen, 'Art. 1 GG' in T Maunz and G Dürig, *Grundgesetz-Kommentar* (Munich, C.H. Beck, looseleaf collection of 2012) paras 41-43; Baldus, 'Menschenwürdegarantie' 548.

13 C McCrudden, 'Human Dignity and Judicial Interpretation' (2008) 19 *EJIL* 655 ff; K Dicke, 'The Founding Function of Human Dignity in the Universal Declaration of Human Rights' in D Kretzmer and E Klein (eds), *The Concept of Human Dignity in Human Rights Discourse* (The Hague et al, Kluwer Law International, 2002) 111 ff.

14 R Dworkin, *Justice for Hedgehogs* (Cambridge et al, Belknap, 2011).

Admittedly, the exact constitutional classification of Art. 1 German Basic Law was never completely undisputed.[15] In particular, there was at no time a solid consensus regarding the question, whether the human dignity standard also is an independent fundamental right in addition to its constitutive effect for the overall legal system.[16] Despite these dissonances, the fundamental importance of Art. 1 German Basic Law as an unconditional limitation with which the entire normative order of the German Basic Law had to conform was never seriously challenged.

In the following, the criticism of the so-called 'dogma of inviolability' will be examined in more detail. The criticism of the claim to absoluteness barely convinces. According to the view developed here, there are good reasons for not grinding down the rough edges of Art. 1 German Basic Law. Ultimately, we should adhere to the claim to absoluteness, which after the adoption of the Basic Law quickly became the identity-forming axiom of German constitutional law.[17] The current battle against the claim to absoluteness of the human dignity standard is – as I will try to demonstrate – based on a problematic normative concept of fundamental and human rights.

In light of the gradually developed thesis of this paper, the claim to absoluteness of the human dignity clause is the expression of an understanding of fundamental and human rights that only arises in the forties of the 20th century; it can first be shown in concrete positive norms in both international law and under the new German Basic Law during this period. Subsequently, the protection of human dignity was anchored particularly strikingly in the German Basic Law, and can be interpreted in this context of origin as an unprecedented and absolute limit, set by the constitutional

---

15 Christoph Goos reconstructs a minimal compromise with regard to the meaning of human dignity as 'internal freedom' of the Christian man for the persons in the 'Committee dealing with Basic Issues' of the Parliamentary Council, C Goos, *Innere Freiheit. Eine Rekonstruktion des grundgesetzlichen Würdebegriffs*, (Göttingen et al, V&R unipress, 2009).

16 For a portrayal of the status of the discussion see Dreier 'Art. 1' paras 39-44, 124 ff.

17 Constitutionalists of the Faculty of Tübingen have laid influential groundwork in this regard. First, of course, by Günter Dürig who formed the constitutional understanding of Art. 1 German Basic Law through major publications and his paradigmatic commentary of Art. 1 in the fifties in 'Maunz-Dürig' like no other; but later in the eighties also by Wolfgang Graf Vitzthum with his work on human dignity in times of genetic engineering, W Graf Vitzthum, 'Die Menschenwürde als Verfassungsbegriff' (1985) *JZ* 201 ff.

legislator. This interpretation is complemented by a new understanding of dignity that differs from the traditional 'Dowry-' and 'Achievement- theories' and adds to these the aspect of the *vulnerability* of the individual. Furthermore, the attempt of the current critics of the claim to absoluteness to force Art. 1 German Basic Law under the yoke of the dogma of balancing can be followed neither for dogmatic reasons nor with a view to the practice of the constitutional court. Even for the so-called hard cases, where a collision of competing dignity claims could arise, the claim to absoluteness of the human dignity clause should therefore be maintained.

II. The Common Beginning

A. Universal Declaration of Human Rights and German Basic Law

During the years 1948 and 1949 there was a common beginning of the German protection of fundamental rights and the international protection of those rights, in which precisely the connection between human dignity and human rights played a central role.[18] In the Parliamentary Council in 1948, drafts of the Universal Declaration of Human Rights, negotiated simultaneously with the German Basic Law, inspired the fathers and mothers of the German Basic Law to anchor a commitment to human dignity at the pinnacle of the constitution.[19] As the protocols show, the 'Committee dealing with Basic Issues' of the Parliamentary Council closely followed the proceedings of the UN Commission on Human Rights.[20] The fact that during the negotiations in New York it was finally agreed to include references to human dignity in a prominent place of the Universal Declaration of Human Rights also brought the breakthrough in negotiations regarding Art. 1 German Basic Law.[21]

---

18   This was carved out by W Vögele, *Menschenwürde zwischen Recht und Theologie* (Gütersloh, Kaiser, 2000) 295 ff and T Rensmann, *Wertordnung und Verfassung. Das Grundgesetz im Kontext grenzüberschreitender Konstitutionalisierung* (Tübingen, Mohr Siebeck, 2007) 25 ff.
19   Rensmann, *Wertordnung und Verfassung* (2007) 25-33.
20   Vögele, *Menschenwürde* (2000) 295 ff; Rensmann, *Wertordnung und Verfassung* (2007).
21   Quotation Mangoldt: 'I am of the opinion one should not leave out these sentences. One also does not need to leave them out. We find them also in that declaration of human rights, which has been developed by the most comprehensive corporation, (...). But if they can do it, we should actually do it as

The Universal Declaration of Human Rights states at the beginning of the preamble:[22]

> Whereas recognition of the inherent **dignity** and of the equal and **inalienable** rights of **all** members of the human family is the foundation of freedom, **justice** and **peace** in the world, [...].

and Art. 1 Universal Declaration of Human Rights starts with the following sentence:

> **All** human beings are born **free** and equal in **dignity** and rights.

Comparing this wording with those of the first two paragraphs of Art. 1 German Basic Law, it clearly shows that the simultaneous start of the German protection of fundamental rights and the international protection of human rights by reference to human dignity at the top of the catalogues also was of a common kind:

> (1) **Human dignity** shall be inviolable. To respect and protect it shall be the duty of all state authority.
>
> (2) The German people therefore acknowledge inviolable and **inalienable** human rights as the basis of every community, of **peace** and of **justice** in the world.

B. Caesura or Return to Tradition?

But was this really something new? Did the texts not just build on the tradition of the great European Civil Rights Declarations? Undoubtedly, the concept of human dignity stood in a long and complex conceptual tradition, which of course was known to the main stakeholders in New York and Bonn. The tradition of the concept of human dignity includes such diverse understandings of dignity as that of the Stoics and Cicero, the medieval status-dignity, the scholastic and late scholastic Imago Dei doctrines, the Renaissance individualism of Pico della Mirandola, right up to Pufendorf's natural law conception of humans as 'morally free persons'.[23] With his understanding of equal dignity, Kant further developed Pufendorf's approach. In the course of this he secularized the conception of dignity as he saw the grounds for dignity solely in the ability of the individual to rea-

---

well.' H von Mangoldt, in Der Parlamentarische Rat (18.11.1948) (Vol. 5/II, Boppard am Rhein, Harald Boldt Verlag, 2010) 586 – my translation –.

22 Highlighting in the following norm quotations by the author.
23 T Stein, *Himmlische Quellen und irdisches Recht* (Frankfurt aM, Campus-Verlag, 2007) 235 ff – my translation –.

son.[24] Additionally, he substantiated the ethical implications of the concept of equal dignity, as he lifted humans, due to their dignity, into the kingdom of ends. Thus the second version of the categorical imperative states: 'Act in such a way that you treat humanity, whether in your own person or in the person of any other, never merely as a means to an end, but always at the same time as an end'.[25] As ends in themselves, men are imponderable. They are of absolute value and as persons have 'dignity'.[26] What this exactly means for Kant's theory of public law is by no means uncontroversial.[27]

Interestingly, in the 19th century Kant's dignity conception is hardly taken note of. In fact, a formalized concept of dignity plays virtually no role during the revolutionary and restorative battles of the 19th century – it does not belong to the core of the conceptual framework of the great Western civil rights declarations. The deliberations over the 'Paulskirchenverfassung' of 1848 mention human dignity only en passant.[28] However, what then explains the new connection between the dignity-term and human rights,[29] that 100 years later leads to the incorporation of the concept in Art. 1 of the Universal Declaration of Human Rights and in the German Basic Law? In the forties of the 20th century, the conceptual link between dignity and rights all of a sudden is ubiquitous.[30] It is also hardly questioned critically. It seems to be evident to contemporaries, though it is new in this form.

The philosopher Arndt Pollmann plausibly examined this novelty from a philosophical point of view.[31] According to him, it is the suffering of

---

24 Stein, *Himmlische Quellen* (2007) 249 ff.
25 I Kant, *Grundlegung der Metaphysik der Sitten*, 1785, 61 – translated by JW Ellington, *Grounding for the Metaphysics of Morals* (3rd edn, Indianapolis and Cambridge, Hacket Publishing Co, 1993) 30.
26 Stein, *Himmlische Quellen* (2007) 251.
27 J Waldron, 'Dignity and Rand – In Memory of Gregor Vlastos (1907-1991)' (2007) 48 *European Journal of Sociology* 211-214 with further references.
28 Negotiations regarding § 139 Paulskirchenverfassung 'A free public even has to respect the dignity of the perpetrator', cited in J Habermas, *Zur Verfassung Europas* (Berlin, Suhrkamp, 2011) 15 – my translation –.
29 A Pollmann, 'Menschenwürde nach der Barbarei. Zu den Folgen eines gewaltsamen Umbruchs in der Geschichte der Menschenrechte' (2010) 4 *ZfMr* 32 ff.
30 For the emergence of the debate about universal rights of man contemporaneous with the US and Great Britain entering the war at the end of the thirties, see JH Burgers, 'The Road to San Francisco: The Revival of the Human Rights Idea in the Twentieth Century' (1992) 14 *Human Rights Quarterly* 447 ff.
31 Pollmann, 'Barbarei' 32.

millions of individuals, caused by the totalitarian excesses of technically upgraded modernity and two world wars, that made the connection to appear so evident for contemporaries. Ex negativo, i.e. out of universally communicated experiences of fundamental injustice,[32] the dignity concept and the idea of universal human rights are conceptually merged.[33] However, it would be short-sighted to trace the new connection only back to the Holocaust. Although the Nazi terror clearly was a central point of reference in New York and at the Parliamentary Council in 1948, the connection between human dignity and human rights becomes a powerful topos as early as the late thirties, at a time when the future extent of the unprecedented Nazi crimes against humanity was not yet foreseeable.[34]

The collective memory of contemporaries was already in the thirties marked by global experiences with state and military violence, discrimination, humiliation and social exclusion, which were directed against 'others', such as national minorities as well as against individuals. From a long series of shocking incidents one might, for instance, think of the genocidal deportations of the Armenians in the Ottoman Empire, the massacre of civilians during World War I, Stalin's political and ethnic 'cleansing policy' or the Japanese mass executions in the war against China. But also systemic violence and injustice soaked into the general consciousness through experiences such as the occasionally excessive tyranny of European colonialists, impoverishment and famine in Asia and Africa, millions of starvation deaths during the 'Holomodor' in Ukraine at the beginning of

---

32 'Experiences of impoverishment, injustice and unfreedom' at J Schwartländer, in id et al (eds), *Menschenrechte: Aspekte ihrer Begründung und Verwirklichung* (Tübingen, Attempto Verlag, 1978) 86; 'Experiences of structural injustice' with regard to Schwartländer at H Bielefeldt, 'Menschenrechtlicher Universalismus ohne eurozentrische Verkürzung' in G Lohmann and G Nooke (eds), *Gelten Menschenrechte universal?* (Freiburg et al, Herder, 2008) 98, 126; 'elementary experiences of injustice' at M Kotzur, *Theorieelemente des internationalen Menschenrechtsschutzes* (Berlin; Duncker & Humblot, 2001) 330; 'Universalism out of common experience' bei H Hofmann, 'Geschichtlichkeit und Universalitätsanspruch des Rechtsstaats' (1995) 34 *Der Staat* 1, 27; interpreted as a specific European access K Günther, 'The Legacies of Injustice and Fear: A European Approach to Human Rights and Their Effects on Political Culture' in P Alston (ed), *The EU and Human Rights* (Oxford, Oxford University Press, 1999) 117 ff – all my translation –.

33 Pollmann, 'Barbarei' 32 ff.

34 For the emergence of the debate contemporaneous with the US and Great Britain entering the war at the end of thirties, see Burgers, 'The Road to San Francisco' 447 ff.

the thirties, the racist lynching of African-Americans in the United States, or the systematic racial discrimination in South Africa. In the first years of the war, but no later than after the liberation of the concentration camps, the call for respect and protection of human rights and human dignity seemed to many contemporaries to be the evident answer to such fundamental experiences of injustice.[35] As it says in the preamble to the Universal Declaration of Human Rights:

> Whereas disregard and contempt for human rights have resulted in barbarous acts which have outraged the conscience of mankind [...].

The theoretical foundation of human dignity itself and its connection with the postulated human rights however seemed to have played a less important role in the thirties and forties. Depending on their intellectual character, authors at this time look at their own tradition, almost as an ex-post validation, for precursors of the now ubiquitous concept of human dignity, for example, as powerful Catholic intellectuals like Jacques Maritain did with Thomas Aquinas. With his personalistic concepts of dignity and rights he sought a third way between fascism and radical market liberalism and professed a neo-scholastic natural law.[36] With the dignity-term Maritain stressed the relationship between individual freedom and community-embedment of the individual. Through the renaissance of the Catholic natural law, this personalistic stream inspired the understanding of Art. 1 German Basic Law of influential German post-war scholars such

---

35   H Joas, *Die Sakralität der Person* (Berlin, Suhrkamp, 2011) 108-115; Morsink shows for the negotiation process of the Universal Declaration of Human Rights several global injustices, which had a shaping impact on the text, among them World War II and the Holocaust (including rights to bodily integrity, legal ability, asylum), the colonial experience, and ethnic and racial discrimination (prohibition of discrimination), impoverishment experiences (social human rights to an adequate standard of living, housing, food, education), and the oppression of women (equality rights), J Morsink, *The Universal Declaration of Human Rights* (Philadelphia, University of Pennsylvania Press, 1999).

36   J Maritain, *Les droits de l'homme et la loi naturelle* (Paris, Hartmann, 1942) 19; with regard to Maritain see: S Moyn, 'Personalismus, Gemeinschaft und die Ursprünge der Menschenrechte' in SL Hoffmann (ed), *Moralpolitik* (Göttingen, Wallstein-Verlag, 2010) 63 ff; with regard to Maritain, Broch and their time in Princeton see: W Graf Vitzthum, ' "L'homme ne doit pas faire de l'homme un esclave!" Les droits de l'homme dans les débats des intellectuels européens émigrés aux Etats-Unis' in M Breuer and A Epiney (eds), *Der Staat im Recht. Festschrift für Eckart Klein zum 70. Geburtstag* (Berlin; Duncker & Humblot, 2013) 1345 ff.

as Dürig and Wintrich, as well as the Protestant Leibholz.[37] Also, it was the politically agile Maritain, who, as a close friend of Pope Pius XII, aligned the Vatican with the human dignity concept during the Second World War.[38] Other authors were seeking explanations for the connection of dignity with human rights in Confucius, the Koran or in Buddhism.[39] Interestingly, during the war, Kant does not play a dominant role.[40]

In this context, it is important that in both Bonn and New York, there was no agreement on a specific and exclusive intellectual tradition of the dignity-term.[41] Both documents lack an explicit explanation for the prominent position of human dignity. Human dignity is neither derived from religion, nor from law of reason, nor from nature. Carlo Schmid during the negotiations on Art. 1 of the German Constitution criticized a proposed blank reference to natural law as a foundation for the dignity concept as being too vague. He drew the attention in the 'Committee dealing with Basic Issues' to the fact that the National Socialist legal theory also was based on natural law, namely on a natural law variation of Social Darwinism.[42] Instead, in Bonn and in New York the fundamental experiences of injustice by contemporaries from the first half of the 20th century serve as an unwritten justification for the inviolability standard of human dignity as

---

37 Dürig stresses that 'consciously or unconsciously the Christian concept of personality was absorbed into the German Basic Law', G Dürig, 'Die Menschenauffassung des Grundgesetzes' in W Schmitt-Glaeser and P Häberle (eds), *Günter Dürig, Gesammelte Schriften 1952-1983*, (Berlin, Duncker & Humblot, 1984) 31 – my translation –; he also emphasizes at this place, that the notion of man of the German Basic Law is not one of an isolated individual, but of a community-bound person (p 32). For the proximity of constitutional scholars towards personalism à la Maritain, who was absorbed by Catholic doctrine of natural law: Moyn, 'Personalismus' 88-89; EM Andries, 'On the German Constitution's Fiftieth Anniversary: Jacques Maritain and the 1949 Basic Law (Grundgesetz)' (1999) 13 *Emory Int'l L Rev* 53; F Günther, *Denken vom Staat her: Die bundesdeutsche Staatsrechtslehre zwischen Dezision und Integration 1949-1970* (Munich, Oldenburg, 2004) 192.
38 Moyn, 'Personalismus' 70-74.
39 See the diverse contributions represented by different world cultures at a UNESCO symposium in 1947; J Maritain, *Um die Erklärung der Menschenrechte – Ein Symposium* (Zürich et al, Europa-Verlag, 1951).
40 Moyn, 'Personalismus' 89-91
41 Morsink, *The Universal Declaration* (1999) 282-295; Rensmann, *Wertordnung und Verfassung* (2007) 29-30.
42 Vierte Sitzung des Grundsatzausschusses (23.09.1948), in *Der parlamentarische Rat* Vol. 5/I (Boppard am Rhein, Harald Boldt-Verlag, 2010) 642 f.

emphasized in 1948.[43] The 'foundation' for human dignity and universal human rights can be found in the abysses of the 'age of extremes'.[44]

In his impressive book on the genealogy of the human rights discourse, Hans Joas, referring to Emile Durkheim, has spoken of a global awareness of the 'sacredness of the person'. Accordingly, this 'sanctification of the individual' – as Durkheim put it, and which Joas references – became at the end of the 19th century the religion of modern society.[45] Relying on Durkheim, Joas goes along with the recent historical thesis by Lynn Hunt that sees the birth of human rights in the new awareness of the European public for the suffering of others as equal individuals in the 18th and 19th century.[46] Joas' and Hunt's observations are illuminating, especially where they call into question the belief that there is a linear trajectory linking European Enlightenment and the idea of universal human rights in the second half of the 20th century.[47] The human rights movement of the 20th century is not simply a resumption of a temporarily forgotten portfolio of enlightened European traditions. On tradition alone, be it Christianity, European Enlightenment or whatever kind, contemporaries could and did not want to rely during the forties. The dark side of European modernity adumbrated the brighter side of the Enlightenment. During this time, Adorno and Horkheimer, while in exile in the U.S., wrote on the dialectic of Enlightenment.

Yet it seems Joas and Hunt are missing a crucial point of the human rights movement of the forties, since this movement demonstrates a veritable historic caesura through its global juridification project. The continuing global movement for a universal catalogue of rights, which first coalesced in the late thirties, aims at a positive codification of absolute limits of what states and governments 'can do' to people.[48] The movement receives its impetus from universally communicated experiences of the vulnerability of the individual by a technologically advanced modernity. Despite various religious and philosophical motives of the main actors, the move to rights constituted a new secular or political project driven by the

---

43 Cf Pollmann, 'Barbarei' 32.
44 The concept of the 'age of extreme' is taken from EJ Hobsbawms, *The Age of Extremes: A History of the World* (New York, Vintage Books, 1996).
45 Joas, *Sakralität* (2011) 81-98 – my translation –.
46 Joas *Sakralität* (2011) 99-101; L Hunt, *Inventing Human Rights* (New York, W.W. Norton & Co, 2007) 102 ff.
47 Joas *Sakralität* (2011) 102 ff.; Hunt, *Inventing* (2007) 176 ff.
48 Pollmann, 'Barbarei' 32, 43 – my translation –.

courage of being horrified, attempting to constrain the unleashed forces of modernity back behind absolute legal limits. Hence the great disappointment of many contemporaries that the Universal Declaration at the United Nations – under pressure from the victorious powers of World War II – initially was negotiated and adopted only as a non-binding declaration. A binding human rights convention, as demanded by civil society movements, was postponed. Thus, the ambitious juridification project initially failed at a universal level.[49]

III. The Importance of the New Connection Between Human Dignity and Human Rights for the Claim to Absoluteness of the Human Dignity Guarantee

In Bonn the Parliamentary Council went juridically a significant step further than the UN General Assembly. It is not just that it explicitly declared the dignity of man as 'inviolable', it also stipulated in Art. 1(3) German Basic Law fundamental rights as directly applicable law, binding all three branches of government. The connection of absolute protection of human dignity and legally secured individual rights, however, makes it not simply a German 'Sonderweg' but a consistent national implementation of a new universal project, which only emerges in this period. Not coincidentally two explanations played a major role in the Parliamentary Council concerning the decision to incorporate Art. 1 German Basic Law:

First, the assumption that the respect for dignity should be a constitutive element of the new order – i.e. that state and social power should be limited by the respect for human dignity from the outset. This explains the term 'inviolability', which the Christian Party ('Zentrum') politician and former Minister of Justice of Württemberg Joseph Beyerle introduced to the negotiations on Herrenchiemsee.[50] The reference to 'inviolable' and 'inalienable' human rights in Art. 1(2) German Basic Law, to which the German people 'confess', also belongs in this context. Human rights are

---

49 J von Bernstorff, 'The Changing Fortune of the Universal Declaration of Human Rights: Genesis and Symbolic Dimensions of the Turn to Rights in International Law' (2008) 19 *EJIL* 903 ff.
50 For proof regarding Herrenchiemsee see FJ Wetz, *Illusion Menschenwürde* (Stuttgart, Klett-Cotta, 2005) 80 ff.

the universal legal institutions that are recognized as the requirement for a decent existence of the German people.

The second element is the concept of legally binding and specific fundamental rights, whose recognition should be judicially controlled by a strong constitutional court. In short: The vulnerability of dignity requires that central spheres of individual freedom be respected irrespective of conflicting state interests. According to a formulation by Habermas – these claims to respect the dignity of the individually are thus institutionally converted into the 'robust shape' of legally guaranteed fundamental rights;[51] and this is not because we are all Catholics, Personalists or Kantians, but because we as the people 'confess' in Art. 1 to the 'inviolability' of dignity and to 'inviolable' and 'inalienable' human rights. It is the juridification of a 'promise' – to pick up a term used by Hasso Hofmann in this context.[52] It is a new legal commitment to mutual respect for the other in an order that defines itself through ultimate limits for state and social powers of disposal over the individual. This commitment is submitted and standardized by the 'pouvoir constituant'.

A. The Vulnerability of the Individual

Historically, this project is explained by the universal experience of the fragility of dignity, i.e. the systematic disregard of dignity.[53] Therefore, one should understand the 'inviolable' dignity as the potential of every human being to live a life in self-respect and respect for the other.[54] We have this potential by being human. Particularly intensive interventions in individual spheres of freedom however, can make it impossible for us to live such a decent life. Examples are profound impairments of physical or psychological integrity, and intensive communicative and social exclusion practices. Thus, the imperative of 'do not violate' prohibits any state order

---

51 Habermas, *Zur Verfassung Europas* (2011) 22 – my translation –.
52 Hofmann, 'Die versprochene Menschenwürde' 353, 369 – my translation –.
53 Pollmann, 'Barbarei' 32; for a social-psychological perspective deriving from the concept of trauma Joas, *Sakralität* (2011) 108-132.
54 For the understanding of dignity as the ability to develop personality, which plays a central role in the debate in the bioethical field, R Spaemann, *Das Natürliche und das Vernünftige* (Munich et al, Piper, 1987) 93-95; Wetz, *Illusion Menschenwürde* (2005) 233 ff; Pollmann, 'Barbarei' 32, 39; M Nettesheim, 'Garantie der Menschenwürde' 93-96 with further references.

that in its actual impact on the individual disregards this potential. Just to be clear, neither a comprehensive 'objective order of values'[55] nor a comprehensive 'system of values'[56] in Dürig's sense can be derived from this. As it has been frequently noted critically, that would be an overstretching of the human dignity clause and – co upled with a strong constitutional jurisdiction – ultimately would result in a gradual disempowerment of the legislator.

Nevertheless, the imperative of 'do not violate' is the codified step towards an order that through fundamental rights constitutes boundaries for certain areas of life, whose exceeding renders a life in both self-respect and respect for others impossible. That order thus makes the concrete definition of these boundaries a societal task for the future. With this understanding, fundamental and human rights are institutionalized requirements for a decent life.[57] These dignity related boundaries are by no means limited to totalitarian state excesses, which are not be feared in Germany at the moment.[58] In modern societies, systemic threats and exclusion practices can also be caused by unregulated levels of freedom in certain social subsystems such as the economic system, violent religious fanaticism, or even by the natural sciences.[59] As the U.S. 'torture memos' and their implementation after the September 11 attacks show, even in established democracies an excessive use of force by public officials against individuals is not utterly out of the question, which moreover points out the importance of insisting on absolute limits prescribed by the human dignity

---

55 BVerfGE 7, 198 [Lüth] – my translation –.
56 G Dürig, 'Der Grundrechtssatz von der Menschenwürde. Entwurf eines praktikablen Wertsystems der Grundrechte aus Art. 1 Abs. 1 i.V.m. Art 19 Abs. II des Grundgesetzes' in W Schmitt-Glaeser and P Häberle (eds), *Günter Dürig, Gesammelte Schriften 1952-1983* (Berlin; Duncker & Humblot, 1984) 127 – my translation –.
57 Pollmann, 'Barbarei' 32, 39.
58 But see Herdegen, 'Art. 1' para 47, who holds the absolute understanding only to be relevant for totalitarian excesses.
59 See G Teubner, 'Die anonyme Matrix. Zu Menschenrechtsverletzungen durch "private" transnationale Akteure' in W Brugger and U Neumann and S Kirste (eds), *Rechtsphilosophie im 21. Jahrhundert* (Frankfurt aM, Suhrkamp, 2008) 440 ff; examples of such 'negative externalities' of self-contained social subsystems are in the words of Gunther Teubner 'killing by chain of command, sweatshops as a consequence of anonymous market forces, martyrs as a result of religious communication, political or military torture as an identity destruction', especially at p 452 – my translation –.

concept; this is primarily a concern of the legislator and only secondarily of the German Federal Constitution Court with its controlling function.

B. Consequences of an Alterity-Centred and Pragmatic Concept of Human Dignity

In summary, the understanding of human dignity that is genealogically derived here, can be referred to as *alterity-centred* and *pragmatic*; *alterity-centred,* insofar as it is based on the emphasis of the 'self-though-reference' of human dignity, which sees dignity as the result of an interpersonal basic experience.[60] In accordance with Emmanuel Lévinas, the understanding of dignity here proposed foregrounds the responsibility for the other. As an ethical postulate, human dignity arises out of the mutual (not-reciprocal) recognition of the irreducible uniqueness and vulnerability of the other, his 'defenceless nakedness' and his 'exposure' to death.[61] Following Lévinas, out of this pre-societal event of sociality arises a responsibility for the other, which is underlying human rights: '*The human right, absolute and original,* only stands to reason within the particular other, as a right of the other'.[62] The *alterity-centred* understanding of human dignity shows a certain proximity to other dignity conceptions focusing on the vulnerability of man.[63] However, neither the above-outlined Kantian nor the Christian Imago Dei conceptions of dignity sufficiently capture this perspective. Among the natural law authors, only Pufendorf highlights the fragility (imbecillitas) of man in particular.[64]

---

60   Dürig stresses the 'self-though-reference' in his paradigmatic commentary of Art. 1(1) German Basic Law, G Dürig, 'Art. 1' in: T Maunz and G Dürig, *Grundgesetz-Kommentar* (looseleaf collection, previous edition, Munich, C.H. Beck) para. 2 – my translation –.
61   E Lévinas, *Verletzlichkeit und Frieden. Schriften über Politik und das Politische* (Zürich and Berlin, Diaphanes, 2007) 119 – my translation –.
62   Lévinas, *Verletzlichkeit und Frieden* (2007) 120 – my translation –.
63   See evidence at Wetz, *Illusion Menschenwürde* (2005); Spaemann, *Das Natürliche* (1987) and Pollmann, 'Barbarei'; also confer Herdegen's reference on 'anthropological basic assumptions' at Thomas Aquinas: Herdegen, 'Art. 1' para. 19; with regard to the problems of final justification due to theories of anthropological need see E Riedel, *Theorie der Menschenrechtsstandards* (Berlin, Duncker & Humblot, 1986) 183 ff.
64   S von Pufendorf, *De iure naturae et gentium* (1744); *De officio hominis et civis secundum legem naturalem* (1753); cited at Wetz, *Illusion Menschenwürde* (2005) 218 f.

Overall, the understanding of human dignity proposed here expands common autonomy conceptions of human rights. Taking account of the vulnerability of the individual thereby gains plausibility not only through the genealogy of human rights discourse in the 20th century, but also allows a better understanding of the dignity relevance of questions regarding needy individuals, such as dementia patients or people with intellectual disabilities, without denying these groups their capacity to autonomy. However, the concept of dignity is not completely absorbed in conceptions of autonomy, as its current discursive use shows.[65]

It is not possible to equate – without any friction – the understanding of the concept of human dignity proposed here with hitherto represented jurisprudential theories of dignity. Recourse to the pre-societal basic experience of the encounter with the vulnerable other differs from the 'Dowry-theory'[66] – somewhat simplified – as the inherent human ability to reason or being created in the image of god is at least not central to the vulnerability approach. On the other hand, this understanding is distinguished from the 'Achievement-theories'[67] since a life in dignity is indeed understood as a result of processes of self-respect and respect for the other, but the focus however is not on individual achievement but on the social preconditions for a decent life (respect and responsibility for the other). In this respect, the understanding shows a certain resemblance to the so-called 'Communication-theories' of human rights, as developed by Hasso Hofmann, which by the term 'solidary recognition' refer to an interpersonal dimension of human dignity.[68] However, this approach lacks the emphasis on the aspect of vulnerability of the other as an ethical basic ex-

---

[65]   Art. 3(a) Convention on the Rights of Persons with Disabilities also mentions dignity as a fundamental principle of the convention on equal footing with the principle of autonomy: 'Respect for inherent dignity, individual autonomy including the freedom to make one's own choices, and independence of persons'.

[66]   H Ottmann, 'Die Würde des Menschen' in J Beaufort and P Prechtl (eds), *Rationalität und Prärationalität. Festschrift für Alfred Schöpf* (Würzburg, Königshausen & Neumann, 1998) 16; Hofmann, 'Die versprochene Menschenwürde' 353; Dreier, 'Art. 1' para 55.

[67]   N Luhmann, *Grundrechte als Institution* (Berlin, Duncker & Humblot, 1965) 68 ff; Dreier, 'Art. 1' para 56.

[68]   Hofmann, 'Die versprochene Menschenwürde' 353 – my translation –; with approval and further development G Frankenberg, 'Die Würde des Klons und die Krise des Rechts' (2000) *Kritische Justiz* 325, 328 f.

perience, and hence it also lacks a universalizable dimension of the human dignity concept.[69]

The understanding of human dignity derived here is pragmatic as it is justified by the performative 'confession' of the German people obtained in Art. 1 German Basic Law, which is in proximity to Hofmann's approach.[70] A (linguistically) pragmatic interpretation of Art. 1 German Basic Law as such has no need for a particular religious or natural law foundation and is able to withstand a missing professional and social consensus regarding the derivation of the dignity concept in terms of the history of ideas.[71] Simultaneously, this pragmatic understanding facilitates the handling of natural scientific attacks on the concept of human dignity. Whatever natural sciences will explore with regard to the biological determination of the human will and its ability to reason, the imperative to respect Art. 1 German Basic Law, which refers to the legal concept of human dignity, remains unaffected.[72] For it is valid – referring to Kelsen – because it can be ascribed to an original positive legislative act,[73] and will last until such time as we jointly decide to write a new constitution.

---

69 This would also be an anchor for a pre-social or universalist understanding of human dignity and human rights, which cannot readily be justified with Hofmann's approach insofar as the latter is too narrow, as dignity is just 'promised'.
70 'Promise' at Hofmann, 'Die versprochene Menschenwürde' 369.
71 That such a metaphysical ultimate foundation, derived from any theoretical tradition whatsoever, can no longer be bindingly defined in a pluralistic society, is rightly stressed by Herdegen, 'Art. 1' para 39; Nettesheim, 'Garantie der Menschenwürde' 71; Dreier, 'Art. 1' para 84.
72 From a system theoretical perspective Ladeur and Augsberg emphasise the constructivist character of Art. 1(1) German Basic Law and appropriately speak of the inviolability of human dignity as 'self-instruction of the law' or a 'legally operable made resistance'; KH Ladeur and J Augsberg, *Die Funktion der Menschenwürde im Verfassungsstaat* (Tübingen, Mohr Siebeck, 2008) 15.
73 H Kelsen, *Reine Rechtslehre* (Leipzig and Wien, Deuticke, 1934) 215 ff; for Kelsen's Basic norm with further references see J von Bernstorff, *Der Glaube an das universale Recht: Zur Völkerrechtstheorie Hans Kelsens und seiner Schüler* (Baden-Baden, Nomos, 2011) 72.

IV. The Criticism of the Claim to Absoluteness

A. Balancing as Supreme Constitutional Principle?

In the Archiv für öffentliches Recht, Manfred Baldus put the thrust of criticism very straight: 'If the guarantee of dignity ought to be transparent and comprehensive in finding of law and law application processes, balancing it against other constitutional interests is inevitable.'[74]

This quote plainly states what the criticism comes down to, and what should step into the spot of an allegedly out-dated dogma. The critics portray human dignity as a fully ponderable value in an allegedly rational constitutional system of balancing, i.e., human dignity as just one individual preference among many others in the market of constitutionally established interests.[75] If necessary, human dignity has to withdraw behind supposedly 'outweighing' individual and collective goods, for instance the protection of public safety, medical progress, or other important community concerns. For it is the 'act of balancing' – quasi as an invisible hand – that is supposed to balance out the particular and collective preferences over and over again with the reliability of the laws of nature.

Ultimately, – that is the basic tenor of the criticism – Art. 1 German Basic Law is a fundamental right like any other.[76] However, the traditional dispute concerning the quality of Art. 1 German Basic Law being a fundamental right is thereby raised to a new, more profound level. According to this criticism, Art. 1(1) German Basic Law is neither a supreme constitutional principle nor an absolute principle regarding the interpretation of fundamental rights, as it is subject to the unwritten 'rule of balancing'. It is remarkable what status the still unwritten balancing principle has gained in parts of German constitutional theory, and by what unbridled methodological optimism 'objective' balancing solutions are assumed. And this at a time when the national and international criticism of the 'rationality' of balancing practices in terms of fundamental and human rights is increasing.[77] Without being able to acknowledge these critical voices in detail

---

74 Baldus, 'Menschenwürdegarantie' 548 – my translation –.
75 Haltern, 'Unsere protestantische Menschenwürde' 93, 122 ff.
76 Baldus, 'Menschenwürdegarantie' 549.
77 With a democratic theory inspired criticism F Schauer, *Playing by the Rules* (Oxford, Oxford University Press, 1991) 137-145; critical from the perspective of separation of powers TA Aleinikoff, 'Constitutional Law in the Age of Balancing' (1987) 96 *Yale Law Journal* 943, 984-986; for the German debate see

here, it should be taken into consideration that the 'balancing principle', now seemingly itself credited with absolute validity, in turn cannot guarantee a privileged access to objective solutions of constitutional conflicts. Even if one admits a limited practical benefit of balancing as a mental operation in fundamental and human rights adjudication, as the author does, there is no need for a scientific exaggeration of this practice as a fundamental principle of German constitutional law. Conceptually, the principle of proportionality, which in fact is central to the fundamental rights jurisdiction, is not necessarily dependent on the balance metaphor.[78]

However, what is the norm-theoretical and dogmatic reasoning underlying the relativization of the claim to absoluteness of Art. 1 German Basic Law? In this regard it should be noted that the semantics of Art. 1 German Basic Law by the term 'inviolability' initially oppose a relativizing approach. Robert Alexy norm-theoretically introduced the relativizing approach to Art. 1 German Basic Law with his theory of fundamental rights. For Alexy, principles are norms commanding that something is to be realized in a relatively large degree. They are simply 'optimization require-

---

instead of many B Schlink, 'Der Grundsatz der Verhältnismäßigkeit' in P Badura and H Dreier (eds), *Festschrift 50 Jahre Bundesverfassungsgericht. Bd. 2: Klärung und Fortbildung des Verfassungsrechts* (Tübingen, Mohr Siebeck, 2001) 445, 460-462; EW Böckenförde, 'Grundrechte als Grundsatznormen' (1990) 29 *Der Staat* 1, 20 ff; critical due to a lack of rationality E Denninger, 'Polizei und demokratische Politik' (1970) *JZ* 145, 152; M Jestaedt, *Grundrechtsentfaltung im Gesetz* (Tübingen, Mohr Siebeck, 1999) 241-248; R Poscher, *Grundrechte als Abwehrrechte* (Tübingen, Mohr Siebeck, 2003) 94 with further references; for the normatively 'untenable' balancing between individual freedom and societal security needs see C Möllers, Judgement Remarks Regarding the State Constitutional Court of Mecklenburg-Vorpommern, from 21.10.1999 – LVerfG 2/98, ThürVBl. (2000), 41, 43; D Neumann, *Vorsorge und Verhältnismäßigkeit* (Berlin, Duncker & Humblot, 1994) 102 ff; for the impossibility of general balancing rules with regard to the principle of equality L Osterloh, 'Art. 3' in M Sachs (ed), *Grundgesetz: Kommentar* (Munich, C.H. Beck, 1999) para 90; for the in the view of the authors failed argumentation theory efforts to objectify balancing confer R Christensen and A Fischer-Lescano, *Das Ganze des Rechts. Vom hierarchischen zum reflexiven Verständnis deutscher und europäischer Grundrechte* (Berlin, Duncker & Humblot, 2007) 357-359; with regard to the value of a 'categorical' (i.e. balancing-resistant) legal practice culture in the field of fundamental and human rights J von Bernstorff, 'Kerngehaltsschutz durch den UN-Menschenrechtsausschuss und den EGMR: Vom Wert kategorialer Argumentationsformen' (2011) 50 *Der Staat* 165 ff.

78   Von Bernstorff, 'Kerngehaltsschutz' 165 ff.

ments'. Their implementation is confined by opposing rules and principles. In contrast, a rule commands, 'to do exactly what it requires, no more no less.'[79] To paraphrase, a rule applies absolutely unless it is confined by an exception clause. With his analysis of the decision of the German Federal Constitutional Court regarding wiretapping (Abhörurteil), Alexy concludes that there are two human dignity standards: a human dignity rule and a human dignity principle. Accordingly, the principle can be implemented (i.e. balanced) in various degrees whereas the human dignity rule is without restraint.

Yet, Alexy did not cease at this distinction that still could be reconciled with the claim to absoluteness, but developed through his 'Law of Balancing' a connection between the assumed human dignity *rule* and the human dignity *principle* according to which the semantically indeterminate human dignity rule is violated, every time human dignity prevails on the principles level (i.e. after balancing)[80]. As a result of this, Alexy devalues the absoluteness of the human dignity rule. Following this construction, human dignity is not absolutely protected, but in the event of prevailing in the balancing process over other constitutionally protected interests, it subsequently has the appearance of absolute primacy.[81] In his commentary on Art. 1 German Basic Law in the Maunz-Dürig, Herdegen offers a similar reasoning. He says that the claim to respect the guarantee of human dignity in the first place is the result of an 'overall balancing evaluation'.[82] Determined as such through balancing, it shall then apply absolutely. The notion of a balancing-resistant human dignity content within fundamental rights is ultimately abolished by this line of thought. If the human dignity rule is to be determined through single case focused ad hoc-balancing, it is no absolute rule but just a standard subject to limitations. For this reason, Alexy's position is unable to theoretically reproduce the 'inviolability' of human dignity as stipulated by Art. 1 German Basic Law.

---

79 R Alexy, *Theorie der Grundrechte* (Frankfurt aM, Suhrkamp, 2001) 76 – my translation –; for the criticism see Jestaedt, *Grundrechtsentfaltung* (1999) 206 f, 222 f; Poscher, *Abwehrrechte* (2003) 73 f.
80 Alexy, *Theorie der Grundrechte* (2001) 96.
81 Critical C Enders, *Die Menschenwürde in der Verfassungsordnung. Zur Dogmatik des Art. 1 GG* (Tübingen, Mohr Siebeck, 1997) 124; KE Hain, 'Konkretisierung der Menschenwürde durch Abwägung?' (2006) 45 *Der Staat* 189, 202.
82 Herdegen, 'Art. 1' para 43.

More convincingly, Enders described the relation of human dignity and balancing processes regarding fundamental rights, even though he unnecessarily engages with Alexy's terminology of 'principles'. Accordingly, human dignity itself is not subject to constitutional balancing, but leads, dominates and confines the balancing process. Hence, human dignity is violated, 'if the preference relation determining the balancing between two principles itself would infringe human dignity.'[83] In that case, human dignity is not balanced against other constitutional positions, but governs and corrects the constitutional decision making from the outside as an absolute limit. It can remain open here whether this boundary is technically conceptualised as a final limitation of constitutionally permitted restrictions or as a balancing-resistant component on the level of the scope of the right. It is fundamental and crucial that the guarantee of human dignity itself is not balanced with other constitutional standards. This understanding of human dignity, which adheres to the concept of an unrestrictable standard, is very close to the apodictic wording of the German Basic Law. Hereby Art. 1 German Basic Law is not only 'supreme constitutional principle',[84] but constitutes at the same time, in connection with the specific fundamental rights, an absolute boundary for infringements. Whether this limit is exceeded by a state measure, is to be determined by the interpretation and application of Art. 1 German Basic Law in conjunction with the relevant fundamental right. This interpretation may not 'weigh' human dignity against other legally protected interests, as it is the case with the principle of proportionality.

B. The Claim to Absoluteness in the Jurisdiction on Art. 1 German Basic Law

According to the German Federal Constitutional Court, Art. 1 German Basic Law applies in a concrete dignity infringement 'without the possibility of balancing competing legal interests.'[85] The Court adheres to this established judicial practice.[86] This tradition of Karlsruhe adjudication

---

83 Enders, *Menschenwürde* (1997) 124 – my translation –.
84 Dürig, 'Grundrechtssatz' 132.
85 BVerfGE 75, 369, 380 – my translation –.
86 BVerfGE 34, 239, 245; 75, 369, 380; 107, 257, 284; 109, 279, 314; 113, 348, 391; 115, 118, 153; as does the predominant literature C Starck, 'Art. 1' in H v. Mangold, F Klein and C Starck (eds), *Grundgesetzkommentar*, 5th edn (Mu-

causes significant difficulties for the critics of the claim to absoluteness. The traditional focus on Karlsruhe by the balancing proponents interferes with their propagated conception of balancing as being a supreme judicial methodology. For them just one solution out of this dilemma is actually remaining: They argue Karlsruhe has abandoned the claim to absoluteness in practice for long. Accordingly, the Court – with its commitments to inviolability – 'veils' that since the decision on wiretapping (Abhörurteil) it balances human dignity as a fully ponderable interest with other interests.[87] Were several generations of constitutional judges from different senates actually just fooling us with their continuous explicit commitments to the claim to absoluteness?

To begin with, it has to be noted that the German Federal Constitutional Court in the vast majority of decisions regarding Art. 1 German Basic Law is very concerned about not including any balancing elements into the reasoning of the decision and instead argues with categorical boundaries. Therefore, the criticism always refers to the same and numerically mar-

nich, Vahlen, 2005) para 34; P Kunig, 'Art. 1' in I v. Münch and P Kunig, Grundgesetz: Kommentar (Munich, C.H. Beck, 2012) para 4; G Robbers, 'Art. 1' in DC Umbach and T Clemens (eds), *Grundgesetz* (Heidelberg C.F. Müller, 2002) para 34; B Pieroth and B Schlink, *Grundrechte Staatsrecht II* (Heidelberg, C.F. Müller, 2001) paras 356-358; V Epping, *Grundrechte*, 2nd edn (Heidelberg, Springer, 2004) para 574; P Lerche, 'Grundrechtlicher Schutzbereich, Grundrechtsprägung und Grundrechtseingriff' in J Isensee and P Kirchhof, Handbuch des Staatsrechts, Vol 5 (Heidelberg, C.F. Müller, 2000) §121 para 19; HD Jarass and B Pieroth (eds), *Grundgesetz* (Munich, C.H. Beck, 2004) Art. 1, paras 2, 12; E Schmidt- Jortzig, 'Systematische Bedingungen der Garantie unbedingten Schutzes der Menschenwürde in Art. 1 GG' (2001) 54 *Die öffentliche Verwaltung* 925 ff; CD Classen, 'Die Forschung mit embryonalen Stammzellen im Spiegel der Grundrechte' (2002) *Deutsches Verwaltungsblatt* 141 ff; W Heun, 'Embryonenforschung und Verfassung – Lebensrecht und Menschenwürde des Embryos' (2002) *JZ* 517 ff; T Hörnle, 'Menschenwürde und Lebensschutz' (2003) 89 *ARSP* 318 ff; R Poscher, '"Die Würde des Menschen ist unantastbar"' (2004) *JZ* 756 ff; W Höfling, 'Unantastbare Grundrechte. Ein normlogischer Widerspruch?' in R Gröschner and OW Lembcke (eds), *Das Dogma der Unantastbarkeit* (Tübingen, Mohr Siebeck, 2009) 111; C Enders, 'Die normative Unantastbarkeit der Menschenwürde' in: R Gröschner and OW Lembcke (eds), *Das Dogma der Unantastbarkeit* (Tübingen, Mohr Siebeck, 2009) 69; B Podlech, 'Art. 1' in E Stein et al (eds), AK-GG, (Neuwied et al, Luchterhand, 2001) para 73; Dreier, 'Art. 1' para 132.

87 T Elsner and K Schobert, 'Gedanken zur Abwägungsresistenz der Menschenwürde – angestoßen durch das Urteil des Bundesverfassungsgerichts zur Verfassungsmäßigkeit der Sicherungsverwahrung' (2007) *Deutsches Verwaltungsblatt* 278 ff.

ginal group of cases in which a remaining balancing semantic can be found in the reasoning.[88] Admittedly, in these exceptional cases, due to ambiguous wording and problematic elements of reasoning, the impression may arise that the affected human dignity of fundamental right holders is balanced with other constitutionally protected positions. But contrary to this first impression, we frequently observe even in these exceptional cases a balancing exercise beyond the narrowly dignity-relevant and therefore balancing-resistant content of the specific position of freedom. In these problematic cases the Court only refers to an overarching relevance of Art. 1 German Basic Law for the particular applicable fundamental right and the case constellation at hand (justification still possible), in order to then however find the dignity-relevant core-content of the fundamental right in the concrete circumstances (absolute protection) not yet infringed.[89] In particular in its judgement on lifelong imprisonment, which is gladly used by critics as a prime example of balancing in the context of Art. 1 German Basic Law,[90] the German Federal Constitutional Court actually does conduct a categorical drawing of boundaries in line with the absoluteness claim. In this decision the senate explicitly explores, within the circumstances first classified as *generally* dignity-relevant, the core-content of the fundamental right that is covered by the human dignity guarantee:

> ... since the core of human dignity is infringed, if the convict has to lose faith in regaining his freedom regardless of the development of his personality.[91]

---

88 Exemplary Baldus, 'Menschenwürdegarantie' 536 ff with reference to BVerfGE 12, 45, 51 – Kriegsdienstverweigerung I; BVerfGE 30, 1, 27 – Abhörurteil; BVerfGE 30, 173, 197 f. – Mephisto; BVerfGE 35, 202, 235 f.; BVerfGE 45, 187, 229 – lebenslange Freiheitsstrafe; BVerfGE 109, 133, 150 – Sicherungsverwahrung; BVerfGE 80, 367, 373 f. – Tagebuch Beschluss; BVerfGE 109, 279, 313 f. – akustische Wohnraumüberwachung; BVerfGE 113, 348, 357– präventive Telekommunikationsüberwachung; BVerfGE 120, 274, 335ff. – Onlinedurchsuchung; BVerfGE 39, 1, 41, 43, 48; 88, 203, 252f. – Schwangerschaftsabbruch; BVerfGE 115, 118, 153, 157, 159 ff. – Luftsicherheitsgesetz.

89 For the absolute protection of the 'core-contents' E Denninger, 'Prävention und Freiheit. Von der Ordnung der Freiheit' in S Huster and K Rudolph (eds), *Vom Rechtsstaat zum Präventionsstaat* (Frankfurt aM, Suhrkamp, 2008) 103 ff; H Bielefeldt, *Auslaufmodell Menschenwürde* (Freiburg et al, Herder, 2011) 132-134.

90 Elsner and Schobert, 'Gedanken zur Abwägungsresistenz' 278 ff.

91 BVerfGE 45, 187, 245 – my translation –.

Thus, the lifelong imprisonment is generally dignity relevant. But the balancing-resistant human dignity content of the second sentence of Art. 2(2) German Basic Law is not infringed as long as certain minimum requirements (including an individual perspective to freedom) are met.[92]

However, the balancing proponents refer to the passage of the judgement that states human dignity is not infringed because the dangerousness of the offender prohibits the pardon.[93] Accordingly, this formulation is proof for a judicial balancing of the human dignity guarantee. Yet, on closer inspection it is just a methodological unfortunate wording for the test of necessity with regard to the imprisonment, which can and should be distinguished from balancing.

Without the dangerousness of the offender, the lifelong imprisonment inherently would not be necessary as an infringement of Art. 2(2) German Basic Law in order to ensure the legislative goal of adequate protection of the population. The infringement would therefore already be classified as disproportionate (unnecessary), independent of balancing. But even if the offender remains dangerous, hence the infringement is necessary, the minimum requirements for a human dignity compliant imprisonment apply, which were derived from Art. 1(1) German Basic Law in the judgement.[94]

Trends among scholars to consider the concretion of human dignity with regard to the particular circumstances of the case as inevitable 'hidden' balancing mix the undoubtedly existing definitional problem with the one of the balancing-resistance.[95] In the end in the discussed judgements, the Court seeks to closer contour the – in its view – absolutely protected freedom positions, and thereby seeks to define the scope of infringements of freedom that it still holds tolerable. In so doing, the claim to absoluteness will be judicially fulfilled, when the judgement ultimately defines the limits for confinements with regard to the concrete effects on the individual of infringements in such a way that they can be applied in similar cases. A categorical formulated standard insofar requires a categorical decision practice. In contrast, the jurisdiction does a disservice to the claim to abso-

---

92   BVerfGE 109, 133, 151.
93   BVerfGE 45, 187, 242; with the argument that the court balances human dignity Alexy, *Theorie der Grundrechte* (2001) 96 f.
94   However, even if the court in individual decisions would treat human dignity as a fully ponderable fundamental right position, it would be unconstitutional from the perspective adopted here, insofar as there would be no adequate justification for the relativist position established in the literature.
95   But see Elsner and Schobert, 'Gedanken zur Abwägungsresistenz' 279-280.

luteness whenever dignity-relevant core-contents are first judicially defined without effectively protecting these against infringements afterwards.[96]

V. Plea for the Retention of the Claim to Absoluteness

Certainly, the here-urged judicial definitions of absolute boundaries cannot be objectified in the sense of a mathematical exercise.[97] Whether the judicially defined limits in a particular case are being drawn convincingly, can and should be debated in a free society. It is only important that it will be argued about the concrete definition of the boundary and not about the existence of absolute boundaries as such. It would also be naïve to prohibit judges from considering the consequences of their decisions with regard to third parties and society as a whole as well as to use these considerations in their personal decision-making.[98] In addition, it does not relativize the claim to absoluteness when the German Federal Constitutional Court considers such thoughts in a decision on Art. 1 German Basic Law, as long as the image of a balancing-resistant last limitation for restrictions is semantically respected.[99]

It is one thing to reflect the potential consequences for society in a judgement with human dignity relevance, and quite another to put the guarantee of human dignity under the general restriction of case-by-case balancing. In the first case, ultimate limitations regarding state enforcement powers can continue to be maintained by the courts. However, under the primacy of ad hoc-balancing also very intensive infringements are only deemed unlawful in the absent of other outweighing societal interests. Precedence and thus the guiding impact of judgements is almost completely abolished. Thus, there can be no meaningful legal discourse regarding

---

96   BVerfGE 109, 279 – großer Lauschangriff; also compare C Möllers, 'Wandel der Grundrechtsjudikatur' (2005) *NJW* 1973, 1976; O Lepsius, 'Der große Lauschangriff vor dem Bundesverfassungsgericht' (2005) *Jura* 433 ff.
97   For the changeability of human dignity understandings see Nettesheim, 'Garantie der Menschenwürde' 87.
98   Legitimately, several voices in the literature refer to such unavoidable valuation processes, cf Gröschner and Lembcke, 'Dignitas absoluta' 15; Nettesheim, 'Garantie der Menschenwürde' 88; U Di Fabio, 'Grundrechte als Werteordnung' (2004) *JZ* 1, 5.
99   But see Baldus, 'Menschenwürdegarantie' 536-540.

last limits for restrictions, independent of individual cases. The problem is not the presumably inevitable deliberative legal reasoning as such,[100] but the lack of rule-like substantiated boundaries concerning particularly severe infringements of fundamental and human rights. Under the primacy of boundless ad-hoc balancing, a deontic (rule-like) understanding of rights will disappear from institutionalised human rights protection. Ultimately, the constitutive pledge of Art. 1 German Basic Law is suspended. It only applies if validated by utilitarian considerations in the individual case, otherwise not.

The result would be a shift in the discourse on human dignity, a utilitarian reassessment of a central concept of the constitution with consequences for our understanding of fundamental rights: state torture would have to be introduced, since rationally being necessary in extreme situations; medical experiments on humans in third parties' interest, even against their will, could then be held reasonable for the good of medical progress and community health; with regard to human genetics, measures of selection and breeding would lose any offensiveness as soon as particular important social interests would let them appear as rationally necessary; also the intentional killing of innocent citizens suddenly emerges untarnished, if high security interests render the killing indispensable. Moreover, what then stands constitutionally firmly against removals of organs of terminally ill and very old individuals without their consent, if four or five fatally ill children may be saved? Welcome to the big market of fully ponderable constitutional preferences, where everything has its price – even human dignity.[101] Precisely because everything is contingent and relative, all 'flows', a social contract based on the continuous definition of absolute limits to what the society can do to the individual remains so central.

The consequences for the systematic position of Art. 1 German Basic Law resulting from all this can be outlined as follows: In the classification favored here, Art. 1 German Basic Law functions, in addition to its 'state founding function',[102] as an absolute limitation of the constitutional exceptions in conjunction with certain fundamental rights.[103] The standard re-

---

100   Gröschner and Lembcke, 'Dignitas absoluta' 15.
101   For the market analogy Haltern, 'Unsere protestantische Menschenwürde' 122 f; for the difference between dignity and price see I Kant, *Grundlegung zur Metaphysik der Sitten*, (1785) 77.
102   Concept from Hofmann, 'Die versprochene Menschenwürde' 368.
103   From a functional perspective, see the helpful term developed by W Graf Vitzthum and E Riedel, one should hold on to a common understanding of the

quires a balancing-stop[104] for particular intensive state infringements of fundamental rights. The fundamental rights contents covered by the clause are also protected from constitutional amendments by Art. 79(3) German Basic Law. From an abstract perspective Art. 1 German Basic Law along with the guarantee of the essence of fundamental rights represents a defense claim of the individual regarding particular intensive infringements, which is to be protected by the jurisdiction *ex negativo* through case constellation orientated categorical (i.e. balancing-resistant) drawings of boundaries within the specific fundamental rights. Thereby, in legal practice the protected positions of freedom should initially be developed out of the specific fundamental rights.[105] For this purpose, the affected fundamental right in conjunction with Art. 19(2) German Basic Law offers the first and correct point of evidence, which is generally dignity-independent.[106] Therefore, human dignity is just a final guardian with regard to the specification of limits of restrictions within the particular fundamental right. The German Federal Constitutional Court has occasionally disregarded this priority for liberty specific determination of the balancing-resistant cores of rights through Art. 19(2) German Basic Law without good cause. As a result of this, Art. 1 German Basic Law was overstressed, the human dignity argument inflated[107] and the guarantee of the

---

constitutive and limiting function of the guarantee of human dignity, compare E Riedel, 'Gentechnologie und Embryonenschutz als Verfassungs- und Regelungsproblem' (1986) *Europäische Grundrechte-Zeitschrift* 469 ff; W Graf Vitzthum, 'Gentechnologie und Menschenwürdeargument' (1987) 20 *Zeitschrift für Rechtspolitik* 33 ff; for the functional approach see T Geddert-Steinacher, *Menschenwürde als Verfassungsbegriff* (Berlin, Duncker & Humblot, 1990) 130 ff.

104 Ladeur and Augsberg speak of a 'function as absolute stop signal'; Ladeur and Augsberg, *Funktion der Menschenwürde* (2008) 10.
105 Höfling, 'Unantastbare Grundrechte' 114; J von Bernstorff, 'Die Wesensgehalte der Grundrechte und das Verhältnis von Freiheit und Sicherheit im Grundgesetz' in F Arndt et al (eds), *48. Assistententagung Öffentliches Recht* (Baden-Baden, Nomos, 2009) 40 ff.
106 In this regard the here developed position clearly differs from Dürig's dogmatic equalisation of Art. 1(1) and Art. 19(2) German Basic Law.
107 R Will, 'Die Menschenwürde: Zwischen Versprechen und Überforderung' in F Roggan (ed), *Mit Recht für Menschenwürde und Verfassungsstaat* (Berlin, Berliner Wissenschafts-Verlag, 2006) 29, 43; D Hömig, 'Menschenwürdeschutz in der Rechtsprechung des Bundesverfassungsgerichts' in R Gröschner and OW Lembcke (eds), *Das Dogma der Unantastbarkeit* (Tübingen, Mohr Siebeck, 2009) 25, 50; CD Classen, 'Die Menschenwürde ist – und bleibt – unantastbar' (2009) 62 *Die öffentliche Verwaltung* 689; C Hillgruber, 'Art. 1' in V Epping

essence of each human right in Art. 19(2) German Basic Law became virtually functionless. Especially if one wishes to adhere to the claim to absoluteness of Art. 1 German Basic Law that through Art. 79(3) German Basic Law is 'double-stitched', the dignity argument requires a sparing dose.[108]

VI. The Claim to Absoluteness in Hard Cases

However, what does adhering to the claim to absoluteness specifically imply for the heavily discussed extreme constellations, for the philosophically intriguing hard cases, to which the constitutional scholars showed much, maybe even too much attention?[109] For instance, what about police torture against the assassin, who should reveal the location of the ticking bomb? These hypothetical scenarios are familiar: without torture by the police the alleged terrorist will not relinquish the bomb prepared by him – a scenario that can result in the killing of many innocent people.[110] Does not in this case the dignity of the terrorist conflict with the lives of many innocent people threatened by the bomb? Must not balancing be allowed at least here, and state torture as a result be re-legalized?[111]

According to the legal philosopher Thomas Nagel, the ethical value of the adherence to absolute prohibitions for such extreme situations can be described as follows: Even if government agencies must do awful things in extreme cases in order to prevent a particular disaster, such as the ill-treatment of the bomb plotter, the measure retains its intuitively adopted flaw. It is understandable, but never quite in order.[112] Precisely this is the essence of a concept of ethics that emanates from moral absolutism. However, translated into the binary-coded language of law this has to mean

---

and C Hillgruber (eds), *Kommentar GG* (Beck Online Kommentar, 2013) para. 11.
108 As here instead of many Dreier, 'Art. 1' para 45 ff.
109 Views deriving from this debate are Brugger, *Menschenwürde*, speech given on 18.07.1996; F Wittreck, 'Menschenwürde und Folterverbot' (2003) 56 *Die öffentliche Verwaltung* 873 ff and the references given in fn 4.
110 This is the bottom line of the argumentation by Brugger, *Menschenwürde*, speech given on 18.07.1996; Wittreck, 'Menschenwürde und Folterverbot' 873 ff.
111 cf Wittreck, 'Menschenwürde und Folterverbot' 873 ff; for the debate see fn 4.
112 T Nagel, *Mortal Questions* (Cambridge, Cambridge University Press, 1979) 73.

that police torture, no matter for what purpose, results in a constitutional violation. Doctrinally, in the event of a dignity-relevant core-content-collision, as occasionally constructed among scholars regarding the state duty to respect the dignity of the assassin and the state duty to protect the dignity of potential victims, a general priority of the duty to respect over the duty to protect has to be assumed. Only then the claim to absoluteness, which derives from the inviolability of the standard, can be doctrinally honored.[113] After all, maintaining the constitutional prohibition of torture does not preclude the judge in a criminal trial to take the existential emergency-situation confronting the acting policemen into consideration when deciding on an appropriate sentence.

According to this understanding, the human dignity standard remains a guarantor of a last residuum of ethical absolutism regarding the protection of fundamental and human rights. Without an appropriate reflection of the ideal of (non-utilitarian) ethical boundaries in judicial practice, human rights law loses its purpose and societal value.

---

113   cf M Hong, 'Das grundgesetzliche Folterverbot und der Menschenwürdegehalt der Grundrechte – eine verfassungsjuristische Betrachtung' in G Beestermöller and H Brunkhorst (eds), *Rückkehr der Folter. Der Rechtsstaat im Zwielicht?* (Munich, C.H. Beck, 2006) 24 ff; I myself have tried to give a more detailed justification of this elsewhere: J von Bernstorff, 'Pflichtenkollision und Menschenwürdegarantie' (2008) 47 *Der Staat* 21, 35 ff.

Developing a Modern Understanding of Human Dignity

Roger Brownsword

I. Introduction

For more than half a century—from the time that Article 1 of the United Nations' Universal Declaration of Human Rights, 1948, famously proclaimed that 'All human beings are born free and equal in dignity and rights', through to the UNESCO Universal Declaration on Bioethics and Human Rights, 2005—we find a seemingly steady consolidation of the cosmopolitan ideal that there should be respect for human rights and human dignity. In post-Lisbon Europe, too, this ideal is explicitly highlighted, Article 2 of the (amended) Treaty on the European Union providing that the EU 'is founded on the values of respect for human dignity, freedom, democracy, equality, the rule of law and respect for human rights';[1] and in legal systems round the world, whether in the Northern or Southern hemisphere, whether in the common law or civilian families, we find prominent constitutional recognition of human dignity as a fundamental value.

Yet, this global consensus that human rights and human dignity are of fundamental value fractures as soon as attempts are made to articulate and apply the concept of human dignity.[2] Whereas, in some articulations, human dignity simply supports the scheme of human rights, in others, it opposes acts or practices that are compatible with human rights. By contrast, although there are many disagreements about the interpretation of particular human rights (such as privacy) or about the priorities between rights when they conflict (such as the priority between privacy and freedom of

---

1   See Consolidated Version of the Treaty on European Union, *Official Journal of the European Union*, C 115/13, 9 May 2008.
2   This was not always the case. See M Düwell, 'Human Dignity: Concepts, Discussions, Philosophical Perspectives' in M Düwell, J Braarvig, R Brownsword, and D Mieth (eds), *The Cambridge Handbook of Human Dignity* (Cambridge, Cambridge University Press, 2014) (noting a general assumption at the time of the UDHR that the meaning and status of human dignity were clear).

expression), the fractures that we find in relation to human rights do not seem to be quite so deep and problematic—no one suggests, for example, that the concept of human rights is useless.

We might respond to this phenomenon by invoking the notion of human dignity as a contested concept. Taking this approach, we would say that many high-level constitutional concepts—for example, 'justice', 'equality', 'freedom', 'solidarity', and so on—are contested; and, to this extent, the concept of human dignity is in good company. The fact that protagonists on both sides of an issue appeal to human dignity is neither pathological nor novel; this happens all the time with contested concepts.[3] Although this is an attractively short way of treating a concept that, in recent times, has been burdened with more than its fair share of criticism,[4] it does not take us much closer to understanding human dignity.

In what follows, I will outline some steps that do promise to take us closer to such an understanding. However, the importance of these steps is not so much that we develop a clearer mapping of the conceptual relationship between human dignity and human rights but that we come to see human dignity as a cornerstone value in communities where interactions and transactions are increasingly mediated by new technologies. Crucially, where regulators turn to new technologies to be used as regulatory tools, it is imperative that communities with moral aspirations remain alert to the implications of such techno-regulatory strategies.

---

3   cp R Dresser, 'Human Dignity and the Seriously Ill Patient' in A Schulman (ed), *Human Dignity and Bioethics: Essays Commissioned by the President's Council on Bioethics* (President's Council on Bioethics, 2008); and R Dworkin, *Justice for Hedgehogs* (Cambridge, Mass, Belknap Press of Harvard University Press, 2011) 204.

4   See, eg, H Kuhse, 'Is there a Tension Between Autonomy and Dignity?' in P Kemp, J Rendtorff and NM Johansen (eds), *Bioethics and Biolaw (vol 2): Four Ethical Principles* (Copenhagen, Rhodos International Science and Art Publishers and Centre for Ethics and Law, 2000) 74: '[H]uman dignity plays a very dubious role in contemporary bioethical discourse. It is a slippery and inherently speciesist notion, it has a tendency to stifle argument and debate and encourages the drawing of moral boundaries in the wrong places. Even if the notion could have some uses as a short-hand version to express principles such as "respect for persons", or "respect for autonomy", it might, given its history and the undoubtedly long-lasting connotations accompanying it, be better if it were for once and for all purged from bioethical discourse.' Famously, to similar effect, see R Macklin, 'Dignity Is a Useless Concept' (2003) 327 *BMJ* 1419.

The paper is in four principal parts, each representing a key aspect of the development of a modern understanding of human dignity. First, I deal with the mapping of human dignity. Secondly, if there is an Archimedean point in the landscape of human dignity, then I suggest that it is to be found in a Gewirthian theory of rights.[5] Thirdly, I draw attention to some significant common ground between those who contest the concept of human dignity: namely, in the way that they attach fundamental importance to agents trying to do the right thing for the right reason. Finally, I develop the latter of these ideas specifically in relation to the modern use of technologies as regulatory tools.

II. Mapping Human Dignity

In this part of the paper, I sketch four steps towards mapping the modern discourse of human dignity. This is not designed to resolve the disagreements but simply to clarify how and why the disagreements arise. The steps are: (i) to emphasise that it is '*human* dignity', not 'dignity' per se, that is to be analysed; (ii) to contrast a liberal conception of 'human dignity as empowerment' with a conservative conception of 'human dignity as constraint'; (iii) to draw out the contrast between the 'rights-based' approaches that underlie the liberal conception and the 'duty-based' approaches that underlie the conservative conception; and (iv) to highlight the importance of consent for the liberal approach and its irrelevance for 'dignitarian' duty-based approaches.

A. Human Dignity Not Dignity

According to Michael Rosen, it is only with Kant that the idea of dignity evolves into that of *human* dignity.[6] Although Rosen emphasises that his project is to analyse dignity, for my purposes it is *human* dignity that is the appropriate focus. The modern cosmopolitan ideal is not that dignity

---

5   The seminal text is A Gewirth, *Reason and Morality* (Chicago, Chicago University Press, 1978).
6   M Rosen: *Dignity—Its History and Meaning* (Cambridge, Mass, Harvard University Press, 2012).

should be respected but that *human* dignity (alongside human rights) should be respected.

That said, and Kant notwithstanding, a discourse of dignity persists in relation to non-humans—dignity being attributed by some both to non-human animals and to the natural environment (or, at any rate, to some parts of it). It follows that, where choices have to be made between pursuing the interests of humans or protecting and preserving non-human animals or the environment, the issue can be presented in terms of choosing the dignity of x over the dignity of y—and without any easy answer being available. For example, some years ago, in the early post-Apartheid years, South African politicians faced such a hard choice: the question was whether coastal land of outstanding natural beauty (lying just South of Cape Town) should be freed for development in order to raise funds for a badly needed social housing programme. Expressing this in terms of rival dignities, the question was: should the (in)dignity of homeless humans prevail over the dignity of the Cape coastline?

If, as I propose, we limit our focus to the concept of human dignity, we can put some of these dignity conflicts beyond the scope of our inquiry. Of course, this does not mean that those conflicts are resolved; the choice between housing humans and degrading the Cape coastline remains. Nor does it mean that, with human dignity as our focus, we will be free of conflicts. Quite to the contrary: as I have indicated already, the concept of human dignity is notorious for being pleaded in support of diametrically opposed positions. Still, as a first step, we can maintain a (narrower) focus on human dignity and not dignity at large.

B. 'Human Dignity as Empowerment' v 'Human Dignity as Constraint'

In a seminal paper, David Feldman cautioned that we should not 'assume that the idea of dignity is inextricably linked to a liberal-individualist view of human beings as people whose life-choices deserve respect'.[7] To the contrary, 'human dignity may subvert rather than enhance choice ... Once it becomes a tool in the hands of lawmakers and judges, the concept of human dignity is a two-edged sword'.[8] In the context of familiar debates about the ethics and legality of abortions, access to modern technologies

---

7   D Feldman, 'Human Dignity as a Legal Value: Part I' (1999) *PL* 682, 685.
8   ibid.

for assisted reproduction, assisted suicide, euthanasia, and the like, where 'pro-choice' positions line up against 'pro-life' positions, we see precisely the dual role of appeals to human dignity—to demand respect for the life-choices that humans make but also to challenge and to set limits on individual choice.

A couple of years after the publication of Feldman's paper, in *Human Dignity in Bioethics and Biolaw*,[9] Deryck Beyleveld and I mapped the discourse of human dignity in rather similar terms. While, on the one side, human dignity functions to support individual choice (the conception of 'human dignity as empowerment'), on the other, it functions to place certain choices off limits (the conception of 'human dignity as constraint'). While the former is closely related to human rights, the latter seems to be quite independent of human rights. Given the conjunction of human rights and human dignity as a cosmopolitan ideal, this division is indicative of serious underlying differences.

Despite such differences, both sides agree that humans should not be instrumentalised. But, again, any apparent consensus soon breaks down. While those who argue for human dignity as empowerment mean that we should respect the rights of others (failing which, we instrumentalise them), those who argue for human dignity as constraint mean that we should not treat others, or ourselves, as things (otherwise humans are instrumentalised). On this latter view, the injunction against instrumentalisation leverages a broad claim that human life should be neither commodified nor commercialised. Some acts of commodification—for example, the use of technologies for social sex selection of babies—do not entail commercialisation. However, in many instances, commodification goes hand-in-hand with commercialisation—this is so, for example, in relation to prostitution and the sale of human organs.

In this light, consider the way that appeals to human dignity play in debates about the use of new technologies for various kinds of human enhancement.[10] On the one side, there is a concern that technologies should

---

9   D Beyleveld and R Brownsword, *Human Dignity in Bioethics and Biolaw* (Oxford, Oxford University Press, 2001).

10   See, eg, R Brownsword, 'Regulating Human Enhancement: Things Can Only Get Better?' (2009) 1 *Law Innovation and Technology* 125; and id, 'A Simple Regulatory Principle for Performance-Enhancing Technologies: Too Good to be True?' in J Tolleneer, P Bonte and S Sterckx (eds), *Athletic Enhancement, Human Nature and Ethics: Threats and Opportunities of Doping Technologies* (Dordrecht, Springer, 2012).

not enhance humans in ways that involve the infringement of human rights; on the other, the argument is that human dignity should not be compromised by technologies that involve commodification of humans. Suppose, following a scenario sketched by Bert Gordijn,[11] nanosensors are fitted in our bodies in order to monitor our health; and, where problems are detected, nanometric drug release systems are activated. Such early warning systems and nano-responses seem to be good for our health, but they might have a downside when viewed through the lens of human dignity as constraint. Thus:

> [S]uch developments will contribute to a more technologically inspired image of the body as something very similar to a machine. The body will increasingly be regarded as a whole, made up of many different components that might be fixed, enhanced or replaced if necessary. Development, functions, and appearance of the body will seem less and less fixed by nature and less frequently accepted without change, and more frequently controllable by technology. Instead of being in charge of our own health we might increasingly trust technology to take over this responsibility. In the process however, the body will be treated almost like the inanimate material of a machine. Hence, the body might become increasingly de-hallowed and de-mystified.[12]

To the extent that nanomedicine adopts or encourages the functional view that is already evident in human genetics and the new brain sciences, this will compound dignitarian concerns about commodification. The promise of in vivo nanosensors and drug release systems, like the promise of regenerative medicine, sounds fine until it is set alongside the disaggregation of humans into their component parts. Is there really no distinction between humans and, say, a motor car or a computer—just so many parts, so many functions, so many models?

C. A Rights-Based Approach v a Duty-Based Approach

The pattern of modern ethical discourse suggests that moral positions are either 'deontological', building from rights or from duties, or 'teleological' (in the way, for example, that utilitarians argue that we do the right thing provided that we act in a way that is calculated to maximise utility).

---

11 B Gordijn, 'Converging NBIC Technologies for Improving Human Performance: A Critical Assessment of the Novelty and Prospects of the Project' (2006) 34 *Journal of Law, Medicine and Ethics* 726–32.
12 ibid 729.

Although utilitarians or other teleologists might find a way of mentioning human dignity, it is not central to their positions. Characteristically, the fiercest debates about human dignity involve protagonists who operate, respectively, with rights-based or duty-based ethics.

For rights-based ethicists, we do the right thing so long as we respect the rights of others. Such a view comports with the conception of human dignity as empowerment. By contrast, for duty-based ethicists, we do the right thing so long as we act in accordance with our duties. Such duties may be to others but also to ourselves. Such a view comports with the conception of human dignity as constraint. Where duty-based ethics is focused on duties to others, it will resemble rights-based ethics; but a major divergence appears when the duties that are argued for are simply to oneself. From a rights-based perspective, it simply does not make sense to talk of a rights-holder having duties to oneself, as though one could divide oneself in this way—including dividing oneself in a way that would allow for one's right-holding self to authorise (by consent) acts to be done by one's duty-bearing self that would otherwise violate one's rights.[13]

Although the contrast between rights-based and duty-based approaches is fundamental to mapping modern ethics, it should not be thought that the two families of approaches are entirely homogeneous—rather, each represents a broad Church. On the rights side, we have both will theories and interest theories, and we have many different positions on the spectrum of negative and positive rights. On the duty-based side, we have what I have previously termed the 'dignitarian alliance'.[14] Here, we have communitarian, Catholic, and Kantian views converging in order to resist the unrelenting push of modern technologies: against this push, the alliance pleads that technologies should be restrained so that they do not compromise human dignity.

---

13 Compare Gewirth, *Reason and Morality* (1978) 334, especially for the contradiction between treating an agent as both a rights-holding self (in which capacity the agent is able to release a duty-bearer from performance of the duty) and a duty-bearing self (in which capacity one cannot release oneself from performance of the duty).

14 See R Brownsword, 'Bioethics Today, Bioethics Tomorrow: Stem Cell Research and the "Dignitarian Alliance"' (2003) 17 *University of Notre Dame Journal of Law, Ethics and Public Policy* 15.

D. Consent and Human Dignity

The mapping of the modern discourse of human dignity is incomplete without an appreciation of the way that consent plays in relation to the rival conceptions.

One of the most striking features of the approach that we are terming 'human dignity as constraint' is that, in many of the duty-based ethics, the consent of the parties cannot redeem an act that otherwise compromises human dignity.[15] So, for example, in the well-known (German) *Peep-Show Decision*,[16] where the Federal Administrative Tribunal denied a licence for a mechanical peep-show on the ground that the performance would violate human dignity, the Tribunal said:

> The consent of the women concerned can only exclude a violation of human dignity if such a violation is based only on the lack of consent to the relevant actions or omissions of the women concerned. However, this is not the situation here because in the case at issue ... the human dignity of the women concerned is violated by the exposition typical of these performances. Here, human dignity, because its significance reaches beyond the individual, must be protected even against the wishes of the woman concerned whose own subjective ideas deviate from the objective value of human dignity.[17]

No doubt, many further illustrations could be given—for example, in *R v Brown*,[18] where the majority of the House of Lords ruled that consent was no defence to the assaults and woundings inflicted during sado-masochistic sexual practices; in another *Brown* case,[19] this time in the US, where the court rejected the defendant's defence that his alcoholic wife consented to the beatings that he administered when she drank; in France, in the famous dwarf-throwing case;[20] and, in Germany, in the more recent

---

15   For an important exception, see NC Manson and O O'Neill, *Rethinking Informed Consent in Bioethics* (Cambridge, Cambridge University Press, 2007).
16   BVerwGE 64 (1981) 274.
17   ibid 277 ff.
18   [1993] 2 All ER 75.
19   *State v Brown* 364 A.2d 27 (NJ Super Ct Law Div 1976), aff'd, 381 A2d 1231 (NJ Super Ct App Div 1977).
20   Conseil d'Etat (October 27, 1995) req nos 136-727 (Commune de Morsang-sur-Orge) and 143-578 (Ville d'Aix-en-Provence).

Omega case,[21] in which the fact that the participants were freely consenting adults failed to salvage the Laserdrome's licence.

By contrast, where liberal thinking prevails, the fact that the parties are consenting is a central (although not sufficient) consideration that pushes towards permission. Thus, in a famous chapter of US constitutional jurisprudence, the Supreme Court, having been divided about the criminalisation of consensual adult homosexual acts, eventually decided in *Lawrence v Texas*[22] that restrictions on sexual freedom violate human dignity. For the majority, the earlier jurisprudence failed to grasp the breadth and depth of the liberty interest at stake and to appreciate that 'adults may choose to enter upon [such a sexual] relationship in the confines of their homes and their own private lives and still retain their dignity as free persons'.[23] Summing up, the majority opinion concludes:

> The case [involves] two adults who, with full and mutual consent from each other, engaged in sexual practices common to a homosexual lifestyle. The petitioners are entitled to respect for their private lives. The State cannot demean their existence or control their destiny by making their private sexual conduct a crime.[24]

While consent does not do all the work here, on the rights-based view of human dignity, it is material; and, other things being equal, it is decisive.

E. Taking Stock

A modern mapping of human dignity reveals a deep division between those who argue for human dignity as empowerment and those who oppose many applications of emerging technologies by appealing to human dignity as constraint. In the former conception, the ethical base is rights-centred and, in practice, human rights (resting on human dignity) do most of the work. In the latter, where the ethical base is duty-centred, human dignity does all the work but it is unclear that it can bear this load—when challenged, dignitarians are prone to asserting, and re-asserting, that hu-

---

21 *Omega Spielhallen-und Automatenaufstellungs-GmbH v Oberbürgermeisterin der Bundesstadt Bonn* (Case C-36/02) (14 October, 2004); OJ C 300, 04.12.2004, 3.
22 123 SCt 2472.
23 ibid 2478.
24 ibid 2484.

man dignity is compromised ... period.[25] The former articulates in a way that is liberal and that treats consent as an authorisation of acts that would otherwise involve a violation of the consenting agent's rights; the latter articulates in a way that tends to be conservative and that treats consent as irrelevant where human dignity is compromised.

III. An Archimedean Vantage Point?

In this part of the paper, I entertain the possibility that, amongst the various approaches to human dignity, there might be one that is to be privileged. Is there, so to speak, an Archimedean vantage point that offers us a clear and correct view? In response, I suggest (not for the first time) that Alan Gewirth's theory of moral rights has superior credentials to its rivals.[26] However, anticipating that this claim will attract limited support, in the next part of the paper, I switch the focus from an arguably privileged position to the lowest common ground in the contested conceptions of human dignity.

Having argued, in previous work, that Alan Gewirth's moral theory has the best credentials as the organising view within practical reason generally—and, a fortiori, within moral reason—it follows that I believe that the Archimedean vantage point is given by Gewirthian rights. Broadly speaking, this would mean that the concept of human dignity as empowerment is correct. However, the philosophical community is deeply sceptical about foundationalist projects and, even if there is a willingness to start with Gewirthian rights (or to operate with human dignity as empowerment), there is likely to be some considerable hesitation in treating this as the rationally-grounded focal standpoint that Gewirthians claim.

---

25   In this way, interlocutors complain that human dignity operates as a 'conversation stopper': see, eg, D Birnbacher, 'Do Modern Reproductive Technologies Violate Human Dignity?' in E Hildt and D Mieth (eds), *In Vitro Fertilisation in the 1990s* (Aldershot, Ashgate, 1998).
26   The root of this view is D Beyleveld and R Brownsword, *Law as a Moral Judgment* (London, Sweet and Maxwell, 1986, repr Sheffield, Sheffield Academic Press, 1994). It explicitly informs the analysis in Beyleveld and Brownsword, *Human Dignity in Bioethics and Biolaw* (2001), and eosdem, *Consent in the Law* (Oxford, Hart, 2007); and, it implicitly guides my thinking about 'a community of rights' in R Brownsword (ed), *Rights, Regulation and the Technological Revolution* (Oxford, Oxford University Press, 2008).

This is not the place to rehearse the arguments that surround the alleged validity of the Gewirthian argument from agency to a supreme moral principle (the so-called 'Principle of Generic Consistency', the 'PGC').[27] However, in the context of disputes about the best understanding of human dignity (where moral reason is already presupposed) coupled with the regulatory direction in which this present discussion will go, it is worth pausing to note how the sting is taken out of the two principal objections.

Briefly, the Gewirthian argument invites those who are pondering what ought to be done (whether for prudential or moral reasons) to view themselves as 'agents'—that is, as beings who have the capacity for free and purposive action. For those who are so pondering, this is surely an invitation that cannot be refused: for, a degree of both freedom and purposivity is implicit in such reflection on what ought to be done. Viewing matters as an agent, it becomes plausible to suppose that some conditions (the so-called 'generic conditions of agency') need to be in place before any particular purpose chosen by an agent can be actualised. Moreover, the logic of viewing oneself as an agent is that one must have a positive and protective attitude towards those generic conditions—after all, if the generic conditions are damaged, this has a negative impact on one's ability to function as an agent. It follows that one must have a negative attitude towards unwilled interferences with one's generic conditions; and, *reasoning strictly as an agent*, one must have a negative view of acts, including one's own acts, that cause damage to the generic conditions.[28] This line of argument results in a code of conduct for agents at the heart of which is the PGC, demanding that there should be respect for the generic conditions of agency (namely, as Gewirth specifies them, the freedom and well-being of agents)—or, that agents have *rights* inter se that the generic conditions should be respected.

There are two recurrent objections to the supposed validity of the Gewirthian argument to the PGC: (1) at some point in the argument, it is said, prudential concepts illicitly become moralised—for example, when an agent's negative attitude to x (interference with the generic conditions)

---

27 For a comprehensive analysis, see D Beyleveld, *The Dialectical Necessity of Morality: An Analysis and Defense of Alan Gewirth's Argument to the Principle of Generic Consistency* (Chicago, University of Chicago Press, 1991).

28 The importance of isolating this agency perspective is clearly drawn out in D Beyleveld and G Bos, 'The Foundational Role of the Principle of Instrumental Reason in Gewirth's Argument for the Principle of Generic Consistency: A Response to Andrew Chitty' (2009) 20 *King's Law Journal* 1.

becomes 'x is not permitted' or 'I have a right that other agents do not do x', and so on; and (2) it is objected that the first person prudential perspective of a particular agent does not translate smoothly into a universalised agency perspective—in other words, it is one thing to have a negative attitude towards acts that interfere with *my* generic conditions, but (contrary to the Gewirthian argument) it does not follow that I must also have a negative attitude to my acts that interfere with *your* generic conditions (implying that 'my generic conditions' and 'your generic conditions' are distinguishable and distinct).[29]

The first of these objections is less challenging where moral discourse is already in play (as it is where the nature of human dignity is under debate). No one debating human dignity is going to object that moral concepts are disallowed. Of course, this does not mean that the objection is irrelevant for Gewirthians, because the ambition of the project is to show that the PGC is entailed by practical reason generally (including amoral reason) not simply that it is entailed by moral reason. Still, if moral reason is conceded, the argument to the PGC is eased.[30]

The second objection persists even where moral reason is conceded. Objectors refuse to allow the agency standpoint ('As a rational being with the prospective capacities of an agent') to take over from the first-person or 'personalised' standpoint ('As John Doe, a rational being with the prospective capacities of an agent'). However, where (as in the present context) we are thinking about the general regulation of agent interactions and transactions, an impartial standpoint is introduced. From a regulatory standpoint, the generic needs of agents are the same; it is irrelevant that one agent is John Doe and another Richard Roe; as potential victims, all agents should rationally subscribe to rules that are designed to protect the generic conditions of agency; and regulators would fail in their responsibilities if they did not take steps to protect those conditions. Once again, then, a contingency that is implicit in the current discussion eases the argument to the PGC.[31]

---

29 See the range of objections in E Regis Jr (ed), Gewirth's *Ethical Rationalism* (Chicago, University of Chicago Press, 1984).

30 For dialectically contingent versions of the argument, see, seminally, D Beyleveld, 'Legal Theory and Dialectically Contingent Justifications for the Principle of Generic Consistency' (1996) 9 *Ratio Juris* 15.

31 Compare the analysis of the 'generic commons' in R Brownsword, 'Friends, Romans, Countrymen: Is There a Universal Right to Identity?' (2009) 1 *Law, Innovation and Technology* 223. If the generic conditions are reduced to a

In short, sceptics might remain unconvinced by the strong Gewirthian claim that, no matter where we start in practical reason, and no matter what our practical standpoint, the PGC is entailed. However, where the question concerns how regulators should best interpret the concept of human dignity, some of the major objections to the Gewirthian argument are significantly weakened. That said, if we operate with a Gewirthian view, *agency* rights do all the work and, although a place for *human* dignity can be found, it no longer seems quite so central.[32]

IV. The Lowest Common Ground

If we set aside any thoughts of finding an Archimedean vantage point, whether Gewirthian or other, we might nevertheless find some common ground that is shared by the protagonists. If there is such common ground, it might offer a basis for building some level of shared understanding of human dignity.

Let me start by assuming that there is a distinction between the project of moral community in a generic sense and particular articulations of moral community—just as there is a distinction between the project of democratic politics (and, concomitantly, governance 'in the public interest') and particular political constituencies, each with their own manifesto for serving the public interest. The organising idea for the moral project is that the community and its members should endeavour to do the right thing relative to the legitimate interests of themselves and others. What counts as a 'legitimate' interest, and who counts as an 'other', are deeply contested matters; and the way in which these questions are answered will determine how a particular moral community is articulated. So, for example if we treat the avoidance of pain and distress as the key *legitimate* interest of others, and if we treat *others* as those who are capable of experiencing pain and distress, then the community will articulate along negative utili-

---

'commons' that *all* agents rely on, then 'my' generic conditions are also 'your' generic conditions, and vice versa.

32 cp A Gewirth, 'Human Dignity as the Basis of Rights' in MJ Meyer and WA Parent (eds), *The Constitution of Rights: Human Dignity and American Values* (Ithaca, NY, Cornell University Press, 1992); and D Beyleveld, 'Human Dignity and Human Rights in Alan Gewirth's Moral Philosophy' in M Düwell, J Braarvig, R Brownsword and D Mieth (eds), *The Cambridge Handbook of Human Dignity* (Cambridge, Cambridge University Press, 2014).

tarian lines. If we treat an agent's freedom and well-being as the relevant *legitimate* interest of others, and if we treat *others* as those who are capable of acting in a purposive way, then the community will articulate along liberal rights-based lines. If we treat human dignity as the key *legitimate* interest, and if we treat all humans as relevant *others*, then the community will articulate as some version of dignitarianism, and so on.[33] These examples could be multiplied many times. However, the point is the simple one that these many different articulations are all examples of moral community in the generic sense; and they are all such examples because they start with a commitment to try to do the right thing relative to the legitimate interests of others.

Accordingly, I take it that, as moralists (in the generic sense), all those who debate human dignity must at least agree on one thing: namely, that it is important that agents should freely try to do the right thing. As we map the discourse of human dignity (as we did in the first part of the paper), we find that, with each moral constituency elaborating its criteria of right action, human dignity becomes more deeply contested, signalling division and dissent rather than agreement. However, if we return to the moral project as one of agents (or humans) trying to do the right thing (rather than acting in a purely self-regarding way) and, moreover, if we extend this into doing the right thing for the right reason, then we might relocate human dignity to this common ground.

If we do this, then we understand human dignity as a virtue that brings together three elements. First, the agent freely chooses to do x. Secondly, the agent, in doing x, tries to do the right thing. Thirdly, the agent does x because it is the right thing to do (even if an agent freely does x and judges that doing x is the right thing to do, the agent might not be primarily motivated by moral reasons).[34] In short, in the ideal-typical case, agents express human dignity when they try to do the right thing for the right reason.

While this common ground does nothing to assist moralists in resolving their differences with regard to the criteria of right action, on this analysis, human dignity signifies the importance of trying to do the right thing for

---

33 See R Brownsword, 'Bioethics Today, Bioethics Tomorrow: Stem Cell Research and the "Dignitarian Alliance"' (2003) 17 *Notre Dame Journal of Law, Ethics and Public Policy* 15.

34 Consider the case where agents are incentivised to do the right thing by 'gamifying' their conduct: see E Morozov, *To Save Everything, Click Here* (London, Allen Lane, 2013), chs 8 and 9.

the right reason and alerts all moralists to the need to preserve the conditions that allow for moral virtue to be developed and expressed. In an age when technologies that have regulatory potential are being rapidly developed (and recognised as such), a shared sense of the fundamental importance of human dignity should unite the moral community in monitoring the way that technological instruments are used by regulators.

To this, let me anticipate a double-barrelled objection. The gist of the objection is that, provided agents do the right thing, it really does not matter whether they do it for the right reason—and, indeed, it is unrealistic to expect anything better of humans. The latter remark picks up on the undeniable fact that, in practice, criminal justice systems employ a mix of moral exhortation and threat of punishment. Where there is compliance, it will not always be for moral reasons; and some might argue that we would be imprudent to do away with the threat and imposition of punishment (incarceration, fines, and so on), relying purely on moral exhortation and censure. Nevertheless, if the ideal-typical moral performance is one in which an agent reflects on the options, determines which option represents doing the right thing, and then acts on that judgment, it does matter that agents act for the right reasons. To suggest otherwise is to assume a moral community that is hierarchical, in which agents are expected to follow the moral precepts laid down by others; or to revert to a morally-threatening risk management mentality.[35]

V. Techno-Regulation and Human Dignity

For communities that have moral aspirations, for communities that take human dignity seriously, it is important that the regulatory environment recognises the right values and puts moral requirements, permissions, and prohibitions in the right place. So much is trite. Much less obviously, though, it is also important that the 'complexion' of the regulatory environment is right in the sense that it allows for humans to express their dignity by freely choosing to do the right thing for the right reason. One of the reasons why we might be nervous about the impact of the surge of new technologies is not so much that their application might compromise hu-

---

35 See R Brownsword, 'Human Dignity, Human Rights, and Simply Trying to Do the Right Thing' in C McCrudden (ed), *Understanding Human Dignity* (Oxford, Proceedings of the British Academy and Oxford University Press, 2013).

man dignity in the instrumentalising ways that we have already mentioned but that, as regulatory tools, they might reduce the scope for the expression of human dignity.

In this part of the paper, we deal first (and briefly) with the nature of the regulatory environment, the modalities available to regulators, and the registers that regulators may employ to engage with the practical reason of their regulatees. This leads to a discussion of the two ways in which the use of technologies as regulatory tools can have negative impacts on the complexion of the regulatory environment: first, by crowding out the moral signals (making it less likely that action will be morally directed); and, secondly, by rendering it impossible for agents to act in a morally directed manner—thereby, compromising the conditions for the expression of human dignity. Finally, I offer some short thoughts on the significance of maintaining the infrastructure for agency—even to the point of employing tools for technological management.

A. The Regulatory Environment, Regulatory Modalities, and Regulatory Registers

It is in the nature of a regulatory environment that there will be various signals that are intended to direct the conduct of regulatees; there will be various means of monitoring conduct to see whether the directions are being followed; and, where deviation is detected, there will be measures for correction. In such environments, regulators signal whether particular acts are permitted (even required) or prohibited, whether they will be viewed positively, negatively, or neutrally, whether they are incentivised or disincentivised, whether they are likely to be praised or criticised, even whether they are possible or impossible, and so on.[36]

One of the key points about the regulatory environment is that we may find regulators employing a range of mechanisms or modalities that are designed to channel the conduct of their regulatees. Some of these modalities may well be of a legal nature (whether in the form of hard or soft law). It is not that regulatory environments never feature legal signals; and, in

---

36 R Brownsword and H Somsen, 'Law, Innovation and Technology: Before We Fast Forward—A Forum for Debate' (2009) 1 *Law Innovation and Technology* 1; and R Brownsword and M Goodwin, *Law and the Technologies of the Twenty-First Century* (Cambridge, Cambridge University Press, 2012).

many instances, it will be the legal signals that have the highest profile. Nevertheless, the regulatory repertoire goes well beyond legal signals—including, for example, social norms, the market, and architecture (or, code).[37] The traditional signals, the signals of law and morality, are normative; but, with new technological instruments, some of the regulatory signals might be non-normative. For example, if regulators decree that cars should be equipped with sensors that can detect alcohol in the driver, such cars might be designed to respond normatively (by advising either that it is not safe for the driver to proceed or that, morally, as a matter of respect for others, the driver ought not to proceed) or non-normatively (by simply immobilising the vehicle).[38] Implicit in these remarks we can detect the following three regulatory registers:

(i) the moral register: here regulators signal that some act, x, categorically ought or ought not to be done relative to standards of right action (as in retributive articulations of the criminal law where the emphasis is on the moral nature of the offence); or

(ii) the prudential register: here regulators signal that some act, x, ought or ought not to be done relative to the prudential interests of regulatees (as in deterrence-driven articulations of the criminal law where the emphasis is on the sanction that will be visited on offenders); or

(iii) the register of practicability or possibility: here regulators signal that it is not reasonably practicable to do some act, x, or even that x simply cannot be done—in which case, regulatees reason, not that x ought not to be done, but that x cannot be done (either realistically or literally).

For moralists, regulators who are eager to improve on the effectiveness of their interventions by grasping new technological opportunities need to be watched carefully. In particular, we need to keep an eye on any changes in the registers that regulators employ because these changes can affect the complexion of the regulatory environment in none-too-obvious but critical ways.

---

37   Seminally, see L Lessig, *Code and Other Laws of Cyberspace* (New York, Basic Books, 1999).
38   cp M Hildebrandt, 'Legal and Technological Normativity: More (and Less) than Twin Sisters' (2008) 12 *TECHNE* 169.

The two particular impacts that should concern moralists are: (i) where technological instruments weaken the moral signal; and (ii) where technological management reduces the options for free action. In the first case, the problem is that, even if regulatees are disposed to try to do the right thing, it becomes more difficult to do it for the right reason. In the second case, the problem is that, even if regulatees succeed in doing (what many would judge to be) the right thing, they do not do so freely. In both cases, human dignity is compromised: regulatees do not freely try to do the right thing for the right reason.

B. Where Technological Instruments Weaken the Moral Signal

With an increasing reliance on regulatory technologies (for example, CCTV, DNA profiling, RFID tracking and monitoring devices, and so on), there is a real likelihood that the strength and significance of the moral signal will fade.[39] Quite simply, with these technological instruments, the dominant signal to regulatees becomes a prudential one, accentuating that the doing of a particular act is contrary to the interests of regulatees (because, in the event of non-compliance, they will be detected and punished).

Without further inquiry, we cannot be confident about the impact of the amplification of prudential signals that comes with an increased reliance on some regulatory technologies. So long as such technologies operate at the fringes of a traditional criminal justice system, there is probably little, if any, overall cost to moral community. However, where the regulatory environment features pervasive surveillance and monitoring technologies (as, of course, is the case in online environments[40]), aspirant moral communities should not be so complacent. In a panopticon environment, how likely is it that moral reason will survive, let alone flourish?

Beatrice von Silva-Tarouca Larsen[41] has suggested that the 'general public [might have] not quite woken up to the potential dangers of

---

[39] cp MA Rothstein and MK Talbott, 'The Expanding Use of DNA in Law Enforcement: What Role for Privacy?' (2006) 34 *Journal of Law, Medicine and Ethics* 153.

[40] cp M Klang, 'The Rise and Fall of Freedom of Online Expression' in Düwell et al, *The Cambridge Handbook of Human Dignity* (2014).

[41] B von Silva-Tarouca Larsen, *Setting the Watch: Privacy and the Ethics of CCTV Surveillance* (Oxford, Hart, 2011).

CCTV'.[42] Her principal concern relates to the loss of anonymity (and privacy) in public places. However, putting her finger on precisely the point that is central to this paper, she says:

> Another reason speaks against pervasive recording in public space as a strategy for crime prevention. Increasing the threat of punishment does not deprive punishment of its moral message, and highlighting the detection risk of offending does not have to dilute the deontological condemnation expressed in punishment. *Nevertheless, one should not rule out the possibility that an over-reliance on CCTV, with its emphasis on the instrumental appeal to desist from crime in order to avoid paying the cost, might entail a dilution of the moral reasons for desistence.* This could become a problem, for it is not possible to record and monitor people all the time. It is important that policy makers realise that CCTV can only ever be a small part of the solution for enforcing the criminal law, and that instrumental obedience is no substitute for moral endorsement of criminal prohibitions. Strengthening, communicating and convincing people of the normative reasons for desistence should always remain a priority.[43]

Accordingly, her recommendation is 'that policy makers should opt for very selective implementation of public CCTV, within a narrow setting, targeted on particular crimes and a particular type of offender'.[44] While such implementation might render CCTV coverage more effective in preventing and detecting crime, this is not really the point. Rather, as Larsen concludes:

> Above all, it is important to remember that surveillance can never be a substitute for frontline crime-prevention work in and with the community, for the normative legitimacy of criminal prohibitions *and the moral incentive to abstain from harming others.*[45]

Insightful though this is, Larsen's point needs to be extended. For, to address the question of the significance of amplified prudential signals, we need to think beyond the impact on individual agents who are already members of a morally aspirant community and to remind ourselves about the project of moral community.

In such an aspirant moral community, the regulatory environment should declare the community's commitment to doing the right thing and it should express its understanding of the guiding principles. At some times and in some places, the process of articulating the community's

---

42 ibid 83.
43 ibid 153 f, emphasis added.
44 ibid 186.
45 ibid, emphasis added.

moral commitments might have been left to an elite group (of philosopher kings or wise men); the commitments so articulated might have been seen as a durable statement (in a world of little change); and the substantive principles articulated might have been viewed with epistemic certainty. However, the project of moral community as I view it for the Twenty-First Century is rather different: it is inclusive, constantly under review, and undertaken with a degree of uncertainty.

To start with *inclusiveness*, the project is one of comprehensive public engagement. On some matters, members of the community might be agreed; and, in all probability, the higher the level of generality at which governing principles are formulated, the easier it will be to agree that these are relevant principles for the guidance of agents who wish to do the right thing. However, there will be many matters that are disputed. Even if the most fundamental of principles are agreed, there might be disagreement about the scope and application of a principle in a particular case, about the priority between competing principles, and about where to draw the line between those who are relevant others and those who are not, and so on.[46] So far as is practicable, there need to be inclusive deliberations about such matters. Once a decision has been made, it should be treated as provisional and open to *review*.[47] The fact that the balance of argument has favoured a particular decision today does not secure it in perpetuity; a moral community must leave open the possibility of revisiting, reviewing, and renewing its decisions. Finally, unless the community claims moral omniscience—which in the Twenty-First Century is hardly a plausible position—it must regard its articulated principles with a degree of epistemic *uncertainty*. This does not have to unravel the project; but it does mean that the current articulation cannot be treated as being set in stone or immune to further debate and discussion.

To the extent that the public life of such a community focuses on constructing an appropriate regulatory environment, it follows that we cannot assess the impact of an amplification of prudential signals simply by checking the impact on the isolated acts (and reasons) of individual regulatees. For, as members of the community, regulatees have a role to play

---

46 See R Brownsword, 'Regulating the Life Sciences, Pluralism, and the Limits of Deliberative Democracy' (2010) 22 *Singapore Academy of Law Journal* 801.

47 ibid; and R Brownsword and J Earnshaw, 'Controversy: The Ethics of Screening for Abdominal Aortic Aneurysm' (2010) 36 *Journal of Medical Ethics* 827.

in debating the regulatory purposes and agreeing the public rules and standards. In other words, before we set aside any concerns about the amplification of prudential signals, we need to check not only whether there is an impact on regulatees at the point of compliance but also on their ability to participate as members of the political (and aspirant moral) community. However, to do this, they must have the capacity to engage in moral discourse and debate—which is to say, there must be no impairment of their moral development.

Taking stock, we can say that the project of moral community (whatever its particular articulation) presupposes that its members will participate in debating the community's best understanding of its moral commitments, in setting public standards that are compatible with those commitments, and in responding to those standards as regulatees who strive to do the right thing for the right reason.[48] Unless we are confident that the amplification of prudential signals has no effect on any part of the project, regulators (as stewards for moral community) should proceed with care.

C. Where Technological Management Reduces the Options for Free Action

The more serious threat to moral community arises when regulatory technologies are employed to manage environments in ways that limit the options that are realistically available to regulatees.[49] In such settings, the signal is no longer normative; rather it becomes that an act is either not practicable (such as trying to board an aircraft for an international flight without going through the security scans, or riding the metro without buy-

---

48 There are also questions for any aspirant moral community about its relationship with and responsibilities towards other communities. See, eg, the discussion in Nuffield Council on Bioethics, *Genetically Modified Crops: The Ethical and Social Issues* (London, Nuffield Council on Bioethics, 1999); and, more recently, Great Britain, Government Office for Science, *Foresight. The Future of Food and Farming: Final Project Report* (London, The Government Office for Science, 2011).

49 See R Brownsword, 'What the World Needs Now: Techno-Regulation, Human Rights and Human Dignity' in id (ed), *Human Rights* (Oxford, Hart, 2004); and id, 'Code, Control, and Choice: Why East is East and West is West' (2005) 25 *Legal Studies* 1.

ing a ticket[50]) or simply not possible.[51] In such strongly managed environments, the space for self-interested (prudential) reason is squeezed, and more importantly it is the opportunities for acting on moral reason that are restricted. In such non-normative managed environments, how are aspirant moral humans to express the *dignity* of their actions? Where the regulatory environment is managed so that 'wrongdoing' is designed out, so that the only possible acts are those that conform to the approved regulatory pattern, how can human agents express the most basic of moral virtues by showing that they are doing the right thing for the right reason?

Where hard technologies are introduced, the pattern of 'respectful' non-harming conduct is not explained by the prudential choices of regulatees, even less by their moral judgments. In a moral community, it is when code and design leave regulatees with no option other than compliance that the legitimacy of the means employed by regulators needs urgent consideration. The problem here is that, even if we concede that the technology channels regulatees towards right action, the technologically secured pattern of right action is not at all the same as freely opting to do the right thing. An agent might be protected from the potentially harmful acts of others, but moral virtue, as Ian Kerr protests, cannot be automated.[52] Expressing this concern in relation to the use of 'digital locks', Kerr says:

> [A] generalized and unimpeded use of digital locks, further protected by the force of law, threatens not merely [various] legal rights and freedoms but also threatens to significantly impair our moral development. In particular, I express deep concern that digital locks could be used in a systematic attempt to 'automate human virtue'—programming people to 'do the right thing' by constraining and in some cases altogether eliminating moral behaviour through technology rather than ethics or law. Originally introduced to improve the human condition, digital locks and other automation technologies could, ironically, be used to control our virtual and physical environments in unprecedented ways, to eliminate the possibility for moral deliberation about certain kinds of action otherwise possible in these spaces by disabling the world in a way that ultimately disables the people who populate it. Not by eliminating their choices but by automating them—by removing people

---

50   cp Morozov, *To Save Everything* (2013) 190–93 ('Why You Should Ride the Metro in Berlin').

51   BJ Koops, 'Technology and the Crime Society: Rethinking Legal Protection' (2009) 1 *Law, Innovation and Technology* 93.

52   I Kerr, 'Digital Locks and the Automation of Virtue' in M Geist (ed), *From 'Radical Extremism' to 'Balanced Copyright': Canadian Copyright and the Digital Agenda* (Toronto, Irwin Law, 2010).

from the realm of moral action altogether, thereby impairing their future moral development.[53]

Applying this analysis to the case of honest action, Kerr detects the irony that a ubiquitous digital lock strategy meant to 'keep honest people honest' is a self-defeating goal since it impairs the development of *phronesis*, stunts moral maturity and thereby disables the cultivation of a deep-seated disposition for honesty. Woven into the fabric of everyday life, digital locks would ensure particular outcomes for property owners but would do so at the expense of the moral project of honesty.[54]

The point is that the shift from law (or ethics) to technological instruments changes the 'complexion' of the regulatory environment in a way that has deep moral significance.[55] Instead of guiding regulatees by prescribing what ought or ought not to be done, regulators might wholly depart from the normative register by signalling what can or cannot be done. To comply or not to comply is no longer the question for regulatees; the only question is what in practice can be done.

Arguably, there is a deep paradox in the idea that, in a community with moral aspirations, the regulatory environment must leave open the option of humans doing the wrong thing so that they can express their dignity by choosing to do the right thing—even perhaps of facilitating moral reflection by confronting agents with the choices available to them.[56] It might also seem absurd that regulators should eschew strategies that are effective in reducing risk to human health and safety by designing-in appropriate technological features; and it might seem implausible that regulating technologies will be used to the point that human dignity is crowded out in this way.[57] Each of these points merits debate. However, unless we have the complexion of the regulatory environment on our radar, we might find that the conditions for simply doing the right thing for the right reason have changed without our noticing that this was happening.

---

53   ibid 254 f.
54   ibid 292.
55   See, further, R Brownsword, 'Lost in Translation: Legality, Regulatory Margins, and Technological Management' (2011) 26 *Berkeley Technology Law Journal* 1321–65.
56   Compare some interesting design possibilities raised by Morozov, *To Save everything* (2013) ch 9.
57   For further reflections, see K Yeung, 'Can We Employ Design-Based Regulation While Avoiding *Brave New World*' (2011) 3 *Law, Innovation and Technology* 1; and R Brownsword, 'Lost in Translation' 1321.

D. Maintaining the Infrastructural Conditions

To the foregoing remarks, I should add an important caveat: the concerns that have been expressed with regard to the complexion of the regulatory environment assume that the regulatory interventions in question are directed at human interactions rather than at the infrastructure presupposed by such interactions. Although the drawing of the line between such interactions and the infrastructure itself is subject to debate, there is a view that regulators may legitimately use a technological fix where their intention is to protect the infrastructure.[58] In other words, if regulators are trying to stage the conditions for moral community, they need not worry about the complexion of the regulatory environment; for, quite simply, until the infrastructure is in place, there is no prospect of any kind of human community.[59]

So long as our understanding of the infrastructure is restricted to the *essential* conditions for human existence (particularly to such vital matters as the availability of food and water, and the preservation of the environment), few regulatory interventions will attract a special dispensation for the use of a technological fix. Concerns about the unwarranted use of techno-regulation and, concomitantly, corrosion of the context for the moral life, will persist. However, if each community adjusts the infrastructural threshold in a way that reflects the stage of its technological development, this might involve characterising many safety features that are designed into, say, everyday transport and health-care facilities, as 'infrastructural'—which, concomitantly, expands the zone of ostensibly legitimate reliance on hard technological management.[60] If these interventions

---

58   See R Brownsword, 'Crimes Against Humanity, Simple Crime, and Human Dignity' in B van Beers, L Corrias, and W Werner (eds), *Humanity Across International Law and Biolaw* (Cambridge, Cambridge University Press, 2013) 106–09.

59   See, further, R Brownsword, 'Responsible Regulation: Prudence, Precaution and Stewardship' (2011) 62 *Northern Ireland Legal Quarterly* 573; and id, 'Criminal Law, Regulatory Frameworks and Public Health' in AM Viens, J Coggon and AS Kessel (eds), *Criminal Law, Philosophy and Public Health Practice* (Cambridge, Cambridge University Press, 2013).

60   Compare Council Directive 2008/114/EC (on the identification and designation of European critical infrastructures and the assessment of the need to improve their protection). Article 2(a) of the Directive defines 'critical infrastructure' as 'an asset, system or part thereof located in Member States which is essential for the maintenance of vital societal functions, health, safety, security,

are judged to be within the special dispensation, this will ease the pressure of the concerns about the complexion of the regulatory environment. A corollary of this is that, for more complex societies, where infrastructural conditions are heavily engineered, where 'the Internet of things' is simply part of the furniture, there is a temptation simply to define away these concerns; but that is obviously no answer for a community that truly retains its moral aspirations.

VI. Conclusion

In this paper, I have suggested four angles from which we might develop a more sophisticated understanding of human dignity. First, we can acknowledge that human dignity is a contested concept; we can map the principal conceptions (human dignity as empowerment and human dignity as constraint); and we can track developments in the discourse of law and ethics by reference to this map. Secondly, drawing on Gewirthian moral theory, we might ascend the heights to argue for the superiority of a rights-driven conception of human dignity. Thirdly, however, we might also set our sights lower to draw out the significance of the agreement that humans should try to do the right thing for the right reason—and, indeed, that they express their dignity by doing just that. Finally, in an age when regulators are discovering a new repertoire of technological tools, we need to keep an eye on the complexion of the regulatory environment. In this context, it would be a serious mistake to think that human dignity is little more than a dogmatic conservative credo that impedes 'progress'; to the contrary, human dignity, as the root aspiration of moral community, and as the deepest expression of moral virtue (indeed, as the locus of 'free will') has an important role to play as a critical benchmark for the use of techno-regulation.

---

economic or social well-being of people, and the disruption or destruction of which would have a significant impact in a Member State as a result of the failure to maintain those functions.'

Problem Areas in the Dignity Debate and the Ensemble Theory of Human Dignity

Eric Hilgendorf*

I. Introduction

In spite of its prominent position as the first human right enumerated in the German Federal Constitution, the provision on human dignity in Article 1 still presents one of the great puzzles of German constitutional theory. As the German model has exerted considerable influence on the formulation of more recent constitutional guarantees of human dignity in Europe,[1] the danger exists that uncertainty and confusion in the concept of human dignity will also be carried over to the European level. The problems commence already in the fact that no general agreement exists as to what the term 'human dignity' is actually supposed to mean. Definitions offered in commentaries on constitutional law are frequently pale and almost bereft of meaning.[2] The same is true for international legal, political and philosophical discourses, where the concept 'human dignity' is given quite varied and often highly ambiguous meanings.[3] The German Federal Constitutional Court has declared that it would not give a general defini-

---

* A German version of this paper appeared in 2013 in *Zeitschrift für evangelische Ethik* 258–71.
1 See particularly Art 1 of the new Charter of Fundamental Rights of the EU, http://www.europarl.europa.eu/charter/pdf/text_en.pdf.
2 P Kunig, 'Art. 1' in I von Münch and P Kunig, *Grundgesetz-Kommentar*, 6th edn, Vol. 1 (Munich, Beck, 2012) Art 1 para 22 suggests that lack of precision in the concept of human dignity is inevitable; see also para 22 et seq for detailed information on various different ways to define the term.
3 For an excellent overview, see the articles in C McCrudden (ed), *Understanding Human Dignity* (Oxford, Oxford University Press, 2013); see also D Shultziner, 'Human Dignity—Functions and Meanings' (2003) 3 *Global Jurist Topics*; see also id, 'A Jewish Conception of Human Dignity. Philosophy and Its Ethical Implications for Israeli Supreme Court Decisions' (2006) 34 *Journal of Religious Ethics*.

tion of human dignity, preferring rather to decide on a case by case basis what actions would or would not infringe on human dignity.[4]

It is also unclear and disputed how human dignity should be protected at law—is it a fundamental right or a bundling of fundamental rights or indeed an ethical ideal without legal effect? What is clear is that the commitment to human dignity was a reaction by the drafters the new German Federal Constitution to the hitherto unprecedented crimes against humanity committed during the period of the National Socialist dictatorship.[5] Pseudo-racially motivated murder, torture, medical experiments on the innocent, the deprivation of rights of entire segments of the population—such crimes should be condemned and forbidden for all time coming.[6]

Sensational new cases—from the threats of torture (by the Deputy Police Chief of Frankfurt) in the '*Daschner* case'[7] up to the debate about the shooting of innocent passengers in the controversy surrounding the passage of the Aviation Security Act[8]—have shown however, that uncertainties about the content and status of human dignity have effects on supposedly clear cases, and that the idea of exceptional justification finds supporters in extreme factual situations. In *Daschner,* a significant minority of law professors held that the threat of torture was not a violation of human dignity, although 'torture' has traditionally been held up as *the* most characteristic example of a violation of Art 1 of the German Constitution. Similarly, during the legal controversy surrounding the possibility of shooting down passenger aircraft in 9/11 situations, a decision was required by the German Federal Constitutional Court to determine that such an action did violate human dignity.[9]

---

4   BVerfGE 30, 1 (25); similarly, M Kriele, *Theorie der Rechtsgewinnung*, 2nd ed (Berlin, Duncker & Humblot, 1976) 213.
5   A Dershowitz, *Rights from Wrongs. A Secular Theory on the Origins of Rights* (New York, Basic Books, 2004) 7 is quite correct when he points out that important rights mostly come into being as a reaction to the experience of extreme wrongs.
6   This can also be interpreted as making certain kinds of infringements 'taboo'.
7   European Court of Human Rights (ECHR), (2008) *Europäische Grundrechte Zeitschrift* 466 (= NJW 2010, 3145); LG Frankfurt NJW 2005, 692.
8   E Hilgendorf, 'Tragische Fälle. Extremsituationen und strafrechtlicher Notstand' in U Blaschke, A Förster, S Lumpp and J Schmidt (eds), *Sicherheit statt Freiheit? Staatliche Handlungsspielräume in extremen Gefährdungslagen*, Schriften zum Öffentlichen Recht Band 1002 (Berlin, Duncker & Humblot, 2005).
9   BVerfGE 115, 118 (157).

In the meantime, pointing to the great vagueness of the concept in terms of content, the seemingly endless possibilities for finding different ways of interpreting what it means, as well as the invitation to abuse resulting from this lack of clarity, belong to the common arguments in the debate on human dignity. Other popular themes in the arsenal of human dignity sceptics[10] include the wide variety of often heterogeneous, sometimes even mutually incompatible explanations of human dignity, and then also the curious intermediate position of the concept in the contentious area between law and morality, which allows it to be subjected to use by such diverse disciplines as Law, Ethics or Moral Theology.

The interdisciplinary aspect leads to the situation that debate about human dignity has been extremely heterogeneous,[11] even though certain standard problems, arguments and accepted positions may have developed within the various individual disciplines, for example within the discipline of Law. In interdisciplinary discussions, the supposed safety of these accepted notions evaporates very quickly. In addition, appeals to human dignity are also easily exploited in the mass media, with the result that the concept of human dignity tends frequently to be employed excessively in the area of political discourse.

Debates on human dignity are often characterised by the highly disordered and unstructured way they are carried out. This is unfortunate because the right of human dignity enumerated in the German Constitution is one of the constitution's most incisive provisions: Human dignity is an absolute right so that any infringement is unconstitutional.[12] It is therefore certainly striking for the debate that not even this finding is undisputed and in point of fact can also be challenged persuasively. Altogether one almost gets the impression that the 'anything goes' argument emerges as victorious. Whoever would prefer a clear and well-structured theory faces the alternatives, either to abandon the term altogether, or to look for ways of structuring and clearly defining the concept of human dignity and its use.

In this article the author seeks to identify the most important questions in the human dignity debate, admittedly at a largely abstract level; the goal

---

10 D Birnbacher, 'Menschenwürde-Skepsis' in JC Joerden, E Hilgendorf and F Thiele (eds), *Menschenwürde und Medizin. Ein interdisziplinäres Handbuch* (Berlin, Duncker & Humblot, 2013).
11 Shultziner, 'Human Dignity' 5.
12 So the still prevailing opinion in constitutional literature, see, eg, Kunig 'Art 1' para 4.

is to provide lawyers and philosophers with, so to speak, both a sort of roadmap of the key issues, and with something of a legal-philosophical toolbox containing instruments for analysis, arguments and possible solutions.

II. Problem Areas in the Human Dignity Debate

A. Reason or Choice?

What is, from the perspective of law, so special about human dignity? My answer is that this concept, as no other, permits normative conflicts in our ever more pluralistic society—and perhaps worldwide from an intercultural perspective—either to be resolved or to be defused. The reason for this is that the concept of human dignity, as it is developed here, is a reaction to the most brutal crimes against humanity, to extreme violations of human interests. No one exists today who would approve of the exceptionally brutal criminal acts committed by the Nazis under the pseudo-legal regime of the Third Reich. Everyone agrees in a complete prohibition (for all time) of such terrible crimes, even people who otherwise have widely disparate moral and political convictions. According to this understanding, Human Dignity provides a 'normative anchor' in the face of an apparently ever expanding world pluralism.

Legal theory supports this moral-political project through conceptual clarification, the identification of problem structures and through the development of suggested solutions to the problems, which can then be tested in practice. If they pass the test, they will be retained for the time being, but if they fail they have to be replaced by other constructs. This interplay of construction and criticism[13] seems to me to be of great importance particularly for the human dignity debate.

That brings us to the first problem, namely the question of what we actually want to achieve by dealing with these conceptual issues. Are we searching for answers that already exist or do we want to find new answers? Methodologically, this question is extremely important, although it appears not to have been explicitly addressed either in Law or in Practical Philosophy. One can characterise the central issue here using the dichoto-

---

13　H Albert, *Konstruktion und Kritik. Aufsätze zur Philosophie des kritischen Rationalismus*, 2nd edn (Hamburg, Hoffmann und Campe, 1975).

my 'reason or choice'. Can we recognise the answer to the question about the 'content' of human dignity, its 'correct' justification and appropriate ways to apply it, because it exists independently of the observer and only needs to be discovered? So does such a thing as an inherent and predetermined meaning to the term 'human dignity' exist? Alternatively, are we talking about answers that we have to first develop ourselves, for which we must make reasoned decisions faced with an inestimably large number of potential choices?

Many philosophers, also philosophers of law and lawyers oriented to basics seem to tend to an essentialist approach. They ask: 'What does human dignity mean?' or 'What is human dignity really?' as if the meaning of the term had been predetermined in some way. This approach, however, is misleading. On closer examination, there is no fixed meaning of 'human dignity' for us to find.[14] Instead, we have to give the term its meaning, i.e. we have to construct the concept. Naturally, when we do this we can draw from a huge pool of suggested definitions from the past, and a proper examination of these potential definitions is a question of reason. Which of these older definitions we actually prefer, and whether or not we want to take over one of these definitions at all, rather than proposing an entirely new definition of 'human dignity', is a matter of choice.

B. Adequacy Requirements for a Definition of 'Human Dignity'

If one shares the goal advocated here of using the concept of human dignity as a normative anchor in an ever more pluralising society, then the next question arises, namely what concept of 'human dignity' is best suited to achieve this goal. This focuses our attention on potential adequacy requirements for a definition of 'human dignity'.

The first requirement that a concept of 'human dignity' must fulfil is its *suitability to achieve the intended goal*. That means that 'human dignity' must be conceived in such a way that the concept can be used as a normative anchor, which all or almost all members of the society can accept, regardless of their cultural background, and regardless of their concrete value systems. The concept must be so sound that, on the one hand, it reveals a reasonably well-defined sphere of protection, but on the other it must be broad enough to be able to reconcile various normative approaches. There-

---

14   Schultziner, 'Human Dignity' 5 *et seq.*

in lies the dilemma: a more precise definition makes the sphere of protection clearer but at the same time narrower so that it covers fewer cases. Therefore, for reasons of utility, one needs to find a suitable balance between a definition that is too precise and one that is too fuzzy.

A second central requirement which 'human dignity' as a legal requirement must fulfil is that it should *conform with the text* of Art 1 of the EU Charter of Rights. If it says there that human dignity shall be 'respected and protected' this can already be interpreted as an indication of what human dignity is supposed to mean, since in constitutional language *rights* must be respected and protected, not ideals or moral values. A closer examination of the issue of the protective functions of human dignity is not possible here; although fundamental rights are traditionally considered primarily to protect the individual from the exercise of state power, our approach is that human dignity should not only bind state organs but everybody. The state has the responsibility to monitor compliance with the guarantee of human dignity, to prevent and where possible to punish infringements.

A third requirement for a suitable definition of human dignity is that it be *compatible with previous jurisprudence* of the courts. It can be said without exaggeration that it was mainly the German Federal Constitutional Court which developed our fundamental rights law, including human dignity, into the form it has now. This law created by the courts has proved itself effective in everyday legal practice. It would, in my opinion, be inexpedient and wrong to set out now to develop a completely new concept of human dignity, which, without ever having proved any practical advantages for itself, would nevertheless compete with the model developed in the court's jurisprudence.

Another central adequacy requirement is *logical rigor and internal consistency* of the concept developed. This precondition, which must always be respected, assumes a certain linguistic transparency, which actually allows the theses and arguments of the concept to be tested. Models which are logically flawed or whose language is abstruse should be excluded from consideration from the very beginning.

A further important requirement for a convincing concept of 'human dignity' is its *compatibility with non-legal concepts*. 'Human dignity' is also an issue which has been and will continue to be dealt with intensively in Practical Philosophy and Moral Theology. Furthermore, this issue is not only very important in Germany, but also internationally throughout the world. A theory of human dignity should therefore be interdisciplinary and culturally compatible at international level. This means it must be conceived in such a way that points of debate both in other disciplines *and* in other countries can be considered in our debate without the necessity of great efforts in transposing unfamiliar ideas.[15]

Finally, the *practical utility of the concept* is very important. Rights should be practically enforceable, so that a concept of 'human dignity' is only convincing if it allows individuals to protect their rights from the deplorable violations discussed *supra*. In this context, it is problematic if the scope of protection, which human dignity affords, is too narrow: Nowadays human rights are frequently infringed by large, private actors, like large multinational companies, rather than by the state. A convincing conception of human dignity does not from the outset exclude protection from the risks posed by such institutions. Effective protection of human dignity has mechanisms in place so that when effected individuals request that their rights be protected, those rights can be enforced.

Finally, it is important to also mention that the concept must be *forward looking* in the sense that it must be able to accommodate societal or technological changes we cannot even anticipate at this time: the concept of human dignity should be tailored to protect us not only from risks posed today but also from those posed by the developments of tomorrow. Ideally the concept of human dignity should be so concrete that it allows societal or technological trends today to be evaluated so that we can steer the future. In this way, the guarantee of human dignity will act as a future-oriented monitoring and control instrument.

Using the approach suggested here, the question of the 'correct' definition of human dignity has, quasi by sleight of hand, been changed into how to define the concept of human dignity in the most effective way in order to attain our goal, namely the anchoring of normative differences in our pluralistic society in a foundation of commonly held values. The teleologically oriented model put forward here is therefore to a certain extent relativistic: Whoever does not share the ultimate goal may prefer a different model of human dignity. Nevertheless, our model is potentially universal, or at least nearly universal, namely if it proves to be true that all or at least nearly all people share the underlying goal advocated here: to put

---

15 I'm not talking here about language translation requirements that result from the use of different languages. The fact that such translations are necessary is sometimes unfortunate, but unavoidable. Restricting discourse to a single scientific language, for example English or German, is neither feasible nor would it be desirable.

an absolute ban on wrongs comparable to atrocities like the Holocaust, genocide, torture and slavery.[16]

C. The Definition of 'Human Dignity' and the Ensemble Theory

This allows the question of 'What is human dignity?' to be posed in a different and more precise way. The question becomes: How shall we define 'human dignity' in order to attain the goal, namely, of creating a normative foundation acceptable to all or nearly all of the many people in our pluralistic society? As developed above, human dignity should serve foremost to protect individuals from extreme forms of attack on their persons and their autonomy as human beings. Such protection can best be achieved through the granting of absolute rights, i.e. rights that may not be restricted under any circumstances. Such a protection model is considerably more powerful and more effective than any concept of human dignity as an 'underlying value' or 'ideal'.

Based on the above-mentioned adequacy requirements, I suggest that the sentence 'A has human dignity' should be equated to mean: 'A has certain rights', namely

The right to a minimum material existence

The right to be free of extreme pain (prohibition of torture)

The right to basic mental integrity (prohibition of brain washing, etc.)

The right to a minimum of autonomous self-development

The right to control one's most intimate information

The right to equality before the law (prohibition of slavery)

The right to a minimum of respect

One would then speak of a violation of human dignity when one or more of this ensemble of rights was infringed. It is important to understand that these rights are an area of core rights which are considered to be absolute, and which are therefore not subject to legal relativisation, meaning they are not subject to legal balancing exercises with other rights or values. The scope of protection of human rights (and not only the human rights enumerated in the EU Charter or Germany's Federal Constitution) taken all

---

16   See section I.

together is considerably wider.[17] Insofar as the scope of protection of these rights is identical with that of human dignity, these rights are also absolute: any impairment of these rights will be regarded as illegal. In contrast, where the scope of protection of human or fundamental rights extends beyond the scope of protection of human dignity, those rights can be limited, for example to make room for some competing right or value. The German Federal Constitution contains many limited rights, for example in Art 2 subsection 1 ('Each person has the right to autonomous self-development as long as he does not infringe the rights of others or endanger the constitutional or moral order').

Any interference with the human dignity of an individual, i.e. with one of the core rights mentioned above, is prohibited; it is not possible to justify the infringement on some exceptional basis. This means, among other things, that torture, as a violation of human dignity, can never be justified, not even where the intent is to save innocent lives.

Creating a definition of 'human dignity' also includes not only addressing conceptually related or historically linked concepts like the human rights touched upon above, for example the right to life or civil liberties, but also 'simple' rights like personal honour. It is important to identify similarities, but also differences. Much work still needs to be done, until we arrive at an even moderately acceptable overview of the wide variety of individual rights as expressions of human dignity or various human rights.

D. The History of Human Dignity and Human Rights

The historical development of the debate on human dignity and human rights, from ancient times (Cicero) through the great international legal

---

17 In many countries, Human Dignity is understood in a much broader sense as a kind of umbrella for rights or even source for all human rights. A good example is Israel, where the Supreme Court considers 'Human Dignity' as a 'Super-Right' from which other human rights, that were lacking in the Israeli Constitution for historical reasons, can be derived. See, eg, M Kremnitzer, 'Human Dignity. An Israeli Perspective' in E Hilgendorf (ed), *Menschenwürde und Demütigung. Die Menschenwürdekonzeption Avishai Margalits* (Baden-Baden, Nomos, 2013).

codifications of the twentieth century up to our present time,[18] are all important sources of the contemporary concept of 'human dignity'. Among the most important insights which can be drawn from an examination of this historical development is that the discourse on human dignity is not coextensive with the discourse on human rights. The passionate resistance of organised Christianity, particularly the Catholic Church, opposing the advancement of ideas on human rights and a secular and egalitarian conception of human dignity,[19] is remarkable and worth considering further. The reason for this was primarily the fact that these rights were formulated and gained support through the Enlightenment, particularly the anti-clerical French Enlightenment at the end of the eighteenth century. Today, the prominent Christian churches in central Europe have not only accepted the ideals of human rights and human dignity, but have committed themselves to their defence and dissemination.[20] This example shows that religions are capable of learning, and that no form of belief should, from the outset, be regarded as incompatible with human rights and human dignity.

E. The Logic of Human Rights and Human Dignity

Another field of research which has received much too little attention is the logic of statements about human dignity and human rights. What does it actually mean to say that this or that right 'follows' from human dignity, or that human dignity 'prohibits' this or that behaviour? What 'consequences' result from human dignity? Is it even permissible to speak of 'consequences'? What logical connections exist between values, or between values and normative rules, or between normative rules themselves? In this context lawyers like to use metaphors, arguing for example that this or that 'flows' from human dignity. It should be obvious that the unre-

---

18   See M Rosen, *Dignity. Its History and Meaning* (Cambridge, Mass, Harvard University Press, 2012) 11–38 for a short history of the concept up to Kant. For the history of human rights see L Meir Friedman, *The Human Rights Culture. A Study in History and Context* (New Orleans, Quid Pro Books, 2011) 25–54.
19   *ibid* 49–54.
20   This does not mean that there are not certain topics that are still highly controversial between secular defenders of Human Dignity and religiously oriented people. A good example is the case of Savita Halappanava (2012) who died because doctors in Ireland refused her an abortion on religious grounds in spite of medical necessity.

flected use of metaphors is not very convincing from an academic point of view. This is an issue in the field of linguistic analysis, but particularly in the area of deontic logic or logic of values and norms. On the legal side, 'legal logic', which has received very little attention in recent years, can claim responsibility for itself.

What is important is that a differentiation is made between logical relationships, between concepts like human dignity and human rights versus the historical genesis of the concepts. The associative links between these normative constructs pose yet a different problem. If one accepts the definition of human dignity proposed here, as a right or collection of rights, it is at least possible to say that individual rights follow from human dignity in a strictly logical sense. In practice the most important logical operations, where rights are concerned, can be represented by a legal syllogism. Taken all together, there are so many unresolved issues in this area that an urgent need for more detailed examination is apparent.

F. Justification of Human Dignity

One of the main problems in the human dignity debate is that many authors do not differentiate clearly enough between the definition of human dignity and its justification. The definition of 'human dignity' answers the question of what we mean when we use the term 'human dignity'. Definitions are linguistic determinations; they are neither right or wrong, but rather only more or less appropriate or suitable. It would be a completely different question, and indeed an empirical one, to ask how a term is used, for example, in German law, or how it is used by a particular philosopher or a particular societal group. The question of the justification for the protection which human dignity affords, goes again in an entirely different direction. The same goes for trying to justify a particular terminological approach to human dignity: Why accept a particular definition of human dignity? How 'good'—plausible, convincing, compelling—are the reasons?[21]

It would seem that the justification or rather the justifiability of our conception of human dignity is one of the central questions in the human

---

21 E Hilgendorf, 'Begründung in Recht und Ethik' in C Brand, EM Engels, A Ferrari and L Kovács (eds), *Wie funktioniert Bioethik?* (Paderborn, Mentis, 2008).

dignity debate. In the German philosophical tradition, and also in the German constitutional tradition, it is very widespread to refer to Immanuel Kant. But recourse to Kant may be insufficient to legitimise central ethical and legal definitions just like that. Mere reference to a suitable passage in one of Kant's major works is certainly not a compelling argument. As an alternative, probably to a certain extent to supplement Kant, Fichte's concept of reciprocal recognition (*Anerkennung*) or Gewirth's concept of conceptual analysis[22] have been discussed, so far, however, without gaining much support. Recourse to the black letter text, a methodology dear in the hearts of lawyers, looking at the wording of the statute or constitution, does not free us from the tasks both of looking for a justification for the establishment of the protection of human dignity in the national legal system, as well as specifying a particular definition of human dignity. Such questions can sometimes be found concealed behind innocently sounding legal phrases such as the 'intention of the legislature' or the 'purpose of the statute'.

The conception of a core area of human autonomy or an area where it is possible to exercise autonomy can be identified as the central idea of almost all justifications of Human Dignity. Therefore, in some respect it is not wrong to hold that Kant is inescapable in the human dignity debate. In my view, however, the catchword 'Kant' should be widened to 'Philosophy of the Enlightenment'[23]: all the important elements of our conception of human dignity and human rights received broad recognition for the first time in the second half of the eighteenth century. In contrast, the conception that man was made in the 'image' of God, and therefore ought to receive special protection, appears to only have a secondary role; it should be clarified whether this conception has ever been at the centre of a serious justification for the human dignity concept.

According to a non-religious understanding, the strong protection human dignity affords to certain fundamental rights can be justified by recourse to similarly fundamental human needs (or 'interests'), for example the universal need for a minimum material existence, freedom from extreme pain, etc. The needs referred to here seem to be universally human,

---

22 For a critical analysis, see A Fagan, *Human Rights. Confronting Myths and Misunderstandings* (Cheltenham, Elgar, 2009) 16–22.

23 J Israel, *A Revolution of the Mind: Radical Enlightenment and the Intellectual Origins of Modern Democracy* (Princeton, Princeton University Press, 2010); P Gay, *The Enlightenment*, vol 1: *The Rise of Modern Paganism* (New York, Knopf, 1966); Vol. 2: *The Science of Freedom* (New York, Knopf, 1969).

like some sort of 'anthropological' constant, which exists across all societies. Even if it is admitted that needs may be modified by different cultures, or change across time, it appears to be justified to speak of some sort of 'minimal natural law'.

G. Bearers of Human Dignity

According to the current and no longer disputed conception, all human beings possess human dignity. 'All human beings' means all human beings after they have been born; only they possess autonomy or have the ability to act autonomously. In the case of human beings who, at any given moment, are non-autonomous, the new-born, the comatose or the mentally ill, however, this approach leads to problems, which up to now have not been resolved in a convincing way. If one accepts the position argued here that the content and scope of the protection of human dignity are not an a priori given, but rather are something we decide on, then it becomes unproblematic to bring people within the scope of protection of human dignity who, in their particular case, are non-autonomous or even unable to ever be autonomous.

At what point an unborn human life, from the moment of conception, or a three month old embryo or a fully developed foetus, possesses human dignity or ought to possess it, continues to be the subject of highly emotional debate. Sometimes even unfertilised human eggs are said to possess Human Dignity. This question of the possession of human dignity before birth is very important in bioethical and bio-legal contexts; one need think only of the controversy surrounding abortion. It is even more controversial when it is already known from the outset that the respective cells or the developing embryos will never be born, as is the case in the therapeutic cloning of human cells.

Whoever shares the view that the protection human dignity provides should be at a very high level, so high indeed, that each and every incursion into the protected area is, without exception, a violation, must confine the scope of protection to a narrow area, so that practically the protection does not extend *ad absurdum*. In the European legal tradition neither the embryo nor the foetus possesses human dignity. If it were otherwise, not only any sort of research involving embryos, but also abortion would without exception be held to be illegal. The protection of certain early stages of human life prior to birth should be accomplished using the general, pre-existing areas of law—from administrative law to criminal law.

The potentiality argument, that is the idea that because a cell or complex of cells has the potential to develop into a living human being, these cells or cell complexes should have certain legal rights, can be taken to the point of absurdity applying the latest human biotechnology research, as almost every human cell apparently possesses this potential.

From time to time we also encounter the idea that the dead should not only be treated with respect but also that they possess dignity. This approach cannot be reconciled with the conception of the protection of autonomy or the capacity to be autonomous. Therefore, the dead as such can only be seen as bearers of human dignity at the high price of considerable conceptual confusion.

Certainly not to be dismissed a priori as out of hand is the question of whether certain animals should enjoy the protection of their 'dignity' or some analogous status. In this question opinions tend to differ widely between those who argue based on the intellectual traditions of Kant and Christianity, as opposed to disciples of other schools of thought such as Utilitarianism or Buddhism. On the issue of autonomy a new-born human child is not very different from an adult non-human primate. Nevertheless making this comparison engenders misunderstanding, often even downright indignation or anger. In such cases we observe the emotional depths of the human dignity debate, which are in urgent need of clarification. I am not advocating here that apes should be granted the ensemble of rights sketched out above.[24] I am only surprised by the vehemence with which the protection of the 'dignity' of animals is rejected. To my mind the reasons for this reaction are in urgent need of clarification.[25]

H. What is a Violation of Human Dignity?

It is a widespread mistake to confound the definition of 'human dignity' with the specification of criteria for its violation. An example of this kind of confusion is the popular statement that 'human dignity' means not being instrumentalised. Expressions like this, which are perfectly common in

---

24   See section II.3.
25   The reason for extremely vehement reactions to such proposals in animal ethics may lie in an apparently deeply rooted need of man to distinguish himself from animals, i.e. to feel a sense of uniqueness. Considering our knowledge of the evolutionary context of all living things, this position will probably not be rationally tenable in the long term.

the 'human dignity' debate, suffer from such serious logical and semantic problems that they can often only be discussed rationally after being completely reframed.

The German Federal Constitutional Court tried for some time to avoid the definitional difficulties by attempting, so to speak, to define the concept of 'human dignity' negatively by defining a list of actions which violate it. Thus, according to a proposal by the constitutional lawyer Günter Dürig, 'human dignity' is violated 'when a concrete human being is degraded into an object, to a simple means (to an end), to something fungible'.[26] Dürig's formula, which is based on the second main formula of Kant's Categorical Imperative, has been subjected for a long time to much criticism.

The topic of 'Instrumentalisation', which is frequently used in connection with possible human dignity violations, is closely related to Dürig's formula. Unfortunately, it is usually not made at all clear what 'instrumentalisation' is supposed to mean. If it is meant, following normal language usage, as nothing more than that one human being uses another human being as a means to achieve some objective, then instrumentalisation cannot simply be characterised as a violation of human dignity. When one person asks another person on the street for directions on how to get somewhere, and therefore 'uses' the other person as a source of information, he certainly is not violating that person's human dignity. It is impossible to imagine everyday life without tiny 'instrumentalisations' such as this, which are not perceived as problematic, illegal or at all denigrating to a person's human dignity.

Defenders of the concept of instrumentalisation point out that a violation of human dignity only takes place when the other person is used 'merely as a means'. But this statement raises more questions than it is able to solve. Thus, using the example above, the person who has been asked for directions has been used exclusively as a means, indeed 'merely as a means' to satisfy the informational needs of the person asking for directions. Nevertheless, no violation of human dignity has taken place. Looked at the other way around, it is certainly possible to think of actions which would generally be considered to be clear violations of human dignity, although one could not sensibly say that the other person was instrumentalised. An example of this is the torture of a prisoner, where the sole

---

26 G Dürig, 'Kommentierung von Art. 1 Grundgesetz' in T Maunz and G Dürig (eds), *Grundgesetz-Kommentar*, 1st edn (Munich, Beck, 1958) paragraph 28.

intention is to torture the prisoner and no other goals are being pursued through the torture. In such a situation it is almost impossible to characterise the action as instrumentalisation, but it is, of course, a human dignity violation. It appears, therefore, that on the one hand, the concept of instrumentalisation is too broad, because it catches too many actions which are not human dignity violations (false positives), but on the other hand it is too narrow, as it fails to catch actions which are clearly human dignity violations (false negatives).[27]

A further concept, which has been under discussion for some time with respect to human dignity violations, is the concept of *humiliation*. It has been suggested that a human dignity violation is committed when a human being is humiliated in a certain way.[28] Some concerns can also be raised about this concept. First of all, the concept of humiliation appears to be too broad, because it catches cases which are generally not considered to be human dignity violations, in which the victim is offended, but is not threatened in his autonomy or in his capacity to be autonomous. In most legal systems of the Civil Law legal tradition, humiliation is placed under the criminal sanction of *insult* so that it is hardly in need of further protection by human dignity. It is also remarkable that even very minor insults, which represent a form of humiliation, would be absolutely forbidden and could not be justified even as exceptions. This seems hardly acceptable. Thus, compulsory vaccination or compulsory military service may be perceived as humiliating, but such compulsory measures can, according to our common understanding, be legitimised by higher purposes. This is not possible for human dignity violations in the strict sense, such as torture, according to the theory presented here. To sum up, it seems to me that 'humiliation' is much too broad a concept to capture the main idea of 'human dignity', if the concept is to be understood in the strict sense developed here.

---

27 For a detailed treatment, see E Hilgendorf, 'Instrumentalisierungsverbot und Ensembletheorie der Menschenwürde' in HU Päffgen (ed), *Strafrechtswissenschaft als Analyse und Konstruktion. Festschrift für Ingeborg Puppe zum 70. Geburtstag* (Berlin, Duncker & Humblot, 2011).

28 T Hörnle, 'Menschenwürde als Freiheit von Demütigungen' (2008) *Zeitschrift für Rechtsphilosophie* 41; *id*, 'Warum sich das Würdekonzept Margalits zur Präzisierung von "Menschenwürde als geschütztes Rechtsgut" gut eignet' in E Hilgendorf (ed), *Menschenwürde und Demütigung. Die Menschenwürdekonzeption Avishai Margalits* (Baden-Baden, Nomos, 2013); see also P Kaufmann et al, *Humiliation, Degradation, Dehumanization. Human Dignity Violated* (Dordrecht et al, Springer, 2011).

I. Loss of Human Dignity?

The possibility of a deprivation of human dignity or, respectively, deprivation of the protection of human dignity, in contrast to the case of the protection of honour, is hardly accepted. Such a possibility of deprivation would frustrate the goal of protecting human dignity. It is not so easy to answer the question of whether it should be possible for a person to renounce his human dignity or at least its protection either completely or partially. The *Dwarf tossing case*[29] and the *Peep show case*[30] are well known examples of controversies in this respect. In both cases the courts held the activities illegal, as violations of the human dignity of the affected persons, respectively, that of the dwarfs and the peep show dancers. This raises the question of the extent to which bearers of human dignity have the power to dispose of, manage or renounce their human dignity protection (for example, in exchange for remuneration). This question, too, is still far from being fully resolved.

It is part of the liberal legal tradition that the individual is granted the power to dispose of his or her rights: *Volenti non fit injuria*. The concept of the protection of human autonomy, the foremost of the underlying values of the protection of human dignity, speaks for the right of the individual to freely decide on such issues. On the other hand, the essential reason for having or recognising a right of human dignity is, so to speak, the creation of a final and inviolable bastion to protect human rights. The unlimited freedom of the individual is certainly a popular position, but it nevertheless needs to be justified. Arguments exist which deny the individual the right to make all possible decisions about his body or his life, particularly as such decisions are sometimes made under circumstances which can hardly be reconciled with the liberal conception of the individual decision maker as judicious, enlightened, free and careful in his deliberations.

One possible solution might be to focus on the central idea of human dignity protection, namely the protection of autonomy, so as to argue that it would be possible for an individual to voluntarily renounce the protection afforded by human dignity, as long as his or her capacity for autono-

---

29   Manuel Wackenheim vs France, Communication No 854/1999, UN Doc CCPR/C/75/D/854/1999 (2002) in United Nations Human Rights Committee, *Selected Decisions under the Optional Protocol, Seventy-Fifth to Eighty-Fourth Sessions* (July 2002–March 2005) 111; for an analysis see Rosen, *Dignity* (2012) 63–70.

30   BVerwGE 64, 274.

my is not threatened with permanent nullification (i.e. a lasting impairment). Temporary slavery would be permitted, but not an agreement whereby a human being would be permanently and irretrievably enslaved. Sexual services provided on a voluntary basis would not be a violation of human dignity, not even those involving consensual torture, but torture which permanently impaired the capacity of the individual to autonomy would be a violation, regardless of whether consent was given by the affected person or not.

In all of these contexts exactly what 'voluntary' is supposed to mean, obviously needs to be clarified. Interesting parallels exist here to *consent to physical injury,* particularly in the criminal law, and, on the other hand, to the issue of what constitutes 'informed consent', which is the subject of much discussion in the context of medical ethics, particularly in countries following the Common Law legal tradition.[31]

J. What Solutions Does Human Dignity Provide for Urgent Public Policy Problems?

This brings us to the last area in the human dignity debate that I want to touch upon, namely the question, what concrete results can we expect from the protection of human dignity? The answer to this question naturally depends on what underlying concept of human dignity one accepts. Whatever impinges on the area protected by human dignity is absolutely prohibited (in any case that is the view proposed here). If one takes this point of departure seriously, the result is that violations of human dignity can be accepted only in exceptional situations, especially in cases where there is a violation of the core area of protection of a fundamental right. Any inflationary use of human dignity would render the concept practically useless in the long run. This means, among other things, that the narrow concept of human dignity advocated here forms only a wide frame for the modern biotechnology industry, medical or biotechnical research or other highly controversial political issues. It is no 'passe-partout' to all our political and moral problems.

---

31   B Greene, *Essential Medical Law* (London, Cavendish Publishing, 2001) 11–38.

III. Summary

Finally, allow me to summarise my remarks in three theses:

In spite of its prominence in numerous legal, philosophical and moral-theological debates, the concept of human dignity leaves as of yet many fundamental questions unanswered.

The key to successfully leading the debate forward lies in also focusing on methodological questions, first of all questioning the widespread conceptual essentialism. The decisive question should not be: 'What is human dignity?' but rather much more 'How shall we define human dignity in order to be able to reach the goals we have taken upon ourselves?'

Whoever agrees with the premise that as a reaction to the unprecedented atrocities of the first half of the twentieth century the goal of the protection of human dignity is the protection, without exceptions, of a core area of humanity and autonomy, as a kind of 'normative anchor', removed from the pros and cons of a pluralistic society, must choose a narrowly defined concept of human dignity. The Ensemble Theory of human dignity put forward here constitutes a proposal for such a concept.

Towards Progressive Human Dignity

Tim Wihl

I. Introductory Remarks

With the specter of war, persecution and industrial killings receding in Europe, the traditional post-1945 German understanding of human dignity has come to a close.[1] The legal debate about dignity seems stuck between a conservative protection of the status quo of bodily and spiritual integrity and the liberal notion of individual autonomy. The first strand of thought can be identified with a 'correspondence' view, which claims that the legal concept of dignity corresponds to certain defined constitutional goods; the second elaborates on the 'coherence' that exists among several implications of dignity in legal cases. In contrast to both these frameworks, the 'consensus' paradigm – which corresponds to a republican as well as forward-looking, progressive idea of human dignity – is mostly missing from the debate. Thus, three classical options in philosophical theories of truth can be aptly transferred to the meta-theoretical ordering of legal theories of human dignity.[2] In particular, this scheme allows for a rediscovery of the third, nowadays vastly neglected consensus paradigm. We can describe it in terms of collective aspirations to a good life, which should not be artificially split off from mere 'life' (or existence). Surprisingly, progressive human dignity reveals itself to be the epitome of collectivity in fundamental rights doctrine, coequal to the principle of democracy. Apart from that the concept of dignity appears reducible and redundant in constitutional doctrine.

The further we distance ourselves from the starting point – the conservative protection of single subjectivity – the more we include commu-

---

[1] I would like to thank Sabine Müller-Mall for her highly valuable comments on the draft of this chapter. Janet Mindes did an excellent job at style-editing this piece.

[2] For theories of truth cf, generally, M Enders and J Szaif (eds), *Die Geschichte des philosophischen Begriffs der Wahrheit* (Berlin, de Gruyter, 2006); G Skirbekk (ed), *Wahrheitstheorien* (Frankfurt, Suhrkamp, 1977); W Künne, *Conceptions of Truth* (Oxford, Oxford University Press, 2005).

nicative, intersubjective parts. And the more we emphasize contingent intersubjectivity, as in the liberal conception, the closer we get to the idealist telos of necessary intersubjectivity, included in the concept of dignity as republican collectivity. To sum it up: Human dignity can only be saved from legal redundancy if we conceive of it, much like Ernst Bloch's seminal 'Natural Law and Human Dignity'[3], as a complex, essentially democratic hope for a collective future of 'aufrechter Gang' (metaphorical 'upright carriage') for all.

II. Conservative Correspondence

The correspondence theory of truth stands for 'adaequatio intellectus ad rem',[4] which creates the ontological obligation to assume that 'objects' (res) exist apart from the intellect – but of which kind they are, and how the intellect expresses their existence, is controversial. So we will only adopt the most basic idea of this theory: the correspondence between entities that belong to two different 'worlds'.[5]

When I use the term 'conservative' here, it is meant to imply a structural idea of conservatism, not so much – though perhaps as a contingent by-effect – the more common notion of political conservatism. Conservative dignity is essentially about a preservation of the status quo ('conservare'). This status quo is, yet again, not defined in a holistic, politically contingent way. Instead, it is applied to single objects, and subject-objects first of all, in a rather atomistic way. Single subjects can have dignity, or so the common wisdom goes. They are thought of as *single*, and regarded as *subjects*, personae/persons. Dignity is about the preservation or protection of (1) singularity, (2) subjectivity, and (3) the resulting mix.

(1) Legal singularity, like every concept, seems to be easily defined with regard to its opposite: plurality. However – and this points to the good sense of this method of definition by opposite – conceptual ambiguities remain, which result from the necessary possibility of different coun-

---

3   E Bloch, *Natural Law and Human Dignity*, transl. DJ Schmidt (Cambridge, MIT Press, 1987).
4   T Aquinas, *Summa theologiae*, I, quaestio 21 a. 2.
5   But cf the pragmatist criticism of this dualism, eg J Habermas, 'Wahrheitstheorien' in id, *Vorstudien und Ergänzungen zur Theorie des kommunikativen Handelns* (Frankfurt, Suhrkamp, 1984) 133.

ter-concepts under the auspices of semantic holism. An alternative counter-concept seems to be collectivity. Let us state, only for the sake of argument, that collectivity and plurality have fixed meanings – which is necessary in that one seeks to break through the wall of the totality of fluid meanings, to reach into the sphere of scientific discourse. Within the humanities we may observe that things are more complicated, and yet as scientists we agree to fix certain meanings in order to advance clear communication and more precise definition. Vagueness granted, it appears nonetheless clear in comparison that collectivity means plurality with a bond, with some index of relative necessity.

Therefore, we need to make clear whether we mean singularity with or without a bond. This may sound theoretical or without legal import. But that is untrue: Since we speak about a spiritual and not a material object, it matters greatly whether we conceive of it as 'objet coupé' or 'objet intouché'. This kind-of-ontological decision might even lead to differing political interpretations of the single subject.

Singularity as non-collectivity, the more demanding idea, is not only a quantitative concept, but also conveys a qualitative meaning. It means an object that has broken, or been deprived of its social or political bonds. It is, in such a very undemanding fashion, an 'emancipated' object. Legally speaking, the single unit disposes of a quality that makes it worth protecting *precisely as* this single object (per se, in itself, as 'free from'). On the other hand, singularity as non-plurality has a purely quantitative meaning. In the legal domain, this translates (only) into the idea that, exclusively, a protection of single units is required, instead of several units together.

(2) Subjectivity is certainly the more complex concept, though we have seen that even seemingly simple notions can reveal themselves to be ambiguous entities. Subjectivity is anti-objectivity: Not being an object, or not being objective. We can easily exclude the second variant here. But what does that mean: Not being an object? In an ontological context, this would point to other entities besides objects – properties perhaps, or activities, or time. This path seems to mislead us here, at first glance. Rather, there appears to be a subclass of objects that are also subjects: subject-objects. These objects should distinguish themselves by a specific property or quality. Yet we cannot do away with the idea of the negation of 'being an object' too abruptly. Maybe there is another ontological entity, which is neither object, nor property, nor activity, nor time, nor space, etc.: the subject.

The implications for the legal arena could be profound. Either we conceive of subjects as objects with determined or determinable qualities, or we try to distinguish them from objects in a more radical manner. This might, in turn, influence the sort of protection we grant: a protection of certain qualities, or a protection of a being per se, in or by virtue of its not being an object.

The second alternative is quite mysterious and cannot be pursued in more detail at this point. The first is more accessible, though. There must be some quality that makes an object a subject, and we call this or the bundle of qualities the object's 'subjectivity'.

Several suggestions have been made in the literature. Most of them are surprisingly detached from the etymological origin of the concept: subiectum, subiungere = to subject someone to something. It is useful, however, to keep this original meaning in mind for there appears to remain a grain of it even in seemingly separated meanings. Most clearly, this is the case in Kantian moral philosophy, which is based on the highly rationalized notion of subjective autonomy that the categorical imperative epitomizes. A subject is an entity that commands a free will, and a will can only be free if it subjects itself to the moral law. One feels some resonance here with Rousseau's teaching of the man who is forced to be free – while the crucial difference lies in Kant's 'Protestant' internalization of this force. In sum, the subject is a free person, or more liberally, in order to avoid the problem of the mentally ill or the minor, the subject belongs to a species of which one can reasonably say that it commands a free will.

Subjectivity, being a subject, seems to be identical with potential freedom of the will, then. As long as biology does not teach us otherwise, we have to limit subjectivity to the human species. What 'makes us human', in contrast to (most?) other animals, is the quintessential source of morality, according to this narrative. Other ideas of subjectivity emphasize the strength, of the physical, psychological, or spiritual variety, that makes us 'good members' of our species, like 'capabilities' (M Nussbaum), or apparent anthropological 'constants', be they conceived of as progressive (C Henning) or truly constant, i. e. fixed (conservative philosophical anthropology). These capacities may or may not be related to reason as the source of 'humanity'-proper. This is relevant insofar as one could easily challenge the ruling rationalist orthodoxy by reference to a more 'emancipated' voluntarism: Human is who wants, who desires, who makes plans, who thinks 'into' the future, in short: who is aware of her mortality. That may make a human being follow her bare, hardly reflexive first-order desires (H Frankfurt) as well as obey her second-order desires. In turn, by extension, one can define subjects as those that obey their wants, needs and desires, thus abandoning moral expectations of 'secularized or egalitarian honor' and defying the systematic devaluation of the 'needy parts' of human subjectivity. Thus, the concept of subjectivity can easily be shown to be self-defeating, if you rightfully do away with undue moralism.

(3) The mix of singularity and subjectivity does not add much to the debate – except a certain emphasis on 'uniqueness'. Every (so far: human) subjectivity – that is, after what I have described above: the human being in her spiritual as well as bodily parts – can claim uniqueness, as was expressed so wonderfully by the Renaissance philosopher Pico della Mirandola. And it seems, in part, this uniqueness we cherish. The source of this liking for difference lies not only in Christian faith, but also in the rise of the natural sciences and the corresponding technological development: We have started to appreciate the complexity of nature, and a sense of miracle has not been lost on the way, but has rather intensified: How is it that we share similar bodily traits and yet look and behave so differently at the same time? And how and why do we develop such diverging talents and capacities? It is certain, after all, that our difference is our strength in strongly differentiated societies. It is no mere coincidence that Emile Durkheim was the first to treat the phenomenon of the sacralization of the self in modern societies from a sociological viewpoint. To put it in a very demystifying, matter-of-fact way: It is simply a result of economic necessity that we love single subjectivity, or human uniqueness, so much today. It is the foundation of our material wealth. And it is a typical sign of a post-Fordist, less homogeneous, individualized and 'neoliberal' society that we are constantly searching for the unique – since we need it for reproduction, and for economic compensation at the same time. We use it as an economic and as an immaterial resource, in our longing for authenticity in the novel conformism that survival dictates. Human dignity, seen from a sociological standpoint, is therefore not much more than the epitome of all the evils we are mired in, voluntarily or not. Durkheim's optimism from the 19th century needs to be severely tempered today. For organic solidarity has liberated us from feudal bonds, but it has never fully set us free. So if we want to remain faithful to the spirit of emancipation that once defined this term, we need to spell out a new 'progressive' concep-

tion, one that reaches beyond Durkheim's and Hans Joas' narrow confines of an advancing sacralization of the 'person'.[6]

In some quarters, we hear a very different diagnosis of the present situation of dignity claims – one that is fueled by a different starting point: the social problems that arise from new biotechnology. Whoever comes to think about dignity from the perspective of bioethics tends to ask different questions than those coming from the 'social justice camp'. Considering the genealogy of the present debate about dignity, one could hardly deny that a new interest in personhood as a potential limit to the naturalization of man is at the beginning of the discourse we observe since the late 1990s.

In an important respect, it is Joas' impressive study, in which he advances the methodological idea of 'affirmative genealogy', that marks a turning point in this discussion: He points out – albeit implicitly, *in actu* – that we increasingly neglect the difference between dignity and rights, thus confirming not only the undertheorized German constitutional doctrine of Art. 1 Basic Law as a 'core' of (which?) other fundamental rights ('Menschenwürdekern der Grundrechte'), but also the doubtful correspondence theory of dignity, which I spell out below. However, Joas deserves some credit for reminding us, especially the German audience, that the emancipation from slavery is the paradigmatic case of the struggle for dignity.[7] Slavery signifies a unique mix of social deprivation, loss of civic status, economic exploitation, physical harm, spiritual degradation, and denial of autonomy – which makes it the quintessential manifestation and experience of lost dignity. Plus, white people could have acknowledged; since even though the American abolitionist movement may have been too small, vocal opponents of slavery have always been around, black and white alike. What the emphasis on slavery adds to the German debate is the insight that economic factors have played a role in the disregard of dignity from the start, and that this has never gone unnoticed. This is sometimes neglected when academics discuss dignity against the background of the irrational racist ideologies that led to the Shoah, a constitutive factor of the German discussion. This discussion, in turn, presaged the

---

6   E Durkheim, *The Division of Labor in Society*, transl. WD Halls (New York, Free Press, 1997); H Joas, *The Sacredness of the Person* (Washington, Georgetown University Press, 2013).
7   cf also J Osterhammel and H Meier, *Sklaverei und die Zivilisation des Westens* (Munich, Siemens Stiftung, 2009).

international debate in a variety of ways, particularly in its focus on current bioethical issues – which, by the way, do not share that many features with the eugenics movements or the Holocaust. In the meantime, the globalization of the discussion, with important contributions from South Africa and other states,[8] has led to an increasing recognition of the social-economic dimension of dignity even in Germany.[9]

What do these different foci of the interpretation of dignity have in common? I want to limit myself to the structural questions here. Structurally, or ontologically if you want, it is striking that the above approaches share the purpose to preserve a certain, often closely defined status quo. This can comprise all sorts of specific rights, conservative (basic property, bodily integrity), liberal (specific parts of the right to individual self-determination, like a communicative private sphere), or progressive (fixed basic income). Apart from the political shades, all these attempts to understand human dignity are – structurally – conservative. Their view of the law is that of the citizen who demands legal certainty, who wishes to cling to something secure in the stormy seas of accelerated modernity. Law appears not as an ideal means to approach something new, unknown, 'utopian', or 'Heimat' (E Bloch), but as a guarantor of concrete-particular achievements of the past. With two important exceptions: Dignity can be used to spur dynamism in legal development when it serves to protect the preconditions of democratic debate (liberal), without specifying them too much, rather as a 'Factor X' of various rights (B Ladwig), or when it denotes the utopian ideals of the teleological constitution themselves as such, per se (progressive). Besides, we advance from conservative correspondence of dignity with specific, concrete, and particular rights, to liberal coherence of rights through the 'Factor X' of dignity and, finally, to progressive consensus on the forever unexhausted content of dignity as the right to collectivity. Contrary to conventional wisdom, we find in dignity the guarantee that nothing should be ultimately guaranteed if we want to adhere to humanist ideals. Everything we want to see guaranteed, such as the abolition of slavery, torture, and extreme poverty, is in fact part of the constitution by way of particular guarantees in more specific rights, such as the right to life and physical integrity.

---

8   D Robertson, *The Judge as Political Theorist* (Princeton, Princeton University Press, 2010).
9   BVerfGE 125, 175 – Hartz IV Judgment of the German Federal Constitutional Court (2010).

Dignity serves as a *bridge concept* that allows us not so much to discover new contents of existing rights,[10] but rather to discover that we have reflected on these rights in an unduly narrow manner. The *'emotional turn'* in philosophy induces us to think about the value of psychological integrity in a new way, for instance.[11] Physical integrity should be joined with psychological health because together they form a conglomerate that deserves unique protection, as the prohibition of torture clearly demonstrates. 'Inner freedom'[12] can be understood in such a naturalizing way, which also subverts the inherited false dichotomy of body and soul, called Cartesian dualism. Ironically, the highly moralist and animality-hostile Kantian idea of dignity thus takes on a wholly new meaning. Autonomy, the concrete ('conservative correspondence') way, is dependent on the revaluation of the body. Not only does dignity bridge the gap between new *naturalism* and fundamental rights, it can also connect *sociology* and rights: the fundamental Marxian insight, borrowed from Hegel, that we are 'the ensemble of the social relations'[13] needs to find some translation in the language of constitutional law. Intricately connected with this idea is the questioning of the allegedly liberalist boundary between life and a good life, between right and good. This is in fact a conservative dichotomy because it is based on existing property, on remnants of the past, in a wide Lockean sense, including the individual body, and not on present autonomy, which always strives to expand, and thereby tear down the boundaries of past property, including contingent cultural conceptions of the body, like the 'necessary' or 'inevitable' link between sex and gender. Thus, it becomes transparent that we need to advance from the narrow conservative conception of dignity, as a rhetorical strengthening of existing rights of the *past*, be they included in national constitutions or international treaties, to the dignity of the *present*.

---

10 But cf J Habermas, 'Das Konzept der Menschenwürde und die realistische Utopie der Menschenrechte' (2010) *Deutsche Zeitschrift für Philosophie* 343.
11 cf R de Sousa, *The Rationality of Emotion* (Cambridge, MIT Press, 1990); MC Nussbaum, *Upheavals of Thought* (Cambridge, Cambridge University Press, 2003).
12 C Goos, *Innere Freiheit* (Göttingen, Vandenhoeck und Ruprecht, 2011).
13 K Marx, Theses on Feuerbach, VI.

III. Liberal Coherence

In a less temporal vocabulary, and once more against the background of theories of truth, we are advancing from correspondence (dignity as a specific, concrete, particular right) to coherence. Correspondence rests on ancient philosophy, most of all (maybe erroneously), on Aristotle's famous and rather vacuous phrase: 'To say of what is that it is not, or of what is not that it is, is false, while to say of what is that it is, and of what is not that it is not, is true.'[14] Coherence goes back to the questioning of metaphysical realism and the development of semantic holism, mostly after the linguistic turn. To sum things up, this theory claims that truth can only arise when networks of meanings are considered – correspondence may be traced back to an event, while coherence appears more demanding, more inclusive. There may be no contradiction with any established true statement. Thus, it is also less easy to localize.

What is it that dignity signifies then? Not simply some single right or a fixed set of rights. Instead, it seems to be a 'Factor X' that somehow connects (1) several or (2) all rights, or a 'quasi-source' of new rights, without being transcendent-idealist, rather (3) tentatively comparable to the phenomenon of supervenience. A set of properties A supervenes on a set of properties B, if and only if any two objects x and y which share all properties in B (are 'B-indiscernible') must also share all properties in A (are 'A-indiscernible'). You can think of a set of rights that is incomplete but can logically be completed with regard to the supervenient set of properties that defines dignity. Only if these rights come together, dignity is possible. But the reverse is not true – dignity can exist without having all the properties, i. e. without containing all the rights of the second set.

(1) Since it is not easy to say positively what defines this Factor X, there is a temptation to combine a certain set of rights under the rubrum of dignity. These can come from the corners of physical or psychological integrity, autonomy (more spiritual), or the social preconditions of liberty. Usually, you can distinguish a specific emphasis on or orientation towards one of these three 'pillars' of dignity. The more vague, less concrete 'head concepts' serve as substitutes for the idea of dignity itself. At the same time, abstraction provides coherence of the often very polymorph sub-concepts. It is decisive to point out whether there is some *surplus value* of the process of abstraction or whether we could identify the term as a sim-

---

14 Aristotle, *Metaphysics* 1011b25.

ple *hedge concept*. In the case of providing coherence for several rights, a class of rights only, a surplus value is probable. The middle level concepts are most fertile in this regard, whereas high level and low level concepts alike are both relatively uninformative because they allow for either contradictory associations, or no association at all.

(2) The comparative lack of fertility is true for a conception of dignity that conceives of it in terms of autonomy, while at the same time covering the whole body of fundamental rights. The totalizing move to regard 'liberal rights' only through the lens of autonomy inevitably provokes a severe reduction of complexity in the reflection of rights.[15] Not only does it confine rights to the liberal program of enhancing individual self-determination, which would be a controversial, yet defensible political premise, it also disregards the internal contradictions that are so characteristic and productive in the realm of constitutional rights. If dignity as autonomy is used to cover these interesting contradictions and tensions, legal discourse gets more silenced, homogeneous, and ideological (= pretending necessity).

(3) It therefore appears that a model trying to distinguish between properties of dignity and an (ontologically lower) set of rights is most promising. It does not confound the system of rights with dignity or a specific subset of rights with a certain property of the concept of dignity, but recognizes the separate value of both levels. Coherence still is possible then, but rather in the sense of providing a heuristic concept that enables us to navigate more safely in the realm of rights – just as psychological ideas facilitate talking about neuronal mental states. Thus, *heuristic* coherence replaces *mereological* coherence. Dignity renders it easier for us to talk about rights in a systematizing manner, the (liberal) 'autonomy-enhancing', (conservative) 'integrity-preserving', (progressive) 'social-animality-emancipating' dimensions of rights.

Dignity as coherence is therefore more polymorph than the more arbitrary, but also more clearly defined dignity as correspondence. It grows from the distinction of different levels of abstraction and the insight that there is not only a mereological fallacy but also a confusion of mereology and heuristics. If we proceed from heuristics to transcendence, we leave the realm of coherence and enter the confines of democratic consensus.

---

15 cf K Möller, *The Global Model of Constitutional Rights* (Oxford, Oxford University Press, 2012).

IV. Progressive Consensus

Progressive human dignity is an attempt at liberating the concept from its reduction in conservative correspondence theories, which identify dignity with *existing*, concrete, particular rights, and its constriction in liberal coherence theories, which facilitate communicating (in a liberal fashion) about rights but either lead to a one-sided, ideological discourse about rights or only structure the terrain of *present* contradictions. What is absent from the debate is: the *future*.

We have grown used to the idea that rights are entities that somehow already exist – written or unwritten, in whichever form – when we speak about them, so that people can trust their stability and rely on them when they act – they might even believe they are 'given' to them and constitute 'a part of them' or, alternatively, that they come into being whenever individuals refer to them in legal proceedings. In other words, rights are supposed to be creatures of the past or the present.

It is imperative to understand that even when, quite naturally, rights are made use of in order to alter the present order of things locally, thereby pointing to the future, they are still not considered creatures of the future. The here proposed perspective on rights that regards them, *stricto sensu*, as future-oriented or aspirational, is more demanding: It insists that rights are never completely fulfilled, that they do not *exist* yet and cannot even be *invoked* fully in the present. Nor can rights be *thought of* as complete, cognitively. They are ever-incomplete concepts in a quasi (!)-Hegelian sense.

Is this doxa, positing without sufficient reason? On the contrary. We never *live* in the past (even when we refer to it in the most nostalgic way), but always in the present, which itself is highly fugitive. In fact, it is the future that determines our present – this is not as counter-intuitive as it first seems. While the past never holds, is ever mortal: 'all that is solid melts into air' (K Marx/ F Engels). It is the future that we live for, that conveys a perspective of sense to our lives. The future is the hermeneutics of the present. This is equally true for rights – they also have to reflect the hermeneutical priority of the things to come. Thus, we regain a sense of the completion of concepts *in time*, the imperfect state of mind and world and its resulting inchoate conceptual vision of this world. Let us take the 'ontology of not-yet' (E Bloch) into consideration. We can distinguish between idealist and materialist progressivism from the start – in order to avoid the closely related term of perfectionism (C Henning), which implies perfection, thus progress, but is primarily directed at its opponent of orthodox liberalism, by stressing an increase in 'good life' (perfect) as opposed to 'the right'. However, there is an undeniable proximity of the concepts because progressivism may be content-neutral at the beginning, but gets transformed into a content-transcendent idea easily. Active neutrality (as opposed to passive neutrality, merely 'looking away') can be understood as a devaluation of boundaries, which is equivalent to their progressive transcendence. Progressivism requires transcendence, thus the approximation of ideals. But following ideals is not the same as idealism. Whether you envision an idealist or a materialist kind of progress depends on where you situate the source of progress: in idealist minds (external) or in minds that reflect on material conditions (immanent). Internal progress, spontaneous transformation of matter, happens, but is certainly exceptional. Even natural evolution does not happen in the vacuum.

V. Idealist Progressivism

Human dignity can appear in the form of a highly abstract concept, like autonomy, as we have seen, and structures the debates of the present then. We can interpret the right to life, under the auspices of dignity = autonomy, as a right to terminate one's life, for example, in coherence with a liberal vision of individual self-determination. Or we can understand the same right against the background of conservative integrity, as an equivalent of the traditional negative right to life. In the latter case, we could also forgo the notion of dignity altogether. The former case does concern and potentially alters a specific interpretation of an existing right in the present. And yet, we cannot ascribe any idealist character to this interpretation – the expansion of individual freedom never comes without cost, which can be discussed and accepted or refused in collective decisions. The constellation is rather horizontal: We shift freedoms and duties (with or without the concept of dignity!) in a group that can be considered to consist of equals, like-powerful people. In order to expand, to 'complete' dignity, to further progress, we need to proceed to the vertical constellations, when power asymmetries exist. Only then can dignity truly grow, which means: only then dignity actually gets into the game. Before, it is just rhetorical masquerade (of correspondent rights) or legal décor (of desired interpretational shifts). While it does have real-world effects in this regard, dignity nevertheless serves as a mere proxy. 'Real' dignity, the progressive exhaustion of the concept, only comes into being when the law rediscovers its liberating – as opposed to liberal – side. This is dependent on republican consensus, in turn. Power relations are necessarily intersubjective and can therefore be abolished collectively only. It takes a republican will to get rid of power.

Dignity can become the epitome of collectivity in the constitution, then, because in contrast to liberal rights it is not immediately attached to normative individualism. Dignity is a more open concept, it is not limited by being interwoven with the basic premise that self-realization is for the individual to achieve. Contrary to common wisdom, however strongly we conceive of the attachment of freedom and equality to individualist thought, it is dignity that manages to open the realm of rights for the structural necessity of collectivity. For dignity is not only coupled with the heterodox notion of a good life – it systematically subverts the liberalist dichotomies of the good and the right, of reason and affect/will, of mind and body – it also bridges the gap between the zero-sum games of the distribution of individual liberties and the idea of solidarity. Ernst Bloch made the point most clearly: For his famous human 'upright carriage', the split between mere survival and a good life needs to be overcome – a free man who barely survives never lives in dignity, and a man who gets everything he wants but lacks freedom does not live in dignity, either. It becomes very transparent that liberty without solidarity is anathema to human dignity, as is solidarity without liberty. There is a grain of revelatory truth in the everyday dilemma the wealthy inhabitant of a city experiences: How should she treat the beggars she encounters? With respect, for sure. But when she gives, she feels she cannot rise up to the challenge of respecting equal liberty at the same time. When she does not give, she feels she has not even done the minimum that solidarity requires. In both cases, dignity has been violated, and she is left with a bad conscience. This bad conscience reminds her that something is wrong with a society that forces people to make this choice between two violations of dignity every day.

It is quite clear what dignity demands from us, then: organizing society in a different way. By way of this analysis, it is evident that dignity, however doubtful its surplus value as a legal term in correspondence and coherence contexts, serves to direct our political objectives towards a new consensus. And from this point of view, it appears obvious that the central position the term has been granted in the German constitution is completely justified. Still, it needs some limited degree of reinterpretation. Since the correspondence and the coherence theories of dignity must be refuted, the provision of Article 1 I Basic Law becomes a political directive of highest rank and honors: 'the *categoric imperative to overthrow all rela-*

tions in which man is a debased, enslaved, abandoned, despicable essence'.[16] Or, in the same mold:

> The Spirit of the Lord God is upon me; because the Lord hath anointed me to preach good tidings unto the meek; he hath sent me to bind up the brokenhearted, to proclaim liberty to the captives, and the opening of the prison to them that are bound. (Isaiah 61:1)
>
> Verily I say unto you, Inasmuch as ye have done it unto one of the least of these my brethren, ye have done it unto me. (Matthew 25:40)

Every generation needs to reach an ethical-political judgment and a successive decision about how to fulfill these imperatives, how to rise up to the challenge to contribute to dignity for all with the limited means of legal transformation. Dignity makes it a constitutional imperative to conceive of the law as an instrument of liberation, not of repressive order, in essence. This also points to the emancipatory understanding of the rule of law as a minimum means against arbitrary power.[17] It is no coincidence that in the Republic of South Africa, which is the global trendsetter in the realm of 'transformative constitutionalism' (P Langa), the notion of dignity plays a decisive role in constitutional adjudication, whenever unjust discrimination needs to be addressed. As a legal argument, dignity can express the new consensus of the Republic that there may never be different classes of people in society again. This also facilitates the legal insight that there is no relevant difference in importance or rank between civil liberties and social rights – in this area, South Africa has been a cautious avant-garde, too.

Richard Rorty has pleaded for a comparable link between dignity, solidarity and affect.[18] He points out that a progress in dignity may not be conceived of in Kantian terms, but needs to turn away from a focus on individual, sometimes solipsist rationality. Instead of centering on 'philosophy', which denotes every representational foundationalism in Rorty's theory, we should take seriously the power of affect, even sentimentality, in gradually expanding our awareness of and sensitivity to pain and suffering. In enlarging our sensitivity, we strengthen our solidarity at the same time. This gradually globalized solidarity – in an optimistic scenario –

---

16 K Marx, *Critique of Hegel's Philosophy of Right*, Introduction (1844).
17 cf EP Thompson, *Whigs and Hunters* (London, Breviary Stuff, 2013) 208.
18 R Rorty, 'Human Rights, Rationality, and Sentimentality' in id, *Truth and Progress* (Cambridge, Cambridge University Press, 1998) 167; id, *Contingency, Irony, and Solidarity* (Cambridge, Cambridge University Press, 1989).

takes the position of the 'end in itself' – combining less dogmatic rationalism, less solipsism, and a better calibrated sense for what truly counts. In Rorty's and Judith Shklar's terms, what really counts is the prevention of cruelty – everyone agrees on that.[19]

The weakness of Rorty's position lies therein: When he takes over Shklar's minimalist account – dignity is roughly equivalent to the absence of cruelty – he adopts the main problem of this position, too. It stems from a very implausible, reductionist account of liberal values which tries to ground them in negative reactions to historical instances of injustice. The bright side of this account is that it deals with history, thus temporality, and the collective, after all. On the other hand, this is a conservatively limited temporality. It lacks the level of the 'not-yet'. If there is no future, there is not even a present that tries to change the past. And in its anti-rationalist furor, Rorty's theory throws out the baby with the bath water. It is right to no longer neglect affects and sentiments, but it is wrong that philosophy per se stands in the way. Solidarity, if conjoined with dignity, is a demanding concept that needs philosophical exploration. And historically, it is this term that bears a huge weight of economic, political, and sociological meanings, which cannot easily be debunked and then thrown away.

It seems, at first glance, that there are two main alternatives for progressive consensus theories of dignity, two ways of reconciling necessary intersubjectivity with contingent truth and the postulate of change.

Though it is allegedly so simple to deconstruct, I would insist that the idealist variant deserves to be revisited. It is not the Kantian origin in the categorical imperative with its dubious, ultimately obscure dependence on the 'Sittengesetz' (Moral Law), but rather the Neokantian renaissance of this thought that deserves closer attention. This is because the Hegelian critique of the formalism of Kant's formula[20] is addressed by Hermann Cohen in his doctrine of human dignity, which shares (or even radicalizes) the Kantian idea of the homo noumenon who complies with the moral law voluntarily, absent any coercion. By this, man 'dignifies' himself. What is really modern about Cohen's conception is the ethical socialism it envisions, by which Cohen avoids Kant's formalism: It is no longer true that

---

19 J Shklar, 'The Liberalism of Fear' in J Shklar and S Hoffmann (eds), *Political Thought and Political Thinkers* (Chicago, University of Chicago Press, 1998) 3.
20 GWF Hegel, *The Philosophy of Right* (1820) § 135.

the categorical imperative is empty and open to all sorts of manipulation. On the contrary, by including the sociality of man, a Hegelian theme, Cohen gets close to Marx' critique of exploitation. If the person is an end in itself, she should not become part of a social 'mechanism' (W 2, 282 f.) in which she stops being this end in itself. Whenever man is reduced to a means or commodity with a price on the job market, the Kantian law is violated (W 7, 322).[21]

If we consider Cohen's idealist solution and Rorty's anti-idealism together, we understand that both can contribute to further understanding of the subject in different ways: They complement each other – Cohen is more rationalist, also more normativist, and therefore more radical in his conclusions. Rorty directs our attention to motivations and the roots of our growing cosmopolitan engagement. Cohen's results point to a transformative future, but remain external to the present. Rorty argues from the inside, from an internal point of view, but needs to invoke some rather unfounded hope to integrate normativity in his account at all. These two examples of strong external critique and weak internal critique remain deficient, but both point to each other's weaknesses and show the necessity to reflect on an immanent transcendence of established notions or levels of dignity in society. This synthesis needs to share the collective basis of the concept as well as its inclusion of the 'not-yet'. However, it seems that it needs to adopt a decidedly more realist stance. Cohen stops short of fundamentally engaging the will of homo phainomenon to realize her moral potential in the material world that surrounds her, though he draws very worldly conclusions. Rorty denies fundaments in theory, but engages sentiments like solidarity born from empathy as a sort of substitute in turn. We need to include the missing third in this (pseudo-) idealist view of dignity: matter.

VI. Materialist Progressivism

The Marxian concept of dignity is in fact very similar to Cohen's with respect to its consequences: the bourgeois class has dissolved human dignity

---

21   Both cited by H Holzhey, 'Hermann Cohen' in R Gröschner et al (eds), *Wörterbuch der Würde* (Munich, Wilhelm Fink Verlag, 2013) 47.

in exchange value.²² Therefore, a very 'manly' notion of honor, in contrast to servitude, needs to be upheld: dignity is like egalitarian honor, without strata and classes. And it can easily be freed from its gender bias, of course. Women need to be elevated (and elevate themselves) to this state of anti-slavery all the more, given their disadvantageous condition to begin with.

There is one striking difference between Marx and Cohen, though, and it points to the heart of the problem. For Marx, the body is the seat of dignity – we could speak, in a somewhat theological diction, of human 'Kreatürlichkeit' (being a creature). For Cohen, it is undeniably the 'pure' (anemic?) sphere of Kantian personhood. Marx likes to engage with 'reality', in an emphatic sense, in a straightforward way, like most proponents of dialectical arguments – this 'reality' partakes in every argument, without filling it completely – unless you are an orthodox materialist, in which case you suffer from the same Cartesian blindness as your idealist opponents.

In fact, reading Marx through a pragmatist lens can help insofar as it saves one from the many wrong discontinuities of the unproductive stand-off between idealism and materialism. The New Realism Movement can be understood as a pointed actualization of this argument. It declares that there is indeed matter, and other real stuff as well (in 'campi di senso'),²³ but that there is no hiatus between this reality, which must be apriorical to some extent, as Quentin Meillassoux demonstrates,²⁴ and 'the human soul'; therefore, it would be wrong to prioritize either of them.

VII. Dialectical Idealist-Materialist Progressivism: Republicanism

If there is something worth preserving and universalizing of the above mentioned 'manly' honor codes of the past, it is certainly the idea of the strong, upright creature that bows down to no authority except the egalitarian rules of the Republic (and to her God). This is close to the ancient Republican ideas of the independent, 'non-dominated' (P Pettit) citizen, and it is necessary to answer to the objections to this vision that played

---

22   MEW 4, 464 f; MEW 2, 123; cited by C Henning, 'Karl Marx' in R Gröschner et al (eds), *Wörterbuch der Würde* (Munich, Wilhelm Fink Verlag, 2013) 46 f.
23   M Gabriel, *Il senso dell'esistenza* (Rome, Carocci, 2012).
24   Q Meillassoux, *After Finitude* (London, Bloomsbury, 2012).

such a big role in the preparation of the French Revolution: the enlightened, 'truly democratic' spirit of 'unbridled', humanist interdependence that d'Holbach preaches so convincingly.[25] It is possible that the Hegelian position offers some kind of reconciliation between the now dominant form of progressivism, human universalism, and the persistent minority strand of thought, the 'deeper layer' of modernism, the not-so-nostalgic longing for 'ethical life'. Since abstract law and morality play their roles, but do not fill the constitutional order in full. Instead, institutions of the 'ethical life' exist, which are no longer of the ancient, heroic sort, but recognize human interdependence, without sufficiently reflecting on it, though. Hegel makes the mistake to transfer the heroic part to the war of nations in history, a result of his overly statist perspective. Marx delegates it to the working class, in the form of class combat, in turn. It would be more appropriate to assign this task of a struggle for relative independence to the order of rights, which needs to ensure the opportunity for everyone to gain that degree of independence which she sees fit for her. Of course, this requires a far greater fluidity in the property order of society, and an inferiority of property rights to speech and equality rights.

In particular, the value of human dignity is exactly the foremost constitutional embodiment of this sublation ('Aufhebung') of classic heroic Republicanism and humanist universalism. Dignity knows no rank, it can no longer be graded as happened in Cicero's classic exclusive Republican view of 'gradus dignitatis'. Dignity protests against all kinds of unjust discrimination – the substance of 'justice' is rather a question of equality, though, and not of dignity. It is sure that dignity precludes first-order discrimination, however.[26] This follows from its core universalist protest against gradation.

Still, dignity is not only a liberal-humanist concept in the vein of d'Holbach. In its insistence on dignity, *as opposed to liberty or equality*, it includes the minority Republican position of modern political philosophy as well – the sanctity of a core independence, whose materiality and whose spirituality are dignified at the same time. This reflects their indissoluble entanglement.

An interesting preliminary result of this analysis is thus: Human dignity is a consensus concept on the purely philosophical level, too. It is getting so much attention these days because with socio-economic dependence

---

25   JF Spitz, *L'amour de l'égalité* (Paris, Vrin, 2000) 78.
26   E Tugendhat, *Anthropologie statt Metaphysik* (Munich, Beck, 2010) 231.

and the partly compensatory individualist ideology on the rise, there is an undeniable need, ever more strongly felt, to refer to the 'other' strand of our constitutional tradition: the 'real', not the fake individualism that contemporary capitalism offers. It is essential to recognize that the constitutional version remains a very reduced republican individualism. If it does not remain unproductive, as in the correspondence view or a one-sided liberal or conservative ideologeme, in accordance with the coherence theory, it needs to be understood as a not-yet realized ideal, future-directed, in order to prevent its ossification as a constitutional symbol. This symbolic reductionism lures as the main problem in every consensus view, especially in times that are as nostalgic and oblivious of the future as ours (in Europe). We need to remind ourselves sometimes that there still are constitutional ideals to fulfill, whose concrete content has to be politically debated and will necessarily be provisional.[27] The directive effect of the constitutional norm is not marginal, however; the obligation to make progress on the realization of dignity, irreducible to existing conservative or liberal liberties, is a very demanding one. When the opportunity will arise for everyone to free herself from unwanted dependence can never be determined. On the contrary, it is conceptually impossible to ever fulfill this ideal completely. We deal with the central political tragedy here: Every consensus excludes and will be contested. 'Real democracy' and 'perfect perfectionism' are incompatible. Real perfectionism – progress – may be tragic, but at least it is achievable.

VIII. Conclusion: Evidence or Redundancy?

The idea that dignity is self-revelatory or evident, that it immediately springs to mind when you see someone in her face, in her actuality ('Menschenantlitz') is certainly ahistorical nonsense. Nor is it convincing that certain deeds violate human dignity in an evident way. On the contrary, the German past should have made the many proponents of this position in Germany think twice. What did not seem evident to too many people in 1933, could engender the same reaction these days – dignity-awareness greatly depends on economic and cultural shifts. In principle,

---

27 cf Carlo Schmid's democratic vision of dignity, elaborated upon by C Möllers, 'Democracy and Human Dignity – Limits of a Moralized Conception of Rights in German Constitutional Law' (2009) *Israel Law Review* 417.

we are not any safer from the erosion of civilization today than we were so many decades ago. On the other hand, even if the fact that rights can never be inferred from wrongs alone is true for the claim to dignity, too, there is still no reason to abdicate this concept in the realm of law altogether. In analogy to the evidence and the redundancy theories of truth, one can find corresponding views of human dignity, too – views that are 'out of time' or temporality. If this amounts to blunt ahistorical reasoning, one should be skeptical – as in the case of the evidence theories that claim to see the angel or the reflection of deity in every man. This is indeed a religious truth, but if you want to transfer it to the realm of politics or law, you should avoid the detour of badly reasoned philosophy of history or other expressions of political theology and take contingency as seriously as possible. It is clear that you can find good reasons for some kind of universalist transcendental equality of humankind, but this should not let you renounce more demanding arguments for the evidence of dignity. Dignity is more complex, it is the *legal synthesis of liberal universalism and republican esteem of particular independence*. Few constitutional concepts are less self-evident and more difficult to explain, and yet few lay to claim so much reverence, not the least for its opaque nature, and perhaps its apparent response to contemporary heartfelt needs.

Redundancy is not such an easy case. It has been shown that correspondence views can be reduced to existing rights, one might therefore see nothing more than a rhetorical reinforcement and an institutional fixation in the recourse to dignity – as can easily be proven for German constitutional adjudication, where dignity was usually referred to in order to strengthen the appeal of highly controversial, unpopular and innovative introductions of new constitutional rights: against imprisonment for life without parole, against the post-9/11 vision of shooting airplanes to save lives, against mass surveillance, against lawful abortion. In essence, these cases were about classic civil liberties and could have been reasoned on the basis of corresponding rights alone (right to self-determination, right to be free from surveillance in one's home, right to be free from unlawful imprisonment, right to life etc.). However, the Federal Constitutional Court sought to bolster its decisions with a recourse to 'eternal' human dignity, thereby having the exceptional 'real' last word on the issue. Besides the institutional aspect, there is certainly a symbolic dimension of these decisions, too. They want to stabilize a certain post-war humanist consensus.

The liberal coherence view, which seems to support the reasoning of the German court at first sight, is not really instructive if you take a closer look. Although there is a tendency to stress the autonomy-enhancing vision of dignity, this is not an undoubted common feature of the respective decisions. Autonomy certainly does not inform the abortion decisions, and it is at least debatable whether it plays any relevant role in the airplane or even the surveillance cases. Conservative coherence does not seem to be a fruitful concept, on the other hand. Integrity is not open or communicative enough a concept. Therefore, it is not stable enough not to immediately coincide with conservative correspondence concepts, because these are so easy to concretize and regularly collapse into particular rights.

Redundancy seems not to hit all kinds of liberal coherence theories, but on the other hand the latter are doubtful for other, normative reasons, as I have shown above. It is also questionable if a clear surplus of these concepts really exists, because they seem to underline the liberal grounds of existing rights only, which can indeed lead to interesting transformations of established interpretations. However, this seems to happen rarely, and almost never if courts or legislators do not refer to egalitarian premises. The impressive jurisprudence of the South African Court is based on a constant synthesis of equality and dignity arguments, and when the US Supreme Court refers to it, it usually attempts to protect particularly vulnerable groups, too ('evolving standards of decency'). In these cases, it is an opening to the future or a progressive consensus view that is clearly at work: an expansive vision of a dignity that is always at risk, not yet achieved and never fully fixed.

IX. A Coda with Bloch

It is perhaps not a coincidence that this theory prospers in Anglo-Saxon or Common Law countries more than in Germany or France. For it is the pragmatist theory of truth that underlies this conception. Developed by Charles S. Peirce in the 19th century, it still exerts considerable influence in the strand of jurisprudence that has been strongly inspired by legal realism. In the formative thought of Oliver Wendell Holmes, both theories merged. So whereas the Common Law tradition was rather conservative in many respects, it got a new orientation in part by means of the idealist and political epistemology of pragmatist jurisprudence. And there are not many good reasons to surrender for this progressive Anglo-Saxon tradition to the more conservative or (sometimes) liberal German dignity doctrine. In fact, there are better grounds for German doctrine to adopt more progressive-republican elements.

How republican, bridging the hiatus of materialist and idealist dignity, can this novel doctrine become? To approach a response, I want to refer to the ever heterodox Ernst Bloch here. The main innovation of his fascinating monograph *Natural Law and Human Dignity* lies in the exposition of the idea that there is a necessary link between the natural right to survive in dignity and the social utopian vision of a good life for all. 'There is just as little human dignity without the end of misery as there is happiness without the end of all old and new forms of subjugation.'[28] Human dignity cannot be conceived of without referring to both traditions: 'political' natural right and 'social' utopia. It can be shown that the ultimate goals of natural law and social utopia collapse into each other, just like freedom, the indispensable, yet ambiguous battle cry, 'symbol' and 'allegory' of real revolutions, and real equality, 'the stable substance' of these.[29] So whereas it is true that, as a matter of historical fact, political and social utopias blossomed at different times, and that the targets of suffering and degradation are not congruent, 'they intertwine in one another'.[30] 'Happiness and dignity (…) sadly never stuck together with the priority of human care and support, and the *primat* of human dignity.'[31]

The triad of human rights, with dignity as a synthesis of contingent individuality and necessary intersubjectivity in republican collectivity, forms a system whose three aspects of correspondence, coherence and consensus structure its different levels of abstraction: dignity as well as its unreasonably alleged correspondent rights. Since correspondence, coherence, and one-sided idealism or materialism fall prey to reductionism, *structural progressivism* demands a sublation of conservative and liberal visions of dignity in a democratic-republican perfection of equal liberty.

---

28 Bloch, *Natural Law* (1987) xxx.
29 Bloch, *Natural Law* (1987) 164 f.
30 Bloch, *Natural Law* (1987) 206.
31 Bloch, *Natural Law* (1987) 208.

Part III

Variations

The Question of Self-Repair: On Discrimination and Dignity

Alexander Somek

I. What is Wrong with Discrimination?

What is wrong with unequal treatment? Instances of haphazard arbitrariness aside, there is, indeed, nothing wrong with it, unless, of course, inequality amounts to discrimination.

Action is supposed to be rational, not least if it is taken by government. In order to behave rationally actors had better make out what they occupy their minds with. Understanding a subject of regulation properly requires, necessarily, that distinctions be drawn for reasons of classificatory accuracy. If government believes that there are reasons to ban firearms in order to minimize what bureaucrats wryly call 'preventable deaths' it would be false if a potential ban included toy revolvers unless there was evidence showing that a straight line of causation leads from playing with guns in the sandbox to high school shooting sprees. The rational pursuit of good reasons for action gives rise to good reasons for drawing one or the other distinction. These reasons for unequal treatment remain good so long as acting upon them does not give rise to discrimination.

But what is wrong with discrimination?

It is submitted, here, that discrimination is wrong because it denies people, without any fault of their own, the social presence that is mediated by enjoying social goods. Blacks are not allowed to sit with whites. Muslims are shunned and can't find jobs. These are paradigmatic instances of discrimination. Spaces on public busses or jobs are social goods. Availing of them is not everything; but enjoying them is indispensable for *being* someone and *counting* as someone for others.[1] Excluding someone from

---

1   See, for a very apt characterisation of what Rousseau called *amour-propre*, F Neuhouser, *Rousseau's Theodicy of Self-Love: Evil, Rationality, and the Drive for Recognition* (Oxford, Oxford University Press, 2008) 36, 73, 83. On the importance of 'counting' in a social context, see also A Honneth, *Unsicht-*

these goods, or limiting access to them, signals that the person is of so little worth that 'counting as someone' is not really an option for her. She is irrelevant. She is admitted to social space only in order to be treated as if she were not here.[2]

Admittedly, the exclusion from the enjoyment of goods seems bad enough to make discrimination wrong; yet, its connection to not giving presence to others becomes obvious when one takes most elementary *rationalizations* of unequal treatment into account. There ought to be freedom of religion. Yeah; but no such liberty must be enjoyed by Catholics. They are dangerous and should not be in the position to proselytize.[3] Public housing should be available to those who are unable to rent a dwelling at market rates. But, of course, Turks must not be included into this group. We do not want to have *them* in our midst.

The link between discrimination and disappearance is possibly ever more clearly revealed when one turns from the face of exclusionary acts to the efforts undertaken by victims in order to *pass* as members of the 'in-group'. What comes into focus, then, are strategies of 'covering' or 'ducking' and other forms of hiding one's self.[4] While the exclusion from the enjoyment of goods may thus be effectively averted, the disappearing of the person continues in subtler from. The discrimination against gays, for example, does not abate simply because gays choose to stay inside the closet. It shows, depressingly, that the victims enlist to the cause.

---

barkeit: Stationen zu einer Theorie der Intersubjektivität (Frankfurt am Main, Suhrkamp, 2003) 15.

2   Concededly, this characterization of discrimination must appear to be similar to Hellman's view of discrimination as 'demeaning' unequal treatment. See D Hellman, *When Is Discrimination Wrong?* (Cambridge, Mass, Harvard University Press, 2008) 31, 33, 35; at 57: 'Demeaning actions are those that put the other down. To demean is to express that the other is less worthy of concern and respect and to do so in a manner that has power.' In my view, this account is a bit too narrow, for it does not take the participation in social goods sufficiently into account. See my *Engineering Equality: An Essay on European Anti-Discrimination Law* (Oxford, Oxford University Press, 2011) 99 f. In addition, it lacks subtlety. Putting another person down is insulting. But it amounts to discrimination only if it is based on an inequality that eliminates someone from social space.

3   See J Locke, *A Letter Concerning Toleration* (James Tully ed, Indianapolis, Hackett, 1985).

4   For a pioneering study, in a legal context, see K Yoshino, 'The Assimilationist Bias in Equal Protection: The Visibility Presumption and the Case of "Don't Ask, Don't Tell"' (1989) 108 *Yale Law Journal* 485–571.

II. Exploring the Link to Dignity

In what follows this view of discrimination will have to be defended precisely because it invites serious objections. Linking discrimination to denying persons—in one way or another—social presence sweeps very broadly. We do not admit persons to our classes that are not enrolled students. Are they discriminated against? This would strike one as odd. Hence, a conception of discrimination that focuses on 'not counting' and 'absence' requires a much more careful elaboration. It needs to be explored, indeed, whether, and under which circumstances, behaviour that is coordinated on markets gives rise to discrimination. We will discuss, in this context, a salient example for being a remarkable person, namely, the case of the composer of *musique concrète instrumental*, Helmut Lachenmann. His works invite listeners 'to hear the conditions under which a sound- or noise-action is carried out'.[5] The resulting sonorities are such that the large majority of ordinary people would not even recognise them as music.

Lachenmann is the embodiment of what it means to be a law unto oneself. He has dignity. But why would it be wrong if he were expected to compose, say, country music if, due to an apparent lack of broad popularity, his complex scores did not earn him a living? He may well find writing country music unbecoming. Should we care? Would not talk of discrimination be out of place in cases where society legitimately expects adaptation? Why should not Lachenmann repair himself and compose for the Grand Ole Opry? Or would even merely to suggest this constitute an offence to his dignity?

The discussion of the core question of where discrimination comes to an end, and where it begins, is preceded by a relatively extended prelude that explores the links connecting discrimination, freedom and human dignity. It is supposed to explain, first, that the exercise of practical reason is tied to the construction and revision of practical identities. Hence, whether people find certain demands to be reasonable depends on who they take themselves to be. Second, linking discrimination to the construction of practical identities helps to understand why a lack of opportunities 'devalues' the self. This is owing to the fact that the value of options reflects what is of value to a 'valuable' self. Withholding for no good reasons options from a self signals that it is of lesser value than others. Final-

---

5 http://slought.org/resources/musique_concrete_instrumentale.

ly, the prelude prepares the ground for exploring the conditions under which pressure to repair one's self or to put up with lesser opportunities indeed constitutes discrimination.

III. Hegelian Persons

There is more than a merely trivial relation between equality and freedom.[6] Moreover, how discrimination *qua* violation of the former affects the latter is also relevant to how it offends human dignity.

In order to understand these conceptual links we need to bear in mind that one's dignity is at least not exhausted by being a person in a Hegelian sense.[7]

A person of this type has freedom of choice. Indeed, such a person has a certain conception of what it takes to be a self-determining being. According to this conception, self-determination is manifest in the act of rising, through choices, above the desired options from among which one chooses. Even though the will of a person is clearly affected by desires, the fact that a person chooses demonstrates that it must be she who resolves on which desire to act.[8] Figuratively speaking, a person in the Hegelian sense is an owner of freedom of choice. This property is circumscribed. Any person living among others needs to accept restrictions on the range of her choices. However, whichever restriction the person may actually be confronted with, it does not affect a person's self-determination; it does not, that is, so long as there remains an opportunity to rise above desires and to pick and choose from among desired options. A person in a Hegelian sense is perfectly at ease with adapting. Her self-determination would not be affected if the consumption of cigarettes, alcohol, fast food, meat and milk chocolate were prohibited for the ominous reasons of health and safety; her self-determination would remain intact so long as she were able to choose, for example, between low fat yoghurt and

---

[6] There is, to be sure, an entirely trivial relation, too. It concerns the fact, for example, that blacks that are not allowed to sit with whites are prevented from sitting with whites.

[7] See GWF Hegel, *Elements of the Philosophy of Right* (A Wood ed, Cambridge, Cambridge University Press, 1991) para 35 pp 67 f.

[8] For an illuminating commentary, see F Neuhouser, *Foundations of Hegel's Social Theory: Actualizing Freedom* (Cambridge, Mass, Harvard University Press, 2001) 24.

tofu. She would thereby remain self-determining and therefore 'free' in the sense envisaged by Hegel for 'persons'.

This explains why this form of freedom of choice is considered to be *formal*. It is indifferent to the substance of choices.

IV. Hegelian Persons in a Hayekian Setting

Intriguingly, persons in the Hegelian sense are the denizens of Hayek's free society.[9] One remains free in the Hayekian sense if one is not forced by another to make choices *and* if the options available for choice do not *themselves* involve acts of coercion. In a culture where having a choice is all there is to freedom, this freedom would only come to an end, for example, when criminal suspects, before an interrogation begins, were given a choice between electroshocks and water-boarding. Within Hayek's universe, however, a choice between either knitting rugs in a stuffy basement for 70 hours a week or suffering malnutrition is qualitatively the *same* as the choice between buying a Porsche Panamera and a Mercedes CLS 500. In Hayek's world, which is inhabited by persons in a Hegelian sense, options are never evaluated.[10] What matters is the spiritual moment in which the will rises above *some* needs or desires.

A conception of self-determination that views choice as the essential factor leaves the choosing agent in the dark. Freedom is supposed to be manifest, and exhausted, in the moment of 'rising above' desires, no matter *how* such a rising might actually take place. A person counts as self-determining even if the choice between and among desires is occasioned by the relatively greater intensity of one particular urge. The transition from perceiving such intensity to an actual choosing does not have to reveal a 'self' standing over and above her choices. This means that the person in the Hegelian sense does not have to be concerned about who she is aside from being a chooser. She may act wantonly.[11]

---

9   See FA von Hayek, *The Road to Serfdom* (London, Routledge, 1991; first edition 1944) 76.

10   See, generally, C Taylor, 'What's Wrong with Negative Liberty' in his *Philosophy and the Human Sciences* (Cambridge, Cambridge University Press, 1985).

11   For the person in the Hegelian sense the existence of a choice is sufficient to demonstrate that a rise above desires has taken place, regardless of whether it merely reflects the temporal ascendancy of one desire over another.

V. Mere Irrationality

The perspective of persons in a Hegelian sense is consistent with a concept of discrimination that views it as inherently *irrational*. Imagine that nationals stand a better chance of finding employment then non-nationals because of widespread prejudice against foreigners. Not employing foreigners is irrational if foreigners actually show comparatively more energy and application than citizens. Society is just in denial. The economic harm of discrimination consists primarily, even though not exclusively, of the harm discriminators inflict upon themselves.[12] If, using a stereotypical example for a stereotype, African Americans are not employed owing to false beliefs about their alleged 'in your face' attitude[13] the net welfare of society is diminished. But none of this affects the self-determination of a person in the Hegelian sense.[14] There is no interference, that is, with freedom.

The question is, of course, whether a freedom that is never affected by *limited* options is of value for the self-determining subject. Put differently, the question is whether we would *choose*, if we could, to be beings for which self-determination amounts to *formal* freedom of choice.

We would, arguably, choose freedom of choice only if we perceived sufficient *value* in its exercise. But the value of freedom of choice depends vitally on the *range* or *value* of options—there is no value for a teetotaller to have a choice between a Margaux and a Pinot Noir from Russian River Valley (poor fellow). Hence, we can endorse being a person in the Hegelian sense only by moving beyond it. Freedom cannot *simply* be about freedom of choice.

---

12 See R Epstein, *Forbidden Grounds: The Case Against Employment Discrimination Laws* (Cambridge, Mass, Harvard University Press, 1992).

13 I owe this example to B Barry, *Freedom and Culture: An Egalitarian Critique of Multiculturalism* (Cambridge, Harvard University Press, 2001) 99.

14 The reduction of discrimination to irrationality quickly comes to an end if, for example, two groups of persons are equally capable of performing a job and members of one group are not hired owing to widespread prejudice. There is no total loss of social welfare as long as there is enough labour supply from members of the other group. Under these conditions it is not irrational to stick to prejudice (unless the members of the disfavoured group were willing to work for less and paying them lower wages would not diminish overall social welfare).

VI. Valuable Options for the Valued Self

Once the *range* of options is taken into account it is possible to see how *freedom* is affected by discrimination, for the latter results in *less opportunities* for the victims of inequality and, a fortiori, less freedom for them than for others. As the late Jerry Cohen memorably pointed out, a lack of opportunities—in particular if caused by a shortage of money—implies a lack of freedom.[15]

With that we arrive at a *different* view of the self-determining self. It presents itself basically as consumer with plenty of stuff to choose from. The greater the range of options, the greater the value of freedom. A glimmer of God's almightiness shines into the choosing self.

But even such a conception of self-determination needs to reach out beyond itself in order to explain the appeal of choices. Even though the self can now choose everything, the choice still remains formal. A wider range of choices does not really make a difference. A choice from among 1000 options is just as indifferent to these options as a choice between merely two. Rather, the chooser has to be able to make out qualitative distinctions. In other words, options have to be evaluated.[16]

The value of the choice, however, cannot *simply* reside in the options either. Otherwise the relevance and value of *choice* would remain inexplicable. It is important that the *chooser* actually identify what is of value. Indeed, this is what a choice is all about. It is a relative evaluative identification and endorsement of options. Since any such identification must be determined by the self it requires relating what is to be chosen to the self for whom something is of value.

We conclude that the value of options would remain unintelligible if it were not for a conception of a valuable *practical identity* that accounts for their value.[17] For a vegetarian, for example, the availability of meat is of

---

15 See GE Cohen, *Freedom, Self-Ownership and Equality* (Cambridge, Cambridge University Press 1995) 58 f.
16 It is not the case that the value of one chosen option stems from the high quantity of options that were not chosen. The model of the self as a potent chooser does not reckon with opportunity cost.
17 On the concept of 'practical identity', see, of course, CM Korsgaard, *The Sources of Normativity* (Cambridge, Cambridge University Press, 1996) 101 where a practical identity is characterised as 'description under which you value yourself, a description under which you find your life to be worth living and your actions to be worth undertaking'.

no value. But this relativity of value demonstrates that the value of options depends on the value of the practical identity that one ventures to enact.[18] If the self—being a vegetarian, for example—were of no value, avoiding meat *qua* path towards self-perfection would be of no value either. The self would not reflexively endorse its own value through not choosing meat.

VII. The Play of Choices

It pays, however, to proceed with circumspection at this point. If one were to say that the value of choice is entirely derivative of the value of options one would clearly create merely a mirror image of a person in the Hegelian sense. It would be equally one-sided. While the person in the Hegelian sense actually has no options to identify because of the absence of the evaluative dimension, its mirror image would really have no choice, but merely have to apply its conception of itself in different situations. The choice would truly be an act of execution or at best amount to an exercise of discretion in cases of doubt.

This misses, however, the value of choice that resides in the fact that it is *oneself*, and not just anybody, who identifies valuable options in an act of endorsement. There is something of value in the *choice* between and among options that is *not* inherited from their evaluation in light of some practical identity. There 'is' something that precedes this identity, and this something, which is indeed neither something nor nothing,[19] leaves its trace in the process of self-constitution.[20] In fact, it is by virtue of a play[21]

---

18   This is, of course, a reference to JD Velleman, *How We Get Along* (Cambridge, Cambridge University Press, 2009), even though it should be noted that Velleman explores self-conceptions as 'descriptions' 'under which your actions and reactions make sense to you in causal-explanatory terms' (ibid 16 fn 8).

19   See G Gamm, *Nicht nichts. Studien zu einer Semantik des Unbestimmten* (Frankfurt am Main, Suhrkamp, 2000).

20   See CM Korsgaard, *Self-Constitution: Agency, Identity, and Integrity* (Oxford, Oxford University Press, 2009) 42. While Korsgaard is quite adamant about the fact that practical identities are not simply adopted and then executed, she does not really elucidate the blind spot that is 'you' when you construct your practical identity. See CM Korsgaard, 'Self-Constitution and Irony' in J Lear, *A Case for Irony* (Cambridge, Mass, Harvard University Press, 2011) 79: 'Your identity is never just a given, but something you are always at work at

between choices and provisional conceptions of who we would like to be that we are self-constituting in actuality. This explains why the *range* of options is not entirely irrelevant to our freedom. It invites recalibration in the face of discrete 'good choices'. Options seduce us. Sometimes we yield to temptations and end up asking ourselves 'Was this really right for me?' Yet we are only over and above our practical identities if we are free to create puzzles for us and to be ahead of ourselves in our choices.

VIII. Free to Be Who You Are

The dependence of valuable options on a positively evaluated practical identity and the dependence of freedom of choice on a *range* of options[22] demonstrate that one can be free only if one is able to attribute value to who one is and is not *required* to overcome it. If freedom of choice were of value only if one had to 'reinvent' oneself before choosing, one would not choose to have choices. This is intuitively plausible.[23] Assume that you happen to be a professor of metaphysics and are confronted with the choice of teaching either 'international trade law' or 'evidence'; such a choice would be valuable to you only if you transformed yourself into a law professor with a penchant for technical subjects. Under this condition, each subject matter would provide you with different opportunities to prove yourself. However, there is no reason for you to become a law professor in the first place because teaching either of these two subjects is of

---

constructing and—within the limits of the demand for your integrity—how you construct it is really up to you.'

21 See HG Gadamer, *Wahrheit und Methode: Grundzüge einer philosophischen Hermeneutik*, 4th edn (Tübingen, Mohr, 1975) 98 f.

22 The range of options is valuable for two reasons. First, it is easier for you to find a place for yourself within the world. Second, a great variety of options offers more clues as to what you may want to do with your life.

23 Here is a transcendental argument (with an eye to Lenin and Lukács): One might want to claim that a person after she had reinvented herself would suddenly perceive the value of options that she had not perceived before. Hence, it may be worth the while to engage in the gamble. Yet, another conception of oneself is presupposed here, namely, that the self has value inasmuch as it creates for itself, possibly through experiment, versions of itself in order to enhance its sphere of experience. Choosing to reinvent oneself in order to perceive valuable choices is valuable for a conception of the self that must not itself be reinvented or abandoned in this process. Hence, one must be allowed to stay the same.

no value to you. If the choice is of no value there is no point in having it. You can enjoy freedom of choice only if you do not *have* to change yourself in order to enjoy it.[24] You may, indeed, venture into new and unchartered territory and open new paths of self-discovery, but this presupposes that you *are* the person with the courage to confront your own fragility. This does not alter the fact that only if you are *someone*, even if someone whom you have not yet recognised, you are in the position to identify valuable options.[25] 'Someonenness' has to be guaranteed to you before you become a chooser.[26] Otherwise, freedom of choice would be reduced to the formal spiritual exercise of rising, without any further reason, above desires.

At its most elementary level, then, to be free means to be free to stay who one is or to pursue who one would like to be.[27] This is where dignity enters the picture. Nobody has dignity to whom it is socially signalled that she is a worthless person because she had better be someone else.

IX. Answering the Obvious Objection

Obviously, the above analysis must raise an objection. Why do we believe that child-molesters have dignity even though they are persons whom we expect to become different from who they have been so far? The explanation is that we ascribe dignity to them because they take it upon themselves to correct an identity that they seem to be *beset* with as if it were an *affliction*. We believe them to have the ability to realise, upon reflection, that there is something deeply troubling and wrong with their self. This presupposes, however, that underneath that practical identity they find themselves thrown into lies a true self that accounts for their worth. This

---

24 Otherwise, you would remain in a state of infancy. But in a state of infancy you do not choose.
25 For a similar argument, see Korsgaard, *Normativity* 121.
26 See ibid 120 f: 'For unless you are committed to some conception of your practical identity, you will lose your grip on yourself as having any reason to one thing rather than another—and with it, your grip on yourself as having any reason to live and to act at all.'
27 The pursuit of the ambition, however, already chances you. You have made yourself into the means to be who you would like to be. For a similar observation, see Korsgaard, *Self-Constitution* 41.

indelibly valuable part of their self is the moral subjectivity that makes them amenable to practical reason.[28]

Being a member of the kingdom of ends is *human dignity's last resort*. As we shall see, however, it represents an impoverished version of dignity. First, it opens the gate to universal agility and adaptability. Second, it does not really pay attention to the *play* between choices and constructs of our practical identity. If anything it is the play between accounting and bewilderment that reveals why we are ultimately of value. Acts of self-constitution may expose us to be erratic; our moral identity forces us to be flexible, for, in all fairness, we have to 'fit in' and 'do our bit'.

With that we can return to discrimination.

X. Trading Off Freedom and Equality

Inequality means less or no access to goods for some. Lack of access means that potentially valuable options remain out of reach. Since selves assert reflexively in their choices their own value, inequality signals that some have no or lesser value than others. They are not 'good enough' to partake of some goods or opportunities.

This explains what makes signs such as 'No Irish need apply' or 'Whites only' offensive. Strategies of segregation affect freedom because they instil in people a sense that they are mistaken about their worth. They suggest that somehow they have to be fixed or, if that is not possible, that they had better remove themselves from the places where the 'better sort' interacts. Not surprisingly, people wearing the badge of second-class status gladly stay among their peers, for this allows them to zoom out their irreparability. They do not show up at the places that matter. They are ashamed of themselves. A free person, by contrast, is free to be incorrigible (incidentally, a sweet fruit of aging) and flamboyant.

Living with the impression that one is somehow defective is constraining. Invariably, people—at least as long as they have not given up on themselves—engage in efforts of self-repair; if this option is unavailable, their life is restricted to what is accessible to second-class people. Conceivably, life is then lived with an attitude of detachment. Perhaps people experience a lingering sense of loss; that they have missed their 'real' life; that they have never made an appearance in their own biography. Not by

---

28   See Korsgaard *Normativity* 121.

accident, some victims of discrimination seem to compensate this loss by developing a sardonic sense of irony.

Hence, discrimination creates unequal freedom not only in a quantitative sense (a narrower range of choices). The freedom is also *qualitatively* unequal. Freedom is invested into repair-efforts or in the detached pursuit of limited opportunities.[29] Having to pass as someone who one is not, nor wants to be, forces people into a *trade-off* between freedom and equality. They either recalcitrantly enact who they are told they have to be or pay the price for who they are. In the former case, they 'reinvent' themselves. They trade presence—at the table of privilege—for internal absence, or, rather, the absence of their own self in the social sphere. This introduces a decidedly undignified element into behaviour. Sycophancy (*Kriecherei*), bootlicking (*Schleimerei*) and servile alacrity (*Eilfertigkeit*) are part of one genre of self-enactment. *Ostensible* self-repair efforts infuse inequality with indignity.

XI. More Objections

Provisionally, we may conclude that discrimination is wrong because it does not give people room to be freely who they are.[30]

This conclusion, however, appears to be guilty of at least two mistakes.

First, it seems to presuppose an 'essentialistic' view of the self. Supposedly, the self is that which it is without activity—choosing—by the self. The self is posited as a given—a non-self. This is inconsistent.

Second, the observations seem to have already branched out into a terrain that is far too general to be relevant to the topic of discrimination. From the perspective adopted above, anyone who feels disrespected in a social context could claim to have been discriminated against. Such a result is, to say the least, overblown, if not outright absurd.

The reply to the first objection will follow further below. The reply to the second requires, indeed, raising the problem of self-repair to the level at which it *has* to be addressed, namely, social co-operation in general.[31]

---

29 In the latter case, as Marx famously noted, all doing becomes enduring. See K Marx, *Ökonomisch-philosophische Manuskripte* (ed M Quante, Frankfurt am Main, Suhrkamp, 2009) 94. R Jaeggi, *Entfremdung: Zur Aktualität eines sozialphilosophischen Phänomens* (Frankfurt am Main, Campus, 2005) 30.

30 Evidently, this covers also cases in which a practical identity is not self-chosen but socially ascribed.

As is well known, discrimination is either behavioural or systemic. In the first case, there is a perpetrator (eg, a racist shopkeeper); in the second case, disadvantage results from a variety of acts that have not been designed to exclude or to demean (eg, the job-market simply has an unequal impact on women).

Social co-ordination on markets *generally* creates *and* adversely affects opportunities. Being a composer of avant-garde contemporary music, such as Helmut Lachenmann, is not easy in a world that listens to Justin Bieber. If Helmut Lachenmann had to hide his lachenmanliness in order to write and sell *Deutsche Schlager* or Country Music, this would undoubtedly affect his dignity *qua* law that he, Helmut Lachenmann, is to himself.

With this hypothetical example in mind we realise why it makes sense to allow the concept of discrimination to sweep broadly, at least *par provision,* and to include systemic discrimination without paying attention to any particular 'forbidden ground'. In Lachenmann's case, it concerns systemic discrimination against contemporary music. It is inherent in allowing the shallow tastes of consumers to determine the viability of artistic pursuits.

XII. Agility and Adaptability

Nevertheless, arguing that Lachenmann falls victim to indirect discrimination is an uphill battle.

A competitive society expects everyone to be flexible and to save for another day many matters that people consider essential to their life. Arguably, various forms of hiding one's self and a great deal of actual self-denial are even essential to individual success. Perplexingly, however, in many cases these attitudes can even provide a path towards self-discovery. We may have no clue who we are and what we are good for. All that is left to us is experimentation with the world in order to determine our place within it. Nothing appears to be better suited for engaging in experiments of this type than a competitive market economy. It creates various and numerous opportunities.

Admittedly, a competitive world is not for the depressed and the inflexible. In such a world, individual *agility* and *adaptability* are virtues that

---

31   Discrimination, as a topic, is fascinating only if one allows the concept to sweep broadly.

individuals are generally expected to develop. Whoever struggles with espousing these in his or her conduct is sooner or later eligible for some form of 'empowering' coaching.

It turns out that we have to re-examine the premise that *seems* to have underlain our discussion so far, namely that who we are is like a substance amenable to appropriation. However, once we revise this premise it becomes very difficult to make sense of the concept of discrimination developed here, notably in its systemic form.[32] Why could temporary self-denial or overcoming stubborn idiosyncrasies (or weakness of the will when it comes to the writing of Country Music) ever pose a normative problem if we are essentially either unfinished or indeterminate and if agility and adaptability are both cardinal virtues of social cooperation *and* keys to unlocking the secret of a meaningful life? Why should the individual responsibility to adjust to market demand not be the universally shared prime directive that we have to recognise from the perspective of our moral identity?

XIII. Immutable Characteristics

Legal reasoning seems to provide us with a clue, even though, as we shall see, it is one of these clues that can easily lead us astray. It directs our attention to so-called 'immutable characteristics'. The complexion cannot be changed, nor can be the country of birth. One is stuck with it. Some of these characteristics, such as complexion, are stereotypical markers of lesser social fitness. Owing to widespread social prejudice they constitute insurmountable obstacles to adaptation for whoever happens to bear them. It makes good sense, therefore, to declare them forbidden grounds of discrimination, at any rate, so long as the relevant characteristic is socially visible, widely used and unrelated to individual performance.

Hence, even though our practical identity may well be one of these postmodernist entities celebrated in modern literature departments—fluid, pliable or even 'hybrid'—we must be immune from suffering disadvantage if we count as someone whom we may have never chosen to be. Thus stated, however, protection from discrimination changes its point. No longer protects it against being shamed, shunned or worse off on the

---

32   We could still try to defend it in the context of direct discrimination with regard to some animus on the part of the perpetrator.

ground of who we are; rather, it turns out to be a type of social insurance against counting as someone if one does not have the power to alter that fact. If there is widespread dislike of Poles in a society, judicial protection from discrimination is designed to remove the obstacle associated with counting as Polish. Some Poles may have abdicated all loyalty to their country. This does not matter. For purposes of protection from discrimination they are still Poles because they count as such.

XIV. Individuality as an Obstacle

One cannot but suspect, however, that the focus on immutable characteristics implicitly harbours a troubling view of the individual self. It is at least perfectly *compatible* with casting the self primarily in object form, namely as a human resource coupled with a set of preferences (which are basically social facts). What is subjective about the self—thinking, willing, judging—is reduced to the exercise of economic rationality. Ideally, the self is a preference driven human resource in the hands of an impersonal planner. Such an impersonal planner is capable of making smart choices for any given set of preferences in light of individual endowments (© Ronald Dworkin). Individual rational selves would be best off it they were mere replicas—indeed, replicants—of the impersonal planner. Whatever imperfection might leave its mark on the planning process it would reveal the influence of mere personal factors (bad breeding, lack of training, interference of emotions, myopia, risk-aversion, confidence-bias, etc.).

Such a view of the self is consistent with a certain view of obstacles to achievement. *External* obstacles result from a lack of resources or unequal opportunities caused by the social relevance of immutable characteristics. *Internal* obstacles stem from being imperfect at personal planning. The *individual* self is thus cast as a root of deficiency. Like a disability it poses the risk of underperformance. Moreover, in a competitive environment imperfect selves need to overcome their internal obstacles themselves. Every single action must therefore always also be an attempt at self-improvement. All doing is supposed to be taking one more step of 'growth'. The goal of growth is the infinitesimal approximation to the mind of the impersonal planner.

Interestingly, seen in this way, a competitive market economy overcomes discrimination by *discriminating against everyone equally*. It casts everyone in a state in which we have to be permanently self-repairing. Actual protection from discrimination is supposed to remove *some* of the obstacles to integration into society that individuals are simply unable to climb themselves. The rest is perennial self-improvement.

Obviously, this is not quite consistent with our prior finding that dignity demands that we be recognised for who we happen to be.

XV. Finding Your Niche

Nevertheless, this view is compatible with how self-repairing selves are supposed to choose their practical identity from a moral point of view.

Identity-choosing subjects understand two things. They realise that if they did not endorse some particular *practical* identity they would never be able to enact a real self and fail to be a self-determining person.[33] They would end up 'drifting through life'[34] and not be determined by their self in their choices. They would not be capable of exercising their practical reason. But they also understand that the market is a medium in which people establish mutuality with regard to what they make of themselves so that each is able to benefit from the life projects of all others. With this in mind, Terry Pinkard mocked Hayek by alluding to Rousseau—that, from this perspective, the market actually forces persons to be *truly* free.[35] Interdependence of supply and demand is a mechanism that constrains people to be free in exactly the manner that is compatible with the equal freedom of all.[36]

Consequently, 'fitting in' by virtue of agility and adaptation is not only a matter of prudence. It appears to be a moral imperative. Morality seems to demand that one's practical identity be shaped and made relevant by the market. Whichever we choose to adopt under conditions of constrained opportunities is morally acceptable so long as one does not, for example, decide to harm people by becoming an assassin.[37]

Opportunities generated by markets count. Morality directs us to identify with whatever might suit us and, more importantly, feed us. The oppor-

---

[33] See Korsgaard *Normativity* 123.
[34] See J Raz, *The Morality of Freedom* (Oxford, Clarendon Press, 1986) 371.
[35] See T Pinkard, *Hegel's Phenomenology: The Sociality of Reason* (Cambridge, Cambridge University Press, 2004) 311.
[36] See L Herzog, *Inventing the Market: Smith, Hegel, and Political Theory* (Oxford, Oxford University Press, 2013) 73.
[37] The example is Korsgaard's. See *Normativity* 126.

tunities arise from collective private self-determination[38], for private individuals can count the circumstances of action that are created by others only as expressions of their own will if they identify with the requisite spontaneous form of cooperation. Admittedly, according to laissez-fair liberals there is a far simpler reason to regard ourselves as free. In their view, we remain free as long as we are not forced to follow the dictates of a particular person. One is, more precisely, not in a situation of dependence if one follows dictates of necessity that result from the unintended consequence of multiple private acts. As is well known, thinkers from Rousseau to Marx viewed this matter very differently.[39]

It must seem, therefore, as though we would have to give Helmut Lachenmann, were he in need, the advice to scrap his intriguing pieces of avant-garde music and to write songs for the Dixie Chicks. In other words, morality—his obligation to live up to what is humanity in him—would dictate that Helmut Lachenmann reinvent himself.

The Grand Ole Opry it is.

XVI. Tragedy

But what if you—or Helmut Lachenmann, for that matter—realised that engaging your agility and adaptability did in no manner help you to arrive at a practical identity that is congruent with being who you divine to be? The question of self-repair then turns into a matter similar to Kierkegaard's 'despair'. On moral grounds you cannot be willing to be enacting what you find yourself thrown into, for this would possibly make you into a useless person. At the same time, since no socially suitable personal identity suits you, you must be unwilling to be a self at all.[40] No morally approved practical identity would ever be compatible with who you sense you are.

---

38   See my 'Europe: From Emancipation to Empowerment' (2013) 60 *LSE 'Europe in Question' Discussion Paper*, www.lse.ac.uk/europeanInstitute/LEQS/LEQSPaper60.pdf.
39   See Neuhouser, *Actualizing Freedom* 71.
40   See S Kierkegaard, *The Sickness Unto Death. Kierkegaard's Writings vol 19* (HW Hong, ed, Princeton, Princeton University Press, 2009); M Kosch, *Freedom and Reason in Kant, Schelling, and Kierkegaard* (Oxford, Clarendon Press, 2006) 154.

The question must arise, therefore, whether you have failed to embrace your moral identity or, conversely, whether your moral identity actually has failed to embrace you.

That the latter is actually the case, is implicitly claimed by Christoph Menke who sees the ancient tragic conflict between family ties and political loyalty recur in modern moral life as a collision between the demands of egalitarian morality, on the one hand, and what may strike you as your individual good, on the other. Egalitarian morality claims to be prior to whatever you deem to be good for you. It does not recognise as inalienable any conception you may happen to entertain of your self.[41] Morality only respects your ability to *choose* between and among practical identities. Your moral identity indeed fails to embrace you—it does not identify with you—inasmuch as you experience who you are as inalienable, not susceptible to choice, or as an outgrowth of your 'inner nature'.[42] In a word, the inalienable individual self is alien to the moral self.[43] Menke concludes, therefore, that modern moral life gives rise to an antinomy (*Entzweiung*) in the relation of moral autonomy in individual self-realisation (*Selbstverwirklichung*).[44] In fact, he could have said that morality collapses because self-determination no longer seems possible. The self appears to be split into a socially compatible 'Me' and a relatively unruly 'I'.[45]

XVII. Moral Estrangement and Stoicism

It might be helpful to summarize the result of our first reading of immutability. The theme became relevant when we began wondering how discrimination could ever be possible in the face of universally demanded

---

41 See C Menke, 'Liberalismus im Konflikt: Zwischen Gerechtigkeit und Freiheit' in M Brumlik and H Brunkhorst (eds), *Gemeinschaft und Gerechtigkeit* (Frankfurt am Main, Fischer, 1993) 237; see also Menke's magisterial study *Tragödie im Sittlichen: Gerechtigkeit und Freiheit nach Hegel* (Frankfurt am Main, Suhrkamp, 1996) 259, 296 f.
42 See J Rebentisch, *Die Kunst der Freiheit: Zur Dialektik demokratischer Existenz* (Berlin, Suhrkamp, 2012) 129.
43 More precisely, your moral identity can only recognise itself as an inalienable self.
44 See Menke, *Tragödie* 241.
45 Readers of American pragmatist philosophy may recognise the reference to Mead.

agility and adaptability. All have to adapt. But this cannot mean that black persons must become white in order to avoid disadvantage. Against such an absurd consequence protects the relevance of immutable characteristics. The exemption of characteristics of this kind, however, reinforces a view of the self as a rational, self-activating and perfectly adaptable agent. The self is completely subordinate to what counts as being a useful member of society with a legitimate interest in its 'success'. What is individual about it is potentially an obstacle to being successful in one's niche.

This amounts to at least an unflattering view of the self.

First, if what makes us distinct from a perfect impersonal planner is our 'bounded' rationality than we are all more or less unfit, and the social persona that we create of ourselves is at best an attempt to cover this up. Worse, still, if what it takes to approximate the powers of the impersonal planner is opaque and eventually manifest only in 'success', than those who have demonstrated their ability to be more successful than others have also established their relatively higher worth. The competitive market society leads thus directly to a society that recognises unequal worth and unequal rank. American oligarchs are increasingly outspoken about how greater wealth bespeaks higher personal worth.

Second, if we, from a moral point of view, do not recognise inalienability we introduce a deep indifference[46] towards the world of action. It results in a two-fold alienation. First, you are alienated from your moral identity, which turns out to be the cousin of the impersonal planner. In no way does it *particularly* represent you. Second, you are also alienated from the practical role that you 'responsibly' put up with. The result is Stoicism. The disengagement from our roles translates into disengagement from the world. It may seem as though you remained 'internally free' vis-à-vis both moral and practical identity, but this freedom can never be realised in practice.[47]

---

46   See R Jaeggi, *Entfremdung: Zur Aktualität eines sozialphilosophischen Problems* (Frankfurt am Main, Campus, 2005) 174.
47   All that, however, if it is conceded that there is a way of accounting of 'inner nature' that does not lead to either essentialism or reification. See Rebentisch, *Kunst der Freiheit* 126.

XVIII. Immutability, Take Two

Fortunately, there is a more appealing way of eliciting the meaning of 'immutability'. It assumes that people are *entitled* to have certain matters *treated* as though they were unchangeable because they, but not others, experience them in this way. This means, evidently, paying respect to the perspective of the first-person. In Rawlsian parlance, it means to regard individuals as 'self-authenticating sources of valid claims'.[48] Immutability, thus understood, creates immunity from agility and adaptability. In contrast to the impersonal planner model, it does not indirectly reinforce these principles.

Religious freedom is a case in point. Religious belief, unless it is shallow, indicates that one has succeeded at becoming a receptacle of insight, revelation or even—lucky you—grace. From within a religious perspective, 'choosing' a religion means demonstrating one's ability to commit oneself to what one recognises to be the *right* faith. A choice of this kind is very different from the type of choice under conditions of substitutability. If the pastry shop is out of one's desired doughnuts and chooses a cupcake instead this does not pose a problem since both are exemplars of 'something sweet'. No such substitution would be reasonable in the case of religion ('Sorry, we are out of Judaism, but we give you a choice between Catholic and Protestant Christianity'). Nobody chooses a religion just in order to have some. In a case like this, self-determining beings are fully invested in what they believe. Owing of their intentionality, they *make* themselves into the *passive* carriers of what they have to rest their faith on. They are free by giving themselves to what they are not and, thereby, realise who they are.[49]

Many of our freedoms expose us publicly as choosing subjects. They suggest that we could, at any time, choose differently. In fact, some of our most important freedoms,—such as the right to marry, the right to profess one's faith or the right to express one's opinion—preserve our ability to hand us over to our emotions and reasons. We enjoy freedom of choice in order to have our self-chosen chains respected and not scrutinised before some social tribunal.

---

48   See J Rawls, *Political Liberalism* (New York, Columbia University Press, 1991) 32.
49   See Jaeggi, *Entfremdung* 243.

That what is at stake in *our* reason-responsiveness leads back to the value of choice. Above, it was pointed out that we constitute ourselves from within the play between choices and shaped practical identities. The builder that pulls ourselves together is someone who is not someone but also not nobody. It is essential that we recognise ourselves in this someone, for otherwise we would not be who we are. This impersonal and yet personal someone is the voice of 'good reasons'. We have to regard it as our own voice. If we, therefore, did not earn social respect for what we regard as indispensable or compelling we would never be able to appear in our actions.

XIX. Protodiscrimination

Where does this leave us with regard to Helmut Lachenmann?

The answer to this question is like any answer to a legal question: it depends.

We have seen above that discrimination develops its full force—comes, in a sense, to full fruition—as soon as its victims participate, either by engaging in self-repair or by hiding away in socially segregated places. Indeed, discrimination exists pervasively in a *prototypical format* in which it is not yet really constituted owing to the pervasive acquiescence on the part of its victims. Proto-discrimination easily passes as rational conduct so long as nobody rebels.

This changes as soon as the victims begin to assert their own worth. No privileged insight into a determinate substantive self is needed for that, just the experience that, as things stand, one is not part of one's life since one is either forced into hiding or shamed for who one is. Going through Hayek's 'tough school of the market' may make people to realise that the hard labour of interdependence denies them an outlet in this world. As soon as they are confident that who they struggle to be is of value they have constituted a case of discrimination. In more than one subtle sense, the victims of discrimination are also *doers*. In a first step, they bring about proto-discrimination through their acquiescence and, in a second step, constitute discrimination by reclaiming their equal worth.

The rest is straightforward. The rebellion against disadvantage can be successful if a life form is amenable to its claims. The validation of 'self-authenticating sources' of claims is a social practice. More is needed, to be sure, than the trite appeals to respect persons or not to deny them their 'self-esteem', which are notoriously filling the pages of contemporary analytic philosophy. Respecting persons is not enough because it is abstract. What matters is the esteem for various aspects of a form of life.

Lachenmann's lachenmanliness would be diminished had he to make money as a doorstep salesman flogging off magazine subscriptions and if he wrote music only during evening hours in order to see it never performed. Nevertheless, engaging in his compositorial pursuits appears to be compatible with expecting him to earn a living as, say, a scholar, a teacher or a conductor. It leaves room for his pursuits and is not too far removed from his calling. This type of flexibility is compatible with what he has 'chosen' to be. Its realisation, however, not only presupposes support and subsidization by others, but also a cultural format that they find accessible. The existence of lachenmanliness has to be part of what they value about their world even if they do not understand it.

In more sombre words this means that freedom in dignity presupposes tradition. This rather Hegelian conclusion suggests that being a law unto oneself is invariably both social and tragic. It is social because rising above the interdependence of markets presupposes a common commitment to a variety of human achievements. What sustains us, as scholars, is a culture that esteems what we are doing. If it were not for the solidarity of others we would already be extinct.

Cultures are, however, particulars. Not everyone can find his place in them. As Rawls wisely realised, there can be no social world without a loss.

XX. Conclusion

Prohibited grounds of discrimination are attempts to reconcile our most personal experiences of inalienability with our moral identity. That is, they signify universalisation. Everyone has to have his or her sexual orientation, religious beliefs or political opinions respected because they make the person into what she is. Such universalisations result from historical struggles. Not by accident, the law has a history. It emerges from the lives of real people.

The validity on the proposed reconstruction of discrimination does not presuppose that people discover their pre-given essence before they can go about claiming respect. Self-constitution in the medium of the play between choices and tinkering with identities may give rise to what Lear has rather enigmatically described as moments of 'ironic disruption'.[50] These are moments at which we wonder if what we believe to have enacted is indeed what we take it to be (eg, 'What does anything of what I have done in my life have to do with being a man?').[51] But self-constitution continues also when we realise that our belief in who we are has concealed from us someone whom we would really like to be. No fixed entity is needed to be self-constituting in these moments.

It may be objected that the proposed understanding of discrimination may well fit the cases when people proudly assert their identity. This is a theory of discrimination for life-affirming gays and lesbians, for fervent religious believers or for culturally recalcitrant foreigners. But what about victims of race discrimination that could not care less to which race they belong? Does not the rejected meaning of immutable characteristics capture more adequately the indignity involved in counting as someone, and suffering disadvantage, even though one has never chosen to be that person?

It is indeed the case that the proposed understanding of discrimination invites us to view victims of race discrimination as people who want to be respected for who they are even if carrying a specific social trait would not matter to their practical identity under more favourable circumstances. But this respect is necessary in order to protect them against a situation in which such a trait is likely to count as a stain on their practical identity.[52]

Often, such respect for the sake of indifference is mistaken for requiring the recognition of pride. The celebration of 'diversity' is based on such a mistake. But perhaps it is a minor flaw of cultures that are trying to cope with deeply entrenched patterns of discrimination.

The final point of the analysis is the most important one and lies beyond the work that has been done here. Living a life in dignity requires more than legal protection from discrimination. We have not even opened the whole chapter of how slower and more contemplative forms of life are to be insulated against the eroding effects of the functional imperatives of universal agility and adaptability. Our age has gone wrong to perceive violations of dignity most paradigmatically expressed in practices of physical

---

50   See Lear, *A Case for Irony* 21, 31, 56, 61.
51   The practical identity is thus measured against itself. See Korsgaard, 'Self-Constituion and Irony' 76.
52   For an exploration of the concept of discrimination from this narrow perspective, see S Moreau, 'What Is Discrimination?' (2010) 38 *Philosophy and Public Affairs* 144, 149.

abuse. Dignity can only be secured when we understand that the full package of human rights—social, economic, civil, political, cultural—is indivisible.

Architecture, Choice Architecture and Dignity

Morag Goodwin[*]

I. Introduction

It is perhaps only a slight exaggeration to suggest that the publication by Richard Thaler and Cass Sunstein of their global bestseller *Nudge* in 2008 has changed the way in which we understand our own behaviour and our expectations of governments to address it.[1] It has become commonplace to note the creation by various governments of 'Nudge Units' to study the possibility of pushing citizens into taking better decisions about their health, financial situation and overall lifestyle. The popularity of nudging amongst regulators is largely due, besides the cost savings that it is claimed to bring about, to the apparent retention of choice and thus the lack of coercion. As such, it chimes perfectly with the acceptance in the Anglo-Saxon world on both sides of the political spectrum that 'the era of big government is over'.[2]

Nudging thus contrasts strongly with another form of regulation that makes use of the architecture metaphor: design-based regulation or code. Much has been written about the moral dangers of this type of regulation since the launch of Lawrence Lessig's seminal work in 1999.[3] Indeed,

---

[*] My thanks to the participants in the Recht im Kontext conference on The Concept of Human Dignity in a Comparative Perspective: Cases and Developments held at the Wissenschaftskolleg zu Berlin, 19-21 June 2013 for their insightful comments and questions. I have also discussed the topic of the paper with Thomas Mertens and am grateful for his insights. Remaining weaknesses are of course my own.

[1] RH Thaler and CR Sunstein, *Nudge. Improving Decisions About Health, Wealth and Happiness* (London, Penguin, 2009).

[2] The phrase is from President Clinton's 1996 State of the Union address, although he used it repeatedly, too, in his second Presidential election campaign. As Thaler and Sunstein say of themselves, 'we are not for bigger government, just for better governance'; ibid 14.

[3] See L Lessig, *Code and Other Laws of Cyberspace* (New York, Basic Books, 1999); and id, 'The Law of the Horse: What Cyberlaw Might Teach' (1999) 113 *Harvard Law Review* 501.

code has become something of a bogeyman in the law and technology field; and the failure of the academic debate to translate into public outcry at the limitations that design-based regulation impose on us has much to do with its integrated, i.e. design-based, nature. Code is often not visible to the normal eye and thus our scope of action is limited without us being even aware of it. Yet the dangers of code to our moral autonomy and to the possibilities of moral community are alleged to be severe. In contrast, while nudging has not escaped criticism, the disquiet expressed has largely been of a liberty-type concern about paternalism. The types of concerns raised are thus very different; nudging is not understood as raising fundamental moral questions. The premise of this paper is that liberty-type concerns fail to capture the moral hazard that nudging represents; the aim is to explore whether a human dignity lens sheds better light on the moral hazards of adopting nudging as a key part of the regulatory toolbox. The suggestion is that the manipulation of choice architecture has more in common with code than the friendly label of 'nudging' would suggest.

Before beginning by examining the types of concerns that have been raised in relation to design-based regulation, it is worth noting that human dignity is a notoriously slippery concept and perhaps a lawyer would be well advised to steer clear of the term. However, the suggestion is that the terminology of human dignity allows us to identify fundamental concerns about certain types of choice architecture that would perhaps otherwise be missed by reflection under the headings of terms such as liberty, equality or welfare. More specifically, where concerns such as those represented by liberty, equality or welfare focus on restrictions to the scope of individual freedom, or on individual well-being, they fail to capture the threat to our understandings of self-worth and respect for the individual posed by the deliberate manipulation of architecture and choice architecture both by public authorities. Such challenges go beyond the complaint of paternalism levelled at nudging. Human dignity is thus used here in a loose way to refer to respect for human agency, both at the level of the self and by others. As I shall attempt to argue, it is the undermining of *respect* for individual human agency and moral autonomy that makes nudging problematic and thus raises human dignity concerns.

II. Dangerous Architecture

To state that our material world conditions our behaviour to a greater extent than we are perhaps comfortable in admitting,[4] or that the manipulation of our social spaces through architecture impacts upon our scope for action on a minute-by-minute basis, is not to reveal anything new. We are born into the world as it is, bound by physical laws and structures. Architecture quite literally gives shape to our world(s) and conditions our experience of it; for example, the faculty building in which I am writing this paper, with its ten self-contained floors to house the different departments, conditions the interaction, or rather lack thereof, between faculty members across departments. Architecture influences, or regulates,[5] our behaviour, whether the effect is intended or not (the lack of cross-departmental contact was presumably an unintended consequence of the faculty building's design). However, social planning has long made use of architecture to constrain our behaviour and our possibility for social interaction in deliberate ways.[6] In cyberspace, Lessig has labelled this form of regulation 'code'. Code—the software and hardware that makes cyberspace the way it is—conditions how we interact with and within cyberspace: certain areas of the internet require a password to enter or apps, such as BBC iPlayer or Netflix, may require an IP address that signifies location in a given territory in order for the user to be able to access content or changes the content depending upon location. Thus, whereas Netflix is not available in Rwanda, the content in Netflix differs widely depending upon whether one is in the Netherlands or in the UK. In the latter example, owners of content use architecture to enforce intellectual property protection.

Architectural or 'design-based' regulatory instruments are not, however, limited to coding the internet. Design-based regulatory instruments are defined as those instruments that are employed at the standard-setting phase of any regulatory cycle and that consist in technical measures designed to influence behaviour by shaping or structuring the practical conditions or preconditions for action. Architectural regulation is also not lim-

---

[4] W Bijker and J Law (eds), *Shaping Technology / Building Society: Studies in Sociotechnical Change* (Cambridge, Mass, MIT Press, 1994); D Vinck, *The Sociology of Scientific Work. The Fundamental Relationship between Science and Society* (Cheltenham, Edward Elgar, 2010).

[5] Lessig, 'The Law of the Horse' 507, for his four modalities of regulation, of which architecture is the fourth.

[6] Langdon Winner, 'Do Artefacts Have Politics?' (1980) 109 (1) *Daedalus* 12.

ited to the regulation of technology but uses technological means to influence or channel behavioural options. Design-based approaches can be employed in three key ways, differing in how they seek to achieve their goal: they can be used to encourage behaviour (e.g. the incessant beeping of the seatbelt alarm once a car is in motion); to mitigate harm (such as Anti-lock Braking Systems (ABS) in modern cars) or to prevent harm-generating activity from occurring altogether (e.g. automatic breaking in cars conditioned by surround sensors of the type that are deployed in driver-less vehicles). The moral alarm occasioned by the growing use of design-based regulation centres around the third type: that which prevents harm by determining a priori hard limits to action. In the first two approaches, it is still possible to drive your car into a tree, if that is what you wish to do, but it is not possible where the vehicle has been programmed to avoid contact with all arboreal objects. In the words of Yeung, 'it is the *action-forcing character* of techno-regulation that makes it a particularly powerful form of control'.[7]

In Lessig's four modalities of regulation, architecture or 'code' is but one form. However, as Lessig suggests, architecture differs from other types of constraint, such as those provided by law or norms or price, in how they are experienced.[8] For example, while other modalities of regulation condition access to a particular place, such as the market through price—if you cannot afford the price of an entrance ticket, you cannot enter the museum—architecture conditions access in a particular way. The now classic example is that of the bridges in the New York beltway that prevented access by poor people, and thus by definition at the beginning of the twentieth century to African-Americans, to the posh beaches in Long Island by being too low to allow buses to pass underneath them.[9] I can know that I cannot access the museum because I cannot afford a ticket. It is much harder to see the regulatory intent behind the architectural barriers that condition my access to places: all I know in the second example is that public buses do not go to the Long Island beaches and that I do not have access to a car; it requires a stretch of imagination to see that my inability to access the beaches is a deliberate regulatory act. One of the paradoxes of architectural regulation is that, in being physically present, it

---

7　K Yeung, 'Can we Employ Design-based Regulation while Avoiding *Brave New World?*' (2011) 3 *Journal of Law, Innovation and Technology* 1, 4.
8　Lessig, 'The Law of the Horse' 509.
9　Winner, 'Do Artefacts Have Politics?' 123.

is harder to 'see' and more difficult to identify as intentional than non-physical forms of regulation such as price or law. This characteristic of architectural regulation has thus been argued to threaten democratic, constitutional and ethical values by eroding transparency and public accountability.[10]

Yet these are not the features of architecture as regulation that have caused most unease among law and technology commentators. Rather, it is the challenge to our self-understanding as moral beings posed by the ability for design-based regulation to be self-enforcing that has generated most concern. Architecture has the potential—particularly with technological advancement[11]—to not only condition behaviour but to prevent it altogether. In the words of Lessig,

> Code['s] ... perfection makes it something different. One obeys these laws as code not because one should; one obeys these laws as code because one can do nothing else. There is no choice about whether to yield to the demand for a password; one complies if one wants to enter the system. In a well implemented system, there is no civil disobedience. Law as code is a start to the perfect technology of justice.[12]

Refusal to obey, for any reason, becomes an impossible option rather than simply an inadvisable one. Compliance becomes the goal.

Roger Brownsword has done more than anyone to raise awareness of the risks that design-based regulation in its third type—as code, or techno-regulation—poses to moral community. As he puts it,

> [t]echno-regulation approaches the problem of social order in a way that does not rely on building a normative consensus; it is amoral; it does by-pass the realm of values; and it does not reply on moral discipline or obedience to authority.[13]

It does all this, according to Brownsword, because it by-passes the process of practical reason. The real threat, therefore, is not to transparency or accountability (although these issues certainly remain), but to the responsi-

---

10 Lessig, *Code and Other Laws of Cyberspace* (1999) 135. Also, R Brownsword, 'Code, control and choice: why East is East and West is West' (2005) 25 *Legal Studies* 1, 14–17.
11 Yeung notes the potential for regulation to be embedded not only in inanimate objects, such as cars, but to be designed into biological organisms, such as plants, animals and human beings. Yeung, 'Design-based Regulation' 3.
12 L Lessig, 'The Zones of Cyberspace' (1996) 48 *Stanford Law Review* 1403, 1408.
13 Brownsword, 'Code, control and choice' 13. See also R Brownsword and M Goodwin, *Law and the Technologies of the Twenty-First Century* (Cambridge, Cambridge University Press, 2012) ch 17.

bility of us as individual moral agents. The existence of a moral community, according to Brownsword, depends upon act morality (concerning the status of the act i.e. whether it permitted and therefore moral, or prohibited and therefore immoral) and agent morality (concerning the motivation for acting). In an ideal scenario, an agent does the right thing for the right reasons; it is, however, possible that someone may do something wrong (immoral) for the right reasons or because they failed to do the right thing whilst still nonetheless trying to do the right thing *because* they believed it to be the right thing to do i.e. for the right reasons. The point is rather that we should care more about whether someone attempted to do the right thing than whether they actually succeeded (although we would of course rather they did both). That we do in fact care more about intent than outcome is demonstrated by the still relative rarity of strict liability within most legal systems.[14] Where the focus shifts to the outcome and away from intention, we cease to be active participants in a moral community. We no longer need to take responsibility for our actions or learn to behave virtuously, the argument runs, because the technology will ensure that we do. In this way, technical fixes that force us to be 'moral' actually destroy the notion of morality they seek to protect. As David Smith has suggested, such use of technology has 'a demoralising effect'; in denying us the opportunity to practice our moral responsibility, our ability to exercise self-control and to act responsibly is weakened.[15] It is the threat to our status as moral agents posed by techno-regulation or architecture, by undermining our ability to be moral agents, that constitutes the challenge to human dignity that Brownsword identifies.[16]

There will, of course, always be individuals who seek to undermine design-based regulatory efforts and may be successful in doing so; it was not long before owners of new cars with seatbelt alarms worked out how to undermine the functioning of the device, either by the technical solution of re-programming the on-board car computer to switch off the alarm or by the considerably less technical solution of fastening the seatbelt and then

---

14 Criminal law is the easiest example, where *mens rea* plays a determining role in how we understand the extent of an agent's wrong-doing. See P Cane, *Responsibility in Law and Morality* (Oxford, Hart Publishing, 2002).
15 DJ Smith, 'Changing Situations and Changing People' 170; cited in Brownsword, 'Code, control and choice' 19.
16 See also R Brownsword, 'What the World Needs Now: Techno-Regulation, Human Rights and Human Dignity' in id (ed), *Global Governance and Human Rights* (Oxford, Hart Publishing, 2004).

sitting on it rather than in it. Techno-regulation avoidance techniques are harder and require more sophisticated responses but they are of course possible.[17] However, we should not dismiss the concerns raised by Brownsword and others too easily: firstly, as suggested above, architecture is frequently difficult to detect and detection is necessary in order to subvert its framing intentions; secondly, the majority of those subject to techno-regulatory efforts do not possess the technical ability to subvert them; thirdly, not all techno-regulation efforts have been successfully subverted, at least not yet;[18] and, finally, bio-technological advances are likely to offer the possibility of embedding regulation *in* biological organisms in the very near future.[19]

The moral hazard identified by Brownsword and by others is thus arguably real. And it is the use of a human dignity approach that allows us to see that the use of technology to condition and to control human conduct threatens the moral and social foundations of community in which our understandings of individual freedom, autonomy and responsibility are rooted.

III. Choice Architecture or Nudging

Nudging has received so much attention, both scholarly and popular, that I will merely sketch its basic features.[20] Choice architecture is the social environment that forms the backdrop to our decision-making processes; it is everywhere and unavoidable (e.g. the bookstore has to put some books closest to the entrance; some candidate's name has to go first on the ballot

---

17   C Fried, 'Perfect Freedom, Perfect Control' (2000) 114 *Harvard Law Review* 606, who provides examples of hackers subverting code in the context of the internet.
18   For example, the 'killer' seeds created by Monsanto. There are reports of farmers in India purchasing the seeds on the black market to avoid the high prices charged by Monsanto but they still need to purchase seeds every season. D Gupta, 'Encroached Commons: Politics of Seeds', Conference Paper for Fourteenth Biennial Conference of the International Association for the Study of the Commons, 3–7 June 2013, Japan; dlc.dlib.indiana.edu/dlc/handle/10535/8904.
19   Yeung, 'Design-based Regulation' note 11.
20   Entering 'Nudging' into google scholar results in thousands of entries across a wide range of disciplines. There is also a nudge blog and an array of popular websites on the phenomenon; eg nudges.org/.

paper). Nudging, then, is the attempt to alter our behaviour by manipulating choice architecture; or, in Sunstein's own words, nudges are 'low-cost, choice-preserving, behaviourally informed approaches to regulatory problems'.[21] What separates nudging from other types of manipulation, such as those by private actors who wish to sell us products or who want to seduce us into a contract that is not in our best interests, is that the modification of the choice architecture around us is done so as to assist us in making the choices that we actually wish to make. As Sunstein notes in his more recent book, 'Nudges consist of approaches that do not force anyone to do anything and that maintain freedom of choice, but that have the potential to make people healthier, wealthier, and happier.'[22]

In addition to maintaining *freedom of choice*, nudging also serves a *public function*, though the 'choice architect' (Sunstein's phrase) does not need to be a public official: a canteen manager who replaces existing plates with smaller ones because she wishes to encourage healthy eating is nudging her patrons into eating less because this is good for them, not because she wishes to make more money.[23] A third central feature of nudging is that it pushes us into making choices that help us realise goals that *we already have*; where we want to give up smoking, nudging helps us make the right decision not to smoke each day, for example by hiding cigarettes from view or by bombarding us with reminders of what we are doing to our bodies with each cigarette.

Nudging is of course a regulatory response to research from the field of behavioural economics. It is based upon the knowledge that individuals do not always act in their own best interests, whether because of laziness, apathy, lack of information, inability to understand information, over-information, myopia, or a lack of self-control. As Kahneman has done so much to bring to the attention of the wider public, human beings procrastinate, are unrealistically optimistic, are frequently unable to identify salient information from background noise and regularly make 'affective

---

21 CR Sunstein, 'Nudges.gov: Behaviourally Informed Regulation' in E Zamir and D Teichmann (eds), *Oxford Handbook of Behavioural Economics and the Law* (Oxford, Oxford University Press, 2014) 719.
22 CR Sunstein, *Simpler. The Future of Government* (New York, Simon and Schuster, 2013) 9.
23 Of course, she may also increase profit by maintaining the same prices. However, it is the public element—the desire to help people be healthier—that makes this an example of nudging. It would otherwise be a more usual corporate tale of maximizing profit.

forecasting errors' i.e. predict that something will have beneficial or adverse effects on their well-being and are wrong.[24] Faced with such a catalogue of human inadequacy, Sunstein and his collaborators have developed

> the first law of behaviourally informed regulation: in the face of behavioural market failures, disclosure of information, warnings, default rules and other kinds of nudges are usually the best response, at least when there is no harm to others.[25]

Nudges, then, are a tool by government to affect human behaviour in order to prevent individuals harming their own interests in situations in which we cannot be trusted to act in our own best interests. An example is smoking or eating the wrong kind of food or failing to save sufficiently throughout our working lives for the retirement that we dream of. Note, nudges are to be limited to situations of self-harm; they are not relevant, according to Sunstein and Thaler, in situations where harm to others is at stake, although they of course overlap, often to a considerable degree. Sunstein's frequently used example is that of texting whilst driving. Such cases should continue to be regulated in a direct manner by government, in the case of driving-whilst-texting by means of both civil and criminal sanctions. Nudging is not then a tool for replacing traditional governance techniques, as the situations in which self-harm alone is an issue are rather limited—prohibitions, requirements and economic incentives all continue to have their place—but is an additional tool in the regulatory toolbox.

Nudges most commonly consist in requirements of disclosure notices, information campaigns, product warnings, reminders and checklists. The aim of these nudges is to raise the salience of helpful or good information and thereby to help individuals make better choices for themselves, both the self of today and that of the future. For example, health campaigns to persuade us to give up smoking or to exercise more provide information on the risks that we run by indulging in unhealthy practices but they do not take the choice away from us. Such information campaigns are even more effective if they not only tell us precisely how harmful (or beneficial depending upon the action desired of us) certain behaviour is but also tell us how to do better; for example, instead of merely extolling the virtues of healthy eating, supplying simple and easily actionable messages on what to do e.g. buy low fat milk instead of full fat.

---

24   D Kahneman, *Thinking, Fast and Slow* (London, Penguin, 2012).
25   CR Sunstein, 'The Storrs Lectures: Behavioural Economics and Paternalism' (2012) 7; papers.ssrn.com/sol3/papers.cfm?abstract_id=2182619.

The framing of information—how that information is presented—has a powerful influence on whether we act upon it. While the reasoning part of our brain—System 2 in Kahneman's language—focuses on the content of information, the automated part of our brain that is programmed to search for associations—System 1—is deeply affected by how information is presented. As most of us do not engage System 2 when doing grocery shopping, we are more likely to buy a product that proclaims itself to be '90% fat-free' on the basis that it sounds healthier than one that carries the label 'contains 10% fat'. We are more likely to buy greener products if we can understand in a simple way which products are indeed greener; the EU energy consumption labelling system is an excellent example of providing information in a way that appeals to our System 1 brain: making use of colour (green for good; red for bad), the alphabet (A–G, where A is most energy efficient: who would not want to strive for an A?), and visual clues (energy inefficient products have larger bars to reflect that they use more energy; A is at the top of the table).[26] We do not need to understand how or why one product is greener or more energy efficient than another; we just need to buy a product labelled with a green A at the top of the table with the smallest bar.

It is not only how information is presented, of course, that can nudge us in a certain direction: *what* information is also important. Campaigns do not present *all* information but select and highlight the information that they want us to absorb and act upon. Anti-smoking campaigns do not provide us with personal stories of individuals who have smoked all their lives and died peacefully in their beds aged 92 but direct our attention to the unfortunate smoker who dies young of lung cancer or heart disease leaving behind a grieving and photogenic family. Similarly, such campaigns do not focus on the reasons that people might choose to smoke—the social side of smoking, the stolen 'me' moment in a busy schedule, the Lauren Bacall coolness of it—but on the negative, health-harming facts about smoking. While an obvious point, it is important to realise that the choice of information is as manipulative as the framing of it (a point that Sunstein openly admits).

---

26   Council Directive 92/75/EEC of 22 September 1992 on the indication by labelling and standard product information of the consumption of energy and other resources by household appliances. See for the visual representation of the guide: en.wikipedia.org/wiki/European_Union_energy_label.

However, inertia is a powerful force and information alone, even where helpfully packaged into a campaign, frequently has little impact on our tendency to procrastinate at all costs. Studies have shown that we are spectacularly bad at actively planning for the future, particularly where it costs us something today. Automatic enrolment in saving schemes or pension plans dramatically increases participation and is more effective than forms of economic incentive, including large tax subsidies.[27] Asking people to check a box if they wish to opt-out of a savings scheme is thus much more effective than asking them to check the box in order to opt-in. Default options rely on our inertia to guide us down certain paths: who but the most technically demanding user changes the default settings on their laptops or mobile phones? Default options, then, are a powerful tool for regulators wanting to help us be better and do better at realising our life's goals.

Nudging thus takes different forms, and these different forms have different levels of invasiveness and impact upon our moral well-being. Although a single regulatory action, such as an information campaign, is likely to make use of two or more of types of nudges, it is helpful for the sake of critique to divide nudging into four categories.

Disclosures address how we process information and are successful where information is not only provided but provided in a way that it is difficult to ignore. They can be extraordinarily effective, as anyone who has stood in a coffee shop in New York after the 2008 calorie posting requirement came into force can attest: a mid-morning snack becomes a lot less attractive when the information that your blueberry muffin contains 450 calories is disclosed alongside the object of your desire.[28] Calorie posting works because it is difficult to ignore and we can no longer fool ourselves that a muffin (even a skinny muffin) is healthy, although of course we need to understand the context of the information (what a calorie is, how many we should be consuming etc.) for this type of information to be salient.

Warnings attempt to alter the framing of information, focusing on the consequences of choices in order to make information more salient. An example would be the graphic warnings attached to cigarette packages. A

---

27   Sunstein, *Simpler* (2013) 58 f.
28   See Section 81.50 of the New York City Health Code; www.nyc.gov/html/doh/downloads/pdf/cdp/calorie_compliance_guide.pdf. For nutritional information on a blueberry muffin in one of the most ubiquitous coffee shops in NYC, see www.starbucks.co.uk/menu/food-list/muffins-pastries-and-doughnuts/classic-blueberry-muffin.

warning in relation to the muffin example above would be to require food establishments to show images of obese individuals next to products with calorie counts over a certain level (just as companies that attempt to sell us trainers or health juices treat us to images of young, skinny people).

A third type of nudge consists in attempting to create a new social norm to promote a certain type of behaviour; for example, advertising campaigns promoting the benefits of a healthy lifestyle (no muffins), or of wearing seatbelts or of not smoking when pregnant. We know that social practices have a profound influence over individual decision-making: we like to do what others think is the right thing to do, so that information about the average consumption of energy per household helps to reduce energy use. Likewise, an individual is more likely to be overweight where others within their social network are also overweight.[29] Informational cascades fall under this type of nudging, as people rely on and amplify in turn certain messages.

The fourth type of nudging is setting a default architecture. This includes automatic enrolment, whether in saving schemes, pension plans or organ donation programmes. It also includes reducing plate sizes in canteens or self-service restaurants. Similarly, a type of default relates to the placement or design of products: plain cigarette packing or the placement of cigarettes below counters where they are not visible but must be specifically requested. In terms of my relationship with muffins, the comparable example would be where the muffin would not be visible behind the counter as I queue for my mid-morning coffee but would be out of sight either behind a solid counter or in the kitchen, available only on request.

If we were to think of these categories of nudges in terms of the types of design-based regulation described in section 2, we would probably conclude that they at most encourage us to mitigate our harmful behaviour (akin to the warning alarm for seatbelts). We can always opt out or ignore information designed to influence us and thus nudging does not begin to approach the draconian nature of Lessig's 'perfect technology' of compliance. Before examining whether we accept this, let us examine the critique that is regularly made of nudging.

---

29   Thaler and Sunstein, *Nudge* (2009) 182 ff; Sunstein, 'Nudges.gov' 740 f.

IV. A Critique of Nudging: The Paternalistic Charge

What could be wrong with the manipulation of information to push us towards doing something that we should be doing anyway and which is in our best interests? Why should we mind that a letter sent to small business owners reminding them to pay their taxes on time contains the sentence that '90% of small business owners pay their taxes on time' as a (apparently very successful) nudge towards compliance?[30] Small business owners *should* be paying their taxes on time (both as a question of legal requirement and moral obligation) and the nudge also helps them avoid a potential penalty for late payment, so what could be wrong with it?

Despite the seeming perfection of nudging as a regulatory tool, a number of criticisms have been raised again the nudging revolution, most related to the charge of paternalism. Some are of a practical or empirical nature and concern questions as to how a regulator (or any choice architect) will know what our real choices are (maybe we really do want to live fast and die young (or at least thin(ner)) and that's why we choose to smoke). Other concerns include the charges that paternalistic approaches may freeze competition or encourage homogeneity by encouraging us to all want to live life according to the same pattern. A similar concern relates to preventing us from learning from our mistakes by infantilising us and protecting us from the consequences of our lethargy or decision-making phobia.[31] These charges are all welfarist in nature and concern the question of whether we are really better off where public authorities intervene in our lives by attempting to correct behavioural market failures. These critiques challenge the idea that the regulator knows best what we really want (they may know best how to ensure a healthy lifestyle but perhaps I get more pleasure from my mid-morning muffin than I would from being that bit healthier and hence prefer the muffin).

The main moral charge made against nudging, however, has been that of nudging as liberty-denying.[32] The libertarian critique views freedom of

---

30   The example is from the UK Government's Behavioural Insights Team (or Nudge Unit) and is described by Sunstein, *Simpler* (2013) 67.

31   See A Burgess, '"Nudging" Healthy Lifestyles: The UK Experiments with the Behavioural Alternative to Regulation and the Market' (2012) 1 *European Journal of Risk Regulation* 3–16.

32   For a good overview, see DM Hausmann and B Welch, 'Debate: To Nudge or Not to Nudge' (2010) 18 *The Journal of Political Philosophy* 123. See also CR

choice as an end in itself, such that even where the government *does* know best what we want, it cannot be legitimate for the government to intrude on our decision-making or, indeed, lack-of-decision-making processes. Here the critique concerns the claim that we have the freedom to make a mess of our lives any which way we want, assuming that we do not directly harm others in the process. A thick version of the autonomy argument sees any form of paternalism as endangering liberty and thus as unacceptable unless for the most compelling reasons. A thinner version of the same argument holds that people want to exercise their autonomy—they want to choose for themselves—and that not allowing them to choose reduces their welfare by making them unhappy; in this version of the argument, freedom of choice is compelling but not necessarily decisive: as Sunstein notes, '[t]he welfare gain of the paternalist action may outweigh the welfare loss'[33], i.e. the frustration caused by the loss of autonomy to choose may not be so great as the reluctantly admitted gain to welfare. It is thus the thick version of the argument that constitutes the chief moral or ethical critique.

Sunstein addresses these charges fairly successfully: there is always choice architecture. How much autonomy do we really have, he asks? Choices are made all the time for us by both public and private authorities, from the design of an alarm clock, to the road layout, to how and when we can take antibiotics. Any claim that we are actually autonomous agents making free choices is delusional. Moreover, as Sunstein notes,

> [t]ime is limited; some issues are complex, boring or both; and if we did not benefit from an explicit or implicit delegation of choice-making authority, we would be far worse off, and in an important sense less autonomous, because we would have less time to chart our own course.[34]

In response to the welfarist charges against nudging, he notes simply that the empirical evidence shows that 'there is real space between anticipated welfare and actual experience';[35] put simply, we do not know better than public officials about how to achieve our desired goals and there are some mistakes that it is impossible to learn from (or where the cost is too high) e.g. saving for retirement or wearing a seatbelt to minimise life-threaten-

---

Sunstein and R Thaler, 'Libertarian Paternalism is Not an Oxymoron' (2003) 70 *The University of Chicago Law Review* 1159.
33   Sunstein, 'The Storrs Lectures' 45.
34   ibid 47.
35   ibid 41.

ing injuries in the event of a car accident. Given the *actual* welfare gain, the paternalistic charge has little teeth. While viewing most nudges as only mildly paternalistic, he is willing to concede that the nature of the threat to individual liberty will depend upon the type of nudging under consideration, as well as the manner in which it is used,[36] and he stresses that paternalist concerns may require the use of active-choice mechanisms rather than default settings, for example. Sunstein does not therefore dismiss the paternalist critique but he is unrepentant in his belief that behavioural market failures justify soft paternalism in order to improve individual welfare.

V. A Dignity-Based Critique

It seems difficult to deny that there is something paternalistic about nudging but the critique misses, I think, the moral hazard that nudging poses. In section 2, we considered one of the leading human dignity-based critiques of architecture or techno-regulation. Brownsword and others suggested that architectural regulation, by making compliance the goal, weakens our ability to act morally and therefore undermines or even excludes our status as moral agents. The similarity to architectural regulation lies in the assumption that the result is what matters. The goal of choice architecture is the results that come from less self-harmful behaviour: the slimmer waistline (and the likely better long-term health prospects) as a result of one less muffin or a more secure future as the outcome of contributing regularly to a pension fund. The difference, as suggested by the term 'choice' architecture, is that, with nudging, we retain the choice to do the right thing for the right reasons—nudging simply helps us to make the right choices.

However, to accept the notion of choice requires us to too quickly overlook how, or perhaps rather *why*, nudging works. Where with architectural regulation or techno-regulation, our choices are conditioned by something external to us, with choice architecture, it is the limits of our brain architecture that conditions our behaviour. We can attempt to train ourselves

---

36   Sunstein is open about default rules being susceptible to bad design, misuse or abuse (See Sunstein, 'Nudges.gov' 735 ff): The basis for selecting a default rule can be that it is what most people would choose, were they to be adequately informed; or a default rule can be chosen in order to promote automatic compliance with the law. As such, they can be used independently or as a facilitating measure.

not to give in so easily to our System 1 instincts and attempt to overcome the natural tendency to inertia and plan properly for our future, but our brain design is working against us. Brain architecture, in this sense, is no less constraining than an actual wall. This is precisely why nudging works. Choice architecture is therefore much more similar to architecture, or the hard-core design-based regulation that concerns law and technology scholars, than the friendlier moniker suggests. There is no doubt, therefore, that the critique that Brownsword and others apply to 'code' applies equally to nudging: it undermines our status as moral agents. My concern here, however, is not that nudging weakens our ability to act morally—behavioural economics demonstrates that we *are* weak: not only can we not do the right thing for the right reason but we can't even be bothered to do the right thing when it is in our best interests—but with the consequences of accepting such weakness.

From a dignity-based perspective, the belief in our ability to choose matters. It matters not because of liberty-type concerns as expressed in the nudging critique, *or* because of concerns about moral community as expressed by Brownsword, but because believing that we can choose speaks to a belief in human agency. And belief in human agency is the basis for our understanding of what it is to be human and to act morally.

In his well-known essay 'What is human agency?', Charles Taylor has asserted that we need an account of human agency to make sense of our identity as humans. Following Frankfurt, Taylor holds that, where we share first-order desires with animals, it is our second-order desires that define us as humans. That is, what is unique to human beings is our capacity to evaluate our desires and choose between them; for example, I may desire a muffin with my coffee (first-order) but I resist because I also want to be fit and healthy, or at least not over-weight (second-order). Let us call this level 1 choosing. Taylor goes on, however, in his account to distinguish between what he terms weak evaluation, where we are concerned with outcomes, and strong evaluation, where we are concerned with the quality of our motivation. I should resist the muffin not because I wish not to gain weight but because to eat the muffin is to be greedy or because I wish to control my desires. In Taylor's terms, I should resist the muffin because to want it is 'unworthy or base, alienating or trivial, or dishonourable, or something of the sort'.[37] Thus even where a drug exists that allows

---

37 C Taylor, *Philosophical Papers vol 1: Human Agency and Language* (Cambridge, Cambridge University Press, 1985) 18.

me to have my muffin and eat it without gaining weight or putting my health at risk, I cannot have my muffin 'and attain the dignity of an autonomous, self-disciplined agent'.[38] I shall call this level 2 choosing.

It is important to Taylor to distinguish between the types of second-order evaluations because of the link he makes to identity: resisting the muffin is not simply, therefore, the assertion of a preference, but the motivation I have to resist the muffin helps to define the kind of person that I want to be and the type of life that I wish to live. Further, he insists that 'the capacity for strong evaluation is essential to our notion of the human subject; that without it an agent would lack a kind of depth we consider essential to humanity'.[39] It is this ability to evaluate qualitatively our desires that incurs our responsibility for our actions. The essential or defining element of human agency, then, is not the freedom to choose but the ability to evaluate the options available to us and to act in a manner that we hold to be consistent with our identity.

One does not need to accept Taylor's argument concerning the authenticity of our identities to accept his account of first- and second-order evaluations (level 1 choosing).[40] As such, one does not need to accept the necessity of level 2 choosing to human identity, at least not in relation to all activities. Perhaps I do not bring strong evaluations to the act of resisting a muffin; perhaps it is enough simply that I am able to resist because I desire the outcome of being thinner more. If this is the case, a drug that would allow me to have my muffin and eat it *and* still fit into my jeans might not be a moral disaster. But assuming that we do at least accept the importance of level 1 choosing to our understanding of what it is to be human, what are the consequences of accepting that nudging works?

My claim is that where we accept the findings of behavioural economists that we are lazy, apathetic and incapable of being trusted to make decisions for ourselves in the furtherance of our own interests i.e. where we accept the need for nudging as a regulatory tool precisely because it does work, the moral distinction between architecture and choice architec-

---

38 ibid 22.
39 ibid 28.
40 See C Taylor, *The Ethics of Authenticity* (Cambridge, Mass, Harvard University Press, 1992); also C Taylor, *Sources of the Self. The Making of Modern Identity* (Cambridge, Cambridge University Press, 1989). I acknowledge that Taylor's virtue ethics can also be characterised as choice-denying at a deeper level and thus as inherently paternalistic, and that as a result I am open to the charge here of attempting to have my theoretical muffin and nonetheless eat it.

ture falls away. Furthermore, following a critique of design-based regulation developed by criminologists in the context of the study of situational crime prevention (SCP),[41] I wish to suggest that the type of human being for whom such regulatory tools can be justified or are needed is one *who cannot be trusted* to act in a manner that takes into account their own, likely longer-term, interests; *who is unable to respond rationally* on the basis of either moral or prudential reasons i.e. either at level 1 or level 2 choosing; and *who is incapable of taking responsibility for their actions*. By accepting that we are incapable of responding to appeals to moral reason or exercising self-control or restraint is to demonstrate a fundamental lack of respect for ourselves as human agents, and therefore, following Taylor's account of human agency, as human beings. Seen in this light, nudging portrays the individual in a manner that not only undermines individual moral responsibility but moral worth. I am not suggesting that it is a moral failing to be misled by my System 1 instincts (any more than it is a moral failing to be forced to comply with IP law) but that accepting that *others* view me in this way undermines my status as a human agent capable of making reasoned (though not necessarily 'rational') choices and thus undermines my human dignity.

The claim, then, is that accepting that behavioural economics paints an accurate picture of human behaviour undermines my status as an agent (both at level 1 and level 2), *whether or not* I actually conform to the image i.e. whether or not I am capable of resisting the muffin by sheer act of will (and whether I resist because I wish to be thinner or because I wish to

---

41   SCP uses situational stimuli to promote lawful behaviour, for example the deliberate placement of CCTV cameras where they are clearly visible on train station platforms combined with signs announcing that the platform is monitored 24hr by CCTV. A less visible intervention are the covered waiting areas at public transport hubs that are not entirely enclosed, with either one side open to the elements or a 5–10 cm gap at the base through which the wind can blow; the aim is to deter rough sleepers and those who would loiter in public spaces for reasons other than those of waiting for transport (of course these design-based forms of regulation are actually highly visible to those whose behaviour is targeted but not to those who are *not* targeted). See RV Clarke, 'Situational Crime Prevention: Its Theoretical Basis and Practical Scope' (1983) 4 *Crime and Justice: An Annual Review of Research* 225; RA Duff and S Marshall, 'Benefits, Burdens and Responsibilities: Some Ethical Dimensions of Situational Crime Prevention' in A von Hirsch, D Garland and A Wakefield (eds), *Ethical and Social Perspectives on Situational Crime Prevention* (Oxford, Hart Publishing, 2000) 20 ff.

have control over my desires), accepts at the very least an impoverished understanding of human agency and thus of human beings as reasoning (level 1) and/or moral agents (level 2). At the extreme end, it denies human agency. This critique is thus not suggesting that behavioural economics has got it wrong or that nudging is identical to preventative design-based regulation in which all choice is taken away. I do not deny that some individuals are demonstrably capable of exercising their will and that nudging allows them to do so where they are so inclined. Rather, it is precisely in speaking to us as at the level of 'human behaviour' that nudging undermines our status as human agents and thus undermines our human dignity. This is why it is the *acceptance* of nudging as a regulatory tool and not the findings themselves that is the moral hazard.

This acceptance has, I think, consequences for the relationship that I have with myself in relation to my self-understanding as an autonomous being. Unlike Sunstein, I think I am likelier to be happier and have a higher self-esteem if I achieve something by working hard for it, for example by exercising self-control. I would undoubtedly get a boost to my self-esteem and be a better 'me' by being thinner, but it would be a shallower sense of achievement where I know the outcome was the result of clever regulatory technique rather than by my resisting mid-morning muffins by force of will. This focus on outcomes at the expense of the motivation and effort of action is arguably cause and consequence of the modern malaise.

However, a greater concern is the harm that follows from others accepting that I am incapable of acting in my own best interests, and in particular the institutional relationship of individuals to public authorities. The real hazard of nudging, I wish to suggest, is in accepting that our own governments having such an impoverished understanding of our status as reasoning, moral beings. This reduced understanding cannot fail to have consequences for the relationship between government and governed and thus to our status as social and political actors. If we cannot be trusted to resist the muffin on display in a coffee shop, or wrestle with the ethical questions of whether or not to donate my organs after my death, how can we be entrusted with deciding on more important matters, like the identity of our next government? If we accept that we are, on the whole, incapable of planning for our own future, how can we be seen by others as capable of deciding jointly on the future of the welfare state? Where I cannot be tasked with making decisions for myself, I cannot expect to be part of a decision-making process that affects the lives of others. This danger is highlighted by Sunstein's assertion that active choosing may impose an unjustified or excessive burden.[42] This claim may resonate where we focus on liberty-type concerns; here, excessive choice may actually reduce our freedom by absorbing time that we could otherwise spend in ways we prefer.[43] However, where we focus on human agency as being at the core of human dignity, viewing choosing as a burden entails serious risks to our status as agents but also to our relationship with those that govern us. If we do not bother to take ourselves seriously, we cannot complain when those that govern us also fail to take us seriously.

The degree to which nudging undermines our status as agents, and thus our human dignity, depends upon the type of nudge and arguably does not apply to some nudges at all. Warnings and disclosure, for example, are actually designed to promote self-control. Such actions appear to trust us to act in our own best interests, whatever we decide those interests are, when we are presented with 'the relevant' facts (even where we accept that the information selection is biased), and are assisting us in doing so. The concern here, then, is with the third and fourth types of nudges: social norms and default settings. Neither are intended to help me in exercising self-control or take me seriously as a self-disciplined, autonomous agent; instead, they are predicated upon my inability to be a (self-)responsible agent and attempt to compensate for it either by setting default norms that I will be too apathetic to change or by changing my behaviour by changing the behaviour of the people around me who I instinctively (blindly) follow. While these types of nudges certainly work, they change our relationship to the institutions that govern us and not in a way that we should lazily accept.

VI. Conclusion

Nudging works precisely because our brains work in the way that Kahneman describes. We *are* lazy, apathetic and slow to act in our own best in-

---

42 Sunstein, 'Nudges.gov' 738 f. For further elaboration of this argument, see CR Sunstein, 'Choosing Not to Choose' (2014) *Harvard Public Law Working Paper* 14-07 available at papers.ssrn.com/sol3/papers.cfm?abstract_id=2377364. His latest book is an elaboration of this argument: CR Sunstein, *Choosing Not to Choose* (Oxford, Oxford University Press, 2015).

43 See Sunstein's response to the paternalist charge in s 4.

terests. The aim of this chapter has not been to challenge the evidence from behavioural economics on which choice architecture is based; it has been to suggest that we should not be so quick to accept the assertions that nudging advocates make about the harm equation, whereby harm is minimised through choice architecture on one side of the equal sign for very little harm done on the other. Instead, the suggestion here has been that the real harm of nudging lies in the acceptance—both of us as moral actors and as political beings—that we are incapable of acting in either a self-interested or in a morally responsible way. This critique is arguably more concerning than that developed by Brownsword and others in the context of code; with code, it is technology that comes to prevent us from exercising our moral agency (level 2 choosing), and thus it represents a moral hazard. With nudging, the suggestion is not that it weakens our ability to act morally but that it betrays an understanding of individuals *as* morally weak. Worse, it entails an acceptance that we (human beings in general) are incapable of even level 1 choosing much of the time!

Just as scientific studies into the role of genetics on our behaviour and the increasing evidence from neuro-studies appear to suggest that we may not be in control of our actions,[44] behavioural economics suggests that we are rarely capable of making the best choices for ourselves. And just as we as individuals are arguably better off ignoring the suggestion that we are only partially in control of our actions, so too we may be best served by refusing to accept the characterisation—so essential to the idea of regulatory nudging—that we are incapable of taking morally responsible action, self-interested or otherwise.

---

[44] eg from the almost daily announcements of new findings, see *BBC News*, Study into gene link in sex attackers, 9 April 2015, www.bbc.com/news/uk-32221589; the story announces the findings of a Swedish study into sex offending that found male relatives of a sex offender were 5 times more likely to commit a similar offence than the general population, suggesting some genetic trait to predatory sexual behaviour.

The Universality of Human Dignity and the Relativity of Social Rights

Stefan Huster

I. Human Dignity as the Foundation of Human Rights

Human dignity can be understood to be the foundation of human rights:[1] The fact that every human being holds inalienable human rights that protect his or her fundamental interests is the highest expression of one's recognition as a legal entity. A person has to be respected with regard to these interests, rather than being considered as a mere object of state power – because this is what would violate human dignity.[2] In the first instance, the German Basic Law (Grundgesetz – GG) follows this link between human dignity and human rights by emphasising the inviolability of human dignity in Art. 1 (1) of the GG. It furthers the link by stating, in the article's second paragraph, that a consequence of the prioritization of human dignity is a commitment to human rights more generally.

This connection between human dignity and human rights has now been widely acknowledged and can be shown clearly for the classical liberal negative rights that are identified in the Universal Declaration of Human Rights and secured by the European Convention on Human Rights. These rights can be understood to be just as universal as the principle of human dignity on which they are based. The substance of some rights that have a distinctly cultural framing – such as the freedom of religion – might require the consideration of the specific social environment in which they operate. But this is ensured by the restrictive clauses that appear in many human rights catalogues. These clauses give the courts that must adjudicate these rights the latitude and discretion justified by the cul-

---

[1] See to this effect the clear and differentiated comments by G Lohmann, 'Menschenwürde als "Basis" von Menschenrechten' in JC Joerden, E Hilgendorf and F Thiele (eds), *Menschenwürde und Medizin. Ein interdisziplinäres Handbuch* (Berlin, Duncker & Humblot, 2013).
[2] On the so-called 'object formula', see BVerfGE 109, 133, 150; 109, 279, 311f.

tural contingence of some human rights.³ Yet, this does not change the fact that human rights as negative rights have a hard core that can only be questioned if the over-arching principle of human dignity were denied. Ignoring the freedom of religion and opinion, disregarding the right to physical integrity, *is* to deny human dignity.

What is less clear is the connection between human dignity and social (human) rights. In at least two respects, social rights seem to contradict human dignity's universality

First, there is a surprisingly wide range of positions, even in political systems that are committed to the principle of human dignity, regarding the question of the state's has social obligations *vis à vis* its citizens. The model of the social-state or welfare-state, as established in continental Europe, has not achieved the same level of acceptance as have the principles of the rule of law and of democracy. It is obvious that not all notions of human dignity result in social obligations for the state and in social rights for citizens. I will refer to this phenomenon as the relativity of the application of social rights.

Even if social rights are acknowledged as human rights, which ultimately are based on the principle of human dignity, their content nevertheless depends on the specific social and economic context. This is also acknowledged by the relevant rights declarations. For instance, Art. 11 (1) 1 of the ICESCR (International Covenant on Economic, Social and Cultural Rights) states that everyone has the right to an 'adequate standard of living.' It is obvious that the question as to what qualifies as an adequate standard of living cannot be answered in a uniform manner for Switzerland and Ethiopia. The Convention's resort to the vague term 'adequate' allows differentiated solutions against the background of the situation in the relevant polity. Similarly, the entitlement to benefits in national constitutions requires political calibration.⁴

---

3 See to this effect, S Huster and A Kießling, 'Religionsfreiheit zwischen menschen- und grundrechtlichem Schutz' in F Bornmüller, T Hoffmann and A Pollmann (eds), *Menschenrechte und Demokratie. Georg Lohmann zum 65. Geburtstag* (Freiburg, Karl Alber, 2013).

4 Regarding the entitlement to a basic income under German law, see BVerfGE 125, 175 para 138: 'However, the scope of this claim in terms of the types of needs and of the means necessary therefor cannot be directly derived from the constitution. It depends on society's views of what is necessary for an existence that is in line with human dignity, and on the concrete circumstances of the person in need of assistance, as well as on the respective economic and

In this chapter I will begin with a discussion of the relativity of the content of social rights (II.). This lays the foundation for the subsequent discussion of the applicability of those rights (III.).

II. The Relativity of the Contents of Social Rights

If social (human) rights are based on the principle of human dignity, then it seems logical that the contents of these rights should be determined by using the universal substantive basic requirements of a dignified existence as a point of reference. In particular, vital goods such as 'food, clothing, household goods, housing, heating, hygiene and health'[5] should be covered by social rights. For various reasons, however, this quasi-anthropological approach to determining a physical subsistence minimum quickly reaches its limits. First, it cannot provide an answer to the question how these basic commodities are to be defined specifically. For example, 'accommodation' can have many different meanings. Second, it is not plausible that a dignified life should amount to nothing more than the fulfilment of the relevant requirements for living (or survival). In its decision identifying a constitutional right to a subsistence minimum income, the German Federal Constitutional Court (BVerfG) went further and also acknowledged a social or socio-cultural subsistence minimum that includes 'ensuring the possibility to maintain inter-human relationships and a minimum of participation in social, cultural and political life.'[6] To a limited extent this helps map the substance of social claims. But it provides an important and correct indication with regard to the necessary 'participation' and its justification – 'given that humans as persons of necessity exist in social relationships.'[7]

The significance of this indication can be explained and clarified by looking at the case law of the administrative courts in the context of the old social welfare law (*Sozialhilferecht*). Here, the courts had to clarify whether, and to what extent, so-called single-instance benefits were a part of the necessary means of subsistence. These benefits were distinct—in

---

technical circumstances, and is to be specifically determined by the legislature in accordance with them.'

5   Enumeration from BVerfGE 125, 175 para 135.
6   ibid.
7   ibid.

their nature and scope—from recurring benefits because they were not scheduled according to standard rates, In order to answer the question whether washing machines, fridges, school trips, children's bicycle helmets, the traditional Schultuete for children who start school, and television sets are a part of the necessary means of subsistence as defined in section 12 of the German Social Welfare Act (BSHG), it was necessary to take recourse to the security obligation under social welfare law, without having a standard more specific than 'human dignity' upon which to rely. The administrative courts have not even attempted to clarify, on a general level, the question as to whether having these objects at one's disposal is a necessary requirement of human dignity. Indeed, the question whether a life in dignity is only possible with a fridge seems strange. Rather, from the beginning, the courts used an approach that is purely 'immanent in society.' They held that it is the task of social welfare to

> counter social discrimination of the person in need of assistance, and to allow such persons to live in the environment of people who do not receive benefits, in a way which is similar to the way they live.[8]

The objective is not held to be the purely biological, but rather an equitable social existence within the community of law, i.e. a 'socio-cultural subsistence level' or the social inclusion of the person in need of assistance – using a term which is commonly used in social sciences and social philosophy. It cannot be determined in the abstract whether somebody is to be included in, or excluded from, a social community. The Federal Administrative Court (BVerwG) has held that this depends on the 'prevailing lifestyle habits and experiences' in the relevant polity. Accordingly, the courts have used, as the decisive basis with regard to specific commodities, the so-called 'furnishing density' in low-income households. If these households consistently owned a specific commodity – such as a fridge or washing machine, then this was considered to be an important indication that that commodity was a part of the necessary living requirements. Ultimately, the courts have found this to be the case for all of the commodities mentioned above.[9]

Taking a step back, one can see the radically relative manner in which social rights relate to human dignity. Whilst torture is a violation of human

---

8 BVerwGE 97, 376, 378 with further references.
9 For a description of these court decisions, see, for all others, E Oestreicher, K Schelter, E Kunz and A Decker (eds), *Bundessozialhilfegesetz*, looseleaf collection, last updated June 2002, § 12 paras 2ff (Munich, CH Beck, 2002).

dignity, everywhere and at all times; but the question whether a television set is a part of a dignified standard of living cannot be answered without taking recourse to the relevant local environment. Ownership of or access to a television set is, as such, irrelevant for human dignity. Lacking a television would only be a violation of human dignity if a television is part of the standard of living in the relevant polity. The link between human dignity and social rights, in this case, does not result from individual fundamental needs. Instead, it derives from a right to inclusion or non-exclusion. The promise of human dignity is unfulfilled if a person is put into a position that is so bad that he or she no longer 'belongs'. With respect to the content of social rights, this may have the consequence that claims that are undoubtedly required to satisfy elementary needs are not protected. This is particularly true in the area of healthcare. If a polity decides that its healthcare system must ration and limit costly life-prolonging measures, then this should not constitute a violation of human dignity and the guaranteed minimum subsistence income, at least as long as this restriction of services is neutral and generally applicable with no discriminatory character. The relativity of the content of social rights might lead to claims that exceed that which is absolutely vital, but nevertheless have effects that restrict the rights. If the ultimate objective is social inclusion, everyone participates in the welfare culture of the relevant polity, with all its advantages, but also with its disadvantages.

III. The Relativity of the Applicability of Social Rights

The fact that the socially-determined content of human dignity ultimately is oriented to the right 'to belong' recalls the famous statement by TH Marshall, who concluded that full citizenship requires not only the granting of civil and political but also social rights.[10] In this way, the three elements seem to intertwine: Human dignity leads to a claim for full citizenship, which, in turn, cannot be realised without social rights. Unfortunately, it is not quite so easy. Marshall's statement is only based on the observation that, at the end of the nineteenth century and during the first half of the twentieth century, social and welfare structures increasingly developed in many states. It does not state, however, that this was the case without

---

10   TH Marshall, 'Citizenship and Social Class' in id, *Citizenship and Social Class and Other Essays* (Cambridge, University Press, 1950).

exception, nor does it attempt to provide a normative justification for this development (even though it undoubtedly shows sympathy for this development).

Rather, the exact conditions for belonging to a political and legal community must be determined by every community on the basis of its own self-conception. Whether, and to what extent, social rights and social equality are constitutive for a community likely cannot be defined in general terms. No doubt, at some point it becomes very difficult to disregard the most minimal social rights whilst at the same time stressing that individuals are 'equal among equals'. But there is a lot of political leeway beyond the extreme cases. Social rights are relative in another respect. If human dignity is aimed at equal belonging, and the substance of inclusion is oriented to the relevant conception within a particular society, then social rights depend on this conception. This is true with regard to both the content and the applicability of social rights.

What's in a Label? Transatlantic Reflections on Health Insurance and Dignity

Nora Markard[1]

Health insurance, or insurance more generally, is a mechanism of solidarity: a risk that would possibly ruin an individual can be spread out on the shoulders of many, and each and every contributor will be protected against that very risk by virtue of the participation of all the others in the scheme. This mechanism is especially attractive in areas where effective self-insurance—i.e. saving up for emergencies—is hardly possible because of the enormity of the cost that the risk involves: car accidents, severe illness, and so on.

Of course, such a system crucially relies on participation across the board; if only those participate who expect they will soon have to take advantage of the system, the contributions will either not be able to cover the cost, or be so high as to defeat the purpose of having the solidarity system in the first place. However, while the possibly disastrous consequences alone may be a strong incentive for obtaining insurance even for low-risk individuals, not everyone will do so; be it for general financial reasons, because the policy is unaffordable on account of the individual's personal risk assessment, or simply because of laziness. When disaster does strike, those without insurance are often unable to pay for the cost of treatment. In some cases, therefore, emergency support for uninsured individuals is guaranteed by the State or, rather, all the other members of the community who, by way of tax contributions, provide the funds necessary to run public affairs, including emergency support. Knowing that this emergency support exists can encourage so-called 'free-riders', a term that could here

---

1   An earlier version of this paper was presented at Yale Law School's 2012 Doctoral Scholarship Conference and at Columbia Law School Associates-in-law Workshop. I am indebted to the participants of the conference workshop, as well as to the 2012–13 Columbia Law School Associates-in-law and to Gillian Metzger and Philip Hamburger, all of whom provided valuable feedback and advice, not all of which could be realized here. All remaining inadequacies are mine alone. Thanks are also due to the DAAD for sponsoring my 2012–13 visiting fellowship at Columbia Law School. This paper is up to date as of 2014.

be applied to individuals who do not purchase health insurance for whichever reason, but who can count on being able to access health benefits, whether or not they can afford them, when they need them.

Legislators in different countries have therefore made health insurance mandatory, not only making coverage accessible to those who had previously been excluded for reasons such as pre-existing conditions ('bad risks'), but also aiming to include many 'good risk' participants who will pay more than they take out, thus broadening the financial basis of insurance schemes while lowering average premiums and making the entire spectrum of health services available to everyone.

This was also the goal of the 2010 US Patient Protection and Affordable Care Act (ACA),[2] and of several state-based reforms preceding it.[3] In Germany too, health insurance was made mandatory in order to reduce the number of uninsured individuals. This reform, passed into law in 2006, went largely unopposed. Solidarity mechanisms are an important element of the German legal fabric, indeed of the constitutional fabric. Here, the very first article of the German constitution, the guarantee of human dignity, has come to be understood as the foundation of the State's obligation to secure the minimum necessary for a humane existence (*Existenzminimum*); an understanding that has partly transformed spheres of (negative) individual liberty into (positive) minimum entitlements directed against the State, and thereby against the community of citizens and tax-payers it represents. Human dignity, thus understood, therefore in a way constitutes an entitlement to a minimal level of solidarity against fellow citizens and residents, a fundamental understanding that also affects health entitlements.

In the US, on the other hand, the ACA's minimum coverage requirement has met fierce opposition, even as the ACA was upheld by the Supreme Court.[4] While the constitutional challenge rested on a federalism issue, it appears that the 'real' opposition was directed against enforced solidarity as an encroachment upon individual liberty. The dignity of those newly included in the US health insurance system, however, had no role to play.

---

2   Publ L No 111–148, 124 Stat 119.
3   eg Massachusetts: An Act Providing Access to Affordable, Quality, Accountable Health Care 2006, Chapter 58 of the Acts of 2006; Vermont: Single-Payer and Unified Health System, H. 202 (2011).
4   *National Federation of Independent Business et al v Sebelius, Secretary of Health and Human Services, et al*, 567 US 519; 132 SCt 2566 (2012).

This paper will first present how health insurance relies on solidarity in the US and in Germany, then outline constitutional issues in terms of federal authority and fundamental rights. It will examine the role of human dignity and liberty for minimum entitlements and solidarity in particular, tracing a discontinued line of dignity jurisprudence in the US. In conclusion, it will discuss how central dignity and the social state are to German minimum entitlements jurisprudence.

I. Health Insurance as a Solidarity Mechanism

The main driving factor for the ACA was cost. In 2011, almost 16 per cent of the population in the US did not participate in any health insurance scheme, but were either self-insuring—i.e. saving up for emergencies—or simply not insured at all.[5] Uninsured individuals only have access to those health services that they can pay for or that they are statutorily entitled to as a matter of emergency care,[6] often effectively excluding them from vital preventive and early care. Of the medical cost generated by uninsured patients in the US before the ACA, 40 per cent was not covered. Instead, it was borne by participants of the existing schemes, as health care providers passed on the cost of uncompensated emergency care to insurers who, in turn, passed it on to the insured—driving up the price of health insurance and thus rendering it even more unaffordable. In 2009, this cost shifting was estimated to result in an average surcharge of $368 per annum for individuals or $1,017 for families.[7]

By comparison, in Germany, the 400,000 uninsured individuals estimated before the 2006 reform only amounted to about half a per cent of

---

[5] C DeNavas-Walt et al, US Census Bureau, *Income, Poverty, and Health Insurance Coverage in the United States: 2011. Current Population Reports* (2012), available at www.census.gov/prod/2012pubs/p60-243.pdf; this includes Medicaid (n 21 below) and Medicare (covering about 94 % of those aged 65 and over). The problem disproportionately affects Blacks and Hispanics, low-income households, individuals in their twenties and thirties, and non-citizens.

[6] Emergency Medical Treatment and Active Labor Act 1986 (EMTALA), amending Medicare statute, 42 USC § 1395dd. Under EMTALA, any Medicare-participating hospital—i.e. virtually all hospitals—must provide standard emergency screening and stabilize an emergency medical condition, irrespective of a patient's ability to pay, citizenship, or legal status.

[7] Families USA, *Hidden Health Tax: Americans Pay a Premium* (2009) 2, 9, and 26, available at familiesusa2.org/assets/pdfs/hidden-health-tax.pdf.

the population.[8] There, the fact that statutory health insurance is automatic for most employees means that coverage has long been near-universal. This is owed to a long tradition of mandatory sectorial public health insurance schemes that goes back to the late nineteenth century;[9] a tradition reflected in the explicit federal powers to regulate both the statutory and the private tier of the German health insurance system.[10] Statutory health insurance[11] covers about 85–90 per cent of all health insurance holders. Only employees whose income exceeds the eligibility ceiling,[12] self-employed individuals and public servants have to obtain private health insurance, which is based on individual risk premiums. Statutory contributions, on the other hand, are income-based; 'bad' risks are spread out among the providers, who are under an obligation to contract, by way of financial transfers.[13] Statutory health insurance thereby ensures a social balance or redistribution (*sozialer Ausgleich*) within the 'solidarity community' (*Solidargemeinschaft*). Unlike Medicaid in the US, it does not only cover the needy[14]—the eligibility ceiling (€ 50,850 or $ 65,700 pa) by far exceeds the federal poverty level (€ 11,278 or $ 14,600 pa). Return options after switching to private insurance are strictly limited[15] in order to prevent individuals from benefiting from low private premiums while they are 'good risks' and coming back to statutory insurance as the risk (and premium) starts going up. The successive introduction in 2006 of a statu-

---

8   See n-tv, 'Arztbesuch ein Luxus? 400.000 ohne Versicherung' (3 September 2007), available at www.n-tv.de/ratgeber/400-000-ohne-Versicherung-article 346320.html.
9   For a historical account, see, eg, M Stolleis, *Geschichte des Sozialrechts in Deutschland* (Stuttgart, Lucius und Lucius, 2003).
10   See at n 47 below.
11   S 5 of the Social Security Code, vol. V (*Sozialgesetzbuch* – SGB V).
12   Mandatory insurance ceiling (*Versicherungspflichtgrenze*), determined annually by the Federal Ministry of Employment and Social Services, s 6(6) SGB V.
13   Affirmed, BVerfGE 113, 167 – *Risk adjustment* (2005).
14   W Rüfner, 'Daseinsvorsorge und soziale Sicherheit' in J Isensee et al (eds), *Handbuch des Staatsrechts*, vol IV (Heidelberg, CF Müller, 2006) § 96, 1049ff.
15   Above the eligibility ceiling, 'voluntary statutory insurance' is only possible if the person was previously insured with a statutory insurance for 12 months, or for 24 months over the previous five years (S 9(1) no 1 SGB V; further cases listed in nos 2–7). As risk premiums can rise quite sharply with age, some therefore choose to forgo income in order to become regularly eligible again.

tory[16] and a private insurance mandate[17] was designed to make this comprehensive system fully universal. And indeed, by 2011, the percentage of uninsured individuals had fallen to less than 0.2 per cent of the population.[18]

The numbers in the US were much higher for a number of reasons: for one, employers do not have to offer health insurance,[19] whereas statutory health insurance in Germany was already largely automatic. Secondly, many did not forego insurance by choice, but because they could not afford it, or because they were denied coverage due to a pre-existing condition[20]—effectively reducing them to emergency care. Finally, for the young and healthy, it may simply be more cost-effective to self-insure.

The ACA was passed with the aims of resolving the financial problems generated by uninsured patients and of providing universal health insurance coverage also for those with pre-existing conditions. It addressed them in two main ways: firstly, it expanded the publicly funded *Medicaid* scheme to all low-income individuals, not just certain groups, and raised the income threshold for Medicaid eligibility.[21] Secondly, it created the

---

16   Section 5(1) no 13 SGB V, in effect since 2007. While employees are automatically insured, this clause addresses students, the jobless and the retired if they do not fall into the categories of private insurance. Welfare recipients can be handled by statutory insurance companies, but their benefits are tax-paid.

17   Section 193 of the Insurance Contract Act (*Versicherungvertragsgesetz*, VVG), since 2009. Private insurance providers have to offer a basic tariff for those unable to join a statutory scheme.

18   Statistisches Bundesamt, 'Weniger Menschen ohne Krankenversicherungsschutz', press release no 285 of 20 August 2012, available at www.destatis.de/DE/PresseService/Presse/Pressemitteilungen/2012/08/PD12_285_122.html.

19   In 2009, about 59 % of employees did receive employer-based coverage; see M Hall, 'A Fiduciary Theory of Health Entitlements' (2014) 35 *Cardozo Law Review* 1729, at 1738–44.

20   DHHS, *Coverage Denied: How the Current Health Insurance System Leaves Millions Behind* (undated), available at www.healthreform.gov/reports/denied_coverage/index.html; the great majority of the states allowed private insurers to deny coverage based on pre-existing conditions or elevated risk: Kaiser Family Foundation, *Health Insurance Market Reforms: Guaranteed Issue* (June 2012), www.kff.org/healthreform/upload/8327.pdf. In several states, it was legal for insurers to reject victims of domestic violence on this basis: National Women's Law Center, *Nowhere to Turn: How the Individual Health Insurance Market Fails Women* (2008) 8, and *Still Nowhere to Turn* (2009), both available at www.nwlc.org/our-resources/reports_toolkits/nowhere-to-turn.

21   Medicaid also used to be limited to selected groups, including children, pregnant women, parents and caretakers earning up to 41 % of the federal poverty

conditions for universal health insurance. To prevent staggering individual premiums for high-risk individuals and denial of insurance on the basis of pre-existing conditions, it provides for *community rating* of premiums and *guaranteed issue* of coverage. At the same time, it avoids the adverse selection problem[22] by introducing a *minimum coverage* requirement for all individuals upwards of the income threshold. Failure to purchase and maintain such coverage is sanctioned by a 'tax penalty' not exceeding the cost of insurance, unless the individual does not file federal income tax returns.[23] Very limited exemptions apply.

II. Constitutional Issues

A. The US: Federal Powers and Individual Liberties

The system created by the ACA requires virtually everyone who can afford it to maintain a minimum level of coverage, while everyone who cannot is covered by Medicaid. Both of these reforms were challenged in the federal courts. The Medicaid expansion attracted opposition because states that refused to go along with the expansion—overwhelmingly, but not wholly federally funded[24]—would lose *all* federal funding for existing Medicaid schemes, something which practically no state could afford.

line (FPL, currently at $14,500 per annum), the medically needy, the elderly and the disabled. From 2014, the ACA is expanding Medicaid to all those earning less than 133 % of the FPL. This expansion is matched by federal tax credits for low-income households (133–400 % of the FPL) purchasing insurance through the new insurance exchanges that the Act introduced.

22 In the area of insurance, adverse selection refers to the fact that the incentive to buy insurance correlates with the risk covered by the insurance, attracting 'bad risks' while providing a low incentive to 'good risks'. This is exacerbated if buying insurance can be put be off until needed, as the guaranteed-issue provision permits.

23 The minimum coverage requirement applies to everyone who is not exempt for religious reasons or because insurance would exceed 8 per cent of the individual's income, see 26 USC § 5000A.

24 The federal government covers 100 % of the added cost throughout the first three years; subsequently, federal funding is phased down to no less than 90 %. For the existing Medicaid programs, federal funding ranges between 50–75 % of the cost, depending on each state's financial situation. See: www.medicaid. gov/Medicaid-CHIP-Program-Information/By-Topics/Financing-and-Reimbursement/Financing-and-Reimbursement.html.

Of central concern for this paper's purposes, the minimum coverage provision, dubbed 'individual mandate', was under attack for exceeding Congress' enumerated powers. In keeping with the legislative statements that sought to play down the fact that the Act introduced taxes,[25] the argument in favour of its constitutionality centred on the Commerce Clause. This argument, however, turned out to be rather risky. Congress obviously has the power to tax categories of the population, such as uninsured individuals, with the goal of providing an incentive to extend coverage while raising revenue to cover the cost of emergency care for uninsured individuals.[26] Not even the conservative dissenters disputed that; they disagreed solely on whether the tax penalty was in fact a tax.[27] And indeed, the Act was finally upheld on this ground.[28] But while Congress can *regulate* commercial activity, the counter-argument of the petitioners ran, it cannot *mandate* the activity that it purports to regulate—in that case, Congress would be regulating commercial *inaction*. The action/inaction distinction, introduced by the libertarian constitutional scholar Randy Barnett,[29] constituted a legalistic distortion of existing precedent, in which the Supreme Court had accepted a 'substantial effect on interstate commerce' even with respect to self-sufficient producers who emphatically *did not* wish to engage in any commerce whatsoever.[30] Nonetheless, this doctrinal innova-

---

25 Congressional findings, sec. 1501(a) of the Act as passed (H R 3590-124, 242 ff).
26 Brief of Constitutional Law Scholars as Amici Curiae in Support of Petitioners (Minimum Coverage Provision), *DHHS et al v State of Florida et al*, no 11-398, available at www.americanbar.org/content/dam/aba/publications/supreme _court_preview/briefs/11-398_petitioner_amcu_conlawscholars.pdf; see also J Balkin, 'That Boring Old Tax Argument Was Always a Winner,' 28 July 2012, www.slate.com/articles/news_and_politics/the_breakfast_table/features /2012/_supreme_court_year_in_review/supreme_court_year_in_review _it_was_always_about_the_tax_.html.
27 *NFIB v Sebelius* 2651, dissent.
28 *NFIB v Sebelius* 2594–2600 Roberts CJ, joined by Ginsburg, Breyer, Sotomayor, and Kagan JJ; 2628f Ginsburg J, rightly questioning why the Chief Justice then pronounced himself on the Commerce Clause at all, instead of practicing judicial minimalism.
29 See, eg, the report on the oral hearing in the 11th Cir, where Barnett was counsel to the NFIB: L Denniston, '*Easy outing for health care law?*', SCOTUSblog (10 May 2011), www.scotusblog.com/2011/05/easy-outing-for-health-care-law/.
30 The substantial effect test can bring an inner-state commercial activity within the scope of the Commerce Clause. In *Wickard v Filburn* 317 US 111 (1942) and *Gonzalez v Raich* 545 US 1 (2005), the Supreme Court accepted such a

tion was adopted both by the Chief Justice and the conservative dissenters on the bench.[31] Had the Chief Justice not changed his mind at the last minute[32] and decided to accept the tax argument, the Act would have been overturned on this ground.

It was surprising to see how much traction the 'newly minted'[33] action/inaction argument managed to gain. The fact that it did suggests that the main opposition against the minimum coverage provision was directed at its interference with the *liberty to choose* if and how to insure against health risks. 'At its core, this dispute is not simply about regulating the business of insurance …[,] it is about an individual's right to choose to participate', a lower court found in a parallel case.[34] Other petitioners put it thus: 'the federal government will have the absolute and unfettered power to create complex regulatory schemes to fix every problem imaginable and to do so by ordering private citizens to engage in affirmative acts, under penalty of law, such as eating certain foods, taking vitamins, losing weight, joining health clubs, buying a GMC truck, or purchasing an AIG policy, among others.'[35] The 'broccoli horrible',[36] as Justice Gins-

---

substantial effect in two cases on wheat and Marijuana production for purely personal use. In *United States v Lopez* 514 US 549 (1995) and *United States v Morrison* 529 US 598 (2000), on the other hand, the Court considered that the economic effects of firearms near schools and of violence against women were too indirect to come within the Commerce Clause.

31 *NFIB v Sebelius* 2586–2591, Roberts CJ; 2644–2650 Scalia, Kennedy, Thomas, and Alito, JJ, dissenting.

32 There has been a lot of speculation over the Chief Justice's change of heart. Two small slips in the judgment seem to me to be strong evidence of the fact that the joint dissent was originally written by Roberts CJ: ibid at 2627, Ginsburg J attacks 'the Chief Justice', an attack to which the dissenters ('we') respond at [2649]; moreover, at [2648], the dissenters misleadingly refer to her partly concurring and partly dissenting opinion as 'dissent'; see N Markard, 'A switch in time: Der Chief Justice hat die Gesundheitsreform in letzter Minute gerettet', *VerfBlog* (30 June 2012), www.verfassungsblog.de/switch-time-der-chief-justice-hat-die-gesundheitsreform-letzter-minute-gerettet/. Scientific analysis appears to suggest otherwise, see W Li, et al, 'Using Algorithmic Attribution Techniques to Determine Authorship in Unsigned Judicial Opinions' (2013) 16 *Stanford Technology Law Review* 503.

33 *NFIB v Sebelius* [2618], Ginsburg J.

34 *Virginia ex rel Cuccinelli v Sebelius* 728 FSupp 2d 768 (ED Va, 2010), reversed, 656 F 3d 253 (4th Cir (Va), 2011), cert denied, 133 SCt 59 (2012).

35 *Thomas More Law Center v Obama* 51 F 3d 529 (6th Cir 2011), cert denied, 133 SCt 61 (Mem); see the Appellate Petition, Motion and Filing, 2011 WL 3136668 (US) 23.

burg called it,[37] came to represent the opponents' fear of a nanny state: if the Government can make people buy insurance, it can also make people buy broccoli to avoid obesity and its costs, and if that is the case, then government power is de facto limitless. After all, as Chief Justice Roberts put it: 'Every day individuals do not do an infinite number of things.'[38] In the end, the dissenters feared, this would mean 'to make mere breathing in and out the basis for federal prescription and to extend federal power to virtually all human activity.'[39]

This is clearly a substantive due process claim[40]—but it is easy to see why the opponents argued on federalism grounds: Not only would an economic due process challenge fail under the post-*Lochner* rational basis review;[41] as Jamal Greene points out, it would also apply to mandates at the state level (including those introduced by conservatives such as Governor Romney in Massachusetts), and it would have to build on pro-choice precedent—both undesirable corollaries for the conservative opposition to the federal mandate.[42]

---

36   The broccoli theme already came up in the first instance, see *Florida ex rel Bondi v DHS,* 780 F.Supp.2d 1256 (ND Fla 2011) [1289]. The constitutionality of a hypothetical 'broccoli mandate' was even discussed in the Senate Judiciary Committee, *see* Transcript of Senate Judiciary Committee Hearing: Constitutionality of the Affordable Care Act (2 February 2011); *see also* Written Testimony of Charles Fried, Beneficial Professor of Law, Harvard Law School, Before the Senate Judiciary Committee on 'The Constitutionality of the Affordable Care Act' (2 February 2011) 4, both cited in *Florida ex rel Bondi* [1311]. At oral argument, the broccoli motif was introduced by Scalia J, see Transcript, 2012 WL 1017220, at 13:8–12, *DHS v Florida et al,* 132 SCt 604 (2012), *sub nom NFIB* 132 SCt 2566 (No 11-398).

37   *NFIB v Sebelius* [2624] Ginsburg J.

38   ibid 2587 Roberts CJ.

39   ibid 2643 Scalia, Kennedy, Thomas, and Alito, JJ, dissenting; a proposition that Ginsburg J calls 'outlandish,' 2625.

40   See, eg, A Koppelman, 'Bad News For Mail Robbers' (2011) 121 *Yale Law Journal Online* 1, 22. Others have proclaimed violations of the Thirteenth Amendment, see J Balkin and S Levinson, 'The Dangerous Thirteenth Amendment' (2012) 112 *Columbia Law Review* 1459.

41   Following *Lochner v New York* 198 US 45 (1905), the Supreme Court invalidated a series of legislation regulating commercial activities, such as labour standards, on the basis of the Due Process Clause. The *Lochner* era ended with *West Coast Hotel Co v Parrish* 300 US 379 (1937), in which the Supreme Court started subjecting such regulatory efforts to mere rational basis review, thereby enabling much of the New Deal legislation.

42   J Greene, 'What the New Deal Settled' (2012) 14 *University of Pennsylvania Journal of Constitutional Law* 265.

Of course, there is also a more principled reason to base the challenge on federalism. The limits of central government power in the federal system are seen as a crucial guarantor of individual liberty. The US Constitution made the federal powers 'few and defined,' leaving powers 'numerous and indefinite' to the states.[43] This balance was established, as the Court highlighted as it struck down a federal firearm regulation based on the Commerce Clause in *Lopez*, 'to ensure protection of our fundamental liberties' and to 'reduce the risk of tyranny and abuse from either front.'[44] In *Bond*, Kennedy J put it succinctly: 'Federalism secures the freedom of the individual.'[45] Leaving most matters to the states allows for a plurality of legal solutions within the Union and seeks to leave issues within the closer reach of local, i.e. state-based legislation.[46]

Still, at heart, this was not an opposition against *federal* overreach, but against *government* overreach *as such*. The broccoli challenge promoted a minimalist, liberal, autonomy-centred model of the US Constitution, a model which pitches individual liberty against (government-imposed) solidarity. No-one, of course, defended the Act on the basis of human dignity, or with reference to minimum entitlements.

B. Germany: Federal Mandates and the Solidarity Community

The way universal health insurance was debated in the US could not have been any more different from how such an issue would be debated in Germany. In fact, in Germany, there would not even have been much of a debate, and indeed there wasn't when mandatory health insurance was introduced in 2006. Constitutionally speaking, the issue of mandatory solidarity is rather straightforward. The federal legislator has express authority to regulate both social security and the private insurance sector under

---

43 J Madison, 'Alleged Danger From the Powers of the Union to the State Governments Considered' *The Federalist* No 45 (26 January 1788).
44 *US v Lopez* [552], quoting *Gregory v Ashcroft* 501 US 452 (1991) [458].
45 *Bond v United States*, 564 US 211, 131 SCt 2355 (2011) [2364], holding that individuals too can rely on the Tenth Amendment; Kennedy J adds, ibid: 'By denying any one government complete jurisdiction over all the concerns of public life, federalism protects the liberty of the individual from arbitrary power. When government acts in excess of its lawful powers, that liberty is at stake.'
46 ibid.

article 74(1) nos. 11 and 12 of the Basic Law.[47] Although the states are in charge by default, there are hardly any areas where the *Bundestag* has not used its concurrent authority.[48]

This federal authority is limited by fundamental rights.[49] Unwanted membership in associations or mandatory contributions constitute interferences with individual liberty (*allgemeine Handlungsfreiheit*) under article 2(1) of the Basic Law, which have to be prescribed by law and be proportionate.[50] These limits are obviously not very strict: it is enough that mandatory associations serve a 'legitimate public function'.[51] This justification also covers elements of social balance as they are typical of social security, and the Federal Constitutional Court has granted the legislator a margin of appreciation in determining membership by what is necessary to establish a working solidarity community and who is in need of its protection:[52]

Statutory health insurance serves to protect those insurance holders regarded as socially vulnerable from the financial risks of an illness. This involves a comprehensive social balancing between the healthy and the sick, the young and the old, insurance holders with low and with higher income, as well as between singles and those with dependents. Since the means necessary to finance such social balancing can obviously not be raised by those typically benefiting from it, the legislator can determine

---

47   In the case of private insurance law, federal legislation is authorized only 'if and to the extent that the establishment of equivalent living conditions throughout the federal territory or the maintenance of legal or economic unity renders federal regulation necessary in the national interest' (art 72(2) BL), a limitation rather easily overcome. See generally JE Schenkel, *Sozialversicherung und Grundgesetz* (Berlin, Duncker & Humblot, 2008).

48   More conservative commentators deplore a 'decline of federalism in the social state': W Schmitt-Glaeser, 'Rechtspolitik unter dem Grundgesetz. Chance – Versäumnisse – Forderungen' (1982) 107 *Archiv des öffentlichen Rechts* 337, 355. Generally on German federalism after the 2006 reform, see A Gunlicks, 'German Federalism Reform: Part One' (2007) 8 *German Law Journal* 111.

49   Few claim that the authority conferred by art 74 BL in itself justifies interferences with fundamental rights.

50   BVerfGE 6, 32 – *Elfes* (1957); literally, art 2(1) BL allows for interferences justified by the 'constitutional order, the rights of others and moral law', but the constitutional order comprises all laws and regulations that are compatible with the Constitution.

51   BVerfGE 10, 89, 102 – *Erft Association* (1959).

52   BSGE 81, 276, 286f (1998); appeal to FCC rejected without decision. See also BVerfGE 113, 167, 220.

the membership of mandatory insurances in the way that is necessary for the establishment and maintenance of an effective solidarity community.[53]

Mandatory insurance schemes in the area of social security are designed to protect the vulnerable by including those who are not vulnerable, in order to have them contribute the basis of the social redistribution within the solidarity community.[54] The Karlsruhe Court even upheld a mandatory contribution of employers to insurance schemes protecting employees on the basis of their bond of solidarity.[55] In the German system, solidarity duties therefore form a constitutional justification for government interferences with individual liberty. What is more, social balancing is a task of the State under article 20(1) of the Basic Law, and this includes basic redistribution measures where necessary, as the Court clarified in a case decided in its first year of operation.[56]

But it is not just that there is an undisputed federal authority in the Basic Law. A German debate around universal health insurance in a setting like the one in the US would have prominently relied on human dignity. Understanding human dignity as relevant to social needs, however, took some time to develop.

Just like the US Constitution, the 1949 German Basic Law does not contain any social rights, only some clauses on the responsibility *of* the community, especially to the family,[57] and *to* the community, eg in rela-

---

53 BVerfGE 113, 167, 220; my translation.
54 See A Wallrabenstein, *Versicherung im Sozialstaat* (Tübingen, Mohr Siebeck, 2009) 361–68.
55 BVerfGE 75, 108, 116 – *Artists' social security* (1987): The legislator can build on existing 'specific relationships of solidarity or responsibility' as they arise (not only) in long-term, integrated work relations or in culturally and historically grown quasi-symbiotic relations. 'The relation between employers and employees is, in modern work and industrial society, the widely typical and, due to the intensity of the social relation at its basis, exemplary case of such a specific responsibility, albeit not the only one' (ibid, my translations).
56 BVerfGE 1, 97, 104 – *Surviving dependants' pension* (1951), where the Court emphasizes that a corresponding individual claim could only arise where the legislator arbitrarily violates this duty.
57 According to art 6(1) BL, '[m]arriage and the family shall enjoy the special protection of the state,' which also watches over the parents in the performance of their duty in caring for their children, art 6(2), while '[e]very mother shall be entitled to the protection and care of the community', art 6(4) BL.

tion to individual property.[58] However, its fundamental commitment to the inviolability of human dignity in its article 1(1) has become the seat of a duty of the state to guarantee the minimum necessary for a humane existence—complemented by minimum entitlements.

Such entitlements were in fact claimed in the mentioned case decided in the Court's first year, in a context marked by dire post-war conditions; however, the Court rejected entitlements on the basis of human dignity.[59] It argued that, while article 1(1) of the Basic Law obliges 'all state authority' to 'respect and protect' human dignity, this does not mean

> protection from destitution, but protection against attacks on human dignity by others, such as debasement, stigmatization, persecution, ostracism, etc.[60]

The first lead case on minimum entitlements came not from Karlsruhe, but from another newly founded court. The Federal Administrative Court, in its second year of operation, found that, under the new Basic Law, public welfare law can no longer treat the individual as a mere recipient of benefits granted, but must envisage her as a rights bearer—'not a subject but a citizen.'[61] Human dignity 'forbids seeing him as a mere object of state action, as far as securing his "bare necessities" ..., that is, his existence as such is concerned.'[62] In the Social State Principle and the social restriction of property,[63] the Court identifies a 'community principle' (*Gemeinschaftsgedanke*) which 'requires that [...] an important part of the people in this community must not be without rights with respect to their existence.'[64] Forging the link between minimum entitlements and human dignity is arguably the work of constitutional law scholar Günter Dürig in his seminal comment on article 1 of the Basic Law.[65] Appealing to the Kanti-

---

58   For example, according to art 14(2) BL, '[p]roperty entails obligations. Its use shall also serve the public good.' Art 14(3) BL allows for expropriations for the public good.
59   BVerfGE 1, 97, 104.
60   ibid; my translation. The Court also rejected such entitlements on the basis of the right to life and physical integrity (article 2(2) BL).
61   BVerwGE 1, 149 – *Entitlements in the area of public welfare* (1954) MN [26]; my translation.
62   ibid MN 28.
63   Art 14(2) BL, '[p]roperty entails obligations. Its use shall also serve the public good.' Art 14(3) BL allows for expropriations for the public good.
64   BVerwGE 1, 149, MN [29].
65   G Dürig, 'Article 1 para 1', in T Maunz and G Dürig (eds), *Grundgesetz. Kommentar* (Munich, Beck, 1958). On Dürig's contribution, see HM Heinig, 'Menschenwürde und Sozialstaat' in P Bahr and HM Heinig (eds), *Menschen-*

an categorical imperative,[66] he wrote, in 1958: 'Human dignity as such is also concerned when, economically, man is forced to exist under living conditions that degrade him to an object.' Under such condition, Dürig argues, man lacks the core of human dignity, 'namely the ability to rise above one's personal environment by free decision'.[67]

The Federal Constitutional Court did not explicitly adopt this line of thinking until the early 1970s, when it affirmed a government duty to provide for societal groups that are obstructed in their personal and social development, securing the minimum conditions of a humane existence.[68] But the Court has always emphasized the legislator's discretion, as long as the absolute minimum is secured.[69]

Only more recently has the Court become more affirmative. In its 2010 judgment on long-term unemployment benefits, the Court clarified that a humane existence encompasses not only physical existence but also social interactions and participation in society. Moreover, it required that the actual needs in these respects must be regularly assessed in a logically consistent and transparent manner.[70] Finally, in 2012, the Court for the first time considered benefits 'manifestly inadequate' to secure a humane existence; in the twenty years since their introduction as separate from general welfare, asylum-seeker benefits had not been adapted to the overall increase in price levels of about 30 per cent.[71]

In the area of medical benefits specifically, the Court has also begun to explore concrete entitlements, albeit not on the basis of human dignity. Here too, the Court has always emphasized legislative discretion, as long

---

würde in der säkularen Verfassungsordnung (Tübingen, Mohr Siebeck, 2006) 264–65.

66   Indeed, the phrasing is even evocative of another version of this imperative, 'to overthrow all relations in which man is a debased, enslaved, forsaken, despicable being'; K Marx, 'Contribution to a Critique of Hegel's Philosophy of Right, Introduction' [1844], in: 1 *MEW* 378, 385; transl. in D McLellan (ed), *Karl Marx: Selected Writings,* 2nd edn (Oxford, OUP, 2000) 71 (emphasis omitted).
67   G Dürig, 'Article 1 para 1' MN 43; my translation.
68   BVerfGE 35, 202 – *Lebach* (1973) MN 72; see also BVerfGE 40, 121, 133 – *Orphans' pension* (1975).
69   BVerfGE 1, 97, 104; 40, 121, 133; 43, 13, 19; 82, 60, 80 – *Child benefits* (1990); 100, 271, 283 – *Difference to income level* (1999): '*Gestaltungsauftrag*' (mandate for design). More recently, see BVerfGE 125, 175 – *Hartz IV* (2010) MN [133]; 132, 134 – *Asylum Seeker Benefits Act* (2012) MN [70].
70   BVerfGE 125, 175, MN [135], [138f].
71   BVerfGE 132, 134, MN [79ff].

as coverage is not entirely inadequate or insufficient to protect life and health.[72] It first affirmed an individual right to coverage for specific health benefits in 2005, if no approved methods are available and alternative methods can improve a terminal condition.[73] In keeping with its earlier jurisprudence on the state's duty to secure life and health and with the *lex specialis* rule, it based this entitlement on article 2(2) of the Basic Law.

III. A Crucial Role of Human Dignity for Minimum Entitlements?

Human dignity, as understood in Germany, thus affirms the duty of the State to secure the minimum conditions of a humane existence, in its physical and also in its social dimensions. This duty translates into minimum entitlements. In the area of medical benefits, such entitlements are more specifically based on the state's duty to protect the right to life and health via insurance claims.

In the US, not only does the Constitution not explicitly guarantee the right to human dignity, a constitutional concept which was only developed by the Supreme Court in the 1940s. Also, neither of the two relevant strands of dignity jurisprudence existing today encompasses minimum entitlements of any sort. Human dignity plays an important role in equality jurisprudence, where inequality is conceptualized as dignitary harm, as in the case of racial[74] and sex discrimination.[75] It is also crucial to the concept of autonomy, in particular the ability to make intimate and personal choices, including issues such as abortion.[76] Neither strand claims a government duty to protect the material basis of liberty or equality, let alone constitutional entitlements.

Nowhere is the contrast to German jurisprudence starker than in *DeShaney*.[77] In that case, concerning a boy subject to domestic violence,

---

72 BVerfGE 46, 160, 164; 77, 170, 215; 79, 174, 202; BVerfG NJW 1997, 3085; NJW 1998, 1775, 1776; NJW 2003, 1236, 1237; NJW 2004, 3100, 3101.
73 BVerfGE 115, 25 – *St Nicolas' Day decision* (2005), MN 65f.
74 *Heart of Atlanta Motel, Inc v US* 379 US 241 (1964).
75 *Roberts v United States Jaycees* 468 US 609 (1984). See L Meltzer Henry, 'The Jurisprudence of Dignity' (2011) 160 *University of Pennsylvania Law Review* 169, 199ff.
76 *Planned Parenthood of Southeastern Pennsylvania v Casey* 505 U.S. 833 (1992) 852.
77 *DeShaney v Winnebago County Department of Social Services* 489 US 189 (1989): no violation of the Due Process Clause by the failure of Social Services

the Supreme Court held that there is no affirmative right to state intervention against private abuse: because the Due Process Clause of the Fourteenth (as well as the Fifth) Amendment requires state action, inaction cannot constitute a substantive due process violation. Unlike in the German system, government inaction in protecting fundamental rights is therefore no constitutional issue, as the US Constitution does not establish a duty to secure core guarantees of human existence.

This line of argument, it seems, would exclude affirmative rights to minimum social standards, also in such areas as welfare or health—and possibly be opposed to state-sanctioned mechanisms that enlist the solidarity of others to secure such minimum entitlements. And would it really be surprising that one of the world's oldest constitutions knows only civil and political rights, when the idea of social rights was not (fully) developed until much later?[78]

IV. Minimum Entitlements in the US: A Different Tradition

A closer look reveals an alternative constitutional tradition in the US that is in fact not that dissimilar to the German conception of dignity-based minimum entitlements—despite the textual absence of human dignity. Cass Sunstein has traced this line of jurisprudence from the early 1940s to the early 1970s, when it was abandoned.[79] He identifies President Franklin Delano Roosevelt's State of the Union Address in 1944,[80] which built on his famous 'Four Freedoms' speech,[81] as a key conceptual foundation.

In his address, President Roosevelt starts out with the two central topics of the time: military security and economic security. He argues that, in light of current economic pressures, political rights do not suffice to pro-

---

to release DeShaney from his violent father's custody. '[O]ur cases have recognized that the Due Process Clauses generally confer no affirmative right to governmental aid, even where such aid may be necessary to secure life, liberty, or property interests of which the government itself may not deprive the individual.' 196, Rehnquist CJ.

78   CR Sunstein, *The Second Bill of Rights: FDR's Unfinished Revolution and Why We Need It More than Ever* (New York, Basic Books, 2004) 105, 109–21.
79   ibid, 149ff.
80   FD Roosevelt, *State of the Union Message to Congress,* 11 January 1944, reproduced online at www.presidency.ucsb.edu/ws/?pid=16518.
81   FD Roosevelt, *State of the Union Message to Congress,* 6 January 1941, facsimile online at www.fdrlibrary.marist.edu/_resources/images/sign/fdr_30.pdf.

tect the modern individual's freedom, thereby linking autonomy and economic security: 'True individual freedom cannot exist without economic security and independence. "Necessitous men are not free men."'[82] To remedy this lack, Roosevelt then goes on to propose a 'second Bill of Rights' and lists the rights it should include—among them the right to a sustainable income, the right to a decent home, to education, and to adequate medical care, as well as the right to social security. To be sure, Roosevelt does not propose a constitutional amendment akin to that which established the 'first' Bill of Rights. This, of course, would have been near impossible to achieve, given how notoriously difficult it is to amend the US Constitution under its Article V—unlike State constitutions, some of which actually have been amended to guarantee minimum entitlements.[83] Instead, Roosevelt puts Congress in charge of implementing this bill of rights, by passing the kind of social rights legislation that the Supreme Court had just made way for in 1937 by giving up its *Lochner* jurisprudence[84] and that had already started with the New Deal. His proposal thus seeks to build not on constitutional *law*, but on *constitutionalism*.

Just a few years before, the Court had in fact begun to explore a *constitutional* basis for minimum entitlements. It started in 1941 with invalidating regulations that discriminated against poor people, such as bans on bringing indigents into a state, emphasizing solidarity between states, which must 'sink or swim together' and 'share the burden'.[85] It continued with requiring government support in criminal[86] and divorce matters[87] where an individual was unable to pay for transcripts or counsel. It justified this duty both with the unequal application of facially neutral laws in

---

82 Sunstein claims that this idea can indeed be traced back to the original Bill of Rights as a means to protect the basics of citizenship, not just a sphere of individual liberty, a much more modern idea; id, *The Second Bill of Rights* (2004) 112–15.
83 eg, Art XVII s 1 of the New York Constitution: 'The aid, care and support of the needy are public concerns and shall be provided by the state and by such of its subdivisions, and in such manner and by such means, as the legislature may from time to time determine.' This has been construed to grant affirmative rights to minimum welfare: *Tucker v Toia* 371 NE 2d 449 (NY 1977).
84 *West Coast Hotel v Parrish* 300 US 379 (1937).
85 *Edwards v California* 314 US 160 (1941).
86 *Griffin v Illinois* 351 US 12 (1956); *Gideon v Wainwright* 372 US 335 (1963); *Douglas v California* 372 US 353 (1963).
87 *Boddie v Connecticut* 401 US 371 (1971).

their operation on poor citizens,[88] but also with liberty concerns: in order to guarantee a fair trial and because of the importance of marriage and the state monopoly on divorce. Equally, the Court struck down a poll tax as a discrimination against poor people in the exercise of their right to vote.[89] The Court then went on to find strong language on the importance of welfare and medical care for human subsistence. In *Shapiro v Thompson*, it still heavily relied on equality arguments, but began to move closer to recognizing a right to minimum benefits.[90] It found a one-year residency requirement for welfare eligibility an impermissible penalty on the fundamental right to interstate travel, stressing the importance of welfare 'upon which may depend the ability of the families to obtain the very means to subsist—food, shelter, and other necessities of life.'[91] A few years later, confirming *Shapiro,* it added that non-emergency 'medical care is as much "a basic necessity of life" to an indigent as welfare assistance.'[92] However, by that time, this line of jurisprudence was already in decline. In *Goldberg v Kelly*, a year after *Shapiro,* the Court had finally crossed the line from equality into due process. It had recognized welfare benefits as 'property' within the Due Process Clause, requiring a hearing before a recipient was struck of the welfare roll.[93] Crucially, the Court used the language of dignity to emphasize the importance of welfare benefits:

> From its founding, the Nation's basic commitment has been to foster the dignity and wellbeing of all persons within its borders. ... Welfare, by meeting the basic demands of subsistence, can help bring within the reach of the poor the same opportunities that are available to others to participate meaningfully in the life of the community. ... Public assistance, then, is not mere charity, but a means to 'promote the general Welfare, and secure the Blessings of Liberty to ourselves and our Posterity.'[94]

88　*Griffin v Illinois*.
89　*Harper v Virginia Board of Elections* 383 US 663 (1966) 668, concluding that '[l]ines drawn on the basis of wealth or property, like those of race, are traditionally disfavored' and that the fee constitutes '"invidious" discrimination.' Douglas J (references omitted).
90　*Shapiro v Thompson* 394 US 618 (1969).
91　ibid 627.
92　*Memorial Hospital v Maricopa County* 415 US 250 (1974): one-year residency period. 'Whatever the ultimate parameters of the *Shapiro* penalty analysis, it is at least clear that medical care is as much "a basic necessity of life" to an indigent as welfare assistance.' 258 Marshall J (footnotes omitted).
93　*Goldberg v Kelly* 397 US 254 (1970).
94　ibid 265.

This passage is notable in a number of ways. The Court connects individual welfare to human dignity and defines both as a main purpose of the existence of the Nation, suggesting a collective responsibility for the welfare of the individual. In the next step, it addresses the significance of a secured subsistence for a meaningful participation in the community. It bases this on the text of the Preamble of the Constitution and, in claiming that public assistance is 'not mere charity', suggests a constitutional duty to provide such assistance in order to secure 'the Blessings of Liberty' mentioned in the Preamble. The similarity to the German idea of protecting 'real freedom' by securing the foundations of liberty is hard to miss. But in connecting liberties and participation in society, the Court arguably goes a small step further, highlighting the significance of social rights (such as education) for the use of political liberties, which in turn are the foundation of democracy, the central value of the US Constitution.[95] Slightly more subtly, Advocate General Verrilli in his concluding statement in *Sebelius* also relied on this line of argument, and on words from the Preamble; recalling the fact that the ACA sought to provide access to insurance for those who could not afford it, he identified 'an important connection, a profound connection, between that problem and liberty.' Among those gaining access, he added,

> there will be millions of people with chronic conditions like diabetes and heart disease, and as a result of the health care that they will get, they will be unshackled from the disabilities that those diseases put on them and have the opportunity to enjoy the blessings of liberty.[96]

Shapiro had raised some expectations[97] that the Court was getting ready to recognize 'minimum welfare' entitlements and to declare welfare a fun-

---

95 F Michelman, 'The Supreme Court 1968 Term. Foreword: On Protecting the Poor Through the Fourteenth Amendment' (1969) 83 *Harvard Law Review* 7, at 9, 14-19; id, 'Welfare Rights in a Constitutional Democracy' (1979) *Washington University Law Quarterly* 659, at 677; see also: Sunstein, *The Second Bill of Rights* (2004) 112–15: the original Bill of Rights protects citizenship.

96 Transcript of the oral argument, 2012 WL 1031485, at 79–80, *DHS v Florida et al,* 132 SCt 604 (2012), *sub nom NFIB* 132 SCt 2566 (No 11-398). In using a reference to shackles, Verrilli may even be alluding to the Thirteenth Amendment; on this, see n 40 above.

97 Michelman thought that the recent Court interventions 'could be more soundly and satisfyingly understood as vindication of a state's duty to protect against certain hazards which are endemic in an unequal society, rather than vindication of a duty to avoid complicity in unequal treatment'; id, 'On Protecting the Poor' (1969) 9.

damental interest for the purposes of Equal Protection review, thereby heightening the standard of scrutiny.[98] But 1970, the year *Goldberg* was decided, already marks the beginning discontinuation of the Court's jurisprudence on indirect discrimination against poor people, when the Court subjected a cap on family aid to the mere rational basis review of economic regulations in *Dandridge*.[99] In 1972, it rejected the argument that housing was a fundamental interest requiring strict scrutiny, stating that the 'Constitution does not provide judicial remedies for every social and economic ill. We are unable to perceive in that document any constitutional guarantee of access to dwellings of a particular quality.'[100] Finally, in 1973, it held in *Rodriguez* that unequal funding for schools based on the respective school area's taxable wealth was no discrimination against the poor since there was no absolute deprivation of education, and declined to find that education was a fundamental right.[101] By that time, President Nixon, who came into office in 1969, had appointed four new Justices in quick succession, effectively changing the face of the Court.[102] All of them formed part of the 5:4 majority in *Rodriguez*.

The three dissents in *Rodriguez* defended a social vision that had been quickly losing ground in the Court. Marshall J protested that 'the literally vital interests of a powerless minority—poor families without breadwinners—[are] far removed from the area of business regulation', and that stricter standards applied to benefits necessary to sustain life: 'Appellees are not a gas company or an optical dispenser, they are needy dependent children and families.'[103] Both he and Brennan J emphasized the importance of education for the exercise of First Amendment rights,[104] re-

---

98 This would have triggered strict scrutiny instead of the mere rational basis review of *Williamson v Lee Optical Co* 348 US 483 (1955) that economic regulations are subject to; *cf*, for the fundamental right to vote: *Harper v Virginia Bd of Elections* 383 US 618 (1969) 670.
99 *Dandridge v Williams* 397 US 471 (1970). The Court of Appeals had found discrimination against poor children of larger families who received less per capita than children of smaller families.
100 *Lindsey v Normet* 405 US 56 (1972).
101 *San Antonio Independent School District v Rodriguez* 411 US 1 (1973).
102 Burger CJ was appointed in 1969, Blackmun J in 1970, and Powell and Rehnquist JJ in 1972.
103 *Dandridge* [529] Marshall J dissenting. The reference to 'optical dispensers' points to *Williamson v Lee Optical Co*.
104 *San Antonio ISD v Rodriguez* 63 and 110ff Marshall J and Brennan J separately dissenting.

minding the Court of the importance of minimum entitlements for Bill of Rights guarantees in order to secure meaningful citizenship.

However, alongside the Court's efforts, Congress had taken charge of implementing the Second Bill of Rights, as envisaged—and promoted—by FDR. This had already started with the 1935 Social Security Act, part of FDR's New Deal legislation, and it included, in 1965, the introduction of Medicare and Medicaid. This is what Eskridge and others call the 'Constitution of statutes', or 'small "c" constitution', without which the constitutional system in the US is not fully understood.[105] This system builds on the model of a minimal Constitution, which is narrowly construed and hard to amend. Constitutional change, thus, is not effected mainly though Amendments, as in Germany, but through statutes built around the Constitution, which can acquire similar weight, such as the Civil Rights Act, the Voting Rights Act, the Americans with Disabilities Act, but also Medicare and Medicaid. The ACA can legitimately be seen as part of this tradition.[106]

V. Dignity: Just a Label?

Looking back, it is startling to realize just how similar the developments were, albeit at very different times. In both systems, the Courts developed an understanding of liberty that included the material foundations necessary to its realization, with a view to participation in society. And, despite the textual absence in the US, both Courts used the concept of human dignity as a foundation of this interpretation—although certainly much more so in Germany than in the US, where this happened at the apex and end of a line of jurisprudence on minimum entitlements. Finally, with the ACA, the US has finally come around to protecting basic health needs in a way that secures the existential minimum for everyone, quite like in Germany, but without basing this on human dignity, or even on the Constitution at all. This begs the question whether human dignity is just the label marking

---

105 WN Eskridge, Jr and J Ferejohn, *A Republic of Statutes: The New American Constitution* (New Haven, YUP, 2010); eiusd, 'Super-Statutes' (2001) 50 *Duke Law Journal* 1215; WN Eskridge, Jr, 'America's Statutory "constitution"' (2007) 41 *UC Davis Law Review* 1; B Ackerman, 'The Living Constitution' (2007) 120 *Harvard Law Review* 1738.

106 See, eg, T Ruger, 'Plural Constitutionalism and the Pathologies of American Healthcare' (2011) 120 *Yale Law Journal Online* 347.

German minimum entitlement jurisprudence, or whether it plays a more integral role.

Critical comparison, if it is to lead to a learning experience, requires distancing and differencing, seeking objectiveness and taking subjectivity into account; the foreign system should neither be presented as the total other, but also not as the same, overlooking important differences.[107] What, then, is a German's learning experience from this comparison? One insight is that human dignity, or the Social State Principle, do not seem to be necessary to developing an understanding of the material conditions of liberty. As the US Supreme Court demonstrated between 1941 and 1970, social rights can even be coaxed out of a Constitution that is all about liberty and not really about human dignity, let alone solidarity. This perspective opens the view to a richer understanding of minimum entitlements in Germany, in a closer connection to the liberties they secure and with a view to the participatory society that these liberties enable. While the Federal Constitutional Court already acknowledges that the minimum necessary to human existence includes 'a minimum of participation in social, cultural, and political life, since man as a person necessarily exists in social relations',[108] the connection to citizenship is still rather subtle.

Another insight might be that not everything that is important to us must necessarily be anchored in the Constitution. Germans tend to get worried if something that they consider crucial to individual welfare or the social fabric could just be changed at the whim of the legislator. But the political process in the US has shown that the 'statutory constitution' can develop a weight quite similar to the Constitution proper. And as a matter of fact, the current level of German health insurance extends far beyond what can safely be considered required by the Basic Law. Should Germans try and trust the constitution of statutes more? Such a changed perspective could incentivize the legislator to take responsibility for such tricky, unpopular, or highly contested decisions, instead of shifting them to Karlsruhe, waiting for the inevitable smack over the head. However, it must be admitted that in the case of universal health insurance in the US, this political process took very long indeed and may well have failed. And

---

107 G Frankenberg, 'Critical Comparisons: Re-thinking Comparative Law' (1985) 26 *Harvard International Law Journal* 411. See now also id, 'Innocence in Context – Comparative Law Revisited', in D Grimm, A Kemmerer, and C Möllers (eds), *Rechtswege. Kontextsensible Rechtswissenschaft vor der transnationalen Herausforderung* (Baden-Baden, Nomos, 2015) 144.

108 BVerfGE 125, 175, 223; 132, 134, 160; my translation.

in Germany, the case of the asylum seeker benefits recently demonstrated just how dangerous it can be to trust in the legislator to protect the subsistence level.[109] Human dignity, by virtue of its inviolability, has proven a reliable line of defence for those forgotten by political process, if only to secure the very minimum. And that can be worth a lot.

---

[109] Thanks to Dieter Grimm for this caveat.

Socioeconomic Rights, Human Dignity, and Constitutional Legitimacy in India

*Rehan Abeyratne**

I. Introduction

Constitutions of new and emerging democracies often enshrine the concept of human dignity in socioeconomic rights. By giving social entitlements the status of 'rights', these constitutions aim to satisfy basic material needs or wants of all citizens so that they may lead (at least) minimally dignified lives. The Indian Constitution does not include socioeconomic *rights*; it sets forth instead 'Directive Principles of State Policy' that direct state lawmakers to reduce inequality and promote greater socioeconomic justice. In theory, the judiciary should have no role in enforcing these principles. Article 37 of the Indian Constitution clearly states that directive principles 'shall not be enforceable by any court'. Moreover, the framers of the Constitution separated directive principles from justiciable rights in the Constitution's structure. While Part III of the Constitution enumerates 'fundamental rights' that the courts may enforce, Part IV lists the aspirational (and non-justiciable) 'Directive Principles'.

However, the Indian Supreme Court has gradually recognised various directive principles as justiciable rights. To overcome the plain meaning of the Constitution's text, the Court has interpreted the fundamental right to life under Article 21 to encompass a 'right to live with human dignity'. Under this capacious interpretation, the Court has identified, inter alia, rights to food, shelter, and education that enforces on behalf of citizens against the central and state governments.

While the Indian Supreme Court is often lauded in the academic literature for proactively protecting the human dignity of the poor and vulnerable, I will explore two objections to the Court's jurisprudence in this area. These objections are not substantive; they do not consider whether it is

---

* This chapter builds on my previous work in 'Socioeconomic Rights in the Indian Constitution: Toward a Broader Conception of Legitimacy' (2014) 39 *Brooklyn Journal of International Law* 1.

morally or politically desirable to confer constitutional status on socioeconomic rights. Rather, drawing from the work of Frank Michelman, they are focused on the proper workings of political and legal institutions in a constitutional democracy.[1]

The first objection, a 'democratic' objection, contends that constitutional socioeconomic rights excessively constrain representative democracy. Elected officials cannot properly deliberate and legislate on any issue involving resource allocation when the Supreme Court is policing their actions to ensure constitutional compliance. The second, 'contractarian', objection posits that constitutional legitimacy might be threatened if citizens cannot understand a Constitution's terms and agree to be governed by them. Because socioeconomic rights require positive action by the government, the extent to which the government 'complies' with these rights depends on an individual citizen's views of distributive justice. This sort of indeterminacy is potentially fatal for contractarian legitimacy.

I contend that only the second, 'contractarian' objection presents a serious threat in the Indian context. In particular, I argue that while the Indian Supreme Court has conferred greater dignity upon India's most vulnerable citizens, it has also undermined the legitimacy of the whole constitutional framework. Courts need to tread cautiously to avoid this contractarian difficulty, which goes beyond the standard separation of powers or judicial review-related concerns to the very core of what a constitution is supposed to do—to provide legitimacy to the system of government it constitutes.

I conclude by placing the Indian Supreme Court's socioeconomic rights jurisprudence in comparative perspective, juxtaposing it with the South African Constitutional Court's case law in this area and its own recent judgment upholding the constitutionality of an anti-sodomy law.[2] In *Koushal v Naz Foundation*, the Court dismissed dignity-based arguments put forth on behalf of the LGBT community, which showed how this law had been misused to discriminate against them. By recognising expansive rights that are not enumerated in the Constitution, while failing to protect core fundamental rights such as equality, privacy and non-discrimination in *Naz Foundation*, the Supreme Court has further damaged constitutional legitimacy.

---

1 See F I Michelman, 'The Constitution, Social Rights, and Liberal Political Justification' in D Barak-Erez and AM Gross (eds), *Exploring Social Rights: Between Theory and Practice* (Portland, Hart, 2007).
2 *Koushal v Naz Foundation*, Civil Appeal No. 10972 (2013) (India).

II. Socioeconomic Rights in India

The concept of human dignity—the notion that all human beings have an inherent worth grounded in their common humanity—lies at the heart of international human rights law.[3] It serves as the foundation of landmark human rights instruments, including the U.N. Charter and the Universal Declaration of Human Rights.[4] While there is debate over the meaning and scope of this concept,[5] it is evident that both international and domestic courts regularly invoke human dignity in their jurisprudence.[6] And though courts may vary in their interpretations such that there is no common understanding of what human dignity substantively requires, the concept may yet have some utility. As Christopher McCrudden argues, context-specific interpretations of human dignity play an important role in enabling local courts to domesticate international human rights norms.[7] Its breadth allows courts to craft judgments recognising a state's human rights obligations, while acknowledging, too, the peculiarities of the local context. In a similar vein, human dignity may serve as a means for courts to declare new rights or to extend the scope of existing rights.[8]

This is precisely what has transpired in India—the Supreme Court has relied on the concept of human dignity to substantially extend the scope of fundamental rights under the Indian Constitution. Over the past thirty years or so, it has expanded the right to life to bring within its ambit a much broader 'right to live with dignity'. I will briefly discuss the history leading up to this development before analysing the landmark cases that recognised socioeconomic rights as justiciable, fundamental rights.

---

3   See D Kretzmer and E Klein (eds), *The Concept of Human Dignity in Human Rights Discourse* (The Hague, Kluwer Law International, 2002).
4   Charter of the United Nations, 26 June 1945, 59 Stat 1031, UNTS 993, 3 Bevans 1153; Universal Declaration of Human Rights, GA Res 217A (III), UN Doc A/810 (1948).
5   See, eg, C O'Mahony, 'There Is No Such Thing as a Right to Dignity' (2012) 10 *International Journal of Constitutional Law* 551; EK White, 'There Is No Such Thing as a Right to Dignity: A Reply to Conor O'Mahony' (2012) 10 *International Journal of Constitutional Law* 575.
6   See C McCrudden, 'Human Dignity and Judicial Interpretation of Human Rights' (2008) 19 *European Journal of International Law* 655.
7   ibid 719 f.
8   ibid 721 f.

447

A. The Drafting of the Indian Constitution and Early Fundamental Rights Cases

Constitutions generally take one of two approaches to socioeconomic rights: the minimalist and the transformative. The minimalist approach is embodied in the U.S. Constitution. It is a concise document whose Bill of Rights seeks to preserve core civil and political liberties.[9] The U.S. Constitution does not, however, enumerate any socioeconomic rights and the U.S. Supreme Court has refrained from reading the Constitution to require the state to take positive measures in order to safeguard individual rights.[10] At the other end of the spectrum is the South African Constitution. It aims to be transformative by seeking not only to protect 'negative' rights (such as the freedom of speech) from government interference, but also to radically alter existing social conditions by establishing justiciable rights to food, shelter, and healthcare, among others.[11] The South African Constitutional Court is empowered to enforce these rights if the state does not take reasonable measures to fulfil them.

The American approach (arguably) views greater social justice as a desirable goal, but one that should be achieved gradually and through the legislative process, not through justiciable rights that would undemocratically hasten the process and limit legislative discretion. The South African view, by contrast, posits (1) that the state is obligated to affirmatively provide a minimum standard of living to its citizens and (2) that it is the province of the judiciary to ensure that the government complies with these obligations. By setting forth justiciable socioeconomic rights, South Africa's Constitution is more ambitious than the minimalist American Constitution. It seeks to hold the government accountable on questions of distributive justice to progressively realise greater substantive (as well as formal) equality.

There are drawbacks, however, to this transformative approach. The principal concern is that it involves the judiciary on complex issues of resource allocation, requiring courts to decide matters on which they arguably lack the expertise or the resources to make sound decisions. Put simply, the judiciary might not be institutionally capable to handle questions of

---

9   See Amendments 1–10, United States Constitution.
10   See *San Antonio Independent School District v Rodriguez*, 411 U.S. 1 (1973); *Dandridge v Williams*, 397 U.S. 471 (1970).
11   See ss 26–27, Constitution of the Republic of South Africa 1996.

socioeconomic justice. And even if courts are able to adjudicate on these difficult questions, they might be required to undertake fact-finding and consult policy experts, which triggers a separation of powers concern: the courts might transgress into the legislative domain. Thus, despite the noble intentions of the transformative approach, it risks giving the judiciary excessive authority at the expense of representative government.

In an effort to reconcile these contrasting approaches, the framers of the Indian Constitution took a middle path. India gained independence from the British in 1947 and adopted its republican Constitution in 1950 after more than two years of debate among members of its Constituent Assembly.[12] Following the Irish model, the framers did not include justiciable socioeconomic rights, but instead set forth a detailed list of directive principles: non-binding guidelines intended to guide the government towards improving socioeconomic conditions.[13] These principles are explicitly non-justiciable—Article 37 of the Constitution states that they 'shall not be enforceable by any court'. One of the reasons directive principles are non-justiciable is that they represent aspirational long-term goals of the state that are not suited for judicial review. For instance, Article 38 (2) declares, 'The State shall, in particular, strive to minimise the inequalities in income', while Article 39 (1) requires the state 'to direct its policy towards securing ... that the citizens, men and women equally, have the right to an adequate means of livelihood'.

The directive principles were placed in Part IV of the Indian Constitution. Part III, entitled 'Fundamental Rights', includes, inter alia, the rights to life, liberty, and equality that courts may enforce. This bifurcated approach between justiciable rights and non-justiciable directive principles arguably adopts the best elements of both the minimalist and transformative constitutional models. In the transformative vein, the Indian Constitution announces the importance of socioeconomic justice and guides political institutions in that direction. As Granville Austin noted, the Indian Constitution is 'first and foremost a social document', as many of its provisions are 'directly aimed at furthering the goals of the social revolution'.[14] However, to avoid concerns of judicial competence and separation of powers, the Constitution gives elected representatives the flexibility to

---

12 See generally G Austin, *The Indian Constitution: Cornerstone of a Nation* (New Delhi, Oxford University Press, 1996).
13 ibid 96 f.
14 ibid 63.

pursue these goals progressively and in light of resource constraints, without having the courts police them for constitutional compliance.

Early Indian Supreme Court jurisprudence reflected this fine balance. Article 32 of the Constitution empowers the Supreme Court to issue 'directions or orders or writs, including writs in the nature of *habeas corpus, mandamus, prohibition, quo warranto* and *certiorari*' to remedy fundamental rights violations. It permits citizens to move the Court via 'appropriate proceedings' to enforce their rights. While this phrase gives the Court some flexibility in deciding which petitions to accept, it was construed narrowly in the early years of the republic. For instance, *G.C. College Silchar v Gauhati University* (1973) involved a challenge to a resolution by Gauhati University's Academic Council to retain English and introduce the native language (Assamese) as the languages of instruction.[15] The university had previously used Bengali alongside English to help students understand the content of English-language lectures. The petitioners, including a Bengali-speaking student, claimed that this resolution violated their constitutional rights as minorities to enrol in any educational institution of their choice and to be free from state discrimination in academic admissions. However, the Supreme Court held that the resolution did not directly affect petitioners and that they therefore lacked standing to challenge its validity under Article 32.[16]

By taking a narrow view of standing, the Court initially adopted a limited role in India's constitutional scheme. This would change following the 1975 Emergency, as the Court liberalised its standing requirements and began to enforce the directive principles. It transformed itself into a more powerful judicial body and arguably into a significant policy-making institution too.

B. The Evolution of Articles 32 and 21—Broader Interpretations of Standing Doctrine and the Right to Life

In 1975, following her conviction in the Allahabad High Court for election fraud in the 1971 general elections, Prime Minister Indira Gandhi declared a state of emergency. Emergency Rule lasted almost two years and wit-

---

15 See *G.C. College Silchar v Gauhati University*, A.I.R. 1973 S.C. 761 1–4 (India).
16 ibid.

nessed severe fundamental rights violations as well as a series of constitutional amendments designed to weaken the judiciary.[17] The most controversial was the Forty-Second Amendment, which prohibited judicial review of the disputed 1971 election and overturned the landmark *Keshavananda Bharati* judgment, which held that the Court could find constitutional amendments unconstitutional if they violated the 'basic structure' of the Constitution.[18] The Forty-Second Amendment barred the Supreme Court from reviewing constitutional amendments, and required a two-third majority of Court benches to hold statutes unconstitutional.[19]

The Supreme Court failed to stand up to the Gandhi regime during the Emergency era. In *A.D.M. Jabalpur v Shiv Shukla* ('Habeas Corpus' Case), the Supreme Court was asked to issue writs of habeas corpus to remove petitioners, including politicians from opposing parties, from government detention.[20] They had been detained pursuant to the Maintenance of Internal Security Act (MISA), which enabled law enforcement agencies to undertake preventative detention as well as searches, seizures and arrests without warrants. A five-judge bench of the Supreme Court convened to hear their appeal. According to Granville Austin, the petitioners expected at least three of these justices, who had reputations for protecting civil liberties, to hold in their favour.[21] However, by a 4–1 majority, the Court dismissed the petitioners' claims and essentially held that the President could deny political detainees access to the courts during periods of emergency rule.[22] The Court in this case had the opportunity to limit the excesses of the Emergency era and provide relief to victims of arbitrary detention, but failed to do so.

The Emergency era ended in March 1977 after Prime Minister Gandhi called for elections and was defeated by the opposition Janata Party. The new government quickly rescinded the controversial constitutional amendments passed by Mrs. Gandhi's regime, and also repealed the

---

17 G Austin, *Working a Democratic Constitution: A History of the Indian Experience* (New Delhi, Oxford University Press, 1999) 309–13.
18 See *Keshavananda Bharati v State of Kerala*, A.I.R. 1973 S.C. 1461 (India).
19 M Mate, 'The Origins of Due Process in India: The Role of Borrowing in Personal Liberty and Preventative Detention Cases' (2010) 28 *Berkeley Journal of International Law* 216, 243.
20 *A.D.M. Jabalpur v Shiv Kant Shukla*, A.I.R. 1976 S.C. 1207.
21 Austin, *Working a Democratic Constitution* (1999) 338.
22 *A.D.M. Jabalpur v Shiv Kant Shukla*, A.I.R. 1976 S.C. 1207.

Emergency Rule-era laws that, inter alia, suspended habeas corpus.[23] It was therefore public pressure and the political institutions—not the judiciary—that restored democracy and fundamental rights in India. Nevertheless, and perhaps chastened by their capitulation during the Emergency, a few Supreme Court judges revolutionised the Court's procedural and substantive approach to fundamental rights in the early 1980s.[24]

The Court became much more accessible to the public and began to accept cases that concerned the rights of large swathes of the Indian population. The procedural innovations it adopted in this period created a new form of litigation commonly referred to as 'public interest litigation' (PIL).[25] The Court's most significant innovation was to relax standing requirements under Article 32. Moving away from the traditional notion of standing—where petitioners had to show that they were directly harmed by an impugned law—the Court began to recognise standing for any member of the public who moved the court for relief on behalf of any 'person or determinate class of persons is by reason of poverty, helplessness or disability or socially or economically disadvantaged position, unable to approach the Court for relief'.[26]

The chief architect of this procedural revolution was Justice P.N. Bhagwati—one of the justices who joined the Court's timorous majority opinion in the Habeas Corpus case. In a 1984 speech delivered at Columbia Law School, Justice Bhagwati set out his views on standing, making the case that procedural formalism inherited from Anglo-American jurisprudence did not suit the Indian context.[27] He said,

> the main obstacle which deprived the poor and disadvantaged of effective access to justice was the traditional rule of standing ... it effectively barred the doors of the Court ... to large masses of people.[28]

---

23   Mate, 'The Origins of Due Process in India' 244.
24   See U Baxi, 'Taking Suffering Seriously: Social Action Litigation in the Supreme Court of India' (1985) 4 *Third World Legal Studies* 107, 113–16; R Dhavan, 'Law as Struggle: Public Interest Law in India' (1994) 36 *Journal of the Indian Law Institute* 302, 306.
25   See generally PP Craig and SL Deshpande, 'Rights, Autonomy and Process: Public Interest Litigation in India' (1989) 9 *Oxford Journal of Legal Studies* 356, 357.
26   *SP Gupta v Union of India*, A.I.R. 1982 S.C. 149 at 17.
27   PN Bhagwati, 'Judicial Activism and Public Interest Litigation' (1984–85) 23 *Columbia Journal of Transnational Law* 561.
28   ibid 570 f.

In response to criticism of the Court's 'judicial activism', Justice Bhagwati argued that it was very much the province of the judiciary to develop new remedies to tackle difficult social problems. In his words, 'unorthodox and unconventional remedies' were needed to 'initiative affirmative action on the part of the state' to 'ensure distributive justice to the deprived sections of the community'.[29]

The case that best illustrates the Court's willingness to experiment with new remedies is *Bandhua Mukti Morcha v Union of India*.[30] Here, a three-judge Supreme Court bench, led by Justice Bhagwati, initiated a PIL in response to a letter they received from an NGO urging the Court to end the practice of bonded labour. Rather than simply issue a judgment declaring bonded labour unconstitutional, the Court adopted a doctrine known as 'continuing mandamus', which permitted it to postpone its final judgment so that it may periodically issue guidelines and interim orders to ensure that the government complies with the relevant constitutional provisions.[31] In addition, the Court appointed two advocates and a doctor as 'special commissioners' to investigate the living and working conditions of bonded labourers, and report their findings to the Court.[32] All told, the Court in this case not only relaxed its standing requirements to allow an NGO to file a writ petition on behalf of bonded labourers, but also expanded the scope of its authority to conduct its own fact-finding and to keep the litigation open so as to monitor compliance with its orders.

This period also saw the Court expanding its substantive jurisdiction. Most notably, it began to enforce the Directive Principles of State Policy by reading them into the fundamental right to life enshrined in Article 21 of the Indian Constitution. Recall that Article 37 explicitly states that directive principles 'shall not be enforceable by any court'. However, given the proclivity of Justice Bhagwati and a few other justices on the Supreme Court to devise new and creative remedies, Article 37 was sidestepped in the larger cause of promoting greater human dignity and distributive justice. In *Francis Coralie Mullin v Union Territory of Delhi* (1981), the Supreme Court was asked to rule on a narrow question: whether a detainee held in preventative detention had the right to meet with his lawyer and

---

29   ibid 575 f.
30   *Bandhua Mukti Morcha v Union of India*, 1984 S.C.R. (2) 67.
31   M Mate, 'Two Paths to Judicial Power: The Basic Structure Doctrine and Public Interest Litigation in Comparative Perspective' (2010) 12 *San Diego Journal of International Law* 175, 196–200.
32   Craig and Deshpande, 'Rights, Autonomy and Process' 362 f.

family.[33] However, Justice Bhagwati took this as an opportunity to substantially enlarge the ambit of Article 21, which provides that 'No person shall be deprived of his life or personal liberty except according to procedure established by law'.

Writing for the Court, Justice Bhagwati declared that this right to life and personal liberty protects a broader right to 'live with human dignity'.[34] He went on to state, 'Article 21 cannot be restricted to mere animal existence'.[35] Rather,

> it must ... include the right to the basic necessities of life and also the right to carry on such functions and activities as constitute the bare minimum expression of the human self.[36]

The Court has since built on this judgment to enforce a number of new socioeconomic rights within the 'right to live with human dignity'. These include the rights to education, food, healthcare, shelter, and a decent livelihood.[37]

In at least three respects, the Court enjoys greater scope for judicial review than it did when the Constitution was adopted in 1950. First, by easing its standing requirements, the Court has become more accessible to the Indian public. NGOs and other concerned citizens now regularly petition the Court for redress of fundamental rights violations on behalf of large affected communities. Second, through a broad reading of the right to life under Article 21, the Court now recognises and enforces a range of socioeconomic rights that were originally thought to be non-justiciable. Third, by keeping cases open and inventing novel remedies in cases dealing with socioeconomic justice, the Court now acts like a quasi-legislature by actively monitoring government compliance with its orders. All told, the Indian Supreme Court today is a significant policymaking institution.

While much has been written on the practical effects of the Indian Supreme Court's jurisprudence in this area, I look at two objections to constitutional socioeconomic rights that are not substantive in nature, but fo-

---

33 *Francis Coralie Mullin v Union Territory of Delhi*, A.I.R. 1981 S.C. 746 (India).
34 ibid 518.
35 ibid 528 f.
36 ibid.
37 See *Unni Krishnan v State of AP*, (1993) 1 S.C.R. 594 (India); *PUCL v Union of India*, Writ Petition (Civil) No. 196 (2001) (India); *Paschim Banga Khet Mazdoor Samity v State of WB*, (1996) 4 S.C.C. 37 (India); *Olga Tellis v Bombay Municipal Corporation*, (1985) 2 S.C.R. Supp. 51 (India).

cus instead on how political and legal institutions should function under a democratic constitutional scheme. These objections are drawn from the work of Frank Michelman; the first will be familiar, the second perhaps less so.

III. The Democratic Objection

The first objection, a 'democratic' objection, is concerned with the effects of socioeconomic rights on representative democracy.[38] Imagine a constitution that establishes a number of socioeconomic rights. In the country that it governs, every citizen is entitled to a minimal food ration, basic accommodation, and access to healthcare. Now imagine that this country is ravaged by a natural disaster—an earthquake, perhaps a hurricane—that requires substantial resources to rescue victims and to rebuild damaged property. However, the state's budget is devoted entirely to ensuring that socioeconomic rights are upheld. The state's legislators, despite their best intentions, are hamstrung by the Constitution and cannot allocate adequate resources to address the devastation caused by this natural disaster.

This illustrates the democratic objection with regard to constitutionalised socioeconomic rights. The fear is that elected officials cannot properly deliberate and legislate on any issue involving resource allocation if the Constitution requires substantial resources to be provided to certain schemes. Put differently, the democratic objector might say that placing socioeconomic rights in a constitution removes so many issues from the legislative agenda that politics becomes, in a certain sense, undemocratic. As Michelman points out, the strength of this objection relies, in part, on how broadly these rights are couched.[39] If a constitution sets forth a comprehensive right to 'social citizenship', ensuring that any citizen 'can make a respectable living through forms of social participation that are themselves a source and support of satisfaction, energy, pride and social respect', this objection becomes quite strong.[40] In this society, Michelman argues, there is potentially no issue of public policy on which legislative

---

38 See Michelman, 'The Constitution, Social Rights, and Liberal Political Justification' 31–35.
39 ibid 24.
40 ibid 31; WE Forbath, 'Constitutional Welfare Rights: A History, Critique and Reconstruction' (2001) 69 *Fordham Law Review* 1821.

deliberation is not limited by the constitution—every policy debate from international trade, to taxes, to public education would be constrained.[41]

It is important to note also that this objection does not depend on the standard conception of separation of powers—where the legislature simply passes laws and the courts are the only (or at least most prominent) institution concerned with the constitutionality of those laws—to retain its force. Even if courts have no scope for judicial review, a constitution that enumerates socioeconomic rights would still place serious limits on democratic deliberation and decision-making as long as legislators and other government officials take constitutional rights seriously in their drafting and enforcement of laws.

Of course, in practice, many constitutional democracies rely on the judiciary, particularly the Supreme Court, to be the final word on matters of constitutional interpretation. This is certainly true in India, where a strong democratic objection can be levelled against the Indian Supreme Court following the dramatic increase in its fundamental rights jurisdiction since the 1980s. The Court today engages in 'something strikingly close to lawmaking',[42] enforcing broad constitutional rights in a way that substantially constrains legislative and executive decision-making.

The ongoing 'Right to Food' litigation in the Indian Supreme Court illustrates this nicely.[43] It began in 2001 as a writ petition alleging that six Indian states failed to provide adequate food to some of their poorest citizens after a famine. Under its new, relaxed standing requirements, the Court allowed an NGO to file for relief under Article 32 of the Indian Constitution on behalf of the famine victims. Relying on *Francis Coralie*, which established that Article 21 protected a right 'to live with human dignity', the petition alleged that the Government of India, the Food Corporation of India (FCI) and six state governments had violated the right to life of millions of Indian citizens under Article 21.[44] Since adequate food is a necessary condition to sustain life, petitioners contended that the state had an affirmative duty to provide and distribute food to citizens affected by the drought. These state actors, according to petitioners, had failed to

---

41 Michelman, 'The Constitution, Social Rights, and Liberal Political Justification' 32 f.
42 L Birchfield and J Corsi, 'Between Starvation and Globalization: Realizing the Right to Food in India' (2010) 31 *Michigan Journal of International Law* 691, 700.
43 See *PUCL v Union of India*, Writ Petition (Civil) No. 196 (2001) (India).
44 ibid.

provide adequate food supplies and employment to the affected population, which they were required to do under the Famine Code of 1962.[45]

On 28 November 2001, the Supreme Court issued an interim order that once again expanded the scope of the right to life and recognised certain food schemes as legal entitlements under Article 21.[46] However, the Court did not end its inquiry there. Much like in *Bandhua Mukti Morcha*, it exercised 'continuing mandamus', keeping the litigation open to retain some oversight on food policy and government compliance going forward.

In 2017, sixteen years after it began, this case was finally closed. Over this period, the litigation expanded to include all twenty-eight Indian states as respondents. The Court issued more than fifty interim orders requiring state governments to implement policies on a range of matters, some of which are only tangentially related to food distribution. For instance, the Court issued guidelines directing governments to act on urban poverty, the right to employment, and general issues of government accountability and transparency.[47] More troublingly from the perspective of the democratic objection, the Court instructed central and state governments on how to implement particular food schemes. Some of these orders resemble legislative statutes more than court judgments. For instance, on the question of how food licenses to the poor should be regulated, the Court instructed state authorities as follows:

> (1) Licensees, who (a) do not keep their shops open throughout the month during the stipulated period, (b) fail to provide grain to BPL families strictly at BPL rates and no higher, (c) keep the cards of BPL households with them, (d) make false entries in the BPL cards, (e) engage in black-marketing or siphoning away of grains to the open market and hand over such ration shops to such other person/organizations, shall make themselves liable for cancellation of their licenses. The concerned authorities/functionaries would not show any laxity on the subject.[48]

This kind of judicial intervention clearly constrains representative decision-making to an extent unimaginable in many constitutional democracies. On what is essentially a policy question—how to distribute licens-

---

45 ibid.
46 See *PUCL v Union of India*, Writ Petition (Civil) No. 196 (2001) (India) (28 November 2001 interim order).
47 'Supreme Court Orders on the Right to Food: A Tool for Action' 3–7 (2005), www.righttofoodindia.org/orders/interimorders.html.
48 *PUCL v Union of India*, Writ Petition (Civil) No. 196 (2001) (India) (2 May 2003 interim order).

es—the Court did not simply rule on the constitutionality of an existing state program, but formulated its own quasi-legislative solution, which it then forced upon state governments. A strong democratic objection clearly arises here.

However, given India's history and political context, the democratic objection is not convincing. Historically, elected officials in India have failed to make any meaningful progress towards improving the lot of its poorest citizens since the Constitution was adopted in 1950.[49] This failure is widely attributed to rampant corruption at all levels of government.[50] In this light, the Supreme Court's broad powers of judicial review and monitoring might be justified since it is one of the few Indian public institutions that has shown the will and capacity to improve social and economic conditions.

Moreover, as David Landau has pointed out, the notion of a legislative space that is out of the judiciary's reach is derived from institutional assumptions—such as a legislature that takes constitutional rights seriously and responds to popular will—that often do not apply in the developing world, including in India.[51] Given India's institutional context—where the elected branches of government are corrupt and dysfunctional—the Indian Supreme Court arguably must step in to ensure that even basic governance and respect for human dignity is maintained. So much, then, for the democratic objection.

IV. The Contractarian Objection

The second, 'contractarian', objection arises out of John Rawls's liberal principle of legitimacy, which holds that political power is justified only when exercised in accordance with a constitution 'the essentials of which all citizens, as reasonable and rational, can endorse in light of their com-

---

49   See J Drèze, 'Democracy and the Right to Food' (2004) 39 *Economic and Political Weekly* 1723.
50   See C Raj Kumar, *Corruption and Human Rights in India* (Delhi, Oxford University Press, 2011) 2 f.
51   See D Landau, 'Political Institutions and Judicial Role in Comparative Constitutional Law' (2010) 51 *Harvard International Law Journal* 319.

mon human reason'.⁵² This legitimacy, therefore depends on whether citizens can understand a constitution's terms; they cannot assent to be governed under a constitution that is too vague or obtuse.

Rawls articulated two principles of justice, setting forth basic rights and regulating socioeconomic inequalities in a just society. The first principle of justice requires that certain fundamental rights and liberties, including free expression, the right to vote, and the provision of a 'social minimum',⁵³ be granted equally to all citizens.⁵⁴ This principle, according to Rawls, is 'constitutionally essential', meaning that any society purporting to comply with the liberal principle of legitimacy must have these rights enshrined in its constitution or basic law.

The second principle of justice states,

> Social and economic inequalities are to satisfy two conditions: first, they are to be attached to offices and positions open to all under conditions of fair equality of opportunity; and second, they are to be to the greatest benefit of the least advantaged members of society.⁵⁵

This principle, unlike the first, is not constitutionally essential. Rawls only requires a 'social minimum'—but not a comprehensive set of socioeconomic rights—to be constitutionally protected. Distributive justice is to be handled by the legislature after a constitution, containing the essentials of the first principle, is already in place. Rawls noted that it is easier to gain consensus on the constitutional essentials, whereas matters of socioeconomic justice are 'always open to reasonable differences of opinion' and depend on 'inference and judgment in assessing complex social and economic information'.⁵⁶ This suggests that Rawls, quite presciently, anticipated difficulties with the interpretation and application of constitutional socioeconomic rights.

Still, Rawls requires that questions of socioeconomic justice are discussed and decided under the 'constraint of public reason'.⁵⁷ This con-

---

52 See J Rawls, *Justice as Fairness: A Restatement* (Cambridge, Belknap Press, 2001) 40 f.; id, *Political Liberalism* (New York, Columbia University Press, 1993) 217.
53 By 'social minimum', Rawls means that the state must provide basic material needs to its citizens to the extent required for them to take effective part in political and social life. See Rawls, *Political Liberalism* (1993) 228 f.
54 Rawls, *Justice as Fairness* (2001) 44.
55 ibid 42 f.
56 ibid 48.
57 Rawls, *Political Liberalism* (1993) 224–28.

straint applies to deliberations over questions of constitutional essentials and basic justice, which includes questions of distributive justice and resource allocation. It requires citizens to present publicly acceptable reasons to each other for their political views.[58] Citizens must also be willing to 'listen to others' and display 'fair-mindedness in deciding when accommodations to their views should reasonably be made'.[59] Public reason applies to citizens, elected representatives, and judges. But the Supreme Court plays a particularly important role here. For Rawls, the Supreme Court is the 'exemplar of public reason'.[60] While citizens and their elected representatives engage with a range of political questions that do not fall under the constraint of public reason, the Supreme Court, in interpreting the Constitution, may only justify and explain its decisions using public reason. In particular, they must fit their judgments into 'a coherent constitutional view over the whole range of their decisions'.[61]

The reason the Supreme Court is held to this higher standard can be traced back to the liberal principle of legitimacy. Recall that this principle requires citizens to be able to understand their constitution so that they can assent to be governed by its terms. If they cannot understand its terms, then the constitution—and the government it establishes—loses legitimacy. Since the Court has the final word on constitutional meaning, it must clearly and cogently explain its decisions in the language of public reason. The legitimacy of the constitution is threatened if it does not do so, since poorly reasoned or articulated Supreme Court judgments may render the constitutional provisions at issue in those judgments inscrutable to ordinary citizens.

How does this contractarian objection apply to socioeconomic rights in India? As discussed, the Indian Supreme Court has somewhat altered the original constitutional structure by reading the directive principles into Article 21's guarantee of the right to life. Article 37 of the Indian Constitution specifically makes these principles non-justiciable, intending them to guide legislators towards ensuring greater socioeconomic justice without the threat of litigation and judicial policing looming over their decisions.

As a matter of constitutional interpretation, clear textual commands cannot be ignored or contravened. Every major theory of constitutional

---

58   See Rawls, *Justice as Fairness* (2001) 90.
59   See Rawls, *Political Liberalism (1993)* 217.
60   ibid 216, 235.
61   ibid 235.

law accepts this basic tenet.[62] Thus, if courts decide to circumvent the plain meaning of the constitution's text, the demands of public reason are raised to a higher—if not extraordinary—level. At the very least, courts must justify their deviations from the plain meaning of constitutional text with well-reasoned and clearly explained judgments. If they do not, then citizens will not be able to understand, much less agree to be governed by, their constitution.

In the Indian context, however, the Supreme Court has not met this high burden. The *Francis Coralie* judgment that established a right to 'live with human dignity' does not even mention Article 37, much less explain how the Court got past its plain meaning to make socioeconomic rights justiciable.[63] In *Bandhua Mukti Morcha*, Justice Bhagwati's majority opinion gives some hints as to the Court's reasoning, but is still unsatisfactory under the high standard demanded by public reason and the contractarian objection. In this case, Justice Bhagwati acknowledged that directive principles 'are not enforceable in a court of law'.[64] He also conceded that the Court cannot compel the government to pass laws or executive orders to further socioeconomic justice. However, he argued that if the state has already passed legislation impacting socioeconomic justice, state actors

> can certainly be obligated to ensure observance of such legislation for inaction on the part of the State in securing implementation of such legislation would amount to denial of the right to live with human dignity enshrined in Article 21.[65]

This is a false distinction, as Article 37 does not merely prevent courts from compelling the state to pass certain laws. Rather, it unambiguously prohibits the enforcement of directive principles, regardless of whether or not the state has implemented legislation concerning socioeconomic justice.

Moreover, even if the Court is permitted to review existing laws affecting socioeconomic policy, it has never clearly set out the standard to

---

62   See, eg, D Strauss, *The Living Constitution* (Oxford, Oxford University Press, 2010) 7 ('Many provisions ... are quite precise and leave no room for quarreling, or for fancy questions about interpretation.').
63   See *Francis Coralie Mullin v Union Territory of Delhi*, A.I.R. 1981 S.C. 746 (India).
64   *Bandhua Mukti Morcha v Union of India*, A.I.R. 1984 S.C. 802 (India).
65   ibid.

which the government is held.⁶⁶ Does the Court rely on a test of proportionality? Reasonableness? Strict scrutiny? No one can say with any certainty. This indeterminacy poses a serious contractarian objection. But it is not just the standard of review that is problematic in this regard—the scope of the right to 'live with human dignity' is also indeterminate.

In the cases thus far discussed, the Court has relied on provisions in the directive principles to flesh out the contours of Article 21. For instance, Article 47 directs the state to 'regard the raising of the level of nutrition' as a 'primary duty', which gives some justification for finding that the right to food constitutes part of the right to 'live with human dignity'.

However, the Court has moved beyond the directive principles to enforce rights that do not appear at all in the Constitution. In a recent case, a group of protestors was given permission to conduct a hunger strike in a public space.⁶⁷ However, the size of the protest group swelled to such an extent that the state withdrew permission and police were dispatched to break up the protest and detain its leaders. The police arrived late at night, waking several of the protestors who were camped out at the site.

The Supreme Court did not wait for a case to be filed—it stepped in *suo motu*. It then held that the 'right to sleep' falls within the ambit of Article 21 and was violated in this case. According to the Court, since sleep is essential 'to maintain the delicate balance of health necessary for ... [human] existence and survival' and without it 'the existence of life itself would be in peril', the right of protestors to sleep had to be protected.⁶⁸

The Court could have resolved this case on narrower and less controversial grounds. The facts indicate that enumerated fundamental rights—such as the freedom of assembly—were violated, but the Court went out of its way to announce a new right. More troublingly, it set a precedent for expanding the scope of the right to 'live with human dignity' without any direct reference to the constitutional text.

The scope of the right to 'live with human dignity' is nebulous and potentially limitless under Indian Constitutional law today. As a result, the contractarian problem is magnified: Indian citizens cannot know with any

---

66   See ibid. See also PB Mehta, 'The Rise of Judicial Sovereignty' (2007) 18 *Journal of Democracy* 70, 74 ('The Court has helped itself to so much power ... without explaining from whence its own authority is supposed to come.').
67   See *In Re Ramlila Maidan Incident Dt. 4/5.06.2011 v Home Secretary, Union of India*, 2012 STPL (Web) 124 S.C. (India).
68   ibid.

clarity or conviction which rights are protected under Article 21. This threatens the legitimacy of India's entire constitutional scheme.

V. India's Socioeconomic Rights Cases in Comparative Perspective

In sum, contractarians have two specific concerns regarding the Indian Supreme Court's case law in the realm of socioeconomic justice: (1) that the Court does not articulate a standard of review and (2) that it has failed to stipulate a limiting principle (or even rough guideposts) to define the contours of the right to 'live with human dignity', rendering this right indeterminate and inscrutable to Indian citizens. To further illustrate both these aspects, it may be useful to place India's socioeconomic rights jurisprudence in broader, comparative perspective.

With respect to standard of review, the South African approach is instructive. Structurally, the South African Constitution differs from India's in two significant ways with regard to socioeconomic justice. First, it includes justiciable socioeconomic *rights*, not merely directive principles. Section 26, for instance, states 'everyone has the right to have access to adequate housing' and Section 27 grants universal access to healthcare, food, water, and social security. Second, it clearly sets forth the standard of review for the Constitutional Court to follow. Both Sections 26 and 27 require the state to take 'reasonable legislative and other measures, within its available resources to achieve the progressive realisation' of these rights. Thus, the Constitutional Court may only strike down government laws or policies on these issues if they are not reasonable in light of resource constraints.

In *Minister of Public Works v Kyalami Ridge Association*,[69] residents of the Kyalami neighbourhood near Johannesburg asked the Minister of Public Works to suspend operations on a transit camp that was being constructed in their vicinity to house flood victims from a nearby area. When the Minister denied their request, the residents filed suit requesting an interdict on this project. They argued that it was *ultra vires*, as it lacked Parliamentary authorization. The Constitutional Court agreed with the residents that South African law requires an Act from Parliament to commence housing works, but nonetheless denied them relief. Relying on its

---

69 *Minister of Public Works v Kyalami Ridge Association* (2001) (7) BCLR 652 (CC).

precedent in *Government of the Republic of South Africa v Grootboom*,[70] which required the government to have resources available to assist victims of natural disasters and other short-term crises, and the reasonableness standard in Section 26 of the Constitution, the Court held that that the government's actions were lawful in the circumstances. In *Grootboom*, the Court had also rejected government-housing measures under Section 26 and ordered the government to submit revised plans for judicial review.[71]

What is significant in both cases is how the Constitutional Court respected its limited jurisdiction. In the first case, it upheld a government scheme that initially appeared unlawful, recognising the state's obligations to provide housing relief under Section 26. In the second case, the Court found that government measures did not meet the standard of reasonableness required by the South African Constitution, but unlike its Indian counterpart, it did not fashion its own remedy. Rather, the Court allowed the government to develop new plans in light of its judgment. No contractarian objection arises here—the South African Constitutional Court is bound by a clear standard of review, to which it respectfully adheres.

With regard to the scope of the right to 'live with human dignity', some commentators have praised the Indian Supreme Court for stepping in to alleviate chronic poverty and inequality where the elected branches have failed. The Court, on this view, has perhaps enhanced the Constitution's legitimacy by giving real effect to its aspirational goals. As Vijayashri Sripati put it,

> If Article 21 has become a living reality for some deprived citizens, it is largely because of the expansive manner in which the Supreme Court has interpreted the clause. The result has been a profound revolution—for social justice—ever achieved by essentially peaceful means.[72]

Sripati acknowledges that the Supreme Court is not the only institution in India concerned with protecting rights, but nonetheless stresses the importance of robust participation by the Court in the task of translating the Constitution's promise into meaningful action … it is … a crucial agency, sometimes perhaps—in the light of a corrupt and an errant executive, an

---

70   *Government of the Republic of South Africa v Grootboom*, 2001 (1) SA 46 (CC).
71   ibid.
72   V Sripati, 'Human Rights in India Fifty Years After Independence' (1997) 26 *Denver Journal of International Law and Policy* 93, 118.

irresponsible Parliament—a virtually indispensable one for the protection of human rights in India.[73]

This sort of consequentialist argument, of course, does not address the process-based concerns set forth in the contractarian objection. But, if for the sake of argument, we adopt this alternative conception of legitimacy, does the Indian Supreme Court fare any better? For the Court to uphold constitutional legitimacy under this paradigm, its jurisprudence would have to consistently promote and rule in favour of greater human dignity in different contexts. As discussed, the Indian Supreme Court has been very open to dignitarian arguments in the realm of socioeconomic rights, even recognising a broad right to 'live with human dignity'. However, the Court has been less receptive to dignity-based claims in the civil rights context. Its recent judgment in *Koushal v Naz Foundation* makes plain this inconsistency.

Naz Foundation concerned the constitutionality of Section 377 of the Indian Penal Code, which criminalises 'carnal intercourse against the order of nature'.[74] The case was initially filed before the Delhi High Court, which found that Section 377 not only compromised HIV/AIDS prevention and treatment, but also damaged the self-esteem and dignity of gay men and other sexual minorities.[75] By criminalising private sexual acts that caused no injury, the Court found that Section 377 was motivated not by any legitimate state purpose, but by animus, and targeted the LGBT community as a class.[76] It was therefore held that Section 377 violated the right to equality under Article 14 and the right against discrimination under Article 15.[77]

However, the Supreme Court reversed the High Court, holding that Section 377 had not violated any fundamental rights of the LGBT community.[78] It relied on the conservative doctrine of judicial restraint, stressing repeatedly that laws enacted Parliament are entitled to strong defer-

---

73 ibid 135 f.
74 *Koushal v Naz Foundation.*
75 *Naz Found. v Gov't of NCT of New Delhi*, WP(C) No.7455/2001, 61–64 (H.C. New Del., 2009).
76 See ibid 91–94; R Abeyratne and N Sinha, 'Insular and Inconsistent: India's Naz Foundation Judgment in Comparative Perspective' (2014) 39 *Yale Journal of International Law Online* 74.
77 *Naz Found. v Gov't of NCT of New Delhi* (n 75) 126.
78 *Koushal v Naz Foundation* 54.

ence and a presumption of constitutionality.[79] This deference seems disingenuous at best in light of the Court's utter lack of deference to other branches of government in its socioeconomic rights cases. It is difficult to square the Court's strong interventionist stance on behalf of those claiming violations of non-justiciable directive principles with its passive retreat in the face of clear violations of justiciable fundamental rights enshrined in Articles 14 and 15.

If human dignity underlies the Court's socioeconomic rights jurisprudence, then it should apply to the rights of sexual minorities as well. The apex courts of other constitutional democracies have relied, at least in part, on dignity-based arguments to rule in favour of the rights of sexual minorities.[80] *Naz Foundation* stands in sharp contrast to judgments from the United States and South Africa that have recognised broad rights for same-sex couples and other sexual minorities, often relying on the concept of human dignity to strike down laws that discriminate on the basis of sexual orientation.[81]

In my view, the Indian Supreme Court's approaches to socioeconomic rights and LGBT rights are irreconcilable. One cannot maintain that the Court's embrace of human dignity in the socioeconomic rights context furthers constitutional legitimacy if it is unreceptive to equally, if not more, compelling dignitarian claims in the context of LGBT rights. The Court's socioeconomic jurisprudence therefore cannot be justified on the grounds that it lends the Constitution legitimacy by championing human dignity. To the contrary, its inconsistency on dignity-based questions casts more doubt on constitutional legitimacy.

VI. Conclusion

This chapter has sought to examine the concept of human dignity in Indian constitutional law, with a focus on socioeconomic rights. It set forth two

---

79 ibid 26 ff.
80 See RB Siegel, 'Dignity and Sexuality: Claims on Dignity in Transnational Debates Over Abortion and Same-Sex Marriage' (2012) 10 *International Journal of Constitutional Law* 335, 374 f.
81 See, eg, *Lawrence v Texas*, 539 U.S. 558 (2003); *United States v Windsor*, 133 S. Ct. 2675 (2013); *National Coalition for Gay and Lesbian Equality v Minister of Justice*, 1999 (1) SA 6 (CC); *Minister of Home Affairs v Fourie*, 2006 (1) SA 524 (CC).

non-substantive objections to the Indian Supreme Court's jurisprudence in this area: a democratic objection and a contractarian objection. While the first objection can arguably be overcome in light of India's history and political dysfunction, the second objection is more problematic. Two aspects stand out: (1) the Court has located and enforced socioeconomic rights in the Indian Constitution using the explicitly non-justiciable directive principles and, in some cases, has declared new rights that do not even appear in the directive principles (like the right to sleep); and (2), the Court has not established a standard of review in these cases to judge the constitutionality of socioeconomic schemes. As a result, Indian citizens cannot know with any clarity or certainty how the Court might rule in future cases on socioeconomic rights. This seriously threatens the Constitution's legitimacy. This threat is exacerbated by the inconsistency in the Court's fundamental rights jurisprudence, where, as in the recent *Naz Foundation* judgment, it trumpets the importance of judicial restraint and the presumption of constitutionality in response to *prima facie* violations of core fundamental rights.

To be sure, the contractarian objection does not inevitably arise in the enforcement of socioeconomic rights. It can be mitigated, even avoided completely, by careful and circumscribed judicial decision-making in this area. Imagine that the Indian Supreme Court clearly explained which directive principles can be read into the right to 'live with human dignity' and defined the scope of this right. Imagine also that the Court limited itself to adjudicating only the reasonableness of government schemes, much like the South African Constitutional Court. In this scenario, the threat to legitimacy would be minimal, as judicial decisions would be more predictable, transparent, and consistent with India's constitutional structure.

The Dignity of the Individual in Irish Constitutional Law

Conor O'Mahony

I. Introduction

Although its precise normative content is famously elusive, the role that is played by the principle of human dignity in international human rights law is relatively clear: it is consistently stated to be the principle from which the human rights of the individual derive. However, in the realm of national constitutional law, the principle can sometimes be used in a rather more haphazard fashion, such that it can be difficult to pin down even its role in the constitutional order, not to mention its normative content. Ireland is a case in point. The Irish Constitution of 1937 was one of the earliest to invoke human dignity as a foundational principle, but case law interpreting and applying that principle has cast dignity in a variety of roles, and as a result has failed to develop in a coherent fashion. This paper will examine the various guises in which human dignity has appeared in Irish constitutional case law,[1] and consider which examples demonstrate the added value that human dignity can bring to constitutional adjudication. The analysis that follows is primarily a legal analysis, and is concerned with the nature of dignity as a legal or constitutional principle, particularly in Irish constitutional law. A detailed engagement with broader philosophical debates is outside the scope of this discussion.

---

[1] Case law from 2002 onwards (ie any of the cases cited using an IEHC or IESC reference) discussed in this paper is freely available online at www.courts.ie or www.bailii.org. Selected decisions from pre-2002 can be accessed at www.bailii.org or www.supremecourt.ie.

II. Human Dignity as a Foundational Principle

A. Dignity in International and Domestic Legal Orders

In international human rights law, the normative justification that is almost invariably given for the protection of human rights is the inherent dignity of all human beings.[2] In domestic law, human dignity plays a key role in the constitutional documents of a wide array of Western States. It has been expressly invoked as a foundational principle in the constitutional documents of at least 14 European countries,[3] as well as others such as South Africa.[4] Dignity has even been afforded a central role in the constitutional law of States that do not expressly give it constitutional recognition, such as in the US,[5] the UK,[6] France,[7] Israel[8] and Canada.[9] I have argued else-

---

[2] The Preambles to the Universal Declaration of Human Rights (UDHR), the International Covenant on Civil and Political Rights (ICCPR), the International Covenant on Economic, Social and Cultural Rights (ICESCR) and the UN Convention on the Rights of the Child (UNCRC) all refer to '... the inherent dignity ... of all members of the human family [as] the foundation of freedom, justice and peace in the world ...'. The Preambles to the ICCPR, ICESCR and UN Convention against Torture state that the 'equal and inalienable rights of all members of the human family ... derive from the inherent dignity of the human person'. Similarly, the Vienna Declaration, World Conference on Human Rights, A/CONF 157/23, 25 June 1993 stated in its Preamble that 'all human rights derive from the dignity and worth inherent in the human person'. See generally D Kretzmer & E Klein (eds), *The Concept of Human Dignity in Human Rights Discourse* (The Hague, Kluwer, 2002); C McCrudden, 'Human Dignity and Judicial Interpretation of Human Rights' (2008) 19 *European Journal of International Law* 655; C O'Mahony, 'There is No Such Thing as a Right to Dignity' (2012) 10 *International Journal of Constitutional Law* 551, and M Neal, 'Respect for Human Dignity as "Substantive Basic Norm"' (2014) 10 *International Journal of Law in Context* 26.

[3] These jurisdictions include Belgium, the Czech Republic, Estonia, Finland, Greece, Hungary, Ireland, Lithuania, Poland, Portugal, the Slovak Republic, Slovenia, Spain and Sweden. See C Dupré, 'Human Dignity and the Withdrawal of Medical Treatment: A Missed Opportunity' (2006) 6 *European Human Rights Law Review* 678, 687n.

[4] Arts 1(a), 10 and 39(1)(a). See I Kroeze, 'Human Dignity in Constitutional Law in South Africa' in *The Principle of Respect for Human Dignity* 88 (Strasbourg, Council of Europe Publishing 1999).

[5] W Brennan, 'The Constitution of the United States: Contemporary Ratification' (1986) 27 *South Texas Law Review* 433, 439, describes the US Constitution as 'a sparkling vision of the supremacy of the human dignity of every individual.' In recent years, the Supreme Court has used the term with an in-

where that the common thread running through all of the examples listed above is the notion that all human beings should be afforded human rights on the basis of equal treatment and respect.[10]

The invocation of human dignity as a foundational value in human rights law, whether international or domestic, has been particularly prevalent since the drafting of the German Constitution and the UDHR in the aftermath the Second World War. An enormous volume of literature has been devoted to these and subsequent developments. In spite of this, it has been mostly overlooked that the express invocation of human dignity in a human rights document had occurred prior to the outbreak of war in at least three countries,[11] one of which was Ireland. The Preamble to the Irish

---

creasing degree of frequency when interpreting provisions of the Bill of Rights; see M Goodman, 'Human Dignity in Supreme Court Constitutional Jurisprudence' (2006) 84 *Nebraska Law Review* 740 and J Resnik & J Chi–hye Suk, 'Adding Insult to Injury: Questioning the Role of Dignity in Conceptions of Sovereignty' (2003) 55 *Stanford Law Review* 1921. Moreover, the constitutions of a number of individual States within the US expressly invoke the concept, while also elaborating on what it entails; see V Jackson, 'Constitutional Dialogue and Human Dignity: States and Transnational Constitutional Discourse' (2004) 65 *Montana Law Review* 15 (2004).

6   In *Ghaidan v Godin–Mendoza* [2004] 2 AC 557, 605, Baroness Hale of Richmond stated: 'Democracy is founded on the principle that each individual has equal value. Treating some as automatically having less value than others not only causes pain and distress to that person but also violates his or her dignity as a human being …'.

7   See J Robert, 'The Principle of Human Dignity' in *The Principle of Respect for Human Dignity* 43 (Strasbourg, Council of Europe Publishing 1999).

8   See Klein, 'Human Dignity in Israeli Jurisprudence' in Kretzmer & Klein (eds), *The Concept of Human Dignity in Human Rights Discourse*.

9   See, eg *Law v Canada (Minister of Employment and Immigration)* [1999] SCR 497, 53.

10 O'Mahony, 'There is No Such Thing as a Right to Dignity', 555.

11 Article 3 of the Mexican Constitution of 1917 (which is still in force) makes a limited reference to human dignity, providing that State education 'shall contribute to better human relationships, not only with the elements which it contributes toward strengthening and at the same time inculcating, together with respect for the dignity of the person and the integrity of the family, the conviction of the general interest of society, but also by the care which it devotes to the ideals of brotherhood and equality of rights of all men, avoiding privileges of race, creed, class, sex, or persons.' More pertinently, Section 1(1) of the Finnish Constitution of 1919 (which has since been replaced by the Constitution of 1999) provided that 'Finland is a sovereign Republic, the constitution of which shall guarantee the inviolability of human dignity and the freedom and rights of the individual as well as promoting justice in society.'

Constitution of 1937, now the oldest existing domestic constitutional provision which invokes the principle of human dignity as an aim of a constitutional order, sets the scene for the document that follows by stating that

> We, the people of Éire ... seeking to promote the common good, with due observance of Prudence, Justice and Charity, so that the dignity and freedom of the individual may be assured ... Do hereby adopt, enact and give to ourselves this Constitution.

Thus it is made clear from the very beginning that one of the primary goals towards which the enactment of the Irish Constitution is directed is the assurance of the dignity of the individual.

Furthermore, it is well established that individual provisions of the Constitution should be interpreted harmoniously with other provisions—which includes not only the other substantive provisions of the Constitution, but also the Preamble.[12] Thus, in interpreting constitutional rights, the Irish judiciary are required to give due weight to the preambular aspiration of assuring the dignity of the individual. In spite of this, the concept has remained somewhat underdeveloped in Irish constitutional law until quite recently, primarily due to the fact that natural law was relied on as the philosophical foundation of the fundamental rights provisions for most of the lifetime of the Constitution.[13] Human dignity was, by comparison,

---

12 See, eg *Buckley v Attorney General* [1950] IR 67 (SC), 80 (O'Byrne J); *McGee v Attorney General* [1974] IR 274 (SC), 322 (Budd J); and *DPP v Best* [2000] 2 ILRM 1 (SC), 35 (Murphy J). Whyte, 'The Role of the Supreme Court in Our Democracy: A Response to Mr. Justice Hardiman' (2006) 28 *Dublin University Law Journal* 1, 20 describes the Preamble as a 'tie–breaker' in a situation where two opposite justifiable courses of constitutional interpretation are open to the court, '... as it sets out the objectives of the new constitutional order formulated by the People in 1937.'

13 The classic statement of this position is the following passage of the judgment of Walsh J in *McGee v Attorney General* [1974] IR 284 (SC), 310: 'Articles 41, 42 and 43 emphatically reject the theory that there are no rights without laws, no rights contrary to law and no rights anterior to law. They indicate that justice is placed above the law and acknowledge that natural rights, or human rights, are not created by law but that the Constitution confirms their existence and gives them protection. The individual has natural and human rights over which the State has no authority: and the Family as the natural primary and fundamental group of society has rights as such which the State cannot control.' See further D Clarke, 'The Role of Natural Law in Irish Constitutional Law' (1982) 17 *Irish Jurist* 187 and A Kavanagh, 'The Irish Constitution at 75 Years: Natural Law, Christian Values and the Ideal of Justice' (2012) 47 *Irish Jurist* 71.

only sporadically and inconsistently invoked by the Irish courts, and as recently as 2003, the authoritative text on Irish constitutional law observed that '[s]uch judicial references to this phrase in the Preamble as exist are not very illuminating.'[14] However, in the decade since, this has begun to change. The Irish courts have recently all but abandoned reliance on natural law;[15] and while only 24 cases made any significant reference to human dignity between 1937 and 1999, the same number did so in just three years in 2011, 2012 and 2013.[16] This recent vein of material has yet to be analysed in academic literature.[17] The remainder of this paper will consider Irish constitutional case law on dignity, identifying thematic areas where the concept has played a particularly prominent role, and analysing differences in the judicial formulation of the concept.

B. The Various Guises of Dignity

At least some of the Irish case law has cast dignity in a role that mirrors the approach taken by international human rights law—namely, as a source of, or normative justification for, human rights. Closely related to this, dignity has been used by the Irish courts as a background principle or

---

14 G Hogan & G Whyte, *JM Kelly: The Irish Constitution*, 4th edn (Dublin, Lexis–Nexis Butterworths, 2003) 60.
15 See *Re Article 26 and the Regulation of Information (Services outside the State for Termination of Pregnancies) Bill 1995* [1995] 1 IR 1 (SC), as discussed in A Twomey, 'The Death of the Natural Law?' (1995) 13 *Irish Law Times* 270; G Whyte, 'Natural Law and the Constitution' (1996) 14 *Irish Law Times* 8, and M De Blacam, 'Justice and Natural Law' (1997) 32 *Irish Jurist* 323.
16 These figures were reached through a comprehensive electronic search of judgments, excluding cases in which dignity was raised in arguments but not relied on by the court in reaching its decision, or in which dignity was used in some other context (eg a reference to the dignity of the court, or to statutory provisions regarding dignity at work).
17 The limited literature on dignity as a constitutional concept in Ireland all pre-dates the recent surge in reliance on the principle by the Irish courts. See TJ O'Dowd, 'Dignity and Personhood in Irish Constitutional Law' in G Quinn, A Ingram and S Livingstone (eds), *Justice and Legal Theory in Ireland* (Dublin, Oak Tree Press, 1995), 163–181; T Iglesias, 'The Dignity of the Individual in the Irish Constitution: The Importance of the Preamble' (2000) 89 *Studies* 19–34, and Binchy, 'Dignity as a Constitutional Concept' in E Carolan & O Doyle (eds), *The Irish Constitution: Governance and Values* (Dublin, Thomson Round Hall, 2008) 307–326.

interpretive aid illuminating the application of the rights provisions of the Irish Constitution to the facts of individual cases. However, judicial reliance on the principle has not been confined to the above: it has taken a variety of other forms also. At times, as will be demonstrated below, this has happened in a coherent and consistent way (such as in the case law on conditions of detention); but at other times, the language of dignity has been used rather loosely, with dignity invoked more as a rhetorical flourish than as a carefully defined legal principle.

A classic example of the latter approach is one of the foremost Irish decisions on dignity, *Re a Ward of Court*,[18] which concerned the withdrawal of artificial nutrition and hydration from a woman who had been in a near–persistent vegetative state for 20 years. The most pertinent judgment on the issue of dignity is that of Denham J (as she then was) in the Supreme Court, who formulated the dignity issue in four different ways in the space of a single judgment. First, she stated that 'invasive medical treatment ... results in a loss of bodily integrity and dignity'.[19] Second, she stated that '[a] constituent of the right of privacy is the right to die naturally, with dignity and with minimum suffering'.[20] Third, Denham J held that '[a]n unspecified right under the Constitution to all persons as human persons is dignity—to be treated with dignity'.[21] Finally, she held that that the Ward had the constitutional right to 'dignity in life and death'.[22] This loose usage of language in relation to dignity was also evident in the judgment of Lynch J in the same case, when he made reference to 'the citizen's right of autonomy or self–determination or privacy or dignity, call it what you will'.[23] Finally, O'Flaherty J referred to the life of the Ward as 'what technically is life but life without purpose, meaning or dignity'.[24]

In *Re a Ward of Court*, dignity arguably played the role of a source of or normative justification for a right—namely, the right to bodily integrity

---

18 [1996] 2 IR 79 (HC and SC).
19 ibid, 158.
20 ibid, 163.
21 ibid.
22 ibid, 169.
23 [1996] 2 IR 79, 94 (HC). See also *F v Clinical Director of Our Lady's Hospital* [2010] IEHC 243 (HC), where Peart J bundled together the rights to autonomy, dignity, privacy and bodily integrity in his analysis, with no attempt to separate or distinguish between them.
24 [1996] 2 IR 79, 134 (SC).

and the concomitant right to refuse medical treatment. It also acted as an interpretive aid to these rights, and assisted the Court in applying them to the facts of the case at hand. However, it was also invoked in several other ways. It was characterised as a free–standing constitutional right in itself—i.e. a right to dignity—with three variations of this appearing, namely, a right to be treated with dignity, a right to dignity in life and a right to dignity in death. Arguably, all of these amount to much the same thing: the right to be afforded treatment or living conditions that are consistent with human dignity. Both Denham J and O'Flaherty J presented dignity as a state to be achieved through the enjoyment of certain conditions and treatment, which can be denied or lost in the absence of such conditions or treatment—hence the references to a 'loss of dignity' and 'life without purpose, meaning or dignity'.

I have argued elsewhere that such a loose and inconsistent approach to the characterization of dignity as a legal (as distinct from philosophical) concept undermines its usefulness in the realm of constitutional law.[25] While accepting that part of the appeal and usefulness of dignity is its malleable nature, it is nonetheless desirable that the concept obeys at least some basic ground rules. If dignity can mean almost anything, the result is that it means nothing, and becomes a conduit for arbitrary and unprincipled decision making. This is why some critics have dismissed the concept as meaningless or even plain stupid.[26] I would not go this far; my position is that the concept can play a valuable role as a normative justification for, and interpretive aid to, human rights. However, if it is to perform this function in a non–arbitrary fashion, it is important that it is conceived and formulated with at least some degree of consistency (as befits any legal principle)—even if that consistent formulation leaves room for disagreement as to its specific application. In particular, I have argued that care should be taken to avoid characterisations of dignity that are out of line with what is consistently found in instruments of international human rights law—namely, the notion of 'inherent dignity' as a source of human rights.

---

25 O'Mahony, 'There is No Such Thing as a Right to Dignity'.
26 See, eg Stephen Pinker, 'The Stupidity of Dignity'. *The New Republic*, 28 May 2008; David Feldman, 'Human Dignity as a Legal Value: Part 1' (1999) *Public Law* 682 and 'Human Dignity as a Legal Value: Part 2' (2000) *Public Law* 61, and Neomi Rao, 'On the Use and Abuse of Dignity in Constitutional Law' (2008) 14 *Columbia Journal of European Law* 201.

As seen above, international law conceives of dignity as a source of rights—as prior to rights, and the reason why rights should be respected. However, since human dignity is described as inherent, it makes no sense to think of dignity as a state to be achieved through the enjoyment of rights. Dignity is prior to rights, and human beings retain their inherent dignity whether their rights are respected or not. Consequently, it also makes no sense to speak of dignity being lost, or of life without dignity, on the basis that rights are being denied to an individual. Such formulations may make sense in a more colloquial usage of the term 'dignity', but they do not cohere with the legal concept of dignity as set down in international human rights law. This need not be a problem if domestic constitutional law stuck to one version of dignity—but as seen above, decisions like *Re a Ward of Court* simultaneously present two conceptions of dignity that are not just different, but are mutually exclusive. This serves only to confuse its meaning and potential application and open the door to arbitrary decision–making, where dignity is invoked as a trump card to defeat other claims in an inconsistent and incoherent manner. Notably, this precise criticism was often levied at the manner in which the Irish courts previously invoked natural law as a source of fundamental rights;[27] if human dignity is to step into the void left by the move away from natural law, it is desirable that the judiciary seek to avoid leaving it open to the same line of attack.

Against this starting point, the following sections will analyse a selection of Irish constitutional case law in which dignity was invoked by a court in making a decision. A comprehensive analysis is not possible in the space available; instead, attention will focus on two manifestations of dignity in the case law. First, the case law in which dignity has been used as an interpretive aid to rights provisions will be examined thematically. Second, the rich vein of case law on the right to be treated with dignity, particularly in the context of conditions of detention, will be discussed. The ultimate aim is to assess whether the principle has been applied with any consistency and established any coherent principles; and to question

---

27   See, eg Clarke, 'The Role of Natural Law in Irish Constitutional Law' 189; G Hogan, 'Constitutional Interpretation' in F Litton (ed.), *The Constitution of Ireland 1937–1987* (Dublin, Institute of Public Administration, 1988) 173, 181; T Murphy, 'Democracy, Natural Law and the Irish Constitution' (1993) 11 *Irish Law Times* 81, 82, and W Duncan, 'The Constitutional Protection of Parental Rights' in *Report of the Constitution Review Group* (Dublin, Stationery Office, 1996) 612, 615.

whether its invocation has added any value to the decision–making process in each instance.

III. Interpretive Aid to Rights Provisions

A. General Principle

On numerous occasions, the Irish courts have emphasised the importance of interpreting the Constitution as a whole in a manner that acknowledges the preambular aspiration of assuring the dignity of the individual. In *Buckley v Attorney General*, O'Byrne J commented:

> In the enacting portion of the Constitution, contained in the Preamble, the people of Ireland, seeking, amongst other things, to promote the common good, with due observance of Prudence, Justice and Charity, so that the dignity and freedom of the individual may be assured . . . adopt, enact and give to themselves the Constitution. These most laudable objects seem to us to inform the various Articles of the Constitution, and we are of opinion that, so far as possible, the Constitution should be so construed as to give to them life and reality.[28]

While the case law shows strong consensus that the Constitution must be interpreted in a manner that respects human dignity, there is significantly less agreement on what exactly this entails. An early glimpse of the inconsistency that the Irish courts have brought to the interpretation of human dignity was provided by some of the first cases in which the concept was invoked. In *Re Article 26 and the Offences Against the State (Amendment) Bill, 1940*, Sullivan CJ, delivering the judgment of the Court, adopted a very communitarian view of the Preamble, holding that the clause that refers to assuring the dignity and freedom of the individual could not be invoked so as to defeat the interests of the common good.[29] A similar approach is evident in a much–cited passage from *In re Philip Clarke*, where the Court invoked dignity to uphold mental health legislation that the Court described as being of a

> paternal character, clearly intended for the care and custody of persons suspected to be suffering from mental infirmity and for the safety and well–being of the public generally ... We do not see how the common good would be promoted or the dignity and freedom of the individual assured by allowing persons, alleged to be

---

28   [1950] IR 67 (SC), 80. See, to similar effect, Budd J in *McGee v Attorney General* [1974] IR 284 (SC), 322.
29   [1940] IR 470 (SC), 478–479.

suffering from such infirmity, to remain at large to the possible danger of themselves and others.[30]

An interesting contrast can be drawn with another of the very earliest cases, *State (Burke) v Lennon*, in which Gavan Duffy J stated: 'As to personal liberty, it is one of the cardinal principles of the Constitution, proclaimed in the Preamble itself, that the dignity and freedom of the individual may be assured'.[31] In this passage, personal liberty is emphasised as being essential to the dignity of the individual, with no reference being made to individual dignity being subsumed by the common good. A number of subsequent cases have seen judges invoke dignity to invalidate measures which purport to be in the interests of the common good. Case law on privacy offers a good example of this approach.

B. Right to Privacy

The right to privacy, although not expressly included in the Irish Constitution, has long been established as an unenumerated right under the guarantee of Article 40.3 of the 'personal rights' of the citizen. This began with the recognition of the right to marital privacy in *McGee v Attorney General*, which Budd J linked to the invocation of the 'dignity and freedom of the individual' in the Preamble.[32] The Supreme Court relied on this right to marital privacy to strike down legislation criminalising importation of contraceptives. Dignity also featured in numerous passages in *Norris v Attorney General*, where laws criminalising sodomy were challenged on several grounds, including the right to privacy. Henchy J recognised the right to privacy as one of 'a range of personal freedoms or immunities as are necessary to ensure his dignity and freedom as an individual in the type of society envisaged [by the Constitution].'[33] In dissenting from the 3–2 majority decision to uphold the laws in question as necessary to uphold public morality, Henchy J held that to seek to legislate the commission of 'sins' out of existence would

> upset the necessary balance which the Constitution posits between the common good and the dignity and freedom of the individual. What is deemed necessary to

---

30   [1950] IR 235 (SC) at 247–248, *per* O'Byrne J.
31   [1940] IR 136 (SC), 143–144.
32   [1974] IR 284 (SC), 322.
33   [1984] IR 36 (SC), 71.

his dignity and freedom by one man may be abhorred by another as an exercise in immorality.[34]

To similar effect, the other dissenting judge, McCarthy J, characterised the dignity of the individual as an essential aspect of the common good:

> I would uphold the view that the unenumerated rights derive from the human personality and that the actions of the State in respect of such rights must be informed by the proud objective of the people as declared in the preamble seeking to promote the common good, with due observance of prudence, justice and charity, so that the dignity and freedom of the individual may be assured, true social order attained, the unity of our country restored, and concord established with other nations. The dignity and freedom of the individual occupy a prominent place in these objectives and are not declared to be subject to any particular exigencies but as forming part of the promotion of the common good.[35]

The classic Irish case on privacy is *Kennedy v Ireland*,[36] in which the tapping of the phones of journalists by a Government Minister for political purposes was found to violate their constitutional right to privacy. Having accepted that the right to privacy is not unqualified and is subject to the constitutional rights of others and to the requirements of public order, public morality and the common good, Hamilton P went on to state:

> The nature of the right to privacy must be such as to ensure the dignity and freedom of an individual in the type of society envisaged by the Constitution, namely, a sovereign, independent and democratic society. The dignity and freedom of an individual in a democratic society cannot be ensured if his communications of a private nature, be they written or telephonic, are deliberately, consciously and unjustifiably intruded upon and interfered with.[37]

Accordingly,

> [t]he action of the executive in this case in 'tapping' the telephones of the plaintiffs without any lawful justification and in interfering with and intruding upon the privacy of the plaintiffs constituted an attack on their dignity and freedom as individuals and as journalists and cannot be tolerated in a democratic society such as ours.[38]

Here, we see dignity playing the dual role of first, being the source or normative justification for the recognition of the unenumerated right to

---

34   ibid, 78.
35   [1984] IR 36 (SC), 99–100.
36   [1987] IR 587 (HC).
37   ibid, 593.
38   ibid, 594.

privacy;[39] and second, as an interpretive aid that helped the Court to reach the decision that the particular interference with privacy complained of was unjustified and unconstitutional. The common thread linking these decisions (and *McGee* and *Norris* in particular) is that dignity was invoked to justify giving preference to individual freedoms over laws that purported to be in the common good. This stands in stark contrast to the manner in which it was invoked in the earlier cases of *Re Article 26 and the Offences Against the State (Amendment) Bill, 1940* and *In re Philip Clarke*.

Kennedy has been influential in subsequent privacy case law, and the appeal to human dignity as a justification for pro–privacy decisions has featured in several other decisions. For example, section 7 of the Criminal Law (Rape) Act 1981 prohibits the publication of any matter likely to lead members of the public to identify a woman as the complainant. In *K (a minor) v Independent Star Ltd*, Hedigan J commented that this statutory provision 'gives expression to a complainant's constitutional right to privacy and dignity'.[40] Accordingly, it was held that a cause of action for damages for breach of the constitutional right to privacy would lie in a case where this provision was violated, notwithstanding the absence of such a remedy having been provided for in the 1981 Act.[41] The protection of anonymity was also at issue in *XY v Clinical Director of St Patricks University Hospital*.[42] The case concerned a *habeas corpus* application to review the legality of detention under the Mental Health Act 2001, and the applicant wished the proceedings to be held *in camera*. Hogan J declined this application, but instead granted an order restricting the media from publishing any matter that might lead to her identification; he held that that this would 'serve an important constitutional value reflected in the Preamble to the Constitution, namely, the assurance of the dignity of the individual'.[43] Both of these decision show how dignity can be used by a court to inform the specific application of a right to the circumstances of the case at hand. This is evident in case law in a number of other fields also.

---

39 Dignity also played this role in the decision of the Supreme Court in *I O'T v B* [1998] 2 IR 321 (SC), 372.
40 [2010] IEHC 500 (HC), 81.
41 ibid.
42 [2012] IEHC 224 (HC).
43 ibid, 17.

C. Value of Human Life

As noted above, the minimum core of human dignity is the notion that all human beings are worthy of equal treatment and respect. Bound up in this is the notion that human life is worthy of such respect, for the simple reason that it is human life. This is reflected in a number of Irish cases in which dignity has been invoked as a constitutional principle. In *Fleming v Ireland*,[44] both the High Court and Supreme Court rejected a challenge to the law making it a criminal offence to assist suicide. The High Court held that

> if physicians were to be permitted to hasten the end of the terminally ill at the request of the patient by taking active steps for this purpose this would be to compromise—perhaps in a fundamental and far–reaching way—that which is rightly regarded as an essential ingredient of a civilised society committed to the protection of human life and human dignity.[45]

The equal treatment and respect aspect of dignity was particularly evident in the Court's observation that '[i]n the eyes of the Constitution, the last days of the life of an elderly, terminally ill and disabled patient facing death have the same value, possess the same intrinsic human dignity and naturally enjoy the same protection as the life of the healthy young person on the cusp of adulthood and in the prime of their life.'[46] As will be discussed further below, the need to respect the inherent dignity of human life was found to outweigh the autonomy of the individual seeking assisted suicide, notwithstanding the invocation of dignity on that side of the argument also.

The respect owed to all human life by virtue of its inherent dignity was again evident in the decision of the High Court in *Byrne v Ryan*.[47] Here, Kelly J rejected an action for damages against a physician for the costs of raising children who were born following a failed sterilization procedure, reasoning that such a decision 'better served' and 'blends more harmoniously' with the value that the Constitution places upon dignity and human life.[48] Similar concerns are evident in Keane J's judgment in *I O'T v B*,[49] which was an action taken by an adoptee seeking to establish the identity

---

44 [2013] IEHC 2 (HC); [2013] IESC 19 (SC).
45 [2013] IEHC 2 (HC), 68.
46 ibid, 74.
47 [2007] IEHC 207 (HC).
48 ibid.
49 [1998] 2 IR 321 (SC).

of her natural mother. The action relied in part on the statement in another decision that each child had the right to 'realise his or her full personality and dignity as a human being';[50] it was argued that this was not possible where the identity of one's natural mother could not be established. Keane J rejected this argument on the following grounds:

> ... to say that a person in the position of the applicants who has been denied that information, and as a consequence the opportunity of getting to know his or her natural parents, has in some sense failed to realise 'his or her full personality and dignity as a human being' could be regarded as a grave overstatement. There have been, no doubt, millions of cases in this and other centuries where, because of individual personal tragedies or widespread social upheavals, people have grown to adulthood without knowing who their real parents were. To say of such people that they have failed in any sense to realise their full personality and dignity as human beings is, it could be argued, to deny the unique value which should be attributed to every human being, irrespective of his or her parentage or ancestry, a value which is surely at the heart of the legal philosophy which underlies the Constitution.[51]

D. Right to Life

If all human life is worthy of equal treatment and respect, then it clearly follows that all humans should have the right to life. The Irish Constitution expressly protects this right, including (rather controversially) for unborn children.[52] In a number of cases in which the courts have been called on to interpret the right to life, dignity has been called on as an interpretive aid. *MEO v Minister for Justice, Equality and Law Reform*[53] was an application for leave for judicial review by a HIV–positive Nigerian asylum seeker (who also suffered from a number of other serious conditions[54]),

---

50 See *G v An Bord Uchtála* [1980] IR 32 (SC), 56.
51 [1998] 2 IR 321 (SC), 370–371.
52 Article 40.3.2° provides general protection for the right to life: 'The State shall, in particular, by its laws protect as best it may from unjust attack and, in the case of injustice done, vindicate the life, person, good name, and property rights of every citizen.' Article 40.3.3° extends this specifically to the unborn child: 'The State acknowledges the right to life of the unborn and, with due regard to the equal right to life of the mother, guarantees in its laws to respect, and, as far as practicable, by its laws to defend and vindicate that right.'
53 [2012] IEHC 5 (HC).
54 In addition to HIV, the applicant suffered from cerebral toxoplasmosis, peripheral neuropathy, ocular complications and significant cognitive impairment.

who sought to resist deportation on the basis that it was unlikely that she would be able to access treatment for her illness in Nigeria. At a preliminary hearing, Hogan J held that the matter merited adjudication at a full hearing, as the applicant had raised

> substantial grounds for contending that her rights under Article 40.3.2 of the Constitution will be breached if deported to Nigeria where, possibly deprived of access to life saving treatment and being indigent, poor and bereft of family and friends while at the same time suffering from impaired mental cognition, she will be condemned to face decline and death over months in circumstances where her human dignity cannot be maintained.[55]

In an earlier decision concerning the right to life and deportation, *Baby O v Minister for Justice*, it was held by the Supreme Court that the fact that deportation might reduce the life expectancy of deportees, or expose unborn children to a higher risk of infant mortality, did not affect the State's power to deport them.[56] Thus, the key issue in *MEO* would seem to have been not the fact that the applicant was more likely to die in Nigeria than in Ireland, but the conditions in which this death would likely occur. The decision in *MEO* was therefore not based solely on the right to life. Given the absence of a justiciable right to healthcare in the Irish Constitution, one view of *MEO* is that the invocation of dignity as a background principle informing the interpretation of the right to life filled a gap that could not have been filled by any other constitutional right or principle.

An alternative interpretation is to say that the decision was not really based on the right to life at all, but on the right to be treated with dignity. Hogan J did not use this formulation here, but (as will be seen below) it has been used in many other cases, and Hogan J's reference to 'circumstances where her human dignity cannot be maintained' is consistent with the notion expressed in *Re a Ward of Court* that certain treatment or living conditions can result in a loss or denial of dignity. As already argued, this formulation is better avoided. In this instance, it makes it difficult to reconcile the various decisions reached in *MEO*, *Baby O* and *Fleming*. *Fleming* suggested that dignity requires that the protection of human life should take precedence over other interests. *Baby O* suggests the opposite, and *MEO* implicitly accepts this. However, *MEO* also suggests that dignity can be violated by allowing a person to die in certain conditions, which appeared to be rejected in *Fleming*. This tension will become even more

---

55   [2012] IEHC 5 (HC) 31.
56   [2002] 2 IR 169 (SC).

apparent when the relationship between dignity and autonomy is discussed below.

Dignity was again invoked as an interpretative aid to the right to life in a deportation case in *Aslam v Minister for Justice, Equality and Law Reform*.[57] Here, the State proposed to deport a heavily pregnant woman, in the middle of winter, by sea (since her pregnancy was too far advanced to allow her to fly). Hogan J made reference to the constitutional obligations to safeguard both her life and that of her unborn child, but stated that 'matters do not stop there':

> The constitutional obligations must be interpreted in a fashion which ensures that, in the words of the Preamble, the 'dignity ... of the individual must be assured.' One cannot therefore readily countenance the mandatory transfer of a heavily pregnant woman by sea, not least during winter conditions, with the prospect of gales and turbulent marine conditions. This would represent a potential test of endurance which no heavily pregnant woman should ever be obliged by State action to face, irrespective of whether she told untruths in the course of an asylum application. There would also be the prospect of the early commencement of labour (or even an early delivery) while at sea, perhaps brought on by turbulent conditions.[58]

Arguably, the invocation of dignity was less necessary in this case than in *MEO*. If the proposed method of deportation posed a direct threat to the life of the mother or the unborn child, that would be sufficient in its own right to block the deportation. The case is distinguishable from *Baby O* as the risk is proximate to the State action and not a generalised risk stemming from higher rates of infant mortality in the receiving country. Alternatively, the case could be viewed as one of exposing the deportee to inhuman treatment, given the unusual combination of a heavily pregnant deportee and turbulent sea conditions.

E. Autonomy

Dignity has always been closely associated with autonomy, and the two concepts are often conflated.[59] I have argued elsewhere that autonomy or self–determination is simply one of many rights that derive from an indi-

---

57   [2011] IEHC 512 (HC).
58   ibid, 34.
59   See, eg McCrudden, 'Human Dignity and Judicial Interpretation of Human Rights' 656–663 and Neal, 'Respect for Human Dignity as "Substantive Basic Norm"', 27–31.

vidual's inherent human dignity. When dignity and autonomy are conflated, the result is disputes where dignity is invoked on both sides of the argument, leaving to court to decide between the equal treatment and respect aspect of dignity and an alleged right to dignity.[60] The Irish case law on end of life has seen this occur, and the result has been inconsistency in the application of the dignity principle.

As seen above, *Re a Ward of Court*[61] concerned the withdrawal of artificial nutrition and hydration from a woman who had been in a near–persistent vegetative state for 20 years. It was held that this treatment should be withdrawn, and that the Ward should be allowed to die a natural death; this decision was justified by reference to the Ward's right to dignity,[62] her right to die a dignified death,[63] and the fact that her life was devoid of dignity.[64] Autonomy also featured in the reasoning, which was partly based on the right to refuse medical treatment.[65] More recently, when the High Court and Supreme Court rejected a challenge by a Multiple Sclerosis sufferer to the law criminalising assisted suicide in *Fleming v Ireland*,[66] *Re a Ward of Court* was distinguished on the basis that allowing a person to die a natural death was not the same as expediting death. Many of the same features were present in both cases—a person living a life that was argued to be devoid of dignity, and that would lead to an undignified death following unnecessary suffering with no hope of recovery. In *Re a Ward of Court*, the Ward's right to a dignified life and dignified death were found to trump the inherent value of preserving her life; her right to autonomy was even invoked by the Court, notwithstanding the fact that the Ward had not been autonomous in any meaningful way for 20 years. Yet in *Fleming*, where the applicant had full mental capacity, the inherent dignity of human life was found to trump any dignity or autonomy interests invoked by the applicant, irrespective of the suffering that would be caused to her by rejecting her challenge.

---

60   O'Mahony, 'There is No Such Thing as a Right to Dignity', 565–574.
61   [1996] 2 IR 79 (HC and SC).
62   See Denham J ibid, 163.
63   See Denham J ibid, 163 and 169.
64   See Denham J ibid, 158 and O'Flaherty J ibid, 134.
65   See Lynch J, ibid, 93–94; Hamilton CJ, ibid, 125; and Denham J, ibid, 160–161 and 167–169.
66   [2013] IEHC 2 (HC); [2013] IESC 19 (SC).

This inconsistent approach to the use of dignity is also evident in other cases on autonomy and personal liberty. In *Attorney General v X*,[67] the High Court had granted an injunction restraining a suicidal rape victim from travelling out of the jurisdiction for an abortion. Article 40.3.3° of the Irish Constitution expressly protects the right to life of the unborn; the effect is that the unborn child is deemed to have its own inherent human dignity as a matter of Irish constitutional law, and its life is worthy of equal treatment and respect. Nonetheless, the Supreme Court overturned the High Court decision, with O'Flaherty J commenting that an injunction that interfered to such an 'extraordinary degree' with the individual's freedom of movement, and carried potential penalties of imprisonment and fines if it were disobeyed, was 'impossible to reconcile with a Constitution one of the primary objects of which, as stated in its Preamble, is to assure the dignity and freedom of the individual.'[68] While this was not the sole basis for the decision (and probably ran contrary to the majority view in the Supreme Court),[69] the suggestion is clearly that autonomy or liberty can sometimes outweigh the need to afford equal treatment and respect to all (constitutionally protected) human life.

Similarly, in *Health Service Executive (Southern Area) v SS (a minor)*, McMenamin J was critical of the repeated detention of a seriously troubled adolescent in secure care, saying that throughout his life, his

> other constitutional rights, to liberty, to dignity, to development as a human being, have been almost entirely subsumed by concerns as to the protection of his life and welfare.[70]

Here, like in the *X* case, we again see the suggestion that the protection and preservation of human life at all costs can reach a point where it violates a person's constitutional 'right to dignity'. This is arguably out of line with the ultimate decision reached in *Fleming*. In any event, it shows the confusion that can be caused when dignity is invoked both as a justifi-

---

67 [1992] 1 IR 1 (SC).
68 Ibid, 88.
69 The key reason why the Supreme Court overturned the decision of the High Court was that it accepted that an established threat of suicide constituted a real and substantial risk to the life of the mother, such that it was permissible to terminate the pregnancy so as to save the life of the mother. The majority of the Court was of the view that the right to travel could not, of itself, take precedence over the right to life of the unborn. See Finlay CJ, ibid, 53–57; Hederman J, ibid, 73; McCarthy J, ibid, 80; and Egan J, ibid, 92.
70 [2007] IEHC 189 (HC), 35.

cation for the protection of life on the basis of equal treatment and respect, and as a free-standing right that can be violated through certain treatment or conditions.

More recently, in *PP v Health Services Executive*,[71] the High Court authorised the withdrawal of life support from a pregnant woman following brain death, as the medical evidence suggested that there was no realistic prospect of successfully maintaining life support long enough to deliver the baby alive. The Court rejected an argument that greater weight should be accorded to the rights of the unborn on the basis that death without indignity was no longer possible. While acknowledging that the unborn had a constitutional right to life, the Court held:

> This does not mean that the Court discounts or disregards the mother's right to retain in death her dignity with proper respect for her autonomy with due regard to the grief and sorrow of her loved ones and their wishes. Such an approach has been the hallmark of civilised societies from the dawn of time. It is a deeply ingrained part of our humanity and may be seen as necessary both for those who have died and also for the sake of those who remain living and who must go on. The Court therefore is unimpressed with any suggestion that considerations of the dignity of the mother are not engaged once she has passed away.

One view might be that this echoes the above-mentioned cases in placing more emphasis on dignity and autonomy than on the preservation of life at all costs. As against this, the case turned on its own particular facts and the absence of any realistic prospect of a live birth. The Court went on to suggest that the mother's dignity may, in a suitable case, take second place to the preservation of life in the event that a live birth was possible, which would come closer to the position seen in *Fleming*:

> However, when the mother who dies is bearing an unborn child at the time of her death, the rights of that child, who is living, and whose interests are not necessarily inimical to those just expressed, must prevail over the feelings of grief and respect for a mother who is no longer living. The question then becomes one of how far the Court should go in terms of trying to vindicate that right in the particular circumstances which arise here.

It would seem, therefore, that the Irish courts are of the view that dignity survives to at least some degree even after death; but the dignity of the dead may sometimes have to give way to the dignity of the living (or potentially even the dignity of the unborn).

---

71 [2014] IEHC 622 (HC) (note: no paragraph numbers are present in the judgment).

Closely related to autonomy is the separate constitutional right to personal liberty, whose interpretation and application by the Irish courts has frequently been informed by reference to human dignity. This may be at least in part due to the phrasing of the Preamble, which joins the two concepts in aspiring that 'the dignity and freedom of the individual may be assured'. Thus, in *State (Burke) v Lennon*, Gavan Duffy J stated:

> As to personal liberty, it is one of the cardinal principles of the Constitution, proclaimed in the Preamble itself, that the dignity and freedom of the individual may be assured.[72]

While personal liberty may obviously be restricted for a variety of reasons, the courts have invoked dignity so as to place limits on the State's powers of detention. Thus, in *Li v Governor of Cloverhill Prison*, Hogan J held that it was impermissible to hold asylum seekers in preventative detention pending the outcome of their asylum application:

> If it is said that there is a compelling State interest in ensuring that persons who happen to have committed breaches of these immigration rules do not remain at liberty and must therefore be detained on a preventative basis pending the outcome of their applications for asylum *simply* by reason of this fact, then I fear that preventative detention would become routine and regular. I refuse to believe that such a state of affairs could be constitutionally sanctioned in a State which is committed to the rule of law and where the words of the Preamble commit the State to ensuring that the 'dignity and freedom of the individual may be assured.'[73]

F. Due Process

Dignity has been invoked to telling effect in Irish case law on due process; in the cases where the concept has featured, constitutional rights have almost invariably been found to have been violated. This raises an interesting contrast with the case law on conditions of detention, where (as will be discussed below) dignity is frequently invoked but rarely found to have been violated. The link between due process and human dignity was first made explicit by O'Higgins CJ in *State (Healy) v Donoghue*:

> ... it is clear that the words 'due course of law' in Article 38 make it mandatory that every criminal trial shall be conducted in accordance with the concept of justice, that the procedures applied shall be fair, and that the person accused will be

---

72   [1940] IR 136 (SC), 143.
73   [2012] IEHC 493 (HC), 13.

afforded every opportunity to defend himself. If this were not so, the dignity of the individual would be ignored and the State would have failed to vindicate his personal rights.[74]

The necessity to safeguard human dignity has loomed large at every stage in the investigation and prosecution of criminal offences, beginning with the very formulation of the criminal offence. In *CC v Ireland*, the Supreme Court struck down the law on statutory rape on the basis that it did not allow for the defence of reasonable mistake as to age.[75] Hardiman J stated that he could not 'regard a provision which criminalises and exposes to a maximum sentence of life imprisonment a person without mental guilt as respecting the liberty or the dignity of the individual'.[76] The same year, for similar reasons, it was found that convicting a person for a crime on the basis of a guilty plea when that person could have pleaded insanity would fail to respect that person's dignity.[77]

In relation to the pre–trial stage, Gannon J held in *Costello v DPP* that the removal of the protection afforded by the judicial preliminary investigation of criminal charges as a prerequisite to the presentation thereof for trial was inconsistent with the 'overriding principle' of assuring the dignity of the individual, as stated in the Preamble to the Constitution.[78] In *People (Attorney General) v O'Brien*, the Attorney General conceded (and the Supreme Court expressly agreed) that 'evidence obtained as a result of gross personal violence or methods which offended against the essential dignity of the human person' should be excluded from trial.[79]

As to the trial itself, the presumption of innocence—perhaps the bedrock of due process—was described by Murray J in *PO'C v DPP* as being 'personal to the dignity and status of every citizen'.[80] The same thinking seems to have informed *DPP v Davis*, where Hardiman J, delivering the judgment of the Court of Criminal Appeal, described the publication of photographs of an unconvicted prisoner wearing shackles as

> a depiction of him in a position of humiliation and indignity ... the dignity of the individual, and the perception that he is a participant in judicial proceedings with

---

74   [1976] IR 325 (SC), 349.
75   [2006] 4 IR 1 (SC).
76   ibid, 44.
77   *DPP v Redmond* [2006] IESC 25 (SC).
78   [1984] IR 436 (HC), 449.
79   [1965] IR 142 (SC), 150 and 159.
80   [2000] 3 IR 87 (SC), 103.

specific rights, and on a footing of equality with other participants, is inconsistent with his appearing there chained, or otherwise manifestly restrained.[81]

Dignity is invoked in each of these cases to broadly similar effect: to emphasise the fundamental importance of a particular principle of due process, and perhaps to justify ruling in favour of a person who may very well have committed the crime in question and for whom many would have little sympathy. Dignity is seen here performing its classic role, as a foundational principle that informs the interpretation and application of rights provisions, but not as a standalone right in itself. Its core message is that all persons are worthy of equal treatment and respect, no matter what crime they have been accused of.

An interesting counterpoint to decisions where human dignity is invoked in defence of a person accused of a crime is the invocation of human dignity to justify the imposition of severe penalties once a person has been convicted of a serious offence. This was most evident in a much–cited passage from *People (DPP) v Tiernan*, where Finlay CJ stated that

> [r]ape is a gross attack upon the human dignity and the bodily integrity of a woman and a violation of her human and constitutional rights. As such it must attract very severe legal sanctions.[82]

Similarly, in *People (DPP) v M*, Denham J described child abuse as 'a gross attack on human dignity, bodily integrity and, a violation of constitutional rights.'[83] By contrast, in *DPP v Murray*, Finnegan J observed that while violent and sexual crime involve an 'affront to human dignity', taxation offences and social welfare fraud are cases where 'the level of moral delinquency will not often approach that particularly elevated level, although, of course, it can do so.'[84]

G. Right to be Treated with Dignity

As noted above, the right to be treated with dignity was recognised by Denham J in *Re a Ward of Court*, and has featured in a large volume of case law since then. This right has been particularly prevalent in case law concerning conditions of detention in prison, either in Irish prisons or in

---

81   [2001] 1 IR 146 (CCA), 151.
82   [1988] IR 250 (SC), 253.
83   [1994] 3 IR 306 (SC), 316.
84   [2012] IECCA 60 (CCA).

prisons in other countries seeking the extradition of a prisoner from Ireland. Thus, while the affront to human dignity involved in committing a crime can justify a lengthy prison sentence, the prisoner nonetheless retains his or her inherent human dignity and has a right to be treated with respect for that dignity once in prison.

The frequent invocation of dignity by prisoners seeking to challenge conditions of detention in the Irish courts is prompted at least in part by the inclusion of an obligation in the Prison Rules for a Prison Governor 'to conduct himself or herself and perform his or her functions in such a manner as to respect the dignity and human rights of all prisoners.'[85] However, the courts do not address the cases solely through the lens of the Prison Rules; the constitutional right to be treated with dignity is consistently invoked. This is presented as standalone constitutional right, albeit one that subsumes (and, in reality, entirely consists of) a number of other rights, most notably freedom from inhuman and degrading treatment, the right to bodily integrity, the right to privacy and the right to freedom of association. Arguably, each of the cases discussed below could have been decided without any reference to the right to be treated with dignity. This raises the question of whether the constitutional right of prisoners to be treated with dignity is really a standalone constitutional right at all, or whether the better view is simply that the inherent dignity of prisoners is a normative justification for other rights whose salience is heightened in a prison environment.

The right of prisoners to be treated with dignity has implications for a whole range of matters involved in running a secure prison. In *Bates v Minister for Justice*, Murphy J commented that

> [n]o doubt prison management is a constant battle between the need to preserve security and safety on the one hand and, on the other hand, the obligation to recognise the constitutional rights of the prisoners and their dignity as human beings.[86]

In that case, the seemingly trivial matter of the service of hot tea to prisoners was one component of this 'constant battle'. Doing so in a manner that

---

85 Rule 75(2)(iii) requires the Prison Governor 'to conduct himself or herself and perform his or her functions in such a manner as to respect the dignity and human rights of all prisoners.'
86 [1998] 2 IR 81 (SC), 86.

minimised the risks associated with distributing hot liquid in a prison,[87] while also maintaining a certain temperature and minimising the restrictions on prisoners' social interaction, was found to be a delicate balancing exercise that risked falling short of the obligation to respect the dignity of prisoners.[88]

If access to a good cup of tea can raise human dignity issues in a prison environment, it is unsurprising that dignity has been invoked before the courts in relation to a range of more pressing issues. Notwithstanding the need to occasionally limit interaction between prisoners or to keep certain prisoners in solitary confinement, it was held in *Devoy v Governor of Portlaoise Prison* that the constitutional right of prisoners to be treated with dignity includes a right to a degree of freedom of association with other prisoners (although not necessarily with any particular prisoners).[89] In *Connolly v Governor of Wheatfield Prison*, Hogan J held that extended periods of solitary confinement (which he said he would 'rather measure in terms of an extended period of months') could 'in some instances at least' fail to respect the human dignity of the prisoner.[90] In cases of indefinite solitary confinement extending over a period of years,

> it would be hard to see how the integrity of the detainee's personality—the very essence of the guarantee of the protection of the person and preservation of the human dignity of the prisoner—could be preserved under such circumstances.[91]

Other matters in respect of which it has been alleged that conditions of detention failed to respect human dignity include the provision of in–cell sanitation;[92] protecting prisoners from physical assault by other prisoners (while avoiding oppressive measures such as intrusive searches or re-

---

[87] The Irish courts have been faced with claims by prisoners deliberately injured by other prisoners using boiling water; see, eg *Breen v Governor of Wheatfield Prison* [2008] IEHC 123 (HC).

[88] Note, however, that the arrangements in the case at hand were found not to be wanting in this respect.

[89] [2009] IEHC 288 (HC).

[90] [2013] IEHC 334 (HC), 22.

[91] ibid; Hogan J continued at p 24 to observe that 'complete sensory deprivation—such as ... placing the prisoner in a padded cell with no access to any facilities whatsoever or to any natural light—will generally be held to compromise the essence of the prisoner's Article 40.3.2 rights if this were to continue beyond a matter of days.'

[92] *Mulligan v Governor of Portlaoise Prison* [2010] IEHC 269 (HC).

strictions on movement);[93] and allowing physical contact with family members on visits.[94] In extradition cases, human dignity has been invoked to challenge extradition not simply by reference to the conditions of detention in the country seeking extradition, but also due to the separation of the prisoner from his family.[95] However, while the above case law has repeatedly emphasised the constitutional right of prisoners to be treated with dignity, it is notable that there has not been a single judgment in which the courts have ruled that conditions of detention in an Irish prison have failed to vindicate this particular right. Many would find this surprising, given that conditions of detention in Irish prisons have been the subject of repeated criticism from the Prison Visiting Committee,[96] civil society groups[97] and international observers such as the UN Committee against Torture[98] and the European Committee for the Prevention of Torture.[99] Instead, the courts have emphasised the deference that should be afforded by the judicial branch to the prison authorities in the difficult and complex task of running a prison system that detains individuals who are often of a dangerous and violent disposition.[100]

There are two cases in which the Irish courts have ruled that conditions of detention violated the rights of prisoners; but curiously, neither judgment expressly referred to human dignity, notwithstanding the common-

---

[93] *Creighton v Ireland* [2010] IESC 50 and *Sage v Minister for Justice* [2011] IEHC 84 (HC).
[94] *Foy v Governor of Cloverhill Prison* [2010] IEHC 529 (HC).
[95] *Minister for Justice Equality and Law Reform v Bednarczyk* [2011] IEHC 136 (HC).
[96] See *Mulligan v Governor of Portlaoise Prison* [2010] IEHC 269, 9.
[97] See, eg Irish Penal Reform Trust, *Submission of the Irish Penal Reform Trust to the European Committee for the Prevention of Torture and Inhuman or Degrading Treatment or Punishment (CPT) in preparation for the 2006 CPT visit to Ireland*, 3 March 2006, http://www.iprt.ie/contents/1312.
[98] See, eg UN Committee against Torture, *Concluding Observations: Ireland*, June 2011, pp 11 to 16, http://www.iprt.ie/files/CAT.C_.IRL_.CO_.1_.doc.
[99] See, eg European Committee for the Prevention of Torture, *Report to the Government of Ireland on the visit to Ireland carried out by the European Committee for the Prevention of Torture and Inhuman or Degrading Treatment or Punishment (CPT) from 25 January to 5 February 2010*, CPT/Inf (2011) 3, http://www.cpt.coe.int/documents/irl/2011-03-inf-eng.htm#_Toc284508910.
[100] See, eg *Walsh v Governor of Midlands Prison* [2012] IEHC 229 (HC) (citing O'Connor J, *Turner v Safley*, 482 US 78 (SC), 89 (1987)) and *Connolly v Governor of Wheatfield Prison* [2013] IEHC 334 (HC), 15. See further M Rogan, *Prison Conditions under Irish Law and the European Convention on Human Rights* (Dublin, Irish Penal Reform Trust, 2012) 7–8.

place invocation of dignity in cases where no violation has been found. In *State (Richardson) v. Governor of Mountjoy Prison*, Barrington J ruled that it was a violation of the constitutional rights of prisoners to be expected to wash their teeth in a basin that contained residue of human excrement due to 'slopping out'.[101] In so ruling, Barrington J made no reference to dignity. However, 30 years later, in *Connolly v Governor of Wheatfield Prison*, Hogan J stated that human dignity had, in essence, been the basis of the *Richardson* decision, and observed: 'What could be more undignified—indeed, degrading—than the obligation to wash in the presence of the human excrement?'[102]

Two years prior to making this observation about *Richardson*, Hogan J ruled on *Kinsella v Governor of Mountjoy Prison*,[103] where the prisoner was detained for 11 days in a padded cell containing nothing but a mattress and a cardboard box for sanitation, with no access to any other facilities apart from a six minute phone call each day. Hogan J found that this amounted to sensory deprivation and constituted a breach of his constitutional rights; but interestingly, based his decision on the right to 'the integrity of the human mind and personality', and made no reference to human dignity whatsoever.[104] This was a curious omission, particularly given that Hogan J is one of a small group of Irish judges who regularly makes reference to human dignity. It was he who made a point in his later decision in *Connolly* of characterising the *Richardson* decision as one essentially based on a violation of human dignity. Moroever, also in *Connolly*, Hogan J described the integrity of the detainee's personality as 'the very essence of the ... preservation of the human dignity of the prisoner'.[105] So, while both of the Irish decisions finding that conditions of detention violated prisoner's rights have been retrospectively characterised as decisions based on human dignity, neither decision invoked dignity at the time.

It is only in one isolated extradition case that a challenge to conditions of detention was upheld on the basis of reasoning that expressly invoked the human dignity of the prisoner. In *Minister for Justice Equality and Law Reform v McGuigan*,[106] Edwards J refused to surrender the respondent for extradition to Lithuania, based on evidence that he would be likely

---

101 [1980] ILRM 82 (HC), 93.
102 [2013] IEHC 334 (HC), 16.
103 [2011] IEHC 235 (HC).
104 ibid, 8 to 10.
105 [2013] IEHC 334 (HC), 22.
106 [2013] IEHC 216 (HC).

to experience conditions of detention in Lithuania that would fail to vindicate his constitutional right to be treated with human dignity. This was due to evidence of the cumulative effect of alleged police mistreatment of detainees; alleged inadequate sanitation; overcrowding and limited access to medical services in Lithuanian prisons; alleged instances of prolonged pre–trial detention; allegedly inhumane and degrading conditions in Lithuanian police stations; and allegations of uncontrolled inter–prisoner violence in prisons.

In summary, the constitutional right to be treated with dignity has featured prominently in Irish case law on conditions of detention, seemingly taking the guise of both a standalone right and a basis for other rights. However, it is questionable whether it has added much value to the decisions. The overwhelming majority of cases demonstrate an extreme reluctance on the part of the courts to substitute their judgment for that of the prison authorities, regardless of any high–sounding appeal to human dignity made on behalf of a prisoner. The courts' assessment that conditions in Irish prisons do not, on the whole, violate the right to be treated with dignity would seem to be out of line with the assessment of a range of highly credible non–judicial bodies. Conversely, the decisions in *Richardson* and *Kinsella* failed to make reference to dignity at all, which demonstrates that conditions of detention can be found to violate other constitutional rights (most notably freedom from inhuman and degrading treatment) without any need to recognise an additional free–standing right to be treated with dignity. Perhaps it could be suggested that the *McGuigan* case shows how dignity can capture the cumulative effect of factors that do not, in isolation, violate individual constitutional rights, but combine in a way that fails to respect human dignity. However, there seems no reason in principle why the right to freedom from inhuman and degrading treatment could not be used to similar effect, as seen in case law from other jurisdictions.[107]

More generally, the notion of a right to be treated with dignity (sometimes phrased as a 'right to dignity') lends itself to confusion. Since it consists of a right to be treated a certain way, it can clearly be denied in the absence of such treatment, giving rise to a situation where it may be

---

107   See, eg *Napier v Scottish Ministers* (2005) 1 SC 307 (CS) (finding a breach of the right to freedom from inhuman and degrading treatment due to the cumulative effect of the 'triple vices' of overcrowding, slopping out and impoverished regime).

said that a person has been stripped of their dignity or is living a life without dignity. But the whole point is that the human dignity of prisoners is inherent—and this is why they have the right to freedom from inhuman and degrading treatment and other rights. Suggesting that they are devoid of dignity is essentially inconsistent with the notion of inherent dignity as a normative justification for rights. This confusing position could be avoided if the notion of a right to dignity or a right to be treated with dignity was abandoned. Instead, dignity could be used as a background principle informing the interpretation of other rights, such as the right to freedom from inhuman or degrading treatment, the right to bodily integrity or the right to privacy. When the State is disinclined to afford certain treatment to convicted murderers or rapists, or the courts are hesitant to interfere in the operation of a prison system, the overarching imperative of respecting the inherent dignity of every human being can provide the normative framework within which specific constitutional rights are protected in such a context. However, this can occur without the need to conceptualise dignity as a freestanding right. It is through the protection of other rights that flow from dignity that dignity is respected.

IV. Conclusion

While the Irish Constitution was one of the earliest to invoke human dignity as a foundational principle, that principle lay relatively dormant for many years. However, human dignity is playing an ever more significant role in the case law interpreting constitutional rights in Ireland, and a small cohort of judges are inclined to invoke it relatively frequently. The Irish case law provides examples of the potential added value that dignity can bring to constitutional adjudication. The due process case law utilised the principle to emphasise the fact that certain rights are of fundamental importance to all individuals, even those who are accused of (and may well have committed) heinous crimes. The *MEO* case on the deportation of a HIV–positive asylum seeker to a country where adequate treatment may not be available arguably used the principle to fill a gap that was not filled by any other constitutional right. The privacy case law used the principle to justify the protection of certain individual interests from being subsumed by an amorphous 'common good'. In each of these instances, dignity may have tipped the balance in a way that another principle might not have managed.

In some other instances, dignity was invoked in a way that arguably made little difference one way or another. The case law on conditions of detention best illustrates this. In the cases where the right to be treated with dignity was invoked, it was not found to have been violated; and in the cases where conditions were found to violate rights, dignity was not invoked. Potentially, dignity could play a similar role in this sphere to the role it plays in due process—namely, reminding us that everyone (even a serious criminal) is worthy of equal treatment and respect. However, other well–recognised rights like the right to freedom from inhuman and degrading treatment have managed this in the absence of any recourse to dignity discourse; and dignity discourse has failed to tip the balance in other cases where it might have been expected to. Thus, these cases show that the recognition of a constitutional right of prisoners to be treated with dignity has been relatively neutral in its impact.

The notion of a right to dignity or a right to be treated with dignity has proven to be a source of inconsistency in other areas, most notably in the end of life cases. Here, dignity has been invoked on one side of the argument as a principle that all life should be respected equally (and therefore protected at the expense of other interests), and on the other side of the argument as a notion that life is undignified in certain conditions and therefore not worth maintaining. The result has been an inconsistent ordering of interests in the relevant case law, particularly as between *Re a Ward of Court* and *Fleming*, but also in other cases.

The lesson of the Irish experience is that dignity has the potential to play a valuable role in constitutional adjudication. However, since its innate vagueness opens the door to accusations of arbitrariness, judges need to minimise this as far as possible by at least formulating and deploying the principle in a consistent manner. This is best achieved by restricting dignity to the role of a background principle that acts as a normative justification for and interpretive aid to rights provisions, by reference to the equal treatment and respect that should be afforded to all human beings. It would be better not to use the language of dignity in the context of a right to dignity, or to be treated with dignity, or life without dignity. As the case law on conditions of detention shows, other rights can frequently fulfill these roles; dignity can help to inform or justify their interpretation, but is best kept in the background rather than the foreground.

Grandma's Dignity: Technology and the 'Elderly'

Christoph Goos

De Hogeweyk is a gated village-style neighborhood in the suburbs of Amsterdam for older people with severe dementia. 152 residents share 23 small and intimate bungalows with seven quite different lifestyle options. The bungalows are equipped with discrete surveillance technology. The care persons wear street clothes and appear as supermarket salespeople, housemates, domestic services staff or family members. They all aim to permit the residents to live an everyday life that is safe, secure and as normal as possible.[1] *Paro*, developed by a Japanese engineer, is a therapeutic robot. The fluffy, big-eyed baby harp seal responds deceptively real to petting, sounds and light. It is used as an artificial companion for people with dementia in nursing homes.[2] *Mindme*, finally, is a small and affordable GPS locator for people who wander because they have dementia. It can be worn around the neck, clipped to the belt or attached to the house key. The Sussex Police was the first force in Britain to buy some of these devices to reduce the number of costly call-outs. The devices are intended to save hundreds of thousands of pounds a year.[3]

---

1   See JW Anderzhon et al, *Design for Aging: International Case Studies of Building and Program* (Hoboken, John Wiley & Sons, 2012) 143–54.
2   See H Robinson et al, 'The Psychosocial Effects of a Companion Robot: A Randomized Controlled Trial' (2013) 14 Journal of the American Medical Directors Association 661; N Subbaraman, 'My robot friend: People find real comfort in artificial companionship' www.nbcnews.com/technology/my-robot-friend-people-find-real-comfort-artificial-companionship-6C10146787; H Dahlkamp, 'Eine Robbe zum Erinnern: Sie kam aus Japan, jetzt soll ein kleiner Roboter auch in Deutschland demente Menschen aufheitern, sie beruhigen und zum Gespräch anregen' www.faz.net/aktuell/rhein-main/hilfe-fuer-demente-menschen-eine-robbe-zum-erinnern-11861191.html.
3   See V Ward, A Philipson and J Bingham, 'GPS tags for dementia patients: Dementia patients are to be fitted with GPS tracking devices for the first time to save police money searching for those who regularly go missing' www.telegraph.co.uk/health/healthnews/10029205/GPS-tags-for-dementia-patients.html; J Bingham and A Philipson, 'Concern over GPS tracking of dementia sufferers: Almost all councils in Britain use GPS devices to track the movements of dementia sufferers, it has emerged, as welfare

De Hogeweyk, *Paro* and *Mindme* are three current examples of assistive and surveillance technologies specifically designed for older people with dementia. It is hardly surprising that all three of them are discussed controversially among nursing scientists.[4] The concept of human dignity, un-

---

        groups accused them of using computer chips as a substitute for carers' www.telegraph.co.uk/health/elderhealth/10031210/Concern-over-GPS-tracking-of-dementia-sufferers.html.

[4]   See, for instance, A Bruhns, '"Die sind nicht bescheuert": Der Pflegeheimleiter und Ethik-Experte Michael Schmieder kämpft gegen den verstörenden Trend, Demenzkranke in einer falschen Realität leben zu lassen' (2014) 11 *Der Spiegel* 134 f; A Niemeijer et al, 'The Place of Surveillance Technology in Residential Care for People with Intellectual Disabilities: Is There an Ideal Model of Application' (2013) 57 *Journal of Intellectual Disability Research* 201; Robinson et al, 'Psychosocial Effects of a Companion Robot'; S Te Boekhorst et al, 'Quality of Life of Nursing-Home Residents with Dementia Subject to Surveillance Technology Versus Physical Restraints: An Explorative Study' (2013) 28 *International Journal of Geriatric Psychiatry* 356; G Petonito et al, 'Programs to Locate Missing and Critically Wandering Elders: A Critical Review and a Call for Multiphasic Evaluation' (2013) 53 *Gerontologist* 17; H Matsuzaki and G Fitzi, 'Menschenwürde und Roboter' in JC Joerden, E Hilgendorf and F Thiele (eds), *Menschenwürde und Medizin: ein interdisziplinäres Handbuch* (Berlin, Duncker & Humblot, 2013); F Habekuß, 'Im Dorf des Vergessens: Im niederländischen De Hogeweyk genießen Menschen mit Demenz maximale Freiheit. Nun wird ein solches Projekt auch in Deutschland geplant' www.zeit.de/2013/05/Demenzdorf-De-Hogeweyk-Alzey; SA Zwijsen, AR Niemeijer and CM Hertogh, 'Ethics of Using Assistive Technology in the Care for Community-Dwelling Elderly People: An Overview of the Literature' (2011) 15 *Aging & Mental Health* 419; AR Niemeijer et al, 'Ethical and Practical Concerns of Surveillance Technologies in Residential Care for People with Dementia or Intellectual Disabilities: An Overview of the Literature' (2010) 22 *International Psychogeriatrics* 1129; M Decker, 'Caregiving Robots and Ethical Reflection: The Perspective of Interdisciplinary Technology Assessment' (2008) 22 *AI & Society* 315; S Cahill et al, 'Technology in Dementia Care' (2007) 19 *Technology and Disability* 55; L Robinson et al, 'Balancing Rights and Risks: Conflicting Perspectives in the Management of Wandering in Dementia' (2007) 9 *Health, Risk & Society* 389; DF Mahoney et al, 'In-Home Monitoring of Persons with Dementia: Ethical Guidelines for Technology Research and Development' (2007) 3 *Alzheimer's & Dementia* 217; A Astell, 'Technology and Personhood in Dementia Care' (2006) 7 *Quality in Ageing and Older Adults* 15; K Eltis, 'Predicating Dignity on Autonomy? The Need for Further Inquiry into the Ethics of Tagging and Tracking Dementia Patients with GPS Technology' (2005) 13 *Elder Law Journal* 387; K Eltis, 'Society's Most Vulnerable under Surveillance: The Ethics of Tagging and Tracking Dementia Patient with GPS Technology: A Comparative View' (2005) 3 *Oxford University Comparative Law Forum* at ouclf.iuscomp.org.

surprisingly, plays a contradictory role in these debates. It is used 'by proponents and critics alike'.[5]

I. Technology and Dignity

As lawyers, specializing in human dignity issues, we are familiar with this phenomenon. Who else, if not us, could try to give the overburdened nursing scientists a hand? We could ask and discuss how these technologies are to be assessed from a legal point of view. If it is the major duty of all state authority to respect and to protect the inviolable dignity of each and every human being,[6] can it then be legally permissible and ethically sound to ghettoize, to deceive and to monitor older people with dementia?

In my opinion, however, a far deeper and more fundamental question would be:[7] What can we, as lawyers, still seeking for a better, clearer and more nuanced understanding of human dignity as a legal concept,[8] learn from these examples and the ongoing ethical discussion of these and other comparable technologies for our understanding of human dignity?

II. Dementia and Dignity

At first glance, it seems profoundly inhumane to lock away people in 'dementiavilles', offering them a bizarre kind of 'Truman show' rather than trying to integrate them into the 'real' world and the 'real' society outside the gates of *De Hogeweyk* and similar institutions. It seems to be more than dubious, as well, to provide the residents of nursing homes with 'cybercompanions', even though many nursing home residents seem to really enjoy the time spent with *Paro*. And it seems, finally, to be totally out of

---

5   Niemeijer et al, 'Ethical and practical concerns of surveillance technologies' 1138.
6   See especially: Art. 1 I Basic Law for the Federal Republic of Germany (official translation at www.gesetze-im-internet.de/englisch_gg/englisch_gg.html): 'Human dignity shall be inviolable. To respect and protect it shall be the duty of all state authority.'
7   cp CM Hertogh, *Technology and dementia—What are the ethical implications?* https://www.youtube.com/watch?v=MQCv-2a5yUg.
8   See C McCrudden (ed), *Understanding Human Dignity* (Oxford, Oxford University Press, 2013).

the question to tag and to track people with dementia with GPS technology as if they were dangerous criminals, even though it might be significantly cheaper to track them then to send out helicopters and police officers again and again.

Nevertheless, each of these examples deserves a closer look:

De Hogeweyk is not much more expensive per resident than more traditional nursing homes. It is fully publicly funded. The residents get individualized 24-hour care tailored to the person that could hardly be provided in their home setting or ordinary nursing homes. They are able to share their day-to-day life with a small group of like-minded people in an environment they are familiar with. The residents can enter the gardens, the streets, and squares without supervision, and they can even leave it accompanied by someone as a matter of course. They are offered a whole range of meaningful activities outside the households such as going out for grocery shopping, visiting a pub or enjoying a concert at the theater. The numerous amenities available at *De Hogeweyk* attract people from the outside community as well. 120 volunteers, not including family members, support the care persons.[9] The residents seem alert, engaged and happy within the make-believe world of *De Hogeweyk*.

Paro, the therapeutic robot, is not used as a substitute for interpersonal relationships in elder care settings. It is used to stimulate interaction between patients and their caregivers. Initial studies show that the cute robot can waken deep emotions even in people who seem to be completely withdrawn in themselves and inapproachable by any other means.[10]

Devices like *Mindme*, finally, can enable people with mild forms of dementia to remain independent for longer, staying in their own homes, as the vast majority prefers. They can ease their fear of getting lost and they also alleviate the burdens of their caregivers by providing them with peace of mind.[11] In nursing home settings, 'smart carpets'[12] and other forms of

---

9   See Anderzhon et al, *Design for Aging* 149–52.
10 See Robinson et al 'The Psychosocial Effects of a Companion Robot: A Randomized Controlled Trial'; Dahlkamp, 'Eine Robbe zum Erinnern'.
11 See R McShane, 'Should Patients with Dementia Who Wander Be Electronically Tagged? Yes' (2013) 346 *British Medical Journal* 3603; Niemeijer et al, 'Place of surveillance technology in residential care' 203; SA Zwijsen et al, 'Surveillance Technology: An Alternative to Physical Restraints? A Qualitative Study among Professionals Working in Nursing Homes for People with Dementia' (2012) 49 *International Journal of Nursing Studies* 212, 216.

discrete surveillance technology can help avoiding more restrictive methods of safeguarding people, like locking doors or physically restraining people.[13]

My impression is that these and other technologies[14] in themselves are less problematic than one would initially assume. It is, as in most cases, crucial how they are designed[15] and how they are used in each individual case.[16]

III. Aging and Dignity

Nevertheless, these technologies are significant[17] because they make us aware of a much more fundamental problem: the challenge of the rapidly aging society. The gates of *De Hogeweyk* are more likely to strike our attention than the often precarious living conditions in ordinary nursing homes.[18] The fake reality of such communities is much more likely to be perceived as a problem than the devastating loneliness of many old people living socially isolated in their own homes. According to a recent study of

---

12   See, most recently, O Tanaka et al, 'A Smart Carpet Design for Monitoring People with Dementia' in H Selvaraj, D Zydek and G Chmaj (eds), *Progress in Systems Engineering* (Cham, Springer International Publishing, 2015).

13   See S Te Boekhorst et al, 'Quality of life of nursing-home residents'; Zwijsen et al, 'Surveillance technology'; A Jerrentrup, 'Technische Hilfen bei der Betreuung Demenzkranker: Definition "Weglaufschutzsystem" und "elektronische Fußfessel"' (2011) 21 *Sozialrecht und Praxis* 479.

14   See, for instance, W Moyle et al, 'Connecting the Person with Dementia and Family: A Feasibility Study of a Telepresence Robot' (2014) 14 *BMC Geriatrics* 7.

15   cp Niemeijer et al 'Ethical and practical concerns of surveillance technologies in residential care for people with dementia or intellectual disabilities' 207.

16   cp M Cash, 'Assistive Technology and People with Dementia' (2003) 13 *Reviews in Clinical Gerontology* 313.

17   cp J. Churchill, quoted by S Gadow, 'Touch and Technology: Two Paradigms of Patient Care' (1984) 23 *Journal of Religion and Health* 63, 65: 'The technological progress of industrial culture has exhibited alienation in a form stark enough for recognition, so we apt to blame technology. This is a mistake. Technology is not the cause of our alienation from the world of our experience. It is the friendly symptom without which our malady would be invisible, and thus beyond treatment. Technology merely exhibits our malady and opens the possibility of cure.'

18   See, for instance, S Moritz, *Staatliche Schutzpflichten gegenüber pflegebedürftigen Menschen* (Baden-Baden, Nomos, 2013) 17–94 and 127 ff.

the British Alzheimer's Society, 250.000 people, almost one third of those having dementia, are now living alone in their own homes. Of those, 29 per cent only see friends or family once a week, while 23 per cent can only expect one weekly phone call. It is not exaggerated to call this an 'epidemic of loneliness'.[19] *Paro* illustrates the enormous difficulty to get access to the world of people with the most serious dementia.[20] *Mindme*, finally, draws our attention to one of the main problems of healthcare provision, namely the delicate balancing act between service-levels and cost[21] that needs to be frankly and emphatically discussed.[22]

The significant increase of the number of older people with dementia, in absolute and relative terms, might be the most challenging aspect of the aging society. The number of people with dementia is expected to nearly double every 20 years.[23] This evolution is also a challenge for lawyers specializing in human dignity issues. I recently finished a book chapter on the dignity of critically ill and dying patients.[24] And I had to learn that this

---

19 L Donelly, 'Thousands of dementia sufferers rarely see loved ones: Tens of thousands of elderly people with dementia see friends or family just once a week, according to a landmark report warning of an "epidemic of loneliness" among Britain's most vulnerable' www.telegraph.co.uk/health/healthnews/9976001/Thousands-of-dementia-sufferers-rarely-see-loved-ones.html.

20 Groundbreaking: TM Kitwood, *Dementia Reconsidered: The Person Comes First* (Maidenhead, Open University Press, 1997).

21 cp A Griffiths, 'Can technology fill the elderly care gap?: With the proportion of over-65s on the increase, Britain is facing a crisis when it comes to care of the elderly. Is technology the answer?' www.telegraph.co.uk/active/9983886/Can-technology-fill-the-elderly-care-gap.html; Eltis, 'Predicating Dignity on Autonomy?' 414.

22 See, eg, S Huster, *Soziale Gesundheitsgerechtigkeit: Sparen, umverteilen, vorsorgen?* (Berlin, Klaus Wagenbach, 2011).

23 M Prince et al, 'The Global Prevalence of Dementia: A Systematic Review and Metaanalysis' (2013) 9 *Alzheimer's & Dementia* 63; M Prince, M Prina and M Guerchet, 'World Alzheimer Report 2013: Journey of Caring' www.alz.co.uk/research/WorldAlzheimerReport2013.pdf; World Health Organization and Alzheimer's Disease International, *Dementia: A Public Health Priority* (Geneva, World Health Organization, 2012) 32. For a more optimistic outlook, see FE Matthews et al, 'A Two-Decade Comparison of Prevalence of Dementia in Individuals Aged 65 Years and Older from Three Geographical Areas of England: Results of the Cognitive Function and Ageing Study I and II' (2013) 382 *The Lancet* 1405.

24 C Goos, '"Innere Freiheit": Der grundgesetzliche Würdebegriff in seiner Bedeutung für die Begleitung Schwerkranker und Sterbender' in N Feinendegen et al (eds), *Menschliche Würde und Spiritualität in der Begleitung am Lebens-*

topic is, at least in Germany, a kind of 'blind spot' in the scholarly literature. While evaluating the commentaries on the German Basic Law, and there are quite a lot of them, one almost gets the impression that the dignity of the embryo and even the dignity of the deceased are much more relevant questions to German constitutional lawyers than the dignity of older people. Some commentaries on Article 1 German Basic Law do not even mention questions of age, sickness, care and dying. Others contain, at least, brief reflections on a death with dignity, but they are, with only one exception, limited to the topic of self-determination about the end of somebody's life.[25] This is without any doubt an enormously important question, but clearly not the full story: We need to think about death with dignity, but we also urgently need to reflect on how we can enable elderly people to live their lives with dignity.[26]

IV. Grandma's Dignity?

It was not until 2013 that the first German handbook on 'Elder Law', edited by Ulrich Becker and Markus Roth, appeared.[27] In the United States, the elder law as a specialty devoted to the legal needs of older people has a longer tradition. The first issue of the *Elder Law Journal* appeared 1993,[28] two years later followed by the first edition of *Elder Law in a Nutshell*.[29]

The 'Elder Law', however, is also subject to fundamental criticism. 'I May Be Older, But I Ain't No "Elder": A Critique of "Elder Law"', for instance, is the title of a remarkable paper, published by Sue Westwood, a gerontologist and legal scholar, in 2012. Westwood criticizes that the notion of 'elder law' perpetuates the myth that older people are somehow

---

ende: *Impulse aus Theorie und Praxis* (Würzburg, Königshausen & Neumann, 2014).
25   For detailed references, see ibid 55 ff.
26   cp IE van Gennip et al, 'The Development of a Model of Dignity in Illness Based on Qualitative Interviews with Seriously Ill Patients' (2013) 50 *International Journal of Nursing Studies* 1080.
27   U Becker and M Roth (eds), *Recht der Älteren* (Berlin, de Gruyter, 2013). See, however, P Häberle, 'Altern und Alter des Menschen als Verfassungsproblem' in P Badura and R Scholz (eds), *Wege und Verfahren des Verfassungslebens: Festschrift für Peter Lerche zum 65. Geburtstag* (Munich, C.H. Beck, 1993).
28   See publish.illinois.edu/elderlawjournal.
29   LA Frolik and RL Kaplan, *Elder Law in a Nutshell*, 5th edn (St. Paul, MN, West Publishing, 2010).

different as a collective identity from the rest of the population, in turn reinforcing the notion that they have distinct special needs, issues, and requirements not shared by those who are younger. The terms 'elder' and 'the elderly' clump all older people together as if they constitute a single homogenous group, which they do not. According to Westwood, the legal profession would better serve people in later life by emphasizing the shared issues among people, young and old, and defining legal practice by its content and function, not by categorizing its clients in a way which involves negatively stereotyping them.[30]

I fully agree with Westwood on that point and have therefore put the 'elderly' in inverted commas in the title of my contribution. There are no 'elderly', and, more importantly, there is no such thing as 'grandma's dignity'.[31] Grandma's dignity is our dignity. Her dignity might be more vulnerable,[32] but it still remains the same dignity we all share.[33]

Over the last few decades, the very old age has become a normal part of life rather than an exception. People aged over 85 are the fastest growing age-group in our population.[34] That implies that the everyday reality of those so-called 'oldest old', ranging from good health and relative independence to frailty and the most severe forms of dementia, has become a normal part of life rather than an exception as well. The complexity and diversity of the reality of these 'oldest old'[35] shows us quite plainly how problematic the common equation of dignity, rationality and autonomy is. Charles Foster quotes Giovanni Pico della Mirandola's 'On Dignity of

---

30　S Westwood, 'I may be older, but I ain't no "elder"': A critique of "elder law"' (2012) 21 *Temple Political & Civil Rights Law Review* 485.

31　cp L Nordenfelt, 'The Concept of Dignity' in L Nordenfelt (ed), *Dignity in Care for Older People* (Wiley-Blackwell 2009).

32　cp D Jopp et al, *Zweite Heidelberger Hundertjährigen-Studie: Herausforderungen und Stärken des Lebens mit 100 Jahren* (Stuttgart, Robert-Bosch-Stiftung, 2013) 67; W Härle, 'Verletzlichkeit im Alter aus ethischer Sicht' in A Kruse, T Rentsch and HP Zimmermann (eds), *Gutes Leben im hohen Alter: Das Altern in seinen Entwicklungsmöglichkeiten und Entwicklungsgrenzen verstehen* (Heidelberg, Akademische Verlagsgesellschaft, 2012); Nordenfelt, 'The Concept of Dignity' 50.

33　cp KF Gärditz, 'Verfassungsrechtliche Grundfragen des Schutzes Dementer' (2010) 19 *Zeitschrift für Lebensrecht* 40; V Wetzstein, 'Alzheimer-Demenz: Perspektiven einer integrativen Demenz-Ethik' (2005) 51 *Zeitschrift für medizinische Ethik* 27, 33.

34　SG Post, *The Moral Challenge of Alzheimer Disease* (Baltimore, Johns Hopkins University Press, 1995) 2.

35　See, most recently, Jopp et al, *Zweite Heidelberger Hundertjährigen-Studie*.

man':[36] 'The gift was a stamp of the divine: its status was dignity, its nature was reason, and its consequence was autonomy.' And he comments:

> This is a pleasingly neat formulation. It pleased the Renaissance, it pleased Kant, and it continues to please many modern bioethicists. But neat formulations don't do well when confronted with the messiness of real humans.[37]

Focusing on just one human faculty, the will, does not only lead to 'a truncated view of humanity and human experience'.[38] It is downright dangerous because it 'wrongly excludes people with dementia from the sphere of human dignity and respect'.[39]

V. Conclusion

Facing the challenge of the aging society, neat formulations are the very last thing we need. What we need instead is a more inclusive, more realistic, more holistic understanding of human dignity.[40] As human beings, we all are embodied selves.[41] The fact that we are embodied selves, unique in

---

36 See Goos, '"Innere Freiheit"' 68–70; R Gröschner, 'Des Menschen Würde – humanistische Tradition eines Verfassungsprinzips' in R Gröschner, S Kirste and OW Lembcke (eds), *Des Menschen Würde – entdeckt und erfunden im Humanismus der italienischen Renaissance* (Tübingen, Mohr Siebeck, 2008); cp also E Cassirer, 'Giovanni Pico Della Mirandola: A Study in the History of Renaissance Ideas' (1942) 3 *Journal of the History of Ideas* 123 (Part I), 319 (Part II).
37 C Foster, *Human Dignity in Bioethics and Law* (Oxford, Hart Publishing, 2011) 34.
38 D Luban, 'Lawyers as Upholders of Human Dignity (When They Aren't Busy Assaulting It)' (2005) *University of Illinois Law Review* 815, 826; see also, criticizing the one-sided fixation on cognition, Wetzstein, 'Alzheimer-Demenz' 34.
39 Post, *Moral challenge of Alzheimer disease* 2.
40 See, eg, C Dupré, 'Unlocking human dignity: Towards a theory for the 21st century' (2009) 2 *European human rights law review* 190, 193; cp also Gärditz, 'Verfassungsrechtliche Grundfragen des Schutzes Dementer' (n 33) 40; J Bullington, 'Being Body: The Dignity of Human Embodiment' in L Nordenfelt (ed), *Dignity in care for older people* (Chichester, Wiley-Blackwell, 2009) 71–75.
41 cp M Coors, 'A Dementalized Body? Reconsidering the Human Condition in the Light of Dementia' (2013) 1 *Geriatric Mental Health Care* 34; AV Campbell, 'Being Mindful of the Body: Enriching the Conceptual Background of Bioethics' (2009) 1 *Law, Innovation and Technology* 171, 175–79; cp also AV Campbell, *The Body in Bioethics* (London, Routledge, 2009); Bullington, 'Be-

space and time, constitutes our dignity.[42] As we are embodied selves, dependence,[43] vulnerability and limitations, change, loss and death, messiness, helplessness and uncertainties are no exceptions. They are integral parts of human life.[44] And as they are integral parts of human life, it is essential to integrate them into a contemporary understanding of human dignity as a legal concept.[45] If we can succeed in this, we will be better prepared for the challenge of the aging society.[46]

---

ing Body' (n 40) 69 ff; G Böhme, *Ethik leiblicher Existenz: Über unseren moralischen Umgang mit der eigenen Natur* (Frankfurt am Main, Suhrkamp, 2008).

42 Bullington 'Being Body: The Dignity of Human Embodiment' 71.
43 See Gadow, 'Touch and technology' 67: '[D]ignity and dependence need not conflict. Dependence upon another for care of the body constitutes an indignity only when the person becomes an object for the caregiver. In reality, physical care from another presents a possibility for dignity greater than if a patient were capable of independent self-care.'
44 cp MC Nussbaum, *Frontiers of Justice: Disability, Nationality, Species Membership* (Cambridge, Mass, Belknap Press of Harvard University Press, 2007) 160; O Bayer, 'Self-Creation? On the Dignity of Human Beings' (2004) 20 *Modern Theology* 275, 285.
45 cp Goos '"Innere Freiheit": Der grundgesetzliche Würdebegriff in seiner Bedeutung für die Begleitung Schwerkranker und Sterbender' 80–91; see also J von Bernstorff, 'Der Streit um die Menschenwürde im Grund- und Menschenrechtsschutz: Eine Verteidigung des Absoluten als Grenze und Auftrag' (2013) 68 *JuristenZeitung* 905, 910 f. cp also HG Gadamer, 'Die Menschenwürde auf ihrem Weg von der Antike bis heute' (1988) 12 *Humanistische Bildung* 95, 98, considering Romano Guardini's view of death as the 'ontological dignity' of man being the starting point for all efforts to get to a cross-cultural conception of human dignity.
46 cp Häberle, 'Altern und Alter des Menschen als Verfassungsproblem' 202, describing the concept of human dignity as the theoretical foundation of any consideration on age and aging as constitutional problems.

Biotechnologies and Human Dignity

Marion Albers

Modern biotechnologies are among the reasons explaining the new focus on the idea of human dignity in public, political and scientific discourses. Topics being debated range from assisted reproduction, cloning, genetic diagnostics and genetic intervention, neuroprosthetics, cyborgs or artificial life all the way to visions of 'transhumanism' or 'posthumanity'. With their potential for bringing about radical transformations, advanced biotechnologies are forcing the notion and boundaries of what is human to be revisited. The biological foundations of humankind are more and more accessible, can be modified in a targeted way, and thus become the object of decisions. Naturalistic self-descriptions are being questioned and replaced by forms of description which are explicitly culturally constructed. We have to rethink the very question of what it means to be human and how we are to construct human boundaries or the difference between human beings and their environment. This creates a new background for the normative concepts of human rights, rights of the individual and human dignity. Through reference to the dignity of a *human being* and to the idea of *dignity*, the concept of human dignity implies notions attached to what constitutes being human. This fundamental meaning is supported by the multifarious traditions of human dignity, by its function as a key concept in interdisciplinary debates and not least by its prominent status in legal texts and discourses. Views of the role of human dignity, though, could not be more divergent. The conviction that dignity is an essential normative concept is juxtaposed with criticism that it is useless, nebulous, incoherent or even reactionary.

This article starts by providing an overview of significant biotechnological fields and visions as well as of essential discussions referring to human dignity. The analysis identifies core problems and new challenges regarding human dignity and its use as an argument (I.). Since biotechnologies and the societal discourse on them develop, approaches to human dignity and potential violations become more nuanced (I. A- H.). The second part examines, particularly with regard to new challenges of biotechnologies, legal contexts of human dignity, especially texts and documents enshrining human dignity (II. A.), legislation (II. B.), the reasoning of courts (II. C.) and scientific discourses (II. D.). In the final part of this article, I will focus on the need to contextualize and differentiate the concept of human dignity – a concept that is probably more obviously than ever before a social construction as well as an extraordinarily complex legal conception (III.). Biotechnologies will prove to be a productive field of reference for discourse about human dignity, and the idea of human dignity is by no means useless.

I. Fields, Visions and Discussions

In public discourse, biotechnologies are often contrasted in a sweeping manner with human dignity as a normative measure. However, biotechnologies cover numerous fields as well as different practices. Considering the word stem 'bíos' their fields encompass all areas of biological organisms or processes, for instance, manufacturing particular products, developing new species of plants, creating novel food, constructing bacteria or cloning animals. Even if the topic of human dignity confines the focus to the human being (while the question of how to describe the boundaries has to be kept in mind), the fields are wide-ranging and quite heterogeneous. At a fundamental level, we can observe groundbreaking developments, such as more and more sophisticated assisted reproduction or the ongoing construction and decoding of DNA structures,[1] followed by the emergence of gene diagnostics or genome editing. Further biotechnologies, data processing and information technologies, neurotechnologies, nanotechnology, robotics and synthetic biology have entered the picture, and the synergies between different technologies are accelerating change. With regard to the increasing accessibility and modifiability of the biological foundations of humankind, which had previously seemed to be a self-evident given, the core of advanced biotechnologies may be described as 'the potential to alter and, to a degree, to control the phenomena of human life'[2] or as the

---

1   The familiar double helix model is a limited scientific construction, see for further developments RN Irobalieva, JM Fogg, DJ Catanese, T Sutthibutpong, M Chen, AK Barker, SJ Ludtke, SA Harris, MF Schmid, W Chiu and L Zechiedrich, 'Structural Diversity of Supercoiled DNA' (2015) 6 *Nature Communications* 8440, DOI:10.1038/ncomms9440.
2   The President's Council on Bioethics (ed), *Beyond Therapy: Biotechnology and the Pursuit of Happiness* (Washington D.C., 2003) 2.

'management of life'[3] and, moreover, as the creation of life in the sense of targeted interventions in previously 'natural' functions. The manufacture of synthetic life shows that even the familiar distinction between technology and life is becoming blurred.[4] At a more concrete level, however, each field involves a wide range of different issues and areas of application.

Beside these requirements for more concrete specification, biotechnologies encompass different praxes. We may distinguish between technical methods or applications and technologies as scientific knowledge, although there is no clear-cut boundary between them. In addition, we can distinguish between technologies which can be applied today and technologies which are envisaged in future scenarios. If we assume that technologies are embedded in society, 'biotechnologies' are not defined in terms of technical knowledge alone. Comprehensive knowledge about biotechnologies is produced in society in general, as well as in various scientific disciplines.[5] This is all the more true when considering practices that are already being applied, scenarios based on available knowledge, and prognoses or futuristic visions. The latter can, even in the form of science fiction novels, promote technical ideas; but they cannot be regarded as scenarios which are certain to become reality in the future. The multitude and convergence of technologies and the broad spectrum ranging from unproblematic to widely rejected applications characterize biotechnologies just as much as the scope extending from applied techniques all the way to futuristic predictions and the plurality of knowledge, which is both a factor in and a product of the discussions.

Precisely this complexity makes biotechnologies one of the most interesting reference fields for discourse about human dignity. Although this is not always the case such questions can involve issues related to the very existence of humankind and also cause matters which had previously been regarded as self-evident truths to be contingent. Additionally, biotechnol-

---

3   T Vidalis, 'Meeting Darwin: The Gradual Emergence of Biolaw' (2009) 6 *Journal of International Biotechnology Law* 221, 222 ff.
4   See, with differentiations, A Grunwald, *Technikzukünfte als Medium von Zukunftsdebatten und Technikgestaltung* (Karlsruhe, KIT Scientific Publishing, 2012) 177 ff.
5   cf A Grunwald, 'Philosophy and the Concept of Technology – On the Anthropological Significance of Technology' in A Grunwald, M Gutmann and E Neumann-Held (eds), *On Human Nature* (Berlin/Heidelberg/New York, Springer, 2002) 179 ff, with broader considerations on the concept of technology.

ogies are advancing, many different fields and areas of application have already been developed, and the discussions are becoming more and more nuanced. Hence, the notion of human dignity and potential violations must also be more clearly delineated. The following analysis explores how human dignity is used in debates about particularly relevant biotechnologies.

A. Assisted Reproduction, Especially Surrogacy

Assisted reproduction suggests itself as a starting point. Discussions can draw upon more or less established practices as well as imaginable ones. Assisted reproduction already encompasses a variety of different approaches: In-vitro fertilization and the subsequent transfer of the embryo into the uterus, cryopreservation of gametes or fertilized egg cells for the purpose of a transfer at a later date ('social freezing'), sperm and egg cell donation or surrogacy. At times, even the technical nature and the artificiality of procreation are regarded as problematic because they are said to lead to a situation where new human life is no longer created in a 'natural' way and as the result of chance, but is instead planned and 'made', or because it is said that no 'natural' mother-child bonding can occur.[6] Mostly, however, it is the way the people involved, their bodies and their psychological and social needs are treated which dominates discussions of human dignity.

In this respect, surrogacy in particular is under discussion. There are different types of surrogacy. A genetic surrogate is inseminated naturally or artificially and carries the baby for the intended parents. In gestational surrogacy, the egg and sperm of the intended parents or of donors are used for in-vitro fertilization, and the embryo is placed into the womb of the surrogate. Globally speaking, surrogacy now numbers among the widely

---

[6] Aside from being socially constructed 'naturalness' and 'artificiality', though, are comparative concepts: Things are more or less natural. Furthermore, the concept of natural can refer to the way something came into existence, its genesis, or to its quality and appearance. Both might diverge: an artificial genesis can lead to a result that is judged to be natural on the basis of its appearance. See D Birnbacher, *Natürlichkeit* (Berlin/New York: de Gruyter, 2006) 4 ff. But cf also for the far-reaching changes due to the 'the artificial recreation of life in the laboratory' C Delaunay, 'The Beginning of Human Life at the Laboratory: The Challenges of a Technological Future for Human Reproduction' (2015) 40 *Technology in Society* 14, 14 ff, 23.

employed reproductive technologies.[7] At the center of issues concerning human dignity is the woman whose body is used for a pregnancy, with all the associated intense relationships in the context of the surrogate motherhood. The scenario, which is by no means far-fetched, of women being held captive and forced to produce children would be classified as a violation of human dignity.[8] Some argue that, in principle, surrogacy undermines the human dignity of the woman carrier, because her body and its reproductive function are brokered as a commodity.[9] The acquirement of an extensive hold over the body of the woman, considering the involvement of the whole body, the relationship between the pregnant woman and the embryo that develops during a pregnancy and the risks associated with pregnancy and giving birth, is highlighted.[10] Others reject a violation of human dignity to the extent that willingness to act as a surrogate mother can be classified as based on a voluntary decision, for example when female family members or female friends volunteer.[11] If the autonomy of the surrogate mother is the focus of attention, considerations in connection with human dignity shift to the conditions that make free decisions possible or impossible and to the conditions of the surrogacy arrangement as a whole.[12] Poverty and commercialization are likely to create economic

---

[7] See the estimate that more than 25000 children are thought to be born to Indian surrogates in P Shetty, 'India's Unregulated Surrogacy Industry' (2012) 380 *The Lancet* 1633, 1633. Cf also AH Elder, 'Wombs to Rent: Examining the Jurisdiction of International Surrogacy' (2014) 16 *Oregon Review of International Law*, 347, 352 ff.

[8] For this scenario see, eg, Hague Conference on Private International Law, Private international law issues surrounding the status of children, including issues arising from international surrogacy arrangements, Preliminary Document No. 11 of March 2011, Sect. 34, http://www.hcch.net/index_en.php?act=publications.details&pid=6175.

[9] See, eg, Parliamentary Assembly of the Council of Europe, Motion for a resolution: Human Rights and ethical issues related to surrogacy, Doc 13562, 1.7.2014, http://assembly.coe.int/nw/xml/XRef/Xref-XML2HTML-en.asp?fileid=21092&lang=en.

[10] Secretariat of the Commission of the Bishop's Conferences of the European Community (COMECE), Opinion of the Reflection Group on Bioethics on Gestational Surrogacy, 2015, 7 f.

[11] See, eg, T Hörnle, 'Menschenwürde und Ersatzmutterschaft' in JC Joerden, E Hilgendorf and F Thiele (eds), *Menschenwürde und Medizin* (Berlin, Duncker & Humblot, 2013) 743, 748 f; P Jofer, *Die Regulierung der Reproduktionsmedizin* (Baden-Baden, Nomos, 2015) 310 ff.

[12] See with different approaches CA Choudhury, 'The Political Economy and Legal Regulation of Transnational Commercial Surrogate Labor' (2015) 48

pressures.[13] Nevertheless, there is disagreement about whether such circumstances are sufficient to cause a violation of human dignity.[14] A further point of discussion is the selection of surrogate mothers on the basis of particular properties. Commercialization and specialized agencies might contribute to circumstances in which surrogates are chosen like goods for sale. As to the child, some emphasize that he or she might be seen as a commodity which has to feature particular properties and to fulfill particular expectations.[15] The scenario that a child might be 'rejected' has become reality in one case in which an Australian couple left a twin boy with Down syndrome ('Baby Gammy') with his Thai surrogate mother and only accepted the healthy baby girl. In addition, scenarios are conceivable in which children are 'produced' for the purpose of sexually abusing them, inflicting violence upon them or for forced labor. However, regarding babies as commodities or objects is in reality not the typical result of surrogacy and the implications depend not least on how surrogacy is regulated. Even this brief overview shows that the blanket assumption that human dignity is being violated by particular reproductive technologies is increasingly being superseded by arguments that can be differentiated in terms of content, reference point and level.

B. Embryo and Stem Cell Research

Techniques used in assisted reproductive technology have resulted in a cascade of new fields of biotechnology. Embryonic and stem cell research

---

Vanderbilt Journal of Transnational Law 1, 50 ff, 63 f; K Galloway, 'Theoretical Approaches to Human Dignity, Human Rights and Surrogacy' in P Gerber and K O'Byrne (eds), *Surrogacy, Law and Human Rights* (Farnham/Burlington, Ashgate Publishing, 2015) 26 ff. For the difficulties of reaching an international regime see Y Ergas 'Babies Without Borders: Human Rights, Human Dignity, and the Regulation of International Commercial Surrogacy' (2013) 27 *Emory International Law Review* 117, 163 ff.

13   This is among the reasons why India aims at restricting the booming surrogacy industry, see The Surrogacy (Regulation) Bill, 2016, http://www.prsindia.org/billtrack/the-surrogacy-regulation-bill-2016-4470/.

14   See Dutch National Rapporteur on Trafficking in Human Beings, *Human trafficking for the purpose of the removal of organs and forced commercial surrogacy* (The Hague, 2012) 17 ff; cf also CA Choudhury, 'The Political Economy' 4 ff.

15   Secretariat of the Commission, Opinion, 13.

in particular have sparked debate on biotechnology and human dignity of varying intensity in different countries.[16] Assisted reproductive technology procedures inevitably result in surplus embryos. In addition, these procedures make it possible to fertilize egg cells in vitro and to allow them to develop into differentiated cell structures to a certain stage. In the initial stages the cells are totipotent, i.e., they can divide and develop into an entire individual provided the necessary conditions exist. This development potential that exists in principle, however, can in the meantime be suppressed from the outset using genetic engineering. Embryos in vitro also open up possibilities for harvesting embryonic stem cells, an area highly interesting to researchers.[17] Given the current state of research such a process results in the embryo being destroyed. Embryonic stem cells themselves are considered pluripotent; however, the extent of their potential for development has only been partly established and this potential can also be manipulated through artificial techniques. More recent research has derived stem cells not only from somatic cells (induced pluripotent stem cells) but also from parthenogenetic blastocysts (parthenogenetic stem cells)[18] and aims at developing effective methods to revert specialized cells back to an embryonic stage (reprogramming).[19]

In debate over this, the first complex of issues revolves around the question of whether embryos are protected by or, going even further, enti-

---

16 See, eg, T Farajkhoda, 'An Overview on Ethical Considerations in Stem Cell Research in Iran and Ethical Recommendations: A Review' (2017), 15 *International Journal of Reproductive BioMedicine* 67, 68 ff; JA Robertson, 'Embryo Stem Cell Research: Ten Years of Controversy' (2010) 38 *Journal of Law, Medicine & Ethics* 191, 191 ff; FS Oduncu, 'Stem Cell Research in Germany: Ethics of Healing vs. Human Dignity' (2003) 6 *Medicine, Health Care and Philosophy* 5, 5 ff.

17 More closely, also regarding the term 'embryo' Jofer, *Regulierung* (2015) 323 ff, 447 ff.

18 The question whether a non-fertilised human ovum whose division and further development have been stimulated by parthenogenesis is 'capable of commencing the process of development of a human being just as an embryo created by fertilisation of an ovum can do so' was the subject matter of a decision of the ECJ, see Case C-364/13 *International Stem Cell Corporation* (2014), accessible under curia.europa.eu.

19 See MZ Ratajczak, T Jadczyk, D Pędziwiatr and W Wojakowski, 'New Advances in Stem Cell Research: Practical Implications for Regenerative Medicine' (2014) 124 *Polskie Archiwum Medycyny Wewnętrznej* 418 ff; D Cyranowski, 'Stem Cells: The Black Box of Reprogramming' (2014) 516 *Nature* 162 ff.

tled to human dignity. As a consequence of the progress of natural sciences this question is increasingly being expanded to cover the – distinguishable but closely linked – question of the prerequisites for it to be possible to speak of an embryo at all, which, given the necessary additional conditions, can develop into a human being. Frequently, the view is expressed that human life and human dignity as its inherent worth begin at the time of the fusion of egg and sperm cell, through which its genetic uniqueness is established.[20] But this apparently 'natural' position either insinuates numerous further presuppositions[21] or is confronted with the problem that its scientific basis is increasingly being eroded, for example as a result of the possibility of cell reprogramming, the suppression of cell development potential, or cloning. In the highly controversial and widely conducted debate over convincing criteria several categories such as species membership, identity, continuity and potentiality are being discussed. The spectrum of development phases being used to define the point where the protection of human dignity begins extends from early cell stages to nidation all the way to birth. The possibilities and results of recent research require further differentiations which are even more difficult to specify. Some proposals for classifying totipotent human artefacts, for example, draw a distinction between transient totipotence and totipotent transience to underline the criterion whether cell entities are or are not embedded in a possibly fictitious context of procreation.[22] Regardless of the stance adopted, it is becoming apparent that recognition of human dignity is a decision which, although in no way arbitrary, must be given reasons for in compliance with criteria accepted as more or less convincing in different cultures and contexts.

The second complex is also controversial, to a certain degree: Provided that the protection of human dignity applies, what is to be regarded as a violation of human dignity? Some people closely connect the protection of dignity with the protection of human life. As a result, they view, for ex-

---

20 cf, eg, EW Böckenförde, 'Menschenwürde als normatives Prinzip' (2003) *JuristenZeitung* 809, 812.
21 Especially in the context of Christian ethics, see Congregation for the Doctrine of the Faith, Instruction on respect for human life in its origin and on the dignity of procreation: replies to certain questions of the day (Donum Vitae) 1987.
22 J Kersten 'Der rechtliche Status totipotenter menschlicher Artefakte – Transiente Totipotenz vs. totipotente Transienz' in T Heinemann, HG Dederer and T Cantz (eds), *Entwicklungsbiologische Totipotenz in Ethik und Recht* (Göttingen, V&R unipress, 2014), 137, 147 ff.

ample, the destruction of human embryos for obtaining stem cells as a violation of human dignity. Usually, however, arguments related to human dignity are based on independent criteria. Regarding the harvesting of stem cells from embryos, it is less the destroying than it is their consumptive use for research purposes benefiting third parties that is the central point.[23] In part, a further differentiation is made here between on the one hand surplus embryos which would not proceed their development anyway under these circumstances, and on the other hand embryos which might have had the chance of being transferred into a womb, for example in the course of an embryo adoption. In addition, there is the conceivable constellation that embryos could be farmed specifically for consumptive embryo stem cell research. In the case of recognition of the right to protection of human dignity, in both of the latter two constellations a violation of human dignity is overwhelmingly recognized based on the argument that a human being is being treated like an object and instrumentalized for purposes benefiting third parties. Here the guiding principle derives from historical experiences with research on living human beings, which contributed to establishing the concept of human dignity.

C. Reproductive Cloning

In addition to embryo and stem cell research, reproductive cloning is a central topic in the human dignity debate. It is based on a future scenario, which, however, can be supported by reference to the already widely established cloning of animals. Meanwhile, techniques beyond cloning have entered the picture, e.g., the derivation of reproductively viable gametes via reprogramming (in vitro gametogenesis).[24] These techniques raise their own problems as well as questions similar to those of cloning.[25]

In the case of human beings, even the necessary research prompts objections on the grounds of human dignity. This is all the more true because cloning research would be a matter of consumptive embryo stem cell research. Human dignity is being discussed in scenarios where cloning takes

---

23 See, eg, Oduncu, 'Stem Cell Research' 11, 14.
24 See IG Cohen, GQ Daley and EY Adashi, 'Disruptive Reproductive Technologies' (2017), 9 (372) *Science Translational Medicine* 1 ff. (DOI:10.1126/scitranslmed.aag2959).
25 SM Suter, '*In Vitro* Gametogenesis: Just Another Way to Have a Baby?' (2016), 3 *Journal of Law and the Biosciences* 87, 91 ff.

place without the cloned person's consent. The requirement for consent is partly based on the use of body cells of the person, partly on the consequences the production and existence of a clone would have for the self-image and the social position of the cloned person. From another perspective, discussion is focused on the human dignity of the clone. Some people reject human dignity as an argument because the clone only exists by virtue of cloning. However, the production of a clone as a potential violation of human dignity and the question of whether an existing clone can claim that a violation of human dignity is responsible for his or her existence are two separate questions. Some people regard the production of a clone as a violation of human dignity because they consider a person to be defined by his or her genetic uniqueness and a clone not to have the preconditions for or the possibility of a sufficient level of autonomy due to social expectations that the clone will resemble the cloned person.[26] Others point out that this perspective is based on genetic determinism which is incorrect and that it would be the inappropriate pressure or social expectations placed on the individual clone that challenge the clone's human dignity.[27] Usually uncontested violations of human dignity are, however, cloning scenarios such as clones bred as human beings that are deliberately stunted to do inferior works, clones bred to be enslaved or clones bred to serve as warriors or as an organ bank.[28] The discussions show that the idea of human dignity is becoming increasingly complex in its construction and is being more clearly delineated. In addition, uncertainty and the assumptions people base their rationale on are playing a major role. In many cases it is assumptions about social or psychological consequences that are caus-

---

26 See, eg, C Kaveny, 'Cloning and Positive Liberty' (1999) 13 *Notre Dame Journal of Law, Ethics & Public Policy* 15, 29 ff.

27 T Caulfield, 'Human Cloning Laws, Human Dignity and the Poverty of the Policy Making Dialogue' (2003) 4 *BMC Medical Ethics*, www.biomedcentral.com/1472-6939/4/3; RG Wright, 'Second Thoughts: How Human Cloning Can Promote Human Dignity' (2000) 35 *Valparaiso University Law Review* 1, 5 ff, 31 ff.

28 Wright, 'Second Thoughts' 18 f; T Hörnle, 'Menschenwürde und reproduktives Klonen' in JC Joerden, E Hilgendorf, F Thiele (eds), *Menschenwürde und Medizin* (Berlin, Duncker & Humblot, 2013) 765, 770 f; for imaginable scenarios and their probability see also A Bühl, 'Reproduktives Klonen in "real life" und in der Science Fiction' in A Bühl (ed), *Auf dem Weg zur biomächtigen Gesellschaft?* (Wiesbaden, VS Verlag für Sozialwissenschaften, 2009) 273, 298 ff, 306 ff.

ing controversy, rather than normative judgments about violations of human dignity made on the basis of certain assumptions.

D. Genetic Diagnostics

The work on the decoding of the human genome and the development of a series of technologies that have the capacity to generate vast quantities of DNA sequence data rapidly and at relatively low cost (next-generation sequencing) have advanced genetic diagnostics in an unprecedented manner. Above all in the US, questions of human dignity are being examined in the context of biobanks, which are classified as research 'on' human beings, although they are a matter of data referring to a person and of bodily materials separated from the body.[29] At times, human dignity is understood as the basis of self-determination, which is reflected in the requirement for 'informed consent'.[30] In this respect, a link is made to the 'concept of human dignity that is predominantly informed by post-Holocaust human-rights deliberations'[31]. In part, reference is made to the argument that with the development of genetic diagnostics, extensive information about human beings is becoming possible in principle. Human dignity is intended to offer protection against people becoming (relatively) transparent to other people – others who with such knowledge would be in a position to block or influence their development prospects. Sometimes reference to

---

29   Biobanks collect samples of bodily materials and medical or genetic data and information as well as general information about the health status or lifestyle of the person in question, in varying combinations, see M Albers, 'Rechtsrahmen und Rechtsprobleme bei Biobanken' (2013) 31 *Medizinrecht* 483, 483 f.

30   T Caulfield and R Brownsword, 'Human Dignity: A Guide to Policy Making in the Biotechnology Era?' (2006) 7 *Nature Review Genetics* 72, 73: '[…] this is the most common application of human dignity – that is, as the foundation for specific legal entitlements, such as informed consent. It is the least contentious use of the concept of human dignity.' More differentiating J Allen and B McNamara, 'Reconsidering the Value of Consent in Biobank Research' (2011) 25 *Bioethics* 155, 156 ff.

31   Caulfield and Brownsword, 'Human Dignity' 72, with references to the Universal Declaration of Human Rights, the Nuremberg Code and the Helsinki Declaration.

human dignity is made to establish protection against fundamental discrimination.[32]

In the case of embryos in vitro, certain genetic characteristics or dispositions can be detected by means of genetic testing prior to implantation in the womb. Whether and to what extent such pre-implantation testing is permissible and the decision to implant may be made dependent upon its results is being vigorously discussed in some countries from the human dignity perspective. In these discussions the central issue is less the possible death of the embryo and more the act of selection.[33] From the point of view of the individual, it is argued that the embryo could be 'discarded' because of its genetic make-up and thus not treated as an 'end in itself'. Looking at the matter more abstractly, objections related to human dignity are raised to the view that a life with certain genetic diseases should be avoided – because it devalues existing people who are living with such an illness, or because it promotes a view of human beings that does not adequately acknowledge imperfection as an element of human existence. The more extensive and refined the possibilities of pre-implantation diagnostics become, the less clearly defined the borders between selection and creation become even at this point in the process. 'Designer babies' is the popular catchword. Extensive selection decisions according to previously specified characteristics or dispositions – going beyond dispositions to illness to include for example, gender, hair and skin color, and intelligence – are being discussed in terms of human dignity. This involves, on the one hand, the individual person: using a distinction between born and made, some fear that fundamental impairments of identity, autonomy and recognition in the social community could be the outcome. On the other hand, human dignity is also taken into consideration in a more abstract way with a view to people who will live in the future or to humankind, which will be shaped by the technology-assisted selection of people living today.

---

32 See, eg, CWL Ho and TSH Khan, 'The Notion of Genetic Privacy' in TSH Khan and CWL Ho (eds), *Genetic Privacy: An Evaluation of the Ethical and Legal Landscape* (London, Imperial College Press, 2013) 1, 1 ff.

33 See, eg, D Birnbacher, 'Menschenwürde und Präimplantationsdiagnostik' in JC Joerden, E Hilgendorf and F Thiele (eds), *Menschenwürde und Medizin* (Berlin, Duncker & Humblot, 2013) 755, 760 ff.

E. Genetic Interventions

In addition to selection on the basis of information obtained through genetic diagnostics, genetic interventions are receiving increasing consideration. Like in other areas, technologies are developing quickly. Modern genome editing techniques, methods or tools allow for alterations of existing DNA sequences or insertion of new ones in a way that is considered to be surprisingly simple, controlled and cost-effective.[34] We can distinguish between interventions involving embryos, especially in case of assisted reproduction, and those involving born human beings who are or who may not be able to decide on their own. Furthermore, we can distinguish between interventions in germ cells and those in somatic cells. In the case of born human beings, genetic interventions via somatic gene therapy, gene transfer techniques or germline alterations are conceivable. Germline interventions affect all future generations. Transhumanist visions or science fiction narratives envisage the reshaping of humankind into a genetically modified post-human species.

Questions concerning violation of the dignity of individual people are being raised in connection with actions realized without their informed consent, even though they are in principle capable of making decisions. Clear cases are covert research on human beings or intervention by force in a person's genetic characteristics. The spectrum is more controversial in the case of genetic interventions in people who by virtue of lack of capacity to make decisions, are not in any way, no longer or not yet able to decide for themselves.[35] Interventions in the germline focus attention on relatively unknown future generations who could be affected by unpre-

---

34   cf, eg, JA Doudna and E Charpentier, 'The New Frontier of Genome Engineering with CRISPR-Cas9' (2014) 346 *Science* 6231, DOI:10.1126/science 1258096; JD Sander and JK Joung, 'CRISPR-Cas Systems for Editing, Regulating and Targeting Genomes' (2014) 32 *Nature Biotechnology* 347 ff. For further developments see F Richter, I Fonfara, R Gelfert, J Nack, E Charpentier, A Möglich, 'Switchable Cas9' (2017), in: 48 *Current Opinion in Biotechnology*, 119 ff.
35   cf, eg, M Salvi, 'Shaping Individuality: Human Inheritable Germ Line Gene Modification' (2001) 22 *Theoretical Medicine* 527, 529 ff; WC Radau, *Die Biomedizinkonvention des Europarates* (Berlin/Heidelberg/New York, Springer, 2006) 341 ff.

dictable mechanisms[36] or whose genes could be edited according to characteristics or dispositions chosen by others. Putting aside concerns about safety, however, despite germline alterations affect people not yet born, without their being able to agree to it, not every constellation raises problems in connection with human dignity. But constellations do exist where there is broad consensus on violations of human dignity. Scenarios include, for example, a situation where people are bred to take over various functions in a society featuring division of labor and people with brain functioning restricted by gene technology are used to carry out low-level work. Over and above the human dignity of individuals, some emphasize threats to humanity.

F. Neurotechnologies

Additional fields are attracting attention due to the convergence of biotechnology, neurotechnology and information technology: the possibilities of observing or intervening in the brain and the development of sophisticated human-machine interfaces.[37] Invasive or noninvasive techniques such as neuroimaging make it possible to examine brain structures and functions thoroughly and in real time and to analyze interrelationships with behavior.[38] Direct brain intervention methods include for example neurogenetic measures, deep brain stimulation, neural prostheses in various forms, or chips implanted in the brain. Neurogenetics involves supplementing or blocking neurotransmitters or replacing defective genes. Deep brain stimulation is less or more invasive in the form of electronic stimulation or implantation of electrodes that carry electrical signals to specific brain locations and cause the brain cells to change their activity.

---

36   cf E Lanphier, F Urnov, SE Haecker, M Werner and J Smolenski, 'Don't Edit the Human Germ Line' (2015) 519 *Nature* 410 f (emphasizing safety concerns).
37   For an overview see R Merkel, G Boer, J Fegert, T Galert, D Hartmann, B Nuttin and·S Rosahl, *Intervening in the Brain. Changing Psyche and Society* (Berlin/Heidelberg/New York, Springer, 2007), 117 ff; RH Blank, *Intervention in the Brain. Politics, Policy, and Ethics* (Cambridge/London, MIT Press, 2013) 25 ff; M Albers, 'Grundrechtsschutz und Innovationserfordernisse angesichts neuartiger Einblicke und Eingriffe in das Gehirn' in J Lindner (ed), *Die neuronale Selbstbestimmung des Menschen* (Baden-Baden, Nomos, 2016) 63 ff.
38   Blank, *Intervention in the Brain* (2013) 49 ff.

Brain implants record, stimulate or block impulses from neurons and could influence sensory or cognitive functions. Advanced research is aiming at creating interfaces between neural and computer systems or even brain-to-brain interfaces.[39] Future scenarios envisage a symbiotic connection between the human biological system and various technical devices. The key word, although it is understood and used in a variety of different ways, is 'cyborg'.[40]

Here too the fundamental question quickly arises of how human beings can be defined when the physical body is no longer the self-evident limit of a human being and criteria of internality and externality are subject to attacks,[41] and which human-machine entity is still a human being who has a right to human dignity. Similar questions from the opposite point of view are emerging in robotics and artificial intelligence.[42] Again, this discourse casts light on questions related to the constructivity of human dignity. At a concrete level, interventions in the human brain or man-machine entities raise the problem of what actually defines the core of a human being and what happens when brain functions can be controlled by external technology or by other people. Many methods have not been sufficiently

---

39 Blank, *Intervention in the Brain* (2013) 38; K Choi and BK Min, 'Future Directions for Brain-Machine Interfacing Technology' in SW Lee, HH Bülthoff and KR Müller (eds), *Recent Progress in Brain and Cognitive Engineering* (Dordrecht, Springer, 2015) 3 ff; see also JB Trimper, PR Wolpe and KS Rommelfanger, 'When "I" Becomes "We": Ethical Implications of Emerging Brain-to-Brain Interfacing Technologies' (2014) 7 *frontiers in Neuroengineering* 2014, Article 4; E Hildt, 'What Will This Do to Me and My Brain? Ethical Issues in Brain-to-Brain Interfacing' (2015) 9 *frontiers in Systems Neuroscience* 17.

40 Cybernetic organism; see R Kurzweil, *Human Body Version 2.0* (2003), www.kurzweilai.net/human-body-version-20; A Clark, *Natural-Born Cyborgs* (Oxford, Oxford University Press, 2003) 3; G Jones and M Whitaker, 'Transforming the Human Body' in C Blake, C Molloy and S Shakespeare (eds), *Beyond Human. From Animality to Transhumanism* (London/New York, Continuum, 2012) 254, 259 ff.

41 cf A Clark, *Natural-Born Cyborgs*, 3 ff.

42 See, eg, MC Gruber, 'Was spricht gegen Maschinenrechte?' in MC Gruber, J Bung and S Ziemann (eds), *Autonome Automaten. Künstliche Körper und artifizielle Agenten in der technisierten Gesellschaft* (Berlin, trafo, 2014) 191, 199 ff. Artificial intelligence and artificial life have become mature interdisciplines and thus demonstrate their complexity and possible significance for future generations, for an overview see W Banzhaf and B McMullin, 'Artificial Life' in G Rozenberg, T Bäck and JN Kok (eds), *Handbook of Natural Computing* (Berlin/Heidelberg, Springer, 2012) 1805, 1806 ff.

investigated in detail and many questions are still open.[43] However, it is widely accepted that complete external neurotechnological control of brain function with the resulting loss of identity and autonomy of the individual is incompatible with human dignity. 'Brainwashing' or destruction through deprivation are the historical parallels that have become known from wartime experiences.

G. 'Patents on Life'

Last but not least, biotechnologies and biotechnical inventions entail questions of patents. A patent gives its holder exclusive rights to the use of the patented invention for a specified time. On one hand, a patent can be granted as a product patent for an invented product or – in the narrower case of a new substance – as a substance patent. As a rule, the patented product is then protected absolutely, i.e., with regard to all known or still unknown functions and uses, regardless of whether the patent holder has specified them or even acknowledged their existence. On the other hand, patent holders can obtain a patent for a process they have invented, a patent also granting fundamental and absolute protection in connection with all applications and purposes with regard to that process. The protection provided by a process patent also extends to products resulting directly from applications. For the manufacture of a patented product or the application of a patented process third parties are required to obtain a license from the patent holder. Being purely an exclusive right, a patent does not grant permission to carry out the invention. But it would not make sense if it were already clear that this embodiment must be prohibited with lasting effect, for instance because it violates human dignity. Apart from this, an exclusive right can also be contrary to normative standards. Patent law and patent protection are by no means ethically neutral.

'Patents on life' is a catchphrase which has resulted in fierce discussions in which human dignity is a key point.[44] Today, the central distinction in patent law is no longer, as was the case in the past, the difference

---

43 cf B Schmitz-Luhn, C Katzenmeier and C Woopen, 'Law and Ethics of Deep Brain Stimulation' (2012) 35 *International Journal of Law and Psychiatry* 130, 130 ff.

44 See more thoroughly M Albers, 'Patente auf Leben' (2003) *JuristenZeitung* 275, 275 ff; C Meiser, *Biopatentierung und Menschenwürde* (Baden-Baden, Nomos, 2006) 15 ff.

between living organisms and lifeless material, but the distinction – no longer based on this difference – between discoveries on the one hand and human inventions on the other.[45] In connection with this, substances that are found in nature but isolated and extracted from their natural environment and thus made readily available are, in principle, just as capable of being patented as are organisms manufactured by means of bioengineering or genetic engineering. Against this background, patent applications have claimed or claim patents for procedures or products involving human DNA sequences, cells, organs or tissue as well as chimeras, embryonic stem cells or embryos themselves. In this discourse, human dignity remains to some extent a vague standard against commodification of humans[46] creeping in by patenting human material.[47] However, the idea of granting a product patent on an embryo is, to the extent that the embryo can develop into a human being, a very clear example where human dignity sets limits for a systematically thought out logic of patent law.

H. Conclusion

In discussions of biotechnologies, human dignity sometimes seems merely to articulate 'a general social unease with a given technology'[48]. Nevertheless, understanding of human dignity is neither entirely indeterminate nor completely heterogeneous, nor is every aspect of it disputed. On the contrary, there is broad and widespread consensus about certain issues.[49] It would be incompatible with human dignity to enslave women for the pur-

---

[45] See the landmark decision Diamond v Chakrabarty, decided 1980 by the US Supreme Court, 447 U.S. 303. See also US Court of Customs and Patent Appeals, in re Bergy, Chakrabarty, 596 F.2d 952 (C.C.P.A. 1979) 975: 'In fact, we see no *legally* significant difference between active chemicals which are classified as "dead" and organisms used for their *chemical* reactions which take place because they are "alive". Life is largely chemistry.'

[46] As to the (non-)commodification with a view to organ markets cf also I Schneider, 'The Body, the Law, and the Market: Public Policy Implications in a Liberal State' in M Albers, T Hoffmann and J Reinhardt (eds), *Human Rights and Human Nature* (Berlin/Heidelberg/New York, Springer, 2014) 197, 197 ff.

[47] See (with criticism and an own approach) DB Resnik, 'DNA Patents and Human Dignity' (2001) 29 *Journal of Law, Medicine & Ethics* 152, 152 ff.

[48] Caulfield and Brownsword, 'Human Dignity' 72.

[49] The point of reference here is current global society. Nothing changes with regard to the existing consensus due to the fact that there are always people and groups who dispute statements or evaluations.

pose of forced surrogate motherhood. Children must never be treated as goods which are produced and required to have certain properties and which need not be accepted in the event of flaws. Once human life enjoys the protection of human dignity, consumptive use for research purposes benefiting third parties becomes a violation of human dignity. Secret gene analyses aimed at ascertaining the full genetic characteristics and dispositions of a particular person and linking these to discriminatory consequences or selling the results of such analysis to interested parties constitute violations of human dignity. An intervention in the brain of a person which leads to the thinking and behavior of this person being externally controlled by others is also a violation of human dignity. A human being cannot be the basis for a product patent.

There is also disagreement on many matters, however. In part, problems regarding knowledge and uncertainties form the basis of the controversy. Because the human is now subject to transformation and transgression in an unprecedented manner, we often do not know what consequences are to be expected. Numerous predictions are highly controversial, for example, whether cloned or genetically altered persons would no longer be able to see themselves as autonomous persons or as the authors of their own biographical histories, or whether social relationships would change if human beings were cloned or genetic engineering conducted intentionally on embryos. Differing underlying assumptions and predictions may explain divergent assessments.

In part, appraisals and value judgments are at the heart of the controversies. When is a living creature a 'human being'? At what point do measures that restrict autonomy reach the point where they violate human dignity? What worth does the human body have and to what extent may body parts or bodily functions be commercialized? And what is the 'human body'? From an analytical perspective, knowledge and value judgments are separate issues, and breaking them down into their components is helpful. In complex biotechnological fields, however, this comes up against the problem that knowledge is no longer broadly shared and fundamental uncertainties are dealt with using values as guidelines.[50] That is among the reasons why discourse about human dignity is partly vague and heterogeneous. It can incidentally also be shown that the point of refer-

---

50 See M Albers, 'Enhancement, Human Nature, and Human Rights', in M Albers, T Hoffmann and J Reinhardt (eds), *Human Rights and Human Nature* (Dordrecht/Heidelberg/London/New York, Springer, 2014) 235, 258 ff.

ence underlying considerations of consequences and evaluations varies. The point of reference is not the individual only. It is also the others who are affected to the same degree and have the same right to be considered; it is future human beings or an even more highly abstracted humanity as such. Human dignity is also being referred to in more abstract lines of argument involving the potential of a technology to change the framework of mutual human interactions in such a way that violations of human dignity are made possible and are increasingly actually occurring. In turn, what is convincing as the point of reference in a given constellation is disputed. But even where there are disagreements, it is not that human dignity offers no help in clarifying matters. On the contrary, the sorting out of the issues in each complex which is among the effects of the discussions contributes as much to understanding those issues as to understanding human dignity. Since the discussions of biotechnologies become more differentiated judgments using human dignity 'as a form of general condemnation'[51] are increasingly being replaced by more nuanced approaches. Human dignity is understood as a requirement calling for regulation, which does not ban the use of biotechnologies entirely but shapes it in such a way that imaginable violations of human dignity are avoided.

Discussions are being carried on in many contexts: throughout society, in the political system, and in various scientific disciplines. However, the theme of human dignity having legal status is, in a form specific to the given context, often implied. Especially in the area of biotechnology, the attractiveness of human dignity as an argument is supported by the fact that its considerable legal value is generally known.

II. Legal Contexts

The legal contexts, with their own independent characteristics, will now become the central focus of the further analysis. Texts establishing norms can serve as crystallization points, although the law is not defined by texts alone and codified norms play differing roles in different legal systems. Human dignity is enshrined in a series of legal documents, for example in the Universal Declaration of Human Rights, in national constitutions, in the European Union Charter of Fundamental Rights or in specific conventions in the field of biomedicine (A.). The picture becomes

---

51   Caulfield and Brownsword, 'Human Dignity' 72.

more complex, because there are several communication contexts within the legal system that operate relatively independently. These include in particular legislation (B.), jurisdiction (C.) and jurisprudence (D.).

A. Establishment of Human Dignity in Catalogues of Human Rights

The now quite widespread establishment of human dignity in legal texts and documents is a recent achievement, primarily a 'postwar constitutional conception'[52] due to the horrendous experiences of the Second World War. The Charter of the United Nations, which was ratified and entered into force on October 24, 1945, declares in its Preamble that, after the scourge of war, the peoples of the United Nations are determined 'to reaffirm faith in fundamental human rights, in the dignity and worth of the human person [...]'. The Universal Declaration of Human Rights, which was proclaimed by the United Nations General Assembly in 1948, enshrines dignity both in its Preamble and in Article 1:

> All human beings are born free and equal in dignity and rights. They are endowed with reason and conscience and should act towards one another in a spirit of brotherhood.

The text is relatively vague both in its contents and in its legal consequences. In addition, there is disagreement concerning the extent to which the Universal Declaration as such has legally binding effects. Some regard it as *ius cogens*, others acknowledge the binding nature in customary international law of at least some of its rights, while still others confine its effects to that of a simple appeal and guideline. Both factors lead to a situation where in this context human dignity can be understood as on the one hand a fundamental, on the other hand a relatively open concept.

It is certain that the Universal Declaration of Human Rights and its enshrinement of dignity have inspired further international declarations in various fields,[53] particularly in bioethics and biotechnologies, as well as bills of rights in constitutional documents of national states. At the inter-

---

52 See LE Weinrib, 'Constitutional Conceptions and Constitutional Comparativism' in VC Jackson and MV Tushnet (eds), *Defining the Field of Comparative Constitutional Law* (Westport, Praeger, 2002) 23 ff.

53 cf K Dicke 'The Founding Function of Human Dignity in the Universal Declaration of Human Rights' in D Kretzmer and E Klein (eds), *The Concept of Human Dignity in Human Rights Discourse* (The Hague, Kluwer Law International, 2002) 111, 111 ff.

national level, human dignity is emphasized in the Convention of the United Nations on the Rights of Persons with Disabilities. The United Nations Declaration on Human Cloning states that Member States are called upon to prohibit all forms of human cloning inasmuch as they are incompatible with human dignity and to adopt measures necessary to prohibit the application of genetic engineering techniques that may be contrary to human dignity.[54] Obviously, the text requires interpretation,[55] and the legal consequences are those of soft law. As a specialized agency of the UN, UNESCO has adopted three influential declarations on bioethical topics: The Universal Declaration on the Human Genome and Human Rights (1997), the International Declaration on Human Genetic Data (2003) and the Universal Declaration on Bioethics and Human Rights (2005). Each of their Preambles refers to human dignity, which is declared to be one of the main bioethical principles.[56] All declarations include general provisions for human dignity to be fully respected and provisions stressing the fundamental equality of all human beings in dignity and rights as well as non-discrimination and non-stigmatization of individuals or groups. Beyond that, the Universal Declaration on the Human Genome and Human Rights makes use of human dignity in further respects: The human genome underlies the fundamental unity of all members of the human family, as well as the recognition of their inherent dignity and diversity, and is, in a symbolic sense, the heritage of humanity.[57] Everyone has a right to respect for their dignity and for their rights regardless of their genetic characteristics. That dignity makes it imperative not to reduce individuals to their genetic characteristics and to respect their uniqueness and diversity.[58] No one shall be subjected to discrimination based on genetic characteristics that is intended to infringe or has the effect of infringing human rights, fundamen-

---

54 UN Resolution A/RES/59/280, adopted 2005.
55 See Caulfield and Brownsword, 'Human Dignity' 75: at least three interpretive opportunities to narrow the scope of the cloning prohibition (by taking 'inasmuch as' to mean 'to the extent that' rather than 'for the reason that'; by adopting the empowerment rather than the constraint conception of human dignity; and by reading human life through a human-rights lens).
56 cf with view to human dignity as a principle of international bioethics R Andorno, 'First Steps in the Development of an International Biolaw' in C Gastmans, K Dierick, H Nys and P Schotmans (eds), *New Pathways for European Bioethics* (Antwerp, Intersentia, 2007) 121, 125 ff.
57 Art. 1 of the UDHGHR.
58 Art. 2 of the UDHGHR, see also Art. 6 of the UDHGHR.

tal freedoms or human dignity.[59] Practices which are contrary to human dignity, such as reproductive cloning of human beings, shall not be permitted.[60] Benefits from advances in biology, genetics and medicine, concerning the human genome, shall be made available to all, with due regard for the dignity and human rights of each individual.[61] A review of these provisions reveals the multifaceted meanings and dimensions of protection in connection with which dignity is discussed and how greatly in need of interpretation it is. Dignity is mostly mentioned in the context of human rights. However, this does not mean that one can simply conclude that it is fundamentally different from a right, for instance merely a guiding principle. All three declarations are of a declaratory nature. This soft law character was explicitly chosen with a view to the constantly changing context, the broadest possible consensus to be reached among signatory countries, and the regulation-promoting effects of awareness raising and public debate.[62]

The European Convention for the Protection of Human Rights and Fundamental Freedoms (1950) contains no express reference to dignity. Nevertheless, the European Court of Human Rights invokes human dignity as the basis of the Convention and its rights.[63] The later Convention on Human Rights and Biomedicine mentions human dignity in its preamble and purpose; the following articles develop more elaborated provisions in a variety of contexts. The preambles and purposes of its Additional Protocols refer to human dignity with regard to the prohibition of any intervention seeking to create a human being genetically identical to another human being,[64] with regard to the prohibition of all forms of discrimina-

---

59 Art. 6 of the UDHGHR; see also Art. 7 of the IDHGD emphasizing non-discrimination and non-stigmatization of individuals, families, groups and communities.
60 Art. 11 of the UDHGHR.
61 Art. 12 of the UDHGHR.
62 For the functions of soft law see F Molnár-Gábor, 'Die Herausforderung der medizinischen Entwicklung für das internationale *soft law* am Beispiel der Totalsequenzierung des menschlichen Genoms' (2012) 72 *Zeitschrift für ausländisches öffentliches Recht und Völkerrecht* 695, 705 ff.
63 See, eg, ECtHR, *Goodwin v UK*, Appl. No. 28957/95, Reports of Judgments and Decisions, 2002-IV, 31 f: '[...] the very essence of the Convention is respect for human dignity and human freedom.'
64 Additional Protocol to the Convention for the Protection of Human Rights and Dignity of the Human Being with regard to the Application of Biology and Medicine, on the Prohibition of Cloning Human Beings, CETS 168.

tion, in particular those based on genetic characteristics,[65] and with regard to research involving interventions on human beings.[66] Unlike the UN or UNESCO declarations, the standards are binding. However, because of the institutional conditions of a framework convention they specify only minimum standards below which States having ratified must not fall.[67]

The Charter of Fundamental Rights of the European Union gives human dignity explicitly highest priority. The title of the first chapter is 'Dignity'. Art. 1 of the EU Charter states that human dignity is inviolable and must be respected and protected.[68] The first chapter further includes the right to life, the right to the integrity of the person, the prohibition of torture and inhuman or degrading treatment or punishment and the prohibition of slavery and forced labor.[69] The right to the integrity of the person, anchored in Art. 3 of the EU Charter, includes rights in the fields of medicine and biology. In particular, the free and informed consent of the person concerned, according to the procedures laid down by law, the prohibition of eugenic practices, in particular those aiming at the selection of persons, the prohibition on making the human body and its parts as such a source of financial gain and the prohibition of the reproductive cloning of human beings must be respected. The fundamental rights of the Charter are binding for all institutions and bodies of the European Union, for the Member States only when they are implementing Union law.[70] Because the law of the European Union is expanding and the European Court of Justice interprets the term 'implementing

---

[65] Additional Protocol to the Convention on Human Rights and Biomedicine concerning Genetic Testing for Health Purposes, CETS 203.

[66] Additional Protocol to the Convention on Human Rights and Biomedicine, concerning Biomedical Research, CETS 195.

[67] For a closer analysis see M Albers, 'Die rechtlichen Standards der Biomedizin-Konvention des Europarats' (2002) *Europarecht* 801, 801 ff.

[68] The enshrinement and the wording have been influenced by Art. 1 para 1 of the German Basic Law. The meaning of human dignity and its inviolability must and will be interpreted, though, in the context of the EU legal order, cf C Dupré, 'Article 1 – Human Dignity' in S Peers, T Hervey, J Kenner and A Ward (eds), *The EU Charter of Fundamental Rights* (Baden-Baden/Munich/Oxford, Nomos/C.H. Beck/Hart Publishing, 2014) 01.18 ff, 01.39 ff.

[69] See Dupré, 'Article 1' 01.05: 'Article 1 EUCFR is clearly related to all the rights enshrined under Title I "Dignity" […].'

[70] Art. 51 para 1 EU Charter.

Union law' broadly, the fundamental rights of the European Union are becoming increasingly important. As far as they are applicable, they are superseding the fundamental rights of the constitutions of Member States.

In many Nation States' constitutions, human dignity is incorporated as a significant norm in a central position.[71] The most prominent and influential example is the German Basic Law, adopted after the Second World War in 1949. Article 1 para. 1 of the German Basic Law establishes the inviolability or, in other words, the indefeasibility ('Unantastbarkeit')[72] of human dignity and the duty of all public authority to respect and to protect it. Hence, no reservation is added permitting limitation by or in terms of legislation. The provision is also safeguarded from constitutional amendment.[73] Although the high rank and the binding character of Article 1 para. 1 of the German Basic Law have been made explicit, many aspects are open to interpretation. This does not apply only to the relatively vague contents. The legal nature and dimensions of the provision have to be developed as well: Is the guarantee of human dignity a founding value or principle, an objective norm serving as a guide to the interpretation of ordinary law, the basis of other human rights or a guideline to their interpretation, an individual right enforceable in the same way as any other right, a 'right to have rights' or a right protecting particular legal goods? Is it plausible to understand it, as the Federal Constitutional Court does, as a combination of several dimensions? Looking at other Constitutions, human dignity can be found in the preamble or in the provisions. The wordings range from a fundamental principle or value, often referred to in conjunction with other values such as freedom, equality, solidarity and social se-

---

71 See the overviews in A Barak, *Human Dignity* (Cambridge, Cambridge University Press, 2015) 49 ff; in C McCrudden, 'Human Dignity and Judicial Interpretation of Human Rights' (2008) 19 *The European Journal of International Law* 655, 664 ff; in H Botha, 'Human Dignity in Comparative Perspective' (2009) 2 *Stellenbosch Law Review* 171, 175 ff; and in D Shulztiner and G Carmi, 'Human Dignity in National Constitutions: Functions, Promises and Dangers' (2014) 62 *American Journal of Comparative Law* 461 ff.
72 cf D Grimm, 'Dignity in a Legal Context: Dignity as an Absolute Right' in C McCrudden (ed), *Understanding Human Dignity* (Oxford, Oxford University Press, 2013) 381, 387.
73 cf Art. 79 para 3 of the German Basic Law. For a comprehensive analysis of the legal background and legal aspects of Art. 1 para 1 of the German Basic Law see M Hong, *Der Menschenwürdegehalt der Grundrechte* (Tübingen, Mohr Siebeck, 2017).

curity,[74] to an individual right that is enforceable before the courts. Interpretation may lead to interdependencies and multi-layered architectures, e.g., if the fundamental principle is understood as a source enabling interpreters to derive rights or if human dignity is understood as a 'mother-right'[75]. Sometimes, multilayered dimensions are already laid down in the document. The Constitution of South Africa, for instance, acknowledges human dignity as a constitutional right, a supreme value and a guide to constitutional interpretation.[76]

In national constitutions, there is seldom any direct mention of modern biotechnological developments. The Swiss Federal Constitution is an exception. Art. 119, adopted by a popular vote in 2015, states that the confederation shall legislate on the use of human reproductive and genetic material and in so doing ensure the protection of human dignity, privacy and the family and adhere to a number of principles. These include making any forms of cloning and interference with the genetic material of human reproductive cells and embryos illegal, forbidding inserting non-human reproductive and genetic material into human reproductive material, banning embryo donations and all forms of surrogate motherhood and safeguarding that a person's genetic material may only be analyzed, registered or made public under certain circumstances. To what extent and how exactly the idea of human dignity substantiates these provisions, however, is a matter of interpretation.

As a result, interdependencies among documents and wordings can be observed, as well as similarities or significant differences in the ways in which human dignity is incorporated as an element of positive law. Closer analysis uncovers the multitude of functions the reliance on human dignity serves. This is true in general terms, but also to the extent that provisions concern themselves specifically with modern biotechnologies.[77] Apart from this already complex picture, law goes be-

---

74 cf Botha, 'Human Dignity' 176, 196 ff.
75 cf A Barak, 'Human Dignity: The Constitutional Value and the Constitutional Right' in C McCrudden (ed), *Understanding Human Dignity* (Oxford, Oxford University Press, 2013) 361, 373 ff; A L Bendor and M Sachs, 'The Constitutional Status of Human Dignity in Germany and Israel' (2011) 44 *Israel Law Review* 25, 44 ff.
76 In more detail Botha, 'Human Dignity' 175 ff.
77 See also M Albers, 'Bioethik, Biopolitik, Biorecht: Grundlagen und Schlüsselprobleme' in id (ed), *Bioethik, Biorecht, Biopolitik: Eine Kontextualisierung* (Baden-Baden, Nomos, 2016) 9, 28.

yond what is stipulated in texts. Instead, texts are consulted and referred to and applied in varying contexts.

B. Dignity in Legislative Processes and Laws

To analyze the role of human dignity in lawmaking a rough distinction can be made between the processes of lawmaking and the laws resulting from lawmaking. At least in democratic transnational or national societies contractual or constitutional rules of procedure define lawmaking processes in such a way that they are open to a greater or lesser extent to the impact of public debate. The forms this takes include participatory forums or platforms, many different forms of communication with members of parliament, coverage in the media and, especially in the fields of modern biotechnologies, participatory procedures initiated by ethics committees. Arguments based on human dignity often come into play here because they are firmly anchored in the public mind. From religious to atheist, from sophisticated to simplifying lines of argument, the range of views in society has a legally recognized place both in the above-mentioned contexts and in parliamentary debates. Beyond that, relevant transnational norms such as the European Convention on Human Rights and Biomedicine – to the extent that they have been ratified – exert legal influence on the lawmaking process as binding or soft law that impacts national law. Relevant rulings of transnational courts can be effective as well, although in strictly procedural terms the impacts of rulings are regularly limited to the case in question. Insofar as human dignity is established in the constitution as a principle or as a right, the resulting binding effects have to be taken into account in lawmaking. The vagueness and complexity of the idea of dignity result in varied interpretations. Whether this devalues its role or even gives it greater value is a question of the theoretical framework and perspective from which analyses and assessments are made. At least in recent decades, human dignity has played a major role in lawmaking processes involving regulation of modern biotechnologies.

Laws, as results of lawmaking, deal with the problems modern biotechnologies have raised within the context of the relevant specialized laws. These are quite different laws regarding the legal issues to be regulated, their legal classification and the contents. The concrete legal provisions are embedded in the specialized legal architecture and terminology of civil or criminal law, of medical or health law, of patent law or laws specific to various other domains. The concept of human dignity is rarely mentioned here; if at all, in preambles or statements of purposes. Nonetheless, particular legal provisions can be influenced by the criterion of human dignity without this concept being mentioned in the text of the law. This applies all the more in view of the fact that the guarantee of human dignity by no means necessarily leads to simple 'Yes/No' decisions. Laws can, of course, specify prohibitions or exception clauses in the context of their area of application. Examples include the prohibition of reproductive cloning in the laws of numerous countries, the prohibition of surrogacy in Switzerland,[78] the frequent prohibition of creating embryos for research purposes,[79] the in-principle prohibition of stem cell importation in Germany[80] or the exemption of processes for modifying the germ line genetic identity of human beings or uses of human embryos for industrial or commercial purposes from being patented.[81] However, prohibitions are not the only imaginable outcome. Frequently, the influence of human dignity is reflected in the fact that a law specifies conditions which are intended to prevent violations of human dignity from taking place. In a number of States, conditions have been laid down for surrogate motherhood as well as for other aspects of assisted reproduction.[82] Preimplantation and genetic diagnosis is often possible under specific condi-

---

78 Art. 119 para 2d of the Swiss Constitution, Art. 4 SwissFMedG (Bundesgesetz über die medizinisch unterstützte Fortpflanzung; Federal Act on Assisted Reproduction). The Explanatory Statement of the Bundesrat states that surrogacy is seen as a instrumentalization of the surrogate mother, see Botschaft über die Volksinitiative 'zum Schutz des Menschen vor Manipulationen in der Fortpflanzungstechnologie (Initiative für menschenwürdige Fortpflanzung, FMF)' und zu einem Bundesgesetz über die medizinisch unterstützte Fortpflanzung (Fortpflanzungsmedizingesetz, FMedG), BBl 1996 III 205, 230, 254 (see also http://www.amtsdruckschriften.bar.admin.ch/viewOrigDoc.do?id=10053942).
79 See, eg, for France Art. L. 2151-2 du code de la santé publique; cf also I Kriari-Catranis, 'Embryo Research and Human Rights – An Overview of Developments in Europe' (1997) 4 *European Journal of Health Law* 43, 55f.
80 cf § 1 StZG (Stammzellgesetz; Stem Cell Act) mentioning human dignity among the purposes.
81 Art. 6 Directive 98/44/EC on the legal protection of biotechnological inventions; cf also recital 38. For a recent survey on the international regulatory landscape regarding human germline gene modification see M Araki and T Ishii, 'International Regulatory Landscape and Integration of Corrective Genome Editing into In Vitro Fertilization' (2014) *Reproductive Biology and Endocrinology* 12:108, 8 ff.
82 For an overview cf the articles in K Trimmings and P Beaumont (eds.), *International Surrogacy Arrangements: Legal Regulation at the International Level* (Oxford/Portland, Hart Publishing, 2013).

tions, but not without restriction or arbitrarily. For genetic and neurotechnological interventions, legal provisions have been enacted to some extent or are to be enacted on the basis of which particular measures are to be possible while maintaining respect for human dignity. Admittedly, appropriate regulation is lacking frequently enough. Human dignity then expressly prompts emphatic calls for regulation in public discourse.

Regardless of whether and to what extent guarantees of human dignity have had an effect, the law provides an independent text that is relatively autonomous from how it came into existence and develops its own binding nature. For the understanding and, not infrequently, acceptance of legal provisions it is often a matter of importance that these provisions are based not merely on issues of human dignity, but also on other grounds.[83] In this way, interpretation of the laws can to a certain extent be kept separate from disagreements related to human dignity. This plays a role especially for courts that are required to apply the laws in specific cases.

C. Dignity in the Reasoning of Courts

When investigating the role of human dignity in the context of court rulings[84] characteristics of and structural limitations to court proceedings and decisions must be kept in mind.[85] Courts are responsible for making binding decisions on cases brought before them as impartial bodies and on the basis of the law. Depending on the particular procedure – civil law dispute, criminal trial, judicial review, a human rights or constitutional com-

---

83 As an example with a view to Germany: § 1 para 1 no. 7 EschG (Embryo Protection Act [1990], for a translation see http://www.auswaertiges-amt.de/cae/servlet/contentblob/480804/publicationFile/5162/EmbryoProtectionAct.pdf) penalizing a person who carries out artificial fertilization in cases of women who are prepared to permanently hand over the child after its birth to a third party or implants an embryo under these circumstances, for instance, is not based on human dignity but on predicted negative consequences for the child and the surrogate and potential conflicts between the intended mother and the surrogate, see the Explanatory Statement, BTDrucks. 11/5460, 6 ff, dip21.bundestag.de/dip21/btd/11/054/1105460.pdf.
84 See, in general, McCrudden 'Human Dignity' 682 ff.
85 See more closely M Albers, 'Höchstrichterliche Rechtsfindung und Auslegung gerichtlicher Entscheidungen' in 71 *Veröffentlichungen der Vereinigung der Deutschen Staatsrechtslehrer* (VVDStRL), *Grundsatzfragen der Rechtsetzung und Rechtsfindung* (Berlin and Boston, de Gruyter, 2012) 257, 259 ff.

plaint, preliminary ruling – procedural rules specify more or less broadly who can bring a complaint before the court and what the matter to be examined is, what additional jurisdictional requirements exist, what standard of proof is to be applied, that reasons must be given for decisions to a particular extent, and what legal consequences decisions have. Among the requirements is, first of all, a plaintiff being able to bring a case before the court and actually doing so. The ruling relates to the particular facts of the case and to the particular object of judicial review. For this reason, the ruling must always be interpreted in terms of the particular constellation or case and the claims brought before the court. The relevant normative measures have to be worked out in the course of the proceedings. The way the guarantee of human dignity comes into play as a normative standard depends on the type of proceedings. Administrative, criminal or civil courts have to interpret statutory laws but when doing so, they must take the binding effects of transnational or constitutional norms as well as those of legally binding rulings of higher courts into account.[86] Hence, the guarantee of human dignity as it applies in law is relevant within a context which is always also shaped by legal norms and legislative decisions. In human rights or constitutional proceedings before the European Court of Human Rights (ECtHR) or constitutional courts, on the other hand, the guarantee of human dignity can be a standard applying directly to the questions of the case. In the relationship between these courts and legislation, however, the scope of the courts' judicial powers is to a greater or lesser extent limited, whether because of the recognition of signatory states' margin of appreciation or because of institutional factors and distribution of powers. Specifically in the case of the guarantee of human dignity, this quite often has an impact in the form of judicial restraint. The way courts reach their legal findings is also determined by legal systems and judicial cultures.[87]

Meanwhile, assisted reproduction and its consequences have been the frequent subject of court rulings. In some rulings human dignity has been applied as a standard. In the landmark case of *Evans v. The United Kingdom*, which was decided by the Grand Chamber of the ECtHR in 2007,[88]

---

86   Albers, 'Rechtsfindung' 265, 267 f.
87   cf for the ECtHR NL Arold, *The Legal Culture of the European Court of Human Rights* (Leiden/Boston, Martinus Nijhoff Publishers, 2007) especially 67 ff.
88   *Evans v The United Kingdom*, Appl. No. 6339/05 (2007), hudoc.echr.coe.int.

the applicant and her former boyfriend had undertaken an IVF treatment before the applicants' ovaries had been removed and six fertilized eggs consigned to storage. A few months later the man withdrew his consent. The applicant commenced proceedings seeking an injunction requiring the man to restore his consent to the use and storage of the embryos and a declaration of incompatibility under the Human Rights Act 1998 to the effect that the domestic law allowing consent to be withdrawn at any stage as long as the embryo created has not been used for treatment breached her rights and neglected the protection embryos were entitled to. The Grand Chamber of the ECtHR considered a wide margin of appreciation of the member States in this field and held that the interests pursued by the legislation are legitimate and consistent with Article 8 ECHR:

> Respect for human dignity and free will [...] underlay the legislature's decision to enact provisions permitting of no exception to ensure that every person donating gametes for the purpose of IVF treatment would know in advance that no use could be made of his or her genetic material without his or her continuing consent.[89]

Contracting States also enjoy a margin of appreciation with regard to the issue of when the right to life begins as a result of the absence of any European consensus on the scientific and legal definition of the beginning of life. Because an embryo does not have independent rights or interests under English law, the Court concluded that the right to life, Article 2 ECHR, was not violated.

Provisions of the Austrian Artificial Procreation Act prohibiting the use of ova from donors and, under further circumstances, of sperm from donors for in-vitro fertilization were the subject matter of the case *S. H. and others v. Austria*.[90] In the course of the procedure a Chamber of the First Section of the ECtHR held that the prohibitions violated rights under Art. 14 in conjunction with Art. 8 of the Convention. It found, inter alia, that concerns based on moral considerations or on social acceptability were not in themselves sufficient reasons for a complete ban on a specific artificial procreation technique, that the legal framework regulating this field must be shaped in a coherent manner and that risks, such as the risk of the exploitation of women or the selection of children, could be addressed by sufficient legal safeguards. In its subsequent ruling handed down in 2011, the Grand Chamber came to the opposite result by stressing that the ques-

---

89   Evans v The United Kingdom, para 89.
90   *S. H. and others v Austria*, Appl. No. 57813/00 (2011), hudoc.echr.coe.int.

tions touch on sensitive moral and ethical issues where there is not yet clear common ground among the member States and that the Austrian legislature did not exceed the wide margin of appreciation. It noted that there is no prohibition under Austrian law on going abroad to seek treatment of infertility that uses assisted reproductive technology not allowed in Austria, and that in the event of a successful treatment the Civil Code rules on paternity and maternity would be applicable. The deliberations do not refer to human dignity. Only the opinion of Judge de Gaetano stated separately, though quite vaguely, that the recognition of the value and dignity of every person may require the prohibition of certain acts in order to uphold the inalienable value and intrinsic dignity of every human being. The joint dissenting opinion of four judges criticized the broad margin of appreciation afforded and questioned the persuasiveness of the argument that there is no prohibition on going abroad.

Precisely the problems of cross-border use of assisted reproductive technologies are increasingly the subject of court rulings on surrogacy. In this respect the courts are dealing with issues arising from the use of surrogates in a foreign country, particularly with the legal status of the child. In the early stages, the famous court rulings in the US[91] and India[92] point-

---

91   *Baby M*, decided 1988 by the Supreme Court of New Jersey, 109 N.J. 396, 537 A.2d 1227, law.justia.com/cases/new-jersey/supreme-court/1988/109-n-j-396-1.html; *Johnson v Calvert*, decided 1993 by the Californian Supreme Court, 5 Cal4th 84, 851 P.2d 776 (1993), law.justia.com/cases/california/supreme-court/4th/5/84.html; cf meanwhile Sec. 7960-7962 California Family Code.

92   In the Baby Manji case the legal status of the child created from the sperm of the Japanese father and an egg harvested from an anonymous Indian woman and born to a surrogate mother was unclear after the Japanese couple got divorced and, in contrast to the father, the woman didn't want the child any more because she felt no genetical, biological, moral or legal obligation to the child. The Indian Supreme Court tried to solve the case which was settled by issuing Baby Manji a travel permission and directed the Indian legislature to enact legal rules governing surrogacy, *Baby Manji Yamada v Union of India & ANR* (2008) INSC 1656, http://indiankanoon.org/doc/854968/. In the landmark Balaz Twins-Decision the Gujarat High Court dealt with the legal status of twins created by using the father's sperm and an anonymous ova donation and given birth by a gestational surrogate; the Court mentioned ethical issues in detail, inter alia the right to privacy of the donor, worries about exploitation of women through surrogacy and the interests of otherwise childless couples; it reached, in the absence of Indian legislation, the decision that the surrogate is the legal mother, see *Balaz v Anand Municipality*, LPA 2151/2009 (Gujarat H.C. 2009), http://www.legalcrystal.com/case/747551/jan-balaz-vs-anand-municipality-6-ors.

ed to the not sufficiently regulated broad range of ethical and legal problems; especially the Indian Courts have stressed that 'a sound and secure legislation to deal with a situation created by the reproductive science and technology'[93] is necessary in order that courts can reach well-founded decisions. In the relevant judgments of the ECtHR this court focused on human rights, in particular on the children's right to respect for private life (Art. 8 ECHR). At least in cases in which one of the intended parents is also the child's biological parent, the court held, Art. 8 ECHR can be infringed by not obtaining recognition under domestic law of the legal parent-child relationship established abroad.[94] The German Federal Court of Justice for Civil Matters (FCJ) discussed, among other, the guarantee of human dignity, Art. 1 para. 1 German Basic Law, in a case in which two male partners sought recognition in Germany of their status as parents, which the Superior Court of the State of California had confirmed in a legally binding decision for a child which had been conceived with the sperm of one of the applicants and anonymously donated eggs; the pregnancy had been carried to term by a surrogate mother from California.[95] Recognition, the FCJ held, does not involve an infringement against the international public policy doctrine: Provided that it is guaranteed that consent to and carrying out of surrogate motherhood are in accordance with laws applied by a foreign court which safeguard the voluntary nature of the decision made by the surrogate mother to bear the child and after its birth to hand it over to the intended parents, the dignity of neither the surrogate mother nor the child is violated. By contrast, the dignity of the surrogate mother, the FCJ further explained, may in fact be violated if the surrogacy arrangement is carried out under circumstances which cast doubt on the voluntary participation of the surrogate mother, or if basic procedural guarantees were ignored in the foreign court process.[96] The legal status of a child from a surrogate mother has also been the subject mat-

---

93 Gujarat High Court, *Balaz v Anand Municipality*, para 19.
94 *Labassee v France*, Appl. No. 65941/11 (2014), *Mennesson v France*, Appl. No. 65192/11 (2014), hudoc.echr.coe.int. See also the far reaching decision of an ECHtR Chamber (Second Section) that has been overruled by the Grand Chamber *Paradiso and Campanelli v Italy*, Appl. No. 25358/12 (2015 and 2017), hudoc.echr.coe.int.
95 Case XII ZB 463/13 (2014), http://www.bundesgerichtshof.de. See also the differentiating decision (against the background of Art. 119 para 2d of the Swiss Constitution) of the Federal Supreme Court of Switzerland, 5A_748/2014, 54 ff.
96 Case XII ZB 463/13 (2014), http://www.bundesgerichtshof.de, 51.

ter of a constitutional complaint; however, the German Federal Constitutional Court (FCC) did not accept the case because the plaintiffs did not present relevant data concerning the status and role of the surrogate mother.[97] The fact that the FCC thus lacked a basis for an appropriate and legally convincing decision illustrates the institutional limitations within which court decisions always operate.

The way in which embryos are handled in assisted reproduction or in embryo and stem cell research is occasionally the subject of court rulings. Considering the lack of consensus on the nature and status of the embryo and differing regulations in the member States of the Council of Europe, the ECtHR is exercising restraint: It explicates that it is not advisable for the Court to intervene in the debate as to who is a person and when life begins and that the issue of when the right to life begins comes within the margin of appreciation that member States enjoy.[98] Quite controversial was the judgment in the case of *Parillo v Italy*.[99] Due to legal prohibitions, the applicant was precluded from donating cryopreserved embryos to scientific research after her partner's death. The majority of the Grand Chamber held that the aim of protecting the "embryo's potential for life" as well as "morals and the rights and freedoms of others" was legitimate and that, against the background of the "delicate moral and ethical questions" and the lack of European consensus, the legal ban did not overstep the margin of appreciation.[100] Prior to this, however, it argued that the right to respect for private life encompasses the applicant's ability to exercise a conscious and considered choice regarding the fate of the embryos – a point of view some of the concurring, partly concurring, partly dissenting and dissenting opinions resolutely rejected on grounds of the respect for human dignity embryos should enjoy.[101]

In France, the Constitutional Council handed down its decision in 1994 on referrals for review of the constitutionality of the Respect for the Hu-

---

97   Case 1 BvR 573/12 (2012), http://www.bundesverfassungsgericht.de. The grounds of the decision imply that the plaintiffs deliberately avoided presenting certain data because they feared the negative effect the information would have.
98   *Vo v France*, Appl. No. 53924/00 (2014) 81 ff.
99   *Parillo v Italy*, Appl. No. 46470/11 (2015), hudoc.echr.coe.int.
100   *Parillo v Italy*, Appl. No. 46470/11 (2015), 162 ff.
101   See *Parillo v Italy*, Appl. No. 46470/11 (2015), 149 ff.; Concurring Opinion of Judge Pinto de Albuquerque, 31 ff.; Partly Dissenting Opinion of Judges Casadevall, Ziemele, Power-Forde, De Gaetano and Yudkivska, 4 ff.; see also the divergent view of Judge Sajó in his Dissenting Opinion.

man Body Act and the Donation and Use of Parts and Products of the Human Body, Medically Assisted Reproduction and Prenatal Diagnosis Act.[102] This statute allowed, under specific conditions and precautions, for instance, the use of particular techniques of artificial reproduction, the selection of embryos to be implanted, donation of surplus embryos to other couples and termination of the preservation of such embryos after at least five years of storage. The Constitutional Council recognized the protection of human dignity against all forms of enslavement or degradation as a principle having constitutional status and as a parameter for review. It then emphasized that the legislature had specified various forms of protection in the event of the conception, implantation and preservation of embryos fertilized in vitro but had advanced the view that the principle of respect for human life and of equality was inapplicable and had not seen a need to provide for the preservation of all embryos, once formed, for all time and under all circumstances. Ultimately, the Constitutional Council did not question the provisions on the grounds that it does not have the same decision-making powers as Parliament.[103] It did not identify any provisions or principles having constitutional status and applicable to embryo selection that address protection of the human genetic heritage.[104] The German FCC has not yet made any decision on the constitutional protection of embryos in vitro. It is true that the protection of embryos was at the center of attention in the abortion decisions in which the FCC declared:

> Wherever human life exists it is entitled to human dignity [...]. The potential capabilities inherent in human existence from the very beginning are adequate to establish human dignity.[105]

But the court restricted these considerations explicitly to the context and the period of pregnancy, and refers to the life developing during pregnancy 'as a human being'[106]. Even so, human dignity is not acknowledged only in the case of those already capable of making autonomous decisions.

In the field of genetic diagnostics human dignity is occasionally mentioned but rarely discussed in detail. At least up until now, practical court rulings have not focused on visions of the future involving conceivably genetically transparent human beings, but on specific genetic analyses. In

---

102   Décision no 94-343/344 DC (1994), www.conseil-constitutionnel.fr.
103   Décision no 94-343/344 DC (1994), www.conseil-constitutionnel.fr, 10.
104   Décision no 94-343/344 DC (1994), www.conseil-constitutionnel.fr, 11.
105   BVerfGE (Decisions of the FCC) 39, 1, 36 ff (1975); 88, 203, 251 ff (1993).
106   BVerfGE 88, 203, 251 f; see also BVerfGE 39, 1, 37.

cases involving provision of information on health prospects to insurance companies, German rulings do not regard human dignity as being affected as long as the genome itself is not made the criterion for legal disadvantages, but symptoms of an existing sickness and its confirmation based on a diagnostic gene test.[107] Pre-implantation diagnostics was the subject of *Costa and Pavan v. Italy*, a case in which the applicants, both asymptomatic carriers of cystic fibrosis, complained that they had no access to PGD for the purposes of selecting an embryo unaffected by the disease.[108] The blanket ban on the use of PGD in Italy was justified, among other reasons, with the interest in precluding a risk of eugenic selection. The ECtHR ruled that the applicants' desire to conceive a child unaffected by the genetic disease of which they are healthy carriers and to use PGD to this end enjoys the protection of Art. 8 ECHR. It further found that prohibiting the use of PGD whilst simultaneously permitting abortion in cases the embryo is affected by the disease violates the right to respect for private and family life.[109] Pre-implantation diagnostics was also the subject of an influential decision by the German Federal Court of Justice for Criminal Matters, according to which a particular method does not constitute a criminal offense as defined by the Embryo Protection Act, and thus cannot be punished.[110] Human dignity is not mentioned in this decision. However, this is attributable to the fact that the disputed breadth of what constitutes a criminal offense was primarily defined according to the normative principle: 'No punishment without law'[111]. The admissibility of pre-implantation diagnosis for the purpose of 'savior siblings' was discussed in a landmark court decision of the Appellate Committee of the House of Lords in terms not of human dignity, but of the objection that this involves a slippery slope leading to 'designer babies' or 'treating the offspring to be

---

107 See Case 5 W 220/11-98 (OLG Saarbrücken, 2011, http://www.rechtsprechung .saarland.de/cgi-bin/rechtsprechung/document.py?Gericht=sl&nr=3798.
108 *Costa and Pavan v Italy*, Appl. No. 54270/10 (2012).
109 *Costa and Pavan v Italy*, Appl. No. 54270/10 (2012), 52 ff. Meanwhile, the Italian Constitutional Court has decided two similar cases and declared that the relevant provisions of Law no 40 are unconstitutional, see Judgment No 96 of 2015, http://www.cortecostituzionale.it.
110 Case 5 StR 386/09 (2010), http://www.bundesgerichtshof.de. The decision was among the causes of an amendment of the ESchG with the result that PGD is explicitly permitted under particular circumstances.
111 cf Article 103 para 2 German Basic Law.

born as a commodity'[112]. The Committee dismissed the appeal against the Human Fertilisation and Embryology Authority's license on the grounds of the specific circumstances of the case to be decided, the conditions imposed in the license, and the decision-making powers granted to the authority by law.

In the case of genetic diagnostics there are also follow-up questions for the courts to answer. These include cases in which incorrect genetic counseling of parents led to the birth of a disabled child. The FCC distinguishes between considering the existence of a child as tantamount to 'damage' to its parents – which would breach the human dignity of the child – and the non-detrimental assumption that the obligation of the parents to meet the costs of rearing the child constitutes damage. The court held that the application of the law on compensation, which aims at achieving just distribution of obligations, to personal relationships and the imposition of the responsibility for child support on the doctor does not lead to any commercialization of the human as a person and does not involve any moral stigma of being worthless being attached to the child. It further found that the human dignity of the child is also not violated by the fact that it could later learn that its birth was to have been prevented. Whether or not psychological harm results from this information is not determined by the economic relief of the parents as a result of damages payments, but depends on the individual parent-child relationship.[113]

Because of the limited competences of the European Union, the European Court of Justice (ECJ) only deals with cases in the field of modern biotechnologies to a certain extent, and only in connection with certain aspects. In the decisions handed down regarding the Directive on the legal protection of biotechnological inventions, however, the ECJ had to interpret Union law in the light of the guarantee of human dignity, Art. 1 EU Charter.[114] The court noted that the context and aim of the Directive show that the EU legislature intended to exclude any possibility of patentability where respect for human dignity could thereby be affected. Against this background it came to the result that the concept of 'human embryo' within the meaning of Article 6 of the Directive must be understood in a wide

---

112 Quintavalle v Human Fertilisation and Embryology Authority (Secretary of State for Health Intervening), 2 A.C. 561 (2005), http://www.publications.parliament.uk/pa/ld200405/ldjudgmt/jd050428/quint-3.htm.
113 Cases 1 BvR 479/92 and 1 BvR 307/94 (1997), BVerfGE 96, 375, 399 ff.
114 Case C-34/10 *Brüstle v Greenpeace e.V.* (2011); Case C-364/13 *International Stem Cell Corporation* (2014), both accessible under curia.europa.eu.

sense and comprises any fertilized human ovum and other organisms that have the inherent capacity of developing into a human being.[115] It is striking, though, what lengths the ECJ goes to to formulate its own decisions following the legislators' value judgments.

In the reasons given for court decisions human dignity thus clearly has a certain relevance, which also depends upon the circumstances of the particular case. Sometimes it is only a vague standard that is merely mentioned in the context of a line of argument supported by other considerations. Sometimes it becomes clear that a legal regulation is required which can prevent conceivable violations of human dignity. Sometimes it becomes apparent that certain behaviors lead to violations of human dignity. The details depend upon the particular understanding of human dignity, which has different normative bases in different legal systems. At the same time, it can be seen that the courts are usually (not always) inclined to exercise restraint in applying the guarantee of human dignity. This has to do with its status and weight, with the fact that where statutory rules are absent, courts have difficulty reaching a decision and try to base their judgments on broad-based grounds, and is related to the fact that if a legal framework exists, several lines of justification can be drawn upon by the courts in their findings. However, courts decide concrete cases with a focus on individual rights and legal entitlements at a later point in time than the passage of laws. Circumstances of the cases to decide, the focus on complaints and individual rights or new scientific developments may result in significant rulings which then trigger legal change, public debate or legislative proposals. Nevertheless, in court decisions human dignity plays a lesser role than in public and parliamentary debates or in scholarly discourse.

---

[115] Case C-34/10 *Brüstle v Greenpeace e.V.* (2011), 24 ff. Shortly after the Brüstle-decision the ECJ had to deal with the question what was meant by being 'capable of commencing the process of development of a human being just as an embryo created by fertilisation of an ovum can do so' and whether a non-fertilised human ovum whose division and further development have been stimulated by parthenogenesis really fulfils that condition, see Case C-364/13 *International Stem Cell Corporation* (2014) 21 ff.

D. Dignity in Scientific Approaches

Jurisprudence understands human dignity in a specifically scholarly and by its very nature varied way. It can be text-oriented and unfold human dignity as a normative measure embedded in catalogues of human rights from a doctrinal point of view. It can analyze the verdicts of courts that use human dignity in their reasoning, strive to guide in methodological terms the way in which 'correct' decisions are reached and then assess case law on this basis. It can also go beyond texts or decisions and focus on, for example, foundations of human dignity with approaches offered by other disciplines in mind. Hence, the context of a particular line of thought must be taken into account.

However, even in terms of specifying duties or rights to be derived from the guarantee of human dignity established in a legal text the spectrum of scientific approaches has always been broad and heterogeneous. For a long time, identifying those who enjoy the protection of human dignity was less problematic than defining what was to be protected. Against the background of differing theoretical foundations and differing legal texts approaches to delineating the contents of the obligation or right are very diverse. The guarantee of human dignity is interpreted as the basis of rights, as the right to have rights[116], or as a principle assisting the further explication of a catalogue of rights generated by the principle. When seen as being a right with specific content, human dignity is understood, e.g., as an inner transcendental kernel or as a person's intrinsic value as a human being, as a basis for autonomy, as the potential of every human being to lead a life marked by self-respect and respect by others, as the capabilities required for performing central human functions or with regard to Kantian ideas that a human being should always be treated as an end and never as a mere means and should neither be made an object nor instrumentalized. According to the 'object formula' which is of considerable significance in Germany, 'human dignity as such is infringed whenever a concrete person is degraded to an object, a mere means, a fungible element'[117]. However, due to its tautologous approach[118] the object formula

---

116 cf with regard to Hannah Arendt C Menke, 'Dignity as the Right to Have Rights: Human Dignity in Hannah Arendt' in M Düwell, J Braarvig, R Brownsword and D Mieth (eds), *The Cambridge Handbook of Human Dignity* (Cambridge, Cambridge University Press, 2013) 332 ff.

117 G Dürig, 'Der Grundrechtssatz von der Menschenwürde' (1956) 81 *Archiv des öffentlichen Rechts*, 117, 127. It would be a misunderstanding of the 'object

elucidates neither what human dignity is nor how it can be violated. Its contribution is to be found in the fact that 'human dignity' is not understood as a characteristic of human beings, but in terms of potential forms of violation. Human dignity is a relational concept. It is worked out in a similar manner when it is concretized with an inductive strategy and through exemplification against the background of the experiences of elementary injustice and the vulnerability of the individual: Practices are identified and categorized which are viewed as breaches of human dignity, such as particular encroachments of the individual's physical and psychological integrity as well as forms of social exclusion.[119] Some debate is centered on whether determining a violation of human dignity has occurred is the result of weighing this against other legally protected interests or whether human dignity resists such relativization.[120] Other discussions deal with how to concretize the multidimensional nature of the guarantee of human dignity: protection against impairments, duties to protect, procedural safeguards, horizontal effects.[121] These discourses refer back to

---

formula' to judge the question of 'degradation' solely in terms of the motivation of the violator or of the State; the matter must rather be examined from an objective viewpoint while considering all circumstances at hand.

118   The concept which is to be defined is already contained in the definition as a prerequisite, see the above cited object formula in German: 'Die Menschenwürde als solche ist getroffen, wenn der konkrete Mensch zum Objekt, zu einem bloßen Mittel, zur vertretbaren Größe *herabgewürdigt* wird', G Dürig, 'Grundrechtssatz' 127.

119   See the contributions in P Kaufmann, H Kuch, C Neuhäuser and E Webster (eds), *Humiliation, Degradation, Dehumanization. Human Dignity Violated* (Dordrecht et al, Springer, 2011), and in A Masferrer and E Garcia-Sánchez (eds), *Human Dignity of the Vulnerable in the Age of Rights* (Dordrecht/Heidelberg/London/New York, Springer, 2016). Cf also O Schachter, 'Human Dignity as a Normative Concept' (1983) 77 *American Journal of International Law* 848, 852; J von Bernstorff, 'Der Streit um die Menschenwürde im Grund- und Menschenrechtsschutz: Eine Verteidigung des Absoluten als Grenze und Auftrag' (2013) *JuristenZeitung* 905, 908 ff; A Pollmann, 'Human Rights Beyond Naturalism' in M Albers, T Hoffmann and J Reinhardt (eds), *Human Rights and Human Nature* (Berlin/Heidelberg/New York, Springer, 2014) 123, 132 f.

120   See, eg, J von Bernstorff, 'Streit' 905 ff.

121   cf M Mahlmann, 'Human Dignity and Autonomy in Modern Constitutional Orders' in M Rosenfeld and A Sajó (eds), *The Oxford Handbook of Comparative Constitutional Law* (Oxford, Oxford University Press, 2012) 370, 383 ff. Elaborating the background and characteristics of the State's duty to protect (with regard to German constitutional law) D Grimm, 'The Protective Function

the fundamental conceptions, the varying textual underpinnings and the heterogeneous content-related ways in which human dignity is made concrete.

The advancement of biotechnologies results in scientific approaches and arguments having to be readdressed in discourse and questions having to be posed in a new or a more salient way. As to legal-philosophical foundations, it is becoming increasingly difficult to found human dignity solely on being human. The self-evident manner in how it had previously been possible to assume a common understanding, to a certain extent, of what characterizes the 'human being' and how to construct human boundaries is clearly disintegrating. As to the understanding of human dignity as a general principle allowing interpreters to derive other particular rights, imaginable scenarios, such as extensive brain intervention, require answers whether and how this principle enables the development of completely new kinds of liberties or rights, for example, cognitive liberty or rights to mental integrity, to emotions or to forget.[122] Regarding the questions who is protected by human dignity and who is a bearer of rights, the answers are no longer relatively clear cut but instead subject to greater and greater difficulties. Ever since artificial reproduction and in-vitro fertilization have made embryos available outside the mother's body, the question of at what point in human development does protection set in is being answered in a heterogeneous way. The spectrum of development phases being used to define the point where the protection of human dignity begins extends from early cell stages to nidation all the way to birth. However, fertilized ova and embryos are at least entities whose fundamental quality as 'human life' is not in question. But biotechnological advances in reprogramming cells or suppressing a particular development potential are increasingly blurring the boundaries.[123] Future visions of genetically and

---

of the State' in G Nolte (ed), *European and US Constitutionalism* (Cambridge et al, Cambridge University Press, 2005) 137, 143 ff.

122 See JC Bublitz, 'My Mind Is Mine!? Cognitive Liberty as a Legal Concept' in E Hildt and AG Franke (eds), *Cognitive Enhancement. An Interdisciplinary Perspective* (Dordrecht, Springer, 2013) 233, 241 ff; BJ Koops, 'Concerning "Humans" and "Human" Rights. Human Enhancement from the Perspective of Fundamental Rights' in BJ Koops, CH Lüthi, A Nelis, C Sieburgh, JPM Jansen and MS Schmid (eds), *Engineering the Human. Human Enhancement Between Fiction and Fascination* (Berlin/Heidelberg, Springer, 2013) 165, 174 ff; Albers, 'Grundrechtsschutz', 82 ff.

123 By no means is the problem resolved by emphasizing that statements based on natural sciences and legal statements must be separated and that latter must be

radically altered human beings, human-machine beings, chimeras or artificially constructed living beings also prompt debate over whether and under what circumstances human dignity includes or can be transferred to such beings[124] or whether and under what circumstances it, conversely, prohibits their development.

Due to these and other challenges, a more precise answer must also be formulated regarding what exact interests or rights worthy of protection actually merit protection on the grounds of human dignity and what can be classified as being a violation of those rights or interests. Here, approaches must contend with the problem that the interests helpful in making human dignity concrete must themselves be carefully thought through again. This is compounded by the problem that partly conceptual and partly empirical aspects are involved, but that quite a few empirical assumptions are uncertain and cannot be researched ex ante. For example, is cloning a problem of human dignity with a view to the cloned person because he or she would not enjoy sufficient autonomy as a 'copy' of someone else, or do such assumptions involve inadmissible genetic determinism? What are 'dignity' and 'autonomy' against the background of the findings of brain research? Do these concepts, in the realm of human rights, have to be linked to a 'natural' person or how far do limits and descriptions change, for instance, in the case of human-machine combinations? Is dignity achieved in evaluations and decisions made by the individual person and does it therefore encompass any voluntarily chosen use of new technologies for 'enhancement', or is it an objectified concept that does not privilege persons own understanding at any rate and under certain circumstances can dispute such decisions?[125] Moreover, with the advent of biotechniques and their potential for intervention the very question arises whether there is a concept of human species which expresses the interest in preserving certain features of the human life-form and which provides

---

supported on their own, see for such an approach Böckenförde, 'Menschenwürde' 810 ff. For despite the fact that they can be differentiated analytically, both forms of statements are intertwined in many ways in concrete assessments.

124 N Bostrom, 'In Defense of Posthuman Dignity' in GR Hansell and W Grassie (eds), *H +/- Transhumanism and Its Critics* (Philadelphia, Metanexus, 2011) 55 ff, 61 ff; MC Gruber, '"Menschenwürde" – Menschlichkeit als Bedingung der Würde?' in H Baranzke and G Duttge (eds), *Autonomie und Würde* (Würzburg, Königshausen & Neumann, 2014) 417, 417 ff; cf also Koops, 'Concerning "Humans"' 179 f.

125 For this debate see Albers, 'Enhancement' 235 ff.

underlying presuppositions for human dignity. Approaches to this question are manifold, answers divergent.[126]

Legal considerations respond to these challenges, among other ways, by constructing the form, statements and effects of legal norms and rights anew. For example, objective legal statements and individual rights are differentiated and decoupled from each other in such a way that not every objective legal statement has a corresponding individual right the protected person can enforce. The duties following from the objective legal guarantee of human dignity can then be broken down in many ways and, if necessary, be tailored to new problems. The construct of an advance objective protection, for instance, attempts to solve the problem arising when the protection of human dignity shall be applied to human beings who do not yet exist. In the case of reproductive cloning, the protection of human dignity would comprise the cloned person and be effective before the protected person exists, since it would apply to the act which produces him or her as a clone.[127] In the constructions of individual rights, proposals such as that of giving a remainder interest to the embryo seek to model protection understood as gradual and increasing protection in the different de-

---

126 Sometimes the concept of a dignity of the human species is not substantiated and introduced to justify prohibitions in an overall manner, see, eg, J Isensee, 'Die alten Grundrechte und die biotechnische Revolution' in J Bohnert, C Gramm, U Kindhäuser, J Lege, A Rinken and G Robbers (eds), *Verfassung – Philosophie – Kirche* (Berlin, Duncker & Humblot, 2001) 243, 253 f, 261 f. In a more elaborated way, the concept aims at preserving an 'ethical self-understanding of the species which is crucial for our capacity to see ourselves as the authors of our own life histories, and to recognize one another as autonomous persons', see J Habermas, *The Future of Human Nature* (Cambridge, Polity Press, 2003) 25. Cf also D Grimm, 'Das Grundgesetz nach vierzig Jahren' (1989) *Neue Juristische Wochenschrift* 1305, 1310; Meiser, *Biopatentierung* (2006) 93 ff; R Andorno, 'Human Dignity and Human Rights as a Common Ground for a Global Bioethics' (2009) 34 *Journal of Medicine and Philosophy* 223; M Nettesheim, 'Biotechnology and the Guarantee of Human Dignity' in S Elm and SN Willich (eds) *Quo Vadis Medical Healing* (Dordrecht, Springer, 2009) 143, 162 ff. For critical considerations see, eg, T Gutmann, '"Gattungsethik" als Grenze der Verfügung des Menschen über sich selbst?' in W van den Daele (ed), *Biopolitik* (Wiesbaden, VS Verlag für Sozialwissenschaften, 2005) 235, 242 ff.

127 See, eg, H Rosenau, 'Reproduktives und therapeutisches Klonen' in K Amelung, W Beulke, H Lilie, H Rüping, H Rosenau and G Wolfslast (eds), *Strafrecht, Biorecht, Rechtsphilosophie* (Heidelberg, C.F. Müller, 2003) 761, 767, 776 ff.

velopmental stages of the embryo by using an appropriate legal construct.[128]

As a result, the scientific approaches to human dignity are becoming even more multifaceted because of the biotechnological challenges. To some extent, they contradict and compete with each other. Considering their self-understanding and their convincibility, they must aim at internal consistency. From the perspective of each particular approach, diverging approaches are mutually irreconcilable. From an external perspective, however, that does not pose an insurmountable problem. Scientific approaches are not integrated within non-academic contexts directly and without change; they are always modified when being used in societal, political or judicial communication.

III. Contextualizing and Differentiating Human Dignity

Biotechnologies have proven to be a productive field of reference for discourse about human dignity and the resulting need to contextualize and differentiate the concept of human dignity becomes clearly evident. The more that, over time and upon closer examination, 'the' biotechnologies differentiate into numerous fields as well as into a broad spectrum of applications and the more nuanced their consequences, both actually observed and potential, are described, the more sophisticated levels, reference points and patterns of argumentation in connection with human dignity are fleshed out. The multifaceted nature of the technologies forces to make arguments related to human dignity more precise. It is no objection that it is not always entirely clear exactly what the features of biotechnology are or what is problematic about them; on the contrary, this is a driving power in the debate. Considered as a whole, discourse about biotechnologies in the various fields provides a substantial contribution to sharpening understanding of human dignity with regard to contexts (A.), functions (B.) or legal constructions (C.). Human dignity is by no means a useless concept.

---

128   Jofer, *Regulierung* (2015) 410 ff.

A. Contexts

Human dignity is discussed in many fields: in society in general, in the political and in the legal system as well as in various scientific disciplines. The idea plays different roles in different contexts, and the particular actors involved contribute in their own ways to how it is understood. To a certain extent, its meaning is shaped by the particular context in which it is used. Of course, there are also interactions. Especially in the area of biotechnology, the juridical conceptualization of human dignity has been a topic of discourse throughout society, and the attractiveness of human dignity as an argument derives not least from the fact that the public is quite familiar with its legal value. Social discourse in various legal systems even differ according to whether human dignity simply has high legal value or whether it goes even further and is considered 'inviolable' in the sense of 'indefeasible' or 'untouchable' ('unantastbar'). For example, in contrast to the United States, questions of informed consent in connection with biobanks are being discussed in Germany – where the Basic Law enshrines the indefeasibility of human dignity – as a problem in terms of personality rights,[129] but regularly not as a problem of human dignity.

When human dignity is used in a legal context, its meaning is shaped by the specific legal environment. Even if the idea has theological or philosophical roots, it is detached from them to a certain extent due to its being transferred to a legal context. Its legal meaning is the result of autonomous legal communication processes.[130] Communication contexts within the legal system are, in their turn, diverse. As this analysis has illustrated, a rough distinction can be drawn between legislation, jurisdiction and jurisprudence. Lawmaking procedures aim at establishing legal rules through procedures that ensure acceptance. In this way they are, to a certain extent, linked to public discourse. They are carried out at the various levels at which norms operate: as procedures for working out an international declaration or convention, as procedures for establishing a constitution, or as legislative procedures. Human dignity can be decisive as a norm or an argument in lawmaking procedures and/or be enshrined as a

---

129 Personality rights are derived from Article 2 para 1 in conjunction with Article 1 para 1 of the Basic Law. The right to freely develop one's personality, Article 2 I of the Basic Law, is the guiding norm. Hence, personality rights do not enjoy the same legal value as human dignity; they are, for example, subject to limiting reservations.
130 See Grimm, 'Dignity' 381 ff, 384.

normative standard in the outcome of the norm-setting procedure. Lawmaking procedures and established legal standards can be interlinked due to the interdependencies between norms and their to some extent hierarchical relationship to each other: The enshrinement of human dignity as the result of a declaration or of the adoption of a constitution affects national legislative procedures in which the provisions of the declaration or constitution exert their influence, whether as soft law or as a binding standard, and are used as an argument in debates. Courts refer to human dignity in the context of decisions on particular cases. As courts are established at different levels and decide in different kind of judicial procedures, the court involved and the particular procedure determine the role human dignity plays as a normative measure. In the case of constitutional courts, the only standard is the constitution; human dignity may be relevant as an objective norm or as an individual right. Other courts apply constitutional standards such as human dignity only by also taking account of legal norms below the level of the constitution. The analysis of the use of human dignity in the reasoning of courts has shown that courts, as a rule, try to base their decisions not on references to human dignity alone, and that they depend, to a certain extent, on legislative guidelines or frameworks when addressing the challenges of biotechnologies. In view of the prospect of as yet unspecified future cases courts are not willing to commit themselves fully to a particular theory or foundation of human dignity but, on the contrary, keep their options open. In contrast, jurisprudence deals with human dignity in a specifically scholarly way. Profundity and consistency are quality standards that require the selection of a particular theoretical framework. Scientific approaches do not need to focus on embodiments of human dignity in texts, but instead can explore foundations or arguments offered by other disciplines. They are by their very nature varied.

Legislation, jurisdiction and jurisprudence differ from each other not simply on the basis of the distinction between theory and practice, but also through the forms of their own independent institutional contexts. The meaning of human dignity does not completely change when it is used in different contexts; however, as a result of its own internal differentiations, the legal system does not offer a uniform understanding of human dignity, but instead a multifaceted one.

B. Functions

Any description of functions depends on approaches, frameworks and perspectives. The use of human dignity in lawmaking or judicial procedures can be analyzed, for instance, from a sociological or political sciences' point of view with emphasis on the function a multi-faceted and ambiguous normative measure such as human dignity plays in 'keeping rival constituencies on board'[131] or in shifting power to courts. From a meta-perspective, the function of the guarantee of human dignity can be seen in offering a basis for ongoing specification and reflection of descriptions how the human should be understood. This function is stimulated by the high rank of human dignity and by follow-up questions like the problem of universalizability of basic values and rights.

As to legal points of view, jurisprudential analyses comprise a wide variety of different approaches. Among other problems, although by no means exclusively, they contend with questions of how normative measures are to be interpreted in a methodologically well-founded manner. Against the background of concepts of the division of power, they might be especially interested in examining the capacity of the legally established guarantee of human dignity to guide regulators and to constrain judicial decision-making. Traditional hierarchical models and ideas of 'steering' in the sense that courts merely subsume their cases under legal provisions, however, have in the meantime been superseded by more complex conceptions of how law functions. In addition, it is part of jurisprudential research interests to analyze, for instance, what legal concepts are suitable for putting the normatively desired influence of the public on legislative decisions into practice, or whether the guarantee of human dignity is, precisely because of its ambiguity and rich implications, helpful for courts to decide cases involving particular challenges of biotechnologies, whether in a situation where statutory rules do not yet exist, or at a later point in time than when laws have been enacted. Functional analyses will, in accordance with their particular approach, come to different results: they may highlight the role the guarantee of human dignity plays for the understanding and enforcement of individual rights as well as for satisfying particular protection needs or criticize that this guarantee fails in giving a clear guidance, 'may obscure the real rationales for, and the lack

---

131   Caulfield and Brownsword, 'Human Dignity' 75.

of consensus about, a given policy approach'[132] or 'is used by courts as a licence to illegitimately overrule democratic authority'[133]. However, even from a legal point of view, human dignity as a normative concept or as a normative measure is by no means in any respect unsuitable just because it is characterized by disparate traditions, by a heuristic character[134], by a 'remarkable plasticity',[135] by specific needs for concretization and by a relative openness to different interpretations.

The results of this article also show that the guarantee of human dignity does not lead to completely arbitrary outcomes. Quite the contrary, there is widespread consensus about the prohibition of, for instance, enslaving women for the purpose of forced surrogate motherhood, breeding human clones that are deliberately stunted to do inferior works, intervening in the brain of a person to gain complete external control or admitting a product patent on a human being. As far as there are disagreements on many matters, the results of this article have elucidated that, from a functional point of view, exactly the 'paradoxical nature'[136] of the guarantee of human dignity might explain its capacities. And even when human dignity is firmly anchored as 'inviolable', it does not present itself as an unchangeable conceptual complex. Biotechnologies are developing, social contexts are changing, in some respects empirical experience is accumulating. Understanding of human dignity is developing along with these, without becoming arbitrary as a result.

---

132   T Caulfield, 'Stem Cells, Clones, Consensus, and the Law' in LP Knowles and GE Kaebnick (eds), *Reprogenetics. Law, Policy and Ethical Issues* (Baltimore, The John Hopkins University Press, 2007) 105, 113 ff.
133   M Rosen, 'Dignity: The Case Against' in C McCrudden (ed), *Understanding Human Dignity* (Oxford, Oxford University Press, 2013) 143, 152.
134   C Dupré, *The Age of Dignity. Human Rights and Constitutionalim in Europe* (Oxford, Hart Publishing, 2016) 16 f.
135   Botha, 'Human Dignity' 217.
136   Botha, 'Human Dignity' 173, 217 ff: 'Dignity is seen as a matter of cosmopolitan right [...] and yet [...] its precise meaning and contours are culturally mediated [...]; it suspends legal decision making between the universal and the particular, between the transcendental and the contingent; [...] dignity constrains legal meaning by excluding a range of interpretations which are incompatible with the inherent worth of the human person. At the same time, it institutes uncertainty by recognising each individual as a unique, self-legislating human being, who has the moral right to question received interpretations and to challenge the normative closure [...].'

C. Legal Constructs

The guarantee of human dignity is enshrined in a series of legal documents, and the forms of text vary, as do the status and role of the various documents. How human dignity is to be understood and what legal effects are linked with it has to be determined in a relatively independent way in the context of a particular document. Interpreting legal guarantees does not stop at simply working out the meaning of texts but also involves and relies on doctrinal systems that can be described as a storehouse of knowledge which consists of, among others, structures, constituent elements and correlations derived from legal or supralegal concepts and to which science, legislation or court rulings contribute.[137] For instance, objective legal statements and individual rights have to be differentiated as well as the legal requirements and legal effects laid down in a provision; additionally, several dimensions of protection can be worked out, such as the protection against impairments, duties to protect or horizontal effects. Hence, appropriate legal responses to social conflicts or new challenges are not only reached by defining the contents of a legal guarantee or the bearer of a right but also by developing a variety of legal constructs and sophisticated legal architectures.

This article has pointed out that, although there have been manifold approaches ever since the legal protection of human dignity was established, the advancement of biotechnologies and their consequences have given rise to an even richer and more highly differentiated diversity of contents and legal constructs. For example, the construct of an advance objective protection derived from the guarantee of human dignity seeks to protect human beings who do not yet exist. Deliberations such as that of giving a remainder interest to embryos aim at introducing an appropriate legal construct to reflect a gradual and increasing protection in the different developmental stages of embryos. Some proposals understand the guarantee of human dignity as a bundle of rights that can be divided into separate elements in order to apply one part or another to artificial entities. Other approaches emphasize that the objective protection of human dignity does not refer to the individual alone, but also to human species. Only infrequently this is meant in the sense that the 'species' as such enjoys the protection of dignity so that 'human nature' must not be altered. More convincing than such a thesis – which leads to unsolvable difficulties of how

---

137 More thoroughly Albers, 'Rechtsfindung' 260 ff.

to find appropriate criteria for defining human 'species' or 'human nature' – is the assumption that there is a concept of human species which provides underlying preconditions for human dignity as a normative idea and which expresses the interest in preserving these preconditions. Such a content-related concept is needed, for instance, for delineating those living beings that are protected by human dignity. It is also needed for applying the protection of human dignity to human beings who do not yet exist and for preventing imaginable developments such as the breeding of people with brain functioning restricted by gene technology for carrying out low-level work. Many other thinkable constellations, though, involve grey zones and finding appropriate answers to them poses new challenges. As a human right that has to be acknowledged and therefore inherently possesses supra-individual values the guarantee of human dignity necessarily goes beyond the individual and transcends individual rights while moving the individual into the center of protection and ensuring that not only his or her interests but also his or her self-understanding of dignity and his or her autonomy are normatively relevant. This reflects once again the 'paradoxical nature'[138] of the guarantee of human dignity and leads to the conclusion that, although species-related arguments might be used for limiting the decisions of the individual, the normative idea of human species, in turn, is relatively variable.

With the development of biotechnologies and the resulting gray areas concerning what a human being is and when a living creature can be said to be human, the image of human dignity as a human being's inner kernel or intrinsic value considered self-evident loses its fundamental basis. More convincing is approaching 'human dignity' not in a way as if it were a characteristic of human beings, but as a relational concept and with a view to social relationships and potential forms of violation. But if we interpret the guarantee of human dignity as a human right that bases on experiences of human vulnerability how can it be handled when we move to biotechnical prospects and new areas characterized by a high level of uncertainties and when the human is subject to transformation and transgression in an unprecedented manner? The description of 'experiences of human vulnerability' – of course always a mixture of hindsight and foresight when used in the context of human dignity violations – will have to focus more on foresight than on hindsight. To a substantial extent, the effects and risks of biotechnologies refer to an unknown future, and the present con-

---

138   Botha, 'Human Dignity' 173, 217.

structions of this future which are continuously being made have to take uncertainties and the unknown, i.e., the constantly generated reverse of knowledge, into consideration.[139] Legal constructions must respond to such challenges by developing forms of proceduralization of law and legally guided decision-making.[140] The legal effects of the guarantee of human dignity are not restricted to prohibiting certain behaviors or to simple 'Yes/No' decisions. In the course of being elaborated in a more differentiated way, these legal effects can extend to providing normative standards such as legislative duties to observe the effects of and to rethink the regulatory approaches chosen or duties to implement risk assessment and evaluation procedures. Considering social and technological change and knowledge or experiences over time, the concrete measures the guarantee of human dignity provides must be regarded as being, to a certain extent, in flux, too.[141] Once again, this guarantee proves to be far from consisting of static statements only.

IV. Outlook

As biotechnologies and the societal discourse on them develop the notion of the guarantee of human dignity is becoming increasingly differentiated. Human dignity does not turn out to be a useless concept.[142] Likewise, it is not 'little other than an umbrella term'[143] or reducible to a mere placeholder for other interests such as autonomy or equal respect. Faced with the potential of advanced biotechnologies for bringing about radical transformations, we need human dignity as a concept forcing us to continuously

---

139   cf Albers, 'Bioethik, Biopolitik, Biorecht', 32 ff.
140   See in more detail M Albers, 'Risikoregulierung im Bio-, Gesundheits- und Medizinrecht' in id (ed), *Risikoregulierung im Bio-, Gesundheits- und Medizinrecht* (Baden-Baden, Nomos, 2011) 13 ff.
141   This has nothing to do with a weighing or balancing of interests which is a specific form of relativizing the protection of the guarantee of human dignity – a relativization human dignity is exempted from in case it is established as being 'indefeasible (unantastbar)'.
142   See, however, R Macklin, 'Dignity Is a Useless Concept' (2003) 327 *British Medical Journal*, 1419 f. Nevertheless, it is true that more precision is required than simply asserting that human dignity is violated.
143   cf U Schüklenk and A Pacholczyk, 'Dignity's Wooly Uplift' (2010) 24 *Bioethics* ii (in the context of patients' needs where claiming 'human dignity', indeed, often might sum up various patients' needs that have to be concretized).

specify and reflect upon what constitutes being human. This is supported by the fact that the idea of human dignity is probably more obviously than ever before a social construction as well as an extraordinarily complex legal concept.

How to Define Human Dignity, and the Resulting Implications for Biotechnology

Tatjana Hörnle

I. Introduction

The aim of this article is to discuss the weaknesses and strengths of different approaches to defining human dignity and to address the implications for judgements about new developments in the area of human reproduction (using the example of surrogate motherhood). It will focus neither on details of international human rights conventions nor on details of German constitutional law and constitutional jurisprudence, but instead discuss conceptual issues. The main question regarding arguments that invoke human dignity to demand legal prohibitions and regulations is: how should we define the concept of human dignity? Pessimists (most famously Arthur Schopenhauer)[1] have argued that talking about human dignity equates to putting empty phrases on show.[2] In contrast to such statements, the following analysis assumes that it is possible to distinguish scenarios that should be classified as a violation of human dignity from those that should not—if one is willing to take a road less travelled. The mainstream approach in the German literature relies heavily on Kant's second categorical imperative.[3] It uses the so-called object formula and asks whether a

---

[1] eg '... shibboleth of all clueless and unthinking moralists', A Schopenhauer, *Über die Grundlage der Moral,* vol VI (Zurich, Diogenes Verlag, Werke in zehn Bänden, 1977) 206.

[2] N Hoerster, *Ethik des Embryonenschutzes* (Stuttgart, Reclam Verlag, 2002) 24; S Pinker, 'The Stupidity of Dignity' (28 May 2008) *The New Republic*; A Lohmar, *Falsches moralisches Bewusstsein: Eine Kritik der Idee der Menschenwürde* (Hamburg, Felix Meiner Verlag, 2017).

[3] In an influential article, Günter Dürig used the formula 'mere object' along with the formula adopted from Kant, 'mere means'. G Dürig, 'Der Grundrechtssatz von der Menschenwürde' (1956), 81 *Archiv des öffentlichen Rechts* 117, 127. See also C Enders, *Die Menschenwürde in der Verfassungsordnung* (Tübingen, Mohr Siebeck Verlag, 1997); G Luf, 'Menschenwürde als Rechtsbegriff' in Rainer Zaczyk et al (eds), *Festschrift für E.A. Wolff* (Berlin, Sprin-

person is treated as 'a mere object'.[4] However, there are problems with this way of operationalising human dignity: the 'mere object' formula is rather vague. I will defend a different approach to human dignity, one that gained prominence in the more recent literature on moral philosophy. According to this approach, the characteristic feature of human dignity violations is that they severely humiliate their victims.

The main part of this article deals with the concept of human dignity from a theoretical, philosophical perspective. However, the starting point is that human dignity figures as an important term within legal contexts, especially in debates about legal policy. In legal systems with a human dignity clause in their constitution,[5] this clause will be cited to demand the prohibition of stem cell research or human cloning, to argue against the shooting down of hijacked aeroplanes or to argue for strict boundaries regarding the interrogation of suspects by police officers, etc. Such legal policy demands to have the state intervene for the sake of human dignity are the background for the need to define this concept. One might, of course, think more abstractly about the notion 'what is dignity?' or describe the evolution of human dignity from a historical and sociological perspective.[6] However, this is not the approach taken here. It is not always possible to step straightforwardly from the descriptive perspective to the normative perspective. The normative approach asks for what reasons and to what extent we *should* acknowledge a legal good called human dignity or human beings' rights (not) to be treated in a certain way. Within normative discourses, the term 'dignity' also appears in different contexts: in our everyday moral judgements as well as in academic moral philosophy and theology. To differentiate between moral philosophy, on the one hand, and legal interpretation and legal politics, on the other hand, does not, of

---

	ger Verlag, 1998) 307; J Hruschka, 'Die Würde des Menschen bei Kant' (2002) 88 *Archiv für Rechts- und Sozialphilosophie* 463.
4	This phrase was applied in the ruling on the German Aviation Security Act (*Luftsicherheitsgesetz*): BVerfGE 115, 118, 154. See O Lepsius, 'Human Dignity and the Downing of Aircraft: The Federal Constitutional Court Strikes Down a Prominent Anti-Terrorism Provision in the New Air-Transport Security Act' (2006) 7 *German Law Journal* 761; T Hoernle, 'Hijacked Airplanes: May They Be Shot Down?' (2007) 10 *New Criminal Law Review* 582.
5	Such as Art 1 I *Grundgesetz* (GG): 'The dignity of man shall be inviolable. To respect and protect it shall be the duty of all state authority.'
6	See, eg JQ Whitman, 'The Two Western Cultures of Privacy: Dignity Versus Liberty' (2003) 113 *Yale Law Journal* 1151; J Waldron, *Dignity, Rank, and Rights* (New York, Oxford, 2012).

course, equate to postulating that there are impermeable barriers between the disciplines. In the following sections, it will be shown that defining human dignity as a legal term cannot be done without drawing on deliberations in other fields. However, one must bear in mind that the *consequences* of invoking human dignity within legal reasoning are different from both colloquial references to dignity and judgements made in moral philosophy. Invoking human dignity as a legal argument means using a heavyweight argument, especially if a constitution grants the protection of human dignity at a prominent position and without reference to countervailing considerations that might justify intrusions. Against such a background, human dignity arguments have the role of trump cards or jokers. Drawing the human dignity joker means suppressing further discussion.

This practical importance of claims about 'violated human dignity' leads me to be sceptical about references to Kant's second categorical imperative. Kant developed this imperative in the context of moral philosophy, in his writings about moral philosophy[7] and not in this treatment of legal philosophy. To adopt the 'mere object' formula (a popular approach in Germany) for a legal concept of human dignity invites the problematic conclusion that every instance of serious disregard of moral rights equates to a violation of human dignity. In a legal discourse, extensive references to human dignity use the trump card too often. The conclusion should not be to abandon the notion of human dignity and its status as a human right altogether, but that it is worth taking a closer look at proposals for defining human dignity beyond the 'mere object' formula.

Prior to approaching the question of how to define human dignity, another point should be mentioned briefly: are attempts to develop a definition necessary at all? In constitutional theory, some authors refrain from definitional efforts, asserting that human dignity constitutes a *mysterium tremendum* that can only 'be sensed in a sacred thrill'.[8] If one interprets a constitutional provision such as Article 1 I GG (*Grundgesetz*, the Basic

---

7 I Kant, 'Grundlegung zur Metaphysik der Sitten' in W Weischedel (ed), *Immanuel Kant: Kritik der praktischen Vernunft. Grundlegung zur Metaphysik der Sitten,* Werkausgabe vol VII,(Frankfurt/M., Suhrkamp Verlag, 2004) 67.

8 *U Haltern,* 'Unsere protestantische Menschenwürde' in P Bahr and HM Heinig (eds), *Menschenwürde in der säkularen Verfassungsordnung* (Tübingen, Mohr Siebeck Verlag, 2006) 117. This is based on the theory proposed by Carl Schmitt that 'all concise concepts of modern political science are secularised theological concepts', in C Schmitt, *Politische Theologie,* 2nd edn (Munich, Duncker & Humblot Verlag, 1934) 49.

Law for the Federal Republic of Germany) as an 'embodiment of the sacred'[9], vagueness and lack of contours become advantageous. They enhance the shimmering aura. Political considerations might also support the conclusion that one should not attempt to define human dignity. Theodor Heuss, one of the fathers of the German Constitution, stated that Article 1 I GG contains an 'uninterpreted proposition'.[10] According to Heuss, it should be left open to interpreters to introduce their own philosophical, ethical or theological notions of human dignity. Proponents of a 'do-not-define' approach point out that widespread and strong identification with the value of human dignity depends on the degree to which it is open to different modes of interpretation.[11] Opinions like these probably contain elements of truth from the perspective of legal sociology and cultural sociology. However, if one argues within a normative context or if one draws legal conclusions from purported violations of human dignity, one cannot opt for the sociologist's detached point of view. Neither a term that cannot be interpreted nor the image of human dignity as a resplendent, yet not clearly visible, object of veneration is useful in a debate on matters of legal policy. If such debates are to proceed in a rational manner, arguments are necessary that establish a connection between human dignity and the conduct to be prohibited, and this requires defining human dignity.

II. Human Dignity as a Quality

A. Dignity

How should one proceed to obtain a workable concept of human dignity? A popular approach attempts to specify those qualities that constitute the dignity of humans. Thinking along these lines, the concept of 'human dignity' could be broken down into its components 'human' and 'dignity'. One starting point for further analysis could be the component 'dignity'. Looking back into the history of ideas, this leads to concepts of 'dignitas',

---

9   Haltern, 'Menschenwürde'.
10 T Heuss, cited in *Jahrbuch des öffentlichen Rechts der Gegenwart* (new edn, 1951), 49.
11 See E Hilgendorf, 'Die missbrauchte Menschenwürde' (1999) 7 *Jahrbuch für Recht und Ethik* 137, 138.

'honestas' and 'nobilitas' in antique societies.[12] Attempts to place dignity into a Christian context use, as a point of reference, the mindset of a person who, supported by his or her faith, finds dignity in situations that are objectively humiliating (such as the crucifixion of Jesus or human martyrdom).[13] In a more general way, a Christian understanding of dignity might be expressed as the ability to distance oneself from one's drives and interests.[14]

However, such approaches are not very helpful for our purpose of defining human dignity as a legal concept that evokes protective claims. They do not presuppose the modern notion of a *right* to human dignity that ought to be protected by the state. Within the framework of the Christian conception, there is no room for a state's duties to respect and protect the human dignity of its citizens against infringements by others. Instead, dignity is seen as an *individual accomplishment*. In cases of abuse, it is the offender, not the victim, who loses dignity.[15] There is also another reason why this way of approaching human dignity leads to a dead end in the context of legal philosophy. The sociological and theological concepts that see dignity as a matter of personal achievement have one feature in common: dignity differs from person to person. This unequal distribution of dignity poses a problem if one is working with a constitutional concept. An *egalitarian understanding* of human dignity is one of the few points on which there is universal consensus.[16] The adoption of the human dignity clause in the German Constitution of 1949 was aimed at distancing postwar Germany from the National Socialist regime of injustice.[17] Perpetra-

---

12 S Schaede, 'Würde – Eine ideengeschichtliche Annäherung aus theologischer Perspektive' in P Bahr and HM Heinig, *Menschenwürde in der säkularen Verfassungsordnung* (Tübingen, Mohr Siebeck Verlag, 2006) 20.
13 Schaede, 'Würde' 28; R Spaemann, 'Über den Begriff der Menschenwürde' in E-W Böckenförde and R Spaemann (eds), *Menschenrechte und Menschenwürde* (Stuttgart, Klett Cotta Verlag, 1987) 299.
14 Spaemann, 'Menschenwürde' 304.
15 TS Hoffman, 'Menschenwürde – ein Problem des konkreten Allgemeinen', in W Schweidler, H Neumann and E Brysch (eds), *Menschenleben – Menschenwürde* (Münster, LIT Verlag, 2003) 111, 121.
16 A Pieper, 'Menschenwürde. Ein abendländisches oder ein universelles Problem? Zum Verhältnis von Genesis und Geltung im normativen Diskurs' in E Herms (ed), *Menschenbild und Menschenwürde* (Gütersloh, Gütersloher Verlagshaus, 2001) 19; H Dreier, in id (ed), *Grundgesetz-Kommentar*, 2nd edn (Tübingen, Mohr Siebeck Verlag, 2004), Art 1 n 59.
17 See Enders, *Menschenwürde in der Verfassungsordnung* (1997) 510.

tors could explain persecutions not only on the basis of (alleged) genetic heredity but also on the basis of (alleged) individual failure and the resulting differences in dignity and rank. Thus, the concept of human dignity should be based on a normative understanding of equality and not on individual achievements.

B. Human

Another starting point for defining 'human dignity' would be the term 'human': by claiming that dignity is not a matter of achievement, but an *inherent quality of all mankind*. One variation of this theme that can be found in theological statements as well as literature on constitutional law refers to 'man as created in God's image'[18]. Its persuasive power is, however, limited to those who believe in the existence of God and his special relationship with the human species. Religious arguments are unsuitable for a contemporary moral or legal discussion on human dignity. In contemporary constitutional and philosophical literature, an approach dominates that is based on a more or less accurate reading of Immanuel Kant's writings. Because such arguments have been presented in numerous articles and books,[19] brief references should suffice here. In his *Groundwork of the Metaphysics of Morals*, Kant refers to the 'dignity of a rational being who obeys no law other than that which he himself also gives'[20]. With regard to self-respect and mutual respect, the *Metaphysics of Morals* states:

> A human being regarded as a person, i.e., as the subject of moral-practical reason, is exalted beyond all price because, as a person (*homo noumenon*), he should be valued not only as means to the ends of other persons, or even as a means to his own ends, but also as an end in and of himself; that is, he possesses a dignity (an absolute inner worth) by which he exacts respect for himself from all rational be-

---

18   For the *imago dei* doctrine, see W Pannenberg, 'Christliche Wurzeln des Gedankens der Menschenwürde' in W Kerber (ed), *Menschenrechte und kulturelle Identität* (Munich, Kindt Verlag, 1991) 61, 72; Schaede, 'Würde' 32, 42; C Starck, 'Menschenwürde als Verfassungsgarantie im modernen Staat' (1981) 36 *JuristenZeitung* 459.
19   See the citations in n 3.
20   Kant, 'Metaphysik' 67 (translation by the author).

ings in the world, with whom he can measure himself and value himself on equal footing.[21]

According to a widespread understanding, the premise of Kant's concept of human dignity is the dual nature of man as 'homo phaenomenon' and 'homo noumenon'.[22] Contemporary authors view the justifiability of such a dual nature with scepticism.[23] As an alternative, in reference to Giovanni Pico della Mirandola's *Oration on the Dignity of Man*, the distinctiveness of man is seen in that he, as opposed to an animal, is not destined to a specific existence, but is capable and free to shape himself.[24] Related ideas with regard to identifying specifically human qualities can be found in modern philosophical literature.[25] Harry Frankfurt views the ability to reflect upon and evaluate one's own desires and motives on a second, higher level as the quality that is characteristic for the status as a person. According to Frankfurt, only a person can develop desires on a second level that allow him to desire not to have a desire on the first level.[26] Similar thoughts can be found in Avishai Margalit's book *The Decent Society*, a publication in which he emphasises the human ability to reflect upon past conduct and to decide about changes.[27]

Unfortunately, many publications on the subject of human dignity end with the development of a quality-based argument. According to the apparent underlying assumption, it suffices to demonstrate distinctive human

---

21   I Kant, 'Metaphysik der Sitten', in: W Weischedel (ed): *Immanuel Kant: Metaphysik der Sitten,* Werkausgabe vol VIII (Frankfurt/M., Suhrkamp Verlag, 2004) 569 (translation by the author).

22   But see also for a different reading O Sensen, *Kant on Human Dignity* (Berlin, Walter de Gruyter Verlag, 2011).

23   WK Frankena, 'The Ethics of Respect for Persons' (1986) 14 *Philosophical Topics* 149, 159; J Raz, *Value, Respect and Attachment* (Cambridge, Cambridge University Press, 2001) 130; R Gröschner, *Menschenwürde und Sepulkralkultur in der grundgesetzlichen Ordnung* (Stuttgart, Boorberg Verlag, 1995) 40; A Leist, 'Ethik der Beziehungen' (2005) 10 *Deutsche Zeitschrift für Philosophie* 597, 601.

24   G Pico della Mirandola, *Über die Würde des Menschen* (Zurich, Manesse Verlag, 1996) 10.

25   See K Bayertz, 'Human Dignity: Philosophical Origin and Scientific Erosion of an Idea' in id (ed), *Sanctity of Life and Human Dignity* (Dordrecht, Kluwer Publishers, 1996) 80.

26   HG Frankfurt, *The Importance of what We Care About. Philosophical Essays* (Cambridge, Cambridge University Press, 1988) 11.

27   A Margalit, *The Decent Society* (Cambridge, Mass., Harvard University Press, 1996) 57, 70.

qualities as the source of human dignity. However, this misses a crucial point. What's critical is not the proof of a special status, but the substantiation of *why a certain action affects this status*. Here one encounters the first of several problems. Qualities that are common to all of humankind must be defined at a high level of abstraction. However, it is difficult to demonstrate why fundamental faculties that constitute the essence of being human can be impacted by the conduct of another person. For example, when a police officer administers electric shocks to a suspect in order to induce a confession, the officer tortures and injures the victim as an empirical being, but he does not affect the victim's status as a 'homo noumenon' and a person capable of forming desires of the second order. The status as a moral person does not require respect and protection: it is invulnerable. If human dignity is interpreted in a quality-focused way, one must take Article 1 I GG literally: that which constitutes human dignity is then indeed inviolable. However, as the basis for legal prohibitions, such a declaration is rather pointless. The statement 'is inviolable' must be translated into a state's effort to protect vulnerable human beings from the actions of others.[28]

Another problem arises for approaches that limit themselves to the search for fundamental human qualities. Sophisticated conceptions of personhood that refer to the status as a 'pure rational being', the ability to freely shape one's life, to control one's first-order desires and the like are empirically contestable. The more ambitious the vision of humanity is formulated, the more people there are in the real world for whom insistence on such qualities clearly clashes with empirical descriptions. The larger the realm of the recognisably fictional, however, the more this undermines the normative equality claim that people are 'the same at their core'.[29] These difficulties are reasons to prefer a somewhat humbler approach. Instead of relying on grand ideals of personhood, one should focus on the question: what kind of conduct is incompatible with *fundamental interests* of people (interests that ought to be protected by the notion of rights)?

---

28 Bayertz, 'Human Dignity' 79 ff.
29 Margalit, *Decent Society* (1996) 64.

III. Interest-Based Arguments

A. Objections Against Interest-Based Arguments

The following parts are based on the assumption that individuals' rights to human dignity should be granted (and protected in legal systems) because such rights safeguard important human interests. The nature of important human interests, especially what humans *do not want to suffer*, can be derived from fundamental conditions of human existence. People do not want others to do evil things to them that disregard fundamentally important interests. This reference to 'evil things' and 'important human interests' is admittedly phrased in a very general fashion and needs further clarification, which will follow in the next section. At this juncture, putative disadvantages of an interest-based approach should be mentioned briefly. First, it could be argued that human interests cannot form a persuasive starting point because they are *too diverse*. If one concentrates on fundamentally important interests, however, a consensus is more likely than if one focuses on traditional quality-based justifications such as 'man as created in God's image' or 'man as homo noumenon'. Those who do not believe in God or are sceptical of the construction 'homo noumenon' will not be persuaded. It is simpler, for example, to develop a consensus on the statement 'humans do not want to be tortured', and this consensus is independent of culturally shaped contexts.

Second, proponents of the traditional concept of human dignity based on specific human qualities criticise reliance on 'fundamental human interests' because this requires discussions and decisions about *which* interests are fundamental (and which are not). If every human being has dignity simply by virtue of belonging to the species 'Homo sapiens', then nobody has to adjudicate the issue. Such arguments are frequently raised in discussions about biotechnology[30] (for instance, with the goal of explaining that human embryos are sacrosanct and may never be used for research that results in their destruction). According to this view, human dignity is an ontological phenomenon, something that every member of the species has after a human egg has been fertilised with human sperm. However, it would be futile to hope that eliminating the notion of interests could spare us discussions and decisions. All concepts delineating the

---

30 See, eg T Stein, 'Recht und Politik im biotechnischen Zeitalter' (2002) 50 *Deutsche Zeitschrift für Philosophie* 855, 861.

scope of application for human dignity require arguments that have to be defended against objections. Ontological claims about human dignity that simply assert 'every human being has human dignity, period' will not convince sceptics.

B. The Relevant Interests

Among those authors who rely on an analysis of fundamental interests to identify violations of human dignity, different variations can be found. One approach is called the 'ensemble theory of human dignity'. It is based on the idea that there is a *cluster of interests* that comprises the *core* of important human interests. These core interests include physical needs (material needs for a minimum subsistence level, freedom from pain) and intellectual-emotional integrity as well as interests in self-determination and fundamental needs regarding social cooperation (privacy, equality before the law).[31] If human dignity is understood in this sense, the consequence for constitutional interpretation is that it overlaps broadly with other fundamental rights. Cases of especially severe violation (for example, the administration of extreme pain) would be a case for human dignity, whereas less severe intrusions would be categorised as violating other human rights. For example, ordinary pain would fall under the right to protection of physical integrity.[32] The drawback of the ensemble theory is that human dignity loses it contours. Many violations of fundamental rights are, according to this theory, violations of human dignity if they are severe enough. Before resorting to this solution, it is preferable to examine whether there is not something more particular about violations of human dignity. The question is whether one can identify *characteristics* that are unique to violations of human dignity.

In his article *Menschenwürde als Ausdruck*, the philosopher Anton Leist describes dignity as the 'quality of dominating the appropriate symbolisation' and human dignity as the 'quality of appropriate symbolisation

---

31 D Birnbacher, 'Mehrdeutigkeiten im Begriff der Menschenwürde' (1995) *Aufklärung und Kritik, Sonderheft* 1, 4, 6; Birnbacher, 'Menschenwürde – abwägbar oder unabwägbar?' in M Kettner (ed), *Biomedizin und Menschenwürde* (Frankfurt/M., Suhrkamp Verlag, 2004) 248, 254; Hilgendorf, 'missbrauchte Menschenwürde' 148.

32 Hilgendorf, 'missbrauchte Menschenwürde' 149.

or symbolic interaction with the necessities of human life'.[33] A violation of human dignity would occur if someone was compelled to act in a manner contrary to his or her own forms of symbolic expression. The key aspect is that the victim is forced into an insufferable self-dilemma by symbolic expression imposed upon his or her person. An example here would be where a victim is forced to perform music as a member of an orchestra in a concentration camp or betray his or her loved ones (as a result of torture). The victim is compelled to assent to or participate actively in symbolisation that is, in his or her view, utterly immoral.[34] Leist excludes actions to which the victim is passively exposed. He presumes that if a person is physically abused or killed, the reference to death, injuries or pain would suffice to characterise the wrongdoing.[35]

Leist's interpretation grasps features of human dignity violations but does not give a comprehensive picture of what it means to violate someone's human dignity. A person who was not in the position to find refuge in a concentration camp's orchestra but instead became a victim of medical experiments at the same place can rightfully claim that his or her human dignity was violated in a much more severe manner. Even if one can argue, from the perspective of moral philosophy, that physical mutilations and physical pain violate rights other than human dignity, an exclusive focus on self-representation and self-symbolisation is not persuasive. Constitutional norms referring to human dignity are typically meant as references to *the worst* that can be done to people. Severe forms of torture, for instance, are an issue of human dignity. Actions that result in injury and death cannot always be properly described merely by means of their physical impact. Such injuries can have an *additional symbolic-expressive meaning* that constitutes or substantially augments wrongdoing. A reference to human dignity is often essential to describe a major dimension of wrongdoing or even its core. For instance, the wrong that is committed in the case of rape cannot be adequately defined if one focuses on physical harm (which can be trivial or even non-existent), freedom of movement and autonomy. Substantial humiliation is the decisive component of the wrong that has been committed.[36]

---

33 Leist, 'Ethik' 607.
34 Leist, 'Ethik' 608.
35 ibid.
36 See for his point also J Gardner and S Shute, 'The Wrongness of Rape' in J Horder (ed), *Oxford Essays in Jurisprudence, Fourth series* (Oxford, Oxford University Press, 2000) 193.

The remaining discussion will focus on a way of thinking about 'human dignity as a fundamental interest' that emphasises the notion of *humiliation*. This type of analysis was promoted by a 1996 publication that has enjoyed major international acclaim: *The Decent Society* by the Israeli philosopher Avishai Margalit. In this work, Margalit explores how a decent society needs to be created. He differentiates between varying levels of societal development, from a 'tamed' or 'bridled' society that, at the very least, abstains from physical atrocities to a 'decent' society and up to a just society. According to Margalit's understanding, the decisive element of a decent society is that its institutions do not humiliate the persons subject to their influence.[37] The phrase 'human dignity' does not play a major role in *The Decent Society* because the author was concerned with outlining the basic structures of a societal organisation and not with addressing a possible human right to respect for human dignity. However, the book contains ideas on the subject of respect and humiliation that can be useful for the discussion on human dignity. In German literature on philosophy, the concept of humiliation is used to define human dignity more precisely (see, for example, Julian Nida-Rümelin).[38]

Margalit shows why humiliation constitutes a violation of fundamental human interests. He refers to mental torture of people, an extension of atrocity from the physical to the emotional.[39] This form of atrocity can coincide with physical torture but must be differentiated from it as an independent wrongdoing. He cites as an example the case of people who survived a concentration camp. They described how the humiliations they suffered were worse than the physical hardships.[40] Whether such a ranking of wrongdoing is persuasive need not be decided (Margalit himself points out that the retrospective narration of the few who survived need not necessarily represent the entire story). This, however, does not mitigate the

---

37 Margalit, *Decent Society* (1996) 1.
38 J Nida-Rümelin, *Über menschliche Freiheit* (Stuttgart, Reclam Verlag, 2005) 131; P Baumann, 'Menschenwürde und das Bedürfnis nach Respekt' and R Stoecker, 'Menschenwürde und das Paradox der Entwürdigung', both in R Stoecker (ed), *Menschenwürde: Annäherung an einen Begriff* (Vienna, öbv Verlag, 2003) 19, 26; 133; P Schaber, *Instrumentalisierung und Würde* (Paderborn, Mentis Verlag, 2010) 120; U Neumann, 'Die Menschenwürde als Menschenbürde – oder wie man ein Recht gegen den Berechtigten wendet' in M Kettner (ed), *Biomedizin und Menschenwürde* (Frankfurt/M., Suhrkamp Verlag, 2004) 61.
39 Margalit, *Decent Society* (1996) 85.
40 Margalit, *Decent Society* (1996) 136.

persuasiveness of the argument that man (Margalit cites Ernst Cassirer's notion of man as *animal symbolicum*[41]) experiences the world not only through physical experience but primarily through symbolic communications.[42] The significance of symbols corresponds to the injurious power of acts of humiliation.

C. Substantial Humiliation as a Violation of Human Dignity

A review of moral-philosophical literature illuminates problems associated with the concept of self-respect, which plays a significant role in Margalit's book. One needs to discuss whether self-respect is a psychological state or whether normative standards need to be developed for adequate self-respect.[43] If we are concerned with defining violations of human dignity from the perspective of legal philosophy, subjective feelings of having been aggrieved cannot be decisive. Whether a person feels humiliated or not depends on his or her temperament and mental state at the time of the incident. Because legal terms need to have stable and clear meanings, it would be problematic to rely on the idiosyncratic reactions of the individuals concerned. Objective standards are needed. This raises the question of whether a non-psychologising understanding of humiliation is possible at all. I believe it is. References to human beings as social beings and to the symbolic importance of modes of interactions depend on socially constructed worlds that can be described and analysed empirically. According to the approach followed here, human dignity is not conceptualised through purely normative visions of personhood, but depends on the meanings of interactions. These meanings depend on cultural backgrounds and culturally constituted understandings that can be reconstructed from a third-person perspective. By a third-person perspective I mean an observer who is familiar with the relevant cultural norms while being free of the resentment and emotional reactions that are to be expected if important cultural norms are disregarded.

---

41 E Cassirer, *Versuch über den Menschen*, 2nd edn (Hamburg, Felix Meiner Verlag, 2007) 51.
42 Margalit, *Decent Society* (1996) 85.
43 See SJ Massey, 'Is Self-Respect a Moral or Psychological Concept?' and DT Meyers, 'Self-Respect and Autonomy', both in R Dillon (ed), *Dignity, Character and Self-Respect* (New York, Routledge, 1995) 198, 218.

Keeping the concept of human dignity narrow enough is a major challenge. Caution is advised against an orientation based on the colloquial use of words such as 'respect' or 'humiliate'. Neither the everyday assessment as 'undignified' nor a moral assessment as 'morally wrong' is sufficient for our purposes. Describing defamation or even mere discourtesies as 'humiliating' is common in our everyday language but not recommendable when considering a legal right to have one's dignity protected. A narrower standard is needed to describe a fundamentally important human right. Within law and legal theory, one has to refrain from using the human dignity joker too often. For this reason, one cannot proceed very far with Margalit's examples. His aim is to describe institutions in a decent society, and in doing so he explores phenomena such as snobbery, bureaucracy and unemployment. It is possible to describe snobbery, for instance, as a societal phenomenon that encourages humiliation,[44] but not every example of snobbish conduct should be classified as a violation of human dignity in the strong legal sense. Not every refusal to recognise and respect another human being is a violation of human dignity. It is advisable to limit the verdict 'violation of human dignity' to cases involving *substantial* or *severe* humiliation.

A way of approaching the phenomenon 'substantial humiliation' consists of calling to mind situations in which there is a broad consensus that the victim's human dignity was violated. Ralf Stoecker suggests that certain National Socialist practices, such as Jewish citizens having to kneel on the street in front of a jeering crowd and clean the pavement with a brush, would fit this category.[45] Further examples include medical experiments on unwilling victims in concentration camps, serious sexual attacks such as rape and racist diatribes where minorities are labelled as 'subhumans' who should be exterminated. Looking at such examples, several elements can be identified that support a classification as substantial humiliation. One feature is the *grossly inappropriate compulsory self-representation* exemplified by the case of street cleaning. As a second and third element, violations of human dignity can be characterised by a *demonstration of disrespect* or by a situation in which the victim is made *entirely powerless* and *totally helpless*. Case scenarios of substantial humiliation are conceivable in which only one or two of the three elements are present. Grossly inappropriate compulsory self-representation is an el-

---

44 Margalit, *Decent Society* (1996) 191.
45 Stoecker, 'Paradox der Entwürdigung' 134.

ement lacking in many cases. Drastic verbal onslaughts directed at the core of the personality are not connected with compulsory false self-representation, and the speaker does not necessarily have to have a position of real power over the victim. The proposal that all of several elements used to describe a phenomenon can be present in a given case while only one or two elements might suffice to apply the term in other cases clashes with the orthodox way of constructing definitions. However, the notion that all elements of a multi-element definition must be present to be able to apply the term is outdated. Complex phenomena call for more flexible ways of working with definitions. In legal theory, the concept of *Typusbegriff* has been adopted to grasp multifaceted states of affairs.[46] This also applies to substantial humiliation: the elements 'grossly inappropriate compulsory self-representation', 'demonstration of disrespect' and 'total helplessness of the victim' need not be present cumulatively.

D. Summary

Although it is widely assumed that human dignity is an acquired or intrinsic quality of human beings, one does not get very far by pursuing this line of thought. Acquired characteristics differ from person to person and can be only partially affected by external sources. Even the approach that emphasises inherent qualities in all human beings leads to a dead end. If dignity is based on faculties that form a person's essence, the problem arises that human dignity is, in a literal sense, inviolable. It is easily declared that we all *have* dignity. The challenge, however, is to define conduct that violates human dignity and to differentiate it from the larger class of offensive and undignified behaviour.

Human dignity as a meaningful legal concept cannot, in my view, be defined positively, but only negatively, i.e., by defining violations of human dignity. The notion of human dignity presented in this article presupposes interactions with other people. Without the presence of another human being, one might invoke the notion of dignity within the context of

---

46 I Puppe, 'Umgang mit Definitionen in der Jurisprudenz' in G Dornseifer et al (eds), *Gedächtnisschrift für Armin Kaufmann* (Cologne, Carl Heymanns Verlag, 1989) 15, 33; G Duttge, 'Zum typologischen Denken im Strafrecht – Ein Beitrag zur "Wiederbelebung" der juristischen Methode' (2003) 11 *Jahrbuch für Recht und Ethik* 103.

virtue ethics. A proponent of virtue ethics will have no difficulty in concluding that even a lonely human being on an island (Robinson) can cope with this situation in a more or less dignified way. However, if one turns to the issue of rights and specifically to human dignity as a *legal right*, it only makes sense as a *relational concept*.[47] A relational understanding of human dignity can be developed by examining fundamental interests that all people share. People are not only vulnerable in their physical integrity, their freedom of movement and other materially tangible interests. They are also highly dependent on recognition from their fellow human beings.[48] Because we live not only in a physical world but also in a symbolic one, and because of the importance this world of social interactions and meanings has, we share an interest in not being exposed to substantial humiliation.

IV. Implications for New Techniques in the Area of Human Reproduction

The question to be addressed in the remaining parts is: could it be convincing to use the argument 'violation of human dignity' in order to demand that legal norms prohibit or regulate new techniques developed in the area of human reproduction? When the term 'dignity' appears in contemporary discussions, it is often in support of criticism directed at an innovation in the area of science or new technologies.[49] This connection is not a necessary one. One could imagine that applied science enhances or supports the dignity of human beings. However, in most discourses, invoking human dignity means criticising a new development and demanding that the legislature interferes by means of prohibitions or restrictions. I will use surrogate motherhood as an example to illustrate the problems. Surrogate motherhood is still prohibited under German law. The so-called 'Embryo Protection Act' (*Embryonenschutzgesetz*, EschG) of 1990[50] sets very narrow margins for doctors in reproductive medicine. It contains,

---

47   H Hofmann, 'Die versprochene Menschenwürde' (1993) 118 *Archiv des öffentlichen Rechts* 353.
48   See A Honneth, *Kampf um Anerkennung* (Frankfurt, Suhrkamp Verlag, 1994).
49   See, eg The President's Council on Bioethics (ed), *Human Cloning and Human Dignity* (Washington D.C., 2002); J Kersten, *Das Klonen von Menschen* (Tübingen, Mohr Siebeck Verlag, 2004); S Vöneky and R Wolfrum (eds), *Human Dignity and Human Cloning* (Berlin, Springer Verlag, 2004).
50   *Embryonenschutzgesetz*, 13 December 1990, BGBl. I, 2746.

among others, criminal law norms that prohibit the artificial fertilisation of an egg cell for any purpose other than bringing about a pregnancy of the woman from whom the egg cell originated (§ 1 Nr. 2 ESchG). In addition, it is a criminal offence to attempt to carry out an artificial fertilisation of a woman who is prepared to give up her child permanently after birth (§ 1 Nr. 7 ESchG). Furthermore, it is a criminal offence to put parents-to-be in contact with a surrogate mother (§ 13c, 14b of the Adoption Placement Act (*Adoptionsvermittlungsgesetz*[51])).

What reasons could be invoked to support this prohibitive stance? At this juncture, we have to turn to arguments that are rather popular in German discourses. Such arguments insist that references to human dignity refer to an objective value beyond individuals' rights. The notion that is commonly invoked is 'dignity of humankind' or 'dignity of the human species' (*Gattungswürde*). It is a common move to use this argument as a joker if attempts to frame human dignity arguments as arguments regarding subjective rights fail, or even as a 'shortcut', that is, without bothering with a rights-based analysis of human dignity. A prominent example in the area of biotechnology where this argument prevails is the cloning of human beings.[52] However, in the case of surrogate motherhood too, one could argue that meddling with the natural laws of human reproduction violates human dignity in the sense of *Gattungswürde*. From a descriptive angle, it is an interesting phenomenon that the notion of *Gattungswürde* appears as an argument in almost any debate about biotechnology (at least in Germany). Clearly, many participants in these discussions share a strong intuition that one should not interfere with the 'natural state of affairs' when it comes to human reproduction. Some decades ago, artificial insemination, which is now a common medical procedure for couples, was deemed a violation of 'human dignity'.[53] But why this commitment to 'naturalness' in the area of human reproduction in particular, and why the strong aversion to human interferences with 'naturalness'? The explanation that seems most plausible to me is that the strong tendency to exaggerate the notion of 'naturalness' goes back to several distinct roots that nourish the intuition that can be described as 'human beings should not play God'. One root for such a statement is clearly a religious one. It is not

---

51   Enacted 2 July 1976, amended 10 December 2008, BGBl. I, 2403.
52   See the references in n 49.
53   G Dürig, 'Der Grundrechtssatz von der Menschenwürde' (1956) 81 *Archiv des öffentlichen Rechts* 117, 130.

surprising to find that movements against cloning and similar practices enjoy the support of the Catholic Church and other conservative, religiously inspired groups. However, it is doubtful whether in contemporary times an open recourse to Christian teaching would on its own be forceful enough to support a strong commitment to 'naturalness'. The overriding importance attributed to 'naturalness' probably also stems from quasi-religious roots. Beyond the nowadays very small group of Christian conservatives, a commitment to 'naturalness' might be driven by a more widespread desire to retain some (ill-reflected, but strongly felt) notions of 'holiness' beyond traditional religious teachings. Another factor that converges with both the Christian and the quasi-religious roots are fears that stem from the awareness of risks as described by the catchword 'risk society'[54]. There is a rational core of fears in 'risk societies' (consider risks connected with, for example, nuclear energy), but it seems likely that anxieties spread beyond this rational core and created a general but somewhat muddy suspicion against anything labelled 'biotechnology'.

If one turns again from the descriptive mode to the normative mode, the question is: could the sociological fact of a strong and widespread desire to support 'naturalness' and the resulting distrust of biotechnology be reason enough to demand legal prohibitions? I don't believe so. There are two problems with turning sociological analyses into normative arguments in our context. First, prohibitions can clash with autonomy rights. In the example of the ban on surrogate motherhood, the German prohibition interferes with the right to reproductive autonomy of would-be parents who cannot have a child 'in the natural way' as well as with the autonomy rights of surrogate mothers. If the state limits autonomy rights in a way that is far from trivial, a high burden of persuasion must be met. Within a weighing of rights and interests, public goods can of course in some cases justify even non-trivial restrictions of autonomy rights. However, such public goods must be shown to have a solid and rational basis. A socio-psychological need for 'naturalness' that is rooted in ill-reflected fears and quasi-religious feelings does not suffice to prohibit reproductive techniques. Another problem is that once reproductive technologies are available, national legal prohibitions will only have the effect of displacement (for many, visiting a centre for reproductive medicine in another country is a feasible option). Any strict ban on reproductive techniques will have

---

54 See U Beck, *Risikogesellschaft. Auf dem Weg in eine andere Moderne* (Frankfurt, Suhrkamp Verlag, 1986).

the effect that chances are missed to regulate and improve their use. Turning to surrogate motherhood again, there is an excellent study by Elly Teman about surrogate motherhood in Israel (where it is legal), one of the findings of which was that surrogate mothers have needs of a non-material kind, namely not to be pushed radically out of the new family's life after delivering the baby.[55] This calls for careful planning and preparation of the processes, which the state could promote by requiring mandatory counselling in preparation of surrogate motherhood and stipulating that surrogate mothers have to be close to the new parents (rather than in far-away countries). If legislatures in the mode of the German Parliament prohibit a reproductive technology in its entirety, they worsen the situation. Simply outlawing a certain practice and displacing it to other countries is not helpful. The true challenge would be to pass regulations that protect the interests of all participants in the best possible way.

Rejecting the notion of *Gattungswürde* is not the end of the analysis. The pertinent question for all discussions about reproductive technology (and other examples of biotechnology) is: would applying this technique violate the human dignity of the individuals involved? In the example of surrogate motherhood, does the child become a commodity with the effect that its human dignity is violated?[56] It is difficult to pinpoint objectionable treatment of the child. The doctor's actions that lead to the fertilisation of the egg cell cannot violate the human dignity of the child due to the fact that a child does not exist at that point in time. The only point in time where a violation of human dignity could be considered to take place is when the baby is transferred after birth. However, it remains unclear why this act should violate the child's right to have its human dignity respected. It is not plausible to argue that the surrogate mother or the future parent humiliates the newborn when the exchange takes place. Nor does one arrive at a different result with the competing 'mere object' formula or references to instrumentalisation. The adults involved do not treat the baby in ways that differ significantly from other cases of adoption or other cases of planned parenthood. In all cases of planned parenthood, the child clearly fulfils some need the parents have, but it is implausible to argue

---

55   E Teman, *Birthing a Mother* (Berkeley, University of California Press, 2010) 205 ff.
56   See MJ Radin, *Contested Commodities* (Cambridge, Mass., Harvard University Press, 1996) 140 ff; M Lehmann, *Die In-vitro-Fertilisation und ihre Folgen* (Frankfurt/M., Peter Lang Verlag, 2007) 174 f.

that this feature of the parent–child relationship suffices to talk about 'humiliation' or 'instrumentalisation'.

Some people may argue that the surrogate mother's right to human dignity is violated.[57] There are extreme versions of 'surrogate motherhood' where this is indeed the case. Consider, for example, biblical stories of female slaves being used to create offspring for their male master.[58] If the surrogate mother is raped or cannot, by virtue of being a slave, give valid consent to artificial insemination, the procedure means severe humiliation and thus violates her human dignity. Consent plays an important role here. Interferences in the intimate sphere, bodily integrity and/or sexual autonomy without the valid consent of all persons concerned severely humiliate the person (on the other hand, the social meaning of an interaction changes radically if the observer who has to decipher its meaning knows that it is a consensual interaction). Deciding whether certain acts severely humiliate or instrumentalise others is highly context-sensitive. However, the non-consensual cases are not typical in modern reproductive medicine. Those who receive treatment at a clinic are not humiliated or treated as a 'mere object' if they enter such institutions based on a free and well-informed decision. If adult women have contacted an agency for surrogate motherhood or decided to take on this role due to a personal relationship with a childless couple, we have to assume that they are autonomous, informed patients. At this point, some argue that such decisions can be based on social or economic pressure and thus question the validity of consent (consider a German case discussed recently where an Indian surrogate mother delivered a baby for a German homosexual couple). The question of 'true' voluntariness on the surrogate mothers' part might indeed deserve some attention. However, the conclusion to be drawn from such doubts would be to consider regulations that protect the interests and rights of surrogate mothers-to-be. A *total* ban on surrogate motherhood is too broad because it includes cases where there is no violation of potential surrogate mothers' human dignity.

To conclude: it is indeed necessary to evaluate the consequences of new technologies in general, and those regarding human reproduction in particular, with respect to human dignity rights. If the application of new technologies would lead to the severe humiliation of human beings, this would be reason to consider legal prohibitions. In the absence of such

---

57 Lehmann, *In-vitro-Fertilisation* 176 ff.
58 See Genesis, 30, 3 and 30, 9.

clashes with human dignity as an individual right not to be severely humiliated, one should not invoke human dignity as an objective value and point to 'dignity of the human species'. References to *Gattungswürde* and the underlying religious or quasi-religious desire to protect 'naturalness' are neither a good reason to curtail autonomy rights nor a convincing strategy when one considers the (displacement) consequences of prohibitions.

Bibliography

Books and Reports

Adelson, BM, *The Lives of Dwarfs: Their Journey from Public Curiosity Towards Social Liberation* (New Brunswick, NJ, Rutgers University Press, 2005).

Albert, H, *Konstruktion und Kritik. Aufsätze zur Philosophie des kritischen Rationalismus*, 2nd edn (Hamburg, Hoffmann und Campe, 1975).

Alexy, R, *A Theory of Legal Argumentation—The Theory of Rational Discourse as Theory of Legal Justification,* trans. R Adler and N MacCormick (Oxford, Oxford University Press, 1989).

Alexy, R, *Theorie der Grundrechte* (Frankfurt aM, Suhrkamp, 2001).

Alexy, R, *Theory of Constitutional Rights* (Julian Rivers trans, Oxford, Oxford University Press, 2002).

Allan, TRS, *Constitutional Justice: A Liberal Theory of the Rule of Law* (Oxford, Oxford University Press, 2001).

Améry, J, *At the Mind's Limits: Contemplations by a Survivor on Auschwitz and Its Realities* (New York, Schocken Books, 1986).

Anderzhon, JW et al, *Design for Aging: International Case Studies of Building and Program* (Hoboken, John Wiley & Sons, 2012).

Appiah, KA, *The Honor Code: How Moral Revolutions Happen* (New York, WW Norton, 2011).

Aquinatis, T, *Summa Theologiae.* Cura Fratrum eiusdem Ordinis, 5 Volumes, Madrid 1978-1985.

Arold, N-L, *The Legal Culture of the European Court of Human Rights* (Leiden/Boston, Martinus Nijhoff Publishers, 2007).

Aschenberg, R, *Ent-Subjektivierung des Menschen. Lager und Shoah in philosophischer Reflexion* (Würzburg, Königshausen & Neumann, 2003).

Austin, A, *The Indian Constitution: Cornerstone of a Nation* (New Delhi, Oxford University Press, 1996).

Austin, G, *Working a Democratic Constitution: A History of the Indian Experience* (New Delhi, Oxford University Press, 1999).

Barak, A, *Human Dignity: The Constitutional Value and the Constitutional Right* (Cambridge, Cambridge University Press, 2015).

Barry, B, *Freedom and Culture: An Egalitarian Critique of Multiculturalism* (Cambridge, Harvard University Press, 2001).

Beck, U, *Risikogesellschaft. Auf dem Weg in eine andere Moderne* (Frankfurt, Suhrkamp Verlag, 1986).

Becker, B von, *Fiktion und Wirklichkeit im Roman: Der Schlüsselprozess um das Buch Esra* (Würzburg, Königshausen und Neumann, 2006).

Becker, EW, *Theodor Heuss. Bürger im Zeitalter der Extreme* (Stuttgart, Kohlhammer, 2011).

Becker, U and Roth, M (eds), *Recht der Älteren* (Berlin, de Gruyter, 2013).

Becking, B, *Ezra, Nehemiah, and the Construction of Early Jewish Identity* (Tübingen, Mohr Siebeck, 2011).

Bibliography

Beestermöller, G and Brunkhorst, H (eds), *Rückkehr der Folter. Der Rechtsstaat im Zwielicht?* (Munich, C.H. Beck, 2006).

Belfort, J, *The Wolf of Wall Street* (New York, Bantam, 2007).

Bergren, TA, *Sixth Ezra: The Text and Origin: The Text and Origin* (Oxford, Oxford University Press, 1989).

Berlin, I, *Liberty. Incorporating Four Essays on Liberty* (Oxford, Oxford University Press, 2002).

Bernstorff, J von, *Der Glaube an das universale Recht: Zur Völkerrechtstheorie Hans Kelsens und seiner Schüler* (Baden-Baden, Nomos, 2011).

Beyleveld, D and Brownsword, R, *Consent in the Law* (Oxford, Hart, 2007).

Beyleveld, D and Brownsword, R, *Human Dignity in Bioethics and Biolaw* (Oxford, Oxford University Press, 2001).

Beyleveld, D and Brownsword, R, *Law as a Moral Judgment* (London, Sweet and Maxwell, 1986, repr Sheffield, Sheffield Academic Press, 1994).

Beyleveld, D, *The Dialectical Necessity of Morality: An Analysis and Defense of Alan Gewirth's Argument to the Principle of Generic Consistency* (Chicago, University of Chicago Press, 1991).

Biedermann, AE, *Christliche Dogmatik*, Vol. 2 (Berlin, Dietrich Reimer Verlag, 1885).

Bielefeldt, H, *Auslaufmodell Menschenwürde* (Freiburg et al, Herder, 2011).

Biller, M, *Esra* (Köln, Kiepenheuer und Witsch, 2007).

Binder, G and Weisberg, R, *Literary Criticism of Law* (Princeton, New Jersey, Princeton University Press, 2000).

Birnbacher, D, *Natürlichkeit* (Berlin/New York: de Gruyter, 2006).

Blank, RH, *Intervention in the Brain. Politics, Policy, and Ethics* (Cambridge/London, MIT Press, 2013).

Bloch, E, *Natural Law and Human Dignity*, transl. DJ Schmidt (Cambridge, MIT Press, 1987).

Bloom, H, *Shakespeare: The Invention of the Human* (New York, Riverhead Books, 1999).

Bloom, H, *The Anatomy of Influence: Literature as a Way of Life* (Yale, Yale University Press, 2011).

Böckenförde, EW, *Recht, Staat, Freiheit* (Frankfurt aM, Suhrkamp, 2006).

Böhme, G, *Ethik leiblicher Existenz: Über unseren moralischen Umgang mit der eigenen Natur* (Frankfurt aM, Suhrkamp, 2008).

Borowski, M, *Grundrechte als Prinzipien*, 2nd edn (Baden-Baden, Nomos, 2007).

Brown, J and Garrido, C, *Velázquez: The Technique of Genius* (New Haven, Yale University Press, 1998) 27, quoted in Edgar, 'Velázquez and the Representation of Dignity' 120.

Brownsword, R (ed), *Rights, Regulation and the Technological Revolution* (Oxford, Oxford University Press, 2008).

Brownsword, R and Goodwin, M, *Law and the Technologies of the Twenty-First Century* (Cambridge, Cambridge University Press, 2012).

Bruckstein, AS, *Die Maske des Moses. Studien zur jüdischen Hermeneutik*, 2nd edn (Berlin, Philo, 2007).

Brugger, W, *Menschenwürde, Menschenrechte, Grundrechte*, speech given on 18.07.1996 (Baden-Baden, Nomos, 1997).

Buckland, WW, *A Text-Book of Roman Law from Augustus to Justinian* (Cambridge, Cambridge University Press, 1932).

Bumke, C and Voßkuhle, A, *Casebook Verfassungsrecht*, 5th edn (Munich, C.H. Beck, 2008).

Bünnigmann, K, *Die Esra-Entscheidung als Ausgleich zwischen Persönlichkeitsschutz und Kunstfreiheit* (Tübingen, Mohr Siebeck, 2013).

Campbell, AV, *The Body in Bioethics* (London, Routledge, 2009).

Cassirer, E, *Versuch über den Menschen*, 2nd edn (Hamburg, Felix Meiner Verlag, 2007).

Christensen, R and Fischer-Lescano, A, *Das Ganze des Rechts. Vom hierarchischen zum reflexiven Verständnis deutscher und europäischer Grundrechte* (Berlin, Duncker & Humblot, 2007).

Clark, A, *Natural-Born Cyborgs* (Oxford, Oxford University Press, 2003).

Cohen, GE, *Freedom, Self-Ownership and Equality* (Cambridge, Cambridge University Press, 1995).

Davidson, M, *The Rage of Caliban: Missing Bodies in Modernist Aesthetics*.

Dershowitz, A, *Rights from Wrongs. A Secular Theory on the Origins of Rights* (New York, Basic Books, 2004).

Des Pres, T, *The Survivor: An Anatomy of Life in the Death Camps* (New York, Oxford University Press, 1976).

Deutscher Bundestag and Bundesarchiv (eds), *Der Parlamentarische Rat 1948–1949. Akten und Protokolle, Band 5, Ausschuss für Grundsatzfragen* (Munich, Boldt im Oldenbourg-Verlag, 1993).

Deutscher Bundestag and Bundesarchiv (eds), *Der Parlamentarische Rat 1948–1949. Akten und Protokolle, Band 9, Plenum*, rev. Wolfram Werner (Munich, Boldt im Oldenbourg-Verlag, 1996).

Deutscher Bundestag and Bundesarchiv (eds), *Der Parlamentarische Rat 1948–1949. Akten und Protokolle, Band 14, Hauptausschuss*, rev Michael F. Feldkamp (Munich, Oldenbourg, 2009).

DHHS, *Coverage Denied: How the Current Health Insurance System Leaves Millions Behind* (undated), available at www.healthreform.gov/reports/denied_coverage/index.html.

Dicey, AV, *Introduction to the Study of the Law of the Constitution*, 8th edn (London, MacMillan, 1924)

Dobbin, R (trans and ed), *Epictetus. Discourses and Selected Writings* (London, Penguin Books, 2008).

Dorner, IA, *System der christlichen Glaubenslehre*, Vol. 1 (Berlin, W.L. Hertz, 1879).

Dorner, IA, *System der christlichen Glaubenslehre*, Vol. 2, part 2 (Berlin, W.L. Hertz, 1881).

Dreier, H (ed), *Grundgesetz. Kommentar,* 1st edn, Vol. 1 (Tübingen, Mohr Siebeck, 1996).

Dreier, H (ed), *Grundgesetz-Kommentar*, 2nd edn (Tübingen, Mohr Siebeck Verlag, 2004).

Dupré, C, *The Age of Dignity. Human Rights and Constitutionalim in Europe* (Oxford, Hart Publishing, 2016) 16 f.

Durkheim, E, *The Division of Labor in Society*, transl. WD Halls (New York, Free Press, 1997).

Dworkin, R, *Justice for Hedgehogs* (Cambridge et al, Belknap, 2011).

Dyzenhaus, D, *Hard Cases in Wicked Legal Systems: Pathologies of Legality*, 2nd edn (Oxford, Oxford University Press, 2010).

Ehrenberg, A, *La société du malaise* (Paris, Odile Jacob, 2010).

Enders, C, *Die Menschenwürde in der Verfassungsordnung. Zur Dogmatik des Art. 1 GG* (Tübingen, Mohr Siebeck, 1997).

Enders, M and Szaif, J (eds), *Die Geschichte des philosophischen Begriffs der Wahrheit* (Berlin, de Gruyter, 2006).

Epping, V, *Grundrechte,* 2nd edn (Heidelberg, Springer, 2004).

Epstein, R, *Forbidden Grounds: The Case Against Employment Discrimination Laws* (Cambridge, Mass, Harvard University Press, 1992).

Eskridge, Jr, WN and Ferejohn, J, *A Republic of Statutes: The New American Constitution* (New Haven, YUP, 2010).

Fagan, A, *Human Rights. Confronting Myths and Misunderstandings* (Cheltenham, Elgar, 2009).

Families USA, *Hidden Health Tax: Americans Pay a Premium* (2009), available at familiesusa2.org/assets/pdfs/hidden-health-tax.pdf.

Feldkamp, MF, *Der Parlamentarische Rat 1948–1949. Die Entstehung des Grundgesetzes* (Göttingen, Vandenhoeck & Ruprecht, 1998).

Feldman, D, *Birth Control in Jewish Law: Marital Relations, Contraception, and Abortion as Set Forth in the Classic Texts of Jewish Law* (New York, New York University Press, 1968).

Felski, R, *Uses of Literature* (Oxford, Backwell Publishing, 2008).

Fensham, CF, *The Books of Ezra and Nehemiah* (Michigan, William B. Eerdmans Publishing Co., 1982).

Finnis, J, *Natural Law and Natural Rights* (Oxford, Clarendon Press, 1980).

Fischer, J, *Theologische Ethik. Grundwissen und Orientierung* (Stuttgart, Kohlhammer, 2002).

Foster, C, *Human Dignity in Bioethics and Law* (Oxford, Hart Publishing, 2011).

Foucault, M, *Les mots et les choses (*trans as *The Order of Things)* (Paris, Gallimard, 1966).

Frank, FHR, *System der christlichen Wahrheit* (Erlangen, Verlag von Andreas Deichert, 1885).

Frankfurt, HG, *The Importance of what We Care About. Philosophical Essays* (Cambridge, Cambridge University Press, 1988) 11.

Friedman, LM, *The Human Rights Culture. A Study in History and Context* (New Orleans, Quid Pro Books, 2011).

Frolik, LA and Kaplan, RL, *Elder Law in a Nutshell*, 5th edn (St. Paul, MN, West Publishing, 2010).

Frye, N, *The Educated Imagination* (Bloomington, Indiana University Press, 1964).

Fuentes, C, *The Buried Mirror: Reflections on Spain and the New World* (Boston, Houghton Mifflin, 1992) 182.

Gabriel, M, *Il senso dell'esistenza* (Rome, Carocci, 2012).

Gadamer, HG, *Truth and Method*, rev 2nd edn (London, Continuum Publishing Group, 2004).

Gadamer, HG, *Wahrheit und Methode: Grundzüge einer philosophischen Hermeneutik*, 4th edn (Tübingen, Mohr, 1975).

Gamm, G, *Nicht nichts. Studien zu einer Semantik des Unbestimmten* (Frankfurt am Main, Suhrkamp, 2000).

Gay, P, *The Enlightenment*, Vol. 1: *The Rise of Modern Paganism* (New York, Knopf, 1966); Vol. 2: *The Science of Freedom* (New York, Knopf, 1969).

Geddert-Steinacher, T, *Menschenwürde als Verfassungsbegriff* (Berlin, Duncker & Humblot, 1990).

Gewirth, A, *Reason and Morality* (Chicago, Chicago University Press, 1978).

Giese, B, Das Würde-Konzept. Eine normfunktionale Explikation des Begriffs Würde in Art. 1 Abs. 1 GG (Berlin, Duncker & Humblot, 1975).

Goerlich, H (ed), *Staatliche Folter: Heiligt der Zweck die Mittel?* (Paderborn, mentis, 2007).

Gombrich, EH, *The Story of Art*, 5th edn (London, Phaidon, 1989).

Goos, C, *Innere Freiheit. Eine Rekonstruktion des grundgesetzlichen Würdebegriffs* (Göttingen, V&R unipress, 2011).

Gottschall, J, *The Storytelling Animal: How Stories Make Us Human* (Boston et al, Houghton Mifflin, 2012).

Gray, J, *Straw Dogs: Thoughts on Humans and Other Animals* 56 (London, Granta Books, 2002).

Great Britain, Government Office for Science, *Foresight. The Future of Food and Farming: Final Project Report* (London, The Government Office for Science, 2011).

Greenblatt, S, *Renaissance Self-Fashioning: From More to Shakespeare* (Chicago, University of Chicago Press, 1980).

Greene, B, *Essential Medical Law* (London, Cavendish Publishing, 2001).

Gröschner, R, *Menschenwürde und Sepulkralkultur in der grundgesetzlichen Ordnung* (Stuttgart, Boorberg Verlag, 1995).

Grunwald, A, *Technikzukünfte als Medium von Zukunftsdebatten und Technikgestaltung* (Karlsruhe, KIT Scientific Publishing, 2012).

Günther, F, *Denken vom Staat her: Die bundesdeutsche Staatsrechtslehre zwischen Dezision und Integration 1949-1970* (Munich, Oldenburg, 2004).

Häberle, P (ed), *Entstehungsgeschichte der Artikel des Grundgesetzes. Neuausgabe des Jahrbuch des öffentlichen Rechts der Gegenwart Band 1* (Tübingen, Mohr Siebeck, 2010).

Habermas, J, *The Future of Human Nature* (Cambridge, Polity Press, 2003).

Habermas, J, *Zur Verfassung Europas* (Berlin, Suhrkamp, 2011).

Halbertal, M and Margalit, A, *Idolatry* (Cambridge, Harvard University Press, 1992).

Halbertal, M, *Interpretative Revolutions in the Making* (Jerusalem: Hebrew University Magnes Press, 1977).

Hayek, FA von, *The Road to Serfdom* (London, Routledge, 1991; first edition 1944).

Hegel, GWF, *Elements of the Philosophy of Right*, ed A Wood (Cambridge, Cambridge University Press, 1991).

Hehl, C von, *Adolf Süsterhenn (1905–1974). Verfassungsvater, Weltanschauungspolitiker, Föderalist* (Düsseldorf, Droste, 2012).

Heidegger, M, *Being and Time*, transl J Macquarrie and E Robinson (New York, Harper and Row, 1962).

Heidegger, M, *Die Grundprobleme der Phänomenologie. Marburger Vorlesung Sommersemester 1927. Gesamtausgabe Bd. 24*, 2nd edn, ed FW von Herrmann (Frankfurt am Main, Klostermann, 1989).

Hell, D, *Soul Hunger. The Feeling Human Being and the Life Sciences* (Einsiedeln, Daimon, 2010).

Hellman, D, *When Is Discrimination Wrong?* (Cambridge, Mass, Harvard University Press, 2008).

Herzog, L, *Inventing the Market: Smith, Hegel, and Political Theory* (Oxford, Oxford University Press, 2013).

Heschel, S, *The Aryan Jesus: Christian Theologians and the Bible in Nazi Germany* (Princeton, New Jersey, Princeton University Press, 2008).

Heun, W, *The Constitution of Germany. A Contextual Analysis* (Oxford, Hart, 2011).

Hewart, L, *The New Despotism* (London, Ernest Benn Ltd, 1929).

Hobbes, T, *Leviathan*, ed R Tuck (Cambridge, Cambridge University Press, 1997).

Hobsbawms, EJ, *The Age of Extremes: A History of the World* (New York, Vintage Books, 1996).

Hoerster, N, *Ethik des Embryonenschutzes* (Stuttgart, Reclam Verlag, 2002).

Hogan, G and Whyte, G, *JM Kelly: The Irish Constitution*, 4th edn (Dublin, Lexis–Nexis Butterworths, 2003).

Hong, M, *Der Menschenwürdegehalt der Grundrechte* (Tübingen, Mohr Siebeck, 2017).

Honneth, A, *Kampf um Anerkennung* (Frankfurt, Suhrkamp Verlag, 1994).

Honneth, A, *Unsichtbarkeit: Stationen zu einer Theorie der Intersubjektivität* (Frankfurt am Main, Suhrkamp, 2003).

Hufen, F, *Staatsrecht II. Grundrechte* (Munich, C. H. Beck, 2007).

Hufen, F, *Staatsrecht II. Grundrechte*, 3rd edn (Munich, C.H. Beck, 2011).

Hunt, L, *Inventing Human Rights: A History* (New York, W.W. Norton & Co, 2008).

Huster, S, *Soziale Gesundheitsgerechtigkeit: Sparen, umverteilen, vorsorgen?* (Berlin, Klaus Wagenbach, 2011).

Hüther, G and Krens, I, *Das Geheimnis der ersten neun Monate. Unsere frühesten Prägungen* (Düsseldorf, Patmos, 2005).

Ignatieff, M, *American Exceptionalism and Human Rights* (Princeton, Princeton University Press, 2005).

Israel, J, *A Revolution of the Mind: Radical Enlightenment and the Intellectual Origins of Modern Democracy* (Princeton, Princeton University Press, 2010).

Jaber, D, *Über den mehrfachen Sinn von Menschenwürde-Garantien. Mit besonderer Berücksichtigung von Art. 1 Abs. 1 GG* (Frankfurt, Ontos, 2003).

Jaeggi, R, *Entfremdung: Zur Aktualität eines sozialphilosophischen Phänomens* (Frankfurt am Main, Campus, 2005).

Jarass, HD and Pieroth, B (eds), *Grundgesetz*, 7th edn (Munich, C.H. Beck, 2004).

Jestaedt, M, *Grundrechtsentfaltung im Gesetz* (Tübingen, Mohr Siebeck, 1999).

Joas, H, *Die Sakralität der Person. Eine neue Genealogie der Menschenrechte* (Berlin, Suhrkamp, 2012).

Joas, H, *Slavery and Torture in a Global Perspective. Human Rights and the Western Tradition* (Leiden, Brill, 2014).

Joas, H, *The Sacredness of the Person* (Washington, Georgetown University Press, 2013).

Jofer, P, *Die Regulierung der Reproduktionsmedizin* (Baden-Baden, Nomos, 2015).

Jopp, D et al, *Zweite Heidelberger Hundertjährigen-Studie: Herausforderungen und Stärken des Lebens mit 100 Jahren* (Stuttgart, Robert-Bosch-Stiftung 2013).

Jüngel, E, *Zur Freiheit eines Christenmenschen. Eine Erinnerung an Luthers Schrift* (Munich, Kaiser, 1991).

Kähler, M, *Die Wissenschaft der christlichen Lehre* (Leipzig, A. Deichert'sche Verlagsbuchhandlung, 1905).

Kaiser Family Foundation, *Health Insurance Market Reforms: Guaranteed Issue* (June 2012), www.kff.org/healthreform/upload/8327.pdf.

Kant, I, *Critique of Practical Reason*, transl M Gregor (Cambridge, Cambridge University Press, 1997).

Kant, I, *Foundations of the Metaphysics of Morals*, 2nd edn, translated by LW Beck (Upper Saddle River/NJ, Prentice-Hall, 1997).

Kant, I, *Grundlegung der Metaphysik der Sitten*, 1785, transl JW Ellington, *Grounding for the Metaphysics of Morals*, 3rd edn (Indianapolis and Cambridge, Hackett Publishing Co, 1993).

Kantorowicz, EH, *The King's Two Bodies* (Princeton, Princeton University Press, 1957).

Katab, G, *Human Dignity* (Cambridge, Mass, Harvard University Press, 2012).

Kaufmann, P, Kuch, H, Neuhäuser, C and Webster, E (eds), *Humiliation, Degradation, Dehumanization. Human Dignity Violated* (Dordrecht et al, Springer, 2011).

Kelsen, H, *Reine Rechtslehre* (Leipzig and Wien, Deuticke, 1934).

Kersten, J, *Das Klonen von Menschen* (Tübingen, Mohr Siebeck Verlag, 2004).

Kettner, MW (ed), *Menschenwürde und Biomedizin* (Frankfurt aM, Suhrkamp, 2004).

Kidd, C, *The Forging of Races: Race and Scripture in the Protestant Atlantic World, 1600-2000* (Cambridge, England: Cambridge University Press, 2006).

Kierkegaard, S, *The Sickness Unto Death. Kierkegaard's Writings*, Vol. 19, ed HW Hong (Princeton, Princeton University Press, 2009).

Kitwood, TM, *Dementia Reconsidered: The Person Comes First* (Maidenhead, Open University Press, 1997).

Kommers, DP and Miller, RA, *The Constitutional Jurisprudence of the Federal Republic of Germany*, 3rd edn (Durham, Duke University Press, 2012).

Korsgaard, CM, *Self-Constitution: Agency, Identity, and Integrity* (Oxford, Oxford University Press, 2009).

Korsgaard, CM, *The Sources of Normativity* (Cambridge, Cambridge University Press, 1996).

Kosch, M, *Freedom and Reason in Kant, Schelling, and Kierkegaard* (Oxford, Clarendon Press, 2006).

Kotzur, M, *Theorieelemente des internationalen Menschenrechtsschutzes* (Berlin, Duncker & Humblot, 2001).

Kretzmer, D, *The Occupation of Justice: The Supreme Court of Israel and the Occupied Territories* (New York, SUNY Press, 2002).

Kriele, M, *Theorie der Rechtsgewinnung*, 2nd edn (Berlin, Duncker & Humblot, 1976).

Künne, W, *Conceptions of Truth* (Oxford, Oxford University Press, 2005).

Bibliography

Kurzweil, R, *Human Body Version 2.0* (2003), www.kurzweilai.net/human-body-version-20.

Ladeur, KH and Augsberg, I, *Die Funktion der Menschenwürde im Verfassungsstaat. Humangenetik – Neurowissenschaft – Medien* (Tübingen, Mohr Siebeck, 2008).

Lange, EHM, *Die Würde des Menschen ist unantastbar. Der Parlamentarische Rat und das Grundgesetz* (Heidelberg, Decker & Müller, 1993).

Lebech, M, *On the Problem of Human Dignity. A Hermeneutical and Phenomenological Investigation* (Würzburg, Königshausen & Neumann, 2009).

Lehmann, M, *Die In-vitro-Fertilisation und ihre Folgen* (Frankfurt/M., Peter Lang Verlag, 2007).

Lessig, L, *Code and Other Laws of Cyberspace* (New York, Basic Books, 1999).

Levi, AW, *Humanism and Politics—Studies in the Relationship of Power and Value in the Western Tradition* (Bloomington, Indiana University Press, 1969).

Levi, AW, *The Humanities Today* (Bloomington, Indiana University Press, 1970).

Lévinas, E, *Jenseits des Seins oder Anders als Sein geschieht* (Freiburg, Alber, 1992).

Lévinas, E, *Totality and Infinity—An Essay on Exteriority*, trans. A Lingis (Pittsburgh, Pa., Duquesne University Press, 1969).

Lévinas, E, *Verletzlichkeit und Frieden. Schriften über Politik und das Politische* (Zürich and Berlin, Diaphanes, 2007).

Lilje, H, *Im finstern Tal* (Nürnberg, Laetare, 1947).

Lipsius, RA, *Lehrbuch der Evangelisch-Protestantischen Dogmatik* (Braunschweig, Schwetschke, 1893).

Locke, J, *A Letter Concerning Toleration*, ed. J Tully (Indianapolis, Hackett, 1985).

Lohmar, A, *Falsches moralisches Bewusstsein: Eine Kritik der Idee der Menschenwürde* (Hamburg, Felix Meiner Verlag, 2017).

Long, AA, *Epictetus. A Stoic and Socratic Guide to Life* (Oxford, Clarendon Press, 2004).

Lorberbaum, Y, *In God's Image: Myth, Theology, and Law in Classical Judaism* (Cambridge, Cambridge University Press, 2014).

Lorz, RA, *Modernes Grund- und Menschenrechtsverständnis und die Philosophie der Freiheit Kants* (Stuttgart, Boorberg, 1993).

Luhmann, N, *Grundrechte als Institution* (Berlin, Duncker & Humblot, 1965).

Maimonides, M, *Mishneh Torah*, Assault and Damages 3.7.

Mangoldt, H von and Klein, F, *Das Bonner Grundgesetz*, 2nd ed (Berlin and Frankfurt aM, Franz Vahlen, 1957).

Manson, NC and O'Neill, O, *Rethinking Informed Consent in Bioethics* (Cambridge, Cambridge University Press, 2007).

Margalit, A, *The Decent Society* (Cambridge, Mass., Harvard University Press, 1996).

Maritain, J, *Les droits de l'homme et la loi naturelle* (Paris, Hartmann, 1942).

Maritain, J, *Um die Erklärung der Menschenrechte – Ein Symposium* (Zürich et al, Europa-Verlag, 1951).

Marx, K, *Critique of Hegel's Philosophy of Right*, Introduction (1844).

Marx, K, *Ökonomisch-philosophische Manuskripte*, ed. M Quante (Frankfurt aM, Suhrkamp, 2009).

Marx, TC, *Disability in Jewish Law* (New York, Routledge, 2002).

Masferrer, A and Garcia-Sánchez, E (eds), *Human Dignity of the Vulnerable in the Age of Rights* (Dordrecht/Heidelberg/London/New York, Springer, 2016).

Mashaw, JL, *Due Process in the Administrative State* (New Haven, Yale University Press, 1985).

McCrudden, C (ed), *Understanding Human Dignity* (Oxford, Oxford University Press, 2013).

Meillassoux, Q, *After Finitude* (London, Bloomsbury, 2012).

Meiser, C, *Biopatentierung und Menschenwürde* (Baden-Baden, Nomos, 2006).

Menke, C, *Tragödie im Sittlichen: Gerechtigkeit und Freiheit nach Hegel* (Frankfurt am Main, Suhrkamp, 1996).

Merkel, R, Boer, G, Fegert, J, Galert, T, Hartmann, D, Nuttin, B and Rosahl, S, *Intervening in the Brain. Changing Psyche and Society* (Berlin/Heidelberg/New York, Springer, 2007).

Merkel, R, *Früheuthanasie. Rechtsethische und strafrechtliche Grundlagen ärztlicher Entscheidungen über Leben und Tod in der Neonatalmedizin* (Baden-Baden, Nomos, 2001).

Merseburger, P, *Theodor Heuss. Der Bürger als Präsident. Biographie* (Munich, Deutsche Verlags-Anstalt, 2012).

Möller, K, *The Global Model of Constitutional Rights* (Oxford, Oxford University Press, 2012).

Moritz, S, *Staatliche Schutzpflichten gegenüber pflegebedürftigen Menschen* (Baden-Baden, Nomos, 2013).

Morozov, E, *To Save Everything, Click Here* (London, Allen Lane, 2013).

Morsink, J, *The Universal Declaration of Human Rights* (Philadelphia, University of Pennsylvania Press, 1999).

Moyn, S, *Christian Human Rights* (Philadelphia, University of Pennsylvania Press, 2015).

Moyn, S, *Origins of the Other: Emanuel Levinas Between Revelation and Ethics* (Ithaca, Cornell University Press, 2005).

Müller-Dietz, H, *Menschenwürde und Strafvollzug* (Berlin, de Gruyter, 1994).

Murdoch, I, *The Sovereignty of Good* (London, Ark Paperbacks, 1985).

Nagel, T, *Mortal Questions* (Cambridge, Cambridge University Press, 1979).

National Women's Law Center, *Nowhere to Turn: How the Individual Health Insurance Market Fails Women* (2008), available at www.nwlc.org/our-resources/reports_toolkits/nowhere-to-turn.

National Women's Law Center, *Still Nowhere to Turn* (2009), available at www.nwlc.org/our-resources/reports_toolkits/nowhere-to-turn.

Neuhouser, F, *Foundations of Hegel's Social Theory: Actualizing Freedom* (Cambridge, Mass, Harvard University Press, 2001).

Neuhouser, F, *Rousseau's Theodicy of Self-Love: Evil, Rationality, and the Drive for Recognition* (Oxford, Oxford University Press, 2008).

Neumann, D, *Vorsorge und Verhältnismäßigkeit* (Berlin, Duncker & Humblot, 1994).

Nida-Rümelin, J, *Über menschliche Freiheit* (Stuttgart, Reclam Verlag, 2005).

Nuffield Council on Bioethics, *Genetically Modified Crops: The Ethical and Social Issues* (London, Nuffield Council on Bioethics, 1999).

Nussbaum, MC, *Cultivating Humanity* (Boston, Harvard University Press, 1994).

Bibliography

Nussbaum, MC, *Frontiers of Justice: Disability, Nationality, Species Membership* (Cambridge, Mass, Belknap Press of Harvard University Press, 2007).

Nussbaum, MC, *Poetic Justice: The Literary Imagination and Public Life* (Boston, Beacon Press, 1995).

Nussbaum, MC, *The Therapy of Desire: Theory and Practice in Hellenistic Ethics* (Princeton et al, Princeton University Press, 1996).

Nussbaum, MC, *Upheavals of Thought* (Cambridge, Cambridge University Press, 2003).

Oestreicher, E, Schelter, K, Kunz, E and Decker, A (eds), *Bundessozialhilfegesetz*, looseleaf collection, last updated June 2002, (Munich, CH Beck, 2002).

Osterhammel, J and Meier, H, *Sklaverei und die Zivilisation des Westens* (Munich, Siemens Stiftung, 2009).

Ousby, I (ed), *Cambridge Paperback Guide to Literature in English* (Cambridge, Cambridge University Press, 1996).

Oyen, RC van and Möllers, MHW (eds), *Das Bundesverfassungsgericht im politischen System* (Wiesbaden, Verlag für Sozialwissenschaften, 2006).

Paton, HJ, *The Categorical Imperative: A Study in Kant's Moral Philosophy* (Philadelphia, University of Pennsylvania Press, 1971).

Perpich, D, *The Ethics of Emanuel Levinas* (Stanford, Stanford University Press, 2008).

Pico della Mirandola, G, *Über die Würde des Menschen* (Zurich, Manesse Verlag, 1996).

Pieroth, B and Schlink, B, *Grundrechte Staatsrecht II*, 17th edn (Heidelberg, C.F. Müller, 2001).

Pieroth, B and Schlink, B, *Grundrechte. Staatsrecht II*, 23th edn (Heidelberg, C.F.Müller, 2007).

Pinkard, T, *Hegel's Phenomenology: The Sociality of Reason* (Cambridge, Cambridge University Press, 2004).

Poscher, R, *Grundrechte als Abwehrrechte* (Tübingen, Mohr Siebeck, 2003).

Post, SG, *The Moral Challenge of Alzheimer Disease* (Baltimore, Johns Hopkins University Press, 1995).

Prauss, G, *Kant über Freiheit als Autonomie* (Frankfurt am Main, Klostermann, 1983).

Probst, P, *Bestirnter Himmel und moralisches Gesetz. Zum geschichtlichen Horizont einer These Immanuel Kants* (Würzburg, Königshausen & Neumann, 1994).

Protokoll der Verhandlungen des Parteitages der SPD vom 21. bis 25. Mai 1950 in Hamburg (Frankfurt am Main, n.d.).

Radau, WC, *Die Biomedizinkonvention des Europarates* (Berlin/Heidelberg/New York, Springer, 2006).

Radin, MJ, *Contested Commodities* (Cambridge, Mass., Harvard University Press, 1996).

Radkau, J, *Theodor Heuss* (Munich, Carl Hanser, 2013).

Raj Kumar, C, *Corruption and Human Rights in India* (Delhi, Oxford University Press, 2011).

Rawls, J, *Justice as Fairness: A Restatement* (Cambridge, Belknap Press, 2001).

Rawls, J, *Political Liberalism* (New York, Columbia University Press, 1991).

Raz, J, *The Morality of Freedom* (Oxford, Clarendon Press, 1986).

Raz, J, *Value, Respect and Attachment* (Cambridge, Cambridge University Press, 2001).

Rebentisch, J, *Die Kunst der Freiheit: Zur Dialektik demokratischer Existenz* (Berlin, Suhrkamp, 2012).

Recki, B, *Ästhetik der Sitten* (Frankfurt am Main, Vittorio Klostermann, 2001).

Regis Jr, E (ed), *Gewirth's Ethical Rationalism* (Chicago, University of Chicago Press, 1984).

Rensmann, T, *Wertordnung und Verfassung. Das Grundgesetz im Kontext grenzüberschreitender Konstitutionalisierung* (Tübingen, Mohr Siebeck, 2007).

Riedel, E, *Theorie der Menschenrechtsstandards* (Berlin, Duncker & Humblot, 1986).

Riedel, M, *Vermutung des Künstlerischen: Der Esra-Beschluss des Bundesverfassungsgerichts – Eine rechts-und literaturwissenschaftliche Untersuchung* (Tübingen, Mohr Siebeck, 2011).

Robertson, D, *The Judge as Political Theorist* (Princeton, Princeton University Press, 2010).

Rogan, M, *Prison Conditions under Irish Law and the European Convention on Human Rights* (Dublin, Irish Penal Reform Trust, 2012).

Rorty, R, *Contingency, Irony, and Solidarity* (Cambridge, Cambridge University Press, 1989).

Rosen-Zvi, I, *Ha-tekes she-lo haya: mikdash, midrash u-migdar be-masekhet Sotah* [The Rite that Was Not: Temple, Midrash and Gender in Tractate Sotah] (Jerusalem: Magnes Press, 2008).

Rosen, M, *Dignity: Its History and Meaning* (Cambridge et al, Harvard University Press, 2012).

Rosenzweig, F, *Der Stern der Erlösung* (Frankfurt am Main, Suhrkamp, 1988).

Rothe, R, *Zur Dogmatik* (Gotha, F.A. Perthes, 1863).

Schaber, P, *Instrumentalisierung und Würde* (Paderborn, Mentis Verlag, 2010).

Schauer, F, *Playing by the Rules* (Oxford, Oxford University Press, 1991).

Scheler, M, *Der Formalismus in der Ethik und die materiale Wertethik. Gesammelte Werke Bd. 2*, 5th edn (Bern, Francke, 1966).

Schenkel, JE, *Sozialversicherung und Grundgesetz* (Berlin, Duncker & Humblot, 2008).

Schmid, C, *Erinnerungen*, 3rd edn (Bern, Munich, Wien, Scherz, 1979).

Schmitt, C, *Politische Theologie*, 2nd edn (Munich, Duncker & Humblot Verlag, 1934).

Scholes, R and Kellogg, R, *The Nature of Narrative* (New York, Oxford University Press, 1966).

Schopenhauer, A, *The World as Will and Idea*, 7th edn, Vol. 1, trans. RB Haldane and J Kemp (London, Kegan Paul, Trench Trübner & Co., 1909; Project Gutenberg EBook 38427, release date: December 27, 2011).

Schopenhauer, A, *Über die Grundlage der Moral*, Vol VI (Zurich, Diogenes Verlag, Werke in zehn Bänden, 1977).

Schwartländer, J, in id et al (eds), *Menschenrechte: Aspekte ihrer Begründung und Verwirklichung* (Tübingen, Attempto Verlag, 1978).

Sensen, O, *Kant on Human Dignity* (Berlin and Boston, De Gruyter, 2011).

Sieckmann, JR, *Regelmodelle und Prinzipienmodelle des Rechtssystems* (Baden-Baden, Nomos, 1990).

Silva-Tarouca Larsen, B von, *Setting the Watch: Privacy and the Ethics of CCTV Surveillance* (Oxford, Hart, 2011).

Bibliography

Simmonds, N, *Law as a Moral Idea* (Oxford, Oxford University Press, 2007).

Skirbekk, G (ed), *Wahrheitstheorien* (Frankfurt/M, Suhrkamp, 1977).

Slaughter, JR, *Human Rights, Inc: The World Novel, Narrative Form, and International Law* (New York, Fordham University Press, 2007).

Somek, A, *Engineering Equality: An Essay on European Anti-Discrimination Law* (Oxford, Oxford University Press, 2011).

Sousa, R de, *The Rationality of Emotion* (Cambridge, MIT Press, 1990).

Spaemann, R, *Das Natürliche und das Vernünftige* (Munich et al, Piper, 1987).

Spitz, JF, *L'amour de l'égalité* (Paris, Vrin, 2000).

Stein, T, *Himmlische Quellen und irdisches Recht. Religiöse Voraussetzungen des freiheitlichen Verfassungsstaates* (Frankfurt/M and New York, Campus, 2007).

Stern, S, *Jewish Identity in Early Rabbinic Writings* (Leiden, Brill, 1994).

Stolleis, M (ed), *Herzkammern der Republik—Die Deutschen und das Bundesverfassungsgericht* (Munich, C.H. Beck, 2011).

Stolleis, M, *Geschichte des Sozialrechts in Deutschland* (Stuttgart, Lucius und Lucius, 2003).

Strauss, D, *The Living Constitution* (Oxford, Oxford University Press, 2010).

Sunstein, CR, *The Second Bill of Rights: FRD's Unfinished Revolution and Why We Need It More than Ever* (New York, Basic Books, 2004).

Teifke, N, *Das Prinzip Menschenwürde* (Tübingen, Mohr Siebeck, 2011).

Teman, E, *Birthing a Mother* (Berkeley, University of California Press, 2010).

The President's Council on Bioethics (ed), *Human Cloning and Human Dignity* (Washington D.C., 2002).

The President's Council on Bioethics (ed), *Beyond Therapy: Biotechnology and the Pursuit of Happiness* (Washington D.C., 2003).

Thompson, EP, *Whigs and Hunters* (London, Breviary Stuff, 2013).

Trimmings K and Beaumont P (eds), *International Surrogacy Arrangements: Legal Regulation at the International Level* (Oxford/Portland, Hart Publishing, 2013).

Tugendhat, E, *Anthropologie statt Metaphysik* (Munich, Beck, 2010).

Velleman, JD, *How We Get Along* (Cambridge, Cambridge University Press, 2009).

Vilmar, AFC, *Dogmatik. Akademie Vorlesungen*, after his death edited by KW Piderit (Gütersloh, Bertelsmann, 1874).

Vögele, W, *Menschenwürde zwischen Recht und Theologie* (Gütersloh, Kaiser, 2000).

Vöneky, S and Wolfrum, R (eds), *Human Dignity and Human Cloning* (Berlin, Springer Verlag, 2004).

Vonnegut, K, *A Man Without a Country* (New York, Random House Trade Paperbacks, 2005).

Waldenfels, B, *Schattenrisse der Moral* (Frankfurt am Main, Suhrkamp, 2006).

Waldron, J, *Dignity, Rank, and Rights*, ed. M Dan-Cohen (Oxford, Oxford University Press, 2012).

Wallrabenstein, A, *Versicherung im Sozialstaat* (Tübingen, Mohr Siebeck, 2009).

Weber, P, *Carlo Schmid 1896–1979. Eine Biographie* (Frankfurt/M, Suhrkamp, 1998).

Wetz, FJ, *Illusion Menschenwürde* (Stuttgart, Klett-Cotta, 2005).

White, JB, *The Legal Imagination: Studies in the Nature of Legal Thought and Expression* (Boston, Little, Brown and Co., 1973).

Wittgenstein, L, *Tractatus Logico-Philosophicus*, ed. and trans. CK Ogden (London, Kegan Paul, Trench, Trubner & Co., New York, Harcourt, Brace & Company, 1922; Project Gutenberg EBook 5740, release date: October 22, 2010)

Wittstock, U, *Der Fall Esra* (Köln, Kiepenheuer und Witsch, 2011).

Wolfe, A, *At Home in Exile: Why Diaspora is Good for the Jews* (Boston, Beacon Press, 2014).

World Health Organization and Alzheimer's Disease International, *Dementia: A Public Health Priority* (Geneva, World Health Organization, 2012).

Žižek, S, *The Ticklish Subject. The Absent Centre of Political Ontology* (London, Verso, 1999).

Zupančič, A, *Das Reale einer Illusion. Kant und Lacan* (Frankfurt/M, Suhrkamp, 2001).

Articles, Book Chapters

Abeyratne, R and Sinha, N, 'Insular and Inconsistent: India's Naz Foundation Judgment in Comparative Perspective' (2014) 39 *Yale Journal of International Law Online* 74.

Ackerman, B, 'The Living Constitution' (2007) 120 *Harvard Law Review* 1738.

Albers, M, 'Bioethik, Biopolitik, Biorecht: Grundlagen und Schlüsselprobleme' in id (ed), *Bioethik, Biorecht, Biopolitik: Eine Kontextualisierung* (Baden-Baden, Nomos, 2016) 9.

Albers, M, 'Die rechtlichen Standards der Biomedizin-Konvention des Europarats' (2002) *Europarecht* 801.

Albers, M, Enhancement, Human Nature, and Human Rights' in M Albers, T Hoffmann and J Reinhardt (eds), *Human Rights and Human Nature* (Dordrecht/Heidelberg/London/New York, Springer, 2014) 235.

Albers, M, 'Grundrechtsschutz und Innovationserfordernisse angesichts neuartiger Einblicke und Eingriffe in das Gehirn' in J Lindner (ed), *Die neuronale Selbstbestimmung des Menschen* (Baden-Baden, Nomos, 2016) 63.

Albers, M, 'Höchstrichterliche Rechtsfindung und Auslegung gerichtlicher Entscheidungen' in 71 Veröffentlichungen der Vereinigung der Deutschen Staatsrechtslehrer (VVDStRL), *Grundsatzfragen der Rechtsetzung und Rechtsfindung* (Berlin/Boston, de Gruyter, 2012) 257.

Albers, M,'Patente auf Leben' (2003) *JuristenZeitung* 275.

Albers, M, 'Rechtsrahmen und Rechtsprobleme bei Biobanken' (2013) *Medizinrecht* 481.

Albers, M 'Risikoregulierung im Bio-, Gesundheits- und Medizinrecht' in id (ed), *Risikoregulierung im Bio-, Gesundheits- und Medizinrecht* (Baden-Baden, Nomos, 2011) 9.

Aleinikoff, TA, 'Constitutional Law in the Age of Balancing' (1987) 96 *Yale Law Journal* 943.

Allen, J and McNamara, B, 'Reconsidering the Value of Consent in Biobank Research' (2011) 25 *Bioethics* 155.

Alpers, S, 'Interpretation Without Representation, or, the Viewing of *Las Meninas*' (1983) 1 *Representations* 31.

Bibliography

Altmann, A, 'Homo Imago Dei in Jewish and Christian Theology' (1968) 48:3 *Journal of Religion* 235.

Altmann, A, 'Moses Mendelssohn as the Archetypical German Jew' in J Reinharz and W Schatzberg (eds), *The Jewish Response to German Culture* (Hanover, University Press of New England, 1985) 17.

Andorno, R, 'First Steps in the Development of an International Biolaw' in C Gastmans, K Dierick, H Nys and P Schotmans (eds), *New Pathways for European Bioethics* (Antwerp, Intersentia, 2007) 121.

Andorno, R, 'Human Dignity and Human Rights as a Common Ground for a Global Bioethics' (2009) 34 *Journal of Medicine and Philosophy* 223.

Andries, EM, 'On the German Constitution's Fiftieth Anniversary: Jacques Maritain and the 1949 Basic Law (Grundgesetz)' (1999) 13 *Emory Int'l L Rev* 53.

Araki, M and Ishii, T, 'International Regulatory Landscape and Integration of Corrective Genome Editing into In Vitro Fertilization' (2014) *Reproductive Biology and Endocrinology* 12:108.

Astell, A, 'Technology and Personhood in Dementia Care' (2006) 7 *Quality in Ageing and Older Adults* 15.

Badura, P, 'Generalprävention und Würde des Menschen', (1964) 19 *JuristenZeitung* 337.

Baer, S, 'Menschenwürde zwischen Recht, Prinzip und Referenz—Die Bedeutung von Enttabuisierungen' (2005) 4 *DZPhil* 571.

Baldus, M, 'Menschenwürdegarantie und Absolutheitsthese' (2011) 136 *Archiv des öffentlichen Rechts* 551.

Balkin, J and Levinson, S, 'The Dangerous Thirteenth Amendment' (2012) 112 *Columbia Law Review* 1459.

Balkin, J, 'That Boring Old Tax Argument Was Always a Winner,' 28 July 2012, www.slate.com/articles/news_and_politics/the_breakfast_table/features/2012/_supreme_court_year_in_review/supreme_court_year_in_review_it_was_always_about_the_tax_.html.

Banzhaf, W and McMullin, B, 'Artificial Life' in G Rozenberg, T Bäck and JN Kok (eds) *Handbook of Natural Computing* (Berlin/Heidelberg, Springer, 2012) 1805.

Barak, A, 'Human Dignity: The Constitutional Value and the Constitutional Right' in C McCrudden (ed), *Understanding Human Dignity* (Oxford, Oxford University Press, 2013) 361.

Barilan, YM, 'From Imago Dei in the Jewish-Christian Traditions to Human Dignity in Contemporary Jewish Law' (2009) 19 *Kennedy Institute of Ethics Journal* 231.

Barilan, YM, 'Judaism, Human Dignity, and the Most Vulnerable Women on Earth' (2009) 9 *The American Journal of Bioethics* 35.

Baumann, P, 'Menschenwürde und das Bedürfnis nach Respekt', in R Stoecker (ed), *Menschenwürde: Annäherung an einen Begriff* (Vienna, öbv Verlag, 2003) 19.

Baxi, U, 'Taking Suffering Seriously: Social Action Litigation in the Supreme Court of India' (1985) 4 *Third World Legal Studies* 107.

Bayer, O, 'Self-Creation? On the Dignity of Human Beings' (2004) 20 *Modern Theology* 275.

Bayertz, K, 'Human Dignity: Philosophical Origin and Scientific Erosion of an Idea', in id (ed), *Sanctity of Life and Human Dignity* (Dordrecht, Kluwer Publishers, 1996) 80.

Bendor, AL and Sachs M, 'The Constitutional Status of Human Dignity in Germany and Israel' (2011) 44 *Israel Law Review* 25.

Bernet, R, 'Subjekt und Gesetz in der Ethik von Kant und Lacan' in HD Gondek and P Widmer (eds), *Ethik und Psychoanalyse* (Frankfurt aM, Fischer Taschenbuch, 1994) 51.

Bernstorff, J von, 'Der Streit um die Menschenwürde im Grund- und Menschenrechtsschutz: Eine Verteidigung des Absoluten als Grenze und Auftrag' (2013) 68 *JuristenZeitung* 905.

Bernstorff, J von, 'Die Wesensgehalte der Grundrechte und das Verhältnis von Freiheit und Sicherheit im Grundgesetz' in F Arndt et al (eds), *48. Assistententagung Öffentliches Recht* (Baden-Baden, Nomos, 2009) 40.

Bernstorff, J von, 'Kerngehaltsschutz durch den UN-Menschenrechtsausschuss und den EGMR: Vom Wert kategorialer Argumentationsformen' (2011) 50 *Der Staat* 165.

Bernstorff, J von, 'Pflichtenkollision und Menschenwürdegarantie. Zum Vorrang staatlicher Achtungspflichten im Normbereich des Art. 1 GG' (2008) 47 *Der Staat* 21.

Bernstorff, J von, 'The Changing Fortune of the Universal Declaration of Human Rights: Genesis and Symbolic Dimensions of the Turn to Rights in International Law' (2008) 19 *EJIL* 903.

Bernstorff, von J, 'Der Streit um die Menschenwürde im Grund- und Menschenrechtsschutz: Eine Verteidigung des Absoluten als Grenze und Auftrag' (2013) *JuristenZeitung* 905.

Bettelheim, B, 'Individual and Mass Behavior in Extreme Situations' (1943) 38 *The Journal of Abnormal and Social Psychology* 417.

Beyleveld, D and Bos, G, 'The Foundational Role of the Principle of Instrumental Reason in Gewirth's Argument for the Principle of Generic Consistency: A Response to Andrew Chitty' (2009) 20 *King's Law Journal* 1.

Beyleveld, D, 'Human Dignity and Human Rights in Alan Gewirth's Moral Philosophy' in M Düwell, J Braarvig, R Brownsword and D Mieth (eds), *The Cambridge Handbook of Human Dign*ity (Cambridge, Cambridge University Press, 2014) 230.

Beyleveld, D, 'Legal Theory and Dialectically Contingent Justifications for the Principle of Generic Consistency' (1996) 9 *Ratio Juris* 15.

Bielefeldt, H, 'Das Folterverbot im Rechtsstaat' in P Nitschke (ed), *Rettungsfolter im modernen Rechtsstaat. Eine Verortung* (Bochum, Kamp, 2005) 95.

Bielefeldt, H, 'Menschenrechtlicher Universalismus ohne eurozentrische Verkürzung' in G Lohmann and G Nooke (eds), *Gelten Menschenrechte universal?* (Freiburg et al, Herder, 2008) 98.

Biletzki, A, 'The Judicial Rhetoric of Morality: Israel's High Court of Justice on the Legality of Torture' (2001) *Occasional Papers of the School of Social Science, Paper no 9.*

Binchy, W, 'Dignity as a Constitutional Concept' in E Carolan & O Doyle (eds), *The Irish Constitution: Governance and Values* (Dublin, Thomson Round Hall, 2008) 308.

Birchfield, L and Corsi, J, 'Between Starvation and Globalization: Realizing the Right to Food in India' (2010) 31 *Michigan Journal of International Law* 691.

Birnbacher, D, 'Do Modern Reproductive Technologies Violate Human Dignity?' in E Hildt and D Mieth (eds), *In Vitro Fertilisation in the 1990s* (Aldershot, Ashgate, 1998) 325.

Birnbacher, D, 'Mehrdeutigkeiten im Begriff der Menschenwürde' (1995) *Aufklärung und Kritik, Sonderheft* 1.

Bibliography

Birnbacher, D, 'Menschenwürde – abwägbar oder unabwägbar?' in M Kettner (ed), *Biomedizin und Menschenwürde* (Frankfurt aM, Suhrkamp Verlag, 2004) 248.

Birnbacher, D, 'Menschenwürde und Präimplantationsdiagnostik' in JC Joerden, E Hilgendorf and F Thiele (eds), *Menschenwürde und Medizin* (Berlin, Duncker & Humblot, 2013) 755.

Birnbacher, D, 'Menschenwürde-Skepsis' in JC Joerden, E Hilgendorf and F Thiele (eds), *Menschenwürde und Medizin. Ein interdisziplinäres Handbuch* (Berlin, Duncker & Humblot, 2013) 159.

Blacam, M De, 'Justice and Natural Law' (1997) 32 *Irish Jurist* 323.

Blidstein, GJ, '"Great is Human Dignity": An Analysis of the History of a Halakha' (Hebrew) (1982-83) 15 *Shnaton ha-Mishpat ha-Ivri* [Annual of the Institute for Research on Jewish Law] 127.

Blythe, JM, 'Family, Government, and the Medieval Aristotelians' (1989) 10 *History of Political Thought* 4.

Böckenförde, EW, 'Die Würde des Menschen war unantastbar' FAZ from 3.9.2003, 33.

Böckenförde, EW, 'Grundrechte als Grundsatznormen' (1990) 29 *Der Staat* 1.

Böckenförde, EW, 'Menschenwürde als normatives Prinzip' (2003) *JuristenZeitung* 809.

Boekhorst, S Te et al, 'Quality of Life of Nursing-Home Residents with Dementia Subject to Surveillance Technology Versus Physical Restraints: An Explorative Study' (2013) 28 *International Journal of Geriatric Psychiatry* 356.

Borowski, M, 'Limiting Clauses: On the Continental European Tradition of Special Limiting Clauses and the General Limiting Clause of Art 52 (1) Charter of Fundamental Rights of the European Union' (2007) 1 *Legisprudence* 197.

Bostrom, N, 'In Defense of Posthuman Dignity' in GR Hansell and W Grassie (eds), *H +/- Transhumanism and Its Critics* (Philadelphia, Metanexus, 2011) 55.

Botha, H, 'Human Dignity in Comparative Perspective' (2009) 2 *Stellenbosch Law Review* 171.

Braun, J, 'Selbstbestimmung und Fremdbestimmung. Über die Schwierigkeit autonomen Handelns in einer heteronom bestimmten Gesellschaft' (2012) 43 *Rechtstheorie* 159.

Brennan, W, 'The Constitution of the United States: Contemporary Ratification' (1986) 27 *South Texas Law Review* 433.

Brownsword, R and Earnshaw, J, 'Controversy: The Ethics of Screening for Abdominal Aortic Aneurysm' (2010) 36 *Journal of Medical Ethics* 827.

Brownsword, R and Somsen, H, 'Law, Innovation and Technology: Before We Fast Forward—A Forum for Debate' (2009) 1 *Law Innovation and Technology* 1.

Brownsword, R, 'A Simple Regulatory Principle for Performance-Enhancing Technologies: Too Good to be True?' in J Tolleneer, P Bonte and S Sterckx (eds), *Athletic Enhancement, Human Nature and Ethics: Threats and Opportunities of Doping Technologies* (Dordrecht, Springer, 2012) 291.

Brownsword, R, 'Bioethics Today, Bioethics Tomorrow: Stem Cell Research and the "Dignitarian Alliance"' (2003) 17 *University of Notre Dame Journal of Law, Ethics and Public Policy* 15.

Brownsword, R, 'Code, Control, and Choice: Why East is East and West is West' (2005) 25 *Legal Studies* 1.

Brownsword, R, 'Crimes Against Humanity, Simple Crime, and Human Dignity' in B van Beers, L Corrias, and W Werner (eds), *Humanity Across International Law and Biolaw* (Cambridge, Cambridge University Press, 2013) 106.

Brownsword, R, 'Criminal Law, Regulatory Frameworks and Public Health' in AM Viens, J Coggon and AS Kessel (eds), *Criminal Law, Philosophy and Public Health Practice* (Cambridge, Cambridge University Press, 2013) 19.

Brownsword, R, 'Friends, Romans, Countrymen: Is There a Universal Right to Identity?' (2009) 1 *Law, Innovation and Technology* 223.

Brownsword, R, 'Human Dignity, Human Rights, and Simply Trying to Do the Right Thing' in C McCrudden (ed), *Understanding Human Dignity* (Oxford, Proceedings of the British Academy and Oxford University Press, 2013) 470.

Brownsword, R, 'Lost in Translation: Legality, Regulatory Margins, and Technological Management' (2011) 26 *Berkeley Technology Law Journal* 1321.

Brownsword, R, 'Regulating Human Enhancement: Things Can Only Get Better?' (2009) 1 *Law Innovation and Technology* 125.

Brownsword, R, 'Regulating the Life Sciences, Pluralism, and the Limits of Deliberative Democracy' (2010) 22 *Singapore Academy of Law Journal* 801.

Brownsword, R, 'Responsible Regulation: Prudence, Precaution and Stewardship' (2011) 62 *Northern Ireland Legal Quarterly* 573.

Brownsword, R, 'What the World Needs Now: Techno-Regulation, Human Rights and Human Dignity' in id (ed), *Human Rights* (Oxford, Hart, 2004) 203.

Bruhns, A, '"Die sind nicht bescheuert": Der Pflegeheimleiter und Ethik-Experte Michael Schmieder kämpft gegen den verstörenden Trend, Demenzkranke in einer falschen Realität leben zu lassen' (2014) 11 *Der Spiegel* 134.

Brunkhorst, H, 'Folter, Würde und repressiver Liberalismus' in G Beestermöller and H Brunkhorst (eds), *Rückkehr der Folter. Der Rechtsstaat im Zwielicht?* (Munich, C.H. Beck, 2006) 88.

Bublitz, JC, 'My Mind Is Mine!? Cognitive Liberty as a Legal Concept' in E Hildt and AG Franke (eds), *Cognitive Enhancement. An Interdisciplinary Perspective* (Dordrecht, Springer, 2013) 233.

Bühl, A, 'Reproduktives Klonen in "real life" und in der Science Fiction' in A Bühl (ed), *Auf dem Weg zur biomächtigen Gesellschaft?* (Wiesbaden, VS Verlag für Sozialwissenschaften, 2009) 273.

Bullington J, 'Being Body: The Dignity of Human Embodiment' in L Nordenfelt (ed), *Dignity in Care for Older People* (Chichester, Wiley-Blackwell, 2009) 54.

Burgers, JH, 'The Road to San Francisco: The Revival of the Human Rights Idea in the Twentieth Century' (1992) 14 *Human Rights Quarterly* 447.

Cahill, S et al, 'Technology in Dementia Care' (2007) 19 *Technology and Disability* 55.

Campbell, AV, 'Being Mindful of the Body: Enriching the Conceptual Background of Bioethics' (2009) 1 *Law, Innovation and Technology* 171.

Carozza, P, 'Human Rights, Human Dignity, and Human Experience' in C McCrudden (ed), *Understanding Human Dignity* (Oxford, Oxford University Press, 2013) 615.

Cash, M, 'Assistive Technology and People with Dementia' (2003) 13 *Reviews in Clinical Gerontology* 313.

Cassirer, E, 'Giovanni Pico Della Mirandola: A Study in the History of Renaissance Ideas' (1942) 3 *Journal of the History of Ideas* 123 (Part I), 319 (Part II).

Caulfield, T and Brownsword, R, 'Human Dignity: A Guide to Policy Making in the Biotechnology Era?' (2006) 7 *Nature Review Genetics* 72.

Caulfield, T, 'Human Cloning Laws, Human Dignity and the Poverty of the Policy Making Dialogue' (2003) 4 *BMC Medical Ethics*, http://www.biomedcentral.com/1472-6939/4/3.

Caulfield, T, 'Stem Cells, Clones, Consensus, and the Law' in L P Knowles/G E Kaebnick (eds), *Reprogenetics. Law, Policy and Ethical Issues* (Baltimore, The John Hopkins University Press, 2007) 105.

Choi, K and Min, BK 'Future Directions for Brain-Machine Interfacing Technology' in SW Lee, HH Bülthoff and KR Müller (eds), *Recent Progress in Brain and Cognitive Engineering* (Dordrecht, Springer, 2015) 3.

Choudhury, CA, 'The Political Economy and Legal Regulation of Transnational Commercial Surrogate Labor' (2015) 48 *Vanderbilt Journal of Transnational Law* 1.

Clark, B, 'Freedom of Art v. Personality Rights: Ban Upheld on the Real Life Novel Esra' (2008) 3 *Journal of Intellectual Property Law and Practice* 221.

Clarke, D, 'The Role of Natural Law in Irish Constitutional Law' (1982) 17 *Irish Jurist* 187.

Classen, CD, 'Die Forschung mit embryonalen Stammzellen im Spiegel der Grundrechte' (2002) *Deutsches Verwaltungsblatt* 141.

Classen, CD, 'Die Menschenwürde ist – und bleibt – unantastbar' (2009) 62 *Die öffentliche Verwaltung* 689.

Clerc, C, 'History and Literature' in SR Serafin (ed), *The Continuum Encyclopedia of American Literature*, 2nd edn (New York/London, The Continuum Publishing Company, 2003) 523.

Cohen, IG, Daley, GW and Adashi, EY, 'Disruptive Reproductive Technologies' (2017), 9 (372) *Science Translational Medicine* 1 (DOI:10.1126/scitranslmed.aag2959).

Coors, M, 'A Dementalized Body? Reconsidering the Human Condition in the Light of Dementia' (2013) 1 *Geriatric Mental Health Care* 34.

Corcoran, S, 'Editor's Introduction' in J Rancière, *Dissensus on Politics and Aesthetics*, ed. and trans. S Corcoran (London and New York, Continuum International Publishing Group, 2010) 5.

Cover, R, 'Obligation: A Jewish Jurisprudence of the Social Order' in M Minow, M Ryan and A Sarat (eds), *Narrative, Violence, and the Law. The Essays of Robert Cover* (Ann Arbor, University of Michigan Press, 1993) 239.

Craig, PP and Deshpande, SL, 'Rights, Autonomy and Process: Public Interest Litigation in India' (1989) 9 *Oxford Journal of Legal Studies* 356.

Cyranowski, D, 'Stem Cells: The Black Box of Reprogramming' (2014) 516 *Nature* 162.

Decker, M, 'Caregiving Robots and Ethical Reflection: The Perspective of Interdisciplinary Technology Assessment' (2008) 22 *AI & Society* 315.

Dederer, G, 'Die Garantie der Menschenwürde (Art. 1 Abs. 1 GG). Dogmatische Grundfragen auf dem Stand der Wissenschaft' (2009) 57 *Jahrbuch des öffentlichen Rechts* 87.

Delaunay, C, 'The Beginning of Human Life at the Laboratory: The Challenges of a Technological Future for Human Reproduction' (2015) 40 *Technology in Society* 14.

Deleuze, G, 'On Four Poetic Formulas That Might Summarize the Kantian Philosophy' in id (ed), *Essays Critical and Clinical*, trans. DW Smith and MA Greco (London, Verso, 1998) 27.

Deleuze, G, 'Sacher-Masoch und der Masochismus' in L von Sacher-Masoch (ed), *Venus im Pelz* (Frankfurt am Main, Insel, 1980) 233.

DeNavas-Walt, C et al, US Census Bureau, *Income, Poverty, and Health Insurance Coverage in the United States: 2011. Current Population Reports* (2012), available at www.census.gov/prod/2012-pubs/p60-243.pdf.

Denninger, E, 'Polizei und demokratische Politik' (1970) *JuristenZeitung* 145.

Denninger, E, 'Prävention und Freiheit. Von der Ordnung der Freiheit' in S Huster and K Rudolph (eds), *Vom Rechtsstaat zum Präventionsstaat* (Frankfurt aM, Suhrkamp, 2008) 103.

Depenheuer, O, 'Das Bürgeropfer im Rechtsstaat' in id (ed), *Staat im Wort: Festschrift für Josef Isensee* (Heidelberg, C.F. Müller, 2007) 43.

Descheemaeker, E, 'Solatium and Injury to Feelings: Roman Law, English Law and Modern Tort Theory' in E Descheemaeker and H Scott (eds), *Inuria and the Common Law* (Oxford, Hart Publishing, 2013) 94.

Dhavan, R, 'Law as Struggle: Public Interest Law in India' (1994) 36 *Journal of the Indian Law Institute* 302.

Dicke, K, 'The Founding Function of Human Dignity in the Universal Declaration of Human Rights' in D Kretzmer and E Klein (eds), *The Concept of Human Dignity in Human Rights Discourse* (The Hague et al, Kluwer Law International, 2002) 111.

Doemming, KB von, Füsslein, RW and Matz, W, 'Entstehungsgeschichte der Artikel des Grundgesetzes' (1951) 1 *Jahrbuch des öffentlichen Rechts der Gegenwart*, new edn, V.

Dominguez, JP, 'El niño de Vallades [Francisco Lezcano]' (1989) 261 *Journal of the American Medical Association* 496.

Dorff, EN, Nevins, DS and Reisner, AI, 'Homosexuality, Human Dignity and Halakha: A Combined Responsum for the Committee on Jewish Law and Standards' *Law Committee of the Rabbinical Assembly of America*, ratified on 6 December 2006, www.rabbinicalassembly.org/sites/default/files/public/halakhah/teshuvot/20052010/dorff_nevins_reisner_dignity.pdf.

Doudna, JA and Charpentier, E, 'The New Frontier of Genome Engineering with CRISPR-Cas9' (2014) 346 Science 6231, DOI:10.1126/science1258096.

Dreier, H, 'Art. 1 Abs. 1', in id (ed), *Grundgesetz. Kommentar*, 3rd edn, Vol. 1, (Tübingen, Mohr Siebeck, 2013).

Dreier, H, 'Art. 1' in id (ed), *Grundgesetz-Kommentar*, 2nd edn, Vol. 1 (Tübingen, Mohr Siebeck, 2004).

Dreier, H, 'Menschenwürdegarantie und Schwangerschaftsabbruch' (1995) 48 *Die Öffentliche Verwaltung* 1036.

Dresser, R, 'Human Dignity and the Seriously Ill Patient' in A Schulman (ed), *Human Dignity and Bioethics: Essays Commissioned by the President's Council on Bioethics* (President's Council on Bioethics, 2008) 508.

Drèze, J, 'Democracy and the Right to Food' (2004) 39 *Economic and Political Weekly* 1723.

Duncan, W, 'The Constitutional Protection of Parental Rights' in *Report of the Constitution Review Group* (Dublin, Stationery Office, 1996) 612.

Dupré, C, 'Article 1 – Human Dignity' in S Peers, T Hervey, J Kenner and A Ward (eds), *The EU Charter of Fundamental Rights* (Baden-Baden/Munich/Oxford, Nomos/C.H. Beck/Hart Publishing, 2014).

Dupré, C, 'Human Dignity and the Withdrawal of Medical Treatment: A Missed Opportunity' (2006) 6 *European Human Rights Law Review* 687.

Bibliography

Dupré, C, 'Unlocking Human Dignity. Towards a Theory for the 21st Century' (2009) 2 *European Human Rights Law Review* 190.

Dürig, G, 'Art. 1' in T Maunz and G Dürig, *Grundgesetz-Kommentar* (looseleaf collection, Munich, C.H. Beck).

Dürig, G, 'Dankrede am 65. Geburtstag' (1987) 36 *Jahrbuch des öffentlichen Rechts der Gegenwart* 91.

Dürig, G, 'Der Grundrechtssatz von der Menschenwürde – Entwurf eines praktikablen Wertsystems der Grundrechte aus Art. 1 Abs. I in Verbindung mit Art. 19 Abs. II des Grundgesetzes' (1956) 81 *AöR* 117.

Dürig, G, 'Der Grundrechtssatz von der Menschenwürde. Entwurf eines praktikablen Wertsystems der Grundrechte aus Art. 1 Abs. I i.V.m. Art. 19 Abs. II des Grundgesetzes' in W Schmitt-Glaeser and P Häberle (eds), *Günter Dürig, Gesammelte Schriften 1952-1983* (Berlin; Duncker & Humblot, 1984) 127.

Dürig, G, 'Die Menschenauffassung des Grundgesetzes' in W Schmitt-Glaeser and P Häberle (eds), *Günter Dürig, Gesammelte Schriften 1952-1983*, (Berlin, Duncker & Humblot, 1984) 31.

Dürig, G, 'Die Menschenauffassung des Grundgesetzes', (1952) 6 *Juristische Rundschau* 259.

Dürig, G, 'Kommentierung von Art. 1 Grundgesetz' in T Maunz and G Dürig (eds), *Grundgesetz-Kommentar*, 1st edn (Munich, Beck, 1958).

Dürig, G, 'Zur Bedeutung und Tragweite des Art. 79 Abs. III GG' in H Spanner et al (eds), *Festgabe für Theodor Maunz zum 70. Geburtstag am 1. September 1971* (Munich, C.H. Beck, 1971) 41.

Duttge, G, 'Zum typologischen Denken im Strafrecht – Ein Beitrag zur "Wiederbelebung" der juristischen Methode' (2003) 11 *Jahrbuch für Recht und Ethik* 103.

Düwell, M, 'Human Dignity: Concepts, Discussions, Philosophical Perspectives' in M Düwell, J Braarvig, R Brownsword and D Mieth (eds), *The Cambridge Handbook of Human Dignity* (Cambridge, Cambridge University Press, 2014) 23.

Dyzenhaus, D, 'Rand's Legal Republicanism' (2010) 55 *McGill Law Journal* 491.

Dyzenhaus, D, 'The "Organic Law" of *Ex Parte Milligan*' in A Sarat (ed), *Sovereignty, Emergency, Legality* (Cambridge, Cambridge University Press, 2010) 16.

Dyzenhaus, D, 'The Politics of Deference: Judicial Review and Democracy' in M Taggart (ed), *The Province of Administrative Law* (Oxford, Hart Publishing, 1997) 286.

Eberle, EJ, 'Human Dignity, Privacy, and Personality in German and American Constitutional Law' in N Knoepffler, P Kunzmann and M O'Malley (eds), *Facetten der Menschenwürde* (Freiburg and Munich, Alber, 2011) 102.

Edgar, A, 'Velázquez and the Representation of Dignity' (2003) 6 *Medicine, Health Care and Philosophy* 111.

Eichner, C and Mix, Y-G, 'Ein Fehlurteil als Maßstab? Zu Maxim Billers Esra, Klaus Manns Mephisto und dem Problem der Kunstfreiheit in der Bundesrepublik Deutschland' (2007) 32 *Internationales Archiv für Sozialgeschichte der deutschen Literatur* 183.

Elder, AH, 'Wombs to Rent: Examining the Jurisdiction of International Surrogacy' (2014) 16 *Oregon Review of International Law* 347.

Elsner, T and Schobert, K, 'Gedanken zur Abwägungsresistenz der Menschenwürde – angestoßen durch das Urteil des Bundesverfassungsgerichts zur Verfassungsmäßigkeit der Sicherungsverwahrung' (2007) *Deutsches Verwaltungsblatt* 278.

Eltis, K, 'Predicating Dignity on Autonomy? The Need for Further Inquiry into the Ethics of Tagging and Tracking Dementia Patients with GPS Technology' (2005) 13 *Elder Law Journal* 387.

Eltis, K, 'Society's Most Vulnerable under Surveillance: The Ethics of Tagging and Tracking Dementia Patient with GPS Technology: A Comparative View' (2005) 3 *Oxford University Comparative Law Forum*, at ouclf.iuscomp.org.

Enders, C, 'A Right to Have Rights – The German Constitutional Concept of Human Dignity', (2010) 3 *NUJS Law Review* 253.

Enders, C, 'Die Menschenwürde und ihr Schutz vor gentechnologischer Gefährdung' (1986) *Europäische Grundrechte-Zeitschrift* 241.

Enders, C, 'Die normative Unantastbarkeit der Menschenwürde' in R Gröschner and OW Lembcke (eds), *Das Dogma der Unantastbarkeit* (Tübingen, Mohr Siebeck, 2009) 69.

Enders, C, 'Die Würde des Staates liegt in der Würde des Menschen – Das absolute Verbot von staatlicher Folter' in P Nitschke (ed), *Rettungsfolter im modernen Rechtsstaat. Eine Verortung* (Bochum, Kamp, 2005) 133.

Ergas, Y, 'Babies Without Borders: Human Rights, Human Dignity, and the Regulation of International Commercial Surrogacy' (2013) 27 *Emory International Law* Review 117.

Eskridge, Jr, WN 'America's Statutory "constitution"' (2007) 41 *UC Davis Law Review* 1.

Eskridge, Jr, WN and Ferejohn, J, 'Super-Statutes' (2001) 50 *Duke Law Journal* 1215.

Fabio, U Di 'Grundrechte als Werteordnung' (2004) *JuristenZeitung* 1.

Farajkhoda, T, 'An Overview on Ethical Considerations in Stem Cell Research in Iran and Ethical Recommendations: A Review' (2017), 15 *International Journal of Reproductive BioMedicine* 67.

Feldman, D, 'Human Dignity as a Legal Value: Part 2' (2000) *Public Law* 61.

Feldman, D, 'Human Dignity as a Legal Value: Part 1' (1999) *Public Law* 682.

Feros, A, '"Sacred and Terrifying Gazes": Languages and Images of Power in Early Modern Spain' in SL Stratton-Pruitt, *Cambridge Companion to Velázquez* (Cambridge, Cambridge University Press, 2002) 83.

Forbath, WE, 'Constitutional Welfare Rights: A History, Critique and Reconstruction' (2001) 69 *Fordham Law Review* 1821.

Frankena, WK, 'The Ethics of Respect for Persons' (1986) 14 *Philosophical Topics* 149.

Frankenberg, G, 'Critical Comparisons: Re-thinking Comparative Law' (1985) 26 *Harvard International Law Journal* 411.

Frankenberg, G, 'Die Würde des Klons und die Krise des Rechts' (2000) *Kritische Justiz* 325.

Frankenberg, G, 'Folter, Feindstrafrecht und Sonderpolizeirecht. Anmerkungen zu Phänomenen des Bekämpfungsrechts' in G Beestermöller and H Brunkhorst (eds), *Rückkehr der Folter. Der Rechtsstaat im Zwielicht?* (Munich, C.H. Beck, 2006) 55.

Frankenberg, G, 'Innocence in Context – Comparative Law Revisited' in D Grimm, A Kemmerer and C Möllers (eds), *Rechtswege. Kontextsensible Rechtswissenschaft vor der transnationalen Herausforderung* (Baden-Baden, Nomos, 2015) 144.

Frankl, VE, 'Der unbedingte Mensch' (1949) in id, *Der leidende Mensch*, 3rd edn (Bern, Huber, 2005) 65.

Frankl, VE, 'Homo patiens' (1950) in id, *Der leidende Mensch*, 3rd edn (Bern, Huber, 2005) 161.

Franz, EB, 'Der Bundeswehreinsatz im Innern und die Tötung Unschuldiger im Kreuzfeuer von Menschenwürde und Recht auf Leben' (206) 45 *Der Staat* 501.

Gadamer, HG, 'Die Menschenwürde auf ihrem Weg von der Antike bis heute' (1988) 12 *Humanistische Bildung* 95.

Gadow, S, 'Touch and Technology: Two Paradigms of Patient Care' (1984) 23 *Journal of Religion and Health* 63.

Galloway, K, 'Theoretical Approaches to Human Dignity, Human Rights and Surrogacy' in P Gerber and K O'Byrne (eds), *Surrogacy, Law and Human Rights* (Farnham/Burlington, Ashgate Publishing, 2015) 13.

Gärditz, KF, 'Verfassungsrechtliche Grundfragen des Schutzes Dementer' (2010) 19 *Zeitschrift für Lebensrecht* 40.

Gardner, J and Shute, S, 'The Wrongness of Rape' in J Horder (ed), *Oxford Essays in Jurisprudence, Fourth series* (Oxford, Oxford University Press, 2000) 193.

Gennip, IE van et al, 'The Development of a Model of Dignity in Illness Based on Qualitative Interviews with Seriously Ill Patients' (2013) 50 *International Journal of Nursing Studies* 1080.

Gewirth, A, 'Are There Any Absolute Rights?' (1981) 31 *The Philosophical Quarterly* 1.

Gewirth, A, 'Human Dignity as the Basis of Rights' in MJ Meyer and WA Parent (eds), *The Constitution of Rights: Human Dignity and American Values* (Ithaca, NY, Cornell University Press, 1992) 10.

Glensky, RD, 'The Right to Dignity' (2011) 43 *Columbia Human Rights Law Review* 65.

Gomes, A, 'Iris Murdoch on Art, Ethics, and Attention' (2013) 53 *British Journal of Aesthetics* 321.

Gondek, HD, 'Vom Schönen, Guten, Wahren. Das Gesetz und das Erhabene bei Kant und Lacan' in HD Gondek and P Widmer (eds), *Ethik und Psychoanalyse. Vom kategorischen Imperativ zum Gesetz des Begehrens: Kant und Lacan* (Frankfurt am Main, Fischer, 1994) 148.

Goodman, M, 'Human Dignity in Supreme Court Constitutional Jurisprudence' (2006) 84 *Nebraska Law Review* 740.

Goos, C, '"Innere Freiheit": Der grundgesetzliche Würdebegriff in seiner Bedeutung für die Begleitung Schwerkranker und Sterbender' in N Feinendegen et al (eds), *Menschliche Würde und Spiritualität in der Begleitung am Lebensende: Impulse aus Theorie und Praxis* (Würzburg, Königshausen & Neumann, 2014) 53.

Goos, C, *'Wirtschaft und Freiheit in den Bauernkriegsartikeln. Verfassungshistorische Anmerkungen zu Artikel 2, 3, 11: Freiheit von Zehnt, Leibeigenschaft und Todfallabgaben'* in GK Hasselhoff and D von Mayenburg (eds), *Die Zwölf Artikel von 1525 und das 'Göttliche Recht' der Bauern – rechtshistorische und theologische Dimensionen* (Würzburg, Ergon, 2012) 77.

Gordijn, B, 'Converging NBIC Technologies for Improving Human Performance: A Critical Assessment of the Novelty and Prospects of the Project' (2006) 34 *Journal of Law, Medicine and Ethics* 726.

Greene, J, 'What the New Deal Settled' (2012) 14 *University of Pennsylvania Journal of Constitutional Law* 265.

Greslé, Y, 'Foucault's Las Meninas and Art-Historical Methods' (2006) 22 *Journal of Literary Studies* 211.

Grimm, D, 'Das Grundgesetz nach vierzig Jahren' (1989) *Neue Juristische Wochenschrift* 1305.

Grimm, D, 'Dignity in a Legal Context: Dignity as an Absolute Right' in C McCrudden (ed), *Understanding Human Dignity* (Oxford, Oxford University Press, 2013) 381.

Grimm, D, 'The Protective Function of the State' in G Nolte (ed), *European and US Constitutionalism* (Cambridge, Cambridge University Press, 2005) 137.

Gröschner, R and Lembcke, OW, 'Dignitas absoluta. Ein kritischer Kommentar zum Absolutheitsanspruch der Würde' in id (eds), *Das Dogma der Unantastbarkeit* (Tübingen, Mohr Siebeck, 2009) 1.

Gröschner, R, 'Des Menschen Würde – humanistische Tradition eines Verfassungsprinzips' in R Gröschner, S Kirste and OW Lembcke (eds), *Des Menschen Würde – entdeckt und erfunden im Humanismus der italienischen Renaissance* (Tübingen, Mohr Siebeck, 2008) 215.

Gruber, MC, '"Menschenwürde" – Menschlichkeit als Bedingung der Würde?' in H Baranzke and G Duttge (eds), *Autonomie und Würde* (Würzburg, Königshausen & Neumann, 2014) 417.

Gruber, MC, 'Was spricht gegen Maschinenrechte?' in M-C Gruber, J Bung and S Ziemann (eds), *Autonome Automaten. Künstliche Körper und artifizielle Agenten in der technisierten Gesellschaft* (Berlin, trafo, 2014) 191.

Grunwald, A, 'Philosophy and the Concept of Technology – On the Anthropological Significance of Technology' in A Grunwald, M Gutmann and E Neumann-Held (eds), *On Human Nature* (Berlin/Heidelberg/New York, Springer, 2002) 179.

Gunlicks, A, 'German Federalism Reform: Part One' (2007) 8 *German Law Journal* 111.

Günther, K, 'The Legacies of Injustice and Fear: A European Approach to Human Rights and Their Effects on Political Culture' in P Alston (ed), *The EU and Human Rights* (Oxford, Oxford University Press, 1999) 117.

Gutmann, T, '"Gattungsethik" als Grenze der Verfügung des Menschen über sich selbst?' in W van den Daele (ed), *Biopolitik* (Wiesbaden, VS Verlag für Sozialwissenschaften, 2005), 235.

Häberle, P, 'Altern und Alter des Menschen als Verfassungsproblem' in P Badura and R Scholz (eds), *Wege und Verfahren des Verfassungslebens: Festschrift für Peter Lerche zum 65. Geburtstag* (Munich, C.H. Beck, 1993) 189.

Habermas, J, 'Das Konzept der Menschenwürde und die realistische Utopie der Menschenrechte' (2010) *Deutsche Zeitschrift für Philosophie* 343.

Habermas, J, 'Das Konzept der Menschenwürde und die realistische Utopie der Menschenrechte' in id, *Zur Verfassung Europas. Ein Essay* (Berlin, Suhrkamp, 2011) 16.

Habermas, J, 'Wahrheitstheorien' in id, *Vorstudien und Ergänzungen zur Theorie des kommunikativen Handelns* (Frankfurt, Suhrkamp, 1984) 133.

Hain, KE, 'Konkretisierung der Menschenwürde durch Abwägung?' (2006) 45 *Der Staat* 189.

Hain, KE, 'Menschenwürde als Rechtsprinzip' in HJ Sandkühler (ed), *Menschenwürde* (Frankfurt aM et al, Lang, 2007) 87.

Hall, M, 'A Fiduciary Theory of Health Entitlements' (2014) 35 *Cardozo Law Review* 1729.

Haltern, U, 'Unsere protestantische Menschenwürde' in P Bahr and HM Heinig (eds), *Menschenwürde in der säkularen Verfassungsordnung* (Tübingen, Mohr Siebeck, 2006) 93.

Bibliography

Hamacher, W, 'Das Versprechen der Auslegung. Zum hermeneutischen Imperativ bei Kant und Nietzsche' in id (ed), *Entferntes Verstehen. Studien zur Philosophie und Literatur von Kant bis Celan* (Frankfurt am Main, Suhrkamp, 1998) 65.

Hamann, B, 'The Mirrors of *Las Meninas*: Cochineal, Silver, and Clay' (2010) 92 *The Art Bulletin* 6.

Hanschmann, F, 'Kalkulation des Unverfügbaren – Das Folterverbot in der Neu-Kommentierung von Art. 1 Abs. 1 GG in Maunz-Dürig' in G Beestermöller and H Brunkhorst (eds), *Rückkehr der Folter. Der Rechtsstaat im Zwielicht?* (Munich, C.H. Beck, 2006) 130.

Härle, W, 'Verletzlichkeit im Alter aus ethischer Sicht' in A Kruse, T Rentsch and HP Zimmermann (eds), *Gutes Leben im hohen Alter: Das Altern in seinen Entwicklungsmöglichkeiten und Entwicklungsgrenzen verstehen* (Heidelberg, Akademische Verlagsgesellschaft, 2012) 239.

Heckel, M, *'Luthers Traktat "Von der Freiheit eines Christenmenschen" als Markstein des Kirchen- und Staatskirchenrechts'* (2012) 109 *Zeitschrift für Theologie und Kirche* 122.

Heinig, HM, 'Menschenwürde und Sozialstaat' in P Bahr and HM Heinig (eds), *Menschenwürde in der säkularen Verfassungsordnung* (Tübingen, Mohr Siebeck, 2006) 264.

Henning, C, 'Karl Marx' in R Gröschner et al (eds), *Wörterbuch der Würde* (Munich, Wilhelm Fink Verlag, 2013) 46.

Henschel, JF, 'Die Kunstfreiheit in der Rechtsprechung des BVerfG' (1990) 32 *NJW* 1937.

Herdegen, M, 'Art 1 (1)' in T Maunz and G Dürig, *Grundgesetz. Kommentar*, Vol. 1 (looseleaf collection, Munich, C.H. Beck).

Heschel, AJ, 'Antwort an Einstein' (September 1940) 20 *Aufbau* 3.

Heschel, AJ, 'Sacred Image of Man' in id, *The Insecurity of Freedom: Essays on Human Existence* (New York, Farrar, Straus and Giroux, 1966) 150.

Heschel, AJ, 'The Individual Jew and His Obligations' in id, *The Insecurity of Freedom: Essays on Human Existence* (New York, Farrar, Straus and Giroux, 1966) 187.

Heun, W, 'Embryonenforschung und Verfassung – Lebensrecht und Menschenwürde des Embryos' (2002) *JuristenZeitung* 517.

Heuss, T, cited in *Jahrbuch des öffentlichen Rechts der Gegenwart* (new ed, 1951) 49.

Hildebrandt, M, 'Legal and Technological Normativity: More (and Less) than Twin Sisters' (2008) 12 *TECHNE* 169.

Hildt, E, 'What Will This Do to Me and My Brain? Ethical Issues in Brain-to-Brain Interfacing' (2015) 9 *frontiers in Systems Neuroscience* 17.

Hilgendorf, E, 'Begründung in Recht und Ethik' in C Brand, EM Engels, A Ferrari and L Kovács (eds), *Wie funktioniert Bioethik?* (Paderborn, Mentis, 2008) 233.

Hilgendorf, E, 'Die missbrauchte Menschenwürde' (1999) 7 *Jahrbuch für Recht und Ethik* 137.

Hilgendorf, E, 'Instrumentalisierungsverbot und Ensembletheorie der Menschenwürde' in HU Päffgen (ed), *Strafrechtswissenschaft als Analyse und Konstruktion. Festschrift für Ingeborg Puppe zum 70. Geburtstag* (Berlin, Duncker & Humblot, 2011) 1653.

Hilgendorf, E, 'Tragische Fälle. Extremsituationen und strafrechtlicher Notstand' in U Blaschke, A Förster, S Lumpp and J Schmidt (eds), *Sicherheit statt Freiheit? Staatliche Handlungsspielräume in extremen Gefährdungslagen*, Schriften zum Öffentlichen Recht Band 1002 (Berlin, Duncker & Humblot, 2005) 107.

Hillgruber, C, 'Art. 1' in V Epping and C Hillgruber (eds), *Kommentar GG* (Beck Online Kommentar, 2013).

Ho, CWL and Khan, TSH, 'The Notion of Genetic Privacy' in TSH Khan and CWL Ho (eds), *Genetic Privacy: An Evaluation of the Ethical and Legal Landscape* (London, Imperial College Press, 2013) 1.

Hoffman, TS, 'Menschenwürde – ein Problem des konkreten Allgemeinen' in W Schweidler, H Neumann and E Brysch (eds), *Menschenleben – Menschenwürde* (Münster, LIT Verlag, 2003) 111.

Höfling, W and Augsberg, S, 'Luftsicherheit, Grundrechtsregime und Ausnahmezustand' (2005) *JuristenZeitung* 1080.

Höfling, W, 'Die Unantastbarkeit der Menschenwürde' (1995) *Juristische Schulung* 857.

Höfling, W, 'Unantastbare Grundrechte. Ein normlogischer Widerspruch?' in R Gröschner and OW Lembcke (eds), *Das Dogma der Unantastbarkeit* (Tübingen, Mohr Siebeck, 2009) 111.

Hofmann, H, 'Die versprochene Menschenwürde' (1993) 118 *Archiv des öffentlichen Rechts* 353.

Hofmann, H, 'Die versprochene Menschenwürde' in id, *Verfassungsrechtliche Perspektiven: Aufsätze aus den Jahren 1980-1994* (Tübingen, Mohr Siebeck, 1995) 104.

Hofmann, H, 'Geschichtlichkeit und Universalitätsanspruch des Rechtsstaats' (1995) 34 *Der Staat* 1.

Hogan, G, 'Constitutional Interpretation' in F Litton (ed), *The Constitution of Ireland 1937–1987* (Dublin, Institute of Public Administration, 1988) 1937.

Holzhey, H, 'Hermann Cohen' in R Gröschner et al (eds), *Wörterbuch der Würde* (Munich, Wilhelm Fink Verlag, 2013) 47.

Hömig, D, 'Menschenwürdeschutz in der Rechtsprechung des Bundesverfassungsgerichts' in R Gröschner and OW Lembcke (eds), *Das Dogma der Unantastbarkeit* (Tübingen, Mohr Siebeck, 2009) 25.

Hong, M, 'Das grundgesetzliche Folterverbot und der Menschenwürdegehalt der Grundrechte – eine verfassungsjuristische Betrachtung' in G Beestermöller and H Brunkhorst (eds), *Rückkehr der Folter. Der Rechtsstaat im Zwielicht?* (Munich, C.H. Beck, 2006) 24.

Hörnle, T, 'Hijacked Airplanes: May They Be Shot Down?' (2007) 10 *New Criminal Law Review* 582.

Hörnle, T, 'Menschenwürde als Freiheit von Demütigungen' (2008) *Zeitschrift für Rechtsphilosophie* 41.

Hörnle, T, 'Menschenwürde und Ersatzmutterschaft' in JC Joerden, E Hilgendorf, F Thiele (eds), *Menschenwürde und Medizin* (Berlin, Duncker & Humblot, 2013) 743.

Hörnle, T, 'Menschenwürde und Lebensschutz' (2003) 89 *ARSP* 318.

Hörnle, T, 'Menschenwürde und reproduktives Klonen' in JC Joerden, E Hilgendorf, F Thiele (eds), *Menschenwürde und Medizin* (Berlin, Duncker & Humblot, 2013) 765.

Hörnle, T, 'Warum sich das Würdekonzept Margalits zur Präzisierung von "Menschenwürde als geschütztes Rechtsgut" gut eignet' in E Hilgendorf (ed), *Menschenwürde und Demütigung. Die Menschenwürdekonzeption Avishai Margalits* (Baden-Baden, Nomos, 2013) 91.

Hruschka. J, 'Die Würde des Menschen bei Kant' (2002) 88 *Archiv für Rechts- und Sozialphilosophie* 463.

Huster, S and Kießling, A, 'Religionsfreiheit zwischen menschen- und grundrechtlichem Schutz' in F Bornmüller, T Hoffmann and A Pollmann (eds), *Menschenrechte und Demokratie. Georg Lohmann zum 65. Geburtstag* (Freiburg, Karl Alber, 2013) 297.

Iglesias, T, 'Bedrock Truths and the Dignity of the Individual' (2001) 4 *Logos: A Journal of Catholic Thought and Culture* 120.

Iglesias, T, 'The Dignity of the Individual in the Irish Constitution: The Importance of the Preamble' (2000) 89 *Studies* 19.

Irobalieva, RN, Fogg, JM, Catanese, DJ, Sutthibutpong, T, Chen, M, Barker, AK, Ludtke, SJ, Harris, SA, Schmid, MF, Chiu, W and Zechiedrich, L, 'Structural Diversity of Supercoiled DNA' (2015), 6 *Nature Communications* 8440, DOI:10.1038/ncomms9440.

Isensee, J, 'Die alten Grundrechte und die biotechnische Revolution' in J Bohnert, C Gramm, U Kindhäuser, J Lege, A Rinken and G Robbers (eds), *Verfassung – Philosophie – Kirche* (Berlin, Duncker & Humblot, 2001) 243.

Isensee, J, 'Menschenwürde: die säkulare Gesellschaft auf der Suche nach dem Absoluten' (2006) 131 *Archiv des öffentlichen Rechts* 173.

Isensee, J, 'Würde des Menschen' in D Merten and HJ Papier (eds), *Handbuch der Grundrechte in Deutschland und Europa, Vol. IV: Grundrechte in Deutschland: Einzelgrundrechte I* (Heidelberg, C.F. Müller, 2011) § 187.

Jackson, V, 'Constitutional Dialogue and Human Dignity: States and Transnational Constitutional Discourse' (2004) 65 *Montana Law Review* 15.

Jarass, HD, 'Art. 1 – Garantie der Menschenwürde' in HD Jarass and B Pieroth, *Grundgesetz für die Bundesrepublik Deutschland. Kommentar*, 9th edn (Munich, C.H. Beck, 2007).

Jarass, HD, 'Art. 1 – Garantie der Menschenwürde' in HD Jarass and B Pieroth (eds), *Grundgesetz für die Bundesrepublik Deutschland – Kommentar*, 10th edn (Munich, C.H. Beck, 2009).

Jarass, HD, 'Art. 2 – Freiheit, Leben, Unversehrtheit' in HD Jarass and B Pieroth (eds) *Grundgesetz für die Bundesrepublik Deutschland – Kommentar*, 10th edn (Munich, C.H. Beck, 2009).

Jarass, HD, 'Art. 5 – Freiheit von Kunst und Wissenschaft (Abs. 3)' in HD Jarass and B Pieroth (eds) *Grundgesetz für die Bundesrepublik Deutschland – Kommentar*, 10th ed (Munich, C.H. Beck, 2009).

Jerrentrup, A, 'Technische Hilfen bei der Betreuung Demenzkranker: Definition "Weglaufschutzsystem" und "elektronische Fußfessel"' (2011) 21 *Sozialrecht und Praxis* 479.

Jones, G and Whitaker, M, 'Transforming the Human Body' in C Blake, C Molloy and S Shakespeare (eds), *Beyond Human. From Animality to Transhumanism* (London/New York, Continuum 2012) 254.

Jouanjan, O, 'Freedom of Expression in the Federal Republic of Germany' (2009) 84 *Ind. L.J.* 867.

Kamir, O, 'Honor and Dignity Cultures: The Case of *Kavod* and *Kvod Ha-Adam* in Israeli Society and Law' in D Kretzmer and E Klein (eds), *The Concept of Human Dignity in Human Rights Discourse* (The Hague et al, Kluwer, 2002) 231.

Kant, I, 'Groundwork of the Metaphysics of Morals' in MJ Gregor (ed and trans), *The Cambridge Edition of the Works of Immanuel Kant: Practical Philosophy* (Cambridge, Cambridge University Press, 1996) 84.

Kant, I, 'Grundlegung zur Metaphysik der Sitten' in W Weischedel (ed): *Immanuel Kant Kritik der praktischen Vernunft. Grundlegung zur Metaphysik der Sitten,* Werkausgabe Vol. VII (Frankfurt aM, Suhrkamp Verlag, 2004).

Kavanagh, A, 'The Irish Constitution at 75 Years: Natural Law, Christian Values and the Ideal of Justice' (2012) 47 *Irish Jurist* 71.

Kavanaugh, JF, 'Lived Humanism: The Aesthetic Education of Albert William Levi' (1991) 25 *Journal of Aesthetic Education* 21.

Kaveny, C, 'Cloning and Positive Liberty' (1999) 13 *Notre Dame Journal of Law, Ethics & Public Policy* 15.

Kemmerer, A, 'Dignified Disciplinarity: Towards a Transdisciplinary Understanding of Human Dignity' in C McCrudden (ed), *Understanding Human Dignity* (Oxford, Oxford University Press, 2013) 649.

Kerr, I, 'Digital Locks and the Automation of Virtue' in M Geist (ed), *From 'Radical Extremism' to 'Balanced Copyright': Canadian Copyright and the Digital Agenda* (Toronto, Irwin Law, 2010) 247.

Kersten, J, 'Die Tötung von Unbeteiligten' (2005) *NVwZ* 661.

Kersten, J, 'Der rechtliche Status totipotenter menschlicher Artefakte – Transiente Totipotenz vs. totipotente Transienz' in T Heinemann, H-G Dederer and T Cantz (eds), *Entwicklungsbiologische Totipotenz in Ethik und Recht* (Göttingen, V&R unipress, 2014), 137.

Klang, M, 'The Rise and Fall of Freedom of Online Expression' in M Düwell et al (eds), *The Cambridge Handbook of Human Dignity* (Cambridge, Cambridge University Press, 2014) 505.

Koops, BJ, 'Concerning "Humans" and "Human" Rights. Human Enhancement from the Perspective of Fundamental Rights' in BJ Koops, CH Lüthi, A Nelis, C Sieburgh, JPM Jansen and MS Schmid (eds), *Engineering the Human. Human Enhancement Between Fiction and Fascination* (Berlin/Heidelberg, Springer, 2013) 165.

Koops, BJ, 'Technology and the Crime Society: Rethinking Legal Protection' (2009) 1 *Law, Innovation and Technology* 93.

Koppelman, A, 'Bad News For Mail Robbers' (2011) 121 *Yale Law Journal Online* 1.

Korsgaard, CM, 'Self-Constitution and Irony' in J Lear (ed), *A Case for Irony* (Cambridge, Mass, Harvard University Press, 2011) 75.

Krawietz, W, 'Gewährt Art. 1 Abs. 1 GG dem Menschen ein Grundrecht auf Achtung und Schutz seiner Würde?' in D Weber und H Wilke (eds), *Gedächtnisschrift für Friedrich Klein* (Munich, Franz Vahlen, 1977) 255.

Kremnitzer, M, 'Human Dignity. An Israeli Perspective' in E Hilgendorf (ed), *Menschenwürde und Demütigung. Die Menschenwürdekonzeption Avishai Margalits* (Baden-Baden, Nomos, 2013) 81.

Kretzmer, D, 'Human Dignity in Israeli Jurisprudence' in D Kretzmer and E Klein, *The Concept of Human Dignity in Human Rights Discourse* (The Hague, Kluwer, 2002) 161.

Kretzmer, D, 'The Law of Belligerent Occupation in the Supreme Court of Israel' (2012) *International Review of the Red Cross* 94:885, 236.

Kriari-Catranis, I, 'Embryo Research and Human Rights – An Overview of Developments in Europe' (1997) 4 *European Journal of Health Law* 43.

Kroeze, I, 'Human Dignity in Constitutional Law in South Africa' in *The Principle of Respect for Human Dignity* (Strasbourg, Council of Europe Publishing 1999) 87.

Kuhse, H, 'Is there a Tension Between Autonomy and Dignity?' in P Kemp, J Rendtorff and NM Johansen (eds), *Bioethics and Biolaw (vol 2): Four Ethical Principles* (Copenhagen, Rhodos International Science and Art Publishers and Centre for Ethics and Law, 2000) 61.

Kunig, P, 'Art. 1' in I von Münch and P Kunig, *Grundgesetz-Kommentar*, Vol. 1, 5th edn (Munich, C.H. Beck, 2000).

Kunig, P, 'Art. 1' in I von Münch and P Kunig, *Grundgesetz: Kommentar*, Vol. 1, 6th edn (Munich, C.H. Beck, 2012).

Landau, D, 'Political Institutions and Judicial Role in Comparative Constitutional Law' (2010) 51 *Harvard International Law Journal* 319.

Lanphier, E, Urnov, F, Haecker, SE, Werner, M and Smolenski, J, 'Don't Edit the Human Germ Line' (2015) 519 *Nature* 410.

Leckey, R, 'Complexifying Roncarelli's Rule of Law' (2010) 55 *McGill Law Journal* 721.

Leist, A, 'Ethik der Beziehungen' (2005) 10 *Deutsche Zeitschrift für Philosophie* 597.

Lepsius, O, 'Der große Lauschangriff vor dem Bundesverfassungsgericht' (2005) *Jura* 433.

Lepsius, O, 'Human Dignity and the Downing of Aircraft: The Federal Constitutional Court Strikes Down a Prominent Anti-Terrorism Provision in the New Air-Transport Security Act' (2006) 7 *German Law Journal* 761.

Lerche, P, 'Grundrechtlicher Schutzbereich, Grundrechtsprägung und Grundrechtseingriff' in J Isensee and P Kirchhof (eds), *Handbuch des Staatsrechts*, Vol. 5 (Heidelberg, C.F. Müller, 2000) §121.

Lerche, P, 'Kunstfreiheit inmitten aktueller Grundrechtskonzepte' in R Jacobs et al (eds), *Festschrift für Peter Raue* (Köln et al, Heymanns, 2006) 215.

Lerche, P, 'Verfassungsrechtliche Aspekte der Gentechnologie' in R Lukes and R Scholz (eds), *Rechtsfragen der Gentechnologie. Vorträge anläßlich eines Kolloquiums Recht und Technik – Rechtsfragen der Gentechnologie in der Tagungsstätte der Max-Planck-Gesellschaft 'Schloß Ringberg' am 18., 19. und 20. November 1985* (Köln, Heymanns, 1986) 88.

Levi, AW, 'Literary Truth' (1966) 24 *The Journal of Aesthetics and Art Criticism* 373.

Levi, AW, 'Literature as a Humanity' (1976) 10 *Journal of Aesthetic Education* 45.

Lévinas, E, 'Reflections on the Philosophy of Hitlerism' (1990) 17 *Critical Inquiry* 62.

Li, W et al, 'Using Algorithmic Attribution Techniques to Determine Authorship in Unsigned Judicial Opinions' (2013) 16 *Stanford Technology Law Review* 503.

Limbach, J, 'Der Mensch wird nie ohne Makel sein' *Frankfurter Allgemeine Zeitung* of 25 February 2002, 51.

Lohmann, G, 'Menschenwürde als "Basis" von Menschenrechten' in JC Joerden, E Hilgendorf and F Thiele (eds), *Menschenwürde und Medizin. Ein interdisziplinäres Handbuch* (Berlin, Duncker & Humblot, 2013) 179.

Lorberbaum, Y, 'Blood and the Image of God' in D Kretzmer and E Klein (eds), *The Concept of Human Dignity in Human Rights Discourse* (The Hague, Kluwer, 2002) 55.

Lorberbaum, Y, 'Human Dignity in the Jewish Tradition' in M Düwell et al (eds), *The Cambridge Handbook of Human Dignity: Interdisciplinary Perspectives* (Cambridge, Cambridge University Press, 2014) 141.

Luban, D, 'Lawyers as Upholders of Human Dignity (When They Aren't Busy Assaulting It)' (2005) *University of Illinois Law Review* 815.

Luf, G, 'Menschenwürde als Rechtsbegriff. Überlegungen zum Kant-Verständnis in der neueren deutschen Grundrechtstheorie' in R Zaczyk et al (eds), *Festschrift für E.A. Wolff zum 70. Geburtstag am 1.10.1998* (Berlin, Springer, 1998) 307.

Luther, M, '*Admonition to Peace*' trans CM Jacobs, revised RC Schultz, in RC Schultz (ed), HT Lehmann (gen ed), *Luther's Works, vol. 46, The Christian in Society III* (Philadelphia, Fortress Press, 1967) 3.

Macklin, R, 'Dignity Is a Useless Concept' (2003) 327 *British Medical Journal* 1419.

Madison, J, 'Alleged Danger From the Powers of the Union to the State Governments Considered,' *The Federalist* No 45 (26 January 1788).

Mahlmann, M, 'Human Dignity and Autonomy in Modern Constitutional Orders' in M Rosenfeld and A Sajó (eds), *The Oxford Handbook of Comparative Constitutional Law* (Oxford, Oxford University Press, 2012) 370.

Mahoney, DF et al, 'In-Home Monitoring of Persons with Dementia: Ethical Guidelines for Technology Research and Development' (2007) 3 *Alzheimer's & Dementia* 217.

Mangoldt, H von, in *Der Parlamentarische Rat (18.11.1948)*, Vol. 5/II (Boppard am Rhein, Harald Boldt Verlag, 2010) 586.

Margalit, A, 'Human Dignity, Between Kitsch and Deification' in C Cordner (ed), *Philosophy, Ethics, and a Common Humanity: Essays in Honour of Raimond Gaita* (London, Routledge, 2011) 106.

Markard, N, 'A switch in time: Der Chief Justice hat die Gesundheitsreform in letzter Minute gerettet' (30 June 2012) *VerfBlog*, www.verfassungsblog.de/switch-time-der-chief-justice-hat-die-gesundheitsreform-letzter-minute-gerettet/.

Marshall, TH, 'Citizenship and Social Class' in id, *Citizenship and Social Class and Other Essays* (Cambridge, Cambridge University Press, 1950) 1.

Marx, K, 'Contribution to a Critique of Hegel's Philosophy of Right, Introduction' (1844) in: 1 *MEW* 378, 385; transl. in D McLellan (ed), *Karl Marx: Selected Writings*, 2nd edn (Oxford, OUP, 2000).

Massey, SJ, 'Is Self-Respect a Moral or Psychological Concept?' in R Dillon (ed), *Dignity, Character and Self-Respect* (New York, Routledge, 1995) 218.

Mate, M, 'The Origins of Due Process in India: The Role of Borrowing in Personal Liberty and Preventative Detention Cases' (2010) 28 *Berkeley Journal of International Law* 216.

Mate, M, 'Two Paths to Judicial Power: The Basic Structure Doctrine and Public Interest Litigation in Comparative Perspective' (2010) 12 *San Diego Journal of International Law* 175.

Matsuzaki, H and Fitzi, G, 'Menschenwürde und Roboter' in JC Joerden, E Hilgendorf and F Thiele (eds), *Menschenwürde und Medizin: ein interdisziplinäres Handbuch* (Berlin, Duncker & Humblot, 2013) 920.

Matthews, FE et al, 'A Two-Decade Comparison of Prevalence of Dementia in Individuals Aged 65 Years and Older from Three Geographical Areas of England: Results of the Cognitive Function and Ageing Study I and II' (2013) 382 *The Lancet* 1405.

McCrudden, C, 'Human Dignity and Judicial Interpretation of Human Rights' (2008) 19 *European Journal of International Law* 655.

McCrudden, C, 'In Pursuit of Human Dignity: An Introduction to Current Debates' in id (ed), *Understanding Human Dignity* (Oxford, Oxford University Press, 2013) 1.

McShane, R, 'Should Patients with Dementia Who Wander Be Electronically Tagged? Yes' (2013) 346 *British Medical Journal* 3603.

Bibliography

Mehta, PB, 'The Rise of Judicial Sovereignty' (2007) 18 *Journal of Democracy* 70.

Menke, C, 'Dignity as the Right to Have Rights: Human Dignity in Hannah Arendt' in M Düwell, J Braarvig, R Brownsword and D Mieth (eds), *The Cambridge Handbook of Human Dignity* (Cambridge, Cambridge University Press, 2013) 332.

Menke, C, 'Liberalismus im Konflikt: Zwischen Gerechtigkeit und Freiheit' in M Brumlik and H Brunkhorst (eds), *Gemeinschaft und Gerechtigkeit* (Frankfurt am Main, Fischer, 1993) 218.

Merkel, R, '§ 14 Abs. 3 Luftsicherheitsgesetz: Wann und warum darf der Staat töten?' (2007) *JuristenZeitung* 373.

Meyers, DT, 'Self-Respect and Autonomy' in R Dillon (ed), *Dignity, Character and Self-Respect* (New York, Routledge, 1995) 218.

Michelman, F, 'The Supreme Court 1968 Term. Foreword: On Protecting the Poor Through the Fourteenth Amendment' (1969) 83 *Harvard Law Review* 7.

Michelman, F, 'Welfare Rights in a Constitutional Democracy' (1979) *Washington University Law Quarterly* 659.

Michelman, FI, 'The Constitution, Social Rights, and Liberal Political Justification' in D Barak-Erez and AM Gross (eds), *Exploring Social Rights: Between Theory and Practice* (Portland, Hart, 2007) 21.

Möller, K, 'Balancing and the Structure of Constitutional Rights' (2007) 5 *ICON* 452.

Möllers, C, 'Democracy and Human Dignity: Limits of a Moralized Conception of Rights in German Constitutional Law' (2009) 42 *Israel Law Review* 416.

Möllers, C, 'Judgement Remarks Regarding the State Constitutional Court of Mecklenburg-Vorpommern, from 21.10.1999 – LVerfG 2/98' (2000) *ThürVBl.* 41.

Möllers, C, 'Wandel der Grundrechtsjudikatur' (2005) *NJW* 1973.

Molnár-Gábor, F, 'Die Herausforderung der medizinischen Entwicklung für das internationale *soft law* am Beispiel der Totalsequenzierung des menschlichen Genoms' (2012) 72 *Zeitschrift für ausländisches öffentliches Recht und Völkerrecht* 695.

Moltke, HJ von, 'Letter of 10 January 1945' in G Brakelmann (ed), *Helmuth James von Moltke. Im Land der Gottlosen. Tagebuch und Briefe aus der Haft 1944/45* (Munich, C.H. Beck, 2009) 328.

Moreau, S, 'What Is Discrimination?' (2010) 38 *Philosophy and Public Affairs* 144.

Moreau, SR, 'The Wrongs of Unequal Treatment' (2004) 54 *University of Toronto Law Journal* 291.

Moyle, W et al, 'Connecting the Person with Dementia and Family: A Feasibility Study of a Telepresence Robot' (2014) 14 *BMC Geriatrics* 7.

Moyn, S, 'Personalismus, Gemeinschaft und die Ursprünge der Menschenrechte' in SL Hoffmann (ed), *Moralpolitik* (Göttingen, Wallstein-Verlag, 2010) 63.

Moyn, S, 'The Secret History of Constitutional Dignity' in C McCrudden (ed), *Understanding Human Dignity* (Oxford, Oxford University Press, 2013) 95.

Müller, F and Richter, T, 'Report on the Bundesverfassungsgericht's (Federal Constitutional Court) Jurisprudence in 2005/2006' (2008) 9 *German Law Journal* 161.

Mureinik, E, 'A Bridge to Where? Introducing the Interim Bill of Rights' (1994) 10 *South African Journal on Human Rights* 31.

Murphy, T, 'Democracy, Natural Law and the Irish Constitution' (1993) 11 *Irish Law Times* 81.

Neal, M, 'Respect for Human Dignity as "Substantive Basic Norm"' (2014) 10 *International Journal of Law in Context* 26.

Nettesheim, M, 'Biotechnology and the Guarantee of Human Dignity' in S Elm and SN Willich (eds), *Quo Vadis Medical Healing* (Dordrecht, Springer, 2009) 143.

Nettesheim, N, 'Die Garantie der Menschenwürde zwischen metaphysischer Überhöhung und bloßem Abwägungstopos' (2005) 130 *Archiv des öffentlichen Rechts* 71.

Neumann, U 'Die Menschenwürde als Menschenbürde – oder wie man ein Recht gegen den Berechtigten wendet' in M Kettner (ed), *Biomedizin und Menschenwürde* (Frankfurt/M., Suhrkamp Verlag, 2004) 61.

Niemeijer, A et al, 'Ethical and Practical Concerns of Surveillance Technologies in Residential Care for People with Dementia or Intellectual Disabilities: An Overview of the Literature' (2010) 22 *International Psychogeriatrics* 1129.

Niemeijer, A et al, 'The Place of Surveillance Technology in Residential Care for People with Intellectual Disabilities: Is There an Ideal Model of Application' (2013) 57 *Journal of Intellectual Disability Research* 201.

Nordenfelt, L, 'The Concept of Dignity' in L Nordenfelt (ed), *Dignity in Care for Older People* (Chichester, Wiley-Blackwell, 2009) 46.

Nussbaum, MC, '"Finely Aware and Richly Responsible": Moral Attention and the Moral Task of Literature' (1985) 82 *Journal of Philosophy* 516.

O'Dowd, TJ, 'Dignity and Personhood in Irish Constitutional Law' in G Quinn, A Ingram and S Livingstone (eds), *Justice and Legal Theory in Ireland* (Dublin, Oak Tree Press, 1995) 163.

O'Mahony, C, 'There Is No Such Thing as a Right to Dignity' (2012) 10 *International Journal of Constitutional Law* 551.

O'Malley, M, 'A Performative Definition of Human Dignity' in N Knoepffler et al (eds), *Facetten der Menschenwürde* (Freiburg and Munich, Alber, 2011) 75.

O'Malley, M, 'Dignity in US Bio-Ethics Debate: Needs Würde' in C Baumbach and P Kunzmann (eds), *Würde – dignité – godnosc – dignity: Die Menschenwürde im internationalen Vergleich* (Munich, Utz, 2010) 253.

Obergfell, EI, 'Der Fall Esra – Eine Neujustierung des Verhältnisses von Persönlichkeitsrecht und literarischer Kunstfreiheit?' (2010) 73 *Amsterdamer Beiträge zur neueren Germanistik* (Justitiabilität und Rechtmäßigkeit. Verrechtlichungsprozesse von Literatur und Film in der Moderne) 65.

Oduncu, FS, 'Stem Cell Research in Germany: Ethics of Healing vs. Human Dignity' (2003) 6 *Medicine, Health Care and Philosophy* 5.

Osterloh, L, 'Art. 3' in M Sachs (ed), *Grundgesetz: Kommentar* (Munich, C.H. Beck, 1999).

Ottmann, H, 'Die Würde des Menschen' in J Beaufort and P Prechtl (eds), *Rationalität und Prärationalität. Festschrift für Alfred Schöpf* (Würzburg, Königshausen & Neumann, 1998) 167.

Palm, U, 'Der wehrlose Staat?' (2007) 132 *Archiv des öffentlichen Rechts* 95.

Pannenberg, W, 'Christliche Wurzeln des Gedankens der Menschenwürde' in W Kerber (ed), *Menschenrechte und kulturelle Identität* (Munich, Kindt Verlag, 1991) 61.

Peters, A, 'Humanity as the A and Ω of Sovereignty' (2009) 20 *European Journal of International Law* 513.

Petonito, G et al, 'Programs to Locate Missing and Critically Wandering Elders: A Critical Review and a Call for Multiphasic Evaluation' (2013) 53 *Gerontologist* 17.

Pfordten, D von der, 'Kants Rechtsbegriff' in id (ed), *Menschenwürde, Recht und Staat bei Kant. Fünf Untersuchungen* (Paderborn, Mentis, 2009) 431.

Pfordten, D von der, 'Zur Würde des Menschen bei Kant' in id (ed), *Menschenwürde, Recht und Staat bei Kant. Fünf Untersuchungen* (Paderborn, Mentis, 2009) 501.

Picker, E, 'Menschenwürde und Menschenleben' in HH Jakobs et al (eds), *Festgabe für Werner Flume* (Berlin et al, Springer, 1998) 155.

Pieper, A, 'Menschenwürde. Ein abendländisches oder ein universelles Problem? Zum Verhältnis von Genesis und Geltung im normativen Diskurs' in E Herms (ed), *Menschenbild und Menschenwürde* (Gütersloh, Gütersloher Verlagshaus, 2001) 19.

Pinker, S, 'The Stupidity of Dignity' (28 May 2008) *The New Republic*, https://newrepublic.com/article/64674/the-stupidity-dignity.

PN Bhagwati, PN, 'Judicial Activism and Public Interest Litigation' (1984–85) 23 *Columbia Journal of Transnational Law* 561.

Podlech, B, 'Art. 1' in E Stein et al (eds), *AK-GG* (Neuwied et al, Luchterhand, 2001).

Pollmann, A, 'Human Rights Beyond Naturalism' in M Albers, T Hoffmann and J Reinhardt (eds), *Human Rights and Human Nature* (Berlin/Heidelberg/New York, Springer, 2014) 123.

Pollmann, A, 'Menschenwürde nach der Barbarei. Zu den Folgen eines gewaltsamen Umbruchs in der Geschichte der Menschenrechte' (2010) 4 *ZfMr* 32.

Poscher, R, '"Die Würde des Menschen ist unantastbar"' (2004) *JuristenZeitung* 756.

Prince, M et al, 'The Global Prevalence of Dementia: A Systematic Review and Metaanalysis' (2013) 9 *Alzheimer's & Dementia* 63.

Prince, M, Prina, M and Guerchet, M, *World Alzheimer Report 2013: Journey of Caring*, www.alz.co.uk/research/WorldAlzheimerReport2013.pdf.

Prior, KS, 'How Reading Makes Us More Human' (June 21, 2013) *The Atlantic Monthly*, http://www.theatlantic.com/national/archive/2013/06/how-reading-makes-us-more-human/277079/.

Puppe, I, 'Umgang mit Definitionen in der Jurisprudenz' in G Dornseifer et al (eds), *Gedächtnisschrift für Armin Kaufmann* (Cologne, Carl Heymanns Verlag, 1989) 15.

Rabe, H, 'Art. Autorität' in J Ritter et al (eds): *Historisches Wörterbuch der Philosophie*, Vol. 1 (Basel, Schwabe Verlag, 1971) col. 727.

Rao, N, 'On the Use and Abuse of Dignity in Constitutional Law' (2008) 14 *Columbia Journal of European Law* 201.

Ratajczak, MZ, Jadczyk, T, Pędziwiatr, D and Wojakowski, W, 'New Advances in Stem Cell Research: Practical Implications for Regenerative Medicine' (2014) 124 *Polskie Archiwum Medycyny Wewnętrznej* 418.

Ravenscroft, J, 'Invisible Friends: Questioning the Representation of the Court Dwarf in Hapsburg Spain' in W Ernst (ed), *Histories of the Normal and the Abnormal: Social and Cultural Histories of Norms and Normativity* (London, Routledge, 2006) 46.

Resnik, DB, 'DNA Patents and Human Dignity' (2001) 29 *Journal of Law, Medicine & Ethics* 152.

Resnik, J and Chi–hye Suk, J, 'Adding Insult to Injury: Questioning the Role of Dignity in Conceptions of Sovereignty' (2003) 55 *Stanford Law Review* 1921.

Richter, F, Fonfara, I, Gelfert, R, Nack, J, Charpentier, E and Möglich, A, 'Switchable Cas9' (2017), in: 48 *Current Opinion in Biotechnology*, 119.

Riedel, E, 'Gentechnologie und Embryonenschutz als Verfassungs- und Regelungsproblem' (1986) *Europäische Grundrechte-Zeitschrift* 469.

Rivers, J, 'Justifying Freedom of Religion: Does Dignity Help?' in C McCrudden (ed), *Understanding Human Dignity* (Oxford, Oxford University Press, 2013) 405.

Robbers, G, 'Art. 1' in DC Umbach and T Clemens (eds), *Grundgesetz* (Heidelberg C.F. Müller, 2002).

Robert, J, 'The Principle of Human Dignity' in *The Principle of Respect for Human Dignity* (Strasbourg, Council of Europe Publishing 1999) 43.

Robertson, JA, 'Embryo Stem Cell Research: Ten Years of Controversy' (2010) 38 *Journal of Law, Medicine & Ethics* 191.

Robinson, H et al, 'The Psychosocial Effects of a Companion Robot: A Randomized Controlled Trial' (2013) 14 *Journal of the American Medical Directors Association* 661.

Robinson, L et al, 'Balancing Rights and Risks: Conflicting Perspectives in the Management of Wandering in Dementia' (2007) 9 *Health, Risk & Society* 389.

Rorty, R, 'Human Rights, Rationality, and Sentimentality' in id, *Truth and Progress* (Cambridge, Cambridge University Press, 1998) 167.

Rosen, M, 'Dignity: The Case Against' in C McCrudden (ed), *Understanding Human Dignity* (Oxford, Oxford University Press, 2013) 143.

Rosen-Zivi, I and Ophir, A, 'Goy: Toward a Genealogy' (2011) 28 *Dine Israel* 69.

Rosenau, H, 'Reproduktives und therapeutisches Klonen' in K Amelung, W Beulke, H Lilie, H Rüping, H Rosenau and G Wolfslast (eds), *Strafrecht, Biorecht, Rechtsphilosophie* (Heidelberg, C.F. Müller, 2003) 761.

Rothstein, MA and Talbott, MK, 'The Expanding Use of DNA in Law Enforcement: What Role for Privacy?' (2006) 34 *Journal of Law, Medicine and Ethics* 153.

Rüfner, W, 'Daseinsvorsorge und soziale Sicherheit' in J Isensee et al (eds), *Handbuch des Staatsrechts*, Vol IV (Heidelberg: CF Müller, 2006) 1049.

Ruger, T, 'Plural Constitutionalism and the Pathologies of American Healthcare' (2011) 120 *Yale Law Journal Online* 347.

Safrai, C, 'Human Dignity in Rabbinical Perspective' in D Kretzmer and E Klein (eds), *The Concept of Human Dignity in Human Rights Discourse*, 99.

Salvi, M, 'Shaping Individuality: Human Inheritable Germ Line Gene Modification' (2001) 22 *Theoretical Medicine* 527.

Sander, JD and Joung, JK, 'CRISPR-Cas Systems for Editing, Regulating and Targeting Genomes' (2014) 32 *Nature Biotechnology* 347.

Scalia, A, 'Judicial Deference to Administrative Interpretations of the Law' (1989) *Duke Law Journal* 511.

Schachter, O, 'Human Dignity as a Normative Concept' (1983) 77 *American Journal of International Law* 848.

Schaede, S, 'Würde – eine ideengeschichtliche Annäherung aus theologischer Perspektive' in P Bahr and HM Heinig (eds), *Menschenwürde in der säkularen Verfassungsordnung. Rechtswissenschaftliche und theologische Perspektiven* (Tübingen, Mohr Siebeck, 2006) 7.

Schleiermacher, FDE, 'Der christliche Glaube. 2. Auflage (1830-31)' § 61, 4 in R Schäfer (ed): *Kritische Gesamtausgabe*, Vol. 13 (Berlin/New York, De Gruyter, 2013) 381.

Bibliography

Schlink, B, 'Der Grundsatz der Verhältnismäßigkeit' in P Badura and H Dreier (eds), *Festschrift 50 Jahre Bundesverfassungsgericht. Bd. 2: Klärung und Fortbildung des Verfassungsrechts* (Tübingen, Mohr Siebeck, 2001) 445.

Schmidt-Jortzig, E, 'Systematische Bedingungen der Garantie unbedingten Schutzes der Menschenwürde in Art. 1 GG' (2001) 54 *Die öffentliche Verwaltung* 925.

Schmitt-Glaeser, W, 'Rechtspolitik unter dem Grundgesetz. Chance – Versäumnisse – Forderungen' (1982) 107 *Archiv des öffentlichen Rechts* 337.

Schmitz-Luhn, B, Katzenmeier, C and Woopen, C, 'Law and Ethics of Deep Brain Stimulation' (2012) 35 *International Journal of Law and Psychiatry* 130.

Schneider, I, 'The Body, the Law, and the Market: Public Policy Implications in a Liberal State' in M Albers, T Hoffmann and J Reinhardt (eds), *Human Rights and Human Nature* (Berlin/Heidelberg/New York, Springer, 2014) 197.

Schopenhauer, A, 'Die beiden Grundprobleme der Ethik' in L Lüdkehaus (ed), *Kleinere Schriften, Werke in fünf Bänden,* Bd. III (Zürich, Haddmans, 1988) 323.

Schroeder, D, 'Human Rights and Human Dignity. An Appeal to Separate the Conjoined Twins' (2012) 15 *Ethical Theory and Moral Practice* 323.

Schüklenk, U and Pacholczyk, A, 'Dignity's Wooly Uplift' (2010) 24 *Bioethics* ii.

Scott, R, 'Dignité/Dignidade: Organizing Against Threats to Dignity in Societies after Slavery' in C McCrudden (ed), *Understanding Human Dignity* (Oxford, Oxford University Press, 2013) 61.

Sedmak, C, 'Human Dignity, Interiority, and Poverty' in C McCrudden (ed), *Understanding Human Dignity* (Oxford, Oxford University Press, 2013) 559.

Sfard, M, 'The Human Rights Lawyer's Existential Dilemma' (2005) 38:3 *Israel Law Review* 154.

Shafer-Landau, R, 'Specifying Absolute Rights' (1995) 37 *Arizona Law Review* 209.

Shetty, P, 'India's Unregulated Surrogacy Industry' (2012) 380 *The Lancet* 1633.

Shklar, J, 'The Liberalism of Fear' in id and S Hoffmann (eds), *Political Thought and Political Thinkers* (Chicago, University of Chicago Press, 1998) 3.

Shultziner, D and Carmi, GE, 'Human Dignity in National Constitutions: Functions, Promises and Dangers' (2014) 62 *American Journal of Comparative Law* 490.

Shultziner, D, 'A Jewish Conception of Human Dignity: Philosophy and Its Ethical Implications for Israeli Supreme Court Decisions' (2006) 34 *Journal of Religious Ethics* 663.

Shultziner, D, 'Human Dignity—Functions and Meanings' (2003) 3 *Global Jurist Topics* 1.

Shulztiner, D and Carmi, G, 'Human Dignity in National Constitutions: Functions, Promises and Dangers' (2014) 62 *American Journal of Comparative Law* 461.

Siegel, RB, 'Dignity and Sexuality: Claims on Dignity in Transnational Debates Over Abortion and Same-Sex Marriage' (2012) 10 *International Journal of Constitutional Law* 335.

Siegel, RB, 'Dignity and the Duty to Protect Unborn Life' in C McCrudden (ed), *Understanding Human Dignity* (Oxford, Oxford University Press, 2013) 509.

Somek, A, 'Europe: From Emancipation to Empowerment' (2013) 60 *LSE 'Europe in Question' Discussion Paper*, www.lse.ac.uk/europeanInstitute/LEQS/LEQSPaper60.pdf.

Sontag, S, 'The Truth of Fiction Evokes our Common Humanity' (April 7, 2014) *Los Angeles Times*, http://www.latimes.com/local/obituaries/la-122804sontag_archives-story.html#page=2.

Sorabji, R, 'Epictetus on *proairesis* and Self' in T Scaltsas and AS Mason (eds), *The Philosophy of Epictetus* (Oxford, Oxford University Press, 2010) 87.

Spaemann, R, 'Über den Begriff der Menschenwürde' in EW Böckenförde and R Spaemann (eds), *Menschenrechte und Menschenwürde* (Stuttgart, Klett Cotta Verlag, 1987) 299.

Sripati, V, 'Human Rights in India Fifty Years After Independence' (1997) 26 *Denver Journal of International Law and Policy* 93.

Starck, C, 'Art. 1' in H von Mangold, F Klein and C Starck (eds), *Grundgesetzkommentar*, 5th edn (Munich, Vahlen, 2005).

Starck, C, 'Behrendt, Gott im Grundgesetz' (1981) *JuristenZeitung* 457.

Starck, C, 'Menschenwürde als Verfassungsgarantie im modernen Staat' (1981) 36 *JuristenZeitung* 459.

Statistisches Bundesamt, 'Weniger Menschen ohne Krankenversicherungsschutz', press release no 285 of 20 August 2012, www.destatis.de/DE/PresseService/Presse/Pressemitteilungen/2012/08/PD12_285_122.html.

Stein, DES, 'Did Maimonides Really Say That?' (2005) 6 *Journal of Religion and Abuse* 1.

Stein, T, 'Recht und Politik im biotechnischen Zeitalter' (2002) 50 *Deutsche Zeitschrift für Philosophie* 855.

Steinberg, L, 'Velázquez's *Las Meninas*' (1981) 19 *October* 45.

Stoecker, R, 'Menschenwürde und das Paradox der Entwürdigung' in id (ed), *Menschenwürde: Annäherung an einen Begriff* (Vienna, öbv Verlag, 2003) 19.

Stratton-Pruitt, SL, 'Introduction: A Brief History of the Literature on Velázquez' in id, *The Cambridge Companion to Velázquez* (Cambridge, Cambridge University Press, 2002) 1.

Stratton-Pruitt, SL, 'Velázquez's *Las Meninas*: An Interpretive Primer' in id, *Velázquez's Las Meninas* (Cambridge, Cambridge University Press, 2003) 124.

Suter, SM, '*In Vitro* Gametogenesis: Just Another Way to Have a Baby?' (2016), 3 *Journal of Law and the Biosciences* 87.

Tanaka, O et al, 'A Smart Carpet Design for Monitoring People with Dementia' in H Selvaraj, D Zydek and G Chmaj (eds), *Progress in Systems Engineering* (Cham, Springer International Publishing, 2015) 653.

Taylor, C, 'What's Wrong with Negative Liberty' in id, *Philosophy and the Human Sciences* (Cambridge, Cambridge University Press, 1985) 211.

Teubner, G, 'Die anonyme Matrix. Zu Menschenrechtsverletzungen durch "private" transnationale Akteure' in W Brugger, U Neumann and S Kirste (eds), *Rechtsphilosophie im 21. Jahrhundert* (Frankfurt/M, Suhrkamp, 2008) 440.

Tollefsen, C, 'The Dignity of Marriage' in C McCrudden (ed), *Understanding Human Dignity* (Oxford, Oxford University Press, 2013) 483.

Trimper, JB, Wolpe, PR and Rommelfanger, KS, 'When "I" Becomes "We": Ethical Implications of Emerging Brain-to-Brain Interfacing Technologies' (2014) 7 *frontiers in Neuroengineering* Article 4.

Twomey, A, 'The Death of the Natural Law?' (1995) 13 *Irish Law Times* 270.

Umberger, E and Bavuso, F, 'Reflections on Reflections' (2010) 92 *The Art Bulletin* 54.

Vesting, T, 'Die innere Seite des Gesetzes. Symbolische Ordnung, Rechtssubjektivität und der Umgang mit Ungewissheit' in I Augsberg (ed), *Ungewissheit als Chance. Perspektiven eines produktiven Umgangs mit Unsicherheit im Rechtssystem* (Tübingen, Mohr Siebeck 2009) 43.

Vidalis, T, 'Meeting Darwin: The Gradual Emergence of Biolaw' (2009) 6 *Journal of International Biotechnology Law* 221.

Vierte Sitzung des Grundsatzausschusses (23.09.1948), in *Der parlamentarische Rat*, Vol. 5/I (Boppard am Rhein, Harald Boldt-Verlag, 2010) 642.

Vitzthum, W Graf, '"L'homme ne doit pas faire de l'homme un esclave!" Les droits de l'homme dans les débats des intellectuels européens émigrés aux Etats-Unis' in M Brauer and E Klein (eds), *Der Staat im Recht. Festschrift für Eckart Klein zum 70. Geburtstag* (Berlin, Duncker & Humblot, 2013) 1345.

Vitzthum, W Graf, 'Die Menschenwürde als Verfassungsbegriff' (1985) *JuristenZeitung* 201.

Vitzthum, W Graf, 'Gentechnologie und Menschenwürdeargument' (1987) 20 *Zeitschrift für Rechtspolitik* 33.

Volkmann, U, 'Nachricht vom Ende der Gewissheit' *Frankfurter Allgemeine Zeitung* of 24 November 2003, 8.

Waldron, J, 'Dignity and Rand – In Memory of Gregor Vlastos (1907-1991)' (2007) 48 *European Journal of Sociology* 211.

Waldron, J, 'Dignity, Rank, and Rights: The 2009 Tanner Lectures at UC Berkeley', papers.ssrn.com/sol3/papers.cfm?abstract_id=1461220.

Walters, MD, 'Jurisdiction, Functionalism, and Constitutionalism in Canadian Administrative Law' in C Forsyth et al (eds), *Effective Judicial Review: A Cornerstone of Good Governance* (Oxford, Oxford University Press, 2010) 302.

Walters, MD, 'Respecting Deference as Respect' (unpublished).

Weinrib, LE 'Constitutional Conceptions and Constitutional Comparativism' in VC Jackson and MV Tushnet (eds), *Defining the Field of Comparative Constitutional Law* (Westport, Praeger, 2002) 23.

Westwood, S, 'I May Be Older, But I Ain't No "Elder": A Critique of "Elder Law"' (2012) 21 *Temple Political & Civil Rights Law Review* 485.

Wetzstein, V, 'Alzheimer-Demenz: Perspektiven einer integrativen Demenz-Ethik' (2005) 51 *Zeitschrift für medizinische Ethik* 27.

White, EK, 'There Is No Such Thing as a Right to Dignity: A Reply to Conor O'Mahony' (2012) 10 *International Journal of Constitutional Law* 575.

Whitman. JQ, 'The Two Western Cultures of Privacy: Dignity Versus Liberty' (2003) 113 *Yale Law Journal* 1151.

Whyte, G, 'Natural Law and the Constitution' (1996) 14 *Irish Law Times* 8.

Whyte, G, 'The Role of the Supreme Court in Our Democracy: A Response to Mr. Justice Hardiman' (2006) 28 *Dublin University Law Journal* 1.

Wicks, R, 'Using Artistic Masterpieces as Philosophical Examples: The Case of *Las Meninas*' (2010) 68 *Journal of Aesthetics and Art Criticism* 259.

Wihl, T, 'Wahre Würde. Ansätze zu einer Metatheorie der Menschenwürdetheorien' in C Bäcker and S Ziemann (eds), *Junge Rechtsphilosophie* (Stuttgart, Steiner, 2012) 187.

Wild, J, 'Introduction' in E Levinas, *Totality and Infinity—An Essay on Exteriority*, trans. A Lingis (Pittsburgh, Pa., Duquesne University Press, 1969) 18.

Will, R, 'Die Menschenwürde: Zwischen Versprechen und Überforderung' in F Roggan (ed), *Mit Recht für Menschenwürde und Verfassungsstaat* (Berlin, Berliner Wissenschafts-Verlag, 2006) 29.

Winkler, D, 'Verfassungsmäßigkeit des Luftsicherheitsgesetzes' (2006) *NVwZ* 536.

Wintrich, J, 'Über Eigenart und Methode verfassungsgerichtlicher Rechtsprechung' in A Süsterhenn (ed), *Verfassung und Verwaltung in Theorie und Wirklichkeit: Festschrift für Wilhelm Laforet* (Munich, Isar-Verlag, 1952) 235.

Wittreck, F, 'Achtungs- gegen Schutzpflicht? Zur Diskussion um Menschenwürde und Folterverbot' in U Blaschke et al (eds), *Sicherheit statt Freiheit? Staatliche Handlungsspielräume in extremen Gefährdungslagen* (Berlin, Duncker & Humblot, 2005) 161.

Wittreck, F, 'Menschenwürde und Folterverbot' (2003) 56 *Die öffentliche Verwaltung* 873.

Wittreck, F, Die aktuelle Entscheidung Esra, Mephisto und Salomo (2010) 128 *JURA* 31.

Wright, RG, 'Second Thoughts: How Human Cloning Can Promote Human Dignity' (2000) 35 *Valparaiso University Law Review* 1.

Yeung, K, 'Can We Employ Design-Based Regulation While Avoiding *Brave New World*' (2011) 3 *Law, Innovation and Technology* 1.

Yoshino, K, 'The Assimilationist Bias in Equal Protection: The Visibility Presumption and the Case of "Don't Ask, Don't Tell"' (1989) 108 *Yale Law Journal* 485.

Zimmermann, J, 'Levinas's Humanism of the Other' in id, *Humanism and Religion: A Call for the Renewal of Western Culture* (Oxford, Oxford University Press, 2012) Ch. 5.

Zwijsen, SA et al, 'Surveillance Technology: An Alternative to Physical Restraints? A Qualitative Study among Professionals Working in Nursing Homes for People with Dementia' (2012) 49 *International Journal of Nursing Studies* 212.

Zwijsen, SA, Niemeijer, AR and Hertogh, CM, 'Ethics of Using Assistive Technology in the Care for Community-Dwelling Elderly People: An Overview of the Literature' (2011) 15 *Aging & Mental Health* 419.

Films and TV

The Simpsons, episode 6, season 8: 'A Milhouse Divided', first broadcast December 1, 1996.

Yasemin (Hamburger Kino-Kompanie, Zweites Deutsches Fernsehen (ZDF) 1988).

Contributors

Rehan Abeyratne
Rehan Abeyratne is an Assistant Professor of Law at the Chinese University of Hong Kong, China.

Marion Albers
Marion Albers is Professor of Public Law, Information and Communication Law, Health Law and Legal Theory, Hamburg University, and Managing Director of the Hamburg Center for Bio-Governance.

Ino Augsberg
Ino Augsberg is Professor of Philosophy of Law and Public Law at Kiel University.

Roger Brownsword
Roger Brownsword is a graduate of the London School of Economics. Currently, he holds professorial positions at King's College London and Bournemouth University; and he is an honorary professor at the University of Sheffield.

Matthildi Chatzipanagiotou
Dr. iur. Matthildi Chatzipanagiotou, LL.M. (NYU) is Dean of Students and Part-time Faculty Member in the School of Business at the American College of Greece, and a member of the Athens Bar Association. She is an alumna of *Graduiertenkolleg Verfassung jenseits des Staates* and of the Faculty of Law at the Humboldt University in Berlin.

Ingolf U. Dalferth
Ingolf U. Dalferth is Danforth Professor of Philosophy of Religion at Claremont Graduate University, Claremont CA, and Professor Emeritus at the University of Zurich, Switzerland, where he directed the Institute for Hermeneutics and Philosophy of Religion from 1998-2012.

David Dyzenhaus
David Dyzenhaus is University Professor of Law and Philosophy at the University of Toronto

Morag Goodwin
Morag Goodwin is Professor of Global Law and Development at Tilburg Law School, the Netherlands. She is series editor of the CUP book series, Global Law.

Christoph Goos
Dr. Christoph Goos is Interim Professor of Public Law at Harz University of Applied Sciences, Halberstadt.

Dieter Grimm
Dieter Grimm, Professor of Public Law at the Faculty of Law at Humboldt-Universität zu Berlin and Yale Law School, 1987 until 1999 Justice of the Federal Constitutional Court, 2001 until 2007 Rector of the Wissenschaftskolleg zu Berlin.

Susannah Heschel
Prof. Dr. Susannah Heschel, a Guggenheim Fellow, holds the Eli Black Professorship in Jewish Studies and is chair of the Department of Jewish Studies at Dartmouth College.

Eric Hilgendorf
Eric Hilgendorf is Professor of Criminal Law, Criminal Procedure and Legal Theory at the Julius-Maximilians-University Würzburg, Germany

Tatjana Hörnle
Prof. Dr. Tatjana Hörnle, M.A. (Rutgers) is Professor of Criminal Law, Legal Philosophy and Comparative Criminal Law at the Faculty of Law, Humboldt-Universität zu Berlin

Stefan Huster
Prof. Dr. Stefan Huster is Professor of Public Law, Social Law, Health Law and Philosophy of Law at the Faculty of Law at Ruhr-University Bochum.

Alexandra Kemmerer

Alexandra Kemmerer is Senior Research Fellow and Academic Coordinator at the Max Planck Institute for Comparative Public Law and International Law in Heidelberg, and Head of the Institute's Berlin Office.

Nora Markard

Prof. Dr. Nora Markard, MA (King's College London) is a Junior Professor for Public Law, International Law and Global Constitutionalism at the University of Hamburg, Germany.

Christopher McCrudden

Christopher McCrudden is Professor of Human Rights and Equality Law, Queen's University Belfast, and William W. Cook Global Law Professor at the University of Michigan Law School. In 2014-2015, he was a Fellow at the Wissenschaftskolleg zu Berlin.

Russell Miller

Russell A. Miller, B.A./M.A./J.D./LL.M., is is the J.B. Stombock Professor of Law at the Washington and Lee University School of Law and the Co-Editor-in-Chief of the German Law Journal.

Christoph Möllers

Prof. Dr. Christoph Möllers, LL.M. (Chicago) is Professor of Public Law and Jurisprudence at the Faculty of Law at Humboldt-Universität zu Berlin and Permanent Fellow at the Wissenschaftskolleg zu Berlin.

Conor O'Mahony

Dr. Conor O'Mahony is Senior Lecturer in constitutional law and children's rights and Deputy Director of the Child Law Clinic at University College Cork.

Stephan Schaede

Dr. Stephan Schaede is director of the Protestant Academy Loccum since 2010. He studied theology and philosophy in Tübingen, Rome and Göttingen, served as a research fellow at the University of Tübingen (1991-1998, with Professor Eberhard Jüngel), as a vicar and pastor in Northern Germany (1999-2004) and as a postdoctoral research fellow and head of the research area "Law and Culture" at the Protestant Institute for Interdisciplinary Research Heidelberg (2004-2010).

Alexander Somek
Alexander Somek is Professor of Legal Philosophy at the University of Vienna and Global Affiliated Professor of Law at the College of Law of the University of Iowa.

Nils Teifke
Dr. Nils Teifke is currently Desk Officer in the Federal Ministry of Labour and Social Affairs (BMAS) in Berlin.

Jochen von Bernstorff
Professor Dr. Jochen von Bernstorff, LL.M. (EUI) holds the Chair for Constitutional Law, International Law and Human Rights at the Eberhard Karls Universität Tübingen (since 2011) and teaches international law as a visiting professor at the German Federal Foreign Office Academy Berlin, Université Panthéon-Assas (institut des hautes études internationales), Université Aix-Marseille and National Taiwan University Taipei. He has acted as a consultant for the German Government and various UN-institutions on human rights, development and international environmental law issues.

Tim Wihl
Tim Wihl is a Junior Research Fellow at the Chair for Public Law and Legal Philosophy (Prof. Christoph Möllers), Humboldt Universität, Berlin.

Index

Abhörurteil 288, 290
abolitionism 47
abortion 122, 143, 337, 365, 486
access to justice 452
Achievement-theories 284
Achtung 56, 57, 60, 61, 64, 67
Adam and Eve 115
administrative law 265
Adoption Placement Act 577
adultery 145
agents 398, 412
   moral agents 407
   rational agents 89
aging society 507
Alexy, Robert 227, 231, 235, 287
Alighieri, Dante 38
Alpers, Svetlana 34, 41
Ambrosius of Milan 120
American Civil Rights Movement 150
Améry, Jean 154
Andrew Edgar 27
animal rationale 87, 98
animality 88
animals 50, 89, 98, 101, 105, 142, 153
Anscombe, Elisabeth 107
anthropomorphism 136
apartheid 246, 265
   Apartheid laws 241
arbitrariness 255
art 27, 47, 48, 171
artistic freedom 171, 176, 187
Ashkenaz 148
assisted reproduction 512, 535, 541
auctoritas 91, 122
Austin, Granville 449
Austria 539

Austrian Artificial Procreation Act 538
autonomy 41, 42, 55, 66, 83, 96, 97, 155, 182, 196, 234, 336, 341, 348, 365, 406, 437, 484, 546, 557
   of the surrogate mother 513, 578
   potential for 90
Aviation Security Act case 198, 211, 214, 221, 269, 326
Badura, Peter 74, 75, 196
Baldus, Manfred 286
Barak, Aharon 156
Barilan, Michael 146
Barnett, Randy 427
Barrington, Donal 494
Bavuso, Francesca 34, 35
Becker, Ulrich 505
Beecher Stowe, Harriet 150
Ben Gurion, David 155
Bentham, Jeremy 71, 72
Bergsträsser, Ludwig 200, 203
Berlin, Isaiah 202
Bernard de Clairvaux 120
Bettelheim, Bruno 203
Beyerle, Joseph 280
Beyleveld, Deryck 303
Bhagwati, Prafullachandra Natwarlal 461
Bible 130, 137, 145
Biedermann, Alois Emanuel 109
Biletzki, Anat 159
Bill of Rights 437
Biller, Maxim 163, 170
bioethics 268, 337, 350, 528
biotechnological developments 533
biotechnology 509, 522, 527,

528, 548, 552, 577
Bloch, Ernst 357, 366
Bloom, Harold 182
Böckenförde, Ernst-Wolfgang 267
Bond case 430
Brennan, William Joseph 440
Brownsword, Roger 397, 407
Budd, Frederick 478
Buddenbrooks 170
Bürgerliches Gesetzbuch (BGB – German Civil Code) 171
burial 133, 139
Calabazas 43
Canada 249
Canadian Charter of Rights and Freedom 261
Canadian Constitution Act, 1867 261
Canadian deference doctrine 259
Carmi, Guy 133, 160
Cassirer, Ernst 573
Charter of Fundamental Rights of the European Union 271, 527, 531
   Article 1 330, 531, 544
   Article 3 531
Charter of the United Nations 528
choice architecture 399, 407
Christianity 92, 119, 148, 334, 578
cloning 549
Closed Circuit Television (CCTV) 317
Code 397
Cohen, Hermann 359
coherence 353
collectivity 347
communication 184
community of persons 79, 80, 90
community principle 433

competitive market economy 383
concentration camps 203
conscience 64
conservative philosophical anthropology 348
Constitution of South Africa 533
constitutional concepts 364
constitutional law
   binding nature of 229
   perspective of 237
constitutional rights 231, 496
constitutionalism 448
continuity 184
contractarian objection 458
Convention on Human Rights and Biomedicine 530
correctness 259
correspondence theory of truth 346
Cover, Robert 66
creation 51
Criminal Law (Rape) Act 1981 480
critical comparison 442
critical reflection 219
criticism 184
Critique of Practical Reason 60
cultural identity 169
Cultural Revolution 96
cyborg 523
Darwin, Charles Robert 93
Daschner case 326
De Hogeweyk 499, 502
de Morra, Sebastián 39, 40, 41, 43
de Pareja, Juan 35, 39
de Ulloa, Doña Marcela 29
de Velasco, Doña Isabel 29
Declaration of Independence, Israel 155
decus 70, 120

default architecture 404
default settings 412
deference 255, 262
  as respect 262, 266
dementia 499, 506
democracy 248, 257, 263
democratic objection 455
Denham, Susan Mary 474, 490
deportation 197
Des Pres, Terrence 154
designer babies 543
detention
  conditions of detention 495
  in prison 490
  preventative detention 488
Diaspora 155
dignified person 45
dignitas 70, 91, 120, 564
dignity
  absoluteness 293
  and human rights 81
  and respect 284
  anthropological accounts of 102
  as a background principle 497
  as a foundation for bioethics 94
  as a foundational principle 490
  as a fundamental right 72
  as a non-interpreted thesis 194, 199
  as a normative justification 491
  as a social construct 135
  as a source of rights 476
  as a value 83
  as an absolute principle 82
  as an expression of self purpose of life 118
  as autonomy 353
  as dignified behavior 51
  as equal status 51
  as Factor X 99
  as fundamental obligation 67
  as hierarchy 51
  as human perception 95
  as maiestas 122
  as nobility 91
  as respect 51
  as right to collectivity 351
  as status 32
  as the equal moral worth of human persons 51
  bearers of 81
  children's 144, 544
  Christian concept of 108, 123, 124
  concept of 108
  conservative 346
  dignity as honor 32
  dignity-fatigue 30
  dignity-talk 30
  Factor X 353
  history of the concept 30
  human 127
  humanistic understanding of 38
  idea of 30, 32, 38, 45, 534
  inviolability of 114
  Kantian idea of 352
  language of 474
  legal concept of 476
  life of 244
  Marxian concept of 360
  meaning of 30, 45
  notion of 27
  of human beings 75, 76
  of Jesus 123
  of moral 66
  of morality 85, 87
  of older people 505
  of subjects 346
  of the individual as a common good 479
  of work 34

627

properties of 354
recognition of 131
religious understandings of 52
representation of 32
right to 239, 263, 265, 270, 496
right to a dignified death 485
right to a dignified life 485
social-economic dimension of 351
ubiquity of the concept 30
understanding of 43
universal validity 130
violation of 142, 247
vulnerability 281
women's 134, 135, 141, 144, 145
dignity discourse 92
directive principles 445, 461
discrimination 369, 374, 389
   against gays 370
   based on genetic characteristics 529
   on the basis of sexual orientation 247
DNA sequence 519
doctrine of radical evil 85
domestic law 470
Doña Margaret Theresa 29
Doña Maria Agustina 29
Donoghue, Denis 31
Dorner, Isaak August 113
Dowry-theory 284
Dreier, Horst 197
Due Process Clause 436
Duffy, George Gavan 488
Duplessis, Maurice 251
Dürig, Günter 73, 195, 196, 208, 213, 267, 278, 288, 339, 433, 547
Durkheim, Emile 279, 349
duty 57

Dwarf tossing case 341
dwarfs 42
Dworkin, Ronald 383
Edgar, Andrew 41, 42, 43
Edwards, John 494
Ehrenberg, Alain 55
elder law 505
Embryo Protection Act (ESchG) 576
embryos 515, 520
emergency support 421
empathy 35, 46, 50
Enders, Christoph 289
enlightenment 70
   philosophy of 55
Epictetus 202
equal treatment 486, 490
equality 116, 241, 274, 566
   and freedom 372
   of opportunity 459
   political 247, 248, 251, 257, 264
   unequal treatment 369
   value of 257
Esra 164, 166, 171
European Convention on Human Rights 530
   Article 8 538
European Court of Human Rights 537
European Court of Justice 544
Evans v. The United Kingdom 537
existence 77
Existenzminimum 422
external theory of rights 232
Factor X 93
federal authority 431
federalism 430
Feldman, David 302
Feros, Antorio 37

fiction 183
fictionalization 177
Finlay, Thomas 490
Finnegan, Joseph 490
food licenses 457
Foster, Charles 506
Foucault, Michel 26, 50
Four Freedoms speech 436
France 42, 541
Frankfurt, Harry 408, 567
Frankl, Viktor 203, 207
freedom 62, 281, 357, 373
  and equality 372
  individual 133
  inner 202, 204, 209
  of choice 372, 377, 388, 400
  of the Christian 201
  of thought 204
  unequal 380
Fuentes, Carlos 53
Fukuyama, Francis 93
fundamental rights 459
future 355
Gaier, Reinhard 175, 189
Gandhi, Indira 450
Gandhi, Mohandas Karamchand 150
Gattungswürde 577
gaze 41, 53
Genesis 51, 130, 136, 152
genesis of values 46
genetic diagnostics 544
genetic diseases 520
genetic engineering 515, 526, 529
Geneva Convention 157
Gentiles 142
German Basic Law
  Article 1 55, 70, 73, 75, 80, 81, 194, 199, 208, 218, 226, 228, 267, 272, 274, 285, 286, 290, 350, 357, 433, 532, 563
    Christian-personalistic interpretation of 208
  Article 19(2) 295
  Article 2 292, 431
    theory of spheres 180
  Article 20 432
  Article 5(3) 171, 172
  Article 74 431
  Article 79(3) 295
  fathers and mothers 273
  genesis of 193
  normative order of 272
German Federal Constitutional Court 82, 163, 165, 171, 290, 431
German Federal Court of Justice for Civil Matters (FCJ) 540
German Social Welfare Act (BSHG) 418
Gewirth, Alan 301, 308
  Gewirthian theory of rights 301
Ginsberg, Ruth Bader 429
God 51, 74, 100, 102, 103, 107, 112, 123, 125, 129, 134, 137, 141, 146, 152, 566, 569
  image of God 110, 114, 118, 130, 136
Goerdeler, Carl Friedrich 203
Gombrich, Ernst Hans 31
Gomes, Anil 54
Gravitas 121
Greene, Jamal 429
Group Areas Act 242
Ha-Am, Ahad 155
Habeas Corpus case 452, 480
Hamann, Bryon 34
Ha-Meiri, Menahem 148
Hamilton, Liam 479
Hardiman, Adrian 489
Hasidism 144
health insurance 421, 423

629

Hegel, Georg Friedrich Wilhelm 362, 372, 376
Heidegger, Martin 56, 61
Hell, Daniel 206
Henchy, Seamus 478
Herdegen, Matthias 267
Herzl, Theodor 154, 155
Herzog, Don 33
Heschel, Abraham Joshua 152, 153, 157
heteronomy 66
Heuss, Theodor 73, 194, 199, 208, 564
Hewart, Gordon 251
High Court of Ireland 481
Hoffmann-Riem, Wolfgang 179
Hofmann, Hasso 284
Hogan, Gerard 484, 488, 492, 494
Hohmann-Dennhardt, Christine 175, 189
Holmes, Oliver Wendell 365
Holocaust 154
Holomodor 276
homo noumenon 62, 64, 89, 568
homo phaenomenon 62, 64, 89
homosexuality 151, 307
honestas 121, 565
honesty 321
honor 31, 70, 122
honor killings 145
human
  human personhood 51
  unborn human life 337, 484
  value of the 43
human agency 409, 411
human dignity
  absolute principle of 235, 237
  as a bundling of fundamental rights 326
  as a consensus concept 362

as a constitutional right 225
as a cosmopolitan ideal 303
as a foundational principle 496
as a foundational value 225, 240, 471
as a fundamental right 326
as a human right 557
as a legal concept 501, 565, 575
as a legal right 576
as a legal term 206, 563
as a moral virtue 323
as a normative anchor 329
as a normative measure 510
as a normative standard 537
as a principle 225, 229, 415
as a relational concept 547, 557, 576
as a right 565
as a virtue 312
as an absolute right 271, 327
as an absolute value 228
as an aim of a constitutional order 472
as an ethical idea 326
as an individual right 553
as an objective norm 553
as an ontological phenomen 569
as the right of rights 240
as the right to have rights 546
balancing 225, 273, 286
Christian understanding of 565
concept of 117, 274, 302, 445, 466, 500, 534, 561, 574
contemporary understanding of 508
definition of 335
ensemble theory of 343, 570
external-theoretic conception of 233

function of 225, 554
guarantee of 267, 537, 546, 554, 556
history of 333
holistic understanding of 507
idea of 509
ideal of 251
impossibility of any limitation of 233
in various scientific disciplines 552
infringement of 226
inviolability 216, 532
  absolute guarantee 220
  tautological proposition of 217
justification of 335
legal idea of 246
legal protection of 556
legal-philosophical foundations 548
minimum core of 481
modern mapping of 307
personalistic understanding of 196
positive definition of 196
protection of 235, 342, 516
rule of 230
scope of 230
sophisticated understanding of 323
source of 568
subjective claim of 175
traditional concept of 569
understanding of 553, 555
violation of 213, 338, 517, 522, 527, 570, 574, 576
  humiliation 340
human rights 71
  autonomy conceptions of 284
  Communication-theories 284
  history of 46, 70, 333
  idea of universal 276, 279
  international human rights law 470, 473
Human Rights Act 1998 538
Human Rights Committee 42
human species 557
human will 63
humane existence 434
humanity 79, 102, 106, 139, 149, 186, 447
  and morality 85
  denials of 79
human-machine entity 523
humiliation 572, 574
Hunt, Lynn 30, 46, 279
Hüther, Gerald 207
idealism 361
identity
  moral identity 379, 386
  practical identity 382
Ignatieff, Michael 160
Illyricus
  Matthias Flacius 111
immigration rules 488
imprisonment
  lifelong 292
inclusion 419
India
  India's history and political context 458
Indian Constitution 445, 449
  Article 2 445
  Article 21 454, 456, 460
  Article 32 450
  Article 37 445, 453, 460
  Article 47 462
  Forty-Second Amendment 451
Indian Supreme Court 445, 451, 456, 460, 465
information 402

Index

information technology 522
insurance 421
integrity 547
  conservative 356
  physical 352
  psychological 352
interests 576
internal theory of rights 231
International Covenant on Economic, Social and Cultural Rights 416
International Declaration on Human Genetic Data 529
international law 476, 528
Irish Constitution 469, 496
  Article 40.3 478
  Article 40.3.2 483
  Preamble 472, 489
Irish Supreme Court 481
Israel 92, 132, 145, 149, 155, 156, 159, 160
  Supreme Court of Israel 156, 157
Israeli Basic Law 156
Israeli High Court of Justice (HCJ) 157
Israeli Supreme Court 147, 159
ius cogens 528
Jabotinsky, Vladimir 155
Jewish law 131, 156
Jews 92, 146
  in Nazi Germany 96
Joas, Hans 27, 46, 47, 50, 52, 279, 350
Judaism 129, 135, 139, 150
judicial intervention 457
juridification
  global juridification project 279
justice
  basic justice 460

  distributive justice 459
  socio-economic justice 459, 463
justification
  culture of 239, 265
Kabbalah 144
Kähler, Martin 117
Kahneman, Daniel 400, 412
Kamir, Orit 155, 156, 160
Kant
  Kantian categorical imperative 57, 434
Kant, Immanuel 55, 56, 58, 64, 70, 83, 85, 86, 87, 88, 90, 91, 93, 98, 113, 117, 148, 149, 208, 213, 245, 274, 301, 336, 348, 359, 546, 561, 566
Kantorowicz, Ernst 37
kavod 136, 137
Keane, Ronan 481
Kidd, Colin 25, 135
King 36, 621
  The King's Two Bodies 37
kitsch 49
Knesset 156, 159
Krens, Inge 207
Kretzmer, David 157, 158
L'Heureux-Dubé, Claire 256, 263
Lacan, Jaques 64
Lachenmann, Helmut 371, 381, 389
Ladeur, Karl-Heinz 56
Ladwig, Bernd 351
Landau, David 458
Language 184
Las Meninas 25, 26, 27, 28, 33, 35, 36, 41, 47, 48, 53
law
  abuse of 243
  administration of 250
  as commandment 58

authority of 258
governing through 254
idea of 237
respect for the 63
supremacy of 258
Law of Competing Principles 231, 234
Lawler, Peter Augustine 96, 97, 98
lawmaking process 534, 552
Lear, Jonathan 390
legal order
  unwritten tradition of 255
legal regime
  administration of 247
legal tradition
  Christian 67
  Jewish 67
  Western 67
Leist, Anton 570
Lemke, Birsel 165
Lerche, Peter 197
Lessig, Lawrence 397
Levi, Albert 183
Levinas, Emmanuel 47, 48, 51, 66, 152, 215, 219, 283
Lezcano, Francisco 43, 45
LGBT rights 466
liberty 71, 459, 478, 488
Lilje, Hanns 203
literature 47, 163, 174, 257, 572
  human elements of 184
  quality of 178
Lochner case 429, 437
Lopez case 430
Lorberbaum, Yair 136, 139
love 151, 167
Luftsicherheitsgesetz 211
Luther, Martin 201
Lutheran theology 111
Lynch, Kevin 474

Macklin, Ruth 94
maiestas 70, 91
Maimonides, Moses 141, 146, 147, 159
Maintenance of Internal Security Act (MISA) 451
Mangoldt, Hermann von 200, 203
Mann, Thomas 170
Margalit, Avishai 27, 47, 49, 567, 572
Marshall, Thomas Humphrey 419
Marshall, Thurgood 440
Marx, Tzvi 138
materialism 361
Maunz, Theodor 267
McCarthy, Niall 479
McCrudden, Christopher 447
Medicaid 426
Mendelssohn, Moses 150
Menschenwürde 31, 42, 76, 195, 203, 206, 209, 615
Meor Hagolah, Gershom 148
metaphysical realism 353
Metaphysics of Morals 57
Michelman, Frank 446, 455
Middle Ages 141, 146
Mindme 502
minimum entitlements 435, 437
Mishnah 139
misogyny 141
Moltke, Helmuth von 204
moral beings 83
moral capacity 84
moral community 311, 317, 394, 397
moral good 62
moral hazard 413
moral imperative 63
moral law 57, 59
moral legitimacy 52
moral life 85

633

moral person 568
moral philosophy 57, 562, 571
moral sentiment 61
moral status 245
moral subject 65
morality 56
   capability of 86
   public morality 478
morally good 84
mortality 348
Moses 136
Moyn, Samuel 152
Murdoch, Iris 27, 54
Murphy, Francis 491
Murray, John Loyola 489
musique concrète instrumental 371
mutual modification 52
Nagel, Thomas 296
National Socialist legal theory 278
nationalism 160
natural law 472
natural rights 71
Naturalists 101
nature-culture-theory 118
Naz Foundation case 465
Nazi era 203
Nazi Germany 134
Nazi regime 209
Nazi system 204
Nazis 328
neurotechnology 522
New Deal 437
New Testament 123
Nietzsche, Friedrich 91, 92, 99
Nixon, Richard 440
nobilitas 91, 121, 565
Nordau, Max 154
norm
   semantic concept of 229

nudging 393, 399, 409, 412
nursing scientists 501
Nussbaum, Martha 47, 182
O'Byrne, John 477
O'Flaherty, Hugh 474, 486
O'Higgins, Tom 488
Obama, Barack 129, 149
obedience 58, 59
object formula 211, 218, 546, 561
objectification 215
Old Testament 115
painting 26, 27, 41, 48, 53
Parliament 257
Parliamentary Council 73, 193, 198, 204, 276, 280
   Committee dealing with Basic Issues 278
Parsons, Talcott 52
patent 524
   patenting human material 525
paternalism 406
   moralistic 42
Patient Protection and Affordable Care Act (ACA) 422, 425, 439
Paulskirchenverfassung 275
Peep show case 306, 341
Peirce, Charles S. 365
personhood 85
   denials of their 79
Pertusato, Nicolasito 29
Philip IV 29
Pico della Mirandola, Giovanni 70, 206, 274, 349, 506, 567
Pinker, Steven 94, 96
Pollmann, Arndt 275
Post-Nazi Germany 193
potestas 70
practical philosophy 56
Prado 26, 39
pragmatism
   pragmatic theory of truth 365

Pre-implantation genetic diagnosis (PGD) 543
President of the United States 149
President's Council on Bioethics 94, 96
Principle of Generic Consistency 309
principles of justice 459
prison 493
  rights of prisoners 493
privacy 479
privative clause 256
progressivism 355
property 362
proportionality
  principle of 287
Protestant theology 107
Public Interest Litigation (PIL) 452, 453
Pufendorf, Samuel von 274
Quebec's Civil Code
  Article 88 252
Rabbi Akiva 144, 146, 153
Rabbi Meir 143, 161
Rabbi Tanhuma 144
racism 135, 141, 149
Rand, Ivan Cleveland 252
rationality 88
Ravenscroft, Janet 38
Rawls, John 388, 458
reasonableness 259
redundancy 364
regulation
  architectural regulation 396, 407
  design-based regulation 393
  of technology 396
regulatory environment 314, 321
regulatory registers
  moral register 315
  prudential register 315
  register of practicability or possibility 315
religion 51, 52, 94, 148
religious traditions 52
renaissance humanism 70
representative democracy 455
reproduction 561
reproductive cloning 517
reproductive medicine 576
respect 57, 61, 490
responsibility 152, 223, 283, 544
Right to Food litigation 456
right to life 447, 454, 460, 482
right to privacy 478
rights
  universal catalogue of 279
Roberts, John 429
Roman à clef 175
roman antiquity 70
Roman Law 32, 240
Romney, Mitt 429
Roosevelt, Franklin Delano 436
Rorty, Richard 358
Rosen, Michael 33, 144, 148, 301
Rosenzweig, Franz 151
Roth, Markus 505
Rothe, Richard 115
Royme, Ayse 178
rule of law 264
  dignitarian conception of 250, 252
  disintegration of 253
  judges conception of 250
  principles of 254, 255
S. H. and others v. Austria 538
Sabbath 142
sacralization of the person 46
Safrai, Chana 144
Schleiermacher, Friedrich Daniel Ernst 108
Schlüsselroman 165

Schmid, Carlo 73, 200, 205, 208, 278
Scholl, Hans 204
Scholl, Sophie 204
Schopenhauer, Arthur 67, 561
scientific culture 97
Second World War 278
security 436
self-constitution 376
self-determination 373, 484, 519
self-respect 573
sensus divinitatis 101
sentimentality 49, 50
servitude 38, 197
sexuality 179
Sfard, Michael 158
shaming 141, 145
Shapiro v. Thompson 438
Shklar, Judith 359
Shultziner, Doron 133, 156, 160
Silva-Tarouca Larsen, Beatrice von 316
singularity 347
Slaughter, Joseph 30
slave 35, 39, 41, 133, 147, 257
  slave-owning society 245
slavery 41, 71, 150, 197, 202
  abolition of 47
  emancipation from 350
Smith, David 398
social balance 424, 431
social class 92
social equality 420
social inclusion 419
social norm 404, 412
social participation 455
social rights 417, 432, 436
social security 431
Social Security Act 1935 441
social status 32
social-state 416

socioeconomic rights 446, 454, 459
solidarity 421
solidarity community 424
solitary confinement 492
Sotah 145
South Africa 150, 241, 263, 302, 358, 448
South African Constitution 448
  Section 26 463
  Section 27 463
South African Constitutional Court 463
SPD 205
Spinoza 60, 154
Sripati, Vijayashri 464
state duties 82
state of emergency 450
State of the Union Address 436
status 31, 48, 134
statute
  implementation of 243
Steinberg, Leo 49
stem cells 515
stigmatization 197
Stoecker, Ralf 574
Stratton-Pruitt, Suzanne 31
subjectivity 347
Sunstein, Cass 393, 400, 406, 411, 436
surrogate motherhood 512, 526, 535, 561, 576, 580
Süsterhenn, Adolf 198
Swiss Federal Constitution 533
synthetic life 511
Tal, Tzvi 156
Talmud 134, 140, 145
Talmudic doctrine 66
Taylor, Charles 408
technology 303, 316, 503, 521
  assistive 500

regulatory 319
reproductive 514
surveillance 499
Thaler, Richard 393, 401
The Simpsons 25
The Wolf of Wall Street 42
theory of competing principles 233
Torah 131, 134
torture 47, 82, 131, 147, 159, 197, 203, 296, 339
constitutional prohibition of 297
mental 572
punitive 146
totalitarian regimes 134
Totality and Infinity 222
Tractatus Logico-Philosophicus 217
Tractatus Theologico-Politicus 154
tradition 92
Umberger, Emily 34, 35
UNESCO 529
United Nations Declaration on Human Cloning 529
United Nations Human Rights Committee 42
United States 150, 160
Universal Declaration of Human Rights 70, 271, 273, 280, 527
Article 1 71, 528
Preamble 274, 528
Universal Declaration on Bioethics and Human Rights 529
Universal Declaration on the Human Genome and Human Rights 529
Upshaw, Dierre 129, 149, 161
US Constitution
Article V 437
Fifth Amendment 436
Fourteenth Amendment 436
Preamble 439
values 83
system of 90
Velázquez, Diego 25, 26, 31, 33, 36, 40, 47, 53
Vilmar, August 112
Vonnegut, Kurt 183
Wackenheim, Manuel 42, 43
Waldron, Jeremy 32, 33
Weber, Helene 200, 206
welfare 438
welfare-state 416
Wessel, Helene 199
Westwood, Sue 505
Wicks, Robert 53
Wintrich, Josef 213
Wittgenstein, Ludwig 217
Wittstock, Uwe 176
World War I 276
Yosef, Ovadiah 151
Zionism 149, 154